Math

Math
ADVANTAGE

HARCOURT
BRACE

Orlando • Atlanta • Austin • Boston • San Francisco • Chicago • Dallas • New York • Toronto • London

http://www.hbschool.com

Grateful acknowledgment is made to Heritage Music Press, a division of The Lorenz Corp., Dayton, OH for permission to reprint "Yankee Doodle" from *The Pianist* by Walter and Carol Noona. Music and lyrics © 1973 by Heritage Music Press, a division of The Lorenz Corp.
(License #414907/Product KM46)

Printed in the United States of America

ISBN 0-15-311436-3

4 5 6 7 8 9 10 048 2000 99

Senior Authors

Grace M. Burton
Chair, Department of Curricular Studies
Professor, School of Education
University of North Carolina at Wilmington
Wilmington, North Carolina

Evan M. Maletsky
Professor of Mathematics
Montclair State University
Upper Montclair, New Jersey

Authors

George W. Bright
Professor of Mathematics Education
The University of North Carolina at Greensboro
Greensboro, North Carolina

Sonia M. Helton
Professor of Childhood Education
Coordinator, College of Education
University of South Florida
St. Petersburg, Florida

Loye Y. (Mickey) Hollis
Professor of Mathematics Education
Director of Teacher Education and Under-
  graduate Programs
University of Houston
Houston, Texas

Howard C. Johnson
Dean of the Graduate School
Associate Vice Chancellor for Academic Affairs
Professor, Mathematics and
  Mathematics Education
Syracuse University
Syracuse, New York

Joyce C. McLeod
Visiting Professor
Rollins College
Winter Park, Florida

Evelyn M. Neufeld
Professor, College of Education
San Jose State University
San Jose, California

Vicki Newman
Classroom Teacher
McGaugh Elementary School
Los Alamitos Unified School District
Seal Beach, California

Terence H. Perciante
Professor of Mathematics
Wheaton College
Wheaton, Illinois

Karen A. Schultz
Associate Dean and Director of Graduate Studies
  and Research
Research Professor, Mathematics Education
College of Education
Georgia State University
Atlanta, Georgia

Muriel Burger Thatcher
Independent Mathematics Consultant
Mathematical Encounters
Pine Knoll Shores, North Carolina

Advisors

Anne R. Biggins
Speech-Language Pathologist
Fairfax County Public Schools
Fairfax, Virginia

Carolyn Gambrel
Learning Disabilities Teacher
Fairfax County Public Schools
Fairfax, Virginia

Lois Harrison-Jones
Education Consultant
Dallas, Texas

Asa G. Hilliard, III
Fuller E. Callaway Professor
  of Urban Education
Georgia State University
Atlanta, Georgia

Marsha W. Lilly
Secondary Mathematics
  Coordinator
Alief Independent School District
Alief, Texas

Judith Mayne Wallis
Elementary Language Arts/
  Social Studies/Gifted Coordinator
Alief Independent School District
Houston, Texas

CONTENTS

Troubleshooting Lesson
Using the Addition Table
H2–H3

Troubleshooting Lesson
Names for Numbers
H4–H5

* Algebra Readiness

iv

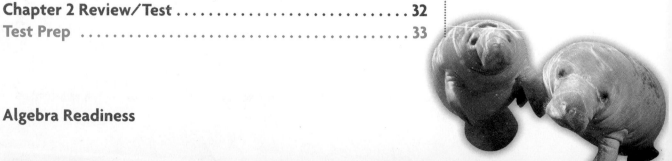

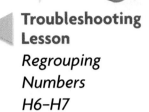

Troubleshooting Lesson
Regrouping Numbers H6–H7

Extension Lesson
Computing Distances H32–H33

* **Algebra Readiness**

v

**Extension
Lesson**
*Time Before
the Hour
H34–H35*

**Troubleshooting
Lesson**
*Using a
Calendar
H8–H9*

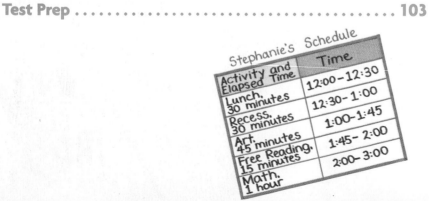

**Troubleshooting
Lesson**
Counting Coins
H10–H11

Chapters 5–7 ✓ Checkpoint

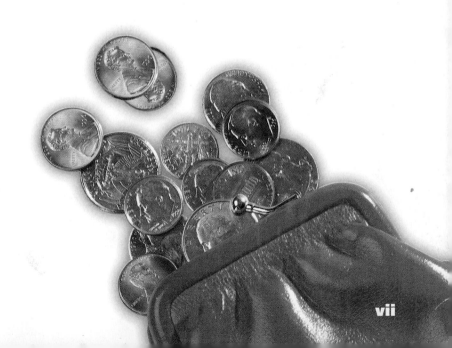

◀ **Troubleshooting
Lesson**
Place Value
H12–H13

◀ **Extension
Lesson**
*Making a
Time Line*
H36–H37

* **Algebra Readiness**

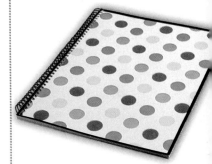

CHAPTER 10 · Compare, Order, and Round Numbers 160

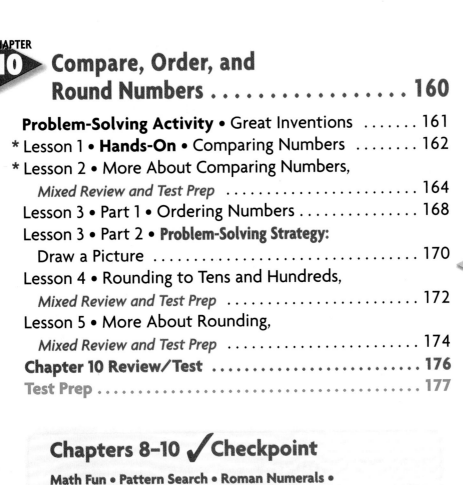

Troubleshooting Lesson
Rounding on a Number Line
H14–H15

Chapters 8–10 ✓ Checkpoint

* Algebra Readiness

**Troubleshooting
Lesson**
*Skip Counting
H16–H17*

**Extension
Lesson**
*Using Arrays to
Find Square
Numbers
H38–H39*

x   *** Algebra Readiness**

**Troubleshooting
Lesson**
Equal Groups
H18–H19

**Troubleshooting
Lesson**
Fact Families
H20–H21

Chapters 11–14 ✓ Checkpoint

* **Algebra Readiness**

Extension Lesson
Making a Survey
H40–H41

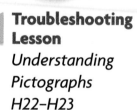

Troubleshooting Lesson
Understanding Pictographs
H22–H23

* **Algebra Readiness**

xii

**Extension
Lesson**
*Predicting
Outcomes
H42–H43*

Chapters 15–17 ✓Checkpoint

Troubleshooting
Lesson
Open and
Closed Figures
H24–H25

Extension
Lesson
Figures That
Tessellate
H44–H45

* Algebra Readiness

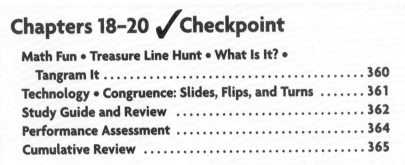

**Extension
Lesson**
*Symmetry by
Turning
H46–H47*

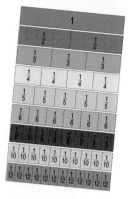

**Extension
Lesson**
*Mixed Numbers
H48–H49*

**Extension
Lesson**
*Fraction of a
Number
H50–H51*

* **Algebra Readiness**

◀ **Extension
Lesson**
*Adding and
Subtracting
Decimals
H52–H53*

Chapters 21–23 ✓Checkpoint

* Algebra Readiness

**Troubleshooting
Lesson**
*Using a Ruler
H26–H27*

**Extension
Lesson**
*Measuring
Greater Lengths
H54–H55*

◀ **Extension
Lesson**
*Multiplying to
Find Area*
H56–H57

Chapters 24–26 ✔ Checkpoint

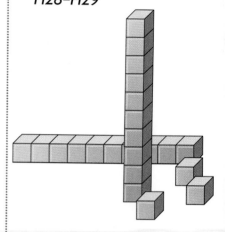

**Troubleshooting
Lesson**
*Multiplication
Facts
H28–H29*

**Troubleshooting
Lesson**
*Division Facts
H30–H31*

* **Algebra Readiness**

STUDENT HANDBOOK

BE A GOOD PROBLEM SOLVER

Good problem solvers need to be good thinkers. This plan can help you think through a problem.

UNDERSTAND the problem

Ask yourself...

- What is the problem about?
- What is the question?

- What information is given?

Then try this.

Retell the problem in your own words.

Say the question as a fill-in-the-blank sentence.

List the information given in the problem.

PLAN how to solve it

Ask yourself...

- What strategies might I use?

- About what will the answer be?

Then try this.

List some strategies you can use.

Predict what your answer will be. Make an estimate if it will help.

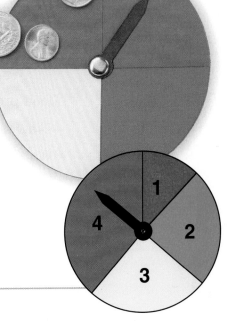

SOLVE it

Ask yourself...	Then try this.
• How can I solve the problem?	Follow your plan and show your solution.
• How can I write my answer?	Write your answer in a complete sentence.

LOOK BACK and check your answer

Ask yourself...	Then try this.
• How can I tell if my answer is reasonable?	Compare your answer to your estimate. Check your answer by redoing your work. Match your answer to the question.
• How else might I have solved the problem?	Try using another strategy to solve the problem.

You can be a good problem solver! Remember these important words—

REMEMBER:

UNDERSTAND

PLAN

SOLVE

LOOK BACK

Ask yourself questions as you think through the problem. Then be proud of your success!

GOOD PROBLEM SOLVERS USE STRATEGIES

Good problem solvers need to know and use these strategies.

- Draw a Picture
- Act It Out
- Make a Model
- Work Backward
- Find a Pattern
- Guess and Check
- Use or Make a Table or Graph
- Make a List
- Write a Number Sentence

Think about how strategies were used to solve these problems:

Samantha, Mark, and Kim were comparing their rock collections. Samantha had 74 rocks. Mark had 73, and Kim had 76. Who had the most rocks? the fewest?

Draw a picture to compare the numbers.

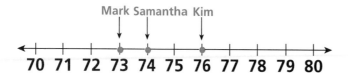

So, Kim had the most rocks. Mark had the fewest rocks.

Jamal and his mother made some cookies on Tuesday. On Wednesday, they made 20 more cookies. Jamal ate 3 of the cookies. He took 35 cookies to a party. How many cookies did Jamal and his mother bake on Tuesday?

Work backward to find the total number of cookies baked.

Start	35	Start with the number of cookies Jamal took to the party.
$35 + 3 = 38$		Add the number of cookies Jamal ate.
$38 - 20 = 18$		Subtract the number of cookies they baked on Wednesday.

So, Jamal and his mother baked 18 cookies on Tuesday.

Susan's mother is making squares for a quilt. She has made the quilt with 6 rows of squares with 5 squares in each row? How many squares are in the quilt?

Make a model to find the total number of squares in the quilt.
Count by fives to find the total, or add 5 + 5 + 5 + 5 + 5 +5 = ?.

So, the quilt has 30 squares in it.

Talk About It

How does using strategies help you become a good problem solver?

1 ADDITION AND SUBTRACTION FACTS

Bananas can grow all year long in countries near the equator. Bananas are the third most popular fruit in the United States. Only apples and oranges are more popular.

Fantastic Fruits

Do you know why some fruits are available only at certain times of the year? Some fruits get ripe in warm seasons and others in cool seasons. Find your favorite fruits on the chart. Which fruits are in season now?

Make a poster about fruit. Use numbers between 0 and 18.

- Make three addition sentences and three subtraction sentences about two fruits, first with pictures and then with numbers.

- Draw pictures of how you think each fruit grows. (HINT: A fruit may grow on a tree, vine, or bush.)

SPRING AND SUMMER FRUITS
peaches
grapes
berries
pineapples

FALL AND WINTER FRUITS
apples
pears
oranges

DID YOU

☑ make three addition sentences with pictures and with numbers?

☑ make three subtraction sentences with pictures and with numbers?

☑ draw pictures of how you think each fruit grows?

Subtraction

Addition

9 apples + 6 oranges = 15 apples and oranges

8 cherries + 9 grapes = 17 cherries and grapes

4 lemons + 7 apricots = 11 lemons and apricots

1

Addition Strategies

VOCABULARY

addend

sum

counting on

make a ten

Why learn this? You can use *counting on* and *make a ten* to find how many pieces of fruit you have.

William saw 3 apples on one shelf and 5 apples on another shelf. How many apples did he see?

Add to find the number of apples.

$3 + 5 = 8$

$$\begin{array}{r} 3 \\ +5 \\ \hline 8 \end{array}$$ ← addend
← addend
← sum

So, William saw 8 apples.

REMEMBER:

Addition is finding the total number of items when two groups of items are joined.

$7 + 3 = 10$

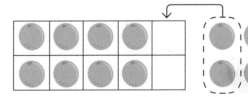

Here are two ways to find sums.

Counting On When one of the addends is 1, 2, or 3, *count on* to find the sum.

$$5 + 3 = \underline{\ ?\ }$$

Begin with the larger number.

Count: 5 . . . 6, 7, 8.
So, $5 + 3 = 8$.

Make a Ten When one of the addends is close to 10, first *make a ten* and then add the rest.

$$8 + 5 = \underline{\ ?\ }$$

Think: $8 + \underline{\ ?\ } = 10$

$8 + 2 = 10$ and $10 + 3 = 13$
So, $8 + 5 = 13$.

▶ CHECK

Copy each problem. Find the sum. Tell if you used *counting on* or *make a ten*.

1. $\begin{array}{r} 3 \\ +6 \\ \hline \end{array}$
2. $\begin{array}{r} 7 \\ +4 \\ \hline \end{array}$
3. $\begin{array}{r} 8 \\ +4 \\ \hline \end{array}$
4. $\begin{array}{r} 7 \\ +6 \\ \hline \end{array}$
5. $\begin{array}{r} 9 \\ +2 \\ \hline \end{array}$

Copy each problem. Find the sum. Tell if you used *counting on* or *make a ten*.

6. 2 +3	**7.** 6 +8	**8.** 5 +7	**9.** 9 +4	**10.** 4 +3

Find the sum.

11. 2 +9	**12.** 8 +3	**13.** 4 +2	**14.** 7 +2	**15.** 3 +9
16. 3 +7	**17.** 6 +3	**18.** 7 +4	**19.** 9 +2	**20.** 5 +9	**21.** 3 +8

22. $6 + 5 = \underline{\ ?\ }$ **23.** $2 + 8 = \underline{\ ?\ }$ **24.** $7 + 3 = \underline{\ ?\ }$

25. $4 + 6 = \underline{\ ?\ }$ **26.** $8 + 5 = \underline{\ ?\ }$ **27.** $9 + 3 = \underline{\ ?\ }$

Problem Solving • Mixed Applications

28. Mr. Perez caught one fish that weighed 4 pounds. He caught a second fish that weighed 5 pounds. How many pounds of fish did he catch?

29. Mental Math Fernando and 5 friends had a picnic lunch. They ate sandwiches and apples. How many children ate a picnic lunch?

30. There are 9 brown ducks and 4 white ducks at the pond. How many ducks are there?

31. ✏ **Write a problem** about people fishing and skating.

Mixed Review and Test Prep

Count by twos or threes. Write the numbers. (taught in Grade 2)

32. 2, _?_, _?_, 8, _?_   **33.** 6, _?_, 12, _?_, 18, _?_   **34.** 12, _?_, 16, _?_, 20, _?_

Count by tens. Choose the letter of the missing number. (taught in Grade 2)

35. 7, 17, _?_, 37   **A** 17   **B** 47   **C** 7   **D** 27

36. 41, 51, _?_, 71   **F** 31   **G** 21   **H** 61   **J** 81

37. _?_, 74, 84, 94   **A** 54   **B** 94   **C** 64   **D** 44

More Addition Strategies

Why learn this? You can use addition strategies to find the total number of animals you see.

Lucy saw 3 sandhill cranes on her way to school. She saw 3 more cranes on her way home. How many cranes did she see in all?

Write a number sentence to find how many cranes Lucy saw.

$$3 + 3 = \underline{?}$$
$$3 + 3 = 6$$

So, Lucy saw 6 sandhill cranes in all.

Here are three ways to find sums.

Doubles	**Doubles Plus One**	**Doubles Minus One**
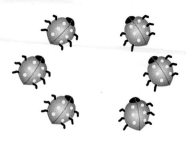		
$3 + 3 = 6$	$3 + 4 = \underline{?}$ Think: $3 + 3 = 6$ and $6 + 1 = 7$	$3 + 2 = \underline{?}$ Think: $3 + 3 = 6$ and $6 - 1 = 5$
When both addends are the *same*, you are adding doubles.	When one addend is *one more* than the other, add the doubles. Then add one more to the sum. So, $3 + 4 = 7$.	When one addend is *one less* than the other, add the doubles. Then take one away from the sum. So, $3 + 2 = 5$.

▶ CHECK

Write an example of a problem that can be solved using these strategies.

1. *doubles* **2.** *doubles plus one* **3.** *doubles minus one*

▶ PRACTICE

Find the sum. Tell if you used *doubles,*
doubles plus one, or *doubles minus one.*

4. 8 +8	**5.** 6 +5	**6.** 5 +5	**7.** 9 +9	**8.** 4 +3	**9.** 6 +7

Find the sum.

10. 6 +6	**11.** 8 +7	**12.** 4 +5	**13.** 7 +7	**14.** 8 +9	**15.** 4 +4

16. 6 + 7 = <u>?</u>   **17.** 8 + 8 = <u>?</u>   **18.** 5 + 6 = <u>?</u>

19. 7 + 8 = <u>?</u>   **20.** 5 + 4 = <u>?</u>   **21.** 9 + 8 = <u>?</u>

22. 3 + 4 = <u>?</u>   **23.** 2 + 3 = <u>?</u>   **24.** 8 + 6 = <u>?</u>

Problem Solving • Mixed Applications

Using Data For Problems 25–28, use the table.

25. How many turtles and frogs in all
    did the students see?

26. How many birds and squirrels
    in all did the students see?

Things We Saw on Our Nature Walk	
Squirrels	4
Birds	9
Turtles	2
Fish	5
Garden Spiders	3
Frogs	6

27. Hiroshi counted the frogs and
    the garden spiders. How
    many did he count in all?

28. **Write a problem** using the
    information in the table.

Mixed Review and Test Prep

Count back by tens. Write the numbers. (taught in Grade 2)

29. 55, 45, <u>?</u>, <u>?</u>, 15, <u>?</u>   **30.** 78, 68, <u>?</u>, <u>?</u>, 38, <u>?</u>

31. 64, <u>?</u>, <u>?</u>, 34, <u>?</u>   **32.** 101, 91, <u>?</u>, <u>?</u>, 61, <u>?</u>

Choose the letter of the missing number in the pattern. (taught in Grade 2)

33. 9, 12, 15, <u>?</u>, 21   **A** 16   **B** 18   **C** 20   **D** 19

34. 12, 16, <u>?</u>, 24   **F** 17   **G** 18   **H** 21   **J** 20

35. 34, 36, <u>?</u>, 40   **A** 35   **B** 38   **C** 39   **D** 40

MORE PRACTICE page H68

5

Order and Zero

Why learn this? You can find the number of pennies you have.

At the school fair, Joey bought a cookie for 5¢ and a pencil for 4¢. Kim bought a whistle for 4¢ and a pretzel for 5¢. How much did each spend?

$$5 + 4 = 9$$
$$4 + 5 = 9$$

So, Joey and Kim each spent 9¢

REMEMBER:

An *addend* is any of the numbers that are added.

$$5 + 4 = 9$$
$$\uparrow \quad \uparrow$$
addends

Changing the order of the addends does not change the sum.

$6 + 3 = 9$	$7 + 2 = 9$	$8 + 1 = 9$
$3 + 6 = 9$	$2 + 7 = 9$	$1 + 8 = 9$

CRITICAL THINKING How do you know that $24 + 56 = 56 + 24$?

Tony found 3 pennies in one pocket and 0 pennies in another pocket. How many pennies did Tony find?

$$3 + 0 = 3$$

So, Tony found 3 pennies.

Any number plus zero equals that same number.

$7 + 0 = 7$	$5 + 0 = 5$	$0 + 9 = 9$

• How can knowing about zero help you?

► CHECK

Copy each problem. Find the sum.

1.	2	9	2.	8	7	3.	6	8	4.	7	9
	+9	+2		+7	+8		+8	+6		+9	+7

► PRACTICE

Find the sum.

5. $6 + 0 = \underline{\ ?\ }$

6. $0 + 8 = \underline{\ ?\ }$

7. $0 + 0 = \underline{\ ?\ }$

8. $7 + 0 = \underline{\ ?\ }$

9. $8 + 3 = \underline{\ ?\ }$

10. $3 + 8 = \underline{\ ?\ }$

11. $3 + 3 = \underline{\ ?\ }$

12. $2 + 0 = \underline{\ ?\ }$

13. $9 + 0 = \underline{\ ?\ }$

14. $6 + 7 = \underline{\ ?\ }$

15. $7 + 6 = \underline{\ ?\ }$

16. $7 + 7 = \underline{\ ?\ }$

17. $8 + 9 = \underline{\ ?\ }$

18. $9 + 8 = \underline{\ ?\ }$

19. $8 + 8 = \underline{\ ?\ }$

20. $0 + 4 = \underline{\ ?\ }$

21. $8 + 0 = \underline{\ ?\ }$

22. $9 + 9 = \underline{\ ?\ }$

Find the sum. Use order in addition to write another addition fact. Example: $5 + 4 = 9$, so $4 + 5 = 9$.

23. $6 + 8 = \underline{\ ?\ }$, so $\underline{\ ?\ } + \underline{\ ?\ } = \underline{\ ?\ }$.

24. $7 + 5 = \underline{\ ?\ }$, so $\underline{\ ?\ } + \underline{\ ?\ } = \underline{\ ?\ }$.

25. $4 + 9 = \underline{\ ?\ }$, so $\underline{\ ?\ } + \underline{\ ?\ } = \underline{\ ?\ }$.

26. $8 + 5 = \underline{\ ?\ }$, so $\underline{\ ?\ } + \underline{\ ?\ } = \underline{\ ?\ }$.

Problem Solving • Mixed Applications

27. **Money** Danny's mother gave him 6¢ on Monday and 5¢ on Tuesday. How much money did Danny have?

28. **Mental Math** Kim put 6 flowers in the white vase and 0 flowers in the blue vase. How many flowers did she put in the vases?

29. **Visual Thinking** Jeff walked 4 blocks to the park and 3 blocks to the store. Tammy walked 3 blocks to the school and 4 blocks to her friend's house. How far did each walk?

30. Pedro bought 9 green pencils and 8 red pencils. How many pencils did Pedro buy?

31. ✏️ **Write a problem** using 7 and 0.

LESSON CONTINUES

Problem–Solving Strategy: Make a Table

▶ **THE PROBLEM** Make a table of all the number sentences that can be written using the numbers 1–4 as addends. Which of the number sentences have the same addends, but show a different order?

REMEMBER:

UNDERSTAND
PLAN
SOLVE
LOOK BACK

UNDERSTAND

• What are you asked to find?

• What information will you use?

• Is there any information you will not use? If so, what?

PLAN

• What strategy can you use to solve the problem?

Make a table like the one below to show all of the number sentences that can be made with the numbers 1–4.

SOLVE

Circle one number sentence from the pair that has the same addends but shows a different order.

Number Sentences			
1 + 1 = 2	2 + 1 = 3	3 + 1 = 4	4 + 1 = 5
1 + 2 = 3	2 + 2 = 4	3 + 2 = 5	4 + 2 = 6
1 + 3 = 4	2 + 3 = 5	3 + 3 = 6	4 + 3 = 7
1 + 4 = 5	2 + 4 = 6	3 + 4 = 7	4 + 4 = 8

LOOK BACK

• How can you decide if your answer makes sense?

• What other strategy can you use?

Make a table to solve.

1. What are all the number sentences that can be written using the numbers 1–5 as addends? Which of the number sentences have the same addends but show a different order?

2. Louise has 423 pennies. She has 243 nickels, 324 dimes, and 102 quarters. Order the numbers of coins from least to greatest.

3. Meadow School students collected newspapers. Order the number of papers collected by each class from least to greatest.

Class	Papers
Mrs. Allen	249
Mr. David	361
Mrs. Ray	196
Mrs. Hope	298
Mrs. Lee	347

Mixed Applications

Solve.

CHOOSE a strategy and a tool.
- **Make a Model**
- **Make a Table**
- **Act It Out**
- **Work Backward**

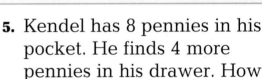

Paper/Pencil   Calculator   Hands-On   Mental Math

4. Sam played soccer for 2 hours. He started playing at the time shown on the clock. At what time did Sam finish playing?

5. Kendel has 8 pennies in his pocket. He finds 4 more pennies in his drawer. How many pennies does Kendel have in all?

6. The third grade had a bake sale. Mr. Keen's class earned $152. Ms. Fu's class earned $125, and Mrs. Day's class earned $251. Order the amounts of money from least to greatest.

7. John bought a large drink for $2.25. He bought a bag of popcorn for $1.00. How much did John spend in all?

8. Grace saw 12 elephants and 5 seals at the circus. How many more elephants than seals did Grace see?

Subtraction Strategies

VOCABULARY

difference

counting back

counting up

sames

zeros

Why learn this? You can find how many you have left when you have used some of them.

Tim bought 5 cans of turkey dinner and 2 cans of tuna dinner for his kitten. How many more cans of turkey dinner than tuna dinner did he buy?

$$5 - 2 = 3 \qquad \begin{array}{r} 5 \\ -2 \\ \hline 3 \end{array} \leftarrow \text{difference}$$

So, Tim bought 3 more cans of turkey dinner.

Here are some ways to find differences.

REMEMBER:

Subtraction is finding how many are left or finding the difference when two groups are compared.

$4 - 1 = 3$

Counting Back When you subtract 1, 2, or 3, *count back* to find the difference.

$$5 - 2 = \underline{}$$

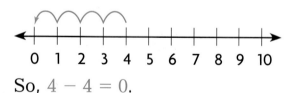

Count: 5 . . . 4, 3.
So, $5 - 2 = 3$.

Counting Up Begin with a smaller number and *count up* to a larger number.

$$9 - 7 = \underline{}$$

Count: 7 . . . 8, 9.
So, $9 - 7 = 2$.

Sames When you subtract a number from the *same* number, the difference is zero.

$$4 - 4 = \underline{}$$

So, $4 - 4 = 0$.

Zeros When you subtract *zero* from a number, the difference is that number.

$$4 - 0 = \underline{}$$

So, $4 - 0 = 4$.

Talk About It

• How do you count back to find $11 - 3$?

CRITICAL THINKING Explain how you know that $56 - 56 = 0$.

▶ CHECK

Find the difference. Tell if you used *counting back, counting up, sames,* or *zeros.*

1. 6
   −2
   ___

2. 7
   −7
   ___

3. 8
   −0
   ___

4. 8
   −6
   ___

5. 9
   −3
   ___

▶ PRACTICE

Find the difference.

6. 5
   −1
   ___

7. 6
   −6
   ___

8. 8
   −5
   ___

9. 7
   −0
   ___

10. 4
    −3
    ___

11. 9
    −0
    ___

12. 7
    −2
    ___

13. 3
    −3
    ___

14. 8
    −4
    ___

15. 6
    −0
    ___

16. 8
    −3
    ___

17. 5
    −0
    ___

18. 9
    −7
    ___

19. 10
    − 1
    ___

20. 9
    −9
    ___

Problem Solving • Mixed Applications

21. **Mental Math** Sharon's mother bought 4 kitten toys. She gave 1 to each of the 4 kittens. How many toys are left?

22. Bob has 6 black mollies and 3 guppies in his fish tank. How many more black mollies than guppies does Bob have?

23. Nick's cat had 7 kittens. He gave away 5 of the kittens and kept the rest. How many kittens did Nick keep?

24. ▭ **Write a problem** about subtracting the number of pets owned by two friends.

Mixed Review and Test Prep

Write the number that is *greater.* (taught in Grade 2)

25. 431 or 393 26. 124 or 214 27. 736 or 756 28. 188 or 818 29. 550 or 505

Choose the letter of the number that is *less.* (taught in Grade 2)

30. 299 or 922   **A** 292   **B** 922   **C** 299   **D** 229

31. 311 or 113   **F** 311   **G** 313   **H** 113   **J** 133

32. 448 or 458   **A** 448   **B** 458   **C** 484   **D** 488

MORE PRACTICE page H69

11

Fact Families

Why learn this? You can find how many you have in all or how many you have left.

Mark had 4 ladybugs. He found 2 more. How many ladybugs does he have now?

$4 + 2 = 6$

So, Mark has 6 ladybugs.

Mark gives 2 of his 6 ladybugs to his sister. How many ladybugs does he have left?

$6 - 2 = 4$

So, Mark has 4 ladybugs left.

Addition and subtraction are **opposite** operations. They undo each other. So, $4 + 2 = 6$ and $6 - 4 = 2$ show opposite operations.

REMEMBER:

Add to find how many in all.

$2 + 2 = 4$

Subtract to find how many are left.

$4 - 2 = 2$

A fact family is a set of related addition and subtraction number sentences using the same numbers.

Fact Family for 2, 4, 6

$4 + 2 = 6$	$2 + 4 = 6$
$6 - 2 = 4$	$6 - 4 = 2$

The same numbers, 2, 4, and 6, are used in each number sentence.

SCIENCE LINK

Many insects are useful. Ladybugs of one kind were brought from Australia in 1888 to control insects that were destroying citrus trees in California. How many spots are on these two ladybugs?

CRITICAL THINKING How many facts are in a fact family for doubles? Why?

▶ CHECK

Write a related subtraction fact.

1. $6 + 3 = 9$ **2.** $7 + 9 = 16$ **3.** $5 + 4 = 9$

4. $8 + 6 = 14$ **5.** $5 + 7 = 12$ **6.** $6 + 9 = 15$

7. $5 + 8 = 13$ **8.** $4 + 9 = 13$ **9.** $7 + 8 = 15$

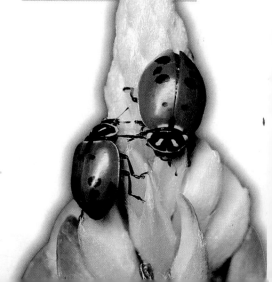

Find the sum. Write a related subtraction fact.

10. $2 + 7 = \underline{\ ?\ }$ **11.** $3 + 9 = \underline{\ ?\ }$ **12.** $7 + 6 = \underline{\ ?\ }$ **13.** $8 + 9 = \underline{\ ?\ }$

Find the difference. Write a related addition fact.

14. $8 - 5 = \underline{\ ?\ }$ **15.** $10 - 6 = \underline{\ ?\ }$ **16.** $12 - 7 = \underline{\ ?\ }$ **17.** $15 - 6 = \underline{\ ?\ }$

Write the missing number to complete each fact in the fact family.

18. $4 + \underline{\ ?\ } = 9$ $5 + \underline{\ ?\ } = 9$ $9 - \underline{\ ?\ } = 4$ $9 - \underline{\ ?\ } = 5$

19. $7 + \underline{\ ?\ } = 15$ $8 + \underline{\ ?\ } = 15$ $15 - \underline{\ ?\ } = 7$ $15 - \underline{\ ?\ } = 8$

Write the fact family for each set of numbers.

20. 3, 4, 7   **21.** 6, 5, 11   **22.** 8, 9, 17

23. 7, 7, 14   **24.** 4, 8, 12   **25.** 6, 7, 13

Problem Solving • Mixed Applications

26. Reasoning Frank had 8 animal stickers. He bought 6 more stickers. Write a number sentence that tells how many stickers he has now. Write the three other facts in the same fact family.

27. **Write About It** Explain how knowing fact families helps you remember facts.

Mixed Review and Test Prep

Write the number just *after* the number that is given.
(taught in Grade 2)

28. 14   **29.** 28   **30.** 37

31. 59   **32.** 70   **33.** 88

Choose the letter of the number which comes just *before* the number that is given. (taught in Grade 2)

34. 20   **A** 21   **B** 22   **C** 18   **D** 19

35. 57   **F** 51   **G** 56   **H** 52   **J** 58

36. 90   **A** 88   **B** 92   **C** 89   **D** 91

Technology Link

In *Mighty Math Carnival Countdown*, the game *Snap Clowns* helps you practice addition and subtraction facts. Use Grow Slide Levels L and O.

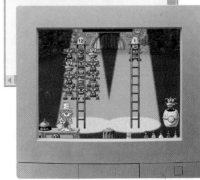

▶ CHECK Understanding

VOCABULARY

1. When one of the addends is close to 10, first _?_ and then add the rest. (page 2)

2. When one of the addends is 1, 2, or 3, you can use _?_ to find the sum. (page 2)

3. When both addends are the same, you are adding _?_. (page 4)

4. When you subtract _?_ from a number, the difference is that number. (page 10)

5. When you subtract 1, 2, or 3, use _?_ to find the difference. (page 10)

Find the sum. Use order in addition to write another addition fact. (pages 6–7)

6. $5 + 7 =$ _?_, so _?_ + _?_ = _?_.   7. $9 + 6 =$ _?_, so _?_ + _?_ = _?_.

▶ CHECK Skills

Find the sum or difference. (pages 2–7, 10–13)

8. $\begin{array}{r} 4 \\ +5 \\ \hline \end{array}$
9. $\begin{array}{r} 15 \\ -\ 9 \\ \hline \end{array}$
10. $\begin{array}{r} 9 \\ +9 \\ \hline \end{array}$
11. $\begin{array}{r} 11 \\ -\ 7 \\ \hline \end{array}$
12. $\begin{array}{r} 7 \\ +8 \\ \hline \end{array}$
13. $\begin{array}{r} 14 \\ -\ 7 \\ \hline \end{array}$

14. $12 - 3 =$ _?_   15. $8 - 8 =$ _?_   16. $6 + 4 =$ _?_   17. $9 - 0 =$ _?_

Write the fact family for each set of numbers. (pages 12–13)

18. 5, 6, 11   19. 8, 9, 17   20. 7, 7, 14

▶ CHECK Problem Solving

Solve. (pages 8–9)

CHOOSE a strategy and a tool.
- Act It Out   • Make a Table
- Write a Number Sentence

Paper/Pencil

Calculator

Hands-On

Mental Math

21. List the addition sentences that can be written using two sets of numbers 1–3. Which sentences have the same addends but show a different order?

22. David has 18 books about birds. His brother has 9 books. How many fewer books does David's brother have?

Test Prep

Choose the best answer.

1. Mrs. Brown made 2 sandwiches for each of her 5 grandchildren. Count how many sandwiches she made.

   A 5   **B** 10
   C 6   **D** 1

2. Mitzi has 3 kittens. Each kitten has 1 bowl for food and 1 bowl for water. How many bowls are there for all the kittens?

   F 7   **G** 6
   H 5   **J** 1

3. David has 9¢. Laura has 6¢. How much more money does David have than Laura?

   A 2¢
   B 1¢
   C 4¢
   D 3¢

4. Jonathan picked 4 apples. His brother picked 9 apples. How many apples did they pick?

   F 15   **G** 16
   H 13   **J** 12

5.   8
     +9

   A 16   **B** 17
   C 18   **D** 19

6. Kim's mother gave him some money. Look at the picture. How much money did she give him?

   F 25¢   **G** 3¢
   H 5¢   **J** 11¢

7. Tyler's dog had 8 puppies. Tyler gave away 5 puppies. How many did he keep?

   A 4   **B** 3
   C 13   **D** 12

8. Beth has 18 books about cats. Her sister has 9 books about birds. How many fewer books does Beth's sister have?

   F 8
   G 10
   H 9
   J 6

9. Mrs. Jackson has $15. She sees a pin for $4 and a picture for $6. If she buys the picture, which shows how to find how much money she will have left?

   A $15 − $4
   B $15 − $4 − $6
   C $15 + $6
   D $15 − $6

2 PLACE VALUE IN ADDITION

The fastest sharks are the great white and the mako. They can swim more than 40 miles an hour. Generally, sharks swim at a slow speed until they see their prey.

Sharks

Imagine that your group has been asked to help select sharks for a new aquarium.

Choose a variety of sharks. The shark tank can hold three sharks. Their combined length should be no more than 50 feet.

- Use the chart on shark lengths to make your selections.

- List at least ten possible combinations of three sharks.

- Add their lengths to show that their total length is no more than 50 feet.

Dogfish Shark		4 ft
Horn Shark		4 ft
Blue Shark		9 ft
Bull Shark		9 ft
Mako Shark		9 ft
Hammerhead Shark		15 ft
Thresher Shark		15 ft
Great White Shark		18 ft
Greenland Shark		18 ft
Basking Shark		25 ft

DID YOU

☑ use the chart on shark lengths to make your selections?

☑ list at least ten possible combinations of three sharks?

☑ add their lengths to show their total length?

☑ share your project with the class?

4 feet Dogfish Shark
9 feet Bull Shark
+15 feet Hammerhead Shark
28 feet

9 feet Blue Shark
9 feet Bull Shark
+18 feet Great White Shark
36 feet

4 feet Dogfish Shark
4 feet Horn Shark
+25 feet Basking Shark
33 feet

More Than Two Addends

Why learn this? You will know how to add three or more numbers when you go shopping.

Sharon went food shopping. She bought 5 pounds of potatoes, 3 pounds of carrots, and 2 pounds of tomatoes. How many pounds of vegetables did she buy?

$$5 + 3 + 2 = \underline{\ ?\ }$$

  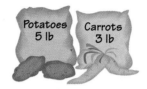

At the market

$5 + (3 + 2) = \underline{\ ?\ }$ $(5 + 3) + 2 = \underline{\ ?\ }$ Add the numbers

$5 + \quad 5 \quad = 10$ $8 \quad + 2 = 10$ in ( ) first.

So, Sharon bought 10 pounds of vegetables.

> Group the addends in different ways. The sum is always the same. $5 + (3 + 2) = 10$ and $(5 + 3) + 2 = 10$

Talk About It

• How many ways can you group three addends to find a sum? Give an example.

• What happens to the sum when you group the three addends in different ways? Why?

CRITICAL THINKING Show all the ways you can group the addends to find $2 + 3 + 4 + 5$.

▶ CHECK
Find the sum.

1. $(4 + 5) + 1 = \underline{\ ?\ }$ **2.** $(3 + 9) + 2 = \underline{\ ?\ }$

3. $5 + (8 + 2) = \underline{\ ?\ }$ **4.** $(7 + 3) + 8 = \underline{\ ?\ }$

5. $6 + (5 + 5) = \underline{\ ?\ }$ **6.** $5 + (6 + 4) = \underline{\ ?\ }$

Technology Link

In **Mighty Math Zoo Zillions**, the game *Fish Stories* challenges you to add and subtract numbers. Use Grow Slide Level I.

Find the sum.

7. $(1 + 4) + 5 =$ ___?___   **8.** $5 + (6 + 2) =$ ___?___   **9.** $(4 + 6) + 4 =$ ___?___

10. $3 + (3 + 7) =$ ___?___   **11.** $(9 + 1) + 5 =$ ___?___   **12.** $(3 + 2) + 9 =$ ___?___

13. $1 + (8 + 8) =$ ___?___   **14.** $(5 + 5) + 7 =$ ___?___   **15.** $5 + (3 + 3) =$ ___?___

Group the addends. Then find the sum.

16. $3 + 1 + 5 =$ ___?___   **17.** $4 + 6 + 5 =$ ___?___   **18.** $2 + 8 + 6 =$ ___?___

19. $7 + 7 + 6 =$ ___?___   **20.** $9 + 1 + 9 =$ ___?___   **21.** $8 + 7 + 3 =$ ___?___

Problem Solving • Mixed Applications

Using Data For Problems 22–23, use the table.

22. Tim's class kept track of rainy days during three months. How many days did it rain in the three months?

Rainy Days		
September	October	November
6	8	4

23. **Science** How many fewer days did it rain in September than in October?

24. Drake rode his bike 6 miles on Monday and 4 miles on Tuesday. He rode 5 miles on Wednesday. How many miles did Drake ride?

25. **Mental Math** At the sea aquarium, Anna saw 2 horn sharks, 3 blue sharks, and 3 mako sharks. How many sharks did she see in all?

26. ✏️ **Write a problem** about the information in this list. Solve it.

6 guppies
4 tetras
6 angelfish

Mixed Review and Test Prep

Find the sum. (pages 2–3)

27. $3 + 7 =$ ___?___   **28.** $5 + 8 =$ ___?___   **29.** $9 + 4 =$ ___?___   **30.** $6 + 6 =$ ___?___

Choose the letter of the correct answer. (pages 10–11)

31. $5 - 3 =$ ___?___   **A** 8   **B** 4   **C** 2   **D** 1

32. $7 - 4 =$ ___?___   **F** 3   **G** 2   **H** 11   **J** 4

33. $9 - 7 =$ ___?___   **A** 1   **B** 3   **C** 0   **D** 2

Using Place Value to Regroup

You will investigate how to add two-digit numbers.

Use base-ten blocks to find the sum.

▶ EXPLORE

MATERIALS: base-ten blocks

MODEL

Find $46 + 27 = $? .

Step 1

Use 4 tens 6 ones to show 46. Use 2 tens 7 ones to show 27.

tens	ones
4	6
+2	7

Step 2

Add the ones. $6 + 7 = 13$. Show how to regroup. Add the tens.

tens	ones
4	6
+2	7

Record

Explain how you used base-ten blocks to regroup to find $46 + 27$.

Talk About It

- What is another name for 13 ones?

- What does it mean to regroup in addition?

- When do you regroup in addition?

▶ **TRY THIS**

1. Use base-ten blocks to find 28 + 93 = _?_ .

2. ▭ **Write About It** How did you use the blocks to find the sum?

▶ **PRACTICE**

Use base-ten blocks. Write *yes* or *no* to tell if you need to regroup. Find the sum.

3.
tens	ones
3	6
+2	3

4.
tens	ones
4	8
+1	2

5.
tens	ones
2	5
+6	6

6.
tens	ones
4	7
+5	2

7.
tens	ones
8	3
+7	9

Find the sum.

8. 24
   +15

9. 18
   +32

10. 36
    +45

11. 53
    +25

12. 65
    +27

13. 78
    +43

14. 12
    +98

15. 63
    +79

16. 94
    +77

17. 99
    +99

Problem Solving • Mixed Applications

18. Tim read 43 animal books and 38 mysteries. How many books did Tim read in all?

19. **Consumer** In Sue's class, 14 students bought hot lunches and 15 students brought lunches from home. How many students ate lunch?

20. **Music** The chorus sang 14 songs in the first program and 16 songs in the second program. How many songs did they sing altogether?

21. ▭ **Write a problem** about a field trip. Use two-digit numbers. Find the sum.

Technology Link

◉ You can add two-digit numbers by using E-Lab, Activity 2. Available on CD-ROM and on the Internet at www.hbschool.com/elab

Adding Two-Digit Numbers

Why learn this? You can find the total distance traveled.

Ruth's family took a trip to Deer Lake. They drove 56 miles each way. How far did Ruth's family travel to the lake and back?

Add to find how far they traveled.

A trip to the lake

MODEL

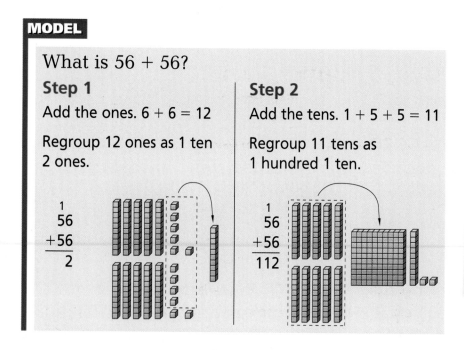

What is 56 + 56?

Step 1

Add the ones. 6 + 6 = 12

Regroup 12 ones as 1 ten 2 ones.

$$\begin{array}{r} 1 \\ 56 \\ +56 \\ \hline 2 \end{array}$$

Step 2

Add the tens. 1 + 5 + 5 = 11

Regroup 11 tens as 1 hundred 1 ten.

$$\begin{array}{r} 1 \\ 56 \\ +56 \\ \hline 112 \end{array}$$

REMEMBER:

When you *regroup* you exchange amounts of equal value.

1 ten = 10 ones

So, Ruth's family traveled 112 miles.

• What is the greatest sum you can get by adding 2 two-digit numbers? Explain.

A trip to the lake

▶ CHECK

Write *yes* or *no* to tell if you need to regroup. Find the sum.

1.

tens	ones
8	7
+2	6

2.

tens	ones
3	2
+4	5

3.

tens	ones
2	4
+6	9

4. $\begin{array}{r} 81 \\ +18 \\ \hline \end{array}$
5. $\begin{array}{r} 7 \\ +17 \\ \hline \end{array}$
6. $\begin{array}{r} 50 \\ +27 \\ \hline \end{array}$
7. $\begin{array}{r} 63 \\ +19 \\ \hline \end{array}$
8. $\begin{array}{r} 28 \\ +\ 4 \\ \hline \end{array}$
9. $\begin{array}{r} 77 \\ +18 \\ \hline \end{array}$

Find the sum.

10. $\begin{array}{r} 49 \\ +99 \\ \hline \end{array}$	**11.** $\begin{array}{r} 47 \\ +\ 8 \\ \hline \end{array}$	**12.** $\begin{array}{r} 72 \\ +16 \\ \hline \end{array}$	**13.** $\begin{array}{r} 85 \\ +30 \\ \hline \end{array}$	**14.** $\begin{array}{r} 29 \\ +40 \\ \hline \end{array}$
15. $\begin{array}{r} 14 \\ +25 \\ \hline \end{array}$	**16.** $\begin{array}{r} 36 \\ +42 \\ \hline \end{array}$	**17.** $\begin{array}{r} 18 \\ +71 \\ \hline \end{array}$	**18.** $\begin{array}{r} 25 \\ +37 \\ \hline \end{array}$	**19.** $\begin{array}{r} 46 \\ +24 \\ \hline \end{array}$
20. $\begin{array}{r} 56 \\ +62 \\ \hline \end{array}$	**21.** $\begin{array}{r} 74 \\ +35 \\ \hline \end{array}$	**22.** $\begin{array}{r} 81 \\ +53 \\ \hline \end{array}$	**23.** $\begin{array}{r} 94 \\ +46 \\ \hline \end{array}$	**24.** $\begin{array}{r} 68 \\ +59 \\ \hline \end{array}$

Problem Solving • Mixed Applications

25. Mental Math Paula used 15 gallons of water to take a shower. Her brother used 20 gallons. How many gallons of water did they use in all for showers?

26. Science You can save up to 9 gallons of water each time you brush your teeth if you run the water only to rinse your brush. About how much water would you save each day if you brushed your teeth two times?

27. Number Sense Tyrone and his friends went fishing. They caught 18 fish. Ten of the fish were bass. The rest were trout. How many trout did they catch?

28. ✏ **Write a problem** using the following information. Then solve it. The Wilson family drove 16 hours to visit their grandparents.

Mixed Review and Test Prep

Find the sum. Use order in addition to write another addition fact. (pages 6–7)

29. $6 + 5 = \underline{\ ?\ }$, so $\underline{\ ?\ } + \underline{\ ?\ } = \underline{\ ?\ }$.

30. $2 + 8 = \underline{\ ?\ }$, so $\underline{\ ?\ } + \underline{\ ?\ } = \underline{\ ?\ }$.

31. $7 + 8 = \underline{\ ?\ }$, so $\underline{\ ?\ } + \underline{\ ?\ } = \underline{\ ?\ }$.

32. $4 + 9 = \underline{\ ?\ }$, so $\underline{\ ?\ } + \underline{\ ?\ } = \underline{\ ?\ }$.

33. $9 + 6 = \underline{\ ?\ }$, so $\underline{\ ?\ } + \underline{\ ?\ } = \underline{\ ?\ }$.

34. $7 + 5 = \underline{\ ?\ }$, so $\underline{\ ?\ } + \underline{\ ?\ } = \underline{\ ?\ }$.

Choose the letter of the correct sum. (pages 4–5)

35. $8 + 9 = \underline{\ ?\ }$ **A** 18   **B** 14   **C** 12   **D** 17

36. $6 + 7 = \underline{\ ?\ }$ **F** 1   **G** 13   **H** 14   **J** 12

Estimating Sums and Differences

VOCABULARY

estimate
round

Why learn this? You can use an estimate to find *about how many* manatees where counted in all and *about how many* more adult than baby manatees were counted.

At Blue Springs, some students counted 28 adult manatees and 15 baby manatees. About how many manatees did the students count in all?

You are finding an **estimate** when you round numbers to find *about how many*.

Use a number line to help you.

When you **round** a number to the nearest ten, you find the ten that is the closest.

Talk About It

- Is 28 closer to 20 or to 30?

- What is the least whole number that rounds to 20?

- What is the greatest whole number that rounds to 20?

- Is 15 closer to 10 or to 20?

When a number is halfway between 2 tens, round to the greater ten. Since 15 is halfway between 10 and 20, round 15 to 20.

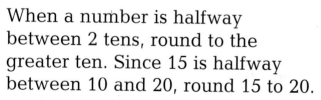

$$28 \rightarrow 30$$
$$\underline{+15} \rightarrow \underline{+20}$$
$$50$$

So, the students counted about 50 manatees.

You can also estimate to find *about how many more*.

About how many more adult manatees than baby manatees did the students count?

$$
\begin{array}{r@{}l}
28 &\rightarrow\ \ \ 30 \\
-15 &\rightarrow -20 \\
\hline
&\ \ \ \ 10
\end{array}
$$

So, the students counted about 10 more adult manatees than baby manatees.

You can round larger numbers to the nearest hundred by finding the hundred each number is closer to.

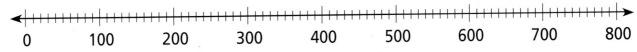

| 0 | 100 | 200 | 300 | 400 | 500 | 600 | 700 | 800 |

EXAMPLES

A
$$
\begin{array}{r@{}l}
180 &\rightarrow\ \ \ 200 \\
-110 &\rightarrow -100 \\
\hline
&\ \ \ 100
\end{array}
$$

B
$$
\begin{array}{r@{}l}
520 &\rightarrow\ \ \ 500 \\
+270 &\rightarrow +300 \\
\hline
&\ \ \ 800
\end{array}
$$

C
$$
\begin{array}{r@{}l}
390 &\rightarrow\ \ \ 400 \\
+440 &\rightarrow +400 \\
\hline
&\ \ \ 800
\end{array}
$$

D
$$
\begin{array}{r@{}l}
430 &\rightarrow\ \ \ 400 \\
+220 &\rightarrow +200 \\
\hline
&\ \ \ 600
\end{array}
$$

- In Example A, why is 180 rounded to 200?

- In Example B, why is it easier to add 500 and 300 than to add 520 and 270?

▶ CHECK

Round each number to the nearest ten or hundred. Use the number lines to help you.

1. 17   **2.** 22   **3.** 29   **4.** 11   **5.** 190   **6.** 210

Estimate each sum or difference by rounding. Show your work.

7. 23
      +12

8. 18
      +14

9. 47
      −26

10. 35
       +15

11. 91
       −13

12. 78
       +19

13. 270
       −210

14. 480
       +320

LESSON CONTINUES

Write the number that is halfway between the 2 tens.

15. 30 and 40   **16.** 60 and 70   **17.** 80 and 90

Round each number to the nearest ten or hundred.

18. 12   **19.** 18   **20.** 24   **21.** 37   **22.** 48

23. 53   **24.** 160   **25.** 280   **26.** 380   **27.** 490

Estimate each sum or difference by rounding.

28.
$$12 \\ +13$$

29.
$$14 \\ +22$$

30.
$$34 \\ -18$$

31.
$$29 \\ +43$$

32.
$$25 \\ +32$$

33.
$$52 \\ -37$$

34.
$$41 \\ -16$$

35.
$$15 \\ +39$$

36.
$$21 \\ +16$$

37.
$$78 \\ -23$$

38.
$$48 \\ +24$$

39.
$$340 \\ -280$$

40.
$$62 \\ +37$$

41.
$$250 \\ +450$$

42.
$$11 \\ +59$$

43.
$$46 \\ -12$$

44.
$$61 \\ -16$$

45.
$$390 \\ -180$$

46.
$$35 \\ -19$$

47.
$$270 \\ +230$$

Problem Solving • Mixed Applications

48. Time The class watched the lions for 30 minutes. Then they spent 15 minutes feeding the monkeys. For how many minutes did they watch the lions and feed the monkeys?

49. Ashley took 25 pictures at the zoo. Christine took 36 pictures. About how many pictures did they take in all?

50. Estimation To the nearest ten, a bag contains 80 pennies. What is the least number of pennies that can be in the bag? the greatest number?

51. Mental Math Jerry is 8 years old. In 9 years he will be as old as his brother is now. How old is his brother now?

52. ▣ **Write About It** Explain how a number line can help you in rounding numbers.

Manatees are mammals that live in warm fresh water and seawater. In Florida, there are laws to protect them.

53. The ranger told the students about manatees. There were 18 students in one group and 17 students in another. About how many students heard the ranger?

54. **Science** Manatees have no front teeth. They have 6 to 7 molars on each side of their jaw, top and bottom. The molars are replaced by new ones as the old ones wear out. About how many molars does a manatee have in all?

55. **Weather** Manatees migrate to areas with warmer waters when the water temperature drops below about 70 degrees. About how many degrees too cold for the manatees is the water if its temperature drops to 59 degrees?

56. **Reasoning** Manatees eat about 100 pounds of wet plants each day. How many pounds of plants do they eat in one week? How can you use skip counting to find the answer?

SCIENCE LINK

Manatees weigh about 1,200 pounds and measure about 10 feet in length. All manatees eat plants. If a manatee eats 89 pounds of plants one day and 91 pounds a second day, how much does it eat in the two days?

Mixed Review and Test Prep

Find the sum. (pages 6–7)

57. $0 + 4 =$? **58.** $7 + 0 =$? **59.** $0 + 9 =$? **60.** $5 + 0 =$?

Write a related subtraction fact. (pages 12–13)

61. $3 + 6 = 9$ **62.** $2 + 8 = 10$ **63.** $5 + 8 = 13$ **64.** $7 + 9 = 16$

Choose the letter of the correct difference. (pages 10–11)

65. $13 - 7 =$?

  A 20   **B** 7

  C 6   **D** 10

66. $15 - 6 =$?

  F 9   **G** 8

  H 7   **J** 11

67. $12 - 5 =$?

  A 6   **B** 9

  C 8   **D** 7

Choosing Addition or Subtraction

Why learn this? You can find the total number of students in your class and how many more boys or girls there are.

Decide if you would add or subtract to solve these problems.

A. Betsy's science class watched *The Curious Wolf*. There are 12 girls and 10 boys in Betsy's class. How many students watched the video?

B. Jim had some baseball cards. His dad gave him 9 more. Then Jim had 17 baseball cards. How many cards did Jim have to begin with?

Talk About It

• In which of the problems would you *add* to find the answer? Why?

• In which of the problems would you *subtract* to find the answer? Why?

• Tell how you solved Problems A and B.

CRITICAL THINKING Give examples of problems where you need to *add* or *subtract.*

▶ CHECK

Tell if you need to *add* or *subtract*. Solve.

1. There are 18 videos on the top shelf. There are 12 videos on the second shelf. How many videos are on the two shelves?

2. Joel has 24 baseball cards. Dana has 12 fewer cards. How many cards does Dana have?

REMEMBER:

Use *addition*
• to join two groups.
• to find how many in all.

$$4 + 8 = 12$$

Use *subtraction*
• to compare.
• to find how many are left.

$$12 - 8 = 4$$

• to find a missing part.

$$12 - \underline{\ ?\ } = 8$$

SCIENCE LINK

A wolf looks like a large dog. It can see and hear very well. It can smell another animal more than a mile away. An adult wolf has 42 teeth. An adult person has 32 teeth. How many more teeth does a wolf have than a person?

Calculator Activities page H66

▶ PRACTICE

Tell if you need to *add* or *subtract*. Solve.

3. Amanda's new computer program has 25 video games. She already had 11 video games. How many video games does she have altogether?

4. There were some flowers in Brittany's garden. Then she planted 15 more flowers. Now she has 28 flowers. How many flowers were in Brittany's garden to begin with?

5. Matthew counted 22 children ice-skating at the rink at one o'clock. He counted 46 children skating at four o'clock. How many more children were skating at four o'clock?

6. Raymond spent 25 minutes on the Internet. Randy was on the Internet for 36 minutes. How many minutes were they on the Internet in all?

Problem Solving • Mixed Applications

Using Data For Problems 7–10, use the scoreboard.

7. **Compare** How many more points did the home team score than the visitors?

8. **Sports** During the first half of the game, the home team scored 15 points. How many points did they score in the second half of the game?

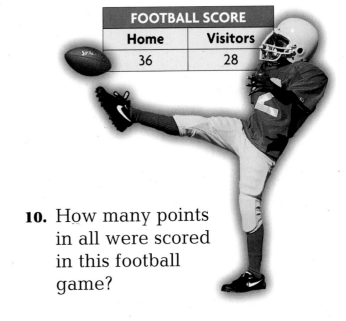

FOOTBALL SCORE	
Home	Visitors
36	28

9. **Visual Thinking** During last week's game, the home team scored 29 points. How many more points did they score in this week's game?

10. How many points in all were scored in this football game?

11. **Reasoning** Lani collected 32 football cards. Harry gave her some cards. Then she had 55 cards. How many cards did Harry give Lani?

12. ▭ **Write About It** What are some ways to get an answer of 20? Write some number sentences.

LESSON CONTINUES ▷

Problem-Solving Strategy: Write a Number Sentence

▶ **THE PROBLEM** Jamie got a fish tank for his birthday. He bought 14 guppies, 10 neon tetras, and 8 swordtails. His sister gave him 3 black mollies. How many fish does Jamie have in all?

REMEMBER:

UNDERSTAND

PLAN

SOLVE

LOOK BACK

UNDERSTAND

• What are you asked to find?

• What information will you use?

• Is there any information you will not use? If so, what?

PLAN

• What strategy can you use to solve the problem?

You know how many fish Jamie bought. You know how many fish his sister gave him. So, *write a number sentence* to find how many fish he has in all.

SOLVE

• What number sentence can you write?

$14 + 10 + 8 + 3 = \underline{\ ?\ }$

$$
\begin{array}{r}
14 \\
10 \\
8 \\
+\ 3 \\
\hline
35
\end{array}
$$

So, Jamie has 35 fish in all.

LOOK BACK

• How can you decide if your answer makes sense?

• What other strategy can you use?

Write a number sentence to solve.

1. For her fish tank, Tanya bought 12 swordtails, 6 neon tetras, and 8 guppies. How many fish does Tanya have in all?

2. Mario's class visited a farm. They saw 6 horses, 4 pigs, 12 cows, and 14 ducks. How many animals did the class see at the farm?

3. Alexis collected 8 bottles the first week and 5 the second week. She collected 11 bottles the third week and 10 the fourth week. How many bottles did she collect in 4 weeks?

4. Jordan rode his bike 6 miles on a bike path. The bike path is 18 miles long. How many more miles does Jordan have to ride his bike to complete the bike path?

Mixed Applications

Solve.

CHOOSE a strategy and a tool.		
• Make a Table • Write a Number Sentence	• Act It Out • Draw a Picture	Paper/Pencil Calculator Hands-On Mental Math

5. Colleen has 3 pets. Laurel has 11 pets. Shannon has 5 pets. How many pets do the three girls have?

6. How many more pets does Laurel have than Colleen? than Shannon?

7. Molly has these coins in her pocket. How much money does Molly have?

8. Corey has 24 football cards. Mike has 14 football cards. How many more cards does Corey have?

9. At the book fair, 187 books were sold to first graders, 212 books to second graders, and 225 books to third graders. Fourth graders bought 178 books, and fifth graders bought 256 books. Which grade bought the most books? the fewest books?

10. On Monday, Edgar read 14 pages of his library book before school. During reading class, he read 12 more pages. After school, he read 9 more pages. How many pages of his library book did Edgar read on Monday?

▶ CHECK Understanding

Group the addends. Then find the sum. (pages 18–19)

1. $5 + 7 + 3 =$?   **2.** $3 + 6 + 4 =$?   **3.** $8 + 5 + 4 =$?

Write *yes* or *no* to tell if you need to regroup.
Find the sum. (pages 22–23)

4. 71	**5.** 45	**6.** 67	**7.** 29	**8.** 23
+26	+37	+66	+19	+71

Round each number to the nearest ten. (pages 24–27)

9. 12   **10.** 25   **11.** 33   **12.** 49   **13.** 57   **14.** 98

▶ CHECK Skills

Find the sum. (pages 18–19, 20–23)

15. $3 + (5 + 5) =$?   **16.** $(6 + 2) + 8 =$?   **17.** $(3 + 7) + 5 =$?

18. 53	**19.** 39	**20.** 45	**21.** 14	**22.** 78
+28	+71	+48	+66	+37

Estimate each sum or difference by rounding. (pages 24–27)

23. 81	**24.** 58	**25.** 65	**26.** 79	**27.** 290
−17	+22	+31	− 8	+170

▶ CHECK Problem Solving

Solve. (pages 28–31)

CHOOSE a strategy and a tool.

- Make a Table
- Draw a Picture
- Act It Out
- Write a Number Sentence

 Paper/Pencil   Calculator   Hands-On   Mental Math

28. One week, Mr. Lewis sold 69 fish. The next week, he sold 87 fish. How many fish did he sell in the two weeks?

29. There are 46 penguins swimming or eating. There are 32 penguins taking naps. How many penguins are there in all?

30. On the bus, Ben is sitting in front of Lisa. Ben is in back of Todd. Lisa is in front of Sue. In what order are the children?

31. James had some baseball cards. Then he got 12 more cards. Now he has 18. How many cards did James have to begin with?

Test Prep

Choose the best answer.

1. Jason set up 75 chairs on Monday. He set up the same number on Tuesday. How many chairs did he set up in two days?

   A 100   **B** 150   **C** 125   **D** 75

2. Amy packed 29 books in a box. Tammy packed 38 books. About how many more books did Tammy pack than Amy?

   F 12   **G** 10   **H** 9   **J** 11

3. Nellie brought 8 apples and 9 oranges to the class party. If every child had one piece of fruit, how many children are in the class?

   A 10   **B** 17   **C** 11   **D** 18

4. Every day, the Grove Bus travels 18 miles on its route. One day, the bus broke down after 9 miles. How many miles were left to finish the route?

   F 8   **G** 9   **H** 7   **J** 6

5. A group of 9 third graders, 8 fourth graders, and 8 adults visited the zoo. How many went to the zoo?

   A 20   **B** 19   **C** 30   **D** 25

6. $\begin{array}{r} 93 \\ +36 \\ \hline \end{array}$

   F 130   **G** 139   **H** 129   **J** 120

7. $9 - 4 = \underline{\ ?\ }$

   A 7   **B** 4   **C** 6   **D** 5

8. The librarian read to the children for 30 minutes. Then the children spent 15 minutes choosing books to read. How many minutes did the children spend at the library?

   F 40 minutes
   G 45 minutes
   H 15 minutes
   J 25 minutes

9. This chart shows the number of votes each video received.

FAVORITE VIDEOS	
Video	Votes
Curious Dog	36
Mystery Spaceship	29
Arnie the Alligator	24
Homerun Kid	32

   Which video received the greatest number of votes?

   A Mystery Spaceship
   B Arnie the Alligator
   C Curious Dog
   D Homerun Kid

10. Carol needs 28 ham sandwiches and 33 tuna sandwiches for the party. About how many sandwiches does she need?

   F 60   **G** 40   **H** 50   **J** 53

3 PLACE VALUE IN SUBTRACTION

34

ART LINK

In 1848 Esther Howland, of Massachusetts, began a business, making handmade valentines. Not many women owned a business then. She set up the work in her parents' house and hired other women.

Greeting Card Assembly Line

Suppose your class wants to make greeting cards using the supplies shown.

Do you have enough supplies to make one greeting card for each person in your class? Will there be supplies left over?

- Design a greeting card using the materials shown.

- Decide how many of each item you need to make a greeting card for each person in your class.

- Figure out how many of each item will be left over.

- Make a table to show what supplies you need and what will be left over.

ART SUPPLIES

106 candies
72 doilies
60 stickers
100 sheets of construction paper

DID YOU

- ✓ design a greeting card?

- ✓ find out how many of each item would be left over after making a greeting card for each person in your class?

- ✓ make a table to show your results?

How many we had	1 student used	2 students used	
106 candies	30	60	
72 doilies	30	60	
60 stickers	30	60	
sheets of	30	60	

Using Place Value to Regroup

You will investigate how to subtract two-digit numbers.

Use base-ten blocks to find the difference.

► EXPLORE

MATERIALS: base-ten blocks

MODEL

Find:

tens	ones
4	2
−1	3

Step 1

Use 4 tens and 2 ones to show 42.

Step 2

Subtract the ones. Since 3 > 2, regroup your blocks to solve the problem.

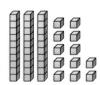

Complete the subtraction.

Record

Explain how you used the base-ten blocks to find the difference.

Talk About It

• What is another name for 3 tens 12 ones?

• How do the blocks help you show regrouping in subtraction?

► TRY THIS

1. Use base-ten blocks to find 31 − 16 = __?__.

2. ✏️ **Write About It** How did you use the blocks to find the difference?

▶ PRACTICE

Use base-ten blocks. Write *yes* or *no* to tell if you need to regroup. Find the difference.

3.
tens	ones
2	3
−1	4

4.
tens	ones
4	4
−3	6

5.
tens	ones
3	1
−1	1

6.
tens	ones
6	3
−2	5

7.
tens	ones
8	8
−4	7

Find the difference. You may wish to use base-ten blocks.

8. 26 −17

9. 21 −14

10. 34 −24

11. 23 −15

12. 35 −18

13. 43 −25

14. 59 −43

15. 43 −32

16. 64 −15

17. 53 −22

18. 73 −47

19. 91 −44

20. 83 −24

21. 91 −12

22. 96 −78

Problem Solving • Mixed Applications

23. Money Christine had 95¢. She bought glitter for 39¢ and stickers for 28¢. How much money does she have left?

24. Collections At the beach Lindsey collected 38 seashells. Bill collected 15 more seashells than Lindsey. How many seashells did Bill collect?

25. Reasoning Josh had 25 stamps in his stamp collection. He traded some stamps for baseball cards. He now has 9 stamps. How many fewer stamps does Josh have now?

26. ✏️ **Write a problem** using subtraction.

Technology Link

💿 You can subtract two-digit numbers by using E-Lab, Activity 3. Available on CD-ROM and on the Internet at www.hbschool.com/elab

Subtracting Two-Digit Numbers

Why learn this? You can subtract to find how many more cupcakes are chocolate than yellow.

For the party Paul's mother made 24 chocolate cupcakes and 18 yellow cupcakes. How many more chocolate cupcakes than yellow cupcakes did she make?

$$24 - 18 = \underline{\ ?\ }$$

Use base-ten blocks to help you subtract.

MODEL

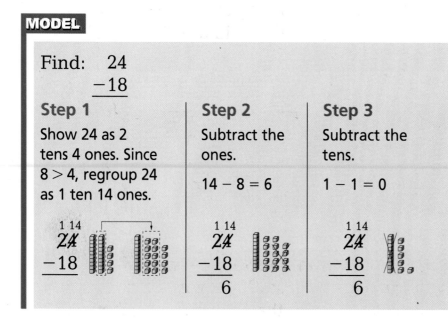

Find: 24
       −18

Step 1
Show 24 as 2 tens 4 ones. Since 8 > 4, regroup 24 as 1 ten 14 ones.

Step 2
Subtract the ones.

$14 - 8 = 6$

Step 3
Subtract the tens.

$1 - 1 = 0$

So, Paul's mother made 6 more chocolate cupcakes than yellow cupcakes.

Talk About It

• In Step 1, how did you regroup 24?

CRITICAL THINKING Why is 39 never regrouped for subtraction?

▶ CHECK

Find the difference. Regroup if needed.

1.	25	2.	88	3.	22	4.	61
	−16		−45		−19		−32

Technology Link

In *Mighty Math Carnival Countdown*, the game *Bubble Band* challenges you to subtract two-digit numbers and use what you are learning about subtraction. Use Grow Slide Level S.

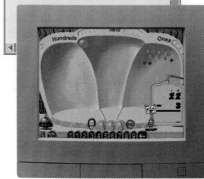

Calculator Activities page H60

Find the difference.

9.	70 −47	**10.**	40 −19	**11.**	90 −78	**12.**	50 −25	**13.**	30 −14
14.	40 −27	**15.**	20 −11	**16.**	60 −12	**17.**	50 −26	**18.**	60 −17
19.	60 −38	**20.**	30 −22	**21.**	70 −24	**22.**	80 −41	**23.**	90 −35

Problem Solving • Mixed Applications

24. Measurement People say Johnny Appleseed walked for miles to take care of his apple trees. Suppose he walked 146 miles one month and 88 miles another month. How many miles did he walk in the two months?

25. Consumer Sarah's mother peeled 16 apples to use for pies. She used all but 3 of the apples. How many apples did she use for pies?

26. Time Sarah and her brother raked leaves for 2 hours. They began at 1:30. At what time did they finish raking leaves?

27. ✏️ **Write a problem** using subtraction and this information. There are 30 jars of apple butter on one shelf and 15 jars on another shelf.

Mixed Review and Test Prep

Round each number to the nearest ten or hundred. (pages 24–27)

28. 14　　**29.** 26　　**30.** 39　　**31.** 41　　**32.** 66　　**33.** 190

Estimate each sum or difference by rounding. Choose the letter of the correct answer. (pages 24–27)

34.	59 +31	**A** 70 **B** 60 **C** 90 **D** 50	**35.**	94 −13	**F** 90 **G** 80 **H** 70 **J** 60	**36.**	46 +18	**A** 40 **B** 50 **C** 60 **D** 70	**37.**	480 −160	**F** 200 **G** 300 **H** 400 **J** 100

Practicing Subtraction

Why learn this? You will be able to find how many more or how many fewer brown horses there are, or how many bales of hay are left in the barn.

The Flying-W Ranch has 24 white horses. It also has 49 brown horses. How many more brown horses than white horses are at the ranch?

Subtract to find *how many more* brown horses than white horses there are.

$$49 - 24 = \underline{\ ?\ } \qquad \begin{array}{r} 49 \\ -24 \\ \hline 25 \end{array}$$

So, there are 25 more brown horses than white horses at the Flying-W Ranch.

REMEMBER:

Compare to find the difference. You can find how many more or how many fewer.

$9 - 3 = 6$

There were 65 bales of hay in the barn. The men loaded 30 bales onto a truck. How many bales of hay are left in the barn?

Subtract to find *how many are left*.

$$65 - 30 = \underline{\ ?\ } \qquad \begin{array}{r} 65 \\ -30 \\ \hline 35 \end{array}$$

So, there are 35 bales of hay left in the barn.

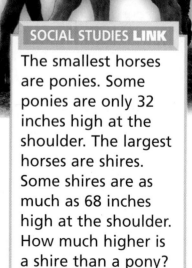

▶ CHECK

1. There are 46 horses in the far pasture and 27 horses in the near pasture. How many more horses are in the far pasture?

2. Sam collected 39 eggs in the hen house. He put 24 eggs into two cartons. How many eggs are left?

SOCIAL STUDIES LINK

The smallest horses are ponies. Some ponies are only 32 inches high at the shoulder. The largest horses are shires. Some shires are as much as 68 inches high at the shoulder. How much higher is a shire than a pony?

Find the difference.

3.	47 −18	**4.** 80 −25	**5.** 99 −70	**6.** 45 −15	**7.** 65 −10
8.	84 −19	**9.** 71 −38	**10.** 23 −14	**11.** 75 −66	**12.** 40 −27

Problem Solving • Mixed Applications

Using Data For Problems 13–14, use the list.

13. **Collecting Data** Joan helps feed the animals on her parents' farm. She made a list of the animals in April. How many fewer horses than cows were on the farm?

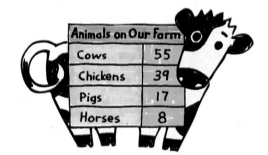

Animals on Our Farm	
Cows	55
Chickens	39
Pigs	17
Horses	8

14. In May Joan's dad bought 6 more cows. He sold 5 pigs. How many cows are now on the farm? How many pigs?

15. Before breakfast Ted collected 21 eggs in the hen house. He collected 14 eggs after school. How many eggs did Ted collect today?

16. **Time** Tom went horseback riding at 2:15 P.M. He rode for 2 hours and 15 minutes. At what time did Tom return?

17. ✏ **Write About It** Write a subtraction problem in which you find how many more or how many are left.

Mixed Review and Test Prep

Compare the numbers. Write <, >, or = for ●. (taught in Grade 2)

18. 45 ● 54   **19.** 67 ● 66   **20.** 41 ● 14   **21.** 25 ● 25   **22.** 17 ● 18

23. 70 ● 70   **24.** 87 ● 78   **25.** 43 ● 34   **26.** 56 ● 65   **27.** 97 ● 98

Count on to find the total. Choose the letter of the correct amount. (taught in Grade 2)

28.   **A** 20¢   **B** 30¢   **C** 45¢   **D** 40¢

29.   **F** 26¢   **G** 31¢   **H** 33¢   **J** 38¢

Using Addition and Subtraction

Why learn this? You can add and subtract to find the number of miles shown on a map from city to city.

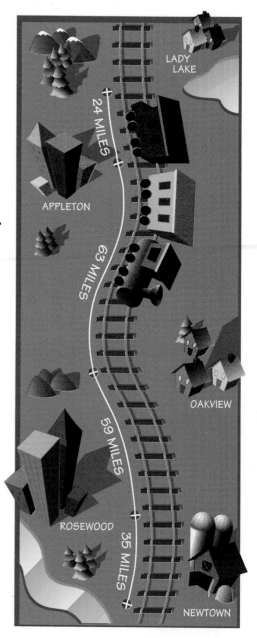

Beth rode the train from Lady Lake to Oakview. How many miles is that?

Add to find the total number of miles.

$$\begin{array}{r} 24 \\ +63 \\ \hline 87 \end{array}\ \begin{array}{l} \text{miles from Lady Lake to Appleton} \\ \text{miles from Appleton to Oakview} \end{array}$$

So, it is 87 miles from Lady Lake to Oakview.

Tom rode the train from Oakview to Rosewood. Sharon rode the train from Rosewood to Newtown. How many more miles did Tom ride the train than Sharon?

Subtract to compare the number of miles.

$$\begin{array}{r} 59 \\ -35 \\ \hline 24 \end{array}\ \begin{array}{l} \text{miles from Oakview to Rosewood} \\ \text{miles from Rosewood to Newtown} \end{array}$$

So, Tom rode 24 more miles than Sharon.

Talk About It

• How many miles is it from Oakview to Newtown?

• How are addition and subtraction different?

▭▷ **Write About It** Write an addition problem and a subtraction problem using information from the map.

▶ CHECK

Solve. For Problems 1–2, use the map.

1. Mike rode his bicycle to Tom's house in the morning. Then he rode to Dan's house for lunch. How many blocks did Mike ride his bicycle?

2. How many blocks farther is it from Price's house to Dan's house than it is from Mike's house to Tom's house?

▶ PRACTICE

Find the sum or difference.

3.	60 −40	4.	16 +49	5.	25 − 9	6.	89 +42	7.	74 −35
8.	40 −15	9.	98 +85	10.	23 −14	11.	73 +17	12.	33 −20

Problem Solving • Mixed Applications

Using Data For Problems 13, 15, and 17, use the table.

13. **Collections** The students in third grade collect the things shown on this table. How many more students collect action figures than baseball cards?

Things We Collect	
Action Figures	37
Stickers	16
Coins	18
Baseball Cards	25

14. Erica has 18 action figures. Bradley has 15 more figures than Erica. How many action figures does Bradley have?

15. **Reasoning** Susan collects stickers. How many fewer students collect stickers than coins?

16. **Sports** Juan had 28 baseball cards. He traded 13 baseball cards for action figures. How many baseball cards does Juan have now?

17. ✏ **Write a problem** using the information in the table.

LESSON CONTINUES

Problem–Solving Strategy: Work Backward

▶ **THE PROBLEM** On Monday Nicholas and his mother made some popcorn balls. On Tuesday they made 10 more balls. Nicholas ate 1 of them. On Wednesday Nicholas took 25 popcorn balls to the school party. How many popcorn balls did Nicholas and his mother make on Monday?

REMEMBER:
UNDERSTAND
PLAN
SOLVE
LOOK BACK

UNDERSTAND

- What are you asked to find?

- What information will you use?

- Is there any information you will not use? If so, what?

PLAN

- What strategy can you use to solve the problem?

  You can *work backward* to solve the problem.

SOLVE

- How can you work backward?

  Start ⇨ 25   Begin with the popcorn balls Nicholas took to the party.

  $25 + 1 = 26$ Add the popcorn ball Nicholas ate.

  $26 - 10 = 16$ Subtract the popcorn balls they made Tuesday.

  So, they made 16 popcorn balls on Monday.

LOOK BACK

- How can you decide if your answer makes sense?

- What other strategy could you use?

Work backward to solve.

1. On Saturday Tina and her mother baked some cookies. She baked 12 more cookies on Sunday. She ate 3 of them. On Monday Tina took 30 cookies to school for the bake sale. How many cookies did Tina make on Saturday?

2. Robert went fishing in the morning. He caught some fish. He caught 8 more in the afternoon. He threw 5 back. At the end of the day, Robert had 16 fish. How many fish did he catch in the morning?

3. Abby had some coins. Her mother gave her 9 coins, but Abby lost 2 of them. Abby now has 20 coins. How many coins did Abby have to start with?

4. Scott had some stamps. He gave 7 stamps to his sister. His brother gave him 14 more stamps. Now he has 36 stamps. How many stamps did Scott have to begin with?

Mixed Applications

Solve.

CHOOSE a strategy and a tool.
• Make a Table • Work Backward
• Act It Out • Write a Number Sentence

 Paper/Pencil Calculator Hands-On Mental Math

5. Wendy went shopping at the mall. She bought a birthday gift. She received these coins as change. How much change did she receive?

6. Tony bought a hot dog for $1.25, a drink for $1.00, and popcorn for $1.75. His mom gave him $1.00. Tony has $1.25 left. How much did he have to begin with?

7. Marcy has two bags of beads. There are 55 beads in each bag. How many beads does Marcy have in all?

8. James is sixth in a line of nine people. How many people are in front of him? How many people are behind him?

9. Ann had some pens. She bought 6 more pens and gave 2 to her friend. She now has 8 pens. How many pens did Ann have to start with?

10. Drew read a book with 95 pages. Justin read a book with 84 pages. How many more pages did Drew read than Justin?

▶ CHECK Understanding

Write *yes* or *no* to tell if you need to regroup.
Find the difference. (pages 36–37)

1. 33 −24	**2.** 51 −11	**3.** 36 −17	**4.** 24 −10	**5.** 63 −24

Find the sum or difference. (pages 44–45)

6. 31 − 7	**7.** 20 −12	**8.** 55 +46	**9.** 70 −17	**10.** 43 +39

▶ CHECK Skills

Find the difference. (pages 40–43)

11. 30 −24	**12.** 50 −33	**13.** 40 −16	**14.** 60 −10	**15.** 80 −24
16. 75 −68	**17.** 91 −82	**18.** 23 −14	**19.** 53 −28	**20.** 65 −10

▶ CHECK Problem Solving

Solve. (pages 44–47)

CHOOSE a strategy and a tool.
- Write a Number Sentence
- Draw a Picture
- Act It Out
- Work Backward

Paper/Pencil   Calculator   Hands-On   Mental Math

21. Becky had a box of stickers. She gave 8 stickers to Will. Jerry gave her 4 more. Now Becky has 24 stickers. How many stickers did Becky have to begin with?

22. Nicholas and his family traveled 65 miles to his grandmother's house. Then they drove back home again. How many miles did they travel in all?

23. Sonia baked 32 cookies. Her family ate 6 of them. How many cookies does Sonia have left?

24. Justin caught 24 fish the first week and 17 fish the second week. How many more fish did he catch the first week?

Test Prep

Choose the best answer.

1. Dad ordered 2 enchilada dinners, 3 taco dinners, and 3 fajita dinners. How many dinners did Dad order?

   A 7   **B** 8   **C** 5   **D** 9

2. This table shows the number of crayons used in the third-grade art class for four weeks.

CRAYONS FOR ART CLASS	
Week	Number of Crayons
One	59
Two	65
Three	76
Four	57

   How many more crayons did students use in week 3 than in week 1?

   F 21   **G** 11   **H** 19   **J** 17

3. Kate delivered 19 newspapers on one street and 22 on another street. How many newspapers did she deliver?

   A 30
   B 41
   C 37
   D 47

4. Marc had 75¢. He bought juice for 55¢. How much money did he have left?

   F 35¢   **G** 20¢   **H** 25¢   **J** 30¢

5. Mr. Davis bought 20 horses for his ranch. He has 50 sheep and 78 cows. How many more cows than horses does Mr. Davis have?

   A 58   **B** 30   **C** 50   **D** 28

6. Jan saved nickels. Her mother gave her 4 nickels. Then Jan lost 2 of them. Now she has 12 nickels. How many did she have to start with?

   F 6
   G 18
   H 16
   J 10

7. Mrs. Jones washed 6 blue socks, 2 green socks, and 4 brown socks and hung them out to dry. Later she found all but 3 socks on the clothesline. How many socks were still on the line?

   A 15   **B** 9   **C** 7   **D** 8

8. Sammy jogged 45 miles one week and 48 miles the next week. How many miles did he jog in the two weeks?

   F 85 mi
   G 73 mi
   H 93 mi
   J 95 mi

4 ADDING AND SUBTRACTING LARGER NUMBERS

LITERATURE LINK

A tall tale is a story, told with lots of exaggeration, about an imaginary person. A legend is a story that may or may not be true about a person who may have actually lived.

PAUL BUNYAN

32 USA

32 USA

S. BILL

SA

JOHN HENRY

50

Problem-Solving Activity

American Tall Tales and Legends

American tall tales and legends have been told since the 1800's. They tell in a colorful and humorous way about the adventures and challenges of life on the frontier.

Choose a character from an American tall tale or legend. Learn more about the character by reading a tall tale or legend.

- Write at least three word problems that use addition or subtraction with numbers in the hundreds.

- Solve your word problems and put the answers on the back of your paper.

- Trade word problems with a classmate and solve.

FAMOUS CHARACTERS

Legends

Johnny Appleseed

Davy Crockett

Paul Revere

Casey Jones

Tall Tales

Pecos Bill

Paul Bunyan

Slue-Foot Sue

Mike Fink

John Henry

DID YOU

☑ learn about a tall tale character?

☑ write and solve at least three word problems with large numbers?

☑ trade and solve word problems written by another classmate?

Presenting TANYA as Annie Oakley

Regrouping to Add

Why learn this? You can add large numbers such as the number of books read in a contest.

One third-grade class read 137 books. Another class read 184 books. How many books did the classes read in all?

Use base-ten blocks to help you.

MODEL

Find 137 + 184 = ___?___.

Step 1
Add the ones. 7 + 4 = 11 ones
Regroup. 11 ones = 1 ten 1 one

Step 2
Add the tens. 1 + 3 + 8 = 12 tens
Regroup. 12 tens = 1 hundred 2 tens
Add the hundreds. 1 + 1 + 1 = 3 hundreds

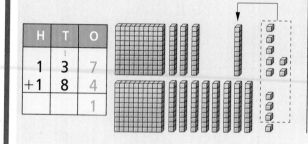

H	T	O
1	3	7
+1	8	4
		1

H	T	O
1	3	7
+1	8	4
3	2	1

So, the third-grade classes read 321 books in all.

Talk About It

• Why is it important to line up the digits in each column?

CRITICAL THINKING How does knowing how to add 2-digit numbers help you add larger numbers?

REMEMBER:
To *regroup*, you exchange amounts of equal value.

1 ten = 10 ones

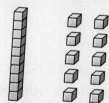

▶ CHECK

Find the sum.

1.

H	T	O
1	5	6
+1	1	6

2.

H	T	O
1	8	8
+1	4	5

3.

H	T	O
2	2	2
+		9	9

4.

H	T	O
4	6	8
+1	3	2

5.

H	T	O
3	6	1
+4	4	2

Find the sum.

6.	H	T	O
	1	2	3
+2	2	4	7

7.	H	T	O
	3	5	8
+4	4	3	4

8.	H	T	O
	6	9	5
+2	2	1	5

9.	H	T	O
	7	3	2
+1	1	8	9

10.	H	T	O
	4	1	6
+3	3	9	6

11.	647
	+178

12.	219
	+763

13.	554
	+257

14.	168
	+692

15.	384
	+586

16.	631
	+189

17.	464
	+446

18.	313
	+649

19.	576
	+265

20.	489
	+511

Problem Solving • Mixed Applications

Using Data For Problems 22, 23, and 25, use the table.

21. **Literature** Joshua read 46 pages about Davy Crockett. Rosa read 29 pages about Paul Bunyan. How many more pages did Joshua read than Rosa?

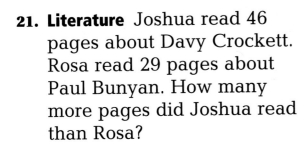

SUMMER BOOK CLUB MEMBERS			
Month	June	July	August
Members	149	117	213

22. **Visual Thinking** How many people joined the book club in June and July?

23. **Compare** In which month did the fewest members join? the most members join?

24. **Logical Reasoning** Sara put 15 more books on the library shelf. Now there are 38 books on the shelf. How many books were there to begin with?

25. ◀▶ **Write a problem** by adding another month and another 3-digit number to the table.

Mixed Review and Test Prep

Estimate each sum or difference by rounding. (pages 24–27)

26.	38
	−31

27.	21
	+36

28.	190
	+290

29.	420
	−330

30.	58
	+18

Choose the letter of the correct difference. (pages 38–39)

31. 50 − 27 = __?__   **A** 21   **B** 32   **C** 23   **D** 33

32. 80 − 42 = __?__   **F** 40   **G** 38   **H** 41   **J** 48

Adding More Than Two Addends

Why learn this? You can solve problems in which you add minutes or amounts of money.

Dave spent 144 minutes at baseball practice one week. He spent 96 minutes at practice the second week and 119 minutes the third week. How many minutes did he spend at baseball practice in the three weeks?

MODEL

Find $144 + 96 + 119 = \underline{\ ?\ }$.

Step 1	Step 2	Step 3
Add the ones.	Add the tens.	Add the hundreds.
$4 + 6 + 9 = 19$ ones	$1 + 4 + 9 + 1 = 15$ tens	$1 + 1 + 1 = 3$ hundreds
Regroup 19 ones as	Regroup 15 tens as	
1 ten 9 ones.	1 hundred 5 tens.	

```
      1                 1 1               1 1
   1 4 4             1 4 4             1 4 4
     9 6               9 6               9 6
  +1 1 9            +1 1 9            +1 1 9
  ───────           ───────           ───────
       9                5 9             3 5 9
```

So, Dave spent 359 minutes at baseball practice.

EXAMPLES

A	**B**	**C**	
``` 1 2```	``` 1 1```	``` 2 2```	• Add money amounts the
``` 3 4 9```	``` 5 5 1```	``` $5.9 8```	same as whole numbers.
``` 6 1 5```	``` 2 7 4```	``` 3.4 9```	• Use a decimal point to
```+ 1 3 9```	```+ 1 1 6```	```+ 9.9 9```	separate dollars and cents.
```1,1 0 3```	``` 9 4 1```	```$1 9.4 6```	• Place a dollar sign and
		``` ↑ ↑```	decimal point in the sum.

▶ CHECK

Find the sum.

	1.	**2.**	**3.**	**4.**	**5.**
	173	271	326	461	$5.58
	61	432	114	351	2.00
	+ 43	+145	+191	+ 32	+ 2.27

 Calculator Activities page H59

Find the sum.

6. 281
    198
    +911

7. $5.46
     6.47
    + 2.72

8. 732
    264
    +735

9. 196
    822
    +566

10. $4.68
     7.85
    + 3.89

11. 654
    356
    +823

12. 929
    573
    +445

13. $4.13
     5.31
    + 6.57

Problem Solving • Mixed Applications

Using Data For Problems 14 and 16, use the price list.

14. **Consumer** Duncan bought lunch for $4.73. Then he went to the store and bought a flashlight and a food cooler. How much more than $20.00 did Duncan spend?

CAMPING ITEMS FOR SALE	
Backpack	$9.98
Flashlight	$8.95
Food Cooler	$6.96
Blanket	$7.89

15. **Time** The Coles began their hike at 2:30 P.M. They hiked for 2 hours and 30 minutes. At what time did the Coles finish hiking?

16. Gloria bought a backpack, a flashlight, and a blanket. How much did she spend for the items?

17. **Money** Chris bought a bicycle for $96. Grace bought a bicycle for $88. How much more did Chris spend than Grace?

18. ▯▭ **Write About It** How is adding money amounts like adding whole numbers? How is it different?

Mixed Review and Test Prep

Find the difference. (pages 42–43)

19. $34 - 25 = $?   20. $46 - 19 = $?   21. $52 - 34 = $?   22. $63 - 16 = $?

23. $27 - 18 = $?   24. $71 - 42 = $?   25. $85 - 66 = $?   26. $92 - 17 = $?

Choose the letter of the correct sum or difference. (pages 44–45)

27. $45 + 67 = $?   **A** 102   **B** 121   **C** 112   **D** Not Here

28. $73 - 26 = $?   **F** 47   **G** 43   **H** 53   **J** 57

Regrouping to Subtract

Why learn this? You can subtract to find how many fewer things, such as videos were sold.

Van's Video Store sold 258 videos one week and 168 videos the next week. How many fewer videos did the store sell the second week than the first week?

Use base-ten blocks to help you.

Choosing a video

MODEL

Find 258 − 168 = _?_ .

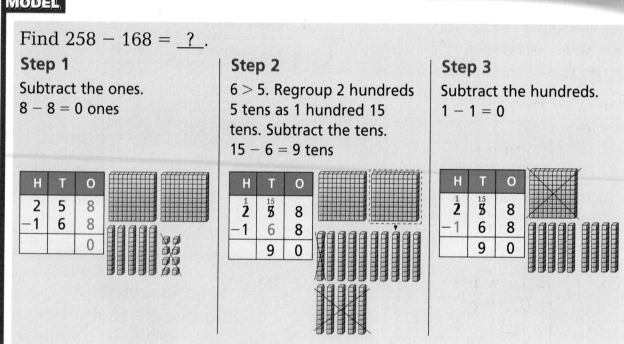

Step 1
Subtract the ones.
8 − 8 = 0 ones

Step 2
6 > 5. Regroup 2 hundreds 5 tens as 1 hundred 15 tens. Subtract the tens.
15 − 6 = 9 tens

Step 3
Subtract the hundreds.
1 − 1 = 0

So, the store sold 90 fewer videos the second week.

- In Step 2 the hundreds and tens are regrouped. Why aren't the ones regrouped?

▶ CHECK

Find the difference.

1.
H	T	O
4	9	2
−2	7	3

2.
H	T	O
5	2	7
−3	4	8

3.
H	T	O
8	1	0
−7	5	7

4.
H	T	O
6	8	2
−4	3	9

5.
H	T	O
4	5	4
−2	4	2

Find the difference.

6.	H	T	O
	4	2	7
−	1	1	8

7.	H	T	O
	3	8	5
−	2	6	7

8.	H	T	O
	5	4	4
−	1	2	9

9.	H	T	O
	2	6	5
−	1	2	8

10.	H	T	O
	4	7	3
−	2	1	2

11.	686 −387	12.	831 −441	13.	342 −167	14.	765 −498	15.	841 −259

16.	912 −575	17.	853 −194	18.	735 −429	19.	885 −396	20.	998 −199

Problem Solving • Mixed Applications

Using Data For Problems 22–24 and 27, use the table.

21. **Mental Math** Sharon bought videos that cost $25.98. She had a coupon for $5.00 off. How much did Sharon spend for the videos?

VIDEOS FOR SALE	
Name	Number of Copies
Aladdin	249
Beauty and the Beast	185
101 Dalmatians	225

22. How many more copies of *Aladdin* are for sale than copies of *Beauty and the Beast*?

23. **Compare** How many fewer copies of *Beauty and the Beast* are for sale than copies of *101 Dalmatians*?

24. **Consumer** How many videos are for sale in all?

25. **Time** Heather has a video that is 115 minutes long. Kyle has a video that is 132 minutes long. How much longer is Kyle's video than Heather's video?

26. **Money** Heather bought a video for $9.97. Kyle bought a video on sale for $7.79. How much more did Heather pay for her video?

27. ✏️ **Write a problem** that uses the information in the table.

Technology Link

💿 In *Mighty Math Number Heroes*, the game *Quizzo* challenges you to solve subtraction puzzles with large numbers. Use Grow Slide Level L.

LESSON CONTINUES ➡

Problem-Solving Strategy: Guess and Check

▶ **THE PROBLEM** The third-grade classes bought 100 containers of food for their field trip. They had 20 more cans than boxes of food. How many boxes and cans did the classes buy?

REMEMBER:

UNDERSTAND

PLAN

SOLVE

LOOK BACK

UNDERSTAND

- What are you asked to find?

- What information will you use?

- Is there any information you will not use? If so, what?

PLAN

- What strategy can you use?

  You can *guess and check* to find the number of boxes and cans the classes bought.

SOLVE

- How can you use the strategy?

  Guess the number of boxes the classes bought. Add 20 to that number for the number of cans. Then check to see if the sum is 100.

Boxes	Cans	Total	Notes
20	20 + 20 = 40	20 + 40 = 60	too low
50	50 + 20 = 70	50 + 70 = 120	too high
40	40 + 20 = 60	40 + 60 = 100	just right

So, the classes bought 40 boxes and 60 cans of food.

LOOK BACK

- How can you use your first two guesses to make a better guess?

► PRACTICE

Use *guess and check* to solve.

1. Nancy helped her teacher for 50 minutes. She worked 10 more minutes in the morning than in the afternoon. How many minutes did Nancy help her teacher in the morning? in the afternoon?

2. Lincoln Elementary School students sold 80 books at the Book Fair. They sold 20 more books on Sunday than on Saturday. How many books did they sell each day?

3. Two numbers have a sum of 15. Their difference is 3. What are the two numbers?

4. James has 170 stamps in his collection. His first book of stamps has 30 more stamps in it than his second book. How many stamps are in each book?

Mixed Applications

Solve.

CHOOSE a strategy and a tool.

- Guess and Check
- Write a Number Sentence
- Make a Table
- Act It Out

 Paper/Pencil   Calculator   Hands-On   Mental Math

5. Irene collected 6 picture postcards from Texas, 14 from New York, and 9 from Florida. How many picture postcards did she collect in all?

6. Shelton has 100 sports cards. He has 30 more baseball cards than basketball cards. How many baseball cards does he have?

7. Maureen's family drove 5 days on vacation. They recorded the miles they drove each day as 528, 418, 485, 582, and 518. Which number of miles was the greatest? the least?

8. Dylan buys a cap, a baseball, and a glove. How much does he spend for the three items?

9. Kim had 48 stickers. She used 10 on cards. She used 22 for an art project. She used 14 more on a present. How many stickers does Kim have left?

Using Place Value to Subtract Across Zeros

You will investigate how to subtract across zeros by using base-ten blocks.

Use base-ten blocks to find the difference.

▶ EXPLORE

MATERIALS: base-ten blocks

MODEL

Find $300 - 149 =$ _?_ .

Use 3 hundreds to show 300.

Since $9 > 0$, regroup the blocks to solve the problem.

H	T	O
3	0	0
−1	4	9

Record

Explain how you regrouped the base-ten blocks to find the difference.

Talk About It

• What is another name for 300?

• Explain why you need to regroup twice to find $300 - 149 =$ _?_ .

▶ TRY THIS

1. Use base-ten blocks to find $406 - 238 =$ _?_ .

2. ⬭▷ **Write About It** How did you use base-ten blocks to find the difference?

Use base-ten blocks to find the difference.

3.	H	T	O
	4	0	4
−	1	5	3

4.	H	T	O
	6	0	3
−	2	6	5

5.	H	T	O
	3	0	0
−	1	6	8

6.	H	T	O
	5	0	5
−	3	1	6

7.	H	T	O
	6	0	0
−	1	3	1

8.   706
    −332

9.   500
    −195

10. 804
    −279

11. 600
    −518

12. 900
    −607

Regroup. Write another name for each.

13. 500   **14.** 700   **15.** 805

16. 604   **17.** 408   **18.** 907

Problem Solving • Mixed Applications

Using Data For Problems 19–21, use the map.

19. Visual Thinking Teresa traveled from Cincinnati to Toledo. Laurel traveled from Cincinnati to Indianapolis. How many more miles did Teresa travel?

20. Logic The Cox family drove from Cincinnati to Indianapolis. The next day, they drove back again. How many miles did they drive?

21. Mental Math Eileen and her family drove from Indianapolis to Cincinnati and then to Toledo. How many miles did they drive in all?

22. Money Jeff needs $300 for the class trip. He saved $178. His grandparents gave him $150. How much money does Jeff have for the trip?

23. ✏️ **Write a problem** about a car trip. Use subtraction in your problem.

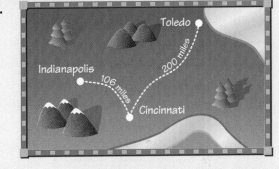

Toledo

Indianapolis

200 miles

106 miles

Cincinnati

Technology Link

💿 You can subtract across zeros by using E-Lab, Activity 4. Available on CD-ROM and on the Internet at www.hbschool.com/elab

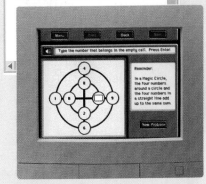

More About Subtracting Across Zeros

Why learn this? You can subtract from numbers with zeros when you subtract photographs or amounts of money.

Rachel is putting 400 photographs in a photo album. Of these, 278 are from her trip to Alaska. How many photographs are not of Rachel's trip to Alaska?

Use base-ten blocks to help you.

MODEL

Find $400 - 278 = $ ___?___ .

Step 1

$8 > 0$. Since there are 0 tens and 0 ones, regroup 4 hundreds as 3 hundreds 10 tens.

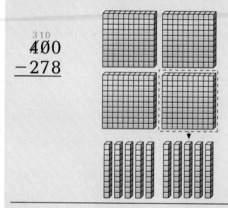

Step 2

Regroup 10 tens 0 ones as 9 tens 10 ones. Subtract the ones.
$10 - 8 = 2$ ones

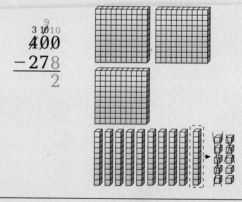

Step 3

Subtract the tens.
$9 - 7 = 2$ tens

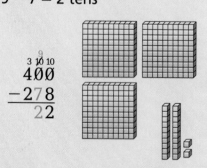

Step 4

Subtract the hundreds.
$3 - 2 = 1$ hundred

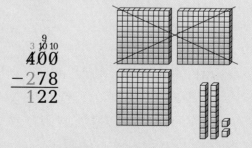

So, 122 photographs are not from Rachel's trip to Alaska.

Talk About It

- Look at Step 1. Why are the hundreds and tens regrouped before the ones are subtracted?

- In Step 2, why are two regroupings shown in the tens column?

CRITICAL THINKING What numbers can you subtract from 400 without regrouping?

_____

Suppose Rachel has $4.00. She spends $1.98 on picture postcards of Alaska. How much money does she have left?

$$\begin{array}{r} \overset{\scriptstyle 9}{} \\ \overset{\scriptstyle 3\ \ \cancel{10}\cancel{10}}{\$4.\cancel{0}\cancel{0}} \\ -\ \ 1.98 \\ \hline \$2.02 \end{array}$$

- How is this problem of Rachel's money like the problem in the model? How is it different?

▶ CHECK

Find the difference.

1.	400 −273	**2.** 500 −338	**3.** 808 −157
4.	601 −239	**5.** 400 −299	**6.** 706 −327
7.	800 −478	**8.** 600 −401	**9.** 203 − 95
10.	607 −419	**11.** 100 − 27	**12.** 410 −203

13. **Estimating** Suppose you have $10.00. How can you use rounding and mental math to decide if you can buy a book about Alaska for $6.79 and postcards for $2.10?

Find the difference.

14.	300 −139	15.	600 −284	16.	200 − 97	17.	500 −262	18.	800 −391
19.	700 −335	20.	$5.00 − 2.41	21.	400 −218	22.	900 −473	23.	$3.00 − 1.96
24.	100 − 98	25.	300 −189	26.	$7.00 − 2.49	27.	$9.00 − 1.16	28.	600 − 74
29.	603 −590	30.	306 −127	31.	800 −637	32.	504 −387	33.	400 −174

Problem Solving • Mixed Applications

Using Data For Problems 34–35, use the table.

34. Compare How much higher is Fairy Waterfall than Nevada Falls? than Bridalveil?

35. List the waterfalls in order from the one with the greatest height to the one with the least height.

FAMOUS WATERFALLS IN THE UNITED STATES	
Name	**Height**
Bridalveil (in California)	620 feet
Fairy (in Washington)	700 feet
Nevada Falls (in California)	594 feet

36. Money A ticket to the park is $6.00. Russ has $4.35. How much more money does Russ need to buy a ticket to the park?

37. Measurement Margaret hiked 950 feet to see the waterfall. Then she hiked back to where she started. How many feet did Margaret hike?

38. Estimation Tim wants to buy a camera that costs about $300. So far he has saved $185 for the camera. About how much more does he need in order to buy the camera?

39. ✐ **Write About It** Explain how subtracting from 400 is like subtracting from $4.00 and how it is different.

Have you ever been to a FireAnt Festival or Punkin Days or a Beautiful Burro Pageant? These are a few of the many festivals and celebrations that are held in the state of Texas.

40. Measurement Mike's burro won 100 pounds of feed at the Beautiful Burro Pageant. If it ate 21 pounds of the feed, how much feed is left?

41. Logical Reasoning At the FireAnt Festival, 407 people entered the bicycle race. Tom came in sixty-seventh. How many racers came in after Tom?

42. Money Shelly took $8.00 to the Texas Cowboy Poetry Gathering. She spent $4.69, 7 dimes, and 4 quarters. How much did she have left?

43. Mr. Louis won a truckload of 256 pumpkins at Punkin Days. He already had 57 pumpkins. How many pumpkins does he have in all?

Mixed Review and Test Prep

Write the number that is halfway between the two tens. You may wish to use a number line. (pages 24–27)

44. 20 and 30   **45.** 50 and 60   **46.** 70 and 80

47. 60 and 70   **48.** 30 and 40   **49.** 90 and 100

Choose the letter of the correct sum. (pages 22–23)

50. $72 + 34 = \underline{\ ?\ }$ **A** 106   **B** 102   **C** 103   **D** 100

51. $87 + 38 = \underline{\ ?\ }$ **F** 115   **G** 105   **H** 111   **J** 125

52. $47 + 61 = \underline{\ ?\ }$ **A** 78   **B** 88   **C** 98   **D** 108

53. $92 + 70 = \underline{\ ?\ }$ **F** 102   **G** 162   **H** 142   **J** 152

54. $85 + 45 = \underline{\ ?\ }$ **A** 120   **B** 130   **C** 145   **D** 150

55. $79 + 58 = \underline{\ ?\ }$ **F** 121   **G** 127   **H** 137   **J** 131

▶ CHECK Understanding

Find the sum. (pages 52–55)

1.	H	T	O
	2	1	3
+1	4	9	

2.	H	T	O
	3	9	1
+2	5	9	

3.	H	T	O
	7	4	9
+1	7	3	

4.
```
  261
  128
+511
```

5.
```
  184
  449
+621
```

Find the difference. (pages 56–57, 62–65)

6.
```
 413
-249
```

7.
```
 572
-357
```

8.
```
 777
-199
```

9.
```
 600
-216
```

10.
```
 800
-673
```

▶ CHECK Skills

Find the sum or difference. (pages 52–57, 62–65)

11.
```
 415
+449
```

12.
```
 600
-168
```

13.
```
$8.88
+ 2.22
```

14.
```
 401
-225
```

15.
```
 254
 249
+327
```

16.
```
$7.00
- 3.31
```

17.
```
 112
+459
```

18.
```
 354
 219
+372
```

19.
```
$5.00
- 2.25
```

20.
```
 710
-447
```

▶ CHECK Problem Solving

Solve. (pages 58–59)

CHOOSE a strategy and a tool.

- **Write a Number Sentence**
- **Draw a Picture**
- **Guess and Check**
- **Make a Table**

 Paper/Pencil   Calculator   Hands-On   Mental Math

21. Cathy and Steve have 26 action figures. Cathy has 2 more figures than Steve. How many figures do Cathy and Steve each have?

22. Martha is 16 years older than her sister. Her sister is 15. How old is Martha?

23. Carmen has 18 marbles. Dan has 14 more marbles than Carmen. How many marbles does Dan have?

24. Keith has 49 stamps in one book. He has 84 stamps in another book. How many fewer stamps are in the first book?

Test Prep

Choose the best answer.

1. In the morning, Marj planted 27 tulip bulbs and 23 daffodil bulbs. By the end of the day, she had planted 62 bulbs. How many did she plant in the afternoon?

   A 22   **B** 12   **C** 10   **D** 25

2. Jan is 10 years old. John is 2 years younger than Jan. What is the sum of their ages?

   F 12   **G** 8   **H** 18   **J** 22

3. Maria rode 3 miles on the school bus when Carmen got on. They rode 6 miles when Paul got on the bus. They rode another 3 miles to school. How many miles is it from Maria's bus stop to school?

   A 12 mi   **B** 9 mi
   C 6 mi   **D** 11 mi

4. Kim practices piano 35 minutes on Wednesday and 50 minutes on Saturday. How many more minutes does she practice on Saturday?

   F 30 min   **G** 35 min
   H 20 min   **J** 15 min

5.   461
    −132

   A 319   **B** 329
   C 331   **D** 333

6. This table shows the number of items each school collected for the city fair.

CITY FAIR COLLECTIONS	
School	Number of Items
Jackson	398
Hale	387
Tobin	390

   How many items did the schools collect in all?

   F 975   **G** 1,175
   H 1,075   **J** 1,050

7. Lily had $150. Her grandmother gave her $125 for her birthday. Her parents gave her $75. How much money does Lily have altogether?

   A $350   **B** $275
   C $325   **D** $400

8. James has 340 baseball cards in his collection. He put 175 cards in a box. How many cards are not in the box?

   F 150   **G** 155   **H** 165   **J** 175

9. The first movie lasted 128 minutes. The second movie lasted 154 minutes. About how long did the two movies last?

   A 100 min
   B 200 min
   C 300 min
   D 400 min

MATH FUN!

DOUBLES GAME

PURPOSE To practice addition strategies for doubles

YOU WILL NEED 2 blank 6-section spinners, set of base-ten blocks

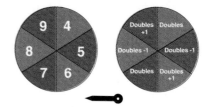

Play this game in small groups. Prepare two spinners as shown. On your turn, spin the two spinners and find the sum as directed by the spinners. Take that number of ones blocks. If you have enough blocks to make a ten, trade them for a tens block. After five turns, compare blocks and see who has the most.

GUESS MY RULE

PURPOSE To practice addition and subtraction

Find the missing numbers on the tables. Look at the numbers on the *In* side. What rule is used to find the numbers on the *Out* side? Make up your own patterns. Have a partner guess your rules.

IN	OUT
3	7
4	9
5	11
6	?
7	?
8	?

IN	OUT
21	12
20	11
19	10
18	?
17	?
16	?

 HOME NOTE Make up some patterns for your family to try at home.

GROUND ZERO

PURPOSE To practice adding and subtracting 3-digit numbers

YOU WILL NEED 3 number cubes of different colors to represent hundreds, tens, and ones; place-value chart; pencil

Play this game with a partner. On your turn, roll the number cubes and record the 3-digit number in the chart. Roll again and record the 3-digit number below the first one. Decide whether to add or subtract. A correct answer gets 1 point.

H	T	O

Adding and Subtracting Larger Numbers

There are 212 zebras, 359 wildebeests, and 1,425 flamingos at the water hole. How many animals in all are at the water hole?

You can use the TI-108 or another calculator to solve the problem.

So, the total number of animals at the water hole is 1,996.

• What can you do to make sure the calculator answer is correct?

How many more flamingos than zebras are there?

So, there are 1,213 more flamingos than zebras.

▶ PRACTICE

Find the sum or difference.

1. 3,178 +2,045	**2.** 6,255 −1,722	**3.** 4,806 +3,977	**4.** 3,178 −2,045

Using the Calculator. Solve.

5. There were 1,124 gazelles grazing. Another 389 arrived. How many gazelles were there in all?

6. The Congo River flows 2,716 miles. The Nile River flows 4,145 miles. How much longer is the Nile River than the Congo River?

Study Guide and Review

Vocabulary Check

Choose a term from the box to complete the sentence.

VOCABULARY
doubles
counting back
counting on
zero

1. When one of the addends is 1, 2, or 3, you can use __?__ to find the sum. (page 2)

2. When both addends are the same, you are adding __?__. (page 4)

3. When you subtract __?__ from a number, the difference is that number. (page 10)

4. When you subtract 1, 2, or 3, use __?__ to find the difference. (page 10)

Study and Solve

CHAPTER 1

EXAMPLE

Find the difference.

$$\begin{array}{r} 11 \\ -\ 3 \\ \hline 8 \end{array}$$

1. Choose a method.
2. Count back to find the difference.
3. Count: 11…10, 9, 8. So, 11 − 3 = 8.

Use order in addition to write another addition fact. (pages 6–7)

5. $4 + 7 = 11$, so __?__ + __?__ = __?__

For Problems 6–7, find the sum or difference. (pages 2–7, 10–11)

6. $\begin{array}{r} 8 \\ +\ 8 \\ \hline \end{array}$

7. $\begin{array}{r} 18 \\ -\ 9 \\ \hline \end{array}$

Solve. (pages 10–11)

8. Mia has 15 crayons. Lani has 9 crayons. How many more crayons does Mia have?

CHAPTER 2

EXAMPLE

Find the sum.

$$\begin{array}{r} \overset{1}{5}9 \\ +35 \\ \hline 94 \end{array}$$

1. Add the ones. $9 + 5 = 14$
2. Regroup. $14 = 1$ ten + 4 ones
3. Add the tens.

Group the addends. Then find the sum. (pages 18–19)

9. $5 + 5 + 8 =$ __?__

For Problems 10–11, find the sum. (pages 20–23)

10. $\begin{array}{r} 29 \\ +71 \\ \hline \end{array}$

11. $\begin{array}{r} 15 \\ +77 \\ \hline \end{array}$

For Problems 12–13, estimate the sum or difference by rounding. (pages 24–27)

12. $\begin{array}{r} 42 \\ +57 \\ \hline \end{array}$

13. $\begin{array}{r} 79 \\ -23 \\ \hline \end{array}$

Solve. (pages 28–31)

14. Mr. Rey has 25 math tests and 26 spelling tests to grade. How many tests does he have to grade in all?

CHAPTER 3

EXAMPLE

Find the difference.

$$
\begin{array}{r}
\overset{7\ 10}{\cancel{8}\cancel{0}} \\
-24 \\
\hline
56
\end{array}
$$

1. Regroup. 80 = 7 tens 10 ones
2. Subtract the ones.
3. Subtract the tens.

For Problems 15–18, find the difference. (pages 38–43)

15.
$$
\begin{array}{r}
40 \\
-26
\end{array}
$$

16.
$$
\begin{array}{r}
64 \\
-37
\end{array}
$$

17.
$$
\begin{array}{r}
90 \\
-85
\end{array}
$$

18.
$$
\begin{array}{r}
51 \\
-26
\end{array}
$$

Solve. (pages 44–47)

19. J.R. gave Dana 8 model cars in a trade. Dana gave him 4 special cars. Now J.R. has 47 cars. How many cars did J.R. have to begin with?

CHAPTER 4

EXAMPLE

Find the sum.

$$
\begin{array}{r}
\overset{1\ 1}{\$7.77} \\
+\ 3.33 \\
\hline
\$11.10
\end{array}
$$

1. Line up decimal points.
2. Add from right to left.
3. Regroup as needed.

For Problems 20–23, find the sum or difference. (pages 52–57, 62–65)

20.
$$
\begin{array}{r}
\$4.54 \\
+\ 5.46
\end{array}
$$

21.
$$
\begin{array}{r}
251 \\
138 \\
+621
\end{array}
$$

22.
$$
\begin{array}{r}
701 \\
-325
\end{array}
$$

23.
$$
\begin{array}{r}
610 \\
-548
\end{array}
$$

Solve. (pages 58–59)

24. Two numbers have a sum of 27. Their difference is 3. What are the two numbers?

25. Laura made 70 key rings. She made 10 more key rings on Saturday than she made on Friday. How many key rings did she make each day?

26. Carly bought three birthday cards. They cost $1.25, $2.35, and $1.50. How much money did Carly spend for birthday cards?

27. Hector had $5.00. He bought milk for $1.59, eggs for $1.89, and bread for $1.49. How much did Hector spend in all? How much change did he receive?

28. There are 120 students in the glee club. There are 34 new members this year. How many students sang last year?

Performance Assessment

Tasks: Show What You Know

1. Explain a strategy you could use to find the difference for each fact. Write the difference.

$$11 - 2 = \underline{?} \qquad 9 - 7 = \underline{?}$$

Explain how knowing $5 + 9 = 14$ can help you solve this fact:

$$14 - 9 = \underline{?}$$

Write the difference.
(pages 10–11, 12–13)

2. Use base-ten blocks to find the sum. Draw a picture to show each step, and name the sum.
(pages 22–23)

$$\begin{array}{r} 35 \\ +28 \\ \hline \end{array}$$

3. Use base-ten blocks to find the difference. Draw a picture to show each step, and name the difference. (pages 40–41)

$$\begin{array}{r} 50 \\ -27 \\ \hline \end{array}$$

4. Explain a strategy you would use to solve this problem and solve. A school has 60 third graders. There are 10 more girls than boys. How many girls and how many boys are third graders? (pages 58–59)

Problem Solving

Solve. Explain your method.

CHOOSE a strategy and a tool.
- **Guess and Check**
- **Make a Table**
- **Work Backward**
- **Write a Number Sentence**

 Paper/Pencil   Calculator   Hands-On   Mental Math

5. Ed has two spinners with numbers 1, 2, and 3. List the number sentences he can write using the numbers on the spinners. (pages 8–9)

6. A bus has 20 seats. There are 9 girls and 8 boys on the bus. How many people are riding in all? How many seats are left? (pages 30–31)

7. Rick gave 6 baseball cards to Len and 5 to Rosa. Now he has 29 cards. How many cards did Rick start with? (pages 46–47)

8. Together Nova and Sam have 35 comic books. Nova has 5 more than Sam. How many comic books does each have? (pages 58–59)

Cumulative Review

Solve the problem. Then write the letter of the correct answer.

1. $7 + 4 + 6 = \underline{\ ?\ }$

    A. 16   **B.** 17

    C. 18   **D.** 70

                               (pages 18–19)

2.   69
    $+24$

    A. 45

    B. 83

    C. 93

    D. 94

                                 (pages 22–23)

3.   56
    $+64$

    A. 12

    B. 100

    C. 110

    D. 120

                                 (pages 22–23)

For Problems 4–6, round each number to the nearest ten. (pages 24–27)

4. 63

    A. 6

    B. 60

    C. 70

    D. 100

5. 35

    A. 4

    B. 10

    C. 30

    D. 40

6. 78

    A. 90

    B. 80

    C. 8

    D. 70

Estimate the sum by rounding.

7.   32
    $+59$

    A. 70

    B. 80

    C. 90

    D. 100

                                 (pages 24–27)

Solve.

8.   50
    -36

    A. 14

    B. 24

    C. 26

    D. 86

                                 (pages 38–43)

9.   65
    -58

    A. 6

    B. 7

    C. 17

    D. 123

                                 (pages 38–43)

10.   675
    $+438$

    A. 237

    B. 1,003

    C. 1,113

    D. 1,114

                                 (pages 52–53)

11. $9.75
    $+\ 4.25$

    A. $14.00

    B. $4.50

    C. $13.00

    D. $5.50

                                 (pages 52–53)

12. $8.00
    $-\ 6.98$

    A. $1.02

    B. $2.02

    C. $2.98

    D. $14.98

                        (pages 56–57, 62–65)

5 TELLING TIME

SCIENCE LINK

An Egyptian water clock is a pot filled with water. Holes in the pot drain the water. Dots that line the side of the pot show the water level and how much time has passed.

Counting the Minutes

Each small mark on a clock is one minute.
Make a clock from paper plates.

YOU WILL NEED: 2 lightweight 9-inch paper plates with ridged edges, scissors, pencil, marker, construction paper, brass fastener, stapler

- Mark a bump. Count 2 dips and mark the next bump. Count 4 dips and mark the next bump. Continue all the way around the plate.

- Cut on the lines, fold back the tabs, and write the numbers 1–12 for each cutout space.

- Attach a blue minute hand and a red hour hand to your clock. Attach the clock to a piece of construction paper. Write a zero above the 12 on your clock. Skip count by fives around the rest of the clock. Record the numbers.

- Show a time on your clock. Write the time.

DID YOU

- ✓ make a paper-plate clock?
- ✓ follow all the directions?
- ✓ show a time on your clock and write the time?

Understanding a Clock

Why learn this? You can use what you know about minutes and hours to tell time.

Andrew must catch the school bus at eight o'clock.

The short hand on a clock is the **hour hand**. It points to the hour. The hour hand moves from one number to the next in one hour.

The long hand on a clock is the **minute hand**. It points to the minute. The minute hand moves around the clock once in one hour.

Look at the clocks. Each shows the same time.

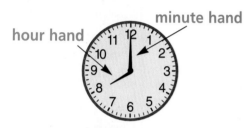
hour hand   minute hand
analog clock

hours minutes
digital clock

Read: eight o'clock   **Write:** 8:00

Talk About It

- How many hours does it take for the hour hand to circle the face of a clock once?

- What happens to the minute hand as the hour hand moves from 8 to 9?

There are five minute marks from one number to the next on a clock. Count by fives to find the number of minutes all the way around the clock from 12 to 12.

▶ **CHECK**

1. How many minutes are in one hour? Explain how you know.

> **REMEMBER:**
> An *analog clock* shows time on the hour when the minute hand is on 12. A *digital clock* shows time on the hour when the minutes show 00.

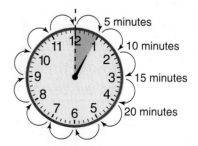
5 minutes
10 minutes
15 minutes
20 minutes

Tell how you would read each time. Write the time.

2.

3.

4.

5.

Write how many minute marks the minute hand has moved. Count by fives.

6.

7.

8.

9.

Problem Solving • Mixed Applications

10. Visual Thinking Carmen looks at the clock. The hour hand is pointing to the 9. The minute hand is pointing to the 2. What time is it?

11. Measurement The Lees drive 269 miles to get to the beach. The Foxes drive 357 miles. How many more miles do the Foxes drive?

12. Luis counted 5 birds in a tree, 4 birds on the grass, and 7 birds in the air. How many birds did Luis count in all?

13. ✏ **Write a problem** about the minute hand moving around the face of a clock for 15 minutes. Draw the clock.

Mixed Review and Test Prep

Find the difference. Regroup if necessary. (pages 38–39)

14. 91
     −16

15. 21
     −11

16. 75
     −43

17. 68
     −59

18. 87
     −46

Choose the letter of the correct sum or difference. (pages 44–45)

19. 42   **A** 51 **B** 60   **20.** 66   **F** 30 **G** 29   **21.** 84   **A** 120 **B** 100
     +29   **C** 61 **D** 71   −37   **H** 20 **J** 21   +26   **C** 110 **D** 125

Estimating Minutes and Hours

VOCABULARY

minutes

hours

Why learn this? You can plan ahead when you know about how long something will take.

Fernando and a friend are going to a movie. Fernando's mother drove the two boys to the movie. Should she return to pick them up in about 2 minutes or 2 hours?

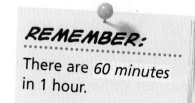

REMEMBER:

There are 60 minutes in 1 hour.

Minutes measure short amounts of time. It takes a class about 1 minute to line up.

Hours measure longer amounts of time. Math class takes about 1 hour.

Since a movie takes a longer amount of time, Fernando's mother should return in about 2 hours.

EXAMPLES

A In about 1 minute you can
  • tie your shoes.
  • brush your hair.

B In about 1 hour you can
  • listen to a CD.
  • get ready for school.

Talk About It

• What are some other things you can do in about one minute? one hour?

• Do you spend minutes or hours in school? brushing your teeth?

Fernando and Ian at the movie

▶ CHECK

Write *minutes* or *hours* to finish each sentence.

1. The fire drill lasted 10 __?__ .

2. The Finns went on a trip. They drove for 2 __?__ .

Write *more than* or *less than* for each.

3. It takes __?__ an hour to give a dog a bath.

4. It takes __?__ a minute to wash the dishes.

Choose the better estimate of time.

5. cook dinner   30 minutes or 30 hours

6. watch a football game   4 minutes or 4 hours

7. sweep the floor   10 minutes or 10 hours

Decide if the estimated time makes sense.
Write *yes* or *no*.

8. It takes about 20 minutes to eat a sandwich.

9. It takes about 2 hours to sharpen your pencil.

10. You sleep for about 8 minutes at night.

Problem Solving • Mixed Applications

11. Sports Rosa played tag for 35 minutes. Then she played baseball for 45 minutes. For how many minutes did she play in all?

12. Mental Math Brent had 15 pencils in his desk. He gave away 6 pencils. How many pencils does Brent have now?

13. Logical Reasoning Jerel rode his bicycle to Dena's house. Did Jerel ride for 15 minutes or 15 hours?

14.  **Write About It** Explain how you can estimate if something takes minutes or hours.

Mixed Review and Test Prep

Find the sum. (pages 54–55)

15.	**16.**	**17.**	**18.**	**19.**
123	424	$1.20	$7.11	811
456	616	2.83	3.48	929
+789	+137	+ 5.44	+ 2.25	+634

Choose the letter of the correct difference. (pages 62–65)

20. 800   **A** 307 **B** 403
        −493   **C** 407 **D** 97

21. $6.00   **F** $4.55 **G** $3.43
        − 2.57   **H** $4.43 **J** $3.55

Time to the Minute

You will investigate telling time to the minute.

Use a clock with hands that move to help you tell time to the minute.

5 minutes

In five minutes the minute hand moves from one number to the next number.

1 minute

In one minute the minute hand moves from one mark to the next mark.

To find the number of minutes after the hour, count by fives and ones to where the minute hand is pointing.

5 minutes
10 minutes
15 minutes
20 minutes
25 minutes
26 minutes

Read: nine twenty-six, or 26 minutes after nine

Write: 9:26

▶ **EXPLORE**

MATERIALS: clocks with movable hands

Find the time shown on each clock.

Record

Record all the ways you could read each time.

Then write each time.

Now, investigate showing the time on your clock.

1. Show 4:33, 12:14, and 7:41 on your clock. Draw clockfaces and show where the hour and minute hands are pointing for each time.

2. How do you say each time you showed on your clock?

3. ✏️ **Write About It** Why do you count by fives and ones to find the number of minutes after the hour?

3:32
This clock shows 32 minutes after three.

► **PRACTICE**

Show each time on your clock. Draw a picture to show where the hour and minute hands are pointing.

4. 1:19   **5.** 8:36   **6.** 7:52   **7.** 4:27

8. 10:49   **9.** 2:44   **10.** 11:13   **11.** 5:28

Write each time.

12.    **13.**    **14.**    **15.**

16.    **17.**    **18.**

Problem Solving • Mixed Applications

19. **Reasoning** The minute hand on a clock shows 16 minutes after the hour. How many minutes after the hour will it show in 15 minutes?

20. **Number Sense** There were 26 players on Dylan's team. Then 11 players left and 8 new players joined the team. How many players are on Dylan's team now?

Technology Link

💿 You can use an analog clock to tell time by using E-Lab, Activity 5. Available on CD-ROM and on the Internet at www.hbschool.com/elab

Time After the Hour

Why learn this? You can be on time when you go places.

These clocks show when Mr. Allen's class has art.

Read: ten thirty,
   or 30 minutes after ten
Write: 10:30

These clocks show when Mr. Allen's class has recess.

Read: eleven fifteen,
   or 15 minutes after eleven
Write: 11:15

These clocks show when Mr. Allen's class goes to lunch.

Read: eleven forty-five,
   or 45 minutes after eleven
Write: 11:45

These clocks show when Mr. Allen's class returns from lunch.

Read: twelve eighteen,
   or 18 minutes after twelve
Write: 12:18

Notice that
⇨ the hour hand moves from one number to the next as the minute hand moves around the face of the clock.

▶ CHECK

Tell where the hour hand points at each of these times.

1. at 30 minutes after ten

2. at 15 minutes after eleven

3. at 45 minutes after eleven

Technology Link

In **Mighty Math Zoo Zillions**, the game *Annie's Jungle Trail* challenges you to skip count. Use Grow Slide Level G.

Write the two ways you can read each time.

4.    **5.**    **6.**    **7.**

Write each time.

8.    **9.**    **10.**    **11.**

Tell where the hour hand should be.

12.    **13.**    **14.**    **15.**

4:05   6:32   3:48   10:56

Problem Solving • Mixed Applications

16. Reasoning Marybeth studied for 60 minutes. Then she read a book for 35 minutes. How much time did she spend studying and reading? How many more minutes did she spend studying?

17. Music Ms. Brennan's class spends 30 minutes in music on Monday. They spend 45 minutes in music on Friday. How many minutes do they spend in music each week?

18. Visual Thinking Mr. Morgan's class has music at two fifteen. Write the time the class goes to music class. Tell where the hour hand is pointing.

19. **Write About It** As the minute hand moves around the face of the clock, how does the hour hand move?

LESSON CONTINUES

Problem–Solving Strategy: Act It Out

▶ **THE PROBLEM** Elena walks her dog every day after school. She and her dog leave the house at four o'clock. They get home at 42 minutes after four. Where are the hands on the clock when Elena and her dog get home from their walk?

UNDERSTAND

- What are you asked to do?

- What information will you use?

- Is there information you will not use? If so, what?

REMEMBER:

UNDERSTAND

PLAN

SOLVE

LOOK BACK

PLAN

- What strategy can you use?

  You can *act it out* using a clock.

SOLVE

- How can you solve the problem?

  Use a clock with hour and minute hands.

  Show 4:00 on your clock.

  Count by fives to 40 while you move the minute hand to each *number*. Count by ones to 42 while you move the minute hand to each *mark*. Move the hour hand between the 4 and the 5, but closer to the 5.

  So, the hands on the clock look like this when Elena and her dog get home from their walk.

LOOK BACK

- How can you decide if your answer makes sense?

- What other strategy could you use?

Act it out to solve.

1. Greg leaves to walk his dog at three o'clock. He gets home at 54 minutes after three. Where are the hands on the clock when Greg and his dog get home?

2. Marla's lunch begins at twelve o'clock. It is over at 12:46. Where are the hands on the clock when Marla's lunch is over?

3. Tony bought an apple for 35¢ and a drink for 55¢. How much money does he need to pay for his food?

4. Four friends are standing in the lunch line. Shawn is ahead of Alex. Nicole is behind Alex. Shawn is behind Kerry. Who is first in line?

Mixed Applications

Solve.

CHOOSE a strategy and a tool.
- Guess and Check
- Write a Number Sentence
- Act It Out
- Work Backward

 Paper/Pencil   Calculator   Hands-On   Mental Math

5. Beth wants to find two numbers with a sum of 11 and a difference of 3. What are the two numbers?

6. Gina has a cat. If you add 4 to her cat's age and double the sum, it equals 16 years. How old is Gina's cat?

7. Felipe got to the bus stop at eight o'clock. He waited 16 minutes for the bus to come. Where were the hands on the clock when the bus came?

8. Ian spent $4.55 at the store. Then he found $2.00. Now Ian has $3.45. How much money did he begin with?

9. Corey left school at three o'clock. The clock shows the time he came home. What time was it when Corey came home from school?

10. At the pet store, Billy counted 18 dogs and 14 cats. How many more dogs than cats were at the pet store?

► **CHECK Understanding**

1. **VOCABULARY** The short hand on a clock is the __?__ .
The long hand on a clock is the __?__ . (page 76)

Write how many minute marks the minute hand has moved.
Count by fives. (pages 76–77)

2.    3.    4.    5.

► **CHECK Skills**

Choose the better estimate of time. (pages 78–79)

6. play with a friend   2 minutes or 2 hours

7. sing a song   5 minutes or 5 hours

Write the two ways you would read each time.
Write each time. (pages 82–83)

8.    9.    10.    11.

► **CHECK Problem Solving**

Solve. (pages 84–85)

CHOOSE a strategy and a tool.
- **Guess and Check**
- **Write a Number Sentence**
- **Act It Out**
- **Work Backward**

 Paper/Pencil   Calculator   Hands-On   Mental Math

12. Jo has dance class at 6:00.
She has to leave home at 13
minutes after five to get there
on time. Where are the hands
on the clock when Jo leaves?

13. Les came home with 11
balloons. He gave away 8
balloons. Then Ana gave him
3 balloons. How many balloons
did Les have to start with?

Test Prep

Choose the best answer.

1. The hour hand on the clock is between the 7 and the 8. The minute hand is pointing to 5. What time is it?

    A 7:05   **B** 5:35

    C 7:25   **D** 5:07

2. Mr. and Mrs. Rose are going to a movie in an hour. Which of these tasks can they do before the movie?

    F paint the house

    G buy some snacks

    H read an encyclopedia from cover to cover

    J drive 500 miles

3. Sandy read a book for 200 minutes. Then she did homework for 89 minutes. For how many more minutes did she read?

    A 100 min   **B** 121 min

    C 111 min   **D** 91 min

4. Ken left home at 25 minutes after eight. Which clock shows the time Ken left?

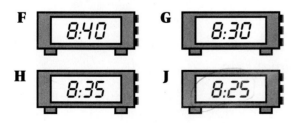

5. Henry needs $400 for a ski trip. He has saved $275. His parents gave him $120. How much money does he have for the trip so far?

    A $359   **B** $309

    C $395   **D** $405

6. School ends at two twenty. Which clock shows the time school ends?

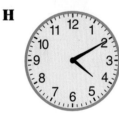 

7. Joe's class collected $280 for the class trip. Sally's class collected $259. How much more did Joe's class collect?

    A $30   **B** $21

    C $40   **D** $39

8. Which clock shows the time 1 hour before 12 o'clock?

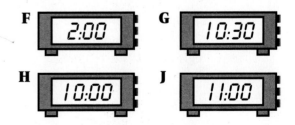

6 SCHEDULES

SPORTS LINK

The earliest recorded form of soccer was played in 1697 B.C. in China. A ball of animal skin was kicked through two bamboo poles. Soccer is the most popular sport in the world.

Problem-Solving Activity

Tournament Time

It's tournament time! Soccer season is ending, and your team, the Blue Jays, will play three 30-minute games on Saturday in the area championships.

Find out your schedule for the day. Check the chart to find when your team will play.

- List the times each of your games will start and end.

- Draw pictures of what your watch will show for the start and end times.

SOCCER TOURNAMENT SCHEDULE	
Time	**Teams**
8:00	Blue Jays vs. Panthers
8:30	Panthers vs. Streaks
9:00	Reds vs. Panthers
9:30	Streaks vs. Reds
10:00	Thunder vs. Reds
10:30	Thunder vs. Blue Jays
11:00	Blue Jays vs. Streaks

DID YOU

✓ list the times each of your games will start and end?

✓ draw pictures of what your watch will show for the start and end times?

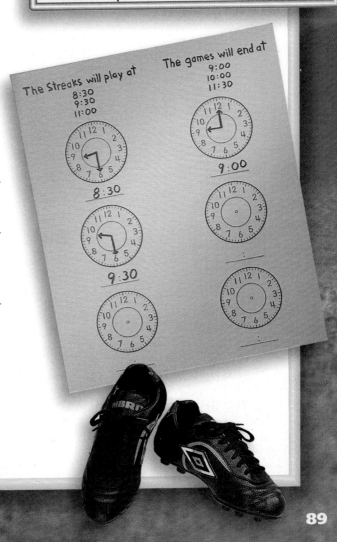

The Streaks will play at
8:30
9:30
11:00

8:30

9:30

The games will end at
9:00
10:00
11:30

9:00

Elapsed Time: Minutes and Hours

VOCABULARY
elapsed time

You will investigate using a clock to measure elapsed time.

Elapsed time is the time that passes from the start of an activity to the end of that activity.

Cameron read a book from 8:15 to 8:45. He can count by fifteens to find the elapsed time.

Start:
8:15

Count:
15 minutes

Count:
30 minutes

REMEMBER:
The *hour hand* moves between two numbers as the *minute hand* moves once around the face of the clock.

So, Cameron read for 30 minutes.

Notice that
⇨ the minute hand moves three numbers every 15 minutes.

▶ EXPLORE

MATERIALS: clocks with hands that move, blank clockfaces

Find the elapsed times from 1:15 to 1:45, 11:30 to 12:15, and 3:45 to 4:30.

Record

Draw pictures to show each starting and ending time. Write the elapsed times.

Now, investigate using elapsed time to find when an activity will end.

If you know how long something takes and when it starts, you can find the ending time.

▶ TRY THIS

Michele has soccer practice at 6:45. Practice will last about 45 minutes.

1. Draw pictures to show the starting and ending times.

2. At about what time will Michele's soccer practice end?

3. How did you find the time that Michele's soccer practice will end?

4. ✏ **Write About It** Explain why people might need to know elapsed time.

Michele at soccer practice

▶ PRACTICE

Use a clock with hands that move. Find the elapsed time.

5. **start:** 3:15
   end: 3:45

6. **start:** 8:30
   end: 8:45

7. **start:** 11:00
   end: 11:30

8. **start:** 7:30
   end: 8:15

9. **start:** 1:45
   end: 2:00

10. **start:** 7:00
    end: 7:45

11. **start:** 9:15
    end: 10:15

12. **start:** 2:30
    end: 3:00

Use a clock with hands that move. Find the ending time.

13. **starting time:** 2:15
    elapsed time: 45 min

14. **starting time:** 6:30
    elapsed time: 30 min

15. **starting time:** 9:45
    elapsed time: 1 hr

16. **starting time:** 10:00
    elapsed time: 1 hr and 15 min

Problem Solving • Mixed Applications

17. **Music** Brandi begins her piano lesson at 3:30. The lesson is 30 minutes long. At what time is Brandi's piano lesson over?

18. Angel's soccer practice begins at 4:15. Practice is over at 5:30. How long is Angel's soccer practice?

19. **Sports** There are 18 boys and 24 girls at soccer practice. How many boys and girls in all are at soccer practice?

Technology Link

💿 You can find elapsed time by using E-Lab, Activity 6. Available on CD-ROM and on the Internet at www.hbschool.com/elab

Using Time Schedules

Why learn this? You can make decisions, such as which movies you want to watch.

A **schedule** is a table that lists activities or events and the times they happen.

Kira and her friend are planning to go to a movie. A movie schedule lists the movies and the times they are playing.

Fly Away Home begins at 2:30. It ends at 4:00. It is shown in Theater A.

Talk About It

- At what time does *Free Willy* begin? end?

- In what theater is *101 Dalmatians* being shown?

- Which movies are shown in Theater B? in Theater C?

- How long is *Beethoven*?

▶ CHECK

For Problems 1–5, use the schedule.

1. At what time does *Pinocchio* begin? end?

2. How long is *Pinocchio*?

3. How long is *Flipper*?

4. Which movie is shown on Saturday from 3:00 to 4:30?

5. What movies are showing on Friday? on Saturday?

MOVIE LAND SATURDAY SCHEDULE		
Movie	**Time**	**Theater**
Fly Away Home	2:30–4:00	A
Free Willy	5:00–6:45	B
Beethoven	6:30–8:15	C
101 Dalmatians	5:00–6:30	A
Babe	7:30–9:00	B

WILTON LIBRARY MOVIE FESTIVAL		
Movie	**Day**	**Time**
The Land Before Time	Fri	2:00–3:30
Flipper	Fri	3:30–5:00
Pinocchio	Fri	5:00–6:45
The Muppet Movie	Sat	3:00–4:30
Homeward Bound	Sat	4:30–6:15

► PRACTICE

For Problems 6–10, use the schedule.

6. At what time does tumbling begin? end?

7. In which studio is the tap dancing class held?

8. How long is ballet 3?

9. Which classes are in Studio A?

ROWENA'S DANCE SCHOOL SCHEDULE		
Class	Time	Studio
Ballet 1	3:00 – 3:45	A
Tap Dancing	3:00 – 3:45	B
Tumbling	4:00 – 4:45	A
Ballet 2	4:00 – 5:00	B
Ballet 3	5:00 – 6:30	A

10. If Francesca takes tap dancing, will she be finished in time to take ballet 2?

Problem Solving • Mixed Applications

11. **Reading** Dana read for 30 minutes after school and for 25 minutes before she went to bed. How long did Dana read?

12. Danielle went skating at 4:30. She skated for 1 hour and 15 minutes. At what time did Danielle finish skating?

13. Brad's favorite television show begins at 7:00 and is over at 7:30. How long is Brad's favorite show?

14. **Using Data** Which class goes to the library at 9:30? How can you tell?

15. **Write About It** Explain how elapsed time is used on a schedule.

THIRD-GRADE LIBRARY SCHEDULE	
Class	Time
Ms. Ortiz	9:00 – 9:30
Mr. Cartier	9:30 – 10:00
Ms. Carr	10:00 – 10:30

Mixed Review and Test Prep

Write each time. (pages 80–81)

16.

17.

18.

19.

Choose the letter of the correct sum. (pages 22–23)

20. 48
   +51
   A 89 **B** 99
   C 97 **D** 87

21. 72
   +16
   F 86 **G** 78
   H 97 **J** 88

22. 67
   +59
   A 122 **B** 136
   C 126 **D** 112

MORE PRACTICE page H77

Scheduling Time: Minutes and Hours

Why learn this? You can plan how to spend your time.

Stephanie is making a schedule for her afternoon at school. She is using this table to finish her schedule.

Activity	Elapsed Time
Art	45 minutes
Free Reading	15 minutes
Math	1 hour

Stephanie's Schedule

Activity and Elapsed Time	Time
Lunch, 30 minutes	12:00 – 12:30
Recess, 30 minutes	12:30 – 1:00

Stephanie will use elapsed time to find each ending time.

Think:

- Art comes after recess. Since recess ends at 1:00, art starts at 1:00. Since art has an elapsed time of 45 minutes, it ends at 1:45.

- Free reading comes after art. Since art ends at 1:45, free reading starts at 1:45. Since free reading has an elapsed time of 15 minutes, it ends at 2:00.

- Math comes after free reading. Since free reading ends at 2:00, math starts at 2:00. Since math has an elapsed time of 1 hour, it ends at 3:00.

Talk About It

- What if Stephanie's class has science for the 45 minutes right before lunch? What will its starting and ending times be?

CRITICAL THINKING Tell about two things you did today. Use elapsed time.

▶ CHECK

1. How much longer is math than art? than free reading? than recess?

Stephanie's Schedule

Activity and Elapsed Time	Time
Lunch, 30 minutes	12:00 – 12:30
Recess, 30 minutes	12:30 – 1:00
Art, 45 minutes	1:00 – 1:45
Free Reading, 15 minutes	1:45 – 2:00
Math, 1 hour	2:00 – 3:00

Copy and complete the schedule.

BASEBALL PRACTICE SCHEDULE			
	Activity	Time	Elapsed Time
2.	Warm-ups	4:00—4:15	?
3.	Batting practice	?	30 minutes
4.	Catching practice	?	15 minutes
5.	Practice game	5:00—6:30	?

For Problems 6–7, use the schedule you made.

6. How much longer is batting practice than catching practice?

7. How much time in all is spent at baseball practice?

Problem Solving • Mixed Applications

Using Data For Problems 10–13, use the schedule below.

8. There are 97 students in third grade, 85 in fourth grade, and 93 in fifth grade. How many students are there in all?

9. Kim's book has 104 pages. Jon's book has 78 pages. How many more pages does Kim's book have?

10. Which activity ends at 10:45? begins at 10:45?

11. Which activities are 30 minutes long?

12. Which activity is the longest?

13. ✏ **Write a problem** using the schedule.

THIRD-GRADE MORNING SCHEDULE	
Activity	Time
Language Arts	8:30–9:15
Physical Education	9:15–9:45
Math	9:45–10:45
Snack	10:45–11:00
Music	11:00–11:30

Mixed Review and Test Prep

Group the addends. Then find the sum. (pages 18–19)

14. $2 + 1 + 4 = \underline{\ ?\ }$ **15.** $5 + 2 + 2 = \underline{\ ?\ }$ **16.** $3 + 4 + 2 = \underline{\ ?\ }$

Round each number to the nearest ten. Choose the letter of the correct answer. (pages 24–27)

17. 25   **A** 20   **B** 25   **C** 30   **D** Not Here

18. 57   **F** 55   **G** 50   **H** 70   **J** Not Here

Scheduling Time: Days and Weeks

Why learn this? You can have a record of what will happen on each day of the week.

Use schedules to list activities and the days or weeks when they happen.

A.

Mr. Ruxton's Class Activity Schedule	
Day	Activity
Monday	Music
Tuesday	P.E.
Wednesday	Computer
Thursday	P.E.
Friday	Art

B.

Kid Land Super Meal Prizes	
Week	Prize
1	sunglasses and hat
2	bug-catching kit
3	bubble wand and bubble mix
4	coloring book and markers

- How are Schedules A and B different?

CRITICAL THINKING Why might you need to use schedules like the ones shown above?

_____

Sometimes a schedule lists activities with the days *and* times that they happen.

EAGLE RIDGE SOFTBALL PRACTICE SCHEDULE		
Activity	Day	Time
Girls 7 to 12 years	Monday	3:30–5:30
Boys 7 to 12 years	Tuesday	3:30–5:30
Teens	Wednesday	2:30–4:30
Women	Thursday	6:30–8:30
Men	Friday	6:30–8:30
Family Softball Day	Saturday	12:00–2:00

▶ CHECK

1. How long is each softball practice?

2. Suki is a girl in third grade. What day and time does she have softball practice?

SPORTS LINK

Softball was first played in Chicago in 1887. Players used an old boxing glove for a ball and a broom handle for a bat. For how many years has softball been played? (HINT: Subtract 1887 from the year it is now.)

▶ PRACTICE

COMPUTER LAB SCHEDULE	
Day	Grade
Monday	kindergarten, first
Tuesday	third
Wednesday	fifth
Thursday	fourth
Friday	second

For Problems 3–4, use the computer schedule.

3. Georgette goes to the computer lab on Wednesday. What grade is she in?

4. Adam is in second grade. What day does he go to the computer lab?

For Problems 5–6, use the activity schedule.

AFTER-SCHOOL ACTIVITY SCHEDULE		
Activity	Day	Time
Play Practice	Mon	3:30–5:30
Chorus	Tue	3:30–4:30
Band	Wed	3:00–5:00
Chorus	Thu	3:30–4:30
Tumbling Team	Fri	4:00–5:30

5. On what days of the week does the chorus practice?

6. Preston is on the tumbling team, and Rafael is in the chorus. What days can they play together after school?

Problem Solving • Mixed Applications

Using Data For Problems 7–9, use the calendar.

October						
Sun	Mon	Tue	Wed	Thu	Fri	Sat
	1	2	3	4	5	6
7	8	9	10	11	12	13
14	15	16	17	18	19	20
21	22	23	24	25	26	27
28	29	30	31			

7. **Sports** Tiffany goes to gymnastics on Mondays and Thursdays. How many days will she go to gymnastics in October?

8. The student council meets on October 1, 15, and 29. The safety patrol meets on October 3, 17, and 31. Make a schedule of these activities.

9. ✍ **Write a problem** about Chandra's uncle. He is coming to visit October 24. He will stay for 5 days.

Mixed Review and Test Prep

Find the sum. (pages 52–53)

10.	11.	12.	13.	14.
345	192	854	426	619
+125	+674	+127	+424	+114

Choose the letter of the correct difference. (pages 62–63)

15. 500   **A** 289
    −321   **B** 179
           C 209
           D 279

16. 800   **F** 303
    −457   **G** 313
           H 333
           J 343

17. 700   **A** 207
    −573   **B** 117
           C 127
           D 107

Elapsed Time: Days, Weeks, and Months

Why learn this? You can tell the elapsed times of activities that are longer than minutes or hours.

The Finns are taking a trip. They are leaving on April 16 and coming home on April 23. How long will they be gone?

Use the calendar to find the elapsed time. Count the number of days from April 16 to April 23.

So, the Finns will be gone for 7 days, or 1 week.

- How long would the Finns' trip be if they came home on April 30?

April						
Sun	Mon	Tue	Wed	Thu	Fri	Sat
			1	2	3	4
5	6	7	8	9	10	11
12	13	14	15	16	17	18
19	20	21	22	23	24	25
26	27	28	29	30		

Units of Time

7 days = 1 week (wk)

12 months (mo) = 1 year (yr)

Use a six-month calendar to find elapsed times longer than one month. Make a six-month calendar by putting 6 one-month calendars together.

1. Start with January. Cut around the outside of the calendar.

1	2	3	4	5	6	7
8	9	10	11	12	13	14
15	16	17	18	19	20	21
22	23	24	25	26	27	28
29	30	31				

2. Cut off the blank rectangles.

1	2	3	4	5	6	7
8	9	10	11	12	13	14
15	16	17	18	19	20	21
22	23	24	25	26	27	28
29	30	31				

3. Glue or tape to the top of a large sheet of paper.

1	2	3	4	5	6	7
8	9	10	11	12	13	14
15	16	17	18	19	20	21
22	23	24	25	26	27	28
29	30	31				

4. Repeat Steps 1 and 2 for February.

		1	2	3	4
5	6	7	8	9	10	11
12	13	14	15	16	17	18
19	20	21	22	23	24	25
26	27	28			

5. Glue or tape so that February 1 is next to January 31. Follow the same steps for March through June.

1	2	3	4	5	6	7
8	9	10	11	12	13	14
15	16	17	18	19	20	21
22	23	24	25	26	27	28
29	30	31	1	2	3	4
5	6	7	8	9	10	11
12	13	14	15	16	17	18
19	20	21	22	23	24	25
26	27	28			

▶ CHECK

1. How many weeks are there from February 26 to April 9?

2. What is the date 3 weeks after April 11?

▶ PRACTICE

For Problem 3, use the calendar at the right.

3. Dennis worked on his science project every day from January 2 to January 16. How many days did he work on his science project? how many weeks?

January						
Sun	Mon	Tue	Wed	Thu	Fri	Sat
1	2	3	4	5	6	7
8	9	10	11	12	13	14
15	16	17	18	19	20	21
22	23	24	25	26	27	28
29	30	31				

For Exercises 4–10, use your six-month calendar. Write the date 4 weeks later.

4. January 13   5. February 28   6. May 5   7. June 1

Write the number of weeks.

8. from January 18 to February 8

9. from March 15 to May 3

10. from April 9 to June 11

Problem Solving • Mixed Applications

Using Data For Problems 11–14, use your six-month calendar.

11. Students return to school after winter break on January 2. Spring break begins March 27. How many weeks are students in school before spring break begins?

12. The last day of spring break is April 7. The students have school for 9 more weeks. When does school end?

13. **Weather** It snowed for 14 days in January, 12 days in February, and 7 days in March. How many days in all did it snow?

14. ⬛ **Write a problem** using your six-month calendar. Ask about an after-school activity.

LESSON CONTINUES

Problem–Solving Strategy: Work Backward

▶ **THE PROBLEM** The date on Crystal's calendar is June 22. She just spent 5 days with her grandparents. Before that, Crystal spent 3 weeks at camp. On what date did Crystal leave for camp?

REMEMBER:

UNDERSTAND

PLAN

SOLVE

LOOK BACK

UNDERSTAND

- What are you asked to find?

- What information will you use?

- Is there information you will not use? If so, what?

PLAN

- What strategy can you use?

  Work backward to find the date on which Crystal left for camp.

SOLVE

- How can you use the strategy to solve the problem?

  Find June 22 on your six-month calendar.

  First, count back 5 days, to June 17, for the time Crystal spent with her grandparents.

  Next, count back 3 weeks, to May 27, for the time Crystal spent at camp.

  So, Crystal left for camp on May 27.

LOOK BACK

- How can you decide if your answer makes sense?

- What other strategy could you use?

Work backward to solve.
For Problems 1–2, use your six-month calendar.

1. The date on Jessica's calendar is June 20. She just spent 6 days in Florida. Before that, Jessica spent 2 weeks at camp. On what date did Jessica leave for camp?

2. The date on Patrick's calendar is June 3. He just spent 5 days at Space Camp. Before Space Camp, Patrick spent 1 week at the beach. On what date did Patrick go to the beach?

3. Shawna was at soccer practice for 45 minutes. Before that, she spent 15 minutes traveling from school to soccer practice. It is now 4:00. At what time did Shawna leave school?

4. It is now 12:00. Heather just spent 30 minutes eating lunch. Before lunch, she was in math class for 1 hour. At what time did math class begin?

Mixed Applications

Solve.

CHOOSE a strategy and a tool.
- Make a Table   • Guess and Check   • Act It Out
- Work Backward   • Write a Number Sentence

 Paper/Pencil   Calculator   Hands-On   Mental Math

5. Keith is thinking of three numbers in a row that are between 1 and 10. The sum of the numbers is 18. What are the three numbers?

6. The Acosta family traveled 236 miles on Saturday and 140 miles on Sunday. How many miles did they travel in all?

7. The clock shows the time right now. Rhonda just spent 45 minutes at lunch. Before that, she spent 15 minutes reading. At what time did Rhonda start reading?

8. The third grade put on a show for their parents. There were 114 parents who went to the show. There were enough seats for 200 people. How many empty seats were there?

9. Yoshi has 3 dimes, 3 nickels, and 5 pennies. How much money does she have?

10. There were 22 birds in a tree. Then 3 birds flew away. How many birds are left?

► CHECK Understanding

VOCABULARY

1. _?_ is the time that passes from the start of an activity to the end. (page 90)

2. A _?_ is a table that lists activities or events and the times they happen. (page 92)

For Problem 3, use the Art Club schedule.
(pages 92–93 and 96–97)

3. What day and time does the Art Club work with clay?

For Problem 4, use the calendar. (pages 98–99)

4. Bill went to Arizona on December 9. He came home on December 23. How long was Bill gone?

ART CLUB SCHEDULE		
Activity	**Day**	**Time**
Clay	Mon	8:15–8:45
Painting	Tue	8:15–8:45
String Art	Wed	8:15–8:45
Weaving	Wed	2:45–3:15

December						
Sun	Mon	Tue	Wed	Thu	Fri	Sat
					1	2
3	4	5	6	7	8	9
10	11	12	13	14	15	16
17	18	19	20	21	22	23
24	25	26	27	28	29	30
31						

► CHECK Skills

Find the ending time. (pages 90–91)

5. **starting time:** 3:30
   elapsed time: 45 minutes

6. **starting time:** 7:15
   elapsed time: 1 hour and 15 minutes

Copy and complete the schedule. (pages 94–95)

GREG'S SATURDAY MORNING SCHEDULE		
Activity	**Time**	**Elapsed Time**
7. Eat breakfast	9:15–9:30	?
8. Shower and get dressed	?	45 min

► CHECK Problem Solving

Solve. (pages 100–101)

CHOOSE a strategy and a tool.

- Make a Table
- Act It Out
- Guess and Check
- Work Backward

 Paper/Pencil   Calculator   Hands-On   Mental Math

9. Bo came home from a 5-day trip on May 17. Before that, he spent 1 week packing for his trip. When did Bo start packing?

10. Three numbers in a row have a sum of 24. The numbers are between 1 and 10. What are the three numbers?

Test Prep

Choose the best answer.

1. The football game starts at 1:15. It ends at 4:30. How long is the game?

   A 1 hr 15 min   **B** 3 hr 45 min

   C 4 hr 25 min   **D** 3 hr 15 min

2. The spelling test took 28 minutes. The math test took 47 minutes. How many minutes longer was the math test?

   F 19 min   **G** 21 min

   H 11 min   **J** 29 min

3. This chart shows the schedule for swimming lessons.

SWIMMING LESSONS	
Group	**Schedule**
Ages 4–6	9:30–10:15
Ages 7–9	10:15–10:45
Ages 10–12	10:45–11:45
Ages 13–14	12:40–1:10

   Which group has the longest class?

   A Ages 4–6   **B** Ages 7–9
   C Ages 10–12   **D** Ages 13–14

4. It took 23 minutes for Ms. Putnam to drive Nathan to play group. They left home at 2:30. Which clock shows the time they arrived at play group?

   F

   H

   G 2:53

   J

5. This chart shows a class schedule.

CLASS SCHEDULE	
Class	**Time**
Reading	8:15–8:55
Math	9:00–9:35
Science	10:15–11:00
Art	2:15–2:45

   Which class is the shortest?

   A Math   **B** Science

   C Reading   **D** Art

6. Use the calendar to find elapsed time.

May						
Sun	Mon	Tue	Wed	Thu	Fri	Sat
				1	2	3
4	5	6	7	8	9	10
11	12	13	14	15	16	17
18	19	20	21	22	23	24
25	26	27	28	29	30	31

   Cindy arrived at her aunt's house on May 8. Two weeks later, she left to visit her cousin. On what date in May did Cindy leave her aunt's house?

   F May 15   **G** May 21

   H May 22   **J** May 23

7. Carrie and her sister made 19 wreaths, 28 bows, and 11 baskets. Which shows how many wreaths and baskets the girls made?

   A 19 + 28   **B** 28 + 11

   C 28 + 19   **D** 19 + 11

7 MONEY

HISTORY **LINK**

One hundred years ago most families bought fabric and sewed their own clothes.

Clothes, Then and Now

Look at the catalog advertisements from 100 years ago. Boys and girls who lived then liked new clothes for special occasions, just like we do today.

Use the price list to find the cost of each item from 100 years ago.

- Draw two ways you could use coins and bills to equal each amount.

- Write a number sentence to check each answer.

- Discuss what these outfits would cost today.

BOYS

Sailor suit, cap.	$1.25
Striped suit.	45¢
White linen suit.	85¢

GIRLS

Skirt, blouse, coat set.	$2.98
Gingham dress.	$1.23
Linen sailor suit.	$1.48

DID YOU

- ✓ find the cost of each item?

- ✓ draw two ways you could use coins and bills to equal each amount?

- ✓ write a number sentence to check each answer?

- ✓ discuss what these outfits would cost today?

Counting Bills and Coins

VOCABULARY
decimal point

Why learn this? You can count larger amounts of money when you're at the store.

Mel bought a T-shirt. He paid the amount shown. How much money did Mel spend?

Count: $5.00 $6.00 $6.25 $6.35 $6.45 $6.46

Write: $6.46

Read: six dollars and forty-six cents

So, Mel spent $6.46.

Notice that

⇨ the number before the decimal point shows the number of dollars.

⇨ the number after the decimal point shows the number of cents.

⇨ the word *and* stands for the decimal point.

REMEMBER:

 half dollar, 50¢, or fifty cents

 quarter, 25¢, or twenty-five cents

 dime, 10¢, or ten cents

 nickel, 5¢, or five cents

 penny, 1¢, or one cent

EXAMPLE

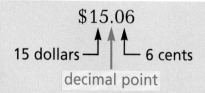

$15.06

15 dollars ⌐ ⌐ 6 cents

decimal point

Read: fifteen dollars and six cents

SOCIAL STUDIES LINK

Around 1850 Isaac Singer invented a machine with a needle that moved up and down. It was powered by a foot pedal. Fabric for a dress cost about $0.65 and thread cost about $0.03. About how much did it cost to sew a dress in the 1850's?

Talk About It

• Why is there a zero after the decimal point in the example?

• What does the zero in $0.83 mean?

• How do you read $0.83?

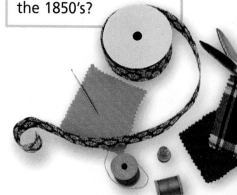

▶ CHECK

Count the money and write the amount.

1.

2.

▶ PRACTICE

Write each amount as you would read it.

3. $2.34   4. $4.26   5. $10.99   6. $18.60

7. $3.07   8. $5.40   9. $16.90   10. $20.01

11. $6.21   12. $8.29   13. $11.11   14. $19.09

Problem Solving • Mixed Applications

For Problems 15–17, use the picture.

15. **Consumer** Carlos has one $1 bill, 2 quarters, and 3 dimes. Which item does he have enough money to buy?

16. **Number Sense** Alex has exactly enough money to buy the pencil box. He has one $1 bill and 5 coins. What coins does he have?

17. ✏ **Write a problem** about money, using the picture.

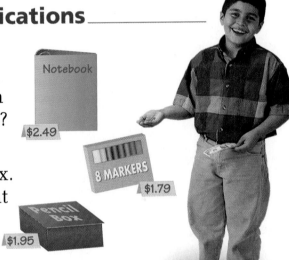

Mixed Review and Test Prep

Copy each problem. Find the sum. Tell if you used *counting on* or *make a ten*. (pages 2–3)

18. 2
    +4

19. 6
    +9

20. 4
    +7

21. 9
    +3

Find the sum. Choose the letter of a related subtraction fact. (pages 12–13)

22. $5 + 6 =$ __?__   **A** $10 - 5 = 5$ **B** $10 - 6 = 4$ **C** $11 - 6 = 5$ **D** Not Here

23. $7 + 9 =$ __?__   **F** $15 - 7 = 8$ **G** $16 - 7 = 9$ **H** $14 - 7 = 7$ **J** Not Here

24. $8 + 6 =$ __?__   **A** $15 - 6 = 9$ **B** $12 - 8 = 4$ **C** $13 - 6 = 7$ **D** Not Here

Making Equivalent Sets

You will investigate making equal amounts of money.

Sets that are **equivalent** name the same amount.

Examples A, B, C, and D are equivalent sets.
Each set of coins has a value of 10¢.

A. **B.** **C.** **D.**

Talk About It

- Which set with a value of 10¢ has the fewest number of coins?

- Which set with a value of 10¢ has the greatest number of coins? Why?

▶ EXPLORE

MATERIALS: play coins and bills

Use play money. Make equivalent sets with a value of $1.25.

Record

Draw pictures of two equivalent sets with a value of $1.25.

List how many of each coin and bill you used for each set.

Now, investigate making three equivalent sets of money.

Use play money to make equivalent sets.

1. Draw three equivalent sets with a value of $3.55 and three equivalent sets with a value of $5.21.

2. List how many of each bill and coin you used for each set.

3. Why might you need to know how to make equivalent sets of money?

4. ✏ **Write About It** Explain how you can show an amount of money by using the fewest bills and coins.

▶ PRACTICE

Make an equivalent set with bills and coins. List how many of each bill and coin you used.

5.

6.

Make two equivalent sets for each amount. List how many of each bill and coin you used.

7. $1.30	**8.** $4.18	**9.** $5.45	**10.** $8.56
11. $6.20	**12.** $9.05	**13.** $7.62	**14.** $10.55
15. $3.65	**16.** $2.98	**17.** $6.49	**18.** $11.14

Problem Solving • Mixed Applications

19. Pat has four $1 bills, 3 quarters, 1 dime, and 2 nickels. Does he have $5.00? Explain.

20. **Logical Reasoning** Tanya has 3 quarters. Evan has an equivalent amount in dimes and nickels. Evan has 9 coins. How many dimes and nickels does he have?

21. **Number Sense** How many combinations of coins can you use to make 12¢? What are the combinations?

Comparing Amounts

Why learn this? You can tell who has more money.

Jo has this much
money in her purse.

Lin has this much
money in her purse.

Who has more money?

Count the money. Jo has $1.75. Lin also has $1.75.

So, they have equivalent amounts of money.

Alan has this much money to
spend at the baseball game.

Ken has this much money to
spend at the baseball game.

Who has more money?

Count the money. Alan has $2.51. Ken has $2.42.

Since $2.51 > $2.42, Alan has more money.

Sara has this much
money to spend at the
school store.

Chris has this much
money to spend at the
school store.

REMEMBER:

The symbol for
greater than is >.
The symbol for
less than is <. The
symbol points to the
smaller number.

52 > 42

Read from left to right.

Say: Fifty-two is
greater than forty-two.

Who has more money?

Count the money. Sara has $2.66. Chris has $2.75.

Since $2.66 < $2.75, Sara has less money.
So, Chris has more money.

▶ CHECK

1. Does the person with more coins always have the greater amount of money? Explain.

▶ PRACTICE

Compare the amounts of money. Write the letter of the greater amount.

2. **a.**   **b.**

3. **a.**    **b.**

4. **a.**    **b.**

Problem Solving • Mixed Applications

5. **Consumer** Lou sells lemonade. Each glass costs 25¢. At the end of the day, Lou has 9 quarters, 6 dimes, and 3 nickels. How many glasses of lemonade did he sell?

6. **Compare** June counts the money in her bank. She has 8 quarters, 10 dimes, and 10 nickels. Isabel has four $1 bills. Who has more money?

7. ✏️ **Write a problem** that compares two amounts of money.

CONSUMER LINK

Have you ever seen this coin? It is called a *half dollar*. A half dollar has a value of fifty cents. How many quarters are equivalent to one half dollar? how many dimes? how many nickels?

Mixed Review and Test Prep

Copy each problem. Find the sum. (pages 6–7)

8. $5 + 0 = \underline{\ ?\ }$ 9. $0 + 9 = \underline{\ ?\ }$ 10. $0 + 0 = \underline{\ ?\ }$

Choose the letter of the correct difference. (pages 10–11)

11. $8 - 3 = \underline{\ ?\ }$ **A** 4   **B** 5   **C** 6   **D** 11

12. $9 - 6 = \underline{\ ?\ }$ **F** 15   **G** 4   **H** 3   **J** 2

MORE PRACTICE page H79

Making Change

You will investigate counting on to make change.

Sandra buys a notebook that costs $0.78. She pays with a $1 bill. How much change will she get?

Count on to find the amount of change Sandra will get. Start at $0.78. Count on to $1.00.

Count on: $0.79 $0.80 $0.90 $1.00

Since 2 pennies and 2 dimes equal $0.22, Sandra will get $0.22 in change.

Notice that
⇨ you begin counting on with coins of least value and continue to coins of greatest value.

Practice counting on to find the amount of change.

▶ EXPLORE

MATERIALS: play coins and bills

Clark pays $1.00 for a pencil that costs $0.27. How much change will he get? Use play money to help you count the change.

Record

Draw a picture of the change Clark will get. Label the picture, as in the example above. Write the amount.

Talk About It

Which coin did you begin with to count on from $0.27 to $1.00?

▶ TRY THIS

Use play money to count the change you will get. Write the amount of change.

1. You pay $1.00 for a drink that costs $0.67.

2. You pay $3.00 for a notebook that costs $2.59.

3. You pay $5.00 for a book that costs $3.75.

4. ✏ **Write About It** When counting change, should you begin with the coin of least or greatest value? Why?

▶ PRACTICE

Use play money. List the coins you could get as change from a $1 bill.

5. $0.45

6.  $0.89

7. CRAYONS $0.39

8. 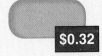 $0.32

Use play money. List the coins and bills you could get as change.

	Amount Paid	Cost of Item	Change
9.	$1.00	$0.26	_?_
10.	$4.00	$3.68	_?_
11.	$5.00	$3.12	_?_

Problem Solving • Mixed Applications

12. **Reasoning** Julio spent $2.18 at the store. He gave the clerk $5.00. List the change he should have received.

13. **Shopping** Emma bought a card for $0.55. She gave the clerk $1.00. The clerk did not have any quarters for change. What is the least number of coins Emma could have received?

Technology Link

💿 In *Mighty Math Zoo Zillions*, the game *Gnu Ewe Boutique* challenges you to make change. Use Grow Slide Level Q.

Adding and Subtracting Money

Why learn this? You can figure out how much money you will spend and how much change you should get.

Ryan bought a dog collar for $4.95 and a leash for $6.54. How much money did Ryan spend?

MODEL

What is $4.95 + $6.54?

Step 1	**Step 2**	**Step 3**
Add money amounts the same as other numbers. Write the problem.	Add to find the sum.	Write the sum in dollars and cents.
$\begin{array}{r} \$4.95 \\ +\ 6.54 \end{array} \rightarrow \begin{array}{r} 495 \\ +654 \end{array}$	$\begin{array}{r} 1 \\ 495 \\ +654 \\ \hline 1149 \end{array}$	$1149 \rightarrow \$11.49$

Since $4.95 + $6.54 = $11.49, Ryan spent $11.49.

Use a calculator to add money.

 Press:

Display: 11.49

MODEL

What is $5.00 − $3.95?

Step 1	**Step 2**	**Step 3**
Subtract money amounts the same as other numbers. Write the problem.	Subtract to find the difference.	Write the difference in dollars and cents.
$\begin{array}{r} \$5.00 \\ -\ 3.95 \end{array} \rightarrow \begin{array}{r} 500 \\ -395 \end{array}$	$\begin{array}{r} 9 \\ 4\ \cancel{10}\ 10 \\ \cancel{5}\ \cancel{0}\ \cancel{0} \\ -3\ 9\ 5 \\ \hline 1\ 0\ 5 \end{array}$	$105 \rightarrow \$1.05$

So, $5.00 − $3.95 = $1.05.

Calculator Activities pages H64–H65

▶ CHECK

1. How is adding and subtracting money amounts different from adding and subtracting other numbers?

2. When adding and subtracting money amounts, why do you need to put a dollar sign and a decimal point in the answer?

CULTURAL LINK

This 1997 ten-cent coin is in memory of the voyage from England to Canada in 1497 by John Cabot. How many years after the voyage was this coin made in its memory?

▶ PRACTICE

Find the sum.

| 3. | $1.35
 + 2.43 | 4. | $4.56
 + 3.27 | 5. | $6.45
 + 0.39 | 6. | $5.42
 + 4.28 | 7. | $2.81
 + 3.79 |

| 8. | $3.09
 + 7.54 | 9. | $8.47
 + 4.61 | 10. | $7.58
 + 5.96 | 11. | $9.50
 + 8.75 | 12. | $6.98
 + 8.85 |

Find the difference.

| 13. | $1.75
 − 0.63 | 14. | $5.78
 − 1.99 | 15. | $4.85
 − 2.93 | 16. | $6.02
 − 3.56 | 17. | $7.41
 − 2.80 |

| 18. | $5.00
 − 2.14 | 19. | $8.67
 − 4.76 | 20. | $10.00
 − 5.85 | 21. | $9.63
 − 2.75 | 22. | $20.00
 − 10.50 |

Problem Solving • Mixed Applications

Using Data For Problems 23–26, use the table.

23. Ming-lei bought a feeding bowl and a circle toy. How much did she spend in all?

24. **Compare** How much more does the scratching post cost than the feeding bowl?

25. Roberto has $5.00 in his wallet. He buys a scratching post for $3.79. How much change will he get?

Cat Items for Sale	
Pet Bed	$7.99
Feeding Bowl	$2.95
Scratching Post	$3.79
Circle Toy	$1.75

26. ✏ **Write a problem** using the information in the table.

LESSON CONTINUES →

Problem–Solving Strategy: Write a Number Sentence

▶ **THE PROBLEM** Alisha is going camping with the Outdoors Club. She needs to buy a flashlight for $5.65, a water bottle for $3.39, and bug spray for $2.73. How much money will Alisha spend in all? How much change will she get if she pays with a $20 bill?

REMEMBER:
UNDERSTAND
PLAN
SOLVE
LOOK BACK

UNDERSTAND

- What are you asked to find?

- What information will you use?

- Is there information you will not use? If so, what?

PLAN

- What strategy can you use?

  You can write *number sentences.*

SOLVE

- How can you use the strategy?

  Write a number sentence to find out how much Alisha will spend in all.

  $5.65 + $3.39 + $2.73 = __?__

$$
\begin{array}{r}
\overset{1\ \ 1}{\$\ 5.65} \\
3.39 \\
+\ \ 2.73 \\
\hline
\$11.77
\end{array}
$$

  So, Alisha will spend $11.77.

  Then write a number sentence to find the change she will get.

  $20.00 − $11.77 = __?__

$$
\begin{array}{r}
\overset{9\ \ 9}{\overset{1\,\cancel{10}\ \cancel{10}\,10}{\$\cancel{20.00}}} \\
-\ 11.77 \\
\hline
\$8.23
\end{array}
$$

  So, Alisha will get $8.23 in change.

LOOK BACK

- How can you check the amount of change?

- What other strategy could you use?

Write a number sentence to solve.

1. Tiffany buys juice for $1.29, apples for $2.18, and a loaf of bread for $1.09. How much does Tiffany spend in all? How much change will she get from $5.00?

2. Ellis buys knee pads for $6.99, elbow pads for $5.98, and wrist guards for $6.95. How much does Ellis spend in all? How much change will he get from $20.00?

3. John buys a game for $4.95, a wallet for $8.29, and a key chain for $5.50. How much does John spend in all? How much change will he get from $20.00?

4. Crystal buys pencils for $1.69, notebook paper for $1.95, and a folder for $0.69. How much does Crystal spend in all? How much change will she get from $10.00?

Mixed Applications

Solve.

CHOOSE a strategy and a tool.
- Write a Number Sentence
- Act It Out
- Guess and Check
- Work Backward

 Paper/Pencil   Calculator   Hands-On   Mental Math

5. The sum of Barbara's and Ed's ages is 15 years. The difference is 5 years. How old are Barbara and Ed?

6. Jamie's science class begins at 10:00. It ends 52 minutes later. Where are the clock hands when science class ends?

7. Chun buys a hat for $3.99, a ball for $2.25, and a T-shirt for $4.49. How much does Chun spend in all? How much change will she get from $15.00?

8. There are 32 students in Gene's class. Of the students, 19 said they have flown in an airplane. How many students have never flown in an airplane?

9. The date is June 23. Leon just spent 4 days at the beach. Before that, he spent 2 weeks with his grandparents. On what date did Leon go to visit his grandparents?

JUNE						
Sun	Mon	Tue	Wed	Thu	Fri	Sat
				1	2	3
4	5	6	7	8	9	10
11	12	13	14	15	16	17
18	19	20	21	22	23	24
25	26	27	28	29	30	

▶ CHECK Understanding

1. **VOCABULARY** Sets that are ⸱?⸱ name the same amount. (page 108)

Make one equivalent set for each amount. List how many of each bill and coin you used. (pages 108–109)

2.

3.

Compare the amounts of money. Write the letter of the greater amount. (pages 110–111)

4. **a.**

   b.

▶ CHECK Skills

Count the money and write the amount. (pages 106–107)

5.

6.

Find the sum or difference. (pages 114–115)

7. $6.16
   + 1.16

8. $9.83
   − 4.24

9. $7.21
   + 9.08

10. $38.13
    − 32.99

11. $31.67
    + 13.79

▶ CHECK Problem Solving

Solve. (pages 116–117)

CHOOSE a strategy and a tool.
- Write a Number Sentence   • Act It Out
- Guess and Check

Paper/Pencil   Calculator   Hands-On   Mental Math

12. Gerard spent $1.65, $2.39, and $5.40. How much did he spend in all? How much change did he get from $10.00?

13. Joelle has some dimes. Kamil has 4 more dimes. They have 10 dimes in all. How many dimes does each one have?

Test Prep

Choose the best answer.

1. Rachel worked on homework for 55 minutes. Then she read a book for 25 minutes. How much time did she spend on homework and reading?

A 95 min   **B** 75 min
C 25 min   **D** 80 min

2. Dan's soccer practice begins at 3:45. It lasts 1 hour and 30 minutes. What time does practice end?

F 4:45   **G** 5:30   **H** 5:15   **J** 4:30

3. Miguel begins to walk to school at 7:30. It takes 35 minutes to get there. Which clock shows the time Miguel arrives at school?

A   **B**

C   **D**

4. Count Emily's money.

How much money does she have?

F $1.65   **G** $1.85
H $1.60   **J** $1.75

5. Tracy has just enough money to buy a headband that costs $1.95. Tracy has $1 and 6 coins. What coins does she have?

A 3 quarters, 2 dimes, 1 nickel
B 1 quarter, 4 dimes, 1 nickel
C 2 quarters, 3 dimes, 1 nickel
D 3 quarters, 1 dime, 2 nickels

6. Keisha had $20.00. She spent $3.17 at the grocery store, $2.45 at the bakery, and $5.35 at the cleaners. How much money does she have left?

F $9.60
G $10.97
H $9.03
J $10.17

7. Fred and Joe went to the movies. The movie started at 8:15. It ended at 10:45. How long was the movie?

A 2 hr 25 min   **B** 2 hr 15 min
C 2 hr 45 min   **D** 2 hr 30 min

8. Ms. Milano has $58. She sees curtains for $35 and pillows for $17. If she buys the curtains, which shows how to find how much money she will have left?

F $58 − $17
G $58 − $35
H $35 − $17
J $35 + $17

MATH FUN!

ON THE JOB

PURPOSE To practice telling time with hours and minutes

YOU WILL NEED paper and pencil, 2 blank spinners, blank clockfaces

Play this game with a partner. Take turns. Make two spinners as shown. Pretend that you each have been hired to baby-sit every afternoon for one week. You start work at noon each day. Use the spinners to see how many hours and minutes you work each day. Draw where the hands on the clocks will point when you finish working. Record your hours for the week. Who worked more hours?

SPENDING GAME

PURPOSE To count change

YOU WILL NEED play money, 2 blank spinners

Play this game in a small group. Make two spinners as shown. Everyone starts with $6. On your turn, spin both pointers to see what you have bought and how much it costs. Pay that amount to the person to your left and ask for the correct change. Make sure that both of you agree the change is correct. See who can keep their money the longest.

WHO HAS MORE?

PURPOSE To practice comparing amounts

YOU WILL NEED play money, pencil, and paper

Write down seven words. Find the value of each by using the alphabet chart. Add up all your words. Find a partner and see whose words cost more.

A		N	
B	1¢		14¢
C	2¢	O	15¢
D	3¢	P	16¢
E	4¢	Q	17¢
F	5¢	R	18¢
G	6¢	S	19¢
H	7¢	T	20¢
I	8¢	U	21¢
J	9¢	V	22¢
K	10¢	W	23¢
L	11¢	X	24¢
M	12¢	Y	25¢
	13¢	Z	26¢

PUZZLES

 HOME NOTE Play this game with a family member.

Making a Schedule

MATERIALS
Microsoft Word® or any other word-processing program

Tommy and his brother made a schedule of TV shows they want to watch this week. Tommy used a word-processing program on their computer to make a table. On which day will they watch the longest TV show?

row →

TV WATCHING SCHEDULE		
Day	**TV Show**	**Time**
Mon	Jungle Journey	6:30–7:30
Tue	Crime Busters	7:00–8:00
Wed	Abracadabra	7:30–8:00
Thu	Animal Mysteries	7:00–8:00
Fri	Lost Planet	7:00–9:00

REMEMBER
row → what you read *across* in a table
column → what you read *down* in a table

↑ column

EXAMPLE

Some word-processing programs have a table icon. Click the icon and then drag to highlight the rows and columns you need for the table.

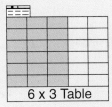

6 x 3 Table

Tommy needs 6 rows and 3 columns for his table. He added another row for the title of the schedule.

PRACTICE

1. Sandy is making a schedule of her classmates' birthdays for the upcoming month, March. Amy's birthday is on the 5th, Joe's is on the 12th, and Cameron's is on the 18th. Make a table to show the March birthday information. Make columns for students' names and for the dates.

2. A swimming class for ages 1–3 is 8:30–9:15 on Mondays and Wednesdays. A class for ages 4–6 is 9:30 to 10:15 on Wednesdays and Fridays. A class for ages 7–10 is at 10:00–11:00 on Tuesdays and Thursdays. Make a table showing the schedule.

3. **Using the Computer** Use a word-processing program and a TV guide to make a schedule of the TV shows you want to watch this week.

4. Make a table that shows a zookeeper's schedule for feeding the animals. Include at least five different animals in the schedule.

Study Guide and Review

Vocabulary Check

Choose a term from the box to complete the sentence.

1. The time that passes from the start of an activity to the end of that activity is __?__. (page 90)

2. A __?__ is a table that lists activities and the times they happen. (page 92)

3. Sets that are __?__ name the same amount. (page 108)

Study and Solve

CHAPTER 5

EXAMPLE

Write the time as you would read it. Write the time.

Read: 32 minutes after 3
Write: 3:32

For Problems 4-5, write *more than* or *less than*. (pages 78-79)

4. It takes __?__ an hour to sing a song.

5. It takes __?__ a minute to watch a whole TV show.

For Problems 6-7, write the time as you would read it. Write the time.
(pages 82-83)

6.

7.

Solve. (pages 84-85)

8. Beth's clock shows 50 minutes after four. Where are the hands on the clock?

CHAPTER 6

EXAMPLE

MARC'S CLASS SCHEDULE		
Subject	Time	Elapsed Time
Reading	9:00– _?_	30 min
Language	9:30–10:00	30 min
Spelling	_?_	30 min
Math	10:30–11:15	_?_

Spelling is after language. It has an elapsed time of 30 minutes. Spelling is from 10:00–10:30.

For Problems 9–10, use the schedule.

9. What time does reading end? (pages 94–95)

10. What is the elapsed time for math? (pages 94–95)

For Problems 11–12, use the calendar to solve. (pages 98–101)

June						
Sun	Mon	Tue	Wed	Thu	Fri	Sat
					1	2
3	4	5	6	7	8	9
10	11	12	13	14	15	16
17	18	19	20	21	22	23
24	25	26	27	28	29	30

11. Rick's Aunt Carol came to visit Rick and his family on June 9. She went home on June 23. How long did Aunt Carol stay?

12. Edy came home from a 1-week trip on June 21. She also spent the 7 days before that on vacation at home. When did her vacation begin?

CHAPTER 7

EXAMPLE

Find the difference.

$8.84   1. Line up decimal points.
− 6.75   2. Subtract as with whole
$2.09   numbers.

Count the money and write the amount. (pages 106–107)

13.

Make an equivalent set of money for the amount shown. List how many of each bill and coin you used. (pages 108–109)

14.

Compare the amounts of money. Write the letter of the greater amount. (pages 110–111)

15.
a.   b.

For Problems 16–19, find the sum or difference. (pages 114–115)

16. $5.15
    + 6.95

17. $21.98
    + 19.25

18. $8.74
    − 2.69

19. $36.15
    − 30.79

Solve. (pages 116–117)

20. Mike buys pens for $1.99, paper for $2.59, and pencils for $4.60. How much does he spend in all? How much change will Mike get from $10.00?

Performance Assessment

Tasks: Show What You Know

1. Name two things it takes you about 1 minute to do. Name two things it takes you about 1 hour to do. Explain how you know. (pages 78–79)

2. Explain how to use the calendar for January at the top of page 99 to solve this problem: Beth ice-skated every day from January 6 to January 27. How many days did she ice-skate? How many weeks? (pages 98–101)

3. Draw these two groups of bills and coins:

Group 1:	**Group 2:**
two $1 bills	one $1 bill
1 quarter	5 quarters
3 dimes	5 dimes
1 nickel	

Explain how to compare the amounts of money in the groups. Tell which group is more.
(pages 110–111)

Problem Solving

Solve. Explain your method.

CHOOSE a strategy and a tool.
- Work Backward
- Write a Number Sentence
- Act It Out

 Paper/Pencil Calculator Hands-On Mental Math

4. Jared starts reading at 3:30 P.M. He reads for 45 minutes. Draw a clock that shows the time Jared finishes reading. Tell what time it is. (pages 84–85)

5. On a trip, the Johnsons will drive for 2 days each way. They will spend 3 days at the beach and 3 days at a state park. They must be home on July 23. On what day should the trip begin? How long will the trip last?

(pages 100–101)

6. Anna buys items for $3.79, $1.50, and $2.25. How much money will she get back if she pays with a $10 bill? Draw one way to show the change she will get back. (pages 116–117)

July						
Sun	Mon	Tue	Wed	Thu	Fri	Sat
	1	2	3	4	5	6
7	8	9	10	11	12	13
14	15	16	17	18	19	20
21	22	23	24	25	26	27
28	29	30	31			

Cumulative Review

Solve the problem. Then write the letter of the correct answer.

1. $6 + 5 + 9 =$ __?__

   A. 10   **B.** 18
   C. 19   **D.** 20

(pages 18–19)

2. Round 94 to the nearest ten.
   A. 9   **B.** 10
   C. 90   **D.** 100

(pages 24–27)

3.   60
   −49

   A. 9
   B. 11
   C. 21
   D. 109

(pages 38–43)

4. $645 + 378 =$ __?__

   A. 267   **B.** 913
   C. 1,023   **D.** 1,025

(pages 52–53)

5.   700
   −469

   A. 231
   B. 241
   C. 331
   D. 341

(pages 56–57, 62–63)

6. Estimate the time it will take to write your name.
   A. less than a minute
   B. about 5 minutes
   C. more than 5 minutes

(pages 78–79)

7. Estimate the time it will take to eat an ice cream cone.
   A. about 10 hours
   B. about 10 minutes
   C. about 10 days

(pages 78–79)

For Problems 8–9, write the letter of the correct time.

8.

   A. 3:27   **B.** 3:52
   C. 4:22   **D.** 4:27

(pages 80–83)

9.

   A. 8:42   **B.** 8:47
   C. 9:22   **D.** 9:27

10. Count the money.

   A. \$8.26   **B.** \$8.31
   C. \$9.21   **D.** \$10.31

(pages 106–107)

11.   \$30.00
   − 25.98

   A. \$4.02
   B. \$4.12
   C. \$5.98
   D. \$55.98

(pages 114–115)

12.   \$9.51
   + 7.68

   A. \$27.19
   B. \$29.17
   C. \$19.17
   D. \$17.19

(pages 114–115)

8 NUMBER CONCEPTS

HEALTH LINK

Your body needs exercise to stay healthy. Exercise gives your body strength by making your muscles work hard. Hard work makes your muscles strong.

Exercise Routines

Slowly stretching our muscles before we exercise helps us do our best. When we release muscle tension and our bodies relax, we move better.

Design a warm-up routine.

- Recall stretches you already know.

- Make a list of ten stretching ideas and name or draw them.

- Practice your exercise routine all the way through 100 stretches to see if you want to make any changes.

STRETCHES

side stretcher   butterfly

back stretcher   hurdler's stretch

arm stretch   leg stretch

DID YOU

☑ recall stretches you already knew?

☑ name ten stretching ideas?

☑ practice exercising 100 stretches?

Ways to Use Numbers

Why learn this? You can use numbers to tell how many people are in line.

Use a **cardinal** number to tell how many. How many people are in line for lunch?

Use an **ordinal** number to show position or order. Cindy is waving at us. Where in the line is Cindy?

Cindy is fifth in line.

So, there are 5 people in line for lunch.

- Which numbers are cardinal numbers? ordinal numbers?

AUGUST						
				1	2	3
4	5	6	7	8	9	10
11	12	13	14	15	16	17
18	19	20	21	22	23	24
25	26	27	28	29	30	31

▶ CHECK

For Exercises 1–4, use the November calendar. Answer each question. Tell if your answer is a *cardinal* or an *ordinal* number.

November						
Sun	Mon	Tue	Wed	Thu	Fri	Sat
1	2	3	4	5	6	7
8	9	10	11	12	13	14
15	16	17	18	19	20	21
22	23	24	25	26	27	28
29	30					

1. How many days are in November?

2. What is the date of the third Monday?

3. Thanksgiving is the fourth Thursday in November. On what date is Thanksgiving?

4. How many Tuesdays are in the month?

5. Give your own examples of cardinal and ordinal numbers.

▶ PRACTICE

For Exercises 6–10, use the words *MATHEMATICS IS FUN*. Answer each question. If your answer is a number, tell if it is a *cardinal* or an *ordinal* number.

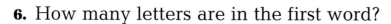

MATHEMATICS IS FUN!

6. How many letters are in the first word?

7. What is the fourth letter of the first word?

8. What is the second letter of the third word?

9. In *FUN*, in which position is the letter *N*?

10. In which position is the second *M* in *MATHEMATICS*?

Problem Solving • Mixed Applications

Using Data The table shows how many medals were won in the 1996 Summer Olympic games by the athletes from five countries. For Problems 11–14, use the table.

11. How many medals did the United States win?

1996 SUMMER OLYMPIC MEDAL WINNERS			
Country	Gold	Silver	Bronze
United States	44	32	25
Russia	26	21	16
Germany	20	18	27
China	16	22	12
France	15	7	15

12. Which country won the fifth-highest number of gold medals?

13. **Compare** In which place is China for gold medal winners?

14. Which country won the second-highest number of silver medals?

15. ▭ **Write About It** Tell the difference between an ordinal number and a cardinal number.

Mixed Review and Test Prep

Find the sum. (pages 18–19)

16. $(2 + 3) + 6 =$?

17. $(5 + 5) + 7 =$?

18. $4 + (8 + 7) =$?

Choose the letter of the correct difference. (pages 56–57)

19. 654
−298
  A 254 **B** 356
  C 354 **D** 456

20. 721
−495
  F 333 **G** 316
  H 326 **J** 226

21. 989
−498
  A 491 **B** 497
  C 511 **D** 411

Understanding 100's

Why learn this? You can use what you know about hundreds to understand amounts of money.

Use what you know about tens and ones to learn about hundreds.

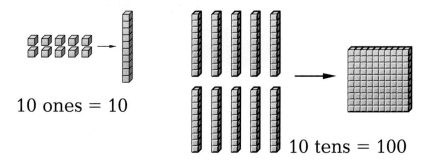

10 ones = 10

10 tens = 100

Talk About It

- How many ones are in 1 ten?

- How many tens are in 1 hundred?

- How many smaller blocks are needed to make the next larger block?

In 1897 saltine crackers cost 5¢ a box, and catsup cost 25¢ a quart. In 1997 the items cost about $1.50 each. How many boxes of crackers could someone have bought for 10¢ in 1897?

Hundreds, tens, and ones can help you understand dollars, dimes, and pennies.

Hundreds	Tens	Ones
1 hundred = 10 tens, or 100 ones	1 ten = 10 ones	1 one
Dollars	**Dimes**	**Pennies**
1 dollar = 10 dimes, or 100 pennies	1 dime = 10 pennies	1 penny

CRITICAL THINKING How are hundreds, tens, and ones like dollars, dimes and pennies?

► CHECK

Answer each question. You may use place-value blocks or play money.

1. How many in ?

2. How many 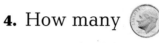 in ?

3. How many  are equal to ?

4. How many  are equal to ?

► PRACTICE

Write *true* or *false*. Change words in the false sentences to make them true.

5. There are 100 ones in a hundred.

6. There are 10 tens in a ten.

7. There are 100 dimes in a dollar.

8. There are 100 pennies in a dollar.

Problem Solving • Mixed Applications

9. **Money** Nash hands a clerk $1.00 for a 69¢ toy. How much change should Nash get? What coins might he get?

10. ✏️ **Write About It** Tell how you would explain to a classmate how you know that 8 dimes and 20 pennies are the same as $1.00.

Mixed Review and Test Prep

Find the difference. Regroup if needed. (pages 38–39)

11.	12.	13.	14.	15.
41	65	78	54	85
−23	−45	−62	−26	−49

Group the addends. Then choose the letter of the correct sum. (pages 18–19)

16. $9 + 6 + 4 =$?   **A** 20   **B** 18   **C** 19   **D** 21

17. $7 + 3 + 8 =$?   **F** 21   **G** 20   **H** 19   **J** 18

18. $5 + 9 + 1 =$?   **A** 16   **B** 15   **C** 17   **D** 14

Number Patterns

VOCABULARY

even

odd

You will investigate number patterns on the hundred chart.

Use number patterns to skip count on a hundred chart.

1	2	3	4	5	6	7	8	9	10
11	12	13	14	15	16	17	18	19	20
21	22	23	24	25	26	27	28	29	30

Talk About It

- What pattern do you notice when you skip count by twos? by threes? by fives?

- Skip count by twos. Move 10 skips. Where are you?

- Skip count by threes. Move 5 skips. Where are you?

Gail is looking for even and odd numbers on the hundred chart. She skip counts by twos and colors each number she says.

Even numbers end with 0, 2, 4, 6, or 8.

Odd numbers end with 1, 3, 5, 7, or 9.

▶ EXPLORE

MATERIALS: hundred charts, crayons
Skip count by twos to 100 and color the boxes yellow. Look for an even and odd number pattern.

Record

Write which boxes on your hundred chart are even and which ones are odd.

Calculator Activities page H58

Talk About It

How do you know which numbers are odd?

I can tell if a number is even or odd by looking at the ones place.

▶ TRY THIS

1. Skip count by threes to 100 on the hundred chart. Color the boxes green. Describe the pattern you see.

2. ✎ **Write About It** How can you use the hundred chart to find 73 + 4?

▶ PRACTICE

Answer each question. Use a hundred chart.

3. Skip count by twos. Move 5 skips. Where are you?

4. Skip count by twos. Move 15 skips. Where are you?

5. Skip count by threes. Move 4 skips. Where are you?

6. Skip count by fives. Move 10 skips. Where are you?

Write the number. Tell whether it is *odd* or *even*.

7. 17	**8.** 11	**9.** 22	**10.** 30
11. 76	**12.** 940	**13.** 315	**14.** 8,135
15. 2,136	**16.** 817	**17.** 1,313	**18.** 999

Problem Solving • Mixed Applications

19. **Money** Geoff has 5 dimes and 2 pennies. He can use only quarters in the snack machine. How many quarters can Geoff get for the coins he has?

20. **Patterns** The houses on Quinn's street are numbered 1, 5, 9, 13, and 17. What are the next three house numbers?

Technology Link

💿 You can discover number patterns by using E-Lab, Activity 8. Available on CD-ROM and on the Internet at www.hbschool.com/elab

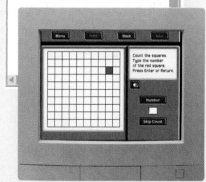

Patterns of Tens

Why learn this? You will use these number patterns to count by tens, such as counting groups of 10 stickers.

Devon had 23 stickers. He bought 3 packs, with 10 stickers in each. How many stickers does Devon have now?

What is 23 + 10 + 10 + 10?

- Add the numbers.
  23 + 10 + 10 + 10 = 53

- Skip count by tens.
  23, 33, 43, 53

- Count by tens on the hundred chart, beginning with 23 and moving down the column to skip count by tens.

So, Devon has 53 stickers.

1	2	3	4	5	6	7	8	9	10
11	12	13	14	15	16	17	18	19	20
21	22	23	24	25	26	27	28	29	30
31	32	33	34	35	36	37	38	39	40
41	42	43	44	45	46	47	48	49	50
51	52	53	54	55	56	57	58	59	60
61	62	63	64	65	66	67	68	69	70
71	72	73	74	75	76	77	78	79	80
81	82	83	84	85	86	87	88	89	90
91	92	93	94	95	96	97	98	99	100

Talk About It CRITICAL THINKING

- If Devon bought 4 more packs of stickers with 10 in each pack, how could he find how many stickers he had in all?

- How could patterns of tens help you subtract five groups of ten from 81? Explain.

▶ CHECK

Use patterns of tens to find the sum or difference.

1. 36 + 10 + 10   **2.** 24 + 20

3. 45 − 10 − 10   **4.** 68 − 30

5. 57 + 30   **6.** 81 − 40

Use patterns of tens to find the sum or difference.

7. $71 + 10 + 10$ **8.** $68 + 10 + 10$ **9.** $32 + 20$

10. $57 + 30$ **11.** $42 + 30$ **12.** $51 + 40$

13. $12 + 40$ **14.** $42 - 30$ **15.** $74 - 20$

16. $56 - 10$ **17.** $87 - 10 - 10$ **18.** $63 - 30$

Problem Solving • Mixed Applications

For Problems 19, 20, and 23, use the pictures of stickers.

19. Val had 13 stickers. Then she bought two sheets of heart stickers. How many stickers does she have now?

20. Val has 57 stickers. If she buys one sheet of star stickers, will she have more than or fewer than 75 stickers?

21. Logical Reasoning Maya is counting backward by tens: 80, 70, 60, 40, 30. Write a sentence to tell the mistake she made.

22. Number Sense I am a number between 40 and 50. If you keep subtracting tens from me, you reach 6. What number am I?

23. ✏️ **Write a problem** using what you know about the heart stickers or the star stickers at the right.

Technology Link

💿 In *Mighty Math Zoo Zillions*, the game *Annie's Jungle Trail* you can learn more about odd and even numbers, skip counting, and number patterns. Use Grow Slide Levels M and R.

Mixed Review and Test Prep

Find the difference. (pages 40–41)

24.
$$\begin{array}{r} 60 \\ -25 \\ \hline \end{array}$$
25.
$$\begin{array}{r} 40 \\ -18 \\ \hline \end{array}$$
26.
$$\begin{array}{r} 50 \\ -37 \\ \hline \end{array}$$
27.
$$\begin{array}{r} 80 \\ -41 \\ \hline \end{array}$$
28.
$$\begin{array}{r} 70 \\ -53 \\ \hline \end{array}$$

Choose the letter of the correct sum. (pages 54–55)

29.
$$\begin{array}{r} 371 \\ 259 \\ +465 \\ \hline \end{array}$$
A 995   **B** 905
C 1,005   **D** 1,095

30.
$$\begin{array}{r} \$2.45 \\ \$4.51 \\ +\$3.72 \\ \hline \end{array}$$
F $11.08   **G** $10.08
H $10.68   **J** $11.68

Using Benchmark Numbers

VOCABULARY
benchmark numbers

Why learn this? You can estimate the number of objects such as pennies, marbles, or beans.

Have you ever tried to estimate the number of beans in a jar?

Compare the beans in these three jars.

Jar A has 10 beans that you can count.

Jar B has 25 beans that you may be able to count.

Jar C has too many beans to count.

Benchmark numbers are useful numbers like 10, 25, 50, and 100 that help you see their relationship to other numbers. They are used to help you estimate about how many objects there are without counting them.

- Do you think Jar C has 14, 31, or 52 beans in it? Explain how you made your estimate.

▶ **CHECK**

1. How many beans would you estimate are in the jar at the right? Explain how you made your estimate.

2. About how many beans will fill the jar at the right? Explain.

► PRACTICE

Estimate the number of beans in each jar.
Use Jars A–C on page 136 as benchmarks.

3.

14, 35, or 70

4.

8, 28, or 60

5.

50, 100, or 200

6.

30, 68, or 95

7.

32, 63, or 91

8.

21, 46, or 70

Write *more than* or *fewer than* for each. Use
Jars A–C on page 136 as benchmarks to help
you estimate.

9. Are there more than or fewer
than 10 beans in Jar X?

10. Are there more than or fewer
than 25 beans in Jar Y?

Problem Solving • Mixed Applications

11. Estimation Look at Jeff's
jar of beans. He needs
50 beans for a project.
Does he have enough
beans? Explain.

Jeff's Jar

12. Tell how Jeff might use a
benchmark of 25 beans to fill
a jar that will hold about 100
beans.

13. Suppose you want to put
about 80 candies into a
piñata. How could you use
10 as a benchmark to help?

14. ✏️ **Write a problem** using a
benchmark and the beans in
Jar X or in Jar Y.

LESSON
CONTINUES ⟹

Problem–Solving Strategy: Make a Model

▶ **THE PROBLEM** Staci and David are saving their pennies for a new game. They have each saved more pennies than they want to count. How can they find how much each one of them has saved?

REMEMBER:

UNDERSTAND

PLAN

SOLVE

LOOK BACK

UNDERSTAND

- What are you asked to find?

- What information will you use?

- Is there information you will not use? If so, what?

David's Pennies   Staci's Pennies

PLAN

- What strategy can you use to solve the problem?

  You can *make a model* to guess how many pennies each one has saved.

SOLVE

- How can you use the strategy to solve the problem?

  Make a model of the same-size jar as Staci's and David's jars.

  Choose a benchmark number of pennies to put into the jar, such as 100.

  Use your benchmark model to guess the number of pennies in Staci's and David's jars.

  So, David has saved about 200 pennies, or about $2.00. Staci has saved about 400 pennies, or about $4.00.

LOOK BACK

- How can you decide if your answer makes sense?

- How can you check your guess?

Make a model to solve.

1. Ana is putting candies into a small box to give to a friend. She can hold about 10 candies in her hand at one time. How can Ana find out about how many candies she used to fill the box?

2. Brian is holding 5 coins in his hand. He tells Abu that the collection is worth 42¢. How can Abu find out which coins Brian is holding?

3. Mary added 3 tens to a set of 9 tens and 4 ones. What number do the tens and ones show?

4. Sheila's birthday is in two weeks. Today is October 8. When is Sheila's birthday?

Mixed Applications

Solve.

CHOOSE a strategy and a tool.
- Make a Model   • Guess and Check   • Act It Out
- Work Backward   • Write a Number Sentence

Paper/Pencil   Calculator   Hands-On   Mental Math

5. Wayne had $9.75. Then he spent $4.98 on a new softball. How much does he have now?

6. Mia removed four handfuls of pennies. She can hold about 25 pennies in her hand at one time. About how much money did she take out?

7. The clock shows the time Alan woke up. He was ready for school 45 minutes later. What time was it then?

8. Sammy and Jenny saved a total of $75. Sammy saved $15 more than Jenny. How much did they each save?

9. Penny has 8 boxes of cookies left to sell. She began with 20 boxes. How many boxes of cookies has Penny sold?

10. Four friends are standing in line to buy tickets. Andrew is ahead of Ben. Renee is behind Ben. Andrew is behind Melanie. Who is first in line?

▶ CHECK Understanding

VOCABULARY

1. A _?_ number tells how many. An _?_ number shows position or order. (page 128)

2. Numbers ending with 0, 2, 4, 6, or 8 are _?_ numbers. Those ending with 1, 3, 5, 7, or 9 are _?_ numbers. (page 132)

3. _?_ numbers are useful numbers like 10, 25, 50, and 100 that help you see their relationship to other numbers. (page 136)

Write the number. Tell if it is *odd* or *even*. (pages 132–133)

4. 16   **5.** 29   **6.** 38   **7.** 68   **8.** 191   **9.** 1,473

▶ CHECK Skills

Use the word *NUMBER* to answer each question.
Tell if it is a *cardinal* or an *ordinal* number. (pages 128–129)

10. How many letters are in the word?

11. In which position is the letter *U*?

Use patterns of tens to find the sum or difference. (pages 134–135)

12. 23 + 10 + 10

13. 48 − 10 − 10

Write *true* or *false*. Make the false sentences true. (pages 130–131)

14. There are 10 ones in a ten.

15. There are 10 pennies in a dollar.

▶ CHECK Problem Solving

Solve. (pages 136–139)

CHOOSE a strategy and a tool.
- Make a Model
- Write a Number Sentence
- Guess and Check
- Work Backward

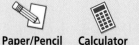

Paper/Pencil   Calculator   Hands-On   Mental Math

16. Trey spent $17 at the ball game. He still had $15 when he got home. How much did Trey have to begin with?

17. Nora has used one box of tiles. About how many more boxes are needed to cover the floor?

Test Prep

Choose the best answer.

1. Mr. Ricardo bought a used bike at a yard sale. It cost $35. He paid for it with two $20 bills. How much change did he get?

   A $20   **B** $25   **C** $15   **D** $5

2. Hannah is putting coins in her bank. She can hold about 20 coins in her hand. About how many coins can she put in the bank with 5 handfuls?

   F 105   **G** 100   **H** 45   **J** 25

3. Jason is fifth in line to buy a movie ticket. How many people are in front of him?

   A 2   **B** 6   **C** 4   **D** 5

4. Mei Ling's house is number 34. The next 3 house numbers are 36, 38, and 40. What is the next house number?

   F 32   **G** 42   **H** 52   **J** 22

5. Jared had 13 stamps. He bought 2 more sheets of stamps with 20 stamps on each sheet. Which number sentence shows how many stamps Jared has now?

   A 13 + 2 + 20
   B 13 + 20 + 20
   C 13 + 20 + 2
   D 20 + 20 + 2

6. Use the calendar to find the elapsed time.

February						
Sun	Mon	Tue	Wed	Thu	Fri	Sat
	1	2	3	4	5	6
7	8	9	10	11	12	13
14	15	16	17	18	19	20
21	22	23	24	25	26	27
28						

   Today is February 4. Sue's vacation begins today and ends in 2 weeks. On what date does her vacation end?

   F Feb 19   **G** Feb 17
   H Feb 18   **J** Feb 25

7. Troy has collected 25 pennies in a jar. Estimate the number of pennies Lisa has collected.

   A 25   **B** 50   **C** 75   **D** 200

8. 800
   −459

   F 331   **G** 339   **H** 439   **J** 341

9. The popcorn vendor filled 32 large boxes and 29 small boxes with popcorn. How many boxes did he fill in all?

   A 57   **B** 41   **C** 61   **D** 51

9 PLACE VALUE OF WHOLE NUMBERS

SCIENCE LINK

A census counts the number of people living in a country. It records facts about people. In 1790 about 4 million people lived in the new United States. In 1990 about 249 million people lived in the United States.

Problem-Solving Activity

The Census

A government needs to know how many people there are in a country in order to know what services they will need. The population of the United States was counted for the first time in 1790. Every ten years since then, a census has been taken.

Draw a number line from 1790 to the present.

- Find out which years were census years by counting by tens from 1790.

- Mark all the census years.

- Identify the census year in which you were first counted.

DID YOU

- ✓ count by tens from 1790?

- ✓ draw and label a number line with the census years, using skip counting?

- ✓ identify the first census in which you were counted?

Value of a Digit

Why learn this? You can understand the value of numbers you use every day, such as those that name distances.

Digits are the symbols 0, 1, 2, 3, 4, 5, 6, 7, 8, and 9. Numbers made up of digits can name distances.

Did you know that it takes Pluto 248 earth years to travel around the sun?

Show 248 with base-ten blocks.

Hundreds	Tens	Ones
2	4	8

Expanded Form: 200 + 40 + 8

Standard Form: 248

Read: two hundred forty-eight

So, 248 means 2 hundreds, 4 tens, and 8 ones, or 200 + 40 + 8, or two hundred forty-eight.

REMEMBER:

Place value is the value given to the place a digit holds in a number.

248
hundreds place ⌐
tens place ⌐
ones place ⌐

Talk About It

- What is the value of 3 in 375?

- What is the expanded form of 527?

▶ CHECK

1. What is the standard form of 800 + 10 + 9?

2. What are the expanded and standard forms of three hundred seventy-five?

3. What is the expanded form of 986?

▶ PRACTICE

Write the expanded form and standard form for the number shown by the base-ten blocks.

4.

5.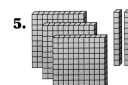

6.

Write the expanded form for each.

7. 349   **8.** 819   **9.** 704   **10.** 625   **11.** 731   **12.** 540

Write the value of the blue digit.

13. 846   **14.** 267   **15.** 493   **16.** 923

17. 191   **18.** 307   **19.** 169   **20.** 850

21. 180   **22.** 418   **23.** 576   **24.** 201

Problem Solving • Mixed Applications

25. Social Studies Yvette lives in a town with a population of 748. Last year there were 10 more people living in the town. How many people lived in the town last year?

26. Reasoning An artist needs 382 tiles to make a wall mosaic. He buys 3 cartons of 100 tiles each and 2 loose tiles. How many 10-tile boxes does he still need?

27. Lee models 453 with blocks. Joy gives her 2 more tens blocks. What is the value of Lee's block collection now?

28. ◁▷ **Write About It** Bev thinks that 300 + 2 is 32. Arthur thinks 300 + 2 is 302. Who is right? Explain.

Mixed Review and Test Prep

Find the sum. (pages 4–5)

29. 6 + 7 = __?__   **30.** 3 + 2 = __?__   **31.** 4 + 4 = __?__

Choose the letter of the correct time. (pages 76–77)

32.
A 12:00
B 12:15
C 3:00
D 3:15

33.
F 9:00
G 8:00
H 8:40
J 12:40

34.
A 12:00
B 2:00
C 11:00
D 1:00

Understanding 1,000's

You will investigate the size of 1,000.

You can show 100 by using a hundreds block or one 10-by-10 paper grid. How can you show 1,000?

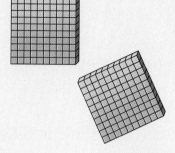

▶ EXPLORE

MATERIALS: base-ten blocks, 10-by-10 paper grids, paste, stapler

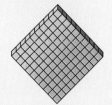

Use base-ten hundreds blocks to build a model for 1,000. Then make a book of 1,000 squares to show what you did.

- Decide how many hundreds blocks you will need.

- Stack the blocks until you have built a cube of 1,000.

- Use one 10-by-10 paper grid for every hundreds block you used.

- Paste each grid on a separate sheet of paper. Staple the sheets together and number the pages at the bottom.

- Number the squares of the grids from 1 to 1,000 any way you like. Be sure that you can find the place of any number in the book.

Record

Explain how you numbered your squares.

Talk About It

- How many hundreds blocks did you need to build a thousands block?

- Why does the number of hundreds blocks equal the number of pages in your book of 1,000 squares?

- If you numbered every square, what would be the first and last numbers on the first page of the book? on the second page?

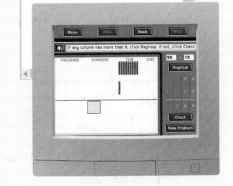

▶ TRY THIS

Combine your book of 1,000 squares with some of your classmates' books to make a book of 3,000 squares.

1. How many books did you use?

2. ▭ **Write About It** How many books would you need to make a book of 4,000 squares? Tell why you think so.

▶ PRACTICE

Look in your book of 1,000 squares. Write the page number on which each number is found.

3. 87	**4.** 148	**5.** 317	**6.** 101
7. 599	**8.** 808	**9.** 618	**10.** 791

Problem Solving • Mixed Applications

For Problems 11–13, use your book of 1,000 squares.

11. **Number Sense** Write three numbers that would be found on page 3.

12. Gina has 701 stickers in an album. On what page in your book is 701?

13. ▭ **Write About It** What is the greatest number on the fifth page of your book? Tell how you know.

Patterns of 100's and 1,000's

Why learn this? You can use number patterns to help you add and subtract collections by using mental math.

How many blocks will Gene have if he adds 2 hundreds blocks to 146?

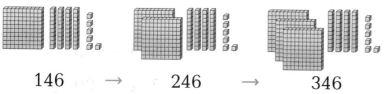

146 → 246 → 346

What is 146 + 200?

- You can add the numbers.
  146 + 100 + 100 = 346

- You can skip count by 100.
  146, 246, 346

So, Gene will have 346 blocks.

Talk About It

CRITICAL THINKING How do patterns of hundreds and mental math help you find the sum?

- If Gene had 2,945 blocks and added 1 thousands block, how many blocks would he have?

EXAMPLES

Patterns of hundreds and thousands can help you subtract.

A
```
  395
− 200
─────
  195
```
Think:
395 − 100 − 100

B
```
  3,430
− 2,000
───────
  1,430
```
Think:
3,430 − 1,000 − 1,000

- In Example A, how does the pattern of hundreds help you subtract 200 from 395? Explain.

Technology Link

In **Mighty Math Zoo Zillions**, the game *Annie's Jungle Trail* can help you practice adding and subtracting 100's. Use Grow Slide Level T.

▶ CHECK

Use patterns and mental math to find the sum
or difference.

1. 212 + 300

2. 498 − 200

3. 2,119 − 1,000

▶ PRACTICE

Use patterns of hundreds or thousands to find the sum
or difference.

4. 612 + 300

5. 226 + 100

6. 515 + 200

7. 456 + 200

8. 887 + 100

9. 702 + 400

10. 804 − 100

11. 761 − 300

12. 299 + 300

13. 624 − 400

14. 598 − 500

15. 946 − 300

16. 3,218 + 1,000

17. 2,914 + 3,000

18. 4,123 + 2,000

19. 5,002 + 4,000

20. 8,217 − 1,000

21. 6,459 − 1,000

22. 9,801 − 8,000

23. 5,305 − 5,000

24. 7,119 − 3,000

Problem Solving • Mixed Applications

25. Mental Math Hank had 200 paper clips. Then
he bought 3 boxes of paper clips. How many
paper clips does Hank have now?

26. ✏️ **Write a problem** using what you
know about the boxes of paper clips.

Mixed Review and Test Prep

Use patterns of tens to find the sum or difference. (pages 134–135)

27. 54 + 10 + 10

28. 76 − 10 − 10

29. 43 − 20

30. 16 + 30

31. 69 − 20

32. 23 + 50

Choose the letter of the correct time. (pages 80–81)

33.
    A 3:30
    B 4:30
    C 5:30
    D 6:20

34.
    F 8:23
    G 6:23
    H 4:35
    J 7:23

35.
    A 11:36
    B 7:52
    C 10:36
    D 9:36

Understanding Larger Numbers

Why learn this? You can understand the size and value of large numbers so you can solve problems about population.

You made a book that shows 1,000. How many books of 1,000 are needed to make a model for 10,000?

Two 📕📕 make 2,000.

Three 📕📕📕 make 3,000.

Six 📕📕📕📕📕📕 make 6,000.

Ten 📕📕📕📕📕📕📕📕📕📕 make 10,000.

So, ten books of 1,000 are needed to make a model for 10,000.

- How many books of 1,000 would you need to model 15,000? 23,000?

You can use a place-value chart to understand large numbers.

In 1990 there were 93,889 children born as a twin in the United States. What does each digit mean?

A comma separates the thousands and hundreds places.

Ten Thousands	Thousands	Hundreds	Tens	Ones
9	3	8	8	9

90,000 + 3,000 + 800 + 80 + 9

Say: ninety-three thousand, eight hundred eighty-nine

Talk About It

- What does the 9 in the first column stand for?

- What is the value of the 3?

- How many books of 1,000 would be needed to show this number? Explain.

Compare this place-value chart to the one on page 150. How is it the same? How is it different?

Hundred Thousands	Ten Thousands	Thousands	Hundreds	Tens	Ones
2	9	3	8	8	9

200,000 + 90,000 + 3,000 + 800 + 80 + 9

Say: two hundred ninety-three thousand, eight hundred eighty-nine

Talk About It

• What does the 2 in the first column stand for?

• What is the value of the 9 in the second column?

• Suppose there was a 3 in the first column. How would you say that number?

CRITICAL THINKING How many books of 1,000 would be needed to show this number? Explain.

► CHECK

Write each number in standard form.

1. 20,000 + 6,000 + 700 + 30 + 4

2. 300,000 + 20,000 + 6,000 + 700 + 40 + 4

3. five hundred sixty-seven thousand

4. two hundred forty-six thousand, one hundred ten

Write each number in expanded form.

	Hundred Thousands	Ten Thousands	Thousands	Hundreds	Tens	Ones
5.				3	4	7
6.		2	5	6	1	3
7.	3	1	4	9	6	1
8.		4	2	9	7	0

LESSON CONTINUES

Write each number in standard form.

9. 50,000 + 4,000 + 300 + 1

10. 30,000 + 9,000 + 200 + 60 + 5

11. 10,000 + 5,000 + 30 + 7

12. 60,000 + 800 + 10 + 6

13. 80,000 + 4,000 + 100 + 5

14. 70,000 + 700 + 7

15. 100,000 + 30,000 + 4,000 + 900 + 20 + 1

16. 600,000 + 70,000 + 1,000 + 400 + 70 + 9

17. fifty-four thousand, nine hundred twenty-six

18. seventy-one thousand, two hundred forty-eight

19. ninety thousand, three hundred sixty-one

20. fourteen thousand, eight hundred twenty

21. thirty-six thousand, seven hundred fifty-five

22. eighty-one thousand, four hundred seventy-nine

Write the value of the blue digit.

23. 81,465

24. 26,817

25. 43,912

26. 9,273

27. 52,391

28. 30,625

29. 16,509

30. 85,098

31. 18,350

32. 48,905

33. 57,623

34. 71,436

35. 62,417

36. 43,901

37. 78,396

38. 90,086

Problem Solving • Mixed Applications

39. Money Tara had 4,053 pennies. Her friend gave her 200 more. How many pennies does Tara have now?

40. Money Mr. Popper owed $3,145 for some work done on his house. He paid $1,000 of the bill. How much more does he owe?

41. Consumer Ed purchased a car for fourteen thousand, nine hundred sixty-eight dollars. Write the amount, using digits.

42. ⬚ **Write About It** How would you describe 10,000 to someone who doesn't know about the size of the number?

Many people live in the cities of the United States and the world. When workers for the census count the people to find the population, they use large numbers.

43. In 1990, Indianapolis had a population of 731,327. Write the number in expanded form.

44. In 1990, Alamo, Texas had a population of 8,352. Huntsville, Texas had a population of 27,925. How much larger was the population of Huntsville than Alamo? Hint: Use a calculator to help you.

45. Guadalupe, Mexico, had a population of 535,332. If 20,000 more people have moved to the city, how many people live there now?

46. ✏️ **Write About It** Find the population of your town or city. Write the number in expanded and standard form.

CULTURAL **LINK**

Each year riders from all over the world enter the Tour de France bicycle race. The race was first run in 1903. It is about 2,500 miles long and loops around France, ending in Paris. If the race leader has ridden 2,000 miles, about how many more miles must he or she ride to complete the race?

Mixed Review and Test Prep

Write the number. Tell whether it is *odd* or *even*.
(pages 132–133)

47. 65   **48.** 44   **49.** 17   **50.** 98

51. 101   **52.** 756   **53.** 1,980   **54.** 3,563

Choose the letter of the correct related *subtraction* fact.
(pages 12–13)

55. $7 + 8 = 15$
  A $15 - 7 = 8$
  B $7 + 1 = 8$
  C $15 - 15 = 0$
  D $15 - 0 = 15$

56. $6 + 7 = 13$
  F $13 - 0 = 13$
  G $13 - 8 = 5$
  H $13 - 7 = 6$
  J $7 + 7 = 14$

57. $5 + 9 = 14$
  A $14 - 14 = 0$
  B $5 + 4 = 9$
  C $14 - 5 = 9$
  D $14 - 0 = 14$

58. $8 + 4 = 12$
  F $12 - 0 = 12$
  G $12 - 8 = 4$
  H $4 + 4 = 8$
  J $12 - 12 = 0$

Using Larger Numbers

Why learn this? You can understand very large numbers, such as those used to tell about the populations of cities.

Would you use thousands or ten thousands to describe the population of each city?

You can use benchmark numbers to help you. Think about the book of 1,000 and the model of 10,000 you made.

Kermit's population is less than 10,000, so a benchmark number of 1,000 might be used to estimate its size.

Sugar Land's population is larger than 10,000, so a benchmark number of 10,000 might be used to estimate its size.

So, use thousands to describe Kermit's population, and ten thousands to describe Sugar Land's population.

> **REMEMBER:**
> A *benchmark* number helps you estimate the size of a number without counting. If you know the size of 1,000 and 10,000, you can estimate the sizes of larger numbers.

Talk About It CRITICAL THINKING

• Would a benchmark of 1,000 or 10,000 be used to estimate or count the population of Edna? Explain.

• Would a benchmark of 1,000 or 10,000 be used to estimate or count the population of Brownsville? Explain.

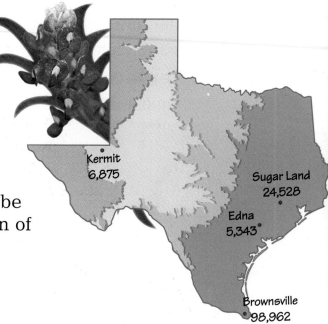

Kermit 6,875

Sugar Land 24,528

Edna 5,343

Brownsville 98,962

► CHECK

Write *yes* or *no* to tell if each number is large enough to be counted by using a benchmark of 1,000 or 10,000.

1. the number of players in a football game

2. the number of people in a football stadium at a professional game

Choose a benchmark of 1,000 or 10,000 to estimate
or count each number.

3. 3,479	**4.** 1,425	**5.** 52,419	**6.** 42,411
7. 18,275	**8.** 2,910	**9.** 30,618	**10.** 61,597
11. 47,613	**12.** 58,342	**13.** 5,173	**14.** 89,056
15. 23,468	**16.** 6,814	**17.** 73,527	**18.** 91,125

Write *yes* or *no* to tell if each number is large enough to
be counted by using a benchmark of 1,000 or 10,000.

19. the number of students in
your class

20. the number of students in
your state

21. the number of cars in the
school's parking lot

22. the population of a city

23. the number of books on a
shelf

24. the number of books in the
library

Problem Solving • Mixed Applications

25. Sports The football team
scored 14 points in the first
half of the game. They scored
17 points in the second half of
the game. How many total
points did they score?

26. Estimation The
population of
Canyon Lake,
Texas, was 9,975
in 1990. Would a
benchmark of 1,000 or
10,000 be used to estimate
the population? Explain.

27. Time A game began at 4:30
and lasted for 3 hours. What
time was the game over?

28. Money Nate has $5.00. He
buys lunch for $2.49. How
much does Nate have now?

29. The population of Tidewater
School is 439. Which
benchmark might be used
to estimate the population?

30. ✏️ **Write a problem** using
a benchmark to estimate
the population of Alice,
Texas, in 1990. It was
19,788.

LESSON
CONTINUES ➡️

Problem–Solving Strategy: Use a Table

▶ **THE PROBLEM** You are a mountain climber. Each year, you climb a higher mountain than you did the year before. Last year you climbed Mount Marcy. The year before, you climbed Black Mountain. How can you decide which mountain to climb this year?

REMEMBER:

UNDERSTAND

PLAN

SOLVE

LOOK BACK

UNDERSTAND

- What are you asked to do?

- What information will you use?

- Is there any information you will not use? If so, what?

PLAN

- What strategy can you use?

  You can *use a table* to help you make a decision.

SOLVE

- How can using a table help you solve the problem?

Mountains in the United States	
Mountain Name	**Height**
Cloud	13,175 feet
Hood	11,235 feet
Washington	6,288 feet
Marcy	5,344 feet
Black Mountain	4,145 feet

Use benchmarks of 1,000 and 10,000 to help you find out which mountains are higher than Mount Marcy.

Mount Washington is close in height to Mount Marcy. A benchmark of 10,000 is needed to estimate the heights of Mounts Hood and Cloud, so they are much higher than Mount Marcy.

So, you can climb Mount Washington this year.

LOOK BACK

- Why is it helpful to use a table?

- What other strategy could you use?

SCIENCE LINK

The highest mountain in North America is Mount McKinley in Alaska. Native Alaskans called this mountain Denali, or The High One. At its peak Mount McKinley is 20,320 feet. Where would it be listed in the table above?

▶ PRACTICE

Use a table to solve.

County Library Books	
Fiction	22,204
History	17,691
Biography	5,924
Science	2,189
Hobbies	1,038

Theme Park Ticket Sales	
April	1,983
May	5,280
June	12,406
July	21,316
August	7,132

1. A computer can read about 10,000 book titles in an hour. Which groups of books need *more* than an hour to scan?

2. The theme park hires extra help when there are more than 10,000 visitors. During which months is extra help needed?

3. Data on about 1,000 books can be stored on one computer disk. How many disks are needed to store information about biographies? Explain.

4. For about every 1,000 tickets sold, a season pass is given away. How many season passes were given away in August? Explain.

Mixed Applications

Solve.

5. How much change will Jen receive from $5.00 if she buys this book?

6. About 10 marshmallows fit in one cup. About how many marshmallows fit in 3 cups?

7. The sum of two numbers is 25. Their difference is 3. What are the two numbers?

8. Ed had 280 toy cars. He gave some to his brother. Now he has 148. How many toy cars did he give away?

9. The arena opens the upper deck when there are more than 10,000 tickets sold. Which days will the upper deck be open?

Concert Ticket Sales	
Thursday	9,136
Friday	11,570
Saturday	12,136
Sunday	10,085

▶ CHECK Understanding

VOCABULARY

1. __?__ are the symbols 0, 1, 2, 3, 4, 5, 6, 7, 8, and 9. (page 144)

Write the expanded form for each. (pages 144–145)

2. 834   **3.** 235   **4.** 306   **5.** 819   **6.** 712   **7.** 270

Write each number in standard form. (pages 150–153)

8. 90,000 + 7,000 + 500 + 30 + 1

9. forty-seven thousand, five hundred thirteen

Choose a benchmark of 1,000 or 10,000 to estimate or count each number. (pages 154–155)

10. 3,479   **11.** 1,425   **12.** 52,419   **13.** 42,411

▶ CHECK Skills

Write the value of the blue digit. (pages 144–145, 150–153)

14. 493   **15.** 620   **16.** 879   **17.** 712

18. 14,037   **19.** 31,952   **20.** 58,916   **21.** 50,743

Use patterns of hundreds or thousands to find the sum or difference. (pages 148–149)

22. 498 + 400   **23.** 415 − 300   **24.** 3,127 + 6,000

▶ CHECK Problem Solving

Solve. (pages 156–157)

CHOOSE a strategy and a tool.
- Act It Out
- Use a Table
- Guess and Check

Paper/Pencil   Calculator   Hands-On   Mental Math

25. I am a number between 5,700 and 5,800. If you keep adding hundreds to me, you reach 6,032. What number am I?

26. Decide if each type of pencil should be shipped in groups of 1,000 or 10,000.

Pencil Type	Amount
Common #2	21,145
Fancy #2	12,107
Push-Top	4,989
Multicolor	1,245

Test Prep

Choose the best answer.

1. Carlos sits at the beginning of the row. Jason is next. Juanita sits behind Jason. Mariel sits behind Juanita. Who is third in the row?

A Mariel   **B** Carlos

C Jason   **D** Juanita

2. What is 667 in expanded form?

F 6 hundreds, 6 tens, 70 ones

G 60 hundreds, 6 tens, 7 ones

H 6 hundreds, 6 tens, 7 ones

J 7 hundreds, 6 tens, 6 ones

3. The table shows the number of games won and lost.

Team	Won	Lost
Blue Jays	8	4
Cardinals	7	5
Hawks	9	3
Roadrunners	6	6

Which team won the most games?

A Blue Jays   **B** Cardinals

C Hawks   **D** Roadrunners

4. Allyson bought a lunch box for $5.75 and a T-shirt for $10.25. How much change did she get from $20.00?

F $1.50   **G** $4.00

H $2.50   **J** $5.50

5. Darryl had 175 sheets of paper. He bought 500 sheets. How can you find how many sheets of paper he has now?

A 175 + 200

B 175 + 500

C 500 − 175

D 175 + 400

6. Which could you find using a benchmark of 10,000?

F the number of people playing a baseball game

G the number of people watching a movie in a theater

H the number of people watching a professional football game

J the number of students in your class

7. Choose 9,000 + 500 + 70 + 6 in standard form.

A 9,756

B 7,965

C 6,759

D 9,576

8. Choose 8 hundreds, 9 tens, and 3 ones in standard form.

F 893

G 983

H 839

J 398

10 COMPARE, ORDER, AND ROUND NUMBERS

Young Inventors Stay Ahead of the School Bus

What's J.C.'s Bus-o-Matic? Two second-graders from New Jersey could tell you. They invented it!

Jordan Wompierski and Carly Snyder missed their school bus one rainy spring day. They came up with a gadget to make sure it didn't happen again.

J.C.'s Bus-o-Matic (named for *Jordan* and *Carly*) signals the children when a school bus is half a mile from the house. On a rainy day, they can stay inside, nice and dry, until their invention lets them know for sure the bus is coming.

SCIENCE LINK

Inventors send their ideas to the U.S. Patent and Trademark Office in Washington, D.C., to be registered. The inventor receives a document to prove that he or she is the owner of the invention.

Great Inventions

An invention is a great idea put to work. We benefit from inventions every day, and sometimes we take them for granted. Learn about the history of inventions.

YOU WILL NEED: list of inventions shown or a list from an almanac or other book, place-value chart, pencil

Select your 10 favorite inventions.

- Enter each invention by age in a place-value chart.

- Order the inventions from oldest to newest in another place-value chart.

- Make a poster showing drawings of your favorite inventions and their ages.

INVENTION	Year of Discovery	Age at Year 2000
Airplane with motor	1903	97
Automobile, gasoline	1889	11
Calculator, pocket	1972	28
Clock, pendulum	1657	313
Computer	1960	10
Parachute	1785	215
Skates, inline	1991	9
Telephone	1876	124
Telescope	1609	391
Television, electronic	1927	73

DID YOU

☑ select 10 inventions and enter them in a place-value chart?

☑ order the inventions from oldest to newest in another chart?

☑ make a poster to share with the class?

Comparing Numbers

You will investigate how to model and compare numbers.

Use base-ten blocks to compare 45 and 62.

MATERIALS: base-ten blocks

- Decide which blocks you will need to model 45.

- Decide which blocks you will need to model 62.

- Make models of each number.

- Compare the tens.

Tens	Ones
4	5
6	2

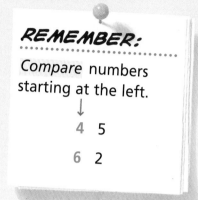

REMEMBER:
Compare numbers starting at the left.

4 5

6 2

Since 6 tens is greater than 4 tens, 62 is greater than 45.

▶ EXPLORE

Use base-ten blocks to compare 316 and 278.
Use a place-value chart to record your work.

Record

Draw your models by tracing around the base-ten blocks.

Explain how you can decide which number is greater.

Talk About It

- How many hundreds did you draw to show 316? 278?

- How can you compare the two numbers?

- What if the two numbers have the same amount of hundreds?

Now investigate making models to compare other numbers.

► TRY THIS

1. Make models to compare 263 and 236. Which number is greater?

2. Why is it necessary to compare the hundreds and the tens?

3. ✏️ **Write About It** Tell how you would use base-ten blocks to compare 527 and 503.

► PRACTICE

Draw base-ten blocks to show your models.
Circle the picture that shows the greater number.

4. 48 and 51

5. 90 and 87

6. 105 and 111

7. 141 and 114

8. 206 and 216

9. 189 and 198

10. 210 and 167

11. 321 and 312

12. 285 and 291

Use models to solve.

13. Sally has 3 hundreds, 2 tens, and 4 ones. Morris has 4 hundreds, 2 tens, and 3 ones. Who has the model with the greater number?

14. Hsu modeled 5 hundreds, 1 ten, and zero ones on a red mat, and 4 hundreds, 9 tens, and 8 ones on a blue mat. Which model shows the greater number?

Problem Solving • Mixed Applications

15. **History** The piano was invented in the year 1709. How many years ago was that?

16. **Measurement** John traveled 285 miles. Tina traveled 185 miles. Who traveled more miles? How many more?

17. **Logical Reasoning** You have 4 hundreds, 9 tens, and 8 ones. With 2 more ones, you can regroup and have just 5 base-ten blocks. How?

Technology Link

💿 You can compare numbers by using E-Lab, Activity 10. Available on CD-ROM and on the Internet at **www.hbschool.com/elab**

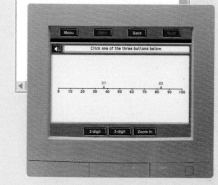

MORE PRACTICE .... page H84

More About Comparing Numbers

Why learn this? You can find the shortest distance or the lowest price.

Beth lives 75 miles from Disney World and 69 miles from Universal Studios. Which theme park is Beth closer to?

Compare 75 and 69.

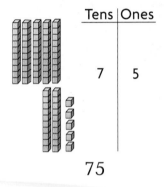

Tens	Ones
7	5

75

Tens	Ones
6	9

69

Compare the number of tens.
Since 7 tens > 6 tens, 75 > 69, or 69 < 75.
So, Beth lives closer to Universal Studios.

A place-value chart can help you compare numbers.

Hundreds	Tens	Ones
8	3	1
8	1	9

Begin at the left.
The hundreds digits are the same.
The tens digits are not the same.
3 tens > 1 ten.
So, 831 > 819,
or 819 < 831.

Talk About It

Suppose you want to compare 427 and 428.

- In which place-value position do you find the greater number?

- How can you compare the numbers by using the *greater than* symbol?

- How can you compare the numbers by using the *less* than symbol?

> **REMEMBER:**
>
> \> means "greater than."
>
> < means "less than." The symbol points to the smaller number.
>
> 25 > 23
>
> **Say:** Twenty-five is greater than twenty-three.

SOCIAL STUDIES LINK

Universal Studios in Hollywood has been giving tours to visitors for more than 30 years. Universal Studios in Orlando has been giving tours for about 10 years. Compare the amount of time tours have been given at Universal Studios in both California and Florida.

A place-value chart can also help you compare greater numbers.

Thousands	Hundreds	Tens	Ones
2 ,	4	8	5
2 ,	6	4	9

Begin at the left.
The thousands digits are the same.
The hundreds digits are not the same.
6 hundreds > 4 hundreds.
So, 2,649 > 2,485 or 2,485 < 2,649.

Talk About It

- How could you compare the numbers above using base-ten blocks?

- If a 4 was in the hundreds place in both numbers, how could you find the greater number?

CRITICAL THINKING Compare 997 and 1,997. Which number is greater? Explain.

▶ CHECK

Compare the numbers. Write < or > for each .

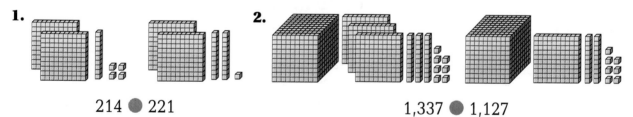

1. 214 ● 221

2. 1,337 ● 1,127

3.

T	O
2	9
9	2

29 ● 92

4.

H	T	O
7	6	4
6	7	4

764 ● 674

5.

Th	H	T	O
5 ,	4	2	9
5 ,	1	4	2

5,429 ● 5,142

6. 46 ● 48

7. 301 ● 299

8. 1,376 ● 1,736

9. 214 ● 241

10. 961 ● 691

11. 3,724 ● 3,427

12. 712 ● 721

13. 141 ● 114

14. 4,291 ● 4,921

LESSON CONTINUES

Compare the numbers. Write < , >, or = for each ●.

15.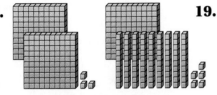
68 ● 98

16.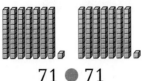
71 ● 71

17.
54 ● 52

18.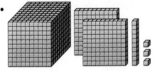
203 ● 195

19.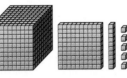
170 ● 159

20.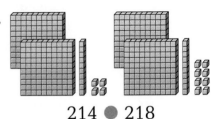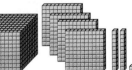
214 ● 218

21.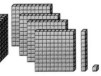
1,213 ● 1,115

22.
1,411 ● 1,421

23.

T	O
9	2
8	3

92 ● 83

24.

H	T	O
1	0	1
1	1	0

101 ● 110

25.

H	T	O
4	2	8
4	2	8

428 ● 428

26. 629 ● 631

27. 758 ● 750

28. 439 ● 438

29. 3,425 ● 3,799

30. 5,712 ● 5,412

31. 2,411 ● 2,412

Problem Solving • Mixed Applications___

32. Money Beth's family spent $17 on dinner and $14 on a movie. How much did they spend on dinner and the movie?

33. Consumer Lori spends $3.75 for a hat, $3.59 for a pin, and $5.00 for a pair of socks. Which costs less, the hat or the pin?

34. Sports Jami can trade 385 tickets for a softball or 402 tickets for a soccer ball. Which ball costs more tickets?

35. ✏ **Write About It** A person needs to be 50 inches tall to ride a roller coaster. Jake is 48 inches tall. Can he ride the roller coaster? Explain.

In some places there are few roads, so a river becomes the highway. In other places, people use a river to have fun.

SOCIAL STUDIES **LINK**

The Mississippi River is 2,348 miles long—the longest river in the United States. It begins as a small stream in north-western Minnesota, and links a series of lakes and rivers as it flows southward into the Gulf of Mexico. The Yukon River in Alaska is 1,979 miles long. Which river is longer?

36. Suppose you took two trips on a Mississippi River paddleboat. In the spring you traveled 237 miles. In the fall you traveled 207 miles. Which trip was longer?

37. The Mississippi River is 2,348 miles long. The Missouri River is 2,315 miles long. If you wanted to travel on the longer river, which one would you choose?

38. **Mental Math** The Rio Grande is 1,885 miles long. Ken traveled the entire length of the river except for 200 miles. How many miles did he travel?

39. **Estimation** Suppose you canoe 95 miles the first year, 120 miles the second year, and 190 miles the third year. About how many miles would you canoe in the three years?

Mixed Review and Test Prep

Find the difference. (pages 114–115)

40. $2.65 − 1.43	**41.** $4.37 − 0.16	**42.** $5.42 − 3.18	**43.** $6.68 − 2.59	**44.** $10.00 − 5.03
45. $8.41 − 3.55	**46.** $7.34 − 3.47	**47.** $8.13 − 4.99	**48.** $7.60 − 5.68	**49.** $8.00 − 0.44

Use patterns of hundreds or thousands to find the sum or difference. Choose the letter of the correct answer. (pages 148–149)

50. $515 + 200 = \underline{\ ?\ }$ **A** 520   **B** 700   **C** 715   **D** 720

51. $775 − 100 = \underline{\ ?\ }$ **F** 700   **G** 577   **H** 675   **J** 765

52. $692 − 200 = \underline{\ ?\ }$ **A** 395   **B** 492   **C** 892   **D** 592

53. $479 + 300 = \underline{\ ?\ }$ **F** 179   **G** 579   **H** 679   **J** 779

Ordering Numbers

Why learn this? You can order numbers such as heights of buildings.

Which building has the most floors?

Use a number line to order numbers.

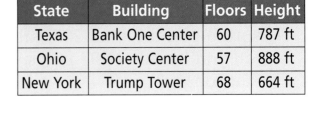

State	Building	Floors	Height
Texas	Bank One Center	60	787 ft
Ohio	Society Center	57	888 ft
New York	Trump Tower	68	664 ft

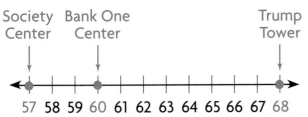

From left to right, the numbers get larger in order from least to greatest.

$$57 < 60 < 68$$

So, Trump Tower has the most floors.

Use a number line to find the tallest building.

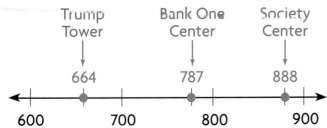

From right to left, the numbers get smaller from greatest to least.

$$888 > 787 > 664$$

So, Society Center is the tallest building.

A very tall building

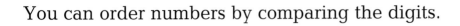

You can order numbers by comparing the digits.

MODEL

Step 1	Step 2
Compare the thousands. 7,613 7,551 7,435 same number of thousands	Compare the hundreds. 7,613 7,551 7,435 $6 > 5 > 4$

So, $7,613 > 7,551 > 7,435$.

► CHECK

Write the numbers in order from *least* to *greatest*.
Use the number lines to help you.

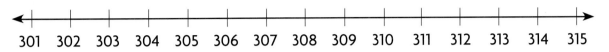

301 302 303 304 305 306 307 308 309 310 311 312 313 314 315

1. 309, 315, 310

2. 301, 312, 308

3. 314, 304, 312

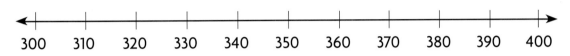

300 310 320 330 340 350 360 370 380 390 400

4. 400, 330, 370

5. 310, 390, 340

6. 339, 394, 349

► PRACTICE

Write the numbers in order from *greatest* to *least*.

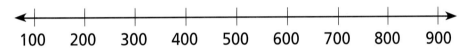

100 200 300 400 500 600 700 800 900

7. 298, 417, 345

8. 684, 799, 701

9. 387, 227, 412

10. 59, 62, 80

11. 107, 99, 111

12. 562, 498, 526

13. 2,500; 4,007; 2,498

14. 3,531; 3,815; 3,726

Problem Solving • Mixed Applications

15. Measurement Three skyscrapers have heights of 594 feet, 612 feet, and 691 feet. Order the heights from tallest to shortest.

16. Money How much change would you get from $5.00 if you purchased a Trump Tower souvenir for $2.95?

17. In two hours 807 people rode to the top of the Sears Tower. The first hour 315 people went to the top. How many people rode to the top during the second hour?

18. On a class trip, Louis spent $8.25 for dinner. His sister Mary spent $8.20. Who spent less? How much less?

19. ✏️ **Write About It** Explain how you know that $56 > 48 > 35$.

LESSON CONTINUES ➡

Problem–Solving Strategy: Draw a Picture

▶ **THE PROBLEM** Samantha, Kyle, and Annie guessed the number of beans in two jars. The small jar held 243 beans. The large jar held 483 beans. Whose guess for the large jar was closest to the actual amount?

REMEMBER:

UNDERSTAND

PLAN

SOLVE

LOOK BACK

| Samantha 412 | Kyle 502 | Annie 444 |

UNDERSTAND

- What are you asked to find?

- What information will you use?

- Is there information you will not use? If so, what?

PLAN

- What strategy can you use?

  You can *draw a picture* to find out whose guess was closest to the actual number.

SOLVE

- How can you solve the problem?

  Draw a number line from 400 to 540.
  Draw dots to show about where the guesses and actual number would be on the number line.

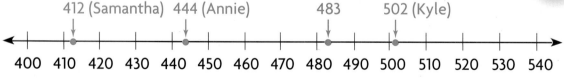

412 (Samantha) 444 (Annie) 483 502 (Kyle)

400 410 420 430 440 450 460 470 480 490 500 510 520 530 540

So, Kyle's guess of 502 was the closest guess.

LOOK BACK

- Why is it helpful to draw a picture?

- What other strategy could you use?

Draw a picture to solve.

1. Craig guesses there are 892 beans in a jar. Roy's guess is 925. There are 900 beans in the jar. Whose guess is closer?

2. At All-Tees, T-shirts are priced at $5.98, $6.50, and $5.75. Order the prices from least expensive to most expensive.

3. Yummies cereal comes in boxes that hold 24, 18, or 30 ounces. Order the box sizes from smallest to largest.

4. Pat lives 257 miles from Grinville, 193 miles from Gladtown, and 204 miles from Smiley. Help Pat order the cities from closest to farthest.

Mixed Applications

Solve.

CHOOSE a strategy and a tool.
• Draw a Picture • Act It Out
• Find a Pattern • Make a Model • Use a Table

Paper/Pencil Calculator Hands-On Mental Math

5. Three houses in a row on Julie's street are numbered 1201, 1205, 1209. What is the next house number on her street?

6. In March a potato plant was 13 centimeters tall. Four weeks later, the plant was 42 centimeters tall. How much did the potato plant grow?

7. Write in order the day the greatest number of tickets was sold to the day the least number of tickets was sold.

8. How many more tickets were sold on Tuesday than on Monday? than on Wednesday?

9. Last year, 219 tickets were sold for Family Fun Night. Were more or fewer tickets sold this year? How many more or fewer?

10. David bought a hotdog for $1.25, lemonade for $0.75, and a cupcake for $0.50. How much change did David get from $5.00?

FAMILY FUN NIGHT TICKET SALES	
Monday	79 tickets
Tuesday	104 tickets
Wednesday	93 tickets

Rounding to Tens and Hundreds

Why learn this? You can use rounding to estimate a size or an amount, such as a number of stuffed toys.

Bette has 25 stuffed toys. About how many stuffed toys does Bette have?

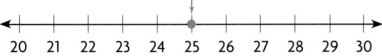

25 is halfway between 20 and 30 on the number line.

When a number is exactly halfway between two tens, round to the greater ten. Say: 25 rounded to the nearest ten is 30.

So, Bette has about 30 stuffed toys.

At Cuddle Toys there are 378 different stuffed toys for sale. To the nearest hundred, how many different stuffed toys are for sale at Cuddle Toys?

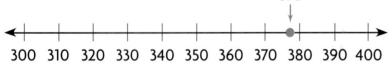

378 is between 300 and 400. It is closer to 400 than to 300. Say: 378 rounded to the nearest hundred is 400.

So, Cuddle Toys has about 400 different stuffed toys for sale.

Talk About It

• Which digit helps you find the hundreds that the number is between?

• Which digit helps you find the closer hundred?

• Suppose Cuddle Toys has 350 different stuffed toys for sale. To the nearest hundred, how many toys do they have for sale?

Technology Link

In **Mighty Math Carnival Countdown**, the game *Giggle Factory* challenges you to compare numbers. Use Grow Slide Levels 0 and U.

► CHECK

Round each number to the nearest hundred.

```
◄─┼──┼──┼──┼──┼──┼──┼──┼──┼──┼──┼──┼──┼──┼──┼──┼──┼──┼──┼──┼──┼─►
  500 510 520 530 540 550 560 570 580 590 600 610 620 630 640 650 660 670 680 690 700
```

1. 521 **2.** 693 **3.** 642 **4.** 561

5. 675 **6.** 599 **7.** 550 **8.** 650

► PRACTICE

Round each number to the nearest hundred.

9. 413 **10.** 256 **11.** 173 **12.** 911

13. 565 **14.** 350 **15.** 750 **16.** 949

Tell which two tens or two hundreds each number is between. Then tell what the number rounds to.

17. 45 **18.** 95 **19.** 750

Problem Solving • Mixed Applications

20. Estimation Hector has 451 tokens. To the nearest hundred, how many tokens does Hector have?

21. Time Cuddle Toys is open 8 hours a day, starting at 10:00 A.M. What time does the store close?

22. Number Sense Evan sold 27 stuffed bears and 74 stuffed lions. Did he sell more than 100 stuffed animals? Explain.

23. ✏️ **Write About It** A building block set has about 200 pieces. Could it have as few as 139 pieces? Explain.

Mixed Review and Test Prep

Write each number in standard form. (pages 150–153)

24. 40,000 + 5,000 + 600 + 5

25. 50,000 + 400 + 80 + 7

26. 70,000 + 3,000 + 20 + 1

27. 60,000 + 6,000 + 60

Use patterns of tens to find the sum or difference.
Choose the letter of the correct answer. (pages 134–135)

28. 52 + 10 + 10 = __?__   **A** 54   **B** 521   **C** 61   **D** 72

29. 45 − 10 = __?__   **F** 44   **G** 35   **H** 40   **J** 36

30. 61 − 20 = __?__   **A** 51   **B** 71   **C** 41   **D** 63

MORE PRACTICE page H85

More About Rounding

Why learn this? You can use rounding in everyday life, such as when you go shopping.

Stephanie buys a camera that costs $47. To the nearest ten dollars, how much does the camera cost?

Rounding to the nearest ten dollars is like rounding to the nearest ten.

Think: 47 is between 40 and 50.
47 is closer to 50 than to 40.

So, Stephanie's camera costs about $50.

ROUNDING RULES
• Decide on the digit to be rounded.
• Look at the digit to its right.
• If the digit to the right is *less than* 5, the digit being rounded stays the same.
• If the digit to the right is 5 *or more*, the digit being rounded is increased by 1.

Mrs. Novak wants to buy a video camera that costs $219. To the nearest hundred dollars, how much does the video camera cost?

Think: 219 is between 200 and 300.
219 is closer to 200 than to 300.

So, the video camera costs about $200.

Talk About It CRITICAL THINKING

• How do the tens and ones digits help you round to the nearest ten dollars?

• Which digits help you find the closer hundred? Explain.

▶ CHECK

Round to the nearest ten or ten dollars.

1. 67	**2.** 44	**3.** $23	**4.** $85
5. 26	**6.** $94	**7.** $15	**8.** $74
9. 58	**10.** $97	**11.** 77	**12.** 19

► PRACTICE

Round to the nearest ten or ten dollars.

13. 59   **14.** 93   **15.** 55   **16.** 31

17. $15   **18.** $22   **19.** $88   **20.** $44

Round to the nearest hundred or hundred dollars.

21. 238   **22.** 919   **23.** 583   **24.** 419

25. $150   **26.** $471   **27.** $660   **28.** $802

Use the digits 1, 3, and 5. Write a number that rounds to the number given.

29. 100   **30.** 200   **31.** 300   **32.** 400

Problem Solving • Mixed Applications

33. Estimation Sue buys a camera case that costs $12. Does she spend about $10 or about $20?

34. Sue wants to buy a camera case and 4 rolls of film. Is $20 enough? Explain.

35. Number Sense I am a number between 345 and 360. When rounded to the nearest 100, I am 300. What numbers could I be?

36. ✐ Write About It When is an exact answer needed? When is an estimate enough? Give an example of each.

Mixed Review and Test Prep

Write the expanded form for each. (pages 144–145)

37. 124   **38.** 235   **39.** 340   **40.** 656   **41.** 904

Choose the standard form shown by the base-ten blocks. (pages 144–145)

42.

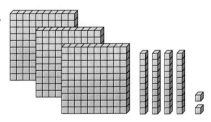

A 332   **B** 242   **C** 341   **D** 342

43.

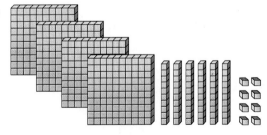

F 456   **G** 466   **H** 468   **J** 478

► CHECK Understanding

Compare the numbers. Write $<$, $>$, or $=$ for each ●. (pages 164–167)

1. 328 ● 289

2. 102 ● 99

3. 243 ● 243

Round each number to the nearest hundred. Use the number line to help you. (pages 172–173)

400 410 420 430 440 450 460 470 480 490 500

4. 450　　　　**5.** 421　　　　**6.** 489　　　　**7.** 444

► CHECK Skills

Write the numbers in order from greatest to least. (pages 168–169)

700 710 720 730 740 750 760 770 780 790 800 810 820 830 840 850

8. 795, 812, 767　　　　**9.** 717, 723, 709　　　　**10.** 811, 802, 816

Tell which two tens or two hundreds each number is between. Then tell what the number rounds to. (pages 172–173)

11. 35　　　　**12.** 75　　　　**13.** 250　　　　**14.** 550

► CHECK Problem Solving

Solve. (pages 170–171)

CHOOSE a strategy and a tool.
- Draw a Picture
- Write a Number Sentence
- Make a Table
- Make a Model

Paper/Pencil　Calculator　Hands-On　Mental Math

15. Anna had $63 before she went shopping. Now she has $16. How much did Anna spend?

16. Anna's bowling scores are 87, 79, and 91. Order the scores from greatest to least.

Test Prep

Choose the best answer.

1. Which shows the numbers in order from *least* to *greatest*?

   A 324   456   423   439

   B 552   455   659   569

   C 393   450   484   540

   D 498   389   524   601

2. The Lu family traveled 8,539 miles on their vacation. What is the value of the 5?

   F 5 thousands

   G 5 tens

   H 5 ones

   J 5 hundreds

3. The table shows the number of visitors to the park.

PARK VISITORS	
Month	Visitors
May	4,559
June	6,845
July	7,850
August	5,500
September	4,295

   Which months have more than 5,000 visitors?

   A May, June, September

   B June, July, August

   C July, August, September

   D May, July, August

4. Mr. Marshall bought a new door. He paid $237. How much money is this rounded to the nearest hundred dollars?

   F $300   G $100   H $200   J $400

5. Which is a group of odd numbers?

   A 23, 25, 27, 29

   B 92, 93, 98, 100

   C 87, 89, 90, 92

   D 41, 43, 48, 51

6. Mikala bought jeans for $25 and a sweatshirt for $12. How much did she spend to the nearest ten dollars?

   F $30   G $40   H $50   J $60

7. Which is correct?

   A 492 < 489

   B 737 > 641

   C 325 = 339

   D 171 < 117

8. Tilly saved 33 dimes. Yvonne saved 28 dimes. Which is the best way to estimate the number of dimes they saved together?

   F 40 + 30

   G 35 + 25

   H 30 + 30

   J 30 + 20

MATH FUN!

PATTERN SEARCH

PURPOSE To use logical reasoning to discover patterns in numbers to 100

1. If you wrote the numbers 1 to 100, how many times would you use the digit 9?

2. If you wrote the numbers 1 to 100, how many times would you use the digit 0?

3. If you wrote the numbers 1 to 100, how many times would you use the digit 1?

ROMAN NUMERALS

PURPOSE To understand the value of a digit

$1 = I$ $5 = V$ $10 = X$

The Romans used letters for numerals. Here are some of the numerals. Other numbers were formed from these by adding or subtracting.

Can you fill in the missing numerals?

| 1 | 2 | 3 | 4 | 5 | 6 | 7 | 8 | 9 | 10 | 11 | 12 | 13 | 14 | 15 | 16 | 17 | 18 | 19 | 20 |
| I | II | | IV | | | | | IX | | | | | | XV | | | | | XX |

1=I
5=V
10=X

Skipping Around

PURPOSE To understand and compare the value of digits

YOU WILL NEED 0–9 spinner, place-value chart or paper, pencil

Make the largest number. Play with a partner. Take turns.

- Spin and write the digit on your place-value chart.
- Spin again and write the digit in another place on your chart.
- Continue until you have made a five-digit number.

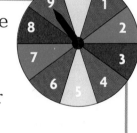

- Read and compare your numbers. The player with the larger number earns a point.
- The first player to earn five points wins the game.

Ten Thousands	Thousands	Hundreds	Tens	Ones

Challenge a family member to make the larger five-digit number.

Technology

Disappearing Digits

Use place value to change one number to another number by making a digit disappear.

EXAMPLES

A Change 1,620 to 1,020.

Think: The thousands, tens, and ones are the same in both numbers. To make the 6 disappear, subtract 6 hundreds, or 600.

B Change 1,970 to 1,000.

Think: The thousands and the ones are the same in both numbers. To make the 9 and 7 disappear, subtract 9 hundreds and 7 tens, or 970.

PRACTICE

Name the amount you subtracted to make the digits disappear.

1. Change 845 to 45.
2. Change 398 to 308.
3. Change 725 to 700.
4. Change 4,297 to 297.
5. **Using the Calculator** Make up a game of Disappearing Digits. Enter a number on a calculator. Your partner enters the same number.

Use place value to make one or more digits disappear. Show your partner the new number. Your partner makes the new number. Take turns.

Study Guide and Review

Vocabulary Check

Choose a term from the box to complete the sentence.

VOCABULARY
cardinal
benchmark
ordinal

1. A(n) _?_ number tells how many. (page 128)

2. A(n) _?_ number shows position or order. (page 128)

3. Useful numbers like 10, 25, 50, and 100 that help you see their relationship to other numbers are _?_ numbers. (page 136)

Study and Solve

CHAPTER 8

EXAMPLE

Use patterns of tens to find the sum.

33 + 10 + 10

⌐————⌐

43 + 10 = 53

For Problems 4–6, use the word LETTER to answer questions. Then tell if your answer is a *cardinal* or an *ordinal* number. (pages 128–129)

4. How many letters are in the word?

5. In what position is the letter L?

6. In what position is the letter R?

For Problems 7–9, write *true* or *false*. Change words in the false sentences to make them true. (pages 130–131)

7. There are 100 ones in 1 hundred.

8. There are 10 pennies in 1 dime.

9. There are 10 ones in 1 hundred.

For Problems 10–12, use patterns of tens to find the sum or difference. (pages 134–135)

10. 22 + 10 + 10

11. 29 − 10 − 10

12. 37 − 10 − 10

Solve. (pages 136–139)

13. A box of pens is half full after Joan takes out 10 pens. About how many pens are in a full box?

CHAPTER 9

EXAMPLE

Write the value of the blue digit.

24,069   4 thousands, or 4,000

For Problems 14–17, write how many hundreds, tens, and ones are in the number. (pages 144–145)

14. 734

15. 805

16. 120

17. 692

For Problems 18–19, use patterns of hundreds or thousands to find the sum or difference. (pages 148–149)

18. $617 - 400$

19. $4{,}135 + 3{,}000$

For Problems 20–23, write the value of the blue digit. (pages 144–145, 150–153)

20. 490   **21.** 683

22. 65,408   **23.** 31,987

For Problems 24–27, write each number in standard form. (pages 150–153)

24. $80{,}000 + 6{,}000 + 400 + 2$

25. $30{,}000 + 7{,}000 + 500 + 60 + 3$

26. twenty-four thousand, six hundred nineteen

27. fifteen thousand, nine hundred ten

For Problems 28–31, choose a benchmark of 1,000 or 10,000 to estimate or count each number. (pages 154–155)

28. 2,531   **29.** 23,650

30. 65,022   **31.** 3,291

CHAPTER 10

EXAMPLE

Round to the nearest hundred.

436 Look at the digit to the right of the one you are rounding.

400 $3 < 5$, so round 436 to 400.

For Problems 32–33, compare the numbers. Write $<$, $>$, or $=$. (pages 164–167)

32.

H	T	O
	9	9
1	0	1

99 ● 101

33.

Th	H	T	O
4,	3	1	2
3,	2	9	8

4,312 ● 3,298

For Problems 34–36, write the numbers in order from least to greatest. (pages 168–169)

34. 495, 513, 476

35. 512, 503, 514

36. 387, 415, 407

For Problems 37–38, round the number to the nearest hundred. (pages 172–173)

37. 419   **38.** 550

For Problems 39–44, tell which two tens or two hundreds each number is between. Then tell what the number rounds to. (pages 172–173)

39. 45   **40.** 320

41. 84   **42.** 760

43. 67   **44.** 440

Performance Assessment

Tasks: Show What You Know

1. Draw 7 dimes and 30 pennies. Use your picture to help explain how you know that 7 dimes and 30 pennies is the same as $1.00. (pages 130–131)

2. Show 359 with base-ten blocks. Use the blocks to explain the expanded form of 359. (pages 144–145)

3. Explain how you could use base-ten blocks or a place-value chart to compare 67 and 64. Then write $<$, $>$, or $=$ to compare the numbers. Read the comparison. (pages 164–167)

67 ● 64

Problem Solving

Solve. Explain your method.

CHOOSE a strategy and a tool.
- Find a Pattern
- Make a Model
- Write a Number Sentence
- Act It Out
- Make a Table
- Draw a Picture

 Paper/Pencil   Calculator Hands-On Mental Math

4. Tina has 2 full jars of marbles. The jars are the same size. Ten marbles fill about half of one jar. Draw a model to show the jars. Tell how many marbles Tina has in all. (pages 136–137)

5. Programs for the baseball games come in boxes of a thousand. How many boxes of programs were needed for each game? (pages 156–157)

PARK CITY SLUGGER TICKET SALES	
Tuesday	4,805
Friday	10,236
Saturday	12,479
Sunday	9,625

6. Four football players weigh 235 pounds, 196 pounds, 228 pounds, and 231 pounds. Put their weights in order from heaviest to lightest. (pages 170–171)

Cumulative Review

Solve the problem. Then write the letter of the correct answer.

Estimate the sum by rounding.

1. 43
    +58

    A. 80
    B. 90
    C. 100
    D. 110

    (pages 24–27)

Find the sum.

2. 648
    +476

    A. 172
    B. 1,014
    C. 1,024
    D. 1,124

    (pages 52–53)

For Problems 3–4, use the schedule.

MONTE'S MEETING SCHEDULE		
Person	Time	Elapsed Time
Ms. Jones	9:00–9:30	30 min
Mr. Sprague	9:30–10:00	?
Ms. Gardi	?	30 min
Mr. Ross	10:30–11:15	45 min

(pages 92–97)

3. What time does Monte meet Ms. Gardi?

    A. 9:00–9:30   B. 9:30–10:00
    C. 10:00–10:30   D. 10:30–11:15

4. What is the elapsed time of Monte's meeting with Mr. Sprague?

    A. 15 minutes   B. 30 minutes
    C. 45 minutes   D. 55 minutes

5. A(n) _?_ number shows position or order.

    A. cardinal   B. ordinal

    (page 128)

6. There are 100 _?_ in a dollar.

    A. pennies   B. nickels
    C. dimes   D. quarters

    (pages 130–131)

Use patterns of thousands to find the difference.

7. 4,254 − 2,000

    A. 2,254   B. 4,054
    C. 4,234   D. 6,254

    (pages 148–149)

What is the value of the blue digit?

8. 54,307

    A. 4 tens
    B. 4 hundreds
    C. 4 thousands
    D. 4 ten thousands

    (pages 144–145, 150–153)

Write the number in standard form.

9. 4,000 + 300 + 5

    A. 4,305   B. 4,355
    C. 40,305   D. 40,350

    (pages 150–153)

10. Round 350 to the nearest hundred.

    A. 300
    B. 350
    C. 360
    D. 400

    (pages 174–175)

11 MULTIPLICATION FACTS 0–5

Most people think that spiders are insects. Spiders have 8 legs, but insects have only 6 legs. A centipede is an animal that has one pair of legs for each of its body segments.

Legs and More Legs

Have you ever wondered what it would be like to have more than 2 legs? Animals use legs to move around to find food, water, and shelter.

Look at the animals on these pages. Count by twos.

- How many groups of 2 legs does each animal have?

- How many legs does each animal have in all?

YOU WILL NEED: poster board, magazines, scissors, paste, markers

Find as many pictures of animals as you can that have 2, 4, 6, 8, or more legs. Group together the animals that have the same number of legs, and make an animal poster.

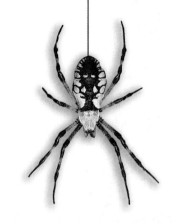

DID YOU

☑ find pictures of animals that have 2, 4, 6, 8, or more legs?

☑ group together the animals that have the same number of legs?

☑ make an animal poster?

Making Equal Groups

You will investigate objects that come in equal groups.

Bicycle tires, shoes, and mittens all are in groups of 2. Your toes and fingers are in groups of 5. Make models to show equal groups.

▶ EXPLORE

MATERIALS: counters, drawing paper

Use counters to show the number of legs on 3 ducks.

MODEL

Make a model by drawing a circle for each duck. Put counters in each circle to show the number of legs.

Record

Draw your model. Write what the model shows. Count to find how many in all.

4 groups of 2 is _?_.

▶ TRY THIS

Make models to show:

1. the number of shoes on 4 people.
2. the number of toes on 2 feet.
3. the number of fingers on 2 hands.
4. the number of fingers on 4 hands.

5. Look at your models. Tell how many groups and how many in each group.

6. ✏ **Write About It** Explain how to draw a model to show the number of shoes worn by 6 soccer players.

► PRACTICE

Use counters to help you find how many in all. Draw a picture of your model.

7. 2 groups of 5   **8.** 3 groups of 5   **9.** 1 group of 2

10. 5 groups of 2   **11.** 7 groups of 2   **12.** 5 groups of 5

Look at the pictures. Write how many there are in all.

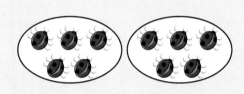
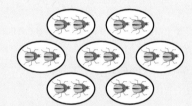

Technology Link

You can use equal groups to multiply by using E-Lab, Activity 11. Available on CD-ROM and on the Internet at www.hbschool.com/elab

13. 2 groups of 5 = _?_   **14.** 7 groups of 2 = _?_

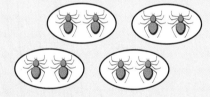
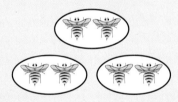

15. 4 groups of 2 = _?_   **16.** 3 groups of 2 = _?_

Problem Solving • Mixed Applications

17. Mental Math Each child has 2 chopsticks. How many chopsticks do 9 children have?

18. Number Sense Tim works in a bike shop. He put new wheels on 5 bicycles. How many new wheels did he put on?

19. Reasoning Alicia needs 12 peaches. Will she have enough peaches if she buys 2 packages with 5 peaches in each package? Explain.

20. Consumer Plums come in packages of 2 or 5 plums. Jason wants to buy 10 plums. How many of each package should he buy?

Multiplying with 2 and 5

Why learn this? You can use multiplication as a quick way to count equal groups of food items.

The 5 people in Brett's family went to a soccer game. Brett packed 2 cans of juice for each person. How many cans did he pack?

Use counters to find the answer.

MODEL

What is 5×2?

Step 1

Draw 5 circles, 1 circle for each person.

Step 2

Put 2 counters in each circle, 1 counter for each can of juice.

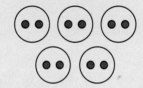

Step 3

There are 5 groups with 2 in each group.

- You can add to find how many in all.
  $2 + 2 + 2 + 2 + 2 = 10$

- You can skip count to find how many in all. **2, 4, 6, 8, 10**

- When the groups have the same number, you can multiply to find how many in all. **5 times 2 equals 10**

So, Brett packed 10 cans in all.

                          factor factor   product
                          ↓   ↓   ↓

The multiplication sentence is $5 \times 2 = 10$.

- The numbers that you multiply are **factors**.

- The answer to a multiplication problem is the **product**.

PHYSICAL EDUCATION LINK

Soccer is the most widely played team sport in the world. If each team has 3 fullbacks, how many fullbacks are on 2 teams?

Talk About It CRITICAL THINKING

- How are addition and multiplication alike? How are they different?

- How can you decide whether to add or multiply to find how many in all?

▶ CHECK

Add and multiply to find how many in all.

1.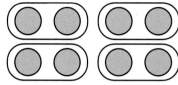

$2 + 2 + 2 + 2 = \underline{\ ?\ }$

$4 \times 2 = \underline{\ ?\ }$

2.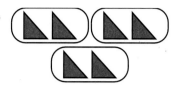

$2 + 2 + 2 = \underline{\ ?\ }$

$3 \times 2 = \underline{\ ?\ }$

3.

$2 + 2 = \underline{\ ?\ }$

$2 \times 2 = \underline{\ ?\ }$

▶ PRACTICE

Add and multiply to find how many in all.

4.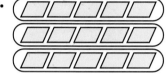

$5 + 5 + 5 = \underline{\ ?\ }$

$3 \times 5 = \underline{\ ?\ }$

5.

$2 + 2 + 2 + 2 + 2 = \underline{\ ?\ }$

$5 \times 2 = \underline{\ ?\ }$

6.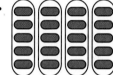

$5 + 5 + 5 + 5 = \underline{\ ?\ }$

$4 \times 5 = \underline{\ ?\ }$

Copy and complete the table.

	×	1	2	3	4	5	6	7	8	9
7.	2	?	?	?	?	?	?	?	?	?
8.	5	?	?	?	?	?	?	?	?	?

Find the product. You may wish to draw a picture.

9. $8 \times 2 = \underline{\ ?\ }$ **10.** $4 \times 5 = \underline{\ ?\ }$ **11.** $2 \times 2 = \underline{\ ?\ }$ **12.** $5 \times 5 = \underline{\ ?\ }$

13. $9 \times 5 = \underline{\ ?\ }$ **14.** $1 \times 2 = \underline{\ ?\ }$ **15.** $6 \times 5 = \underline{\ ?\ }$ **16.** $7 \times 5 = \underline{\ ?\ }$

Problem Solving • Mixed Applications

17. Consumer Sal bought 3 packages of toy cars. There are 2 cars in each package. How many cars did he buy?

18. Rebecca bought 2 red apples and 5 green apples. How many apples did she buy?

19. Drew has 5 pairs of white socks and 2 pairs of black socks. How many more pairs of white socks than black socks does he have?

20. ✏ **Write a problem** about 5 children on each relay team. There are 6 relay teams.

LESSON CONTINUES ▶

Problem–Solving Strategy: Draw a Picture

▶ **THE PROBLEM** Before the soccer game, 6 players practiced kicking the ball into the goal. They each made 5 practice kicks. How many practice kicks were made in all?

UNDERSTAND

- What are you asked to find?

- What information will you use?

- Is there information you will not use? If so, what?

REMEMBER:

UNDERSTAND

PLAN

SOLVE

LOOK BACK

PLAN

- What strategy can you use to solve the problem?

  You can *draw a picture* to find how many kicks were made in all.

SOLVE

- How can you use the strategy to solve the problem?

  You can draw a picture to show the 6 players and the 5 kicks made by each player.

- Draw 6 circles for the 6 players.

- Put 5 dots in each circle for the 5 kicks made by each player.

  So, 30 practice kicks were made.

$5+5+5+5+5+5=30$ $6 \times 5 = 30$

LOOK BACK

- How did you decide if your answer makes sense?

- What other strategy could you use?

Draw a picture to solve.

1. Suppose 8 players practiced kicking the ball into the goal. They each made 5 practice kicks. How many practice kicks were made in all?

2. Beth and her mother made a tile tabletop. They used 5 rows of tiles with 5 tiles in each row. How many tiles did they use?

3. Ted read 7 books in August, 4 books in September, and 9 in October. How many books did he read in the three months?

4. Melanie has 7 coins in her pocket. The coins equal 33¢. What coins are in Melanie's pocket?

Mixed Applications

Solve.

CHOOSE a strategy and a tool.
• Draw a Picture • Act It Out • Find a Pattern   • Make a Model • Write a Number Sentence

Paper/Pencil   Calculator   Hands-On   Mental Math

5. Julie is making 5 costumes. She needs 2 buttons for each costume. How many buttons does Julie need?

6. Anna tells a riddle to 3 friends. Each friend tells it to 2 different friends. How many people are told the riddle?

7. There are 12 people on the bus. When the bus stops, 4 people get off and 8 people get on. How many people are on the bus now?

8. Pat bought a book that cost $2.59. He gave the store clerk $5.00. How much change did he receive?

9. Sam reads for 2 hours each day and plays computer games for 1 hour each day. For how many hours does he read in 5 days?

10. How many cubes would you need to build these steps?

11. Sari used this pattern to make a bead necklace: 1 black bead and then 4 silver beads. She used 20 beads to make the necklace. How many black beads did she use?

Multiplying with 3

Why learn this? Using the Order Property will help you memorize the multiplication facts.

Lea and Kim practiced for the spring swim meet.

Lea practiced 2 hours each day for 3 days. How many hours did she practice in all?

For 2 hours, move 2 spaces. For 3 days, make 3 jumps of 2 spaces.

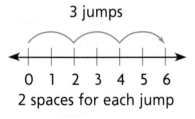

3 jumps

0 1 2 3 4 5 6
2 spaces for each jump

Multiply. $3 \times 2 = 6$

Kim practiced 3 hours each day for 2 days. How many hours did she practice in all?

For 3 hours, move 3 spaces. For 2 days, make 2 jumps of 3 spaces.

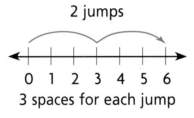

2 jumps

0 1 2 3 4 5 6
3 spaces for each jump

Multiply. $2 \times 3 = 6$

Did Lea or Kim practice more hours?

So, each girl practiced for 6 hours.

The **Order Property of Multiplication** allows two numbers to be multiplied in any order. The product is the same.

EXAMPLE

Multiply. $3 \times 5 = 15$

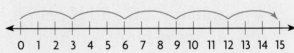

0 1 2 3 4 5 6 7 8 9 10 11 12 13 14 15

Multiply. $5 \times 3 = 15$

0 1 2 3 4 5 6 7 8 9 10 11 12 13 14 15

So, the product for 3×5 and 5×3 is the same.

Talk About It

- Does the order of factors affect the product? Give an example.

- Does the order of addends affect the sum? Give an example.

- Can you subtract numbers in any order? Give an example.

REMEMBER:

Addends are numbers you add. The answer is the *sum*.

addend addend sum
↓ ↓ ↓
5 + 2 = 7

Kim and Lea are learning to dive.

Lea dives 4 times each day for 3 days. Kim dives 3 times each day for 4 days. Which number line below shows Lea's dives? Kim's dives? How many dives did each girl make?

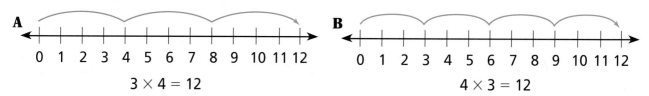

A
0 1 2 3 4 5 6 7 8 9 10 11 12
3 × 4 = 12

B
0 1 2 3 4 5 6 7 8 9 10 11 12
4 × 3 = 12

So, number line A shows Lea's dives. Number line B shows Kim's dives. Each girl made 12 dives.

Talk About It

CRITICAL THINKING Suppose Kim made 8 dives on each of 3 different days. Lea made 3 dives each day for 8 days. How many dives did each girl make?

• How could you use a number line to find the number?

▶ Check

Complete each number sentence using the number line.

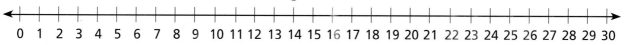

0 1 2 3 4 5 6 7 8 9 10 11 12 13 14 15 16 17 18 19 20 21 22 23 24 25 26 27 28 29 30

1. 3 × 6 = __?__

2. 6 × 3 = __?__

3. 3 × 9 = __?__

4. 9 × 3 = __?__

5. 3 × 7 = __?__

6. 7 × 3 = __?__

7. 3 × 5 = __?__

8. 5 × 3 = __?__

9. 2 × 3 = __?__

10. 3 × 8 = __?__

11. 1 × 3 = __?__

12. 8 × 3 = __?__

Copy each number line. Draw the jumps to find each product.

13.
0 1 2 3 4 5 6 7 8 9 10

2 × 4 = __?__

14.
0 1 2 3 4 5 6 7 8 9 10

4 × 2 = __?__

15. 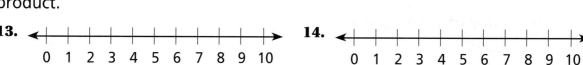 **Write About It** Use a number line to explain how you know 1 × 5 = 5 × 1.

LESSON CONTINUES

Complete the multiplication sentence for each number line.

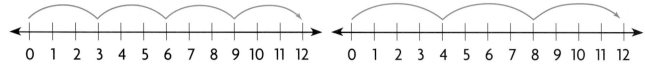

16. $4 \times 3 =$? **17.** $3 \times 4 =$?

Use the number line. Find the product.

18. $6 \times 3 =$? **19.** $5 \times 4 =$? **20.** $9 \times 3 =$? **21.** $2 \times 9 =$?

22. $3 \times 3 =$? **23.** $4 \times 3 =$? **24.** $8 \times 2 =$? **25.** $5 \times 2 =$?

26. $5 \times 5 =$? **27.** $3 \times 9 =$? **28.** $5 \times 1 =$? **29.** $2 \times 3 =$?

30. $3 \times 6 =$? **31.** $8 \times 3 =$? **32.** $9 \times 2 =$? **33.** $3 \times 4 =$?

34. $2 \times 8 =$? **35.** $1 \times 8 =$? **36.** $3 \times 2 =$? **37.** $3 \times 7 =$?

38. $2 \times 4 =$? **39.** $7 \times 3 =$? **40.** $4 \times 2 =$? **41.** $3 \times 8 =$?

Problem Solving • Mixed Applications

42. Visual Thinking How many tennis balls will you have if you buy 4 cans of tennis balls?

43. Reasoning Jody needs 25 Ping-Pong® balls. There are 5 balls in one package. If she buys 5 packages of Ping-Pong® balls, will she have enough? Explain.

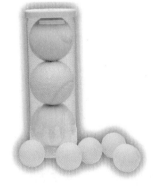

44. Time Sam played tennis for 2 hours and 30 minutes. He began playing at 3:30. At what time did he finish playing tennis?

45. Money Jody spent $6.35 at the sports store. She paid with $10.00. How much change did Jody receive?

46. Logic Carl has $4 more than Susan. Susan has $6. Ray has $5 more than Carl. How much money does Ray have?

47. ⬛ **Write a problem** using the information about the tennis balls or the Ping-Pong® balls.

The Olympic Games were held in Atlanta in 1996. Amy Van Dyken became the first American woman to win 4 gold medals in a single Olympics.

48. Third-grade students collected pictures of Amy Van Dyken. They found 3 different pictures of Amy winning each of the 4 different medals. How many pictures do they have in all?

49. History The first modern Olympic Games were held in 1896. How many years ago was that?

50. Time Amy Van Dyken trained for the backstroke, the freestyle, and the butterfly swimming races. If she practiced 7 hours a week for each race, how many hours each week did she practice for the 3 races?

Mixed Review and Test Prep

Use patterns of hundreds or thousands to find the sum or difference. (pages 148–149)

51. $200 + 709$ **52.** $3,218 - 2,000$

Find the sum. (pages 22–23, 52–53)

53.
$$\begin{array}{r} 53 \\ +28 \\ \hline \end{array}$$

54.
$$\begin{array}{r} 235 \\ +173 \\ \hline \end{array}$$

55.
$$\begin{array}{r} 475 \\ +288 \\ \hline \end{array}$$

56.
$$\begin{array}{r} 540 \\ +\ 68 \\ \hline \end{array}$$

57.
$$\begin{array}{r} 765 \\ +\ 39 \\ \hline \end{array}$$

58.
$$\begin{array}{r} 605 \\ +276 \\ \hline \end{array}$$

Choose the letter of the correct sum. (pages 22–23, 52–55)

59.
$$\begin{array}{r} 35 \\ 14 \\ +26 \\ \hline \end{array}$$
   A 76
   B 75
   C 65
   D 85

60.
$$\begin{array}{r} 165 \\ 192 \\ +422 \\ \hline \end{array}$$
   F 799
   G 780
   H 779
   J 789

61.
$$\begin{array}{r} 649 \\ 398 \\ +231 \\ \hline \end{array}$$
   A 1,278
   B 1,168
   C 1,478
   D 1,268

Multiplying with 1 and 0

Why learn this? You can find how many apples you have in all.

Karl put 1 apple in each of 5 bags. How many apples in all did he put in bags?

Draw a picture to find the answer.

- Draw 5 bags.

- Draw 1 apple in each bag.

So, Karl put 5 apples in bags.

Talk About It

- What multiplication sentence can you write for 5 apples in 1 bag?

- How can you use the Order Property to write the related multiplication sentence?

5 groups of 1 = 5 $5 \times 1 = 5$

Suppose Karl has 3 bags with 0 apples in each bag. How many apples does he have now?

3 groups of 0 = 0 $3 \times 0 = 0$

So, Karl has 0 apples.

Talk About It

- What multiplication sentence can you write for 9 bags with 0 apples in each bag?

- If you have 0 bags of apples, how many apples are there?

CRITICAL THINKING What happens when you multiply any number by 1? by 0?

HEALTH LINK

You should have 2 to 4 servings of fruit each day to stay healthy. If you eat 2 servings each day, how many servings will you eat in a week?

▶ CHECK

Complete the multiplication sentence.

1. $4 \times 1 = \underline{?}$ **2.** $5 \times 0 = \underline{?}$ **3.** $1 \times 3 = \underline{?}$

▶ PRACTICE

Find the product.

4. $4 \times 0 = \underline{?}$ **5.** $6 \times 0 = \underline{?}$ **6.** $8 \times 1 = \underline{?}$ **7.** $1 \times 5 = \underline{?}$

8. $0 \times 3 = \underline{?}$ **9.** $1 \times 7 = \underline{?}$ **10.** $2 \times 0 = \underline{?}$ **11.** $9 \times 1 = \underline{?}$

12. $1 \times 4 = \underline{?}$ **13.** $0 \times 0 = \underline{?}$ **14.** $0 \times 7 = \underline{?}$ **15.** $1 \times 1 = \underline{?}$

16. $7 \times 3 = \underline{?}$ **17.** $3 \times 5 = \underline{?}$ **18.** $5 \times 4 = \underline{?}$ **19.** $8 \times 2 = \underline{?}$

20. $3 \times 2 = \underline{?}$ **21.** $4 \times 3 = \underline{?}$ **22.** $9 \times 0 = \underline{?}$ **23.** $3 \times 3 = \underline{?}$

Problem Solving • Mixed Applications

24. Money Craig has 6 nickels. Each nickel is 5 cents. How much are Craig's nickels worth?

25. Reasoning Ara put 1 muffin and 2 cookies on each of 5 plates. How many muffins did she put on plates?

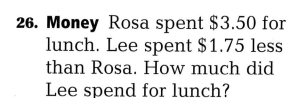

26. Money Rosa spent $3.50 for lunch. Lee spent $1.75 less than Rosa. How much did Lee spend for lunch?

27. ✎ **Write About It** Explain how to draw a model to find a product when you multiply by 1.

Mixed Review and Test Prep

Compare the numbers. Write $<$ or $>$ for each ●. (pages 164–167)

28. 470 ● 407   **29.** 635 ● 536   **30.** 442 ● 424   **31.** 1,409 ● 1,501

Choose the letter that shows the numbers in order from least to greatest. (pages 168–169)

32. 68, 52, 75, 57, 71
   A 57, 52, 68, 71, 75   **B** 75, 71, 68, 57, 52
   C 52, 57, 68, 71, 75   **D** 52, 57, 71, 75, 68

33. 468, 642, 486, 624
   F 468, 642, 624, 486   **G** 486, 468, 624, 642
   H 624, 642, 468, 486   **J** 468, 486, 624, 642

Multiplying with 4

Why learn this? It will help you count groups of coins and other items.

Aaron counted the pennies in his bank. He made 8 stacks with 4 pennies in each stack. How many pennies did he count?

Multiply to find how many pennies.

$$8 \times 4 = 32$$

↑ stacks of pennies   ↑ pennies in each stack   ↑ pennies in all

$$\begin{array}{r} 4 \leftarrow \text{factor} \\ \times 8 \leftarrow \text{factor} \\ \hline 32 \leftarrow \text{product} \end{array}$$

So, he counted 32 pennies.

You can use a multiplication table to find products.

CONSUMER LINK

A penny is 1 cent. What are some things you can buy with 32 pennies?

EXAMPLE

$6 \times 4 = 24$

The product is found where the factor 6 row and the factor 4 column meet.

Talk About It [CRITICAL THINKING]

- Look across the factor 6 row and down the factor 4 column. What patterns do you see?

- Look across the factor 0 row and down the factor 0 column. What does this show you about multiplying by 0?

- How can you use the multiplication table to find 8×4?

Multiplication Table

column ↓

×	0	1	2	3	4	5	6	7	8	9
0	0	0	0	0	0	0	0	0	0	0
1	0	1	2	3	4	5	6	7	8	9
2	0	2	4	6	8	10	12	14	16	18
3	0	3	6	9	12	15	18	21	24	27
4	0	4	8	12	16	20	24	28	32	36
5	0	5	10	15	20	25	30	35	40	45
6	0	6	12	18	24	30	36	42	48	54
7	0	7	14	21	28	35	42	49	56	63
8	0	8	16	24	32	40	48	56	64	72
9	0	9	18	27	36	45	54	63	72	81

row→ (at row 6)

Suppose Aaron has 5 stacks of pennies with 7 pennies in each stack. How many pennies does he have?

$$5 \times 7 = 35 \qquad \begin{array}{r} 7 \\ \times 5 \\ \hline 35 \end{array}$$

✕	0	1	2	3	4	5	6	7	8	9
0	0	0	0	0	0	0	0	0	0	0
1	0	1	2	3	4	5	6	7	8	9
2	0	2	4	6	8	10	12	14	16	18
3	0	3	6	9	12	15	18	21	24	27
4	0	4	8	12	16	20	24	28	32	36
5	0	5	10	15	20	25	30	35	40	45
6	0	6	12	18	24	30	36	42	48	54
7	0	7	14	21	28	35	42	49	56	63
8	0	8	16	24	32	40	48	56	64	72
9	0	9	18	27	36	45	54	63	72	81

The 5 stands for the number of stacks. The 7 stands for the number of pennies in each stack.

Talk About It

• How could Aaron use a multiplication table to solve the problem?

• How would you complete the table below?

• How is it different from Aaron's table?

✕	0	1	2	3	4	5	6	7	8	9
5	0	5	10	?	?	?	?	?	?	?

▶ CHECK

Copy and complete the table.

1.

✕	0	1	2	3	4	5	6	7	8	9
4	?	?	?	?	?	?	?	?	?	?

Find the product.

2. $\begin{array}{r} 2 \\ \times 3 \\ \hline \end{array}$ 3. $\begin{array}{r} 3 \\ \times 4 \\ \hline \end{array}$ 4. $\begin{array}{r} 8 \\ \times 2 \\ \hline \end{array}$ 5. $\begin{array}{r} 8 \\ \times 3 \\ \hline \end{array}$ 6. $\begin{array}{r} 4 \\ \times 3 \\ \hline \end{array}$ 7. $\begin{array}{r} 3 \\ \times 3 \\ \hline \end{array}$ 8. $\begin{array}{r} 4 \\ \times 6 \\ \hline \end{array}$

9. $\begin{array}{r} 0 \\ \times 3 \\ \hline \end{array}$ 10. $\begin{array}{r} 4 \\ \times 7 \\ \hline \end{array}$ 11. $\begin{array}{r} 9 \\ \times 4 \\ \hline \end{array}$ 12. $\begin{array}{r} 2 \\ \times 4 \\ \hline \end{array}$ 13. $\begin{array}{r} 4 \\ \times 0 \\ \hline \end{array}$ 14. $\begin{array}{r} 1 \\ \times 4 \\ \hline \end{array}$ 15. $\begin{array}{r} 4 \\ \times 4 \\ \hline \end{array}$

16. $\begin{array}{r} 4 \\ \times 9 \\ \hline \end{array}$ 17. $\begin{array}{r} 8 \\ \times 4 \\ \hline \end{array}$ 18. $\begin{array}{r} 3 \\ \times 5 \\ \hline \end{array}$ 19. $\begin{array}{r} 3 \\ \times 2 \\ \hline \end{array}$ 20. $\begin{array}{r} 5 \\ \times 4 \\ \hline \end{array}$ 21. $\begin{array}{r} 3 \\ \times 8 \\ \hline \end{array}$ 22. $\begin{array}{r} 6 \\ \times 4 \\ \hline \end{array}$

LESSON CONTINUES

Find the product. You may wish to use the
multiplication table.

23. 4   **24.** 4   **25.** 5   **26.** 7   **27.** 0   **28.** 4   **29.** 9
     ×2   ×8   ×4   ×4   ×4   ×5   ×4

30. 6   **31.** 4   **32.** 2   **33.** 8   **34.** 2   **35.** 1   **36.** 0
     ×4   ×3   ×3   ×5   ×7   ×9   ×6

37. 6   **38.** 3   **39.** 9   **40.** 6   **41.** 1   **42.** 5   **43.** 7
     ×3   ×4   ×1   ×0   ×8   ×8   ×5

44. $2 \times 8 = \underline{?}$ **45.** $7 \times 2 = \underline{?}$ **46.** $3 \times 1 = \underline{?}$ **47.** $0 \times 2 = \underline{?}$

48. $1 \times 5 = \underline{?}$ **49.** $9 \times 5 = \underline{?}$ **50.** $8 \times 3 = \underline{?}$ **51.** $0 \times 0 = \underline{?}$

52. $5 \times 2 = \underline{?}$ **53.** $4 \times 4 = \underline{?}$ **54.** $9 \times 3 = \underline{?}$ **55.** $6 \times 5 = \underline{?}$

Problem Solving • Mixed Applications

Using Data Use the graph for Exercises 56–58 and 61.

56. Sports How can you use
multiplication to find the
total number of goals
scored in each game?

57. Compare How many more
goals were scored in Game 2
than in Game 3?

58. What was the total number of
goals scored in all three games?

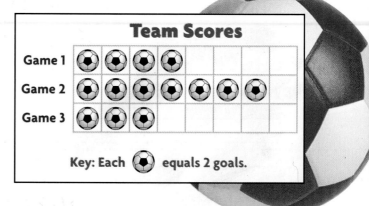

Team Scores

Game 1
Game 2
Game 3

Key: Each ⚽ equals 2 goals.

59. Money Rosa spent $1.75 for a
hot dog, $1.25 for a lemonade,
and $5.50 for a ticket to the
game. How much did Rosa
spend?

60. Time David goes to soccer
practice from 3:00 until 4:30
on Wednesdays and Fridays.
For how long does David have
soccer practice each week?

61. Camron scored 4 goals in
Game 1, 5 goals in Game 2,
and 7 goals in Game 3. How
many goals did he score in
the 3 games?

62. ✐ **Write a problem** using the
data in the graph.

In-line skating or rollerblading is one of the most popular sports. It is also one of the best exercises for helping you keep healthy and strong.

63. In-line skates can have three wheels, four wheels, or five wheels. Suppose 5 friends have skates with 4 wheels each. How many wheels do the 5 skaters have?

64. History In-line skates were invented in 1980. For how many years have people been rollerblading?

65. Estimation The sport of roller hockey began on old-fashioned skates in 1870. To the nearest hundred years, for how long have people been playing roller hockey?

66. The roller hockey rink is 200 feet in length and 85 feet wide. If 175 students went skating on Friday and 268 went skating on Saturday, how many students skated in the 2 days?

67. ✏️ **Write a problem** using in-line skating and multiplication.

When you exercise, you need to drink lots of liquids. Water is in all the liquids you drink as well as in most of the foods you eat.

Your body needs at least 8 glasses of water every day. If a glass holds 8 ounces of water, and you drink 8 glasses a day, how many ounces of water do you drink in a day?

Mixed Review and Test Prep

Find the sum. (pages 52–55)

68. 234 + 167 = _?_   **69.** 25 + 25 + 25 = _?_   **70.** 563 + 217 = _?_

71. 14 + 35 + 46 = _?_   **72.** 818 + 79 = _?_   **73.** 315 + 495 = _?_

74. 48 + 10 + 59 = _?_   **75.** 681 + 127 = _?_   **76.** 367 + 150 = _?_

77. 36 + 14 + 16 = _?_   **78.** 325 + 219 = _?_   **79.** 220 + 719 = _?_

Choose the letter that shows the value of the blue digit. (pages 144–145)

80. 32,984   **A** 2 tens   **81.** 25,345   **F** 2 tens

             B 2 hundreds   **G** 2 hundreds

             C 2 thousands   **H** 2 ten thousands

             D 2 ten thousands   **J** 2 hundred thousands

▶ CHECK Understanding

VOCABULARY

1. In the number sentence $3 \times 5 = 15$, the numbers 3 and 5 are called the __?__ and the 15 is called the __?__. (page 188)

2. Since $8 \times 3 = 24$, then $3 \times 8 = 24$ because of the __?__. (page 192)

Write the addition sentence and the multiplication sentence for each picture. (pages 188–189)

3.    4.    5.

Complete the multiplication sentence for each number line. (pages 192–195)

6.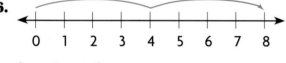

$2 \times 4 =$ __?__

7.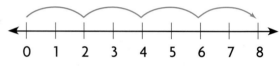

$4 \times 2 =$ __?__

▶ CHECK Skills

Find the product. (pages 188–189, 196–201)

8. $3 \times 7 =$ __?__   9. $9 \times 2 =$ __?__   10. $7 \times 4 =$ __?__   11. $5 \times 5 =$ __?__

12. $\begin{array}{r} 1 \\ \times 6 \\ \hline \end{array}$ 13. $\begin{array}{r} 2 \\ \times 8 \\ \hline \end{array}$ 14. $\begin{array}{r} 9 \\ \times 4 \\ \hline \end{array}$ 15. $\begin{array}{r} 3 \\ \times 3 \\ \hline \end{array}$ 16. $\begin{array}{r} 0 \\ \times 7 \\ \hline \end{array}$ 17. $\begin{array}{r} 5 \\ \times 2 \\ \hline \end{array}$

18. $\begin{array}{r} 6 \\ \times 2 \\ \hline \end{array}$ 19. $\begin{array}{r} 4 \\ \times 4 \\ \hline \end{array}$ 20. $\begin{array}{r} 5 \\ \times 0 \\ \hline \end{array}$ 21. $\begin{array}{r} 1 \\ \times 9 \\ \hline \end{array}$ 22. $\begin{array}{r} 4 \\ \times 6 \\ \hline \end{array}$ 23. $\begin{array}{r} 1 \\ \times 8 \\ \hline \end{array}$

▶ CHECK Problem Solving

Solve. (pages 190–191)

CHOOSE a strategy and a tool.

- Draw a Picture
- Write a Number Sentence
- Make a Model
- Act It Out

  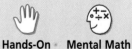

Paper/Pencil   Calculator   Hands-On   Mental Math

24. Paulo bought peanuts for 47¢. He paid for them with five coins. What coins?

25. There are 4 shelves, each with 6 plants. How many plants are there?

Test Prep

Choose the best answer.

1. What is the value of the blue digit? 37,829

   A seven hundreds

   B seventy thousands

   C seventy-eight hundreds

   D seven thousands

2. On Saturday, Mr. Yen sold 223 boxes of popcorn. On Sunday, he sold 375 boxes. About how many boxes did Mr. Yen sell in all?

   F 300   G 400   H 600   J 800

3. Madison has 4 sisters. She gave 2 balloons to each sister. Which number sentence shows how many balloons Madison gave in all?

   A $8 - 4 = 4$ B $4 \times 2 = 8$

   C $4 + 2 = 6$ D $8 + 2 = 10$

4. Melinda put her books in 3 piles. Each pile has 5 books. How many books does Melinda have in all?

   F 10   G 15   H 8   J 20

5.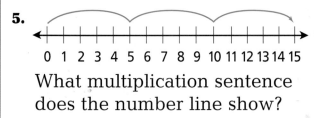

   What multiplication sentence does the number line show?

   A 3×3 B 4×3

   C 1×15 D 3×5

6. The hour hand on the clock is between the 6 and the 7. The minute hand is pointing to the 9. What time is it?

   F 6:09   G 7:45

   H 6:45   J 6:15

7. This table shows Bob's Saturday schedule.

BOB'S SATURDAY SCHEDULE	
Chore	Time
Mowing the lawn	9:30–10:05
Walking the dog	10:10–10:30
Cleaning his room	10:45–12:15
Washing his bike	12:20–12:35

   Which chore takes Bob the longest?

   A mowing the lawn

   B walking the dog

   C cleaning his room

   D washing his bike

8. Jerry has 2 boxes of CDs. There are 8 CDs in each box. Which picture shows how many CDs Jerry has?

   F

   G

   H

   J

SOCIAL STUDIES LINK

Native Americans planned ahead for winter by drying meat and fish. Meat was cut into strips and dried in the sun and wind or over a fire. Fish was salted and hung to dry.

Winter Food

Fruit leather and beef jerky are popular lunch items, but they are not new foods. Native Americans prepared for the winter by drying beef, fish, berries, and nuts.

Find out what the Native Americans in your area ate and what they might have preserved for winter.

- Draw two drying racks for a Native American food.

- Draw on one rack food drying in four rows with six items in each row.

- Draw on the other rack food drying in three rows with eight items in each row.

- Find how many items are on each rack.

- Draw a larger drying rack that could hold all the food in equal rows.

DID YOU

☑ learn about Native American food sources in your area?

☑ draw two drying racks?

☑ find the total food items?

☑ draw a larger rack that could hold all the food in equal rows?

Multiplying with 6

You will investigate how to use factors to make arrays.

An **array** shows objects in rows and columns.
Use square tiles. Make arrays to find products.

> **REMEMBER:**
>
> The numbers that you multiply are *factors*. The answer to a multiplication problem is the *product*.
>
> factor factor product
>
> 6 × 3 = 18

▶ **EXPLORE**

MATERIALS: square tiles

MODEL

Find $5 \times 6 =$ __?__ .

Step 1

Use tiles.

Step 2

Arrange them in 5 rows of 6 tiles.

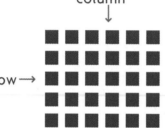

column

row →

Record

Record the multiplication fact that your array shows. Explain how you found the product.

Talk About It

- How can using tiles to make an array help you find a product?

- How would you make an array to show 6×6?

- How could you use a number line to show 6×6?

▶ **TRY THIS**

1. Use eight tiles. What four arrays can you make with the eight tiles?

2. ✎ **Write About It** How are the arrays for 2×4 and 4×2 different? How are they alike?

▶ PRACTICE

Use tiles to make arrays. Find the product.

3. $4 \times 6 =$?

4. $3 \times 5 =$?

5. $5 \times 2 =$?

6. $4 \times 4 =$?

7. $6 \times 3 =$?

8. $6 \times 6 =$?

9. $5 \times 5 =$?

10. $6 \times 5 =$?

11. $6 \times 2 =$?

12. $6 \times 7 =$?

Technology Link

You can use equal groups to solve multiplication problems by using E-Lab, Activity 12. Available on CD-ROM and on the Internet at www.hbschool.com/elab

Write the multiplication fact that is shown by each array.

13. ▪▪▪▪▪
▪▪▪▪▪

14. ▪▪▪▪
▪▪▪▪
▪▪▪▪

Copy and complete the table.

15.

×	1	2	3	4	5	6	7	8	9
6	?	?	?	?	?	?	?	?	?

Name all the arrays you can make with each set of tiles.

16. 6 tiles

17. 10 tiles

18. 12 tiles

Problem Solving • Mixed Applications

19. Arlene put 3 rows of 5 pictures on her bulletin board. How many pictures did she put up in all?

20. The Boyds are laying tiles. They bought 5 boxes of tiles. There are 8 tiles in each box. How many tiles did they buy?

21. Logic Michael has these coins in his pocket. Anthony has the same amount of money, but twice the number of coins. What coins could Anthony have?

22. Sheila has 9 clay pots on each of 3 shelves. How many clay pots does she have in all?

Multiplying with 7

Why learn this? You can solve problems about the number of vacation days in several weeks.

Collin's family is going on a vacation in 6 weeks. There are 7 days in 1 week. In how many days is Collin's family going on vacation?

You can make an array and break it into smaller arrays to help you find the product.

MODEL

What is 6×7?

Step 1
Make an array that shows 6 rows of 7.

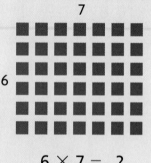

$6 \times 7 = \underline{\ ?\ }$

Step 2
Break the array into two smaller arrays whose products you know.

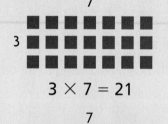

$3 \times 7 = 21$

$3 \times 7 = 21$

Step 3
Add the products of the two arrays.

$$\begin{array}{r} 21 \\ +21 \\ \hline 42 \end{array}$$

$6 \times 7 = 42$

So, Collin's family is going on vacation in 42 days.

Talk About It

• How does an array show multiplication?

• How can breaking a larger array into smaller arrays help you find its product?

CRITICAL THINKING Name two smaller arrays you could make to find $8 \times 7 = \underline{\ ?\ }$.

Collin is making a summer vacation picture diary. He needs 1 sheet of paper for every day. How many does he need for 9 weeks?

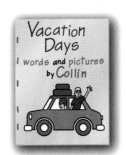

To find the product, you can make an array.

MODEL

Find. $\begin{array}{r} 7 \\ \times 9 \\ \hline \end{array}$

Step 1
Make an array that shows 9 rows of 7.

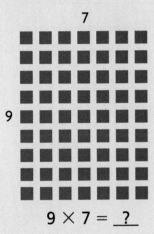

$9 \times 7 = \underline{\ ?\ }$

Step 2
Break the array to use products you know.

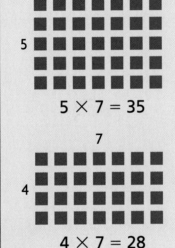

$5 \times 7 = 35$

$4 \times 7 = 28$

Step 3
Add the products of the two arrays.

$\begin{array}{r} 1 \\ 35 \\ +28 \\ \hline 63 \end{array}$

$\begin{array}{r} 7 \\ \times 9 \\ \hline 63 \end{array}$

So, Collin needs 63 sheets of paper for his diary.

CRITICAL THINKING How is Step 2 in the model above different from the one on page 208?

▶ CHECK

Make two smaller arrays to find each product.

1.

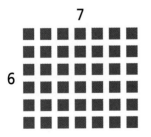

2.

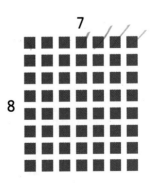

Find the product.

3. $2 \times 7 = \underline{\ ?\ }$ **4.** $5 \times 7 = \underline{\ ?\ }$ **5.** $3 \times 7 = \underline{\ ?\ }$

▶ PRACTICE

Make two smaller arrays to find each product.

6.

7.
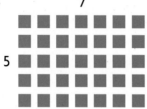

8.
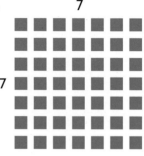

Copy and complete the table.

9.

×	1	2	3	4	5	6	7	8	9
7	?	?	?	?	?	?	?	?	?

Find the product.

10. $3 \times 8 = \underline{\ ?\ }$ **11.** $6 \times 6 = \underline{\ ?\ }$ **12.** $6 \times 9 = \underline{\ ?\ }$ **13.** $5 \times 5 = \underline{\ ?\ }$

14. $7 \times 6 = \underline{\ ?\ }$ **15.** $8 \times 4 = \underline{\ ?\ }$ **16.** $7 \times 7 = \underline{\ ?\ }$ **17.** $7 \times 8 = \underline{\ ?\ }$

18. $\begin{array}{r} 7 \\ \times 5 \\ \hline \end{array}$ **19.** $\begin{array}{r} 5 \\ \times 3 \\ \hline \end{array}$ **20.** $\begin{array}{r} 6 \\ \times 9 \\ \hline \end{array}$ **21.** $\begin{array}{r} 8 \\ \times 3 \\ \hline \end{array}$ **22.** $\begin{array}{r} 9 \\ \times 7 \\ \hline \end{array}$ **23.** $\begin{array}{r} 0 \\ \times 7 \\ \hline \end{array}$

Problem Solving • Mixed Applications

Using Data For Problems 26–28, use the schedule.

24. Number Sense A movie is shown 6 times each day. How many times is the movie shown in 1 week?

25. Mental Math The room has 7 rows of seats with 9 seats in each row. How many seats are in the room?

26. Time How long is the program *The Night Sky? Exploring Space?*

27. How many times is the program *The Night Sky* shown each day?

28. Compare Which program is longer than 30 minutes?

29. ✏ Write a problem that uses this information. In a book about space, Joe read 7 pages each day for 7 days.

PLANETARIUM SCHEDULE

The Night Sky	9:00 - 9:30
Exploring Space	9:45 - 10:30
The Night Sky	11:00 - 11:30
Exploring Space	11:45 - 12:30
The Night Sky	1:30 - 2:00
Exploring Space	2:15 - 3:00
The Night Sky	3:30 - 4:00

Moving pictures made from drawings are called animation. One of the oldest types of animation is found in a flip book. The same object appears on each page, but in a slightly different spot. When the pages are flipped, the object appears to move.

30. **Visual Thinking** Christie traces the outline of her family car once on each of 4 sheets of paper. How many cars does she have altogether?

31. **Number Sense** Christie decides to make the flip book longer. It will be 40 pages. On how many more pages will Christie need to trace her car?

32. Each car is traced on one page of the flip book. So far 19 pages have cars. How many more cars need to be traced to fill the 40 pages?

33. **Reasoning** You have $1.00. You want to buy 10 sheets of paper at $0.12 a sheet. Will you have enough money? Explain.

34. **Estimation** Suppose everyone in your class makes a 7-page flip book. Will your class need about 50 pages in all, about 100 pages, or about 1,000 pages?

Mixed Review and Test Prep

Write the value of the blue digit. (pages 150–153)

35. 42,875   **36.** 35,154   **37.** 85,971   **38.** 68,326

Round to the nearest hundred. Choose the letter of the correct answer. (pages 172–173)

39. 184 **A** 140   **40.** 559 **F** 500   **41.** 335 **A** 400   **42.** 819 **F** 850
          B 180   **G** 600   **B** 435   **G** 900
          C 200   **H** 800   **C** 300   **H** 800
          D 100   **J** 900   **D** 325   **J** 700

LESSON 3

Multiplying with 8

Why learn this? You can multiply to find the number of apples in several boxes.

Mr. Donald bought 5 boxes of apples for his class to use at their party. There are 8 apples in each box. How many apples are in the 5 boxes?

Make an array. Break it into smaller arrays to help you find the product.

MODEL

What is 5×8?

Step 1	**Step 2**	**Step 3**
Make an array that shows 5 rows of 8.	Break the array into two smaller arrays whose products you know.	Add the products of the two arrays.

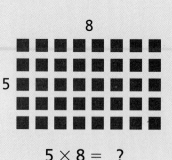

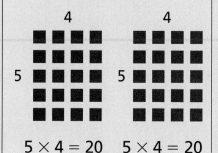

$5 \times 8 = \underline{?}$ $5 \times 4 = 20$ $5 \times 4 = 20$

$$\begin{array}{r} 20 \\ +20 \\ \hline 40 \end{array}$$

$5 \times 8 = 40$

So, there are 40 apples in the 5 boxes.

Talk About It

• Name two other smaller arrays that you could use to find $5 \times 8 = \underline{?}$.

• What smaller arrays could you use to find the product for 8×8?

▶ CHECK

Find the product. You may want to make arrays to help you.

1. $3 \times 8 = \underline{?}$ **2.** $6 \times 8 = \underline{?}$

3. $4 \times 8 = \underline{?}$ **4.** $2 \times 8 = \underline{?}$

SCIENCE LINK

Apple growers must take care of their trees. They make sure the trees have sunlight and water. Healthy apples grow best about 5 inches apart. If a branch has 8 apples spaced about 5 inches apart, about how long is the branch?

Write two smaller arrays for each array. Find the product.

5.   8

6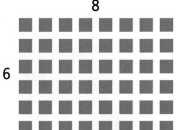

6.   8

4

7.   8

7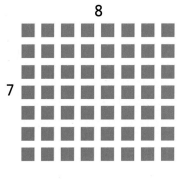

Copy and complete the table.

8.

×	1	2	3	4	5	6	7	8	9
8	?	?	?	?	?	?	?	?	?

Find the product.

9. $8 \times 8 = $?　　　**10.** $4 \times 6 = $?　　　**11.** $9 \times 8 = $?　　　**12.** $6 \times 7 = $?

Problem Solving • Mixed Applications

Using Data For Problems 13–15, use the picture.

13. Consumer Joy got 1 bag of apples, 1 bag of oranges, and 1 bunch of bananas. How many pieces of fruit did she get?

8 apples $2.89

8 oranges $2.25

5 bananas $0.89

FRUIT for SALE

14. Money Andrew bought 1 bag of apples. How much change did he receive from $5.00?

15. ✏️ **Write a problem** about Jeff and the 5 bags of apples he bought.

Mixed Review and Test Prep

Find the sum. (pages 114–115)

16.　$2.43
　　　$+ 3.54$

17.　$5.72
　　　$+ 1.26$

18.　$6.45
　　　$+ 5.61$

19.　$5.38
　　　$+ 7.42$

Choose the letter that shows the number in expanded form. (pages 144–145)

20. 432　　**A** 4 hundreds, 3 tens, 3 ones　　**B** 3 hundreds, 4 tens, 2 ones
　　　　　　C 2 hundreds, 2 tens, 3 ones　　**D** 4 hundreds, 3 tens, 2 ones

21. 905　　**F** 5 hundreds, 0 tens, 9 ones　　**G** 0 hundreds, 9 tens, 5 ones
　　　　　　H 9 hundreds, 0 tens, 5 ones　　**J** 5 hundreds, 5 tens, 0 ones

Multiplying with 9

Why learn this? You can use patterns of 9 when you play games.

Sarah plays on the Bluebirds baseball team. She has played in 9 games. She played 7 innings in each game. How many innings did Sarah play?

$$7 \times 9 = \underline{\ ?\ }$$

Use patterns in the products of nine to help you.

Playing ball

Facts of Nine
1 x 9 = 9
2 x 9 = 18
3 x 9 = 27
4 x 9 = 36
5 x 9 = 45
6 x 9 = 54
7 x 9 = 63
8 x 9 = 72
9 x 9 = 81

Talk About It

- What pattern do you see in the products in the ones column?

- What pattern do you see in the tens column?

- Add the digits in each product. What pattern do you see in the sums?

CRITICAL THINKING Why do you already know most of the facts of nine?

So, Sarah played 63 innings.

Here is another way to remember facts of nine.

EXAMPLE

$$4 \times 9 = \underline{\ ?\ }$$

First, multiply by 10 instead of 9. Think: $4 \times 10 = 40$

Next, subtract the first factor so you have 4 nines.

Since $40 - 4 = 36$, $4 \times 9 = 36$.

- How can you use this way to find 5×9?

- How can you use this way to find 7×9?

Technology Link

In *Mighty Math Calculating Crew*, the game *Intergalactic Trader* challenges you to solve problems by using what you are learning about multiplication. Use Grow Slide Levels C and D.

► CHECK

Copy and complete the table.

1.

×	1	2	3	4	5	6	7	8	9
9	?	?	?	?	?	?	?	?	?

► PRACTICE

Find the product.

2. 8
   ×7

3. 5
   ×3

4. 9
   ×2

5. 5
   ×5

6. 9
   ×0

7. 3
   ×8

8. 9
   ×5

9. 7
   ×4

10. 6
   ×8

11. 9
   ×9

12. 5
   ×7

13. 9
   ×3

14. 1
   ×9

15. 9
   ×7

16. 8
   ×9

17. $2 \times 9 = \underline{\ ?\ }$

18. $5 \times 8 = \underline{\ ?\ }$

19. $4 \times 9 = \underline{\ ?\ }$

20. $6 \times 6 = \underline{\ ?\ }$

21. $5 \times 6 = \underline{\ ?\ }$

22. $7 \times 7 = \underline{\ ?\ }$

23. $5 \times 4 = \underline{\ ?\ }$

24. $9 \times 6 = \underline{\ ?\ }$

Problem Solving • Mixed Applications

Using Data For Problem 27, use the calendar.

25. Mental Math David scored 3 runs in each of 9 games. How many runs in all did he score?

26. Money At the baseball game, Adam bought a slice of pizza for $1.65 and a small drink for $0.95. How much did he spend on snacks?

27. Elapsed Time Bonnie went to a baseball game on April 9. Two weeks later she went roller skating. On what date did she go roller skating?

April						
S	M	T	W	T	F	S
					1	2
3	4	5	6	7	8	9
10	11	12	13	14	15	16
17	18	19	20	21	22	23
24	25	26	27	28	29	30

28. Time The baseball game lasted 3 hours and 30 minutes. It began at 2:00. At what time was it over?

29. Jody is 9 years old. Her coach is 28 years older. How old is Jody's coach?

30. ✏ **Write About It** Explain how you can use tens to find a product when 9 is one of the factors.

LESSON CONTINUES

Problem–Solving Strategy: Make a Model

▶ **THE PROBLEM** Danielle is making an afghan. She has made it 6 squares wide and 8 squares long. How many squares has Danielle made so far?

UNDERSTAND

- What are you asked to find?

- What information will you use?

- Is there any information you will not use? If so, what?

REMEMBER:
UNDERSTAND
PLAN
SOLVE
LOOK BACK

PLAN

- What strategy can you use to solve the problem?

  You can *make a model* to find the number of squares Danielle has made so far.

SOLVE

- How can you use the strategy to solve the problem?

  Use tiles to make a model of the afghan. Use one tile for each square of the afghan.

  8 rows of 6 squares
  $8 \times 6 = 48$

  So, Danielle has made 48 squares for her afghan.

LOOK BACK

- How can you decide if your answer makes sense?

- What other strategy could you use?

► PRACTICE

Make a model to solve.

1. Charlene is tiling the roof of her doll house. She has glued 8 rows of tiles. There are 9 tiles in each row. How many tiles has she used so far?

2. For the party, Carl has put 6 rows of muffins on a plate. There are 6 muffins in each row. How many muffins did he put on the plate?

3. Daphne is setting up a game of Concentration. She has put 7 cards in each row. There are 6 rows of cards. How many cards are there in all?

4. Ms. Adams is hanging up her students' pictures. The display is 5 pictures wide and 6 pictures long. How many pictures are in the display?

Mixed Applications

Solve.

CHOOSE a strategy and a tool.
- Draw a Picture
- Guess and Check
- Write a Number Sentence
- Make a Model
- Act It Out
- Work Backward

 Paper/Pencil   Calculator   Hands-On   Mental Math

5. It is now 12:30 P.M. Pedro has music class for 1 hour. Then he has math class for 45 minutes. What time will it be when he finishes his math class?

6. Kenesha knitted for 90 minutes. She knitted 10 more minutes in the afternoon than in the morning. How many minutes did she knit in the morning? in the afternoon?

7. Francine has this amount of money in her wallet. She just spent $1.25 at the school store. How much money did she have to begin with?

8. Megan's quilt is blue, green, and pink. She used 3 different shades of each color. How many different shades of color are in her quilt?

9. The Gordons' kitchen floor is 5 tiles wide and 9 tiles long. How many tiles are on the Gordons' kitchen floor?

10. Megan began working on her quilt on Monday, May 4. She worked on it for 3 weeks. On what day did she finish?

Completing the Multiplication Table

Why learn this? You can find products and see patterns on a multiplication table.

While at the airport, Justin saw 7 jets waiting to take off. Each jet had 3 engines. How many engines were there in all?

$$7 \times 3 = \underline{\ ?\ }$$

Use the multiplication table. Find where factor 7 row and factor 3 column meet.

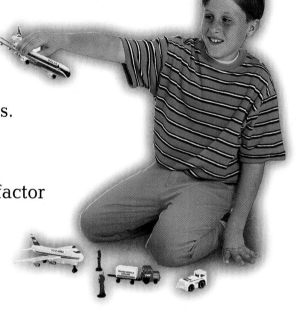

MULTIPLICATION TABLE

↓ column

×	0	1	2	3	4	5	6	7	8	9
0	0	0	0	0	0	0	0	0	0	0
1	0	1	2	3	4	5	6	7	8	9
2	0	2	4	6	8	10	12	14	16	18
3	0	3	6	9	12	15	18	21	24	27
4	0	4	8	12	16	20	24	28	32	36
5	0	5	10	15	20	25	30	35	40	45
6	0	6	12	18	24	30	36	42	48	54
row→ **7**	0	7	14	21	28	35	42	49	56	63
8	0	8	16	24	32	40	48	56	64	72
9	0	9	18	27	36	45	54	63	72	81

So, there were 21 engines in all.

Make a multiplication table.

>
> **REMEMBER:**
> On a multiplication table, a *product* is found where a *row* and a *column* meet.
>
> **EXAMPLE:** $4 \times 5 = \underline{\ ?\ }$
> column
> 5
> ↓
> row 4 → **20**
> product

Talk About It

• What is the product when one factor is zero? when one factor is 1?

• How does the Order Property help you record products on the table? Give an example.

CRITICAL THINKING Draw a line from the × symbol to 81 on the table you made. Color the products on the line. What products are these?

Calculator Activities page H61

The multiplication table on page 218 shows the product for the factors 7 and 3. Compare the table with other ways to find 7 equal groups of 3.

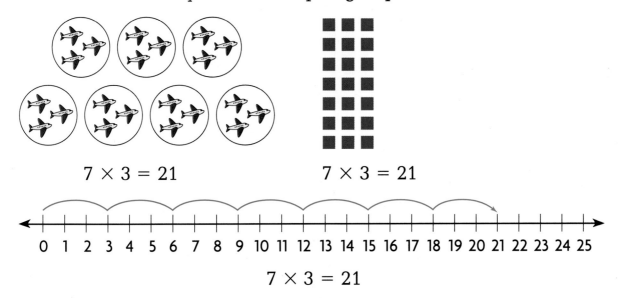

$7 \times 3 = 21$ $7 \times 3 = 21$

$7 \times 3 = 21$

To find a product, you can use the multiplication table, equal groups, arrays, or a number line.

Talk About It

- Tell how you would find the product for $2 \times 7 = \underline{\ ?\ }$ and for $9 \times 7 = \underline{\ ?\ }$.

- How would you find $4 \times 6 = \underline{\ ?\ }$ on a number line? in a multiplication table? with items in equal groups? with an array?

CRITICAL THINKING Find the products 21 and 12 on the multiplication table. Which one appears more often? Why?

- When can a multiplication table be more helpful for finding a product than an array or a number line?

▶ CHECK

Find the product by using a multiplication table, equal groups, an array, or a number line.

1. $5 \times 4 = \underline{\ ?\ }$ **2.** $8 \times 7 = \underline{\ ?\ }$ **3.** $9 \times 3 = \underline{\ ?\ }$

4. $6 \times 7 = \underline{\ ?\ }$ **5.** $7 \times 5 = \underline{\ ?\ }$ **6.** $8 \times 9 = \underline{\ ?\ }$

LESSON CONTINUES

Write a multiplication sentence for each picture.

7.

8.

9.

10.

```
0  1  2  3  4  5  6  7  8  9  10 11 12 13 14 15 16 17 18 19 20 21 22 23 24 25
```

Use the multiplication table to find the products.

| **11.** 4 ×3 | **12.** 6 ×7 | **13.** 8 ×5 | **14.** 2 ×9 | **15.** 9 ×9 |

| **16.** 7 ×9 | **17.** 8 ×6 | **18.** 9 ×4 | **19.** 6 ×0 | **20.** 8 ×8 |

For Exercises 21–24, use a copy of a multiplication table.

21. Find the products of each set of odd numbers. Color the products red.

22. Find the products of each set of even numbers. Color the products blue.

23. Color the products of one odd number and one even number green.

24. How are the patterns alike? different?

Problem Solving • Mixed Applications

25. Money Hector paid $149 for his airplane ticket. David paid $168 for his ticket. How much more did David pay than Hector?

26. Reasoning Four friends are in line. Julie is ahead of Elaine. Carol is behind Elaine. Julie is behind Marlene. Who is first in line?

27. Mental Math There are 9 seats in one row of the airplane. How many seats are in 6 rows?

28. ⬛▷ **Write a problem** about the number of seats on an airplane. Use multiplication to solve.

The 747 jumbo jet is one of the biggest planes flying today. The inside of a 747 looks like a large movie theater.

29. **Mental Math** A 747 has 3 sections of seats. The middle section has 5 seats in each row. How many seats are in 8 rows?

30. Suppose 9 rows of 5 seats and 8 rows of 2 seats are filled. How many people altogether are traveling in those rows?

31. **Visual Thinking** Draw arrays to show seating for your class on a 747 jumbo jet. Use as many rows of 5 as you need. How many will that be? How many rows of 2 will you need? If anyone in your class still needs a seat, show where it will be. Write multiplication sentences to show your plan.

32. **Mental Math** The fastest airliner is the Concorde, but it only carries 100 people. The 747 can carry 5 times that many people. How many people can the 747 carry?

The center of Australia is called the Outback. Because towns are very far apart in the Outback, airplanes are the main means of transportation. Planes are used to deliver mail and library books, as well as being used for medical emergencies. Suppose 6 boxes of library books were delivered each week for 9 weeks. How many boxes of books were delivered in all?

Outback
AUSTRALIA
Brisbane
Sydney
Melbourne

Mixed Review and Test Prep

Write *true* or *false*. Change words in the false sentences to make them true. (pages 130–131)

33. There are 10 tens in 1 hundred.

34. There are 100 pennies in 1 dime.

35. There are 100 dimes in 1 dollar.

36. There are 100 ones in 1 hundred.

Find a benchmark to estimate each number.
Choose the letter of the correct answer. (pages 154–155)

37. 2,465
   A 100
   B 1,000
   C 10,000
   D 100,000

38. 162,580
   F 100
   G 1,000
   H 10,000
   J 100,000

39. 42,904
   A 100
   B 1,000
   C 10,000
   D 100,000

▶ CHECK Understanding

VOCABULARY

1. An __?__ shows objects in rows and columns. (page 206)

Make two smaller arrays to find each product. (pages 208–215)

2.

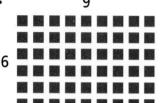

3.

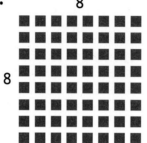

4.

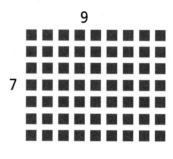

Copy and complete the tables. (pages 208–215)

5.

×	4	5	6	7
7	?	?	?	?

6.

×	5	6	7	8
6	?	?	?	?

7.

×	6	7	8	9
8	?	?	?	?

▶ CHECK Skills

Find the product. (pages 208–215, 218–221)

8.   6
     ×7

9.   9
     ×6

10.   5
      ×5

11.   9
      ×9

12.   5
      ×8

▶ CHECK Problem Solving

Solve. (pages 216–217)

CHOOSE a strategy and a tool.
- **Make a Model**
- **Act It Out**
- **Write a Number Sentence**
- **Work Backward**

 Paper/Pencil   Calculator   Hands-On   Mental Math

13. Joe's dad is putting tiles on the bathroom wall. He has put up 7 rows of 9 tiles. How many tiles has Joe's dad used so far?

14. At 3 o'clock Dana began to play the piano. She played for 45 minutes. Then she had a snack for 15 minutes. At what time did she finish her snack?

15. There are 7 desks in each row. There are 5 rows. How many desks are there?

16. There are 4 softball teams with 9 players. How many players are there?

Test Prep

Choose the best answer.

Use this table for Problems 1 and 2. It shows money Sara earned.

Money Earned	
Week 1	● ● ●
Week 2	● ● ● ●
Week 3	● ● ●
Week 4	● ● ● ● ●

Key: Each ● equals 25¢.

1. How much money did Sara earn in Week 4?

  A $1.00   **B** $1.50

  C $1.25   **D** $.75

2. How much money did Sara earn in Weeks 2 and 4?

  F $1.50   **G** $1.00

  H $2.25   **J** $1.25

3. There are 6 movie screens. A movie is shown 4 times a day on each screen. How many movies are shown in all?

  A 12   **B** 24   **C** 10   **D** 14

4. Mrs. Smith teaches art to 3 groups of students. There are 8 students in each group. How many students does Mrs. Smith teach?

  F 11   **G** 16

  H 24   **J** 20

5. It is 1:30. Luis has music class for 1 hour, and then he has math class for 50 minutes. What time will he finish math class?

  A 4:00   **B** 3:30

  C 2:30   **D** 3:20

6. Nadia has 7 dimes. How much money does Nadia have?

  F $7

  G $70

  H $0.50

  J $0.70

7. Maya is setting the table for 9 guests. Every guest gets 2 forks, 1 knife, and 1 spoon. How many forks, knives, and spoons will Maya put on the table in all?

  A 36

  B 38

  C 27

  D 19

8. William planted 5 seeds in each row of the garden. There are 6 rows. Which number sentence shows how many seeds William planted?

  F $6 \times 2 = 12$

  G $5 \times 1 = 5$

  H $6 \times 5 = 30$

  J $5 \times 5 = 25$

13 CONNECTING MULTIPLICATION AND DIVISION

There are at least 8,800 kinds of ants. Some ants are an inch long. Ants store their food in different places.

Storerooms for Ants

Ants' tunnels are very narrow—less than the width of a pencil. Each storeroom can hold only a few grains of food. How can ants store all they collect?

Plan storerooms for ants so they can keep their grain in equal groups.

YOU WILL NEED: large drawing paper, pencil, glue, corn kernels

- Choose a number of ants between 6 and 9, and choose an equal number of corn kernels for each ant.

- Write a number sentence that tells how many corn kernels the ants have to store.

- Decide how many storerooms are needed. Remember to store the corn kernels in equal groups.

- Draw a tunnel with storerooms to show your work and glue the corn kernels in each room.

DID YOU

✓ find how many corn kernels need to be stored?

✓ decide how many storerooms there will be?

✓ decide how many corn kernels to put in each storeroom?

✓ draw a picture and show your work?

Exploring Division

You will investigate how to find equal groups or how many are in each group.

Multiply to put equal groups together.
Divide to separate into equal groups.

▶ EXPLORE

MATERIALS: 20 counters

MODEL

Find how many counters will be in each of 4 groups.

Step 1
Use 20 counters.

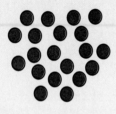

Step 2
Draw 4 circles. Put the same number of counters in each circle. Use all of the counters.

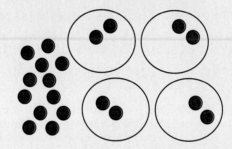

Record

Explain how you used the 20 counters to find how many counters are in each of 4 groups.

Talk About It

• Are the 4 groups equal? How do you know?

• The symbol ÷ means *divided by*. What division sentence can you write to record what you did with the 20 counters?

• What does each part of your division sentence mean?

▶ TRY THIS

1. Use 12 counters. How many different ways can you make equal groups?

2. What equal groups did you make?

3. How did you use the counters to find all the equal groups?

4. What division sentences can you write to record your groups?

▶ PRACTICE

5. Use 10 counters. Put them into as many equal groups as you can. Write division sentences to record your groups.

Copy and complete the table. Use counters to help you.

	Counters	How many equal groups?	How many in each group?
6.	12	3	?
7.	15	?	5
8.	18	6	?
9.	20	?	5
10.	24	3	?
11.	24	?	4

Problem Solving • Mixed Applications

12. **Mental Math** There are 9 ants that are going to move 27 kernels of corn. The ants each will carry the same number of kernels. How many corn kernels will each ant carry?

13. There are 36 kernels of corn in 4 piles. How many kernels are in each pile?

14. **Money** Dale spent $9.87 for lunch. She paid with $20.00. How much change did she receive?

15. ✐ **Write a problem** about 16 puzzle books. Use division in your problem.

Technology Link

💿 You can solve division problems by using E-Lab, Activity 13. Available on CD-ROM and on the Internet at www.hbschool.com/elab

Connecting Subtraction and Division

VOCABULARY
division

Why learn this? You can subtract equal groups, such as when you share game pieces with your friends.

Kevin and his friends want to play a game of Sorry®. There are 16 game pieces in the game. Each player needs 4 pieces. How many groups of 4 game pieces are there?

$$16 \div 4 = \underline{\ ?\ }$$

Division is like repeated subtraction. You can start with 16 and subtract 4 until you reach 0.

$$\begin{array}{cccc} 16 & 12 & 8 & 4 \\ -\ 4 & -\ 4 & -4 & -4 \\ \hline 12 & 8 & 4 & 0 \end{array}$$

You can subtract 4 from 16 four times since there are four 4's in 16.

Write: $16 \div 4 = 4$
Read: Sixteen divided by 4 equals 4.

So, there are 4 groups of 4 game pieces.

Talk About It

- How is division like repeated subtraction?

- When are some times that you use division?

▶ CHECK

1. Tell how you can use subtraction to find how many groups of 3 are in 12.

2. Tell how you can use subtraction to find how many groups of 5 are in 30.

CULTURAL LINK

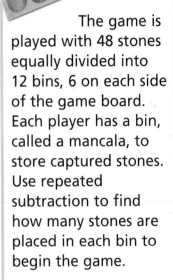

Mancala is an Egyptian game. It was created about 3,000 years ago.

The game is played with 48 stones equally divided into 12 bins, 6 on each side of the game board. Each player has a bin, called a mancala, to store captured stones. Use repeated subtraction to find how many stones are placed in each bin to begin the game.

$$48 \div 12 = \underline{\ ?\ }$$

Show how you can use subtraction to solve.

3. $10 \div 2 = $ _?_   **4.** $15 \div 3 = $ _?_   **5.** $16 \div 4 = $ _?_

6. $8 \div 2 = $ _?_   **7.** $18 \div 3 = $ _?_   **8.** $21 \div 3 = $ _?_

Write the division sentence shown by the repeated subtraction.

9.
$$\begin{array}{cccc} 12 & 9 & 6 & 3 \\ -3 & -3 & -3 & -3 \\ \hline 9 & 6 & 3 & 0 \end{array}$$

10.
$$\begin{array}{ccccc} 20 & 16 & 12 & 8 & 4 \\ -4 & -4 & -4 & -4 & -4 \\ \hline 16 & 12 & 8 & 4 & 0 \end{array}$$

11.
$$\begin{array}{cccc} 20 & 15 & 10 & 5 \\ -5 & -5 & -5 & -5 \\ \hline 15 & 10 & 5 & 0 \end{array}$$

12.
$$\begin{array}{ccccc} 30 & 24 & 18 & 12 & 6 \\ -6 & -6 & -6 & -6 & -6 \\ \hline 24 & 18 & 12 & 6 & 0 \end{array}$$

Problem Solving • Mixed Applications

13. Reasoning There are 6 students making a book about animals. Each student needs 6 magazines. How many do the 6 students need in all?

14. Mental Math Felicia made a necklace. She had 12 red beads left over. She gave 2 beads to each of her friends. How many friends got 2 red beads?

15. Time Mr. Johnson's class worked 2 hours each day on a project. It took 10 days for the class to complete the project. How many hours did the class work in all?

16. ✏️ **Write a problem** about making animals with 45 paper strips. Use division in your problem.

Mixed Review and Test Prep

Find the product. (pages 214–215)

17.
$$\begin{array}{r} 9 \\ \times 9 \\ \hline \end{array}$$

18.
$$\begin{array}{r} 8 \\ \times 9 \\ \hline \end{array}$$

19.
$$\begin{array}{r} 7 \\ \times 9 \\ \hline \end{array}$$

20.
$$\begin{array}{r} 5 \\ \times 9 \\ \hline \end{array}$$

21.
$$\begin{array}{r} 6 \\ \times 9 \\ \hline \end{array}$$

Choose the letter that tells the value of the blue digit. (pages 144–145)

22. 856
A 5 ones
B 5 tens
C 5 hundreds
D 5 thousands

23. 975
F 9 ones
G 9 tens
H 9 hundreds
J 9 thousands

24. 8,346
A 8 ones
B 8 tens
C 8 hundreds
D 8 thousands

Relating Multiplication and Division

Why learn this? You can use division to find how many items are in each group or how many groups there are.

You can use division to find $30 \div 5 = \underline{\ ?\ }$.

MODEL

Step 1

Start with 30 shown as an array.

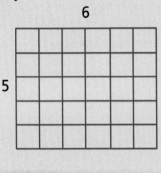

Step 2

Separate into 5 equal groups of 6.

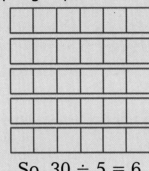

So, $30 \div 5 = 6$.

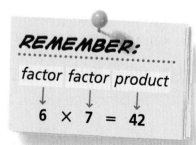

A division sentence has 3 parts. The **dividend** is the number being divided. The **divisor** is the number that divides the dividend. The answer is the **quotient**.

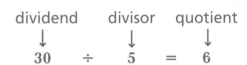

dividend   divisor   quotient
$$30 \div 5 = 6$$

You can use multiplication to solve a division problem by finding the missing factor.

$42 \div 6 = \underline{\ ?\ }$ Think: $6 \times \underline{\ ?\ } = 42$
   ↑
  missing factor

REMEMBER:

factor factor product
$$6 \times 7 = 42$$

Multiplication and division are opposites, or inverse operations. Since $6 \times 7 = 42$, then $42 \div 6 = 7$.

• How are multiplication and division related?

CRITICAL THINKING How can you multiply to check division?

► CHECK

Use the array to find the quotient.

1.

$12 \div 3 = \underline{\ ?\ }$

2.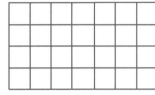

$28 \div 4 = \underline{\ ?\ }$

3.

$18 \div 3 = \underline{\ ?\ }$

► PRACTICE

Write the missing factor for each number sentence.

4. $4 \times \underline{\ ?\ } = 20 \quad 20 \div 4 = \underline{\ ?\ }$

5. $7 \times \underline{\ ?\ } = 21 \quad 21 \div 7 = \underline{\ ?\ }$

Check each division with multiplication. Show your work.

6. $14 \div 2 = \underline{\ ?\ }$

7. $15 \div 5 = \underline{\ ?\ }$

8. $20 \div 5 = \underline{\ ?\ }$

Problem Solving • Mixed Applications

Using Data For Problems 9–12, use the list.

9. Ms. Duncan is getting the fishing line for the experiment. How many feet does she need?

10. **Mental Math** How many drinking glasses in all are needed for the experiment?

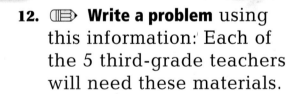

Science Experiment on Sound

Materials needed:

4 lengths of fishing line, each 7 feet long
8 wood blocks
4 sets of 3 drinking glasses
4 metal spoons

11. **Science** The materials for the experiment will be shared equally among 4 groups. How many of each item will each group use?

12. ▭▷ **Write a problem** using this information: Each of the 5 third-grade teachers will need these materials.

Mixed Review and Test Prep

Compare the numbers. Write $<$, $>$, or $=$ for each ●. (pages 164–165)

13. 81 ● 91

14. 67 ● 67

15. 166 ● 616

16. 988 ● 889

Choose the letter of the correct product. (pages 212–213)

17.
$\begin{array}{r} 5 \\ \times 8 \\ \hline \end{array}$
A 35
B 13
C 40
D 45

18.
$\begin{array}{r} 8 \\ \times 7 \\ \hline \end{array}$
F 49
G 56
H 15
J 52

19.
$\begin{array}{r} 9 \\ \times 8 \\ \hline \end{array}$
A 64
B 17
C 75
D 72

20.
$\begin{array}{r} 6 \\ \times 8 \\ \hline \end{array}$
F 48
G 36
H 14
J 42

Fact Families

Why learn this? You can solve problems by using multiplication and division to find how many people are in a group.

There are 18 students working on art projects. They are working in groups of 3. How many groups of students are working on art projects?

$$18 \div 3 = \underline{\ ?\ }$$

Since division is the opposite of multiplication, you can use a multiplication table to find a quotient.

> Think: $\underline{\ ?\ } \times 3 = 18$

You know one factor, 3. Find it in the top row. Look down to find the product, 18. Look to the left to find the missing factor, 6.

Since $6 \times 3 = 18$, $18 \div 3 = 6$.

So, 6 groups of students are working on art projects.

Multiplication Table

×	0	1	2	3	4	5	6
0	0	0	0	0	0	0	0
1	0	1	2	3	4	5	6
2	0	2	4	6	8	10	12
3	0	3	6	9	12	15	18
4	0	4	8	12	16	20	24
5	0	5	10	15	20	25	30
6	0	6	12	18	24	30	36

A fact family shows how multiplication and division are related.

A *fact family* is a set of related multiplication and division sentences that use the same numbers.

Fact Family for 3, 6, 18

factor		factor		product		dividend		divisor		quotient
3	×	6	=	18		18	÷	3	=	6
6	×	3	=	18		18	÷	6	=	3

CRITICAL THINKING The fact family for 3, 3, and 9 has only two number sentences. Why?

▶ CHECK

1. What multiplication and division sentences make up the fact family for 2, 8, and 16?

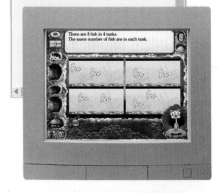

Write the other three sentences in the fact family.

2. $3 \times 4 = 12$ **3.** $2 \times 5 = 10$ **4.** $6 \times 4 = 24$

Write the fact family for each set of numbers.

5. 2, 6, 12   **6.** 4, 8, 32   **7.** 3, 5, 15

8. 7, 4, 28   **9.** 9, 3, 27   **10.** 6, 6, 36

Problem Solving • Mixed Applications

Using Data For Problems 11–15, use the list on the art kit.

Art Kit
Includes:
3 packs glitter
8 stencils
18 crayons
24 sheets of paper
12 stamps
3 craft scissors

11. The 15 members of the Art Club are sharing an art kit. The same number of students are sharing each pair of craft scissors. How many students are sharing each pair?

12. Of the art projects, 3 need to have glitter put on them. How many packs of glitter can be put on each of the 3 projects?

13. Mental Math Patti and Samantha each have an art kit. How many stencils do they have in all?

14. Renaldo, Brad, and Katya are sharing the crayons. How many crayons can each use?

15. ✐ **Write a problem** about items in the art kit. Use division in your problem.

Mixed Review and Test Prep

Write each number in standard form. (pages 150–153)

16. $50,000 + 8,000 + 400 + 50 + 3$ **17.** $20,000 + 500 + 70 + 9$

18. $70,000 + 7,000 + 80 + 8$ **19.** fifteen thousand, four hundred sixty-two

Choose the letter that shows the numbers in order from least to greatest. (pages 168–169)

20. 833, 338, 383   **A** 383, 338, 833
                 B 338, 833, 383
                 C 338, 383, 833
                 D 833, 388, 383

21. 919, 909, 990   **F** 909, 919, 990
                 G 990, 909, 919
                 H 919, 909, 990
                 J 919, 990, 909

Practicing Division Facts Through 5

Why learn this? You can find how many buttons will be in each group.

June has collected 24 buttons. She put them in groups of 4. How many groups did she make?

$$24 \div 4 = ?$$

| number of buttons | number in each group | number of groups |

Talk About It

• What multiplication fact can you use to find the quotient?

• How can you use subtraction to find the quotient?

Ken put 15 cars in 5 groups. How many cars did he put in each group?

$$15 \div 5 = ?$$

| number of cars | number of groups | number in each group |

Talk About It CRITICAL THINKING

• What multiplication fact can you use to find the quotient?

• How can you use subtraction to find the quotient?

▶ CHECK

Copy and complete the tables.

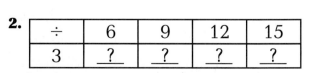

1.

÷	6	8	10	12
2	?	?	?	?

2.

÷	6	9	12	15
3	?	?	?	?

Copy and complete the tables.

3.

÷	16	20	24	28
4	?	?	?	?

4.

÷	20	25	30	35	40
5	?	?	?	?	?

Write the multiplication fact you can use to find each quotient. Write the quotient.

5. $20 \div 4 = \underline{\ ?\ }$

6. $24 \div 3 = \underline{\ ?\ }$

7. $18 \div 2 = \underline{\ ?\ }$

8. $12 \div 3 = \underline{\ ?\ }$

9. $35 \div 5 = \underline{\ ?\ }$

10. $28 \div 4 = \underline{\ ?\ }$

11. $30 \div 5 = \underline{\ ?\ }$

12. $16 \div 4 = \underline{\ ?\ }$

13. $27 \div 3 = \underline{\ ?\ }$

14. $45 \div 5 = \underline{\ ?\ }$

15. $36 \div 4 = \underline{\ ?\ }$

16. $21 \div 3 = \underline{\ ?\ }$

17. $40 \div 5 = \underline{\ ?\ }$

18. $28 \div 7 = \underline{\ ?\ }$

19. $5 \div 5 = \underline{\ ?\ }$

Problem Solving • Mixed Applications

20. Elapsed Time Nicole saves 4 cans each day from her pets' food. She now has 28 cans. For how many days has Nicole been saving the cans?

21. Jessica has 12 games in her closet. There are the same number of games on each of 3 shelves. How many games are on each shelf?

22. Time The lunchroom line serves 8 people each minute. How many people can it serve in 5 minutes?

23. ◀▣ **Write About It** Write an example of each of the two kinds of problems that use division.

Mixed Review and Test Prep

Use patterns of hundreds or thousands to find the sum or difference. (pages 148–149)

24. $415 + 300$

25. $725 - 100$

26. $687 - 300$

Choose the letter of the number that is *odd* or *even*.
(pages 132–133)

27. odd
A 24
B 18
C 29
D 46

28. even
F 21
G 39
H 47
J 58

29. even
A 99
B 40
C 73
D 85

30. odd
F 66
G 78
H 54
J 21

Choosing Division or Multiplication

Why learn this? You will know which operation to use to solve problems, such as how many times a week the goldfish need to be fed.

Before you can choose an operation to solve a problem, you must decide what the problem asks you to find.

Jordan feeds his goldfish 2 times each day. How many times does he feed his fish in one week?

a. $2 \times 7 = \underline{\ ?\ }$ **b.** $7 \div 2 = \underline{\ ?\ }$

Talk About It

- What does this problem ask you to find?

- Should you multiply or divide? Why?

- Which number sentence can you use to solve the problem?

So, Jordan feeds his fish 14 times in one week.

There are 18 students going to the nature park. If 6 students ride in each van, how many vans will the students need?

a. $6 \times 18 = \underline{\ ?\ }$ **b.** $18 \div 6 = \underline{\ ?\ }$

Talk About It

- What does this problem ask you to find?

- Should you multiply or divide? Why?

- Which number sentence can you use to solve the problem?

So, the students will need 3 vans to go to the park.

SCIENCE LINK

Goldfish are originally from China and Eastern Europe. In nature, goldfish like shallow and cool freshwater ponds and creeks. Some goldfish live for 25 to 30 years. Goldfish living in bowls need their water changed and their bowls cleaned about 2 times a week. About how many times does a goldfish bowl need to be cleaned in 4 weeks?

Write *a* or *b* to show which number sentence you would use to solve each problem and then solve.

1. Each week, Quan learns 3 new songs for the piano. How many new songs will he learn in 8 weeks?

   a. $3 \times 8 = 24$

   b. $24 \div 3 = 8$

2. Each day, Brittany plays 3 new pages from her piano book. How many days does it take her to play 24 pages? .

   a. $3 \times 8 = 24$

   b. $24 \div 3 = 8$

3. There are 20 children playing in groups on the playground. There are 4 children in each group. How many groups of children are playing?

   a. $4 \times 5 = 20$

   b. $20 \div 4 = 5$

4. There are 4 areas in which to play on the playground. There are 5 children in each area. How many children are on the playground?

   a. $4 \times 5 = 20$

   b. $20 \div 4 = 5$

Problem Solving • Mixed Applications

Using Data For Problems 5, 6, and 9, use the Big Tree Park sign.

BIG TREE PARK
Nature Trail   2 miles
Bike Trail   3 miles
Jogging Trail   4 miles

5. **Measurement** On Monday, Wednesday, and Friday, Rosa rode her bike the length of the bike trail. How many miles did Rosa ride in all?

6. **Mental Math** In one week, Preston jogged 20 miles. Each time that he jogged, he went the length of the jogging trail 1 time. How many times did he use the jogging trail?

7. **Time** Melinda arrived at the park at 10:30. She rode her bike for 1 hour and 30 minutes. She had a picnic lunch for 30 minutes before she left. At what time did Melinda leave the park?

8. **Money** Jake bought a bike helmet for $24. He gave the clerk three $10 bills. How much change did he receive?

9. ▭▷ **Write a problem** using this information. Danielle walked the length of the nature trail 4 times.

LESSON CONTINUES

Problem–Solving Strategy: Write a Number Sentence

▶ **THE PROBLEM** Kyle is playing a trumpet solo in the band concert 4 weeks from today. In how many days is Kyle's solo?

UNDERSTAND

- What are you asked to find?

- What information will you use?

- Is there any information you will not use? If so, what?

REMEMBER:
- UNDERSTAND
- PLAN
- SOLVE
- LOOK BACK

PLAN

- What strategy can you use to solve the problem?

  You can *write a number sentence* to find the number of days in 4 weeks.

SOLVE

- How can you use the strategy to solve the problem?

  Since there are 7 days in one week, you can multiply to find the number of days in 4 weeks.

  $$4 \quad \times \quad 7 \quad = \quad 28$$

  | number of weeks | days in one week | days in 4 weeks |

  So, Kyle will play his trumpet solo in 28 days.

LOOK BACK

- How can you decide if your answer makes sense?

- What other strategy could you use?

Write a number sentence to solve.

1. Tyler begins clarinet lessons 3 weeks from today. In how many days does Tyler begin his lessons?

2. Chelsea has 4 boxes of markers. There are 8 markers in each box. How many markers does Chelsea have?

3. Ricky goes to karate class 2 times each week. How many classes does he go to in 8 weeks?

4. Shelly earned $9 baby-sitting. She baby-sat for 3 hours. How much money did she earn each hour?

Mixed Applications

Solve.

| **CHOOSE** a strategy and a tool. |
| • Write a Number Sentence • Make a Model |
| • Draw a Picture   • Act It Out |
| • Guess and Check |

Paper/Pencil   Calculator   Hands-On   Mental Math

5. Timor buys a cap, a poster, and a baseball. How much does he spend in all? How much change will he get from $20.00?

$5.99

$2.75

$8.95

6. Jennifer is in line before Frank but after Heather. Tommy is after Frank but before Amanda. In what order are the students in line?

7. There are 4 rows of students singing in the concert. There are 9 students in each row. How many students are singing in the concert?

8. Stacey is thinking of two numbers. The sum of the numbers is 18. The difference of the numbers is 6. What are the two numbers?

9. Megan's computer printer can print 4 pages each minute. How many pages can it print in 3 minutes?

10. There are 58 marbles on the floor. Kirk owns 12 more of the marbles than Randy. How many marbles does each own?

11. Pia and Martin are playing a board game. They each have 3 turns. Pia moves 6, 5, and 3 spaces. Martin moves 4, 4, and 6 spaces. Who is ahead?

► CHECK Understanding

VOCABULARY

1. Multiplication and division are _?_, or opposite, operations. (page 230)

2. A _?_ is the number that is being divided. (page 230)

3. A _?_ is the number that divides the dividend. (page 230)

4. A _?_ is the answer in a division problem. (page 230)

5. A _?_ is a set of related multiplication and division sentences that use the same numbers. (page 232)

► CHECK Skills

Write the missing factor for each number sentence. (pages 230–231)

6. $7 \times \underline{\,?\,} = 14$ $14 \div 7 = \underline{\,?\,}$

7. $6 \times \underline{\,?\,} = 24$ $24 \div 6 = \underline{\,?\,}$

Write the fact family for each set of numbers. (pages 232–233)

8. 4, 9, 36

9. 3, 7, 21

10. 5, 8, 40

Write the multiplication fact you can use to find each quotient. Write the quotient. (pages 234–235)

11. $30 \div 6 = \underline{\,?\,}$

12. $16 \div 2 = \underline{\,?\,}$

13. $27 \div 9 = \underline{\,?\,}$

► CHECK Problem Solving

Solve. (pages 238–239)

CHOOSE a strategy and a tool.
- Write a Number Sentence
- Draw a Picture
- Guess and Check
- Make a Model
- Act It Out

 Paper/Pencil   Calculator   Hands-On   Mental Math

14. Terry bought 2 puzzles for his sister. Each puzzle has 9 pieces. How many puzzle pieces are there in all?

15. John and 3 classmates are going to share 36 marbles equally. How many marbles can each student have?

16. Mr. Davis is 8 times as old as his grandson. His grandson is 8 years old. How old is Mr. Davis?

17. Jessica's trumpet solo is 3 weeks from today. In how many days is Jessica's trumpet solo?

Test Prep

Choose the best answer.

1. Chad has music lessons 3 times a week. How many lessons will he have in 8 weeks?

A 15   **B** 24   **C** 16   **D** 11

2. Dottie bought 3 colors of yarn to knit a sweater. She needed 5 balls of yarn in each color. Which number sentence tells how many balls of yarn she bought?

F $3 \times 5 = 15$

G $3 \times 3 = 9$

H $5 \times 1 = 5$

J $5 \times 5 = 25$

3. Sheila had 20 cookies. She put 5 cookies on each plate. How many plates of cookies did she have?

A 10   **B** 5   **C** 4   **D** 2

4. Mr. Hardy has 9 students who are drawing book covers for the book fair. If each student draws 3 covers, how many book covers will Mr. Hardy have?

F 24   **G** 27

H 32   **J** 30

5. What is the missing factor in these sentences?

$3 \times \underline{\ ?\ } = 21$ $21 \div 3 = \underline{\ ?\ }$

A 8   **B** 6   **C** 7   **D** 9

6. Susan bought paper for $1.79, colored pencils for $4.30, and an eraser for $0.59. How much change did she get from $10.00?

F $4.89   **G** $3.32

H $6.09   **J** $6.68

7. It is about 200 miles from Boston to New York City. On Thursday the Nixons drove from Boston to New York City. They drove home to Boston on Saturday. About how many miles did they drive in all?

A 300 mi

B 200 mi

C 400 mi

D 100 mi

8. There were 4 tables, with 3 chairs at each one. Which picture shows the tables and chairs?

F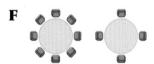

G

H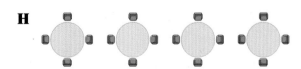

J

14 DIVISION FACTS THROUGH 9

SCIENCE LINK

In 1994 a Boeing 747-400 jet could travel at a speed of about 538 miles per hour and carry 396 passengers. Each jet used about 3,420 gallons of fuel each hour. The cost of operating one aircraft for one hour was $6,686.

Vehicles Moving Many

Design a vehicle to transport many passengers by land, air, or sea. Each seat must have a seatbelt. Use the table to choose a vehicle for your project.

YOU WILL NEED: drawing paper and pencil To find quotients you do not remember, use manipulatives or a multiplication table.

- Choose a type of vehicle.

- Use the number of passengers and the number of seats to find how many rows to fit in your vehicle.

- Draw a top view of your vehicle showing each seat.

- Draw a side view of your vehicle showing one window for each row of seats.

- Trade drawings with a classmate and check each other's designs.

LAND VEHICLE
6 seats each row
Number of Passengers
36 42 48 54

AIR VEHICLE
7 seats each row
Number of Passengers
49 56 63

SEA VEHICLE
8 seats each row
Number of Passengers
64 72

SPACE VEHICLE
9 seats each row
Number of Passengers
81

DID YOU

- ✓ choose a type of vehicle to draw?

- ✓ determine how many rows to draw?

- ✓ draw a top view and a side view of your vehicle?

- ✓ trade drawings with a classmate and check the design?

Land Vehicle: Bus

36 Passengers

6 rows of 6 seats

Modeling Division Using Arrays

You will investigate how to use arrays to find equal groups.

You can use arrays to find equal groups.

▶ EXPLORE

MATERIALS: square tiles

MODEL

Find $35 \div 7 =$ __?__ .

Step 1
Use 35 tiles.

Step 2
Place 7 tiles in each row.
Use all the tiles.

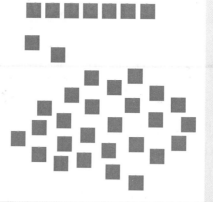

Record
Explain how you used the 35 tiles to find
how many groups of 7 are in 35.

Talk About It
- How many rows of 7 tiles are there?

- What division sentence can you
  write to record what you did?

- What multiplication sentence
  can you use to check your
  division?

▶ TRY THIS

1. Use 30 tiles. Make an array that has 6 rows. Put all the tiles in the 6 rows. Draw a picture of your array.

2. How many tiles are in each row?

3. What division sentence can you write to record what you did?

4. What multiplication sentence can you use to check your division?

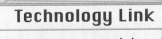

▶ PRACTICE

For Exercises 5–10, use square tiles to make an array. Write the division sentence that records what you did.

5. How many groups of 6 are in 24?

6. How many groups of 5 are in 25?

7. How many groups of 4 are in 32?

8. How many groups of 3 are in 27?

9. Use 36 tiles. Make an array that has 6 rows.

10. Use 40 tiles. Make an array that has 8 rows.

Problem Solving • Mixed Applications

11. **Using Data** How many more points does Tamisha have than Andrew?

SCORECARD	
Tamisha	Andrew
85	68

12. Rebecca has 18 school pictures of her friends. She puts them on her mirror. She places 6 pictures in each row. How many rows of pictures are there?

13. **Reasoning** Alfredo and Louis designed a sea vehicle with 5 rows of 5 seats. How many people can ride on their sea vehicle?

14. ✏️ **Write a problem** about 4 friends playing a game with 36 cards. Each player receives the same number of cards.

Dividing Using 0 and 1

Why learn this? You have fewer division facts to learn when you understand the patterns with 0 and 1.

There were 8 runners in 8 lanes at the track meet. How many runners were in each lane?

Use 8 counters. Divide them into 8 groups.

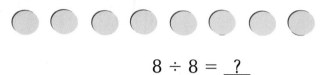

$$8 \div 8 = \underline{\ ?\ }$$

When a number is divided by itself, the quotient is always 1. $\qquad 8 \div 8 = 1$

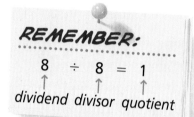

REMEMBER:

$$\underset{\text{dividend}}{8} \div \underset{\text{divisor}}{8} = \underset{\text{quotient}}{1}$$

So, there was 1 runner in each lane.

• What happens when you divide a number by itself?

_____

Next, put your 8 counters into 1 group.

$$8 \div 1 = \underline{\ ?\ }$$

When a number is divided by 1, the quotient is always that number. $\qquad 8 \div 1 = 8$

• What happens when you divide a number by 1?

_____

Now, put your 8 counters away.

• How many counters are on your desk?

Divide them into 8 groups.

$$0 \div 8 = \underline{\ ?\ }$$

When zero is divided by any number, the quotient is always zero. $\qquad 0 \div 8 = 0$

• What happens when you divide zero by a number?

► CHECK
Find the quotient.

1. $6 \div 6 = \underline{\ ?\ }$ **2.** $0 \div 3 = \underline{\ ?\ }$ **3.** $5 \div 1 = \underline{\ ?\ }$

4. $9 \div 1 = \underline{\ ?\ }$ **5.** $7 \div 7 = \underline{\ ?\ }$ **6.** $0 \div 4 = \underline{\ ?\ }$

► PRACTICE

Find the quotient.

7. $5 \div 5 = \underline{\ ?\ }$ **8.** $0 \div 5 = \underline{\ ?\ }$ **9.** $8 \div 1 = \underline{\ ?\ }$

10. $0 \div 9 = \underline{\ ?\ }$ **11.** $6 \div 1 = \underline{\ ?\ }$ **12.** $9 \div 9 = \underline{\ ?\ }$

13. $8 \div 8 = \underline{\ ?\ }$ **14.** $0 \div 1 = \underline{\ ?\ }$ **15.** $7 \div 1 = \underline{\ ?\ }$

Problem Solving • Mixed Applications

For Problems 16–18, use the drawing of the building.

16. Logic Each floor of the building has 9 offices. Each of the offices has 1 window. How many windows are on each floor? How many offices are in the building?

17. Visual Thinking The elevator takes 6 seconds to move from one floor to the next. How long does it take to go from the first floor to the top floor of the building?

18. ✏️ **Write a problem** about the number of people in the office building.

Mixed Review and Test Prep

Copy and complete the tables. (pages 234–235)

19.

÷	20	12	16	4	32
4	?	?	?	?	?

20.

÷	30	15	20	40	5
5	?	?	?	?	?

Use a multiplication fact to help you find each quotient. Choose the letter of the correct quotient. (pages 234–235)

21. $27 \div 9 = \underline{\ ?\ }$ **A** 9 **B** 3 **C** 7 **D** 2 **22.** $28 \div 7 = \underline{\ ?\ }$ **F** 4 **G** 7 **H** 8 **J** 5

23. $32 \div 8 = \underline{\ ?\ }$ **A** 3 **B** 2 **C** 5 **D** 4 **24.** $54 \div 6 = \underline{\ ?\ }$ **F** 7 **G** 6 **H** 4 **J** 9

Using the Multiplication Table to Divide

Why learn this? You can find how many players are on each team.

There were 72 students who signed up to play softball. The coach put them into teams of 9 players each. How many teams did the coach make?

You can use a multiplication table to find a quotient.

72 ÷ 9 = _?_

Think of the missing factor.

9 × _?_ = 72

You know one factor, 9.
Find it in the top row.
Look down the column to find the product, 72. Look left across the row to find the quotient, or missing factor, 8.

72 ÷ 9 = 8

So, the coach made 8 teams.

×	0	1	2	3	4	5	6	7	8	9
0	0	0	0	0	0	0	0	0	0	0
1	0	1	2	3	4	5	6	7	8	9
2	0	2	4	6	8	10	12	14	16	18
3	0	3	6	9	12	15	18	21	24	27
4	0	4	8	12	16	20	24	28	32	36
5	0	5	10	15	20	25	30	35	40	45
6	0	6	12	18	24	30	36	42	48	54
7	0	7	14	21	28	35	42	49	56	63
8	0	8	16	24	32	40	48	56	64	72
9	0	9	18	27	36	45	54	63	72	81

Talk About It

- Why can you use a multiplication table to find a quotient?

- What multiplication fact can you use to find the quotient for 42 ÷ 6?

CRITICAL THINKING You have learned facts through 5. Where on the table are the new facts located? How many are there?

Technology Link

In *Mighty Math Calculating Crew,* the game *Intergalactic Trader* challenges you to practice division facts. Use Grow Slide Levels F and J.

► **CHECK**

Use the multiplication table to find each quotient.

1. $14 \div 2 = \underline{\ ?\ }$ **2.** $12 \div 4 = \underline{\ ?\ }$ **3.** $20 \div 5 = \underline{\ ?\ }$

4. $36 \div 6 = \underline{\ ?\ }$ **5.** $56 \div 8 = \underline{\ ?\ }$ **6.** $45 \div 5 = \underline{\ ?\ }$

► **PRACTICE**

Find the quotient.

7. $64 \div 8 = \underline{\ ?\ }$ **8.** $54 \div 9 = \underline{\ ?\ }$ **9.** $72 \div 8 = \underline{\ ?\ }$

10. $27 \div 3 = \underline{\ ?\ }$ **11.** $36 \div 4 = \underline{\ ?\ }$ **12.** $48 \div 6 = \underline{\ ?\ }$

13. $35 \div 5 = \underline{\ ?\ }$ **14.** $49 \div 7 = \underline{\ ?\ }$ **15.** $56 \div 7 = \underline{\ ?\ }$

16. $72 \div 9 = \underline{\ ?\ }$ **17.** $54 \div 6 = \underline{\ ?\ }$ **18.** $42 \div 7 = \underline{\ ?\ }$

Problem Solving • Mixed Applications

Using Data For Problems 19–21, use the table.

19. At the basketball tournament, 30 players are playing on the courts. How many teams are playing?

20. Ms. Wilcox has 12 students who want to play on 2 teams. In which sport would all 12 students be able to play?

21.  **Write a problem** using the information in the table.

TEAM MEMBERS	
Basketball	5 players
Volleyball	6 players
Baseball	9 players

Mixed Review and Test Prep

Write the multiplication fact that is shown by each array. (pages 206–207)

22.   **23.**   **24.**   **25.**

Count the money. Choose the letter of the correct amount. (pages 106–107)

26.

   A $2.60
   B $3.65
   C $4.65
   D $3.85

27.

   F $5.51
   G $5.71
   H $5.31
   J $6.41

MORE PRACTICE page H92

Practicing Division Facts Through 9

Why learn this? You can make equal groups of cards from a deck of cards.

Carlos and some classmates want to play a card game. They have 54 cards. Each player needs 9 cards. How many students can play the game?

$$54 \div 9 = \underline{\ ?\ }$$

Here are four ways to find the quotient of $54 \div 9$.

A. Use counters.

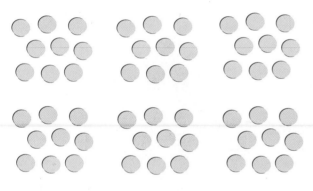

$$54 \div 9 = 6$$

B. Use tiles and an array.

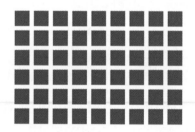

$$54 \div 9 = 6$$

C. Make a row for nines from the multiplication table or skip count by nines. Then fill in all the quotients.

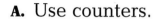

÷	0	9	18	27	36	45	54	63	72	81
9	0	1	2	3	4	5	6	7	8	9

$$54 \div 9 = 6$$

D. Use repeated subtraction.

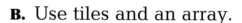

$$
\begin{array}{cccccc}
54 & 45 & 36 & 27 & 18 & 9 \\
-\ 9 & -\ 9 & -\ 9 & -\ 9 & -\ 9 & -9 \\
\hline
45 & 36 & 27 & 18 & 9 & 0
\end{array}
$$

$$54 \div 9 = 6$$

So, 6 students can play the game.

• Choose one of these four ways and tell how you can find $56 \div 8$.

▶ CHECK

Copy and complete the table.

1.

÷	48	72	40	32	64
8	?	?	?	?	?

2.

÷	81	18	63	72	54
9	?	?	?	?	?

3.

÷	21	35	49	28	63
7	?	?	?	?	?

4.

÷	18	42	54	30	6
6	?	?	?	?	?

▶ PRACTICE

Find the quotient.

5. $24 \div 6 = \underline{?}$

6. $45 \div 9 = \underline{?}$

7. $18 \div 6 = \underline{?}$

8. $21 \div 7 = \underline{?}$

9. $27 \div 9 = \underline{?}$

10. $30 \div 6 = \underline{?}$

11. $56 \div 7 = \underline{?}$

12. $35 \div 7 = \underline{?}$

13. $81 \div 9 = \underline{?}$

14. $63 \div 9 = \underline{?}$

15. $72 \div 8 = \underline{?}$

16. $49 \div 7 = \underline{?}$

Problem Solving • Mixed Applications

Using Data For Problems 17 and 21, use the ticket price list.

17. Money Cecilia bought 2 tickets for the roller coaster. How much change did she receive from $5.00?

18. Entertainment The simulator ride has 7 rows of seats. There are 8 seats in each row. How many people can be seated in the simulator ride at one time?

19. Mental Math The roller coaster can carry 48 people at one time. There are 8 cars. How many people can ride in each car?

20. Time The merry-go-round ride lasts 5 minutes. There are 4 minutes between rides. How many times does it run in 45 minutes?

21. ✏️ **Write a problem** using the information in the table. Use division.

CARNIVAL TICKETS	
Merry-go-round	$0.75
Roller coaster	$1.50
Simulator ride	$1.75
Ferris wheel	$1.00

LESSON CONTINUES

Problem–Solving Strategy: Make a Table

▶ **THE PROBLEM** Heather and Donna are going to sell lemonade. The three pitchers hold 32 ounces, 48 ounces, and 64 ounces. How many 8-ounce glasses of lemonade can be filled from each pitcher?

REMEMBER:
UNDERSTAND
PLAN
SOLVE
LOOK BACK

UNDERSTAND

- What are you asked to find?

- What information will you use?

- Is there any information you will not use? If so, what?

PLAN

- What strategy can you use to solve the problem?

  You can *make a table* to show how many 8-ounce glasses can be filled from each pitcher.

SOLVE

- How can you use the strategy to solve the problem?

  Make a table to show the number of 8-ounce glasses that can be filled from each pitcher.

÷	0	8	16	24	32	40	48	56	64	72
8	0	1	2	3	4	5	6	7	8	9

So, the pitchers can fill 4, 6, and 8 glasses.

LOOK BACK

- How can you decide if your answer makes sense?

- What other strategy could you use?

Make a table to solve each problem.

1. Mrs. Shuman is deciding which size cereal box to buy. The sizes are 12, 15, and 18 ounces. Her children each eat 3 ounces for breakfast. How many 3-ounce servings are in each box?

2. Jabbar has three plastic bags of different sizes. They hold 16, 32, and 64 ounces. How many 8-ounce servings of trail mix will each bag hold?

3. The students are giving 5-minute speeches. The class will use 20 minutes in the morning, 30 minutes at noon, and 45 minutes in the afternoon for the speeches. How many speeches can be given at each time?

4. Kim's school collected papers. The second grade collected 365 papers, the third grade 465 papers, the fourth grade 356 papers, and the fifth grade 456 papers. Order the number of papers collected from the least to the greatest.

Mixed Applications

Solve.

> **CHOOSE** a strategy and a tool.
> - **Write a Number Sentence**
> - **Make a Table**
> - **Act It Out**
> - **Make a Model**
> - **Guess and Check**
>
> Paper/Pencil   Calculator   Hands-On Mental Math

5. The boxes are 12, 20, and 28 ounces. How many 4-ounce servings are in each box?

6. The sum of two friends' ages is 21. The difference is 3. How old are the two friends?

7. Stefanie has 32 feet of red ribbon, 40 feet of blue ribbon, and 48 feet of white ribbon. How many 8-foot-long pieces can she cut from each color?

8. Lindsey put a cake in the oven at 3:30. It baked for 45 minutes and cooled for 30 minutes. Then it took her 15 minutes to frost the cake. What time is it now?

9. Mike bought lunch for $3.46. He gave the clerk $10.00. He received these bills and coins in change. Did he receive the correct change? Explain.

Choosing the Operation

Why learn this? You can know what to do when planning a garden.

Before you can solve a problem, you must decide what the problem asks you to find.

A. Susan watered her mother's plants. There were 6 plants on the top shelf. There were 4 plants on the middle shelf and 5 plants on the bottom shelf. How many plants did Susan water?

B. Last year Susan's parents planted 36 strawberry plants. This year they planted 45 strawberry plants. How many fewer strawberries did they plant last year?

C. In the garden, Susan's father planted 4 rows of tomato plants. He put 5 plants in each row. How many tomato plants did he put in the garden?

D. Susan's mother bought 12 tulips. She planted them in 2 rows. How many tulips did she plant in each row?

Talk About It

- What is being asked for in Problems A–D?

- What operation can you use to solve each problem? Explain your choice.

- What two operations could you use to solve Problem C? Why?

CRITICAL THINKING   What ways could you use to solve Problem D?

▶ CHECK

What operation will you need? Choose *multiply* or *divide*.

1. 15 seeds in equal rows
How many in each row?

2. 9 rows of 7 tiger lilies
How many in all?

Calculator Activities page H63

▶ PRACTICE

Write *a* or *b* to show which number sentence you would use to solve each problem.

3. There are 6 apples in each basket. Mariah bought 3 baskets of apples. How many apples did she buy?

    a. $6 \times 3 = 18$
    b. $6 \div 3 = 2$

4. There are 8 carrots in each bag. Chris needs 24 carrots. How many bags should he buy?

    a. $24 - 8 = 16$
    b. $24 \div 8 = 3$

5. The store clerk washed and set out 48 cucumbers. In the morning, 8 cucumbers were sold. How many were left?

    a. $48 \div 8 = 6$
    b. $48 - 8 = 40$

6. Nicole bought 9 ears of white corn and 3 ears of yellow corn. How many ears of corn did she buy altogether?

    a. $9 + 3 = 12$
    b. $9 - 3 = 6$

Problem Solving • Mixed Applications

Using Data For Problems 7–10, use the recipe.

7. Consumer How many oranges will Jon need to serve the fruit salad to 8 people?

8. Nick has 12 apples. How many apples will he have left if he makes enough fruit salad for 4 people?

FRUIT SALAD

4 apples, cut up
4 bananas, sliced
6 oranges, in sections
3 grapefruits, in sections

Mix all ingredients, Chill and serve.
Serves 4.

9. How many pieces of fruit are needed to make the fruit salad?

10. ✏️ **Write About It** Explain why you can't multiply to find the total pieces of fruit needed to make the salad.

Mixed Review and Test Prep

Write the missing factor for each number sentence. (pages 230–231)

11. $4 \times \underline{\ ?\ } = 24$ $24 \div 4 = \underline{\ ?\ }$

12. $4 \times \underline{\ ?\ } = 32$ $32 \div 4 = \underline{\ ?\ }$

Choose the letter for the correct product. (pages 208–211)

13.   5   **A** 21
    $\times 7$ **B** 50
        C 35
        D 45

14.   9   **F** 36
    $\times 7$ **G** 54
        H 72
        J 63

15.   7   **A** 28
    $\times 4$ **B** 21
        C 35
        D 42

16.   8   **F** 46
    $\times 7$ **G** 56
        H 86
        J 64

▶ CHECK Understanding

Find the quotient. (pages 246–247)

1.

$6 \div 6 =$ _?_

2.

$6 \div 1 =$ _?_

Copy and complete the table. (pages 250–251)

3.

÷	21	35	7	42	56
7	?	?	?	?	?

4.

÷	16	8	56	32	24
8	?	?	?	?	?

5.

÷	24	36	48	6	54
6	?	?	?	?	?

6.

÷	18	36	27	45	72
9	?	?	?	?	?

▶ CHECK Skills

Find the quotient. (pages 246–247, 250–251)

7. $8 \div 4 =$ _?_

8. $6 \div 6 =$ _?_

9. $5 \div 1 =$ _?_

10. $0 \div 7 =$ _?_

11. $27 \div 3 =$ _?_

12. $30 \div 6 =$ _?_

13. $56 \div 7 =$ _?_

14. $4 \div 4 =$ _?_

15. $63 \div 7 =$ _?_

16. $9 \div 1 =$ _?_

17. $35 \div 5 =$ _?_

18. $72 \div 8 =$ _?_

▶ CHECK Problem Solving

Solve. (pages 252–255)

CHOOSE a strategy and a tool.
- Write a Number Sentence
- Make a Model
- Make a Table
- Act It Out
- Guess and Check

 Paper/Pencil   Calculator   Hands-On   Mental Math

19. Popcorn comes in 18, 24, and 36 ounces. How many 6-ounce servings are in each?

20. Mary put zero flowers into 4 vases. How many flowers did she put into each vase?

21. There are 27 students. They sit in 3 equal rows. How many students are in each row?

22. Karen has 5 leashes for 5 puppies. The same number are on each puppy. How many leashes are on each one?

Test Prep

Choose the best answer.

1. Jenny had 3 pages of homework. She spent about 20 minutes on each page. About how long did she spend on homework?

A 30 min   **B** 3 hr

C 1 hr   **D** 2 hr

2. Which sentence does not belong in the fact family for 7, 4, 28?

F $7 \times 4 = 28$

G $4 \times 7 = 28$

H $28 - 4 = 24$

J $28 \div 7 = 4$

3. This table shows the number of lunch tickets sold in 1 week.

TICKETS SOLD	
Day	**Number**
Monday	▬ ▬ ▬ ▬
Tuesday	▬ ▬
Wednesday	▬ ▬ ▬
Thursday	▬ ▬ ▬ ▬
Friday	▬ ▬ ▬

Key: Each ▬ equals 2 tickets.

How many tickets were sold on Monday and Friday?

A 8   **B** 14   **C** 32   **D** 6

4. There are 8 bowling teams. Each team has 2 bowlers. How many people are bowling?

F 10   **G** 16   **H** 4   **J** 12

5. Lisa is filling 6 bins with vegetables. It takes 3 baskets of vegetables to fill one bin. How many baskets of vegetables does Lisa need to fill all the bins?

A 18   **B** 20

C 16   **D** 2

6. A train leaves the station every 20 minutes starting at 8:00 o'clock. Paolo gets to the station at 9:10. What time can Paolo get a train?

F 9:20

G 9:00

H 9:30

J 8:20

7. What is the value of 3 in 1,367?

A 3 ones   **B** 3 tens

C 3 hundreds **D** 3 thousands

8. Melissa has 24 pictures. Her album has 8 pages. She will put an equal number of pictures on each page. Which number sentence shows how many pictures Melissa will put on each page?

F $24 + 8 = 30$

G $24 - 8 = 16$

H $24 \div 8 = 3$

J $24 \times 8 = 192$

MATH FUN!

RINGS AND THINGS

PURPOSE To practice making equal groups and finding the total number

YOU WILL NEED number cube 0–5, paper and pencil

Play with a partner. Take turns.

- Toss the number cube. Draw that number of **rings**.

- Toss the cube again. Draw that number of **things** in each ring.

- Write the total number of things in rings below the drawing.

- Now it's your partner's turn to toss the cube and draw rings.

The player who has drawn the most things altogether after 5 rounds wins the game.

HOME NOTE Play this game with someone in your family.

THE LAST WORD

PURPOSE To practice connecting subtraction with division

YOU WILL NEED hundred chart, markers or crayons in 2 colors, number cube

Play this game with a partner. Pick a number between 10 and 50. Mark it on your hundred chart. Now, roll the cube and divide your number by that number. Take turns skip counting backward by that number, and circle the numbers as you count. The player who circles the last group of numbers wins a point.

STARS IN YOUR EYES

PURPOSE To practice multiplication and division facts

YOU WILL NEED paper and pencil, a way to time 1 minute

How many stars can you draw in one minute? Work with a partner to find out. Time each other. Now, circle groups of stars. Put the same number of stars in each circle. Were any left over? How many groups did you make? How many were in each group?

Making a Pictograph

Seabreeze Elementary had a contest to see which class could sell the most tickets to the school's annual concert. The sales were recorded using a computer graphing program. The data were entered in a table, a picture was chosen for the pictograph, and the pictograph icon was clicked. The data changed into a pictograph!

MATERIALS
Graph Links Plus or any other graphing program

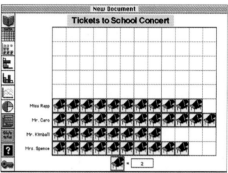

TICKETS SOLD	
Mrs. Spence	20
Ms. Kimball	16
Mr. Caro	24
Miss Rapp	22

EXAMPLE

Graphing programs may have a selection of pictures for making pictographs. In *Graph Links Plus* the Symbol Library includes pictures of foods, sports, and other subjects. Click on a picture in the Symbol Library and the picture name appears in the Data Center. Then enter the data.

Data Center	Tickets sold
Mrs. Spence	20
Mr. Kimball	16
Mr. Caro	24
Miss Rapp	22

► PRACTICE

1. There were 16 students from 1st grade, 30 students from 2nd grade, 36 from 3rd grade, 34 from 4th grade, and 28 from 5th grade who came to the skating party. Make a pictograph to show the skating party attendance.

2. **Using the Computer** Use a graphing program and the table below to make a pictograph showing the number of points scored by Kyle's basketball team in the first four games. HINT: You may need a different key than 2.

BASKETBALL SCORES	
Game 1	55
Game 2	60
Game 3	75
Game 4	80

Study Guide and Review

Vocabulary Check

Choose a term from the box to complete the sentence.

VOCABULARY
divisor
factors
inverse
product
quotient

1. The numbers you multiply in a multiplication problem are called ___?___. (page 188)

2. The answer to a multiplication problem is the ___?___. (page 188)

3. Multiplication and division are ___?___, or opposite, operations. (page 230)

4. The number that divides the dividend is a ___?___. (page 230)

5. The answer in a division problem is a ___?___. (page 230)

Study and Solve

CHAPTER 11

EXAMPLE

$3 \times 4 = $ ___?___

This is 3 groups of 4, or $4 + 4 + 4 = 12$, so $3 \times 4 = 12$.

For Problems 6–7, complete the multiplication sentence for each number line. (pages 192–195)

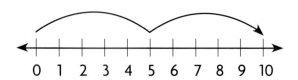

6. $2 \times 5 = $ ___?___

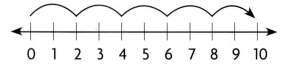

7. $5 \times 2 = $ ___?___

For Problems 8–11, find the product. (pages 198–201)

8. $4 \times 5 = $ ___?___

9. $6 \times 3 = $ ___?___

10. $\begin{array}{r} 5 \\ \times 7 \\ \hline \end{array}$

11. $\begin{array}{r} 2 \\ \times 6 \\ \hline \end{array}$

Solve. (pages 190–191)

12. Marie plays tennis 3 times a week. How many times does she play in 7 weeks?

13. Tim has 4 nickels in his pocket. How much money does Tim have?

14. Marty tacked 6 papers on the board. He used 4 tacks on each paper. How many tacks did Marty use?

CHAPTER 12

EXAMPLE

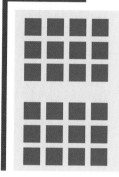

$6 \times 4 = 24$

An array can help you multiply.

You can divide it into 2 smaller arrays.

Complete the table.

15. (pages 208–215)

×	5	6	7	8	9
9	45	?	?	?	?

For Problems 16–19, find the product.
(pages 208–215)

16. $6 \times 6 = \underline{\ ?\ }$ **17.** $7 \times 8 = \underline{\ ?\ }$

18. $\begin{array}{r} 7 \\ \times 9 \\ \hline \end{array}$ **19.** $\begin{array}{r} 8 \\ \times 9 \\ \hline \end{array}$

Solve. (pages 216–217)

20. Matt bought 4 packs of sports cards. Each pack had 8 cards. How many cards did he get?

CHAPTER 13

EXAMPLE

$12 \div 4 = \underline{\ ?\ }$

Division is repeated subtraction.

$\begin{array}{ccc} 12 & 8 & 4 \\ -4 & -4 & -4 \\ \hline 8 & 4 & 0 \end{array}$ so $12 \div 4 = 3$.

Write the division sentence shown by the repeated subtraction.
(pages 228–229)

21. $\begin{array}{cccc} 20 & 15 & 10 & 5 \\ -5 & -5 & -5 & -5 \\ \hline 15 & 10 & 5 & 0 \end{array}$

For Problems 22–23, write the fact family for the set of numbers.
(pages 232–233)

22. 6, 2, 12   **23.** 9, 4, 36

For Problems 24–25, write the multiplication fact you can use to find the quotient. Write the quotient.
(pages 234–235)

24. $24 \div 3 = \underline{\ ?\ }$ **25.** $25 \div 5 = \underline{\ ?\ }$

Solve. (pages 238–239)

26. Bob had 12 pens. He put the same number of pens in each of 3 boxes. How many pens were in each box?

CHAPTER 14

EXAMPLE

An array can help you divide.

$28 \div 7 = 4$

For Problems 27–28, find the quotient. (pages 244–245, 250–251)

27. $72 \div 8 = \underline{\ ?\ }$ **28.** $45 \div 5 = \underline{\ ?\ }$

Solve. (pages 252–255)

29. Ana has 3 cousins. She baked 2 cupcakes for each of them. How many cupcakes did Ana bake for her cousins?

Performance Assessment

Tasks: Show What You Know

1. Write an addition and a multiplication sentence for the picture. Explain how the sentences are related. (pages 188–190)

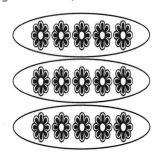

2. Use tiles to make arrays to show the product of each basic fact. Explain your method. (pages 206–213)

$3 \times 6 = \underline{?}$ $6 \times 7 = \underline{?}$
$5 \times 8 = \underline{?}$ $4 \times 5 = \underline{?}$

3. Explain how you can use subtraction to solve.

$12 \div 2 = \underline{?}$ (pages 228–229)

4. Explain what these facts illustrate about using 0 and 1 in division. (pages 246–247)

$7 \div 7 = 1$
$7 \div 1 = 7$
$0 \div 7 = 0$

Problem Solving

Solve. Explain your method.

CHOOSE a strategy and a tool.
- Find a Pattern • Draw a Picture • Make a Model
- Make a Table • Write a Number Sentence

 Paper/Pencil   Calculator   Hands-On   Mental Math

5. There are 4 basketball teams at King School. Each team has 5 players. How many basketball players are there altogether? (pages 190–191)

6. There are 9 rows of desks in a classroom. There are 6 desks in each row. How many desks are in the classroom? (pages 216–217)

7. Mrs. Palmer bought 4 six-packs of soda. How many cans of soda did she buy? (pages 238–239)

8. Sugar Tops Cereal comes in 3 different-size boxes—12, 20, and 36 ounces. How many 4-ounce servings are in each box? (pages 252-253)

Cumulative Review

Solve the problem. Then write the letter of the correct answer.

1. $7 + 5 + 5 = \underline{\ ?\ }$

A. 16   **B.** 17
C. 18   **D.** 27

(pages 18–19)

2. $\begin{array}{r} \$8.00 \\ -\ 5.95 \\ \hline \end{array}$

A. $2.05
B. $2.15
C. $3.95
D. $13.95

(pages 56–57, 62–65)

3. What time is shown?

A. 3:27   **B.** 3:52
C. 4:27   **D.** 5:17

(pages 82–83)

4. $\begin{array}{r} \$2.46 \\ +\ 3.52 \\ \hline \end{array}$

A. $5.78
B. $5.98
C. $5.99
D. $6.98

(pages 114–115)

5. Which is an ordinal number?

A. 5th   **B.** 7
C. 28   **D.** 413

(pages 128–129)

Choose the number.

6. ten thousand, nineteen

A. 1,019   **B.** 10,009
C. 10,019   **D.** 10,190

(pages 150–153)

7. $5 \times 0 = \underline{\ ?\ }$

A. 0   **B.** 1
C. 5   **D.** 50

(pages 196–197)

8. What two smaller arrays can you use to find $8 \times 3 = 24$?

A. 3×3 and 2×3
B. 5×3 and 2×3
C. 4×3 and 4×1
D. 4×3 and 4×3

(pages 212–213)

9. $\begin{array}{r} 7 \\ \times 9 \\ \hline \end{array}$

A. 16
B. 54
C. 63
D. 78

(pages 214–215)

Write the missing number for each number sentence.

10. $5 \times \underline{\ ?\ } = 45$
$45 \div 5 = \underline{\ ?\ }$

A. 6, 6   **B.** 7, 7
C. 8, 8   **D.** 9, 9

(pages 230–231)

Write the multiplication fact you can use to find the quotient.

11. $24 \div 4 = \underline{\ ?\ }$

A. $24 \div 3 = 8$ **B.** $4 \times 5 = 20$
C. $4 \times 6 = 24$ **D.** $4 \times 20 = 80$

(pages 234–235)

12. $72 \div 9 = \underline{\ ?\ }$

A. 8   **B.** 9
C. 63   **D.** 81

(pages 250–251)

15 COLLECTING AND RECORDING DATA

An acre of soil may be home to as many as one million earthworms. They break up hard soil and bring nutrients up to the top. Earthworms eat decayed leaves and plants and replace them with nutrients for plants.

Soil Scientists

Soil is composed of dirt particles, small stones, and living and decaying things.

Work as a soil scientist to investigate a soil sample from your school or nearby.

YOU WILL NEED: paper cup of soil, tweezers or plastic forks and spoons, paper plates

- Slowly and carefully take apart the soil sample with tools.

- Sort the sample into four categories: stones, plants (grass, weeds), decaying things (roots, twigs), and other (insects, nutshells).

- Count or measure each element, and tally.

- Organize your data into a frequency table.

- Put the soil sample back where you found it.

DID YOU

✓	collect and sort the sample into four categories?
✓	tally each element?
✓	organize your data into a frequency table?
✓	share your results with the class?

Our Soil Sample
stones   old plants
new plants   other

Collecting and Organizing Data

VOCABULARY
data
tally table
frequency table

You will investigate how to collect data and organize them into a table.

Information about people or things is called **data**. Data can be organized and sorted for many purposes.

One way to organize data is in a **tally table**. It uses tally marks to show how often something happens.

Another way to organize data is in a **frequency table**. It uses numbers to show how often something happens.

> **REMEMBER:**
>
> *Tally marks* are grouped by fives for easy counting. Make four lines with one line across them for each group of five.

OUR SHOE FASTENERS	
Type	**Tallies**
Shoelaces	~~||||~~ ||
Buckles	|||
Velcro®	~~||||~~ ||||
No fastener	||

OUR SHOE FASTENERS	
Type	**Numbers**
Shoelaces	7
Buckles	3
Velcro®	9
No fastener	2

- How are the two tables alike? different?

▶ EXPLORE

Collect data about your classmates. Organize the data in a tally table. Then make a frequency table.

MODEL

Step 1

Decide on a question to ask your classmates. Make a tally table to record their answers. In the tally table, list the choices classmates can give as answers.

Step 2

Ask everyone in your class the question. Each time you get an answer, make a tally mark beside that answer. Then make a frequency table of the data.

▶ TRY THIS

1. Describe in words what you found out about your classmates. Explain what you put in your tables.

2. How is a tally table good for recording data?

3. ✏ **Write About It** Why is a frequency table a good way to show data?

▶ PRACTICE

Make a tally table of five after-school activities. Ask each classmate which activity he or she likes best. Make a tally mark beside the activity. Then make a frequency table of the same data.

4. Which after-school activity did the most classmates choose? the fewest choose?

Ride bikes IIII
Watch TV ℍℍ II
Play Video Games ℍℍ
Draw II
Play Sports ℍℍ IIII

5. Compare your tables with those of your classmates. Did everyone get the same results?

Problem Solving • Mixed Applications

For Problems 6, 7, and 9, use the tally table.

6. Change this tally table into a frequency table.

7. How many people answered the question about their favorite sandwich?

8. Tania has 12 slices of bread to make sandwiches. She uses 2 slices of bread for each sandwich. How many sandwiches can she make?

9. ✏ **Write a problem** using the information in the tally table.

MORE PRACTICE page H93

SCIENCE LINK

Creatures such as earthworms, ants, moles, and chipmunks dig tunnels beneath the surface of the soil. How could you record data about the number of creatures in an area of land?

Technology Link

You can collect and organize data by using E-Lab, Activity 15. Available on CD-ROM and on the Internet at www.hbschool.com/elab

FAVORITE SANDWICHES	
Sandwich	Tallies
Peanut Butter & Jelly	ℍℍ III
Grilled Cheese	ℍℍ ℍℍ I
Tuna Fish	IIII
Ham & Cheese	ℍℍ I

Recording Data

Why learn this? You can see what happens when you do an experiment.

An **experiment** is a test done in order to find out something.

Greg and Emma did an experiment with a spinner. They wanted to know what number they would spin the most often and the least often.

They spun the pointer 50 times. They recorded each number the pointer landed on by placing a tally mark beside that number in a table.

SPINNER EXPERIMENT	
Number	**Number of Times Spun**
1	卌 ||
2	卌 卌 卌
3	卌 卌 |
4	卌 卌 卌 ||

Talk About It

- What number did Greg and Emma spin the most often? the least often?

- Was the tally table a good choice to record the spins? Explain.

CRITICAL THINKING What kind of table would you use to report the results of an experiment? Why?

▶ CHECK

1. Sarah is doing an experiment. She will toss a penny 50 times and record whether it lands heads up or tails up. Make a table she could use to record what happens.

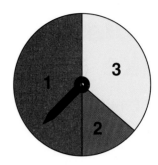

2. Colin wants to show what happened when he did an experiment with this spinner. What type of table should he use to show the results to his class? Why?

▶ PRACTICE

For Problems 3–6, tell what kind of table should be used. Write *tally table* or *frequency table*.

3. Denise did an experiment with a number cube. Now she wants to show what happened.

4. Jim is getting ready to do a spinner experiment. He will record the color the pointer lands on each time he spins.

5. Mrs. Putnam is about to show her class how to do an experiment with a number cube and a coin. She wants to show them how to record what happens.

6. Alec has just finished an experiment. He tossed a two-color counter and spun a pointer. He wants to show the class how the experiment turned out.

Problem Solving • Mixed Applications

7. Bobby did an experiment with a four-color spinner. He spun the pointer 20 times. He spun red 5 times, yellow 4 times, green 8 times, and blue 3 times. Make a frequency table showing what happened.

8. Mariah rolled a number cube 25 times. She rolled a 1 three times, a 2 four times, a 3 two times, a 4 five times, a 5 seven times, and a 6 four times. Make a tally table showing what happened.

9. ✏️ **Write About It** Explain when to use a tally table and when to use a frequency table.

LESSON CONTINUES ➡️

Problem–Solving Strategy: Make a Table

▶ THE PROBLEM Greg and Emma are rolling two number cubes to find out what difference they will roll the most often and the least often. They will roll the pair of cubes 50 times. Each time, they will subtract the two numbers they roll. What would be the best way to organize and record what happens in their experiment?

REMEMBER:
UNDERSTAND
PLAN
SOLVE
LOOK BACK

UNDERSTAND

- What are you asked to find?

- What information will you use?

- Is there information you will not use? If so, what?

PLAN

- What strategy can you use to solve the problem?

  You can *make a table* to organize the data.

SOLVE

- What should you put in the table?

  Greg and Emma are recording differences in this experiment. So, label one column of the table *Differences*. In this column, list all the differences they can get from rolling two number cubes. Label another column *Number of Times Rolled.* Use a tally mark to record each difference as it is rolled.

 $4 - 2 = 2$

| NUMBER CUBE EXPERIMENT ||
Differences	Number of Times Rolled
0	
1	
2	I
3	
4	
5	

LOOK BACK

- How can you check your answer?

- What other strategy could you use?

Make a table to solve.

1. Jeremy and Kate are doing an experiment with these two spinners. They spin the pointers on the spinners. Then they record the sum of the two numbers they spin. They will spin the pointers 20 times. Show how they could organize a table about their experiment.

2. Heather and Sam are doing an experiment with a spinner. One section of the spinner is red, one is blue, one is green, and one is yellow. In the experiment, they spin the pointer and record the results 30 times. Show how they could organize a table about the experiment.

Mixed Applications

Solve.

CHOOSE a strategy and a tool.
- Work Backward
- Guess and Check
- Write a Number Sentence
- Make a Table
- Act It Out

 Paper/Pencil   Calculator   Hands-On   Mental Math

3. In a board game, Allen is behind Marie. Pam is ahead of Steve. Pam is between Allen and Steve. What is the order of the children in the game?

4. Carol rode her bike 3 miles farther than Connie. Together, they rode 19 miles. How many miles did each girl ride?

5. What time was it 2 hours and 15 minutes ago?

6. Lauren spent $5 at the movies. She still had $7 when she got home. How much did Lauren have to begin with?

7. Ashley is doing an experiment with two number cubes. She will roll the cubes 25 times and add the two numbers to find the sum. Show how she could organize and record her experiment.

8. There are 8 teddy bears on each of 3 shelves. How many teddy bears in all are on the shelves?

Understanding Collected Data

Why learn this? You can find out what people like and don't like.

A **survey** is a set of questions that a group of people are asked. The answers from a survey are the **results** of the survey.

Bruce and Gina took a survey to find out their classmates' favorite holiday. The tally table shows the choices and votes of their classmates.

Taking a survey

OUR FAVORITE HOLIDAYS	
Holiday	Votes
Presidents' Day	$\cancel{||||}$
Memorial Day	
The 4th of July	||||
Thanksgiving	$\cancel{||||}$ $\cancel{||||}$	
Labor Day	$\cancel{||||}$ ||

Talk About It CRITICAL THINKING

• List the holidays in order from the most favorite to the least favorite.

• How many students answered Bruce and Gina's survey? How do you know?

• Why do you think Bruce and Gina chose to use a tally table to take their survey?

• What would be a good way for Bruce and Gina to share the results of their survey with others? Why?

SOCIAL STUDIES LINK

In November 1621, the Pilgrims celebrated the first Thanksgiving with Native Americans. On October 3, 1863, Abraham Lincoln set aside a national Thanksgiving holiday in November. How many years after the first celebration did Thanksgiving become a national holiday?

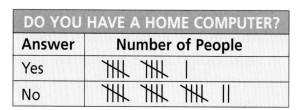

▶ CHECK

1. Make two statements about the survey results shown in the table at the right.

DO YOU HAVE A HOME COMPUTER?	
Answer	Number of People
Yes	$\cancel{||||}$ $\cancel{||||}$	
No	$\cancel{||||}$ $\cancel{||||}$ $\cancel{||||}$ ||

► PRACTICE

For Problems 2–5, use the survey results in the tally table.

2. List the cereals in order from the most to the least favorite.

3. How many people answered the survey?

4. How many more people like Krispy Kritters than Fruity Puffs?

5. How many more people like Krispy Kritters than Tasty Flakes?

OUR FAVORITE CEREAL	
Cereal	Votes
Yummy Pops	卌 丨
Oat Squares	卌 丨丨
Krispy Kritters	卌 卌 卌
Fruity Puffs	卌 卌 丨丨
Tasty Flakes	卌 卌

For Problems 6–9, use the frequency table.

6. How many more people play the drums than the piano?

7. What musical instrument do the most people play?

8. How many people answered this survey?

9. ✏ **Write a problem** using the information in the table.

WHAT MUSICAL INSTRUMENT DO YOU PLAY?	
Musical Instrument	Number of People
Piano	24
Guitar	38
Violin	11
Flute	16
Drums	30

Problem Solving • Mixed Applications

10. **Measurement** Jenny ran around a 440-yard track 2 times in 1 day and 1 time the next day. How many yards did she run in both days?

11. **Money** Each of four students bought 8 color pencils for 5¢ each. How much money did each student spend?

Mixed Review and Test Prep

Find the product. (pages 198–201)

12.	13.	14.	15.	16.	17.
1	4	2	3	7	5
×8	×3	×6	×5	×2	×4

Choose the letter of the correct quotient. (pages 246–247)

18. $5 \div 5 = \underline{\ ?\ }$ **A** 0   **B** 5   **C** 1   **D** 3

19. $0 \div 2 = \underline{\ ?\ }$ **F** 2   **G** 0   **H** 1   **J** 20

20. $4 \div 1 = \underline{\ ?\ }$ **A** 4   **B** 1   **C** 0   **D** 2

Grouping Data in a Table

Why learn this? You can organize data in a way that lets you show differences, such as color and size.

Data can be grouped in ways in which they are the same. Data can be grouped by size, color, shape, and in many other ways.

Mr. Davis gave each pair of students in his class a cup of buttons. He told the students to think of a way to group the buttons. Then he told them to find a way to show their data so that others could easily see what they had.

Corey and Evan recorded the groupings in this table.

CUP OF BUTTONS			
	Small	**Medium**	**Large**
Yellow	3	2	5
Blue	2	1	3
Red	2	2	5

Talk About It CRITICAL THINKING

- How many buttons are in Corey and Evan's cup? How do you know?

- How many small yellow buttons are there? How many blue buttons? How many large buttons?

- How are the data grouped in more than one way?

▶ CHECK

1. What are some ways in which you could group your classmates?

Technology Link

In *Graph Links Plus* Computer *Software* you can practice making a table to group data.

▶ PRACTICE

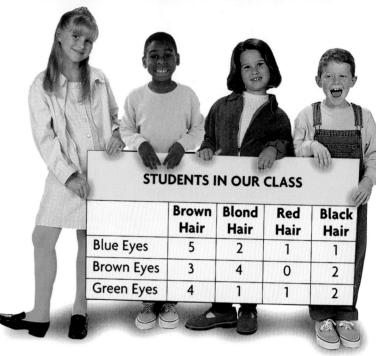

For Problems 2–6, use the table.

2. How many students have blond hair and brown eyes?

3. How many students have blue eyes?

4. How many students have brown hair?

5. What color hair do only two students have?

6. How many students are in the class?

7. Look at the figures at the right. Make a table to group the figures.

STUDENTS IN OUR CLASS

	Brown Hair	Blond Hair	Red Hair	Black Hair
Blue Eyes	5	2	1	1
Brown Eyes	3	4	0	2
Green Eyes	4	1	1	2

Problem Solving • Mixed Applications

8. Sports On Courtney's softball team, there are 8 girls and 10 boys. Of the girls, 5 are good hitters and the rest are good fielders. Of the boys, 8 are good hitters and the rest are good fielders. Make a table to group the players on the softball team.

9. ✏ **Write a problem** about the data in this table.

PICTURES IN THE ART SHOW

	Chalk	Crayon	Paint
Pictures of People	4	5	2
Pictures of Nature	9	7	8

Mixed Review and Test Prep

Find the quotient. (pages 250–251)

10. $18 \div 6 =$?

11. $40 \div 8 =$?

12. $35 \div 5 =$?

13. $27 \div 3 =$?

14. $16 \div 4 =$?

15. $56 \div 8 =$?

Choose the letter of the correct product. (pages 196–197)

16. $4 \times 8 =$?
- **A** 16
- **B** 12
- **C** 36
- **D** 32

17. $7 \times 6 =$?
- **F** 21
- **G** 54
- **H** 42
- **J** 13

18. $9 \times 7 =$?
- **A** 63
- **B** 72
- **C** 81
- **D** 47

MORE PRACTICE page H94

► CHECK Understanding

VOCABULARY

1. You can organize data in a __?__ using tally marks or in a __?__ using numbers to show how often something happens. (page 266)

2. Information about people or things that can be organized and sorted is called __?__. (page 266)

3. A test done in order to find out something is an __?__. (page 268)

4. A set of questions that a group of people are asked is a __?__. The set of answers from a survey are the __?__. (page 272)

► CHECK Skills

For Problems 5–8, use the survey results in the tally table. (pages 272–273)

5. What question was asked in this survey?

6. How many people answered the survey?

7. List the breakfasts in order from the most favorite to the least favorite.

8. How many more people like cereal than pancakes?

FAVORITE BREAKFAST	
Breakfast	**Votes**
Pancakes	卌 |||
French Toast	||||
Cereal	卌 卌
Eggs and Bacon	卌	
Bagels and Cream Cheese	||

► CHECK Problem Solving

Solve. (pages 270–271)

CHOOSE a strategy and a tool.

• Write a Number Sentence • Make a Table
• Work Backward • Find a Pattern

 Paper/Pencil   Calculator   Hands-On   Mental Math

9. A spinner has red, green, and blue sections. Show how you could organize the results of an experiment with the spinner.

10. Draw the next four figures in the pattern.

Test Prep

Choose the best answer.

1. A class of 25 children went on a field trip with 5 parents as guides. The same number of children went with each parent. How many children did each parent guide?

   A 10   **B** 5

   C 20   **D** 25

2. The students washed 9 cars. They charged $3 for each car. How much money did they earn?

   F $18   **G** $12

   H $30   **J** $27

3. Dave buys a camera that costs $86. To the nearest ten dollars, how much does the camera cost?

   A $60   **B** $10

   C $90   **D** $70

4. What is the value of 3 in 1,367?

   F 3 ones

   G 3 tens

   H 3 hundreds

   J 3 thousands

5. The bus has 9 rows of seats. Each row has 2 seats. How many people can sit on the bus?

   A 9   **B** 36   **C** 18   **D** 27

6. You want to put about 60 candies in a piñata. Which jar of candies would you use as a benchmark?

   F jar with 50 candies

   G jar with 500 candies

   H jar with 5,000 candies

   J jar with 5 candies

7. This table shows the 4 most popular dogs in one town.

POPULAR DOGS	
Dog	**Number**
Shepherd	26
Retriever	58
Poodle	65
Cocker Spaniel	42

   Which breed is most popular?

   A poodle   **B** retriever

   C shepherd   **D** cocker spaniel

8. This table shows how students get to school.

GETTING TO SCHOOL	
Transportation	**Students**
Car	43
Bus	335
Bicycle	85
Walk	167

   What way do most students get to school?

   F walk   **G** bicycle

   H bus   **J** car

16 REPRESENTING DATA

SOCIAL STUDIES **LINK**

In 1909 the profile of Abraham Lincoln was first used on the face of the penny to celebrate the one hundredth anniversary of his birth.

Collecting Pennies

Collecting pennies is fun. Collectors look at the date, whether the coin is worn or new, and the mint mark (an initial under the date) to decide if they want to keep a coin. Pennies are minted in Philadelphia (no mint mark) and in Denver (D). Up until 1975, they were also minted in San Francisco (S).

Use a handful of pennies and find the date and mint mark for each one. Make a table and a graph that shows information about your coins.

YOU WILL NEED: hand lens, 25 pennies, paper, and pencil

- Make a tally table for dates.

- Make a tally table for the mint marks. Which mint appeared most often?

- Make a vertical bar graph using your data on mint marks.

- Discuss and compare your findings as a class.

DID YOU

✓	make a tally table for dates and mint marks?
✓	make a vertical bar graph?
✓	participate in a discussion of results?
✓	share your results with the class?

Pictographs and Multiplication

Why learn this? You can understand pictographs you see in magazines and newspapers.

A **pictograph** shows data by using pictures. The **key** at the bottom of a pictograph tells how many each picture stands for. The pictograph below shows how all the third-grade students at Ocean View Elementary get to school.

HOW WE GET TO SCHOOL

Walk	✹ ✹ ✹
Ride a Bike	✹ ✹ ✹ ✹
Ride the Bus	✹ ✹ ✹ ✹ ✹ ✹
Ride in a Car	✹ ✹

Key: Each ✹ = 10 students.

SOCIAL STUDIES LINK

Before there were cars, people traveled in carriages pulled by horses. In 1896 Henry Ford built a quadricycle. This was a car on bicycle wheels. In 1908 he built the first gas-run car, the Model T. How do you think most students got to school in 1908?

Notice that

⇨ in the key, each picture stands for 10 students.

⇨ each row has a label such as *Walk* that tells the ways students get to school.

Talk About It

• How many students walk to school? How do you know?

• How many students ride a bike to school? ride the bus? ride in a car?

▶ Check

1. If 50 students ride the bus to school, how would you show that in the pictograph?

▶ PRACTICE

For Problems 2–6, use the pictograph.

2. How many students does each juice-box picture stand for?

3. How many students like each type of juice the best?

4. Which type of juice do the most students like the best? the fewest students?

OUR FAVORITE JUICE	
Orange	🧃🧃🧃
Grape	🧃🧃🧃🧃🧃🧃
Apple	🧃🧃🧃🧃
Fruit Punch	🧃🧃🧃
Grapefruit	🧃

Key: Each 🧃 = 5 students.

5. How many more students like orange juice better than fruit punch? apple juice better than grapefruit juice?

6. ✏️ **Write About It** Suppose *Pineapple Juice* is added to the pictograph. There are 6 pictures in that row. Tell how many students these pictures would stand for. How do you know?

Problem Solving • Mixed Applications

7. Money For the party, Miss Hale spent $6.85 on apple juice and $4.56 on grape juice. How much did she spend in all on juice?

8. Time The party started at 1:30. It ended 1 hour and 15 minutes later. At what time did the party end?

9. Number Sense The key in a pictograph shows that each picture stands for 4 students. There are 7 pictures in one row. How many students does that stand for?

10. In one class 17 students collect pennies. In another class 18 students collect pennies. How many students collect pennies?

Mixed Review and Test Prep

Write *true* or *false*. Change words in the false sentences to make them true. (pages 130–131)

11. There are 100 dimes in a dollar.

12. There are 10 tens in a hundred.

Choose the letter of the correct product. (pages 214–215)

13. $8 \times 7 = \underline{\ ?\ }$
 A 72 **B** 35
 C 56 **D** 54

14. $9 \times 5 = \underline{\ ?\ }$
 F 36 **G** 54
 H 18 **J** 45

15. $6 \times 3 = \underline{\ ?\ }$
 A 18 **B** 15
 C 12 **D** 14

16. $7 \times 6 = \underline{\ ?\ }$
 F 36 **G** 42
 H 54 **J** 63

Making a Pictograph

You will investigate how to show data in a pictograph.

> **REMEMBER:**
>
> A *frequency table* is a table that uses numbers to show how often something happens.

▶ EXPLORE

Make a pictograph that shows the data from this frequency table.

MATERIALS: crayons, ruler

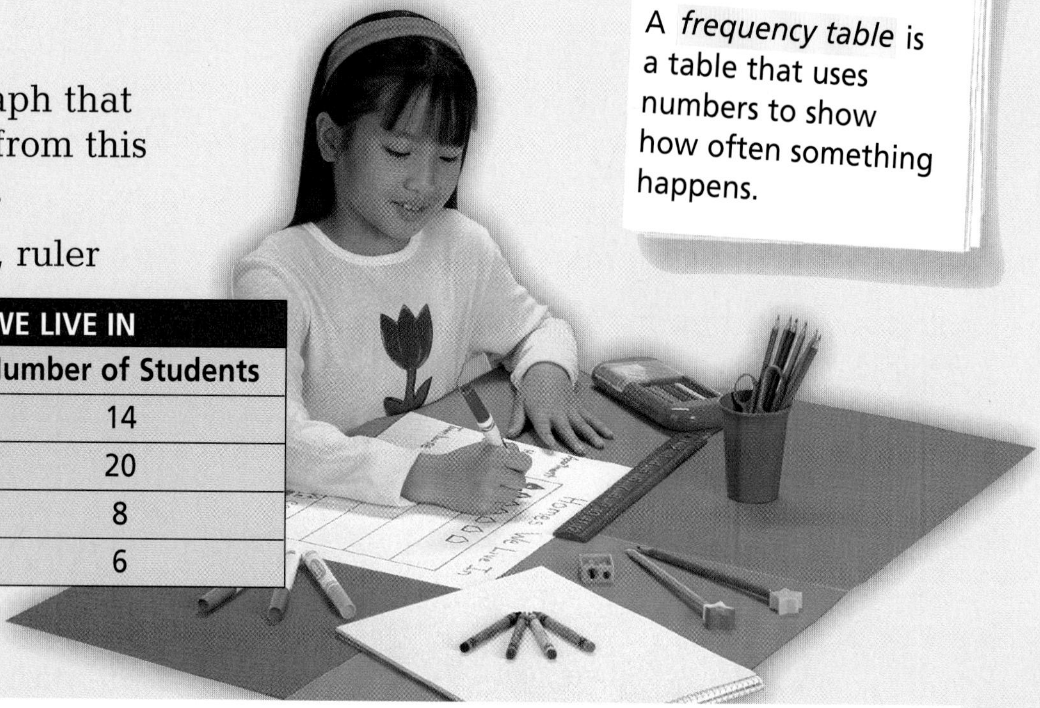

HOMES WE LIVE IN	
Type of Home	**Number of Students**
Apartment	14
House	20
Condominium	8
Townhouse	6

MODEL

Step 1

Copy the graph below. Include the title, the labels, and the key. Notice that since all the numbers in the table are even, a key of 2 was chosen.

HOMES WE LIVE IN	
Apartment	
House	
Condominium	
Townhouse	

Key: Each ⌂ = 2 students.

Step 2

The key tells you that each picture stands for 2 students. Think about how many pictures to draw for each type of home. Then complete the pictograph.

HOMES WE LIVE IN	
Apartment	⌂ ⌂ ⌂ ⌂ ⌂ ⌂ ⌂
House	
Condominium	
Townhouse	

Key: Each ⌂ = 2 students.

Record

Explain how you decided how many pictures to draw for each type of home.

Talk About It

• How is a key useful in a pictograph?

• How was each part of the table used in the pictograph?

Now, investigate how to show in a pictograph the number of tickets sold for the school play.

▶ TRY THIS

1. Make a pictograph to show the data in the table. Think of a symbol to stand for tickets in the key. Let each symbol stand for 5 tickets. Give your graph a title and labels.

2. ✎ **Write About It** Explain how a pictograph is like a frequency table and how it is different.

NUMBER OF SCHOOL PLAY TICKETS SOLD	
Day	Number of Tickets
Monday	20
Tuesday	35
Wednesday	50
Thursday	40
Friday	25

▶ PRACTICE

3. Think of an idea for making a pictograph. Take a survey, or collect data, about a subject that interests you. Then make a pictograph. Decide on a symbol and key for the graph. Include a title and labels.

4. Tell how you decided on the subject of your pictograph.

5. Explain how you chose a symbol and key for your pictograph.

"Pictograph Ideas"
1. Our Favorite Books
2. Sizes of Our Families
3. Our Favorite Colors

Problem Solving • Mixed Applications

6. **Money** Mike paid for a magazine with a $10 bill. His change was $6.84. How much did the magazine cost?

7. **Logical Reasoning** In a race Lisa beat Frank. Alan came in after Jill. Frank beat Alan and Jill. In what order did they finish?

8. **Mental Math** Jeremy is 4 times as old as Tom. Tom is 2 years old. How old is Jeremy?

9. **Money** Larry earned $6 raking leaves for 2 hours. How much money did he earn per hour?

MORE PRACTICE page H95

Reading Bar Graphs

Why learn this? You can understand bar graphs that you see in magazines and newspapers.

VOCABULARY

bar graph
scale
horizontal
vertical

Bar graphs use bars to stand for data. A bar graph has a **scale** of numbers that helps you read the number each bar shows.

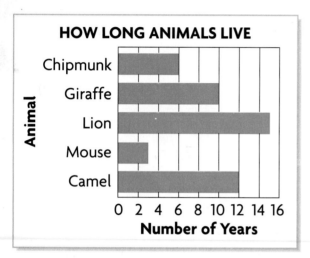

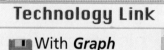

In a **horizontal** bar graph, the bars go across from left to right.

In a **vertical** bar graph, the bars go up.

Notice that

⇨ both bar graphs show the same data.

⇨ the labels and the scale are in a different place on each graph.

⇨ the bar for *Mouse* ends between the lines that mark the scale. Since it is halfway between 2 and 4, the bar shows 3.

Technology Link

With *Graph Links Plus* computer software, you can change the graph to either a horizontal or vertical bar graph.

▶ CHECK

1. What scale is used on the bar graphs?

2. How long does a chipmunk live? a giraffe? a camel?

3. How long does a lion live? How can you tell?

▶ PRACTICE

For Problems 4–8, use the bar graph.

4. What type of bar graph is this?

5. How many students named the monkey bars as their favorite playground activity? jumping rope? hopscotch?

6. Which activity is liked the best by the most students? Which activity is liked the best by the fewest students?

7. Suppose the graph is made into a vertical bar graph. How would the graph change?

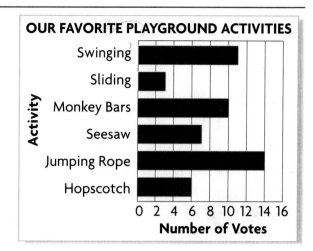

8. ◀▭ **Write About It** Tell how many students named swinging as their favorite activity. Explain.

Problem Solving • Mixed Applications

9. Samantha has written 3 stories. Donna has written 3 times as many stories. How many stories has Donna written?

10. **Patterns** Find the next three numbers in the pattern: 3, 8, 13, 18, 23, 28, _?_, _?_, _?_.

11. **Time** Melissa played the piano from 3:30 until 4:15. Sylvia played from 4:00 until 4:40. Who played longer? How much longer?

12. **Consumer** Hassan has a coupon for $5 off his purchase. He buys glue for $4, paints for $6, and a booklet for $2. How much does Hassan pay after using his coupon?

Mixed Review and Test Prep

Write the division sentence shown by the repeated subtraction. (pages 228–229)

13.
$$
\begin{array}{cccc}
20 & 15 & 10 & 5 \\
-5 & -5 & -5 & -5 \\
\hline
15 & 10 & 5 & 0
\end{array}
$$

14.
$$
\begin{array}{cccc}
16 & 12 & 8 & 4 \\
-4 & -4 & -4 & -4 \\
\hline
12 & 8 & 4 & 0
\end{array}
$$

Choose the letter of the correct product. (pages 188–189)

15. $2 \times 7 =$ _?_   **A** 9   **B** 18
                          C 14   **D** 12

16. $6 \times 5 =$ _?_   **F** 25   **G** 35
                          H 11   **J** 30

Making Bar Graphs

You will investigate how to show data in a bar graph.

▶ EXPLORE

Make a horizontal bar graph of the data in this frequency table. Use the title of the table as the title of the graph. Label the bars with the names of the sports. The number of votes can help you choose the scale.

MATERIALS: grid paper, markers

OUR FAVORITE SPORTS	
Sport	**Votes**
Football	12
Basketball	6
Soccer	4
Baseball	8
Volleyball	6

MODEL

Step 1

Copy the graph below on grid paper. Include the title, the labels, and the numbers on the scale.

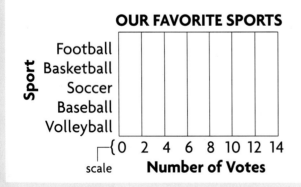

Step 2

Complete the bar graph by drawing the bar for each sport. Make the length of each bar equal to the number of votes for that sport.

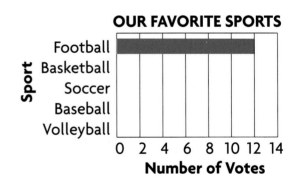

Record

Explain how you knew how long to draw the bar for basketball.

Talk About It

- Explain how a pictograph can be used to show the favorite sports data.

- Look at the frequency table at the top of page 286. How is each part of the table used in the bar graph?

Now, investigate how to show what some third-grade students want to be when they grow up.

▶ TRY THIS

▶ TRY THIS

1. Make a bar graph of the data in the table showing the career choices of some third-grade students. Use a scale numbered by twos (0, 2, 4, 6, 8). Remember to title and label the graph.

2. What other scale could you use for the data in the graph above?

▶ PRACTICE

Find a bar graph in a magazine or newspaper. Cut out the graph and mount it on a sheet of notebook paper. Use the graph to answer Problems 3–5.

3. What does the graph show?

4. What scale is used in the graph?

5. Is there anything different about the graph compared with the bar graphs you have studied in the past two lessons?

Technology Link

You can make bar graphs by using E–Lab, Activity 16. Available on CD-ROM and on the Internet at www.hbschool.com/elab

WHAT WE WANT TO BE	
Career	**Number of Students**
Teacher	6
Dentist	2
Actor	6
Doctor	7
Nurse	5
Lawyer	4

Problem Solving • Mixed Applications

6. **Number Sense** Dana's book has 45 pages. Each story in it is 5 pages long. How many stories are in the book?

7. **Money** Sam spent $1.75 for lunch. He got $3.25 in change. How much money did Sam have before lunch?

8. **Time** It is 3:20. The next bus comes at 4 o'clock. How many minutes until the next bus?

9. **Mental Math** Jose has 36 coins. He makes groups of 4. How many groups does he make?

Comparing Data

Why learn this? You can compare heights and weights of animals.

Blake made this bar graph showing the heights of animals.

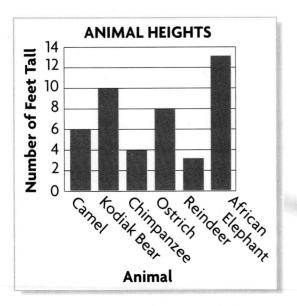

6 ft

Talk About It CRITICAL THINKING

• Is this a horizontal or vertical bar graph?

• How many feet tall is a chimpanzee? a camel? a reindeer?

• Which animal in this group is the shortest? the tallest?

▶ CHECK

For Problems 1–3, use the bar graph.

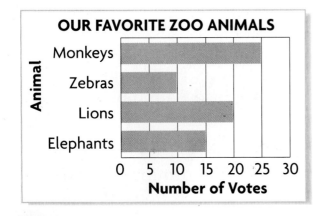

1. How many students like monkeys the most? like lions the most?

2. Do more students like zebras or lions the best?

3. How many more students like monkeys better than elephants?

▶ PRACTICE

For Problems 4–8, use the pictograph.

4. How many baseball cards does Chaz have in his collection? Chris? Ira?

5. Who has the most baseball cards in his collection? the fewest?

6. Who has more baseball cards— Chris or Ira?

7. How many baseball cards do Chaz and Marc have altogether?

BASEBALL CARD COLLECTIONS

Jake	🃏🃏🃏🃏🃏
David	🃏🃏🃏
Chris	🃏🃏🃏🃏🃏
Chaz	🃏🃏🃏🃏🃏🃏🃏
Marc	🃏🃏🃏🃏
Ira	🃏🃏🃏🃏🃏🃏🃏

Key: Each 🃏 = 10 cards.

8. ✏️ **Write a problem** using the information in the pictograph.

Problem Solving • Mixed Applications

9. Logical Reasoning At the petting farm, there are 6 pigs in one pen. There are twice as many chickens in another pen. How many chickens are there?

10. Time Lacey arrived at the party 1 hour late. The time was 8:15. At what time did the party begin?

11. Reasoning The Springdale Sports Club has 63 students signed up for baseball teams. There are 7 equal-size teams. How many students are on each team?

12. Sports In one game Kristi scores 4 more runs than Jon. Jon scores one run less than Carlos. Carlos scores 3 runs. How many runs do Jon and Kristi each score?

13. Logic There are 8 people in a line. Maria is at the front of the line. There are 3 people between Maria and Jeff. Max is behind Jeff. There is one person between Max and Jeff. What is Max's position in line?

14. ✏️ **Write a problem** about the plants, bushes, and trees at Julio's plant nursery.

LESSON CONTINUES

Problem–Solving Strategy: Use a Graph

▶ **THE PROBLEM** Suppose you have taken a survey to find out what vegetables the students in your school like. You have made a graph to show what you have found out. What vegetables are liked by the most and the fewest students?

REMEMBER:

UNDERSTAND

PLAN

SOLVE

LOOK BACK

UNDERSTAND

- What are you asked to find?

- What information will you use?

- Is there information you will not use? If so, what?

PLAN

- What strategy can you use to solve the problem?

You can *use a graph* to find out which vegetable is liked by the most students and which is liked by the fewest students.

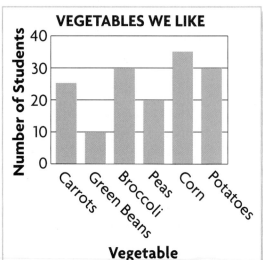

VEGETABLES WE LIKE

Number of Students

Vegetable

Carrots, Green Beans, Broccoli, Peas, Corn, Potatoes

SOLVE

- How can you use the graph to solve the problem?

Look at the bars in the graph at the top of the page.

The tallest bar is the bar for corn. So, corn is the vegetable that is liked by the most students.

The shortest bar is the bar for green beans. So, green beans is the vegetable that is liked by the fewest students.

LOOK BACK

- How else could you solve this problem?

For Problems 1–4, use the graphs.

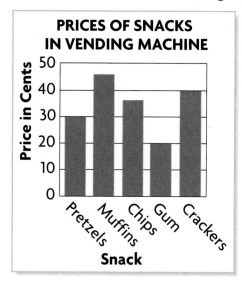

PRICES OF SNACKS IN VENDING MACHINE

Price in Cents: 50, 40, 30, 20, 10, 0

Snack: Pretzels, Muffins, Chips, Gum, Crackers

BOXES OF COOKIES SOLD

Tammy	🍪🍪🍪🍪
Julia	🍪🍪🍪🍪🍪🍪🍪🍪
Tasha	🍪🍪🍪🍪🍪🍪
Katelyn	🍪🍪🍪
Felicia	🍪🍪🍪🍪🍪🍪

Key: Each 🍪 = 5 boxes.

1. Which snack costs the most? the least?

2. How much would it cost to buy 2 packages of chips and 1 package of crackers?

3. How many boxes of cookies did Julia sell?

4. How many more boxes of cookies did Felicia sell than Tammy?

Mixed Applications

Solve.

CHOOSE a strategy and a tool.

- Write a Number Sentence
- Use a Graph
- Act It Out
- Find a Pattern

Paper/Pencil   Calculator   Hands-On   Mental Math

5. It was 4:00 when Val and Theresa began a math project. Val finished it in 15 minutes. Theresa finished 8 minutes later than Val. At what time did Theresa finish the math project?

6. Carol bought a puzzle book for $1.80. She gave the cashier 9 coins. What coins did she use?

7. Draw the two shapes that will come next.

8. How many more nonfiction books were sold than poetry?

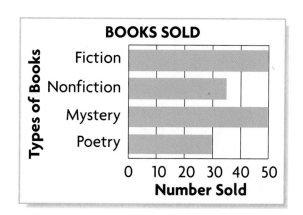

BOOKS SOLD

Types of Books: Fiction, Nonfiction, Mystery, Poetry

Number Sold: 0 10 20 30 40 50

▶ CHECK Understanding

1. A graph that shows data by using pictures that stand for more than one thing is a ?. (page 280)

2. The ? at the bottom of a pictograph tells how many each picture stands for. (page 280)

3. A ? is a graph that uses bars to stand for data. (page 284)

4. The bars on a ? bar graph go up. (page 284)

5. The ? of numbers on a bar graph helps you read what the length of each bar stands for. (page 284)

6. The bars on a ? bar graph go across from left to right. (page 284)

▶ CHECK Skills

For Problems 7–9, use the bar graph. (pages 284–287)

7. Who has the most compact discs? the fewest?

8. How many compact discs does Sarah have?

9. How many more compact discs does Zach have than Leslie?

COMPACT DISC COLLECTIONS

Bar graph titled "COMPACT DISC COLLECTIONS". Y-axis: Number of Compact Discs (0 to 30 by 5s). X-axis: Student — Sarah 15, Zach 20, Leslie 10, Cole 25.

▶ CHECK Problem Solving

Solve. (pages 290–291)

CHOOSE a strategy and a tool.
- Use a Graph   • Make a Model
- Guess and Check

 Paper/Pencil   Calculator   Hands-On   Mental Math

10. How many students chose blue as their favorite color?

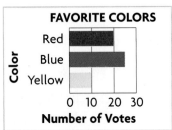

FAVORITE COLORS
Bar graph. Color (Red, Blue, Yellow) vs Number of Votes (0 10 20 30).

11. A gameboard has 27 squares. Each square is red or blue. The number of red squares is two times the number of blue squares. How many squares of each color are there?

Test Prep

Choose the best answer.

1. Mrs. Dennis put 5 toys on each of 3 shelves. Which number sentence shows how many toys there were?

A $5 + 3 = 7$ **B** $5 - 3 = 2$

C $3 \times 5 = 15$ **D** $15 \div 3 = 5$

2. This table shows some school lunches.

| SCHOOL LUNCHES ||
Lunch	Votes
Taco	87
Pizza	98
Salad	55
Hot Dog	65

Which list shows most favorite to least favorite lunches?

F hot dog, pizza, taco, salad

G pizza, taco, hot dog, salad

H taco, salad, pizza, hot dog

J salad, hot dog, taco, pizza

3. This pictograph shows high school sports.

| SCHOOL SPORTS ||
Sport	Number of Students
Softball	🧍 🧍 🧍
Field Hockey	🧍 🧍
Basketball	🧍 🧍 🧍 🧍
Gymnastics	🧍
Key: Each 🧍 = 10 students.	

How many students play softball?

A 30 **B** 40 **C** 20 **D** 10

4. Matthew asked 5 friends to his party. He has 3 hats and 4 whistles. Which shows how many more hats he will need so that everyone can have one?

F $5 + 3 = 8$ **G** $5 - 4 = 1$

H $5 + 4 = 9$ **J** $6 - 3 = 3$

5. At the baseball tournament there are 36 players playing on the field. If each team has 9 players, how many teams are playing?

A 9 **B** 4 **C** 27 **D** 45

6. What is the place value of the blue digit in 26,917?

F 2 tens

G 2 hundreds

H 2 thousands

J 2 ten thousands

7. Gina did a survey to show how many students use the public library.

| STUDENTS USING PUBLIC LIBRARY ||
Day	Students
Monday	12
Tuesday	16
Wednesday	25
Thursday	10
Friday	3

What did she make to show the results?

A tally table **B** frequency table

C pictograph **D** bar graph

17 PROBABILITY

When your stomach is empty, it needs food and starts to contract. It starts with a rhythm of contractions that come more often and last longer until you eat.

Problem-Solving Activity

The Lunch List

Suppose that you and a parent are trying to decide what to fix for lunch by using two spinners to select a menu. If you use these two spinners, lunch looks pretty good!

Design a spinner with your favorite lunch foods and a spinner with your favorite lunch drinks.

- Divide each spinner into 2, 3, 4, or 5 sections each.

- Make a list of all the possible lunch choices.

- Share your lunch menus with the class.

DID YOU

✓ design two spinners?

✓ make a list of lunch choices?

✓ share your lunch ideas with the class?

sandwich + milk
sandwich + juice
sandwich + fruit smoothie

pizza + milk
pizza + juice
pizza + fruit smoothie

bagel + milk
bagel + juice
bagel + fruit smoothi

Certain and Impossible

VOCABULARY

event
certain
impossible

Why learn this? You can decide what is certain and impossible when you pull marbles from a bag or spin the pointer on a spinner.

An **event** is something that happens.

An event is **certain** if it will always happen.

An event is **impossible** if it will never happen.

1. You will go to the moon today.
2. You will see a live dinosaur in your school yard.
3. The ground will get wet if it rains.
4. An ice cube is cold.
5. Dropping a brick on the floor will make a noise.

- In this list of events, which are certain? Which are impossible?

Talk About It CRITICAL THINKING

- Is it certain or impossible that you will pull a yellow marble from this bag?

- Are you certain to pull a blue or green marble? How do you know?

▶ CHECK

1. On this spinner, is it certain or impossible that you will spin red, blue, or yellow? spin green?

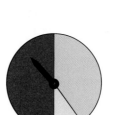

2. Is a spin of orange certain or impossible? Why?

Technology Link

In *Mighty Math Number Heroes*, the game *Probability* challenges you to choose certain and impossible events. Use Grow Slide Level A.

▶ PRACTICE

Read each event. Tell whether the event is *certain* or *impossible* to happen.

3. Touching a hot stove will burn you.

4. You will go to Mars tomorrow night.

5. pulling a purple or green marble from this bag

6. spinning yellow, orange, or green on this spinner

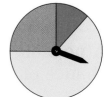

For Exercises 7–9, use the spinner. Tell if each event is certain or impossible.

7. spinning an odd number

8. spinning an even number

9. spinning a number greater than one

Problem Solving • Mixed Applications

10. Money Daniel has 2 quarters, 2 dimes, and 4 pennies. How much more money does he need to have 90¢?

11. Reasoning A spinner has the numbers 1 through 4. Is it certain or impossible that you will spin a number less than 6?

12. Collecting Data Sandy is going to do an experiment tossing two coins. How can she record what happens?

13. ✏ **Write About It** Think about your eating habits. List two events that are certain to happen tomorrow and two events that are impossible.

Mixed Review and Test Prep

Write the number. Tell whether it is *odd* or *even*. (pages 132–133)

14. 13　　**15.** 26　　**16.** 44　　**17.** 51　　**18.** 77　　**19.** 98

20. 17　　**21.** 31　　**22.** 58　　**23.** 67　　**24.** 84　　**25.** 93

Use patterns of hundreds or thousands. Choose the letter of the correct sum or difference. (pages 148–149)

26. $412 + 300$
  A 442
  B 430
  C 700
  D 712

27. $841 + 100$
  F 741
  G 941
  H 900
  J 951

28. $335 - 100$
  A 235
  B 325
  C 324
  D 435

Recording Possible Outcomes

| VOCABULARY |
| possible outcome |
| most likely |
| least likely |

Why learn this? You can see how events, such as spinning the pointer on a spinner, can have possible outcomes.

A **possible outcome** is something that has a chance of happening.

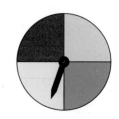

Lisa and Trevor are doing an experiment with this spinner. What are the possible outcomes of spinning the pointer on the spinner?

One way to record outcomes is by making a tally table. As Lisa and Trevor spin, they keep track of the color they spin each time.

Color	Tallies
Red	IIII
Yellow	卌I
Green	卌
Blue	III

An event is **most likely** to happen if it has a greater chance of happening than other events. An event is **least likely** to happen if it has a lesser chance of happening than other events.

Talk About It CRITICAL THINKING

- What are the possible outcomes of pulling a marble from this bag?

- What color marble are you most likely to pull from this bag? least likely?

▶ CHECK

1. What are the possible outcomes for this spinner?

2. Which color are you most likely to spin? least likely?

3. Make a table for recording the possible outcomes of tossing this counter.

► PRACTICE

List the possible outcomes of each event.

4. playing a board game with a friend

5. trying on a pair of shoes at the store

6. rolling a number cube

7. pulling a block from a box containing 2 yellow blocks and 5 purple blocks

Tell which outcome is *most likely* to happen.

8.

You spin the pointer on this spinner.

9.

You pull a marble from this bag.

10.

You spin the pointer on this spinner.

Problem Solving • Mixed Applications

11. **Reasoning** There were 28 students in Laura's class. During the year, 6 students left and 4 new students joined the class. How many students were in the class at the end of the year?

12. **Data Collection** Make a table for recording the possible outcomes of spinning the pointer on this spinner.

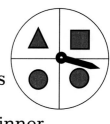

13. **Logic** The numbers on a six-section spinner are the even numbers less than 14. What are the numbers?

14. **Time** Lisa and Trevor began a spinner experiment at 1:30. They finished it 15 minutes later. At what time did they finish their experiment?

15. **Money** Larry gave the clerk a $1 bill. The clerk gave Larry 3 dimes and a nickel in change. How much change did Larry get? How much was his purchase?

16. ✏ **Write a problem** about the possible outcomes of this event. Andrew measured himself and his friend, Joe, and compared their heights.

LESSON CONTINUES

Problem–Solving Strategy: Make a List

REMEMBER:

UNDERSTAND

PLAN

SOLVE

LOOK BACK

▶ **THE PROBLEM** Tony and Anita are doing an experiment with two coins. They are tossing the coins 50 times and recording the outcome of each toss. They want to see if one outcome happens more often than the other possible outcomes.
What are the possible outcomes of tossing two coins?

UNDERSTAND

- What are you asked to find?
- What information will you use?
- Is there information you will not use? If so, what?

PLAN

- How will you solve the problem?

  You can *make a list* to find the possible outcomes of tossing two coins.

SOLVE

- How can you make a list of the possible outcomes?

  You know that the possible outcomes of tossing one coin are heads or tails. List the possible combinations for tossing two coins together.

Penny	Nickel	Outcomes
Coin 1	Coin 2	
Heads	Heads	H, H
Heads	Tails	H, T
Tails	Heads	T, H
Tails	Tails	T, T

LOOK BACK

- How can you decide if your answer makes sense?
- What other strategy can you use?

Make a list to solve.

1. Camille and Marty are doing an experiment. They are tossing a coin and pulling a marble from a bag. What are the possible outcomes of tossing a coin and pulling a marble from this bag?

2. In an experiment Michelle spins the pointer on each of two spinners. She records each outcome. What are the possible outcomes of spinning the pointer on these two spinners?

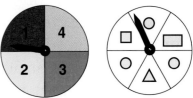

Mixed Applications

Solve.

CHOOSE a strategy and a tool.
- Find a Pattern • Make a Model • Make a List
- Act It Out • Use a Graph
- Write a Number Sentence

Paper/Pencil   Calculator   Hands-On   Mental Math

3. Holly spent 25 minutes making a spinner. She spent 10 minutes doing an experiment with it. She spent 12 minutes writing a report about what happened. How long did it take Holly to do everything?

4. In this marble experiment, what color marble was pulled most often? least often?

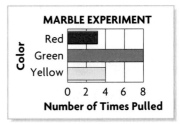

5. Find the next three numbers in the pattern: 101, 110, 119, 128, 137, _?_, _?_, _?_.

6. Lynn started reading at 2:00. She read for 45 minutes. After reading, she painted for 30 minutes. At what time did she finish?

7. Sabrina goes to soccer practice 3 times each week. How many times does she go to soccer practice in 6 weeks?

8. Candy is doing an experiment. She pulls a marble from each of two bags. What are the possible outcomes?

Recording Results of an Experiment

You will investigate how to record the results of an experiment.

▶ EXPLORE

Make one of these spinners. Decide which outcomes are most likely and least likely for that spinner. Spin the pointer on the spinner 20 times and record the results in a table. Then spin the pointer 50 times and record the results in another table.

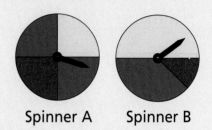

Spinner A   Spinner B

MATERIALS: 3- or 4-section spinners; a penny and a nickel; marbles, colored blocks, or colored tiles; brown paper bag

MODEL

Step 1

Choose a spinner. Then make a table. With your partner, decide which outcome you think will happen the most and which you think will happen the least. Record your guesses.

EXPERIMENT 1	
Color	Tallies
Blue	
Red	
Yellow	

Step 2

Spin 20 times. Each time, put a tally mark beside the color on which the pointer lands.

EXPERIMENT 1	
Color	Tallies
Blue	||
Red	|||
Yellow		

Repeat the experiment by making another table and spinning 50 times. Title the table *Experiment 2*.

Record

Compare the results of Experiment 1 with Experiment 2.

• Did your guess of the most likely outcome happen the most often?

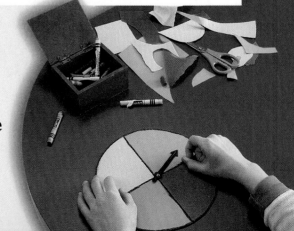

▶ TRY THIS

Outcome	Tallies
H, H	
H, T	
T, H	
T, T	

1. Toss two coins together 20 times. Record the results in a tally table.

2. In the coin experiment, was there an outcome that was the most likely to happen? least likely?

3. Suppose you tossed the coins 50 times. Would you expect the results to be different? Explain.

4. ▢ **Write About It** How was the spinner experiment like the coin experiment? How was it different?

▶ PRACTICE

Technology Link

You can experiment with spinners by using E-Lab, Activity 17. Available on CD-ROM and on the Internet at www.hbschool.com/elab

Set up an experiment for a classmate. Use marbles, colored blocks, or colored tiles. Choose ten objects in two or three different colors, and put them in a bag.

5. Make a table for recording. Ask a classmate to pull an object, record each pull, and replace it in the bag 20 times. Guess which color there is the most of in the bag. Repeat the experiment, pulling, recording, and replacing an object 50 times. Your classmate may change the guess.

6. Did your classmate correctly guess which color there was most of in the bag after 20 pulls?

7. Was the guess changed after 50 pulls? Why or why not?

Problem Solving • Mixed Applications

8. **Logic** Four friends are in line at the movies. Rafael is ahead of Erin. Paul is behind Erin. Rafael is behind Jeremy. Who is first in line?

9. **Time** Erin was at the movie theater 10 minutes before the movie started. The movie started at 6:30. At what time did Erin get there?

10. **Money** Paul bought a hat for $8.25. How much change did he get from $10.00?

11. **Mental Math** There are 7 rows of 8 cans on the shelf. How many cans are on the shelf?

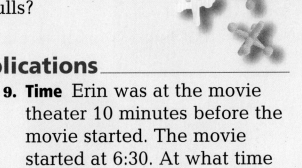

Fair or Unfair Games

Why learn this? You can choose a game to play that you know is fair.

A game is **fair** if every player has an equal chance to win. Students in Evelyn's class made math games. Evelyn made a spinner game in which three bicycles move around a path. Each time a color is spun, the bicycle of that color moves forward a space. Which spinner would make Evelyn's game fair?

Spinner A   Spinner B

Talk About It

• What makes the spinner fair?

• Why is the other spinner unfair?

In Greg's game, two players take turns pulling a marble from a bag to move their game piece. Which bag of marbles will make Greg's game fair?

Bag A   Bag B

Talk About It CRITICAL THINKING

• What makes one bag of marbles fair?

• Why is the other bag of marbles unfair?

▶ CHECK

1. Which of these spinners are fair? Why?

Spinner A   Spinner B   Spinner C   Spinner D

2. For each unfair spinner in Exercise 1, what are the most likely and least likely outcomes?

3. Which of these bags of marbles are fair?

| Bag A | Bag B | Bag C | Bag D |

4. For the unfair bags of marbles, what are the most likely and the least likely outcomes?

▶ PRACTICE

Choose the spinner or bag of marbles that is fair.
Write *A* or *B*.

5.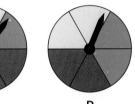

   A   B

6.

   A   B

7.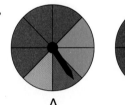

   A   B

8.

   A   B

Problem Solving • Mixed Applications

9. Logical Reasoning I am a number between 60 and 70. If you keep subtracting tens from me, you reach 2. What number am I?

10. ✏ **Write About It** Choose an unfair spinner or bag of marbles from above. Tell how to make it fair.

Mixed Review and Test Prep

Find the product. (pages 196–197)

11. $3 \times 0 = \underline{\ ?\ }$ **12.** $7 \times 1 = \underline{\ ?\ }$ **13.** $1 \times 9 = \underline{\ ?\ }$ **14.** $0 \times 5 = \underline{\ ?\ }$

Choose the letter that shows the value of the blue digit. (pages 144–145)

15. 144   **A** 4 ones   **16.** 279   **F** 7 ones   **17.** 836   **A** 8 ones
            B 4 hundreds   **G** 7 tens   **B** 8 hundreds
            C 4 tens   **H** 7 hundreds   **C** 8 tens
            D 4 thousands   **J** 7 thousands   **D** 8 thousands

▶ CHECK Understanding

VOCABULARY

1. An __?__ is something that happens. (page 296)

2. An event is __?__ if it will always happen and __?__ if it will never happen. (page 296)

3. A __?__ is something that has a chance of happening. (page 298)

4. A game is __?__ if every player has an equal chance to win. (page 304)

5. An event is __?__ to happen if it has a greater chance of happening than other events. It is __?__ to happen if it has a lesser chance of happening than other events. (page 298)

▶ CHECK Skills

For Exercises 6–10, use the spinner. (pages 296–299, 304–305)

6. What are the possible outcomes of spinning the pointer on this spinner?

7. Is it certain or impossible that you will spin blue?

8. Is it certain or impossible that you will spin red, orange, or yellow?

9. Are you most likely or least likely to spin yellow? Explain why.

10. Is the spinner fair? Explain.

▶ CHECK Problem Solving

Solve. (pages 300–301)

CHOOSE a strategy and a tool.
- Make a Model
- Make a List
- Act It Out
- Use a Table
- Work Backward

 Paper/Pencil   Calculator   Hands-On   Mental Math

11. Paul tosses a coin and spins the pointer on a spinner having blue, green, red, and yellow sections. What are the possible outcomes?

12. Some coins are arranged in a pattern of 1 quarter, 3 pennies. What type of coin is the tenth coin?

Test Prep

Choose the best answer.

1. This graph shows vacation places.

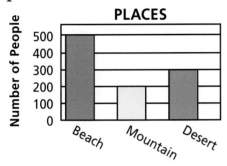

PLACES

How many more people go to a beach than go to a desert?

A 200   **B** 300
C 100   **D** 400

2. The elevator takes 6 seconds to move from one floor to the next. How many seconds does it take to go eight floors?

F 14 seconds   **G** 48 seconds
H 40 seconds   **J** 42 seconds

3. Look at this bar graph.

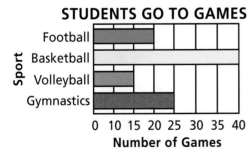

STUDENTS GO TO GAMES

Which sport have students been to the least?

A gymnastics   **B** football
C volleyball   **D** basketball

4. There are 20 children who want to play basketball. If the coach places 5 children on each team, how many teams will there be?

F 5   **G** 15   **H** 6   **J** 4

5. Amy goes to karate class 3 times each week. How many classes does she go to in 9 weeks? Choose the correct number sentence.

A $3 \times 7 = 21$ **B** $27 \div 9 = 3$
C $9 \times 3 = 27$ **D** $27 - 21 = 6$

6. Which is the most likely outcome?

F choosing red
G choosing blue
H choosing yellow
J choosing green

7. Three skyscrapers have heights of 550 feet, 620 feet, and 592 feet. Order the heights from shortest to tallest.

A 550 feet, 592 feet, 620 feet
B 620 feet, 592 feet, 550 feet
C 550 feet, 620 feet, 592 feet
D 620 feet, 550 feet, 592 feet

8. A spinner is red, blue, and orange. Which event is impossible?

F The spinner lands on blue.
G The spinner lands on red.
H The spinner lands on orange.
J The spinner lands on yellow.

MATH FUN!

ALL MIXED UP

PURPOSE To practice collecting data and organizing them into a table

Suppose you came into your school one day and the furniture in all the rooms was mixed up. Would you know what belongs in your classroom? Make a table of what is in your room. Show your results in a frequency table.

My Classroom
Desks
Chairs
Computers
Bookshelves

HOME NOTE Make a table of the items in your room at home. Ask a member of your family to make a table of the items in your room that are the most important. Compare your tables.

NOW YOU SEE IT

PURPOSE To practice predicting outcomes and recording results

YOU WILL NEED paper and pencil, small object

Hide a small object in one hand behind your back. Ask a partner to guess which hand it is in. Predict how many out of ten times your partner will guess correctly. Make a table to record your results. Is there a way to be sure to predict the correct hand? If you try ten more times, will your prediction be better? Try and see. Switch roles, play again, and compare your predictions.

MISSION IMPOSSIBLE

PURPOSE To better understand certain and impossible events

Work with a partner. Each of you writes as many certain or impossible events as you can. Give one point for each event. Now, switch papers with your partner and decide if you agree with his or her list. Put a *C* for certain or an *I* for impossible next to each event. Give one point for each correct answer.

Eat breakfast   C
Travel to Mars   I

Making a Table to Organize Data

MATERIALS
Graph Links Plus or any other graphing program

Carly spun the pointer on the spinner 30 times and recorded the outcomes in a tally table. When she was ready to change the data to a frequency table, she used a graphing program on the computer. After the data were entered in the table, she printed it. How many times did the pointer land on yellow?

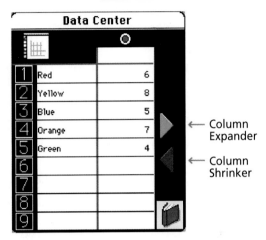

← Column Expander

← Column Shrinker

EXAMPLE

Computer graphing programs have a place to enter data in table form. *Graph Links Plus* has a Data Center for this. The Data Center has 9 rows and up to 5 columns for entering data. Click the Column Expander for more columns and the Column Shrinker to reduce the number of columns.

Data Center	Exp. 1	Exp. 2	Exp. 3	Exp. 4
Red	6	5	7	6
Yellow	8	5	8	5
Blue	5	6	6	7
Orange	7	9	4	7
Green	4	5	5	5

▶ PRACTICE

1. The tally table shows the results of Allen's marble experiment. Make a frequency table of the data.

TALLY TABLE	
Color	**Times Pulled**
Blue	ЖЖ I
Yellow	ЖЖ III
Orange	ЖЖ ЖЖ I

2. **Using the Computer** In Ronda's shell collection, there are 10 small and 15 large shells. Of the small shells, 6 are white and the rest are multi-colored. Of the large shells, 9 are white and the rest are multi-colored. Use a graphing program to organize the shell collection data in a table.

Study Guide and Review

Vocabulary Check

Choose a term from the box to complete the sentence.

1. You can organize data in a(n) _?_, using numbers to show how often something happens. (page 266)

2. A test done in order to find out something is a(n) _?_. (page 268)

3. The _?_ at the bottom of a pictograph tells how many each picture stands for. (page 280)

4. The _?_ of numbers on a bar graph helps you read what the lengths of the bars stand for. (page 284)

5. The bars on a(n) _?_ bar graph go across from left to right. (page 284)

6. A game is _?_ if each player has an equal chance at winning. (page 304)

Study and Solve

CHAPTER 15

EXAMPLE

FAVORITE SPORTS

Sport	Votes
Football	IIII III
Soccer	IIII
Basketball	IIII IIII
Baseball	IIII I
Golf	II

What question was asked in this survey? (What is your favorite sport?)

For Problems 7–10, use the survey results in the tally table in the example. (pages 272–273)

7. How many people answered the survey?

8. How many more people chose basketball than golf?

9. How many more people chose baseball than soccer?

10. What were the favorite sports in order from most votes to least votes?

11. In an experiment, you are rolling two number cubes numbered 1–6 to see what sums are rolled most often. Show how you could organize the results of your experiment. (pages 270–271)

CHAPTER 16

EXAMPLE

On what two days were 10 tickets sold?

CONCERT TICKETS SOLD

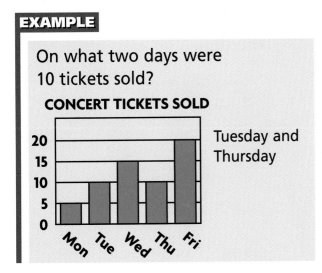

Tuesday and Thursday

For Problems 12–16, use the bar graph in the example. (pages 284–285)

12. On what day were the most concert tickets sold? the fewest?

13. How many tickets were sold on Wednesday?

14. How many more tickets were sold on Tuesday than on Monday?

15. On what day were 20 tickets sold?

16. How many tickets were sold in all?

CHAPTER 17

EXAMPLE

Which color are you least likely to spin? yellow

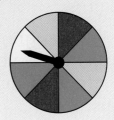

For Problems 17–20, use the spinner in the example. (pages 296–299, 304–305)

17. What are the possible outcomes of spinning the pointer on this spinner?

18. Is it certain or impossible that you will spin brown?

19. Are you most likely or least likely to spin green?

20. Is the spinner fair? Explain.

21. Tonya tosses two coins. What are all the possible outcomes? (pages 300–301)

22. Ron tossed 3 red-and-yellow counters. What are all the possible outcomes? (pages 300–301)

Performance Assessment

Tasks: Show What You Know

1. Draw 20 figures. Make some squares, some circles, and the rest triangles. Color some of the figures red, some green, and the rest blue. Make a table that shows how to group your figures. (pages 274–275)

2. Look at the bar graph on page 285. Explain how you would use the graph to answer these questions.

   • What scale is used on this graph?

   • How many students named sliding as their favorite activity? (pages 284–285)

3. Suppose you have a bag of yellow cubes. Describe each event as certain or impossible. Explain your choices. (pages 296–297)

   • pulling a green cube from the bag

   • pulling a yellow cube from the bag

Problem Solving

Solve. Explain your method.

CHOOSE a strategy and a tool.
• Use a Graph • Act It Out • Make a List
• Make a Table • Write a Number Sentence

 Paper/Pencil   Calculator   Hands-On   Mental Math

4. Becky flips both a nickel and a penny at the same time. She records whether they landed heads or tails. Show how Becky could record what happens. (pages 270–271)

5. Write 2 questions that can be answered by using the graph. Then answer the questions. (pages 290–291)

6. Leon rolled a number cube labeled with numbers 1 through 6. At the same time, he flipped a coin with heads and tails. List all the possible outcomes of this experiment. (pages 300–301)

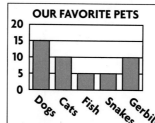

OUR FAVORITE PETS

20
15
10
5
0

Dogs Cats Fish Snakes Gerbils

Cumulative Review

Solve the problem. Then write the letter of the correct answer.

1. Round 35 to the nearest ten.

  A. 10   **B.** 30
  C. 40   **D.** 50

(pages 24–27)

2. What time is it?

  A. 35 minutes after 5
  B. 5 minutes after 7
  C. 7 minutes after 5
  D. 1 minute after 7

(pages 82–83)

3. Which shows the numbers in order from least to greatest?

  A. 377, 395, 412
  B. 377, 412, 395
  C. 395, 377, 412
  D. 412, 395, 377

(pages 168–169)

4. Round 408 to the nearest hundred. Use a number line to help you.

  A. 400   **B.** 410
  C. 500   **D.** 800

(pages 172–173)

5. $1 \times 9 = \underline{\ ?\ }$

  A. 0   **B.** 1
  C. 9   **D.** 19

(pages 214–215)

6. $\begin{array}{r} 8 \\ \times\ 7 \\ \hline \end{array}$

  A. 1
  B. 15
  C. 56
  D. 64

(pages 212–213)

7. $20 \div 4 = \underline{\ ?\ }$

  A. 3   **B.** 4
  C. 5   **D.** 80

(pages 250–251)

For Problems 8–10, use the bar graph.

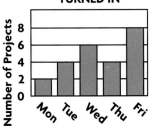

8. How many projects were turned in on Wednesday?

  A. 2 projects   **B.** 3 projects
  C. 4 projects   **D.** 6 projects

(pages 284–285)

9. On which day were the fewest projects turned in?

  A. Monday   **B.** Tuesday
  C. Thursday   **D.** Friday

10. On which day were the most projects turned in?

  A. Monday   **B.** Wednesday
  C. Thursday   **D.** Friday

18 CLASSIFYING PLANE AND SOLID FIGURES

SCIENCE LINK

In the 1880's, steel girders and concrete made it possible to build tall buildings called skyscrapers. The first skyscraper was built in Chicago.

Anytown, U.S.A.

Have you ever thought about the buildings in your town or city and what they are used for?

Use three-dimensional building blocks to make a building. As a class, put all the buildings together to make a model town. Use directions of north, south, east, and west to tell where your buildings are located.

YOU WILL NEED: crayons, scissors, tape, and nets of solid figures; one sheet of tagboard for the base

- Color, cut, and put together each net to make the solid figures.

- Put the figures together to design a building using tape or a glue stick.

- Write a paragraph telling what your building is used for, who uses it, and where it is in the model town.

DID YOU

☑ color, cut, and tape the nets?

☑ make a building from the figures?

☑ add your building to the class model?

☑ write a paragraph about your building?

Sorting and Comparing Solids

Why learn this? You can identify solid figures in objects such as buildings.

Solid figures are all around you. Each has a name.

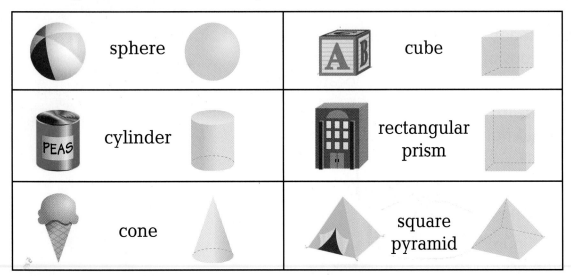

sphere		cube	
cylinder		rectangular prism	
cone		square pyramid	

Some solid figures have faces, edges, and corners.

A **face** is a flat surface of a solid figure.

An **edge** is a straight line where 2 faces meet.

A **corner** is where 2 or more edges meet.

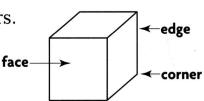

- How many faces does a cube have? how many edges? how many corners?

▶ CHECK

1. How many edges does a rectangular prism have? a sphere?

2. How many corners does a square pyramid have? a cylinder?

3. How are a sphere, a cylinder, and a cone alike? different?

Technology Link

In *Mighty Math Calculating Crew*, you can explore solid figures in *Dr. Gee's 3D Lab.* Use Grow Slide Levels B, H, and M.

4. Which of the solid figures on page 316 roll? Explain how they are different from each other.

▶ PRACTICE

Copy and complete the table.

	Figure	Faces	Edges	Corners
5.	Sphere	?	?	?
6.	Cube	?	?	?
7.	Cylinder	?	?	?
8.	Rectangular prism	?	?	?
9.	Cone	?	?	?
10.	Square pyramid	?	?	?

Name the solid figure that each looks like.

11.

12.

13.

14.

15.

16.

17.

18.

Problem Solving • Mixed Applications

19. Visual Thinking A figure has 1 face and no edges or corners. What solid figure is it?

20. ✏️ **Write About It** Explain how a cube and a rectangular prism are alike and different.

Mixed Review and Test Prep

Use patterns of tens to find the sum or difference. (pages 134–135)

21. $33 + 10 + 10$ **22.** $46 - 10 - 10$ **23.** $69 + 20$ **24.** $74 - 30$

Write the letter of the expanded form for each. (pages 144–145)

25. 245
  A $500 + 40 + 2$
  B $500 + 30 + 5$
  C $200 + 40 + 5$
  D $200 + 50 + 4$

26. 369
  F $300 + 60 + 9$
  G $300 + 90 + 6$
  H $900 + 90 + 3$
  J $600 + 90 + 3$

27. 506
  A $500 + 10 + 6$
  B $500 + 0 + 6$
  C $600 + 10 + 6$
  D $500 + 60 + 0$

Tracing and Naming Faces

You will investigate how to name the faces that make up solid figures.

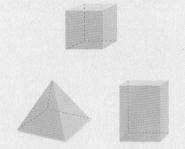

Most solid figures have one or more faces.

▶ EXPLORE

Trace the faces of several solid figures. Then name the faces that make up each solid figure.

MATERIALS: solid figures (cube, rectangular prism, square pyramid), paper, crayons, scissors, tape, variety of boxes and bags

MODEL

Step 1

On a large sheet of paper, make a chart like the one below. Take a square pyramid. Use a crayon to trace around one face at a time until you have traced all the faces. Do the same with the other solid figures.

Name of Figure	Faces
Square Pyramid	□ △ △ △ △
Cube	

Step 2

Make a table like the one below. Record the number of faces and the names of the faces for each figure.

Name of Figure	Names and Number of Faces
Square pyramid	1 square, 4 triangles
Cube	

Record

Do any of the solid figures that you traced have more than one kind of face? If so, which ones?

Now, investigate making a solid figure from its faces.

► TRY THIS

Cut out the faces, or shapes, that you traced from a cube, a rectangular prism, or a square pyramid. Tape the faces together to form the solid figure.

1. Was a sphere one of the solid figures you traced? Explain why or why not.

2. How is a cube different from a rectangular prism?

► PRACTICE

Take an object, such as a cereal box or a bag, that you can easily cut and flatten. Cut the object along the edges. Be careful *not* to cut into a face of the object. Cut only along the edges. After you finish cutting, flatten the object.

3. What is the name of each face of your object?

4. How many faces does the flattened shape have?

5. Can you refold your flattened object into its original shape?

Mixed Applications

6. **Reasoning** Laura has 5 quarters. Tracy has an equal amount in dimes and nickels. Tracy has 16 coins. How many dimes and nickels does she have?

7. **Number Sense** The quotient is 2 more than the divisor. The dividend is 15. What are the quotient and the divisor?

8. **Mental Math** Each package holds 6 rolls. If you buy 4 packages, how many rolls do you get?

Technology Link

You can identify solid figures by using E–Lab, Activity 18. Available on CD-ROM and on the Internet at www.hbschool.com/elab

MORE PRACTICE page H98

Matching Faces to Solids

Why learn this? You can visualize the shapes used to make sculptures.

Mrs. Cooke drew a square on the board. She asked the class to name solid figures that have at least one face that is a square.

Kevin named the cube and square pyramid.

- Do you agree with Kevin's answer? Explain why or why not.

Mrs. Cooke drew more shapes on the board. She asked the class to name solid figures that have at least one or more faces of each shape.

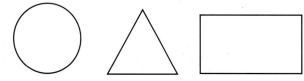

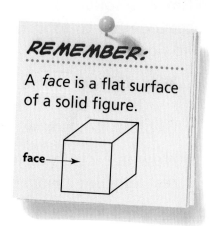

REMEMBER:

A *face* is a flat surface of a solid figure.

face →

Talk About It CRITICAL THINKING

- Which solid figure or figures have a circle as one or more of their faces?

- Which solid figure or figures have a triangle as one or more of their faces?

- Which solid figure or figures have a rectangle as one or more of their faces?

▶ CHECK

Write the name of the figure that answers each riddle.

1. I am a solid figure with no edges and 2 faces. My faces are circles. What am I?

2. I am a solid figure with 5 corners and 5 faces. Four of my faces are triangles. What am I?

3. I am a solid figure with 6 faces, 12 edges, and 8 corners. My faces are squares. What am I?

ART **LINK**

Sculptures are sometimes carved out of solid wooden cylinders made from tree trunks. Sometimes they are carved from rectangular or square blocks of stone. What figure can you see on the face of this sculpture?

Tell which solid figure has each set of faces.
Write *a*, *b*, or *c*.

4.

   a. rectangular prism
   b. cube
   c. square pyramid

5.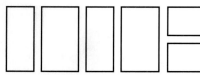

   a. cube
   b. rectangular prism
   c. square pyramid

6.

   a. cube
   b. square pyramid
   c. rectangular prism

Problem Solving • Mixed Applications

7. **Time** Cliff started playing a computer game at 4:30. He stopped playing 45 minutes later. What time was it?

8. **Measurement** One window is 5 panes wide and 7 panes long. How many panes make up the window?

9. **Elapsed Time** Larry looked at his watch at 1:30 and again at 2:45. How much time passed between the first and second times Larry looked at his watch?

10. ✏ **Write About It** Explain how you know a cube and a rectangular prism are different solid shapes.

Mixed Review and Test Prep

Find the sum. (pages 114–115)

11. $1.25
   + 2.63

12. $4.16
   + 3.01

13. $5.44
   + 4.20

14. $6.34
   + 0.35

Find the value of the blue digit. Write the letter of the correct answer. (pages 150–153)

15. 118,385
  A 8 ones
  B 8 tens
  C 8 hundreds
  D 8 ten thousands

16. 34,964
  F 4 hundreds
  G 4 thousands
  H 4 ten thousands
  J 4 hundred thousands

17. 93,642
  A 9 hundreds
  B 9 thousands
  C 9 ten thousands
  D 9 hundred thousands

Plane Figures

Why learn this? You can recognize the shapes of plane figures on flowers, sidewalks, and designs.

A **plane** is a flat surface that goes on and on. A sheet of paper is like part of a plane.

A **plane figure** is a closed figure in a plane. The figure on this sheet of paper is a plane figure.

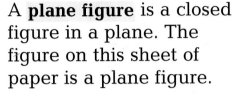

- What other things that are like planes can you name?

A plane figure is formed by lines that are curved, straight, or both.

These are plane figures.

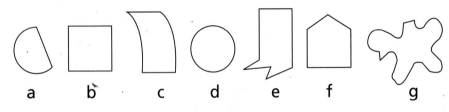

a   b   c   d   e   f   g

Talk About It CRITICAL THINKING
- Which of the figures above have all straight lines?

- How are plane figures different from solid figures?

REMEMBER:

A *closed figure* begins and ends at the same point.

▶ CHECK

Tell if each figure is formed by only straight lines, only curved lines, or both straight and curved lines.

1.   **2.**    **3.**   **4.**

Tell if each figure is formed by only straight lines, only curved lines, or both straight and curved lines.

5.

6.

7.

8.

9.

10.

11.

12.

Problem Solving • Mixed Applications

13. Time The hour hand points to 5. The minute hand points to 1. What time is it?

14. Measurement Carol is 45 inches tall. Ann is 8 inches taller. How tall is Ann?

15. Nancy has 12 crayons and Lenore has 8. Joe has 15 crayons and Jason has 10. How many more crayons do Joe and Jason have than Nancy and Lenore?

16. Number Sense Rebecca passed out 16 markers. She gave the same number of markers to each of 4 classmates. How many markers did each classmate get?

17. Money Brian spent $3.32 at the store. He gave the clerk $5.00. List the change he should get.

18. 🖉 **Write About It** Explain how you know the figure in Exercise 12 is a closed plane figure.

Mixed Review and Test Prep

Find the difference. (pages 114–115)

19. $1.74
    − 0.21

20. $5.92
    − 2.80

21. $8.34
    − 2.33

22. $10.00
    − 2.65

Use patterns of hundreds or thousands to find the sum or difference. Choose the letter of the correct answer. (pages 148–149)

23. $621 + 200$
  A 921
  B 800
  C 641
  D 821

24. $479 − 300$
  F 449
  G 179
  H 279
  J 476

25. $5,117 − 5,000$
  A 5,112
  B 617
  C 117
  D 1,117

Patterns with Plane Figures

Why learn this? You can find interesting patterns in clothing.

Mrs. Wright's class used pattern blocks to make patterns.

hexagon   rhombus   trapezoid   triangle

Stefan made this pattern.

- What two shapes come next?

_____

Cindy made a pattern with pattern blocks. Then she removed two of the blocks.

Talk About It

- What shapes are missing?

- How can you tell which two blocks were removed by Cindy?

CRITICAL THINKING   How is identifying the missing shapes different from looking for the shape that comes next?

REMEMBER:

To find a *shape pattern*, look for the place where the pattern repeats. Then you can easily tell what shape is missing.

▶ CHECK

1. Draw the next two shapes in this pattern.

2. Make a pattern with pattern blocks. Remove the last two blocks. Exchange patterns with a classmate and complete them.

▶ PRACTICE

Draw the next two shapes in each pattern.

3.
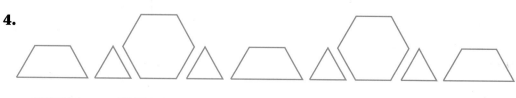

4.

5.
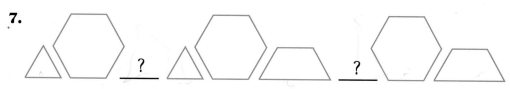

Tell what shapes are missing in each pattern.

6.

7.

8.

Problem Solving • Mixed Applications

9. Logic For a portrait, Lauren is between Dale and Roger. Sophie is on the right end. Dale is between Lauren and Anita. How are they arranged from left to right?

10. Reasoning Mel and Bob play a pattern game. Mel says 3, and Bob says 9. Mel says 4, and Bob says 12. Mel says 5, and Bob says 15. What does Bob say when Mel says 7? says 9?

11. ✏️ **Write About It** Explain to a first grader how to find the patterns in this lesson.

LESSON CONTINUES

Problem–Solving Strategy: Find a Pattern

▶ **THE PROBLEM** Marianne is a member of the Pueblo people. She is painting a design on a piece of pottery. Her design has a pattern. What will be the next 3 shapes in the pattern she is painting?

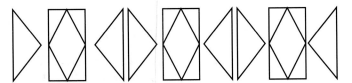

REMEMBER:

UNDERSTAND
PLAN
SOLVE
LOOK BACK

UNDERSTAND

- What are you asked to find?

- What information will you use?

- Is there information you will not use? If so, what?

PLAN

- How will you solve the problem?

  You can *find a pattern*.

SOLVE

- How can you find a pattern?

  Use the order of the shapes in the design to identify a pattern.

  The shapes of the design in order are triangle, rhombus inside a rectangle, and triangle.

  So, the next three shapes in the pattern are these.

Making a pattern

LOOK BACK

- How can you check your answer?

- What other strategy could you use?

326 Chapter 18

Find a pattern to solve.

1. Valerie is coloring a pattern around the border of a picture frame. What will be the next three shapes in her pattern?

2. Mrs. Becker is painting a border around her kitchen. What will be the next three shapes in the pattern?

3. Kenny sees a pattern in the set of numbers 4, 11, 18, 25, 32. He is going to write the next three numbers. What numbers will he write?

4. Ellen placed 1 card in the first row, 3 cards in the second row, 5 cards in the third row, and 7 cards in the fourth row. If she continues this pattern, how many cards will she place in the fifth row?

Mixed Applications

Solve.

CHOOSE a strategy and a tool.
- Act It Out
- Guess and Check
- Make a List
- Make a Model
- Find a Pattern

Paper/Pencil Calculator Hands-On Mental Math

5. David spent 6 more minutes on homework than Daniel. Together, they spent 36 minutes. How many minutes did each spend?

6. What are the possible outcomes of tossing a coin and pulling a marble from this bag?

7. Alex's birthday is in three weeks. Today is March 6. When is Alex's birthday?

8. A coin is tossed 100 times. It lands heads up 56 times. How many times does it land tails up?

9. Lisa put a border around the birthday card she was making. What will be the next three shapes in her pattern?

10. Create-It! craft store is having a sale on fabric paint. For every 3 tubes of paint you buy, you get 1 tube of paint free. You need 16 tubes of fabric paint. How many will be free?

▶ CHECK Understanding

VOCABULARY

1. A flat surface of a solid figure is a __?__ . (page 316)

2. The place where 2 or more edges of a solid figure meet is a __?__ . (page 316)

3. An __?__ of a solid figure is a straight line where 2 faces meet. (page 316)

4. A __?__ is a flat surface. A __?__ is a closed figure in a plane. (page 322)

Identify the solid figure. Write *a*, *b*, or *c*. (pages 316–317)

5.

6.

7.

a. cone

b. square pyramid

c. cube

▶ CHECK Skills

For Problems 8–10, use the figure at the right. (pages 316–317, 322–323)

8. Is the figure a solid or a plane figure?

9. Is it open or closed?

10. Is it formed by straight lines, curved lines, or both?

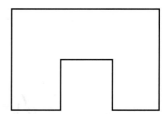

▶ CHECK Problem Solving

Solve. (pages 326–327)

CHOOSE a strategy and a tool.
- **Act It Out**
- **Find a Pattern**
- **Work Backward**
- **Guess and Check**

 Paper/Pencil   Calculator   Hands-On   Mental Math

11. Nicole is painting a pattern on a T-shirt. What will be the next three shapes in her pattern?

12. Stuart is going to write the next three numbers in the pattern 7, 14, 21, 28, 35. What numbers will he write?

13. The divisor is 7. The dividend is 28. What is the quotient?

14. Louis started working at 5:20. He worked for 30 minutes. What time did he finish?

Test Prep

Choose the best answer.

1. This bar graph shows concert tickets sold in part of one week.

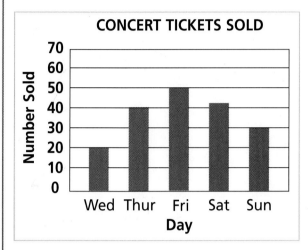

CONCERT TICKETS SOLD

On what day were the most tickets sold?

A Thursday **B** Friday
C Saturday **D** Sunday

2. Helen made a tally table of the class's favorite books.

FAVORITE BOOKS	
Book	Tallies
Danger Along the Ohio	ℍℍ ℍℍ I
Breath of the Dragon	ℍℍ ℍℍ ℍℍ
Spider Boy	ℍℍ ℍℍ III
Wild Horse Summer	ℍℍ III

How many children chose *Spider Boy*?

F 11 **G** 15 **H** 13 **J** 8

3. How many edges does the sphere have?

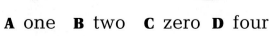

A one **B** two **C** zero **D** four

4. Six girls want to enter the track event. There are 6 lanes on the track field. How many girls will run in each lane?

F 36 **G** 1 **H** 0 **J** 6

5. Mr. Davis is buying cereal. The box weighs 32 ounces. How many 4-ounce servings are in that box?

A 28 **B** 16 **C** 8 **D** 6

6. There are 4 shelves in the closet. Sarah stores 8 games on each shelf. How many games does she store in the closet?

F 32 **G** 12 **H** 2 **J** 36

7. Barbara cut a pattern for a quilt.

What will be the next three shapes in her pattern?

A ○ □ △
B □ □ ◇
C □ ◇ ◇
D ◇ □ ◇

8. Look at the figure.

How many faces does the figure have?

F 2 **G** 6 **H** 4 **J** 8

Tangram puzzles were invented in China more than 4,000 years ago. Chinese storytellers arranged the seven pieces, called tans, to show a character or an object to illustrate a story.

Trade a Tangram

Make your own tangram puzzle. Use all seven pieces without overlapping.

YOU WILL NEED: two sets of paper tangrams, two envelopes to store puzzle pieces, scissors, one sheet of construction paper, one sheet of white paper, pencil, glue

- Cut out two tangrams, keeping the two sets in separate envelopes.

- Arrange the pieces of one tangram to make a design. Glue it onto construction paper. Cut out the tangram design.

- Trace the outline of your tangram design onto white copy paper.

- Trade puzzles with a classmate.

- Use your second set of tangram pieces to solve each other's puzzles.

barn   cat

rocket   goose

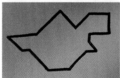

DID YOU

☑ cut out two tangrams?

☑ make a tangram puzzle and trace it?

☑ trade and solve tangram puzzles?

Line Segments and Angles

VOCABULARY
line
line segment
angle
right angle

Why learn this? You will be able to see line segments and angles in shapes around you.

A **line** is straight. It continues in both directions. It does not end. Arrows show a line continues.

A **line segment** is straight. It is the part of a line between two points, called endpoints.

Carlos uses craft sticks to make shapes. He says that the craft sticks are like line segments.

• How many line segments are in the triangle? in the square?

An **angle** is formed where two line segments cross or meet.

A **right angle** is a special angle. The corners of a sheet of paper are right angles.

• Use a corner of a paper to find right angles. Name three things in your classroom that have right angles.

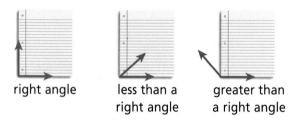

right angle — less than a right angle — greater than a right angle

Technology Link

In *Mighty Math Carnival Countdown*, the game *Pattern Block Roundup* challenges you to identify figures in a design. Use Grow Slide Level L.

▶ CHECK

1. How many angles does a triangle have? does a square have?

2. How are the angles different in the square and the triangle above?

3. What do you notice about the number of line segments and the number of angles in a figure?

Write the number of line segments in each figure.

4. 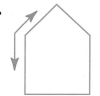 **5.**  **6.**   **7.**

Write the number of angles in each figure.

8.  **9.**   **10.**   **11.**

Write if each angle is a *right angle, less than* a right angle, or *greater than* a right angle. Use a corner of your paper to help you.

12.   **13.**   **14.**  **15.**

Problem Solving • Mixed Applications

16. Mrs. Lee picked 12 roses from her garden. She divided them equally among 4 vases. How many roses are in each vase?

17. ✏️ **Write About It** Choose a figure. Write about the number of line segments and angles in that figure.

Mixed Review and Test Prep

Choose a benchmark of 1,000 or 10,000 to estimate or count each number. (pages 154–155)

18. 2,643   **19.** 44,781   **20.** 6,386   **21.** 89,527

Choose the letter of the correct product. (pages 214–215)

22. $3 \times 9 = $ _?_   **A** 25   **23.** $6 \times 9 = $ _?_   **F** 54   **24.** $9 \times 5 = $ _?_   **A** 36
                  B 19   **G** 64   **B** 45
                  C 30   **H** 57   **C** 40
                  D 27   **J** 63   **D** 81

Locating Points on a Grid

VOCABULARY

grid

ordered pair

Why learn this? You can locate places on a map.

Josh and his family are at the zoo. They are using this map to help them find the animals. Josh wants to see the tigers first. How can you use this map to help Josh find the tigers?

Start at 0.
Move 4 spaces to the right.

• On what number are you?

Now, move 2 spaces up. The tigers are located at (4,2) on the map.

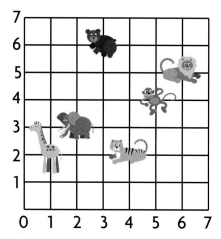

A **grid** is a map divided into equal squares.

An **ordered pair** of numbers names a point on a grid. The first number tells how many spaces to move to the right from zero. The second number tells how many spaces to move up. The ordered pair (4,2) means 4 spaces to the right and 2 spaces up.

CRITICAL THINKING Does (4,2) show the same place on the grid as (2,4)? Explain.

▶ CHECK

1. At which ordered pair are the elephants?

2. Which animals are at (5,4) on the grid?

3. At which ordered pair are the lions?

4. Look at the path from the giraffe at (1,2) to the tiger at (4,2). What is another name for this path between the two animals?

SCIENCE LINK

The San Diego Zoo has the largest collection of mammals, birds, and reptiles in North America. The zoo has about 4,240 animals. Which ordered pair shows where the zoo is located?

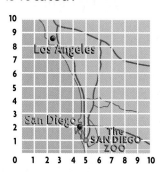

▶ PRACTICE

Use a grid. Make a map of the zoo. Use the ordered pairs below to place animals on your map. Record the first letter of the animal's name on the correct point.

5. (2,5) deer　　　**6.** (4,7) snake

7. (3,4) parrot　　**8.** (5,3) zebra

For Exercises 9–14, use the grid.
Write the ordered pair for each vegetable.

9. carrots　　　**10.** tomatoes

11. onions　　　**12.** green beans

13. peas　　　　**14.** cucumbers

Problem Solving • Mixed Applications

15. Reasoning Preston planted peas at (2,3) on a grid. Edgar planted corn at (2,5). What ordered pair names the point between the peas and corn?

16. Science Susan has 6 tomato plants. Each plant has 4 tomatoes on it. How many tomatoes does Susan have?

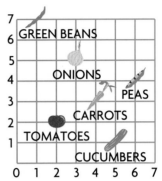

17. Visual Thinking Mrs. Meyer's garden is shaped like a rectangle. How many angles does the garden have? What kind of angles?

18. 🖉 **Write a problem** about the location of two animals at the zoo. Give the ordered pair for each animal.

Mixed Review and Test Prep

Write the fact family for each set of numbers. (pages 232–233)

19. 3, 6, 18　　　**20.** 4, 5, 20　　　**21.** 7, 5, 35

22. 6, 9, 54　　　**23.** 8, 7, 56　　　**24.** 4, 9, 36

Choose the letter that shows the expanded form for each. (pages 144–145)

25. 659　**A** 900 + 50 + 6
　　　　B 500 + 60 + 9
　　　　C 600 + 50 + 9
　　　　D 600 + 90 + 6

26. 854　**F** 800 + 50 + 4
　　　　G 500 + 60 + 4
　　　　H 800 + 40 + 5
　　　　J 400 + 50 + 8

Congruent Figures

Why learn this? You can find congruent figures around you.

Congruent figures have the same *size* and *shape*.
Figures that are turned can also be congruent.

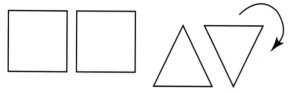

These pairs of figures are congruent.   These pairs of figures are not congruent.

You can tell if two figures are congruent by comparing the lengths of their line segments.

Trace and cut out rectangle A. Place it over rectangle B.

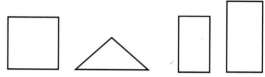

- Are all the line segments in rectangle A the same lengths as those in rectangle B?

So, rectangles A and B are congruent.

Trace and cut out triangle A. Place it over triangle B.

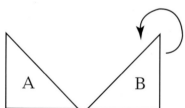

- What did you have to do to triangle A to match it to triangle B?

- Are the line segments in triangle A the same lengths as those in B?

So, triangles A and B are congruent.

▶ CHECK

1. What do you notice about the angles in the congruent triangles A and B?

2. Compare figures A and B.

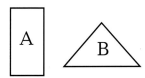

Are they congruent? Explain.

3. Compare figures C and D.

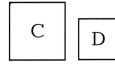

Are they congruent? Explain.

Tell whether the two figures are congruent. Write *yes* or *no*.

4.

5.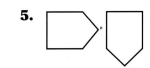

6.

Name each figure.

7. I am a figure with 4 sides, not all the same length, and 4 right angles. What am I?

8. I am a solid figure with 0 edges, 0 faces, and 0 corners. What am I?

Problem Solving • Mixed Applications

9. Time The minute hand on a clock shows 21 minutes after the hour. How many minutes after the hour will it show in 19 minutes?

10. Probability A spinner has the first six even numbers, beginning with 2. Is it certain or impossible that you will spin a number greater than 12?

11. Money Brian hands a clerk $2.00 for a book that costs $1.59. How much change should he get?

12. ✏️ **Write About It** Explain how you can tell if two figures are congruent.

Mixed Review and Test Prep

List the possible outcomes of each event. (pages 298–299)

13. flipping a coin

14. playing a game

15. rolling a number cube

Choose the letter that shows the value of the blue digit. (pages 150–153)

16. 25,793

A 7 ones
B 7 tens
C 7 hundreds
D 7 thousands

17. 78,026

F 8 hundreds
G 8 thousands
H 8 ten thousands
J 8 hundred thousands

18. 263,173

A 2 hundreds
B 2 thousands
C 2 ten thousands
D 2 hundred thousands

Using Congruent Figures

You will investigate how to use figures to make designs.

▶ EXPLORE

Use the pattern blocks to make a design on triangle dot paper.

MATERIALS: pattern blocks, crayons, triangle dot paper, white paper

MODEL

Step 1

Choose 1 or 2 pattern blocks. Spend a few minutes turning the blocks and putting them together. Plan a design you can make.

Step 2

On triangle dot paper, trace and turn the pattern blocks to make a design.

Make sure the blocks are next to each other without any spaces or overlapping.

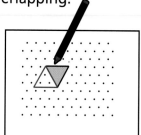

Record

After you have finished your design, count the number of pattern block figures in it. Record the numbers in a table like the one at the right. How many are there?

Block	Number of Congruent Figures
◆	?
▲	?

Talk About It

• Why are the same figures in the design congruent?

• How did you make a design from the pattern blocks?

▶ TRY THIS

1. Make another design with pattern blocks. This time, use blocks different from the ones you used in your first design. Again, trace the blocks on triangle dot paper and record the number of congruent figures in your design.

2. ▭ **Write About It** Do two figures have to be in the same position in order to be congruent? Explain.

▶ Technology Link

You can make congruent figures by using E–Lab, Activity 19. Available on CD-ROM and on the Internet at www.hbschool.com/elab

▶ PRACTICE

3. Trace and cut out figures A through D below. Then use each cutout figure to find the number of figures in the design that are congruent with that figure. Record your findings in a table.

A B C D

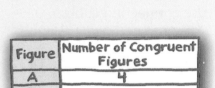

Figure	Number of Congruent Figures
A	4
B	

Problem Solving • Mixed Applications

4. **Logic** In the video game, Kate scored higher than Jay. Sue's score was between Jay's and Al's scores. Omar scored higher than Kate. Al scored the lowest. List the players in order from highest to lowest score.

5. Amanda's class is going on a field trip to the Science Center. There are 27 students in her class. If 3 students go with each parent, how many parents are needed for the field trip?

6. **Visual Thinking** Chantal drew a figure on the board. It had 4 right angles and 4 line segments all the same length. What figure did she draw?

7. **Time** Earl painted for 12 minutes more than Jack. Together, they painted for 58 minutes. How many minutes did each boy spend painting?

Congruent Solid Figures

You will investigate how to identify solid figures that are congruent.

You can use connecting cubes to build and find congruent figures.

► EXPLORE

MATERIALS: 30 connecting cubes

MODEL

Build these figures. Compare ways they are alike and ways they are different. **A.** **B.** **C.**
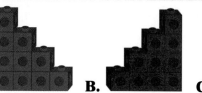

Step 1
Use connecting cubes.

Step 2
Build the bottom layer first.

Record
Explain how you used the connecting cubes to make the three figures.

Talk About It
- How are figures A, B, and C alike? How are they different?

- Which of the three figures are congruent? Explain.

▶ TRY THIS

Use connecting cubes. Make a figure that has at least three layers. Then make a second figure that is congruent to the first figure.

1.  **Write About It** Explain how you know that your figures are congruent.

▶ PRACTICE

For Exercises 2–4, use cubes to build each figure. Tell how many cubes make up each figure.

2.

3.

4.

5. Are the solid figures in Exercises 2 and 3 congruent? Explain why or why not.

Write the letter of the solid figure that is congruent with the first solid figure.

6.

A.

B.

Problem Solving • Mixed Applications

7. **Patterns** The numbers on the first three houses are 1517, 1519, and 1521. Troy lives in the fourth house. What is his house number?

8. **Money** Lana has four $1 bills, 8 dimes, 7 nickels, and 23 pennies. Does she have enough money to buy a new wallet for $5.16?

9. **Visual Thinking** I have 4 sides and 4 corners. My sides are not all the same length. What figure am I?

10. **Sports** Mark swam 27 laps last week. He swam 36 laps this week. How many laps did he swim?

LESSON CONTINUES ▶

Problem–Solving Strategy: Make a List

▶ **THE PROBLEM** Tara and Brett each made a solid figure with blocks. Are the two solid figures congruent?

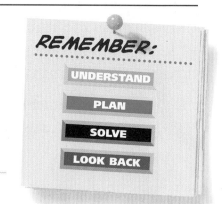

UNDERSTAND

• What are you asked to find?

• What information will you use?

• Is there information you will not use? If so, what?

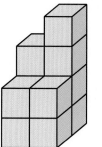 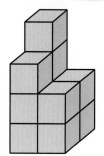

Tara's figure   Brett's figure

PLAN

• What strategy can you use to solve the problem?

You can *make a list* of the number of cubes in each layer. Then check if the figures match.

SOLVE

• How can you use the strategy to solve the problem?

You can make a list of the cubes in each layer.

Tara's figure	Brett's figure
Layer 1 — 4 cubes	Layer 1 — 4 cubes
Layer 2 — 4 cubes	Layer 2 — 4 cubes
Layer 3 — 2 cubes	Layer 3 — 2 cubes
Layer 4 — 1 cube	Layer 4 — 1 cube

$4 + 4 + 2 + 1 = 11$ cubes $4 + 4 + 2 + 1 = 11$ cubes

So, the two figures are congruent because they have the same number of cubes and have the same shape.

LOOK BACK

• How else could you solve this problem?

Make a list to solve.

1. These solid figures were made with connecting cubes. Are the two solid figures congruent? Explain why or why not.

2. Kyle built a solid figure with connecting cubes. There are 6 cubes in the first layer, 1 cube in the second layer, and 1 cube in the third layer. Could the solid figure below be the one Kyle made? Explain.

Mixed Applications

Solve.

CHOOSE a strategy and a tool.
- **Guess and Check**
- **Write a Number Sentence**
- **Draw a Picture**
- **Make a List**

Paper/Pencil   Calculator   Hands-On   Mental Math

3. What are the possible outcomes of tossing a coin and spinning the pointer on this spinner?

4. Su Yen's group has 36 pencils to share. Including Su Yen, there are 4 members in the group. How many pencils will each member receive?

5. Ed watched television for 1 hour and 30 minutes. He started watching at 3:45. At what time did he stop watching television?

6. The art teacher gave 28 jars of paint to the class. She gave 4 jars to each group working on the mural. How many groups are working on the mural?

7. Anton's solid figure had 5 cubes in the first layer, 2 in the second layer, and 1 in the third layer. Did Anton make the figure at the right? Explain why or why not.

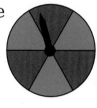

8. Jean bought a box of crayons for $2.49. She paid with $3.00. How much change did she receive?

▶ CHECK Understanding

VOCABULARY

1. An __?__ is formed where two line segments meet. (page 332)

2. An __?__ of numbers names a point on a grid. (page 334)

3. A __?__ is straight and does not end. (page 332)

4. A __?__ is straight and is the part of a line between two endpoints. (page 332)

5. A __?__ is a map divided in equal squares. (page 334)

6. Since these two circles are the same size and the same shape, they are __?__. (page 336)

▶ CHECK Skills

For Exercises 7–9, use the figure at the right. (pages 332–333, 336–337)

7. How many line segments are in the figure? How many angles?

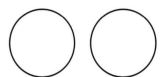

8. Is the angle shown on the figure a *right angle*, *less than* a right angle, or *greater than* a right angle?

9. Is this figure congruent with the figure above? Explain why or why not.

▶ CHECK Problem Solving

Solve. (pages 342–343)

CHOOSE a strategy and a tool.

- **Make a List**
- **Write a Number Sentence**
- **Draw a Picture**
- **Make a Model**

Paper/Pencil   Calculator   Hands-On   Mental Math

10. Are these two solid figures congruent? Explain why or why not.

11. Ellen handed the clerk $4.00 for a box of markers that cost $3.68. How much change should Ellen get?

Test Prep

Choose the best answer.

1. Emanuel is cutting paper shapes.

What shape is missing in his pattern?

A △ **B** (trapezoid)

C ◇ **D** □

2. Look at this figure.

What fact tells about it?

F It is formed only by straight lines.

G It is formed only by curved lines.

H It is formed by straight and curved lines.

J It is not a plane figure.

3. This table shows the number of people at a restaurant.

PEOPLE SERVED	
Table	**Tallies**
Table 1	⊮⊮ II
Table 2	⊮⊮ ⊮⊮
Table 3	⊮⊮ ⊮⊮
Table 4	⊮⊮

How many people were served in all?

A 24 **B** 30 **C** 32 **D** 26

4. Jason made a shape with sticks.

How many angles does his shape have?

F 4 **G** 3 **H** 5 **J** 6

5. Carol and Ken made a grid of the flowers they planted.

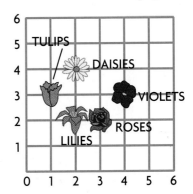

What is the ordered pair for the violets?

A (2,3) **B** (4,3) **C** (3,2) **D** (2,4)

6. Which multiplication fact can you use to find the quotient for $36 \div 9 = \underline{\ ?\ }$

F $36 \div 1 = 36$

G $36 \times 0 = 0$

H $3 \times 9 = 27$

J $4 \times 9 = 36$

7. How many line segments are in this figure?

A 3 **B** 4 **C** 5 **D** 8

20 MOVING PLANE FIGURES

Repeated patterns of basic shapes
are part of America's art history.
Native American pottery, baskets,
blankets, and beadwork show
geometric designs. Pioneer
quilts display geometric
designs in their patterns.

Decorate with Designs

Choose an object to decorate with a patterned border: a picture frame, a place mat, a book jacket, or a special award!

YOU WILL NEED: scissors, sponges, grid paper, stamp pads or paint, object to decorate

Plan a design that uses a pattern of one or two simple figures.

- Choose two colors for your design.

- Try out some ideas on paper, and choose one.

- Make a stamp out of a sponge. You will need as many stamps as there are figures and colors in your design.

- Stamp your pattern to decorate an object.

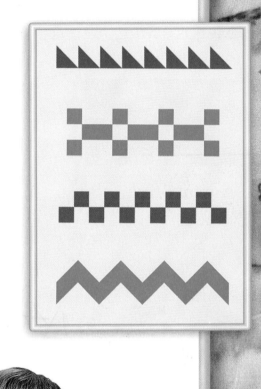

DID YOU

☑ plan a design, using figures and two colors?

☑ make a stamp for each color?

☑ decorate an object?

Sliding, Flipping, and Turning

VOCABULARY
slide
flip
turn

Why learn this? You will be able to recognize these motions in actions and in designs you see.

Objects can be moved in different ways.

Meg is *sliding* a book across the table.

Jon is *flipping* a pancake.

Amanda is *turning* a puzzle piece.

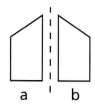

A plane figure can be moved in three ways.

You can **slide** it.

You can **flip** it.

You can **turn** it.

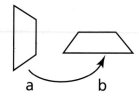

Talk About It CRITICAL THINKING

- When you slide a plane figure, does its size or shape change? How do you know?

- When you flip or turn a plane figure, does its size or shape change? Explain.

▶ CHECK

Look at Figures *a* and *b*.

Technology Link

In *Mighty Math Number Heroes*, the game *GeoComputer* shows you how to slide, flip, and turn different plane figures. Use Grow Slide Levels F and N.

1. What kind of motion was used to change Figure *a* to Figure *b*?

2. Is Figure *b* congruent with Figure *a*? Explain.

3. Trace this triangle and cut it out. Trace the cutout triangle onto a sheet of paper. Then move the cutout triangle and trace it again as **a.** a slide. **b.** a flip. **c.** a turn.

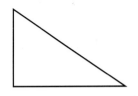

▶ PRACTICE

Tell what kind of motion was used to move each plane figure. Write *slide, flip,* or *turn.*

4.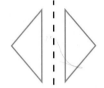

5.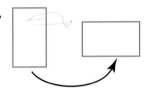

6.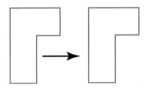

7.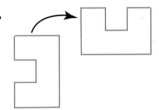

8.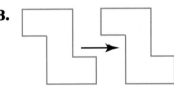

9.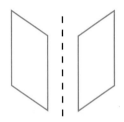

Problem Solving • Mixed Applications

10. Time David was 10 minutes late for karate class. The class began at 6:15. At what time did David arrive?

11. Visual Thinking Akiko used triangles and squares to make a pattern for a border. Draw a pattern Akiko could use.

12. Patterns Write the next three numbers in the pattern 202, 215, 228, 241, 254, __?__, __?__, __?__.

13. ▭ **Write About It** What motion or motions do you see in this figure?

starting point
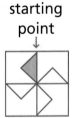

Mixed Review and Test Prep

Copy and complete the table. (pages 208–211)

14.

×	1	2	3	4	5	6	7	8	9
7	?	?	?	?	?	?	?	?	?

Choose the letter that shows the number of line segments. (pages 332–333)

15.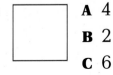
A 4
B 2
C 6
D 8

16.
F 2
G 3
H 4
J 5

17.
A 5
B 6
C 4
D 3

18.
F 4
G 3
H 5
J 6

Symmetry

You will investigate making plane figures that have a line of symmetry.

▶ EXPLORE

Make a figure that has a line of symmetry.
A **line of symmetry** is an imaginary line that
divides a figure in half. If you fold a figure
along a line of symmetry, both sides match.

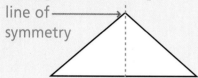
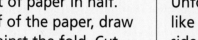

MATERIALS: paper, scissors, crayons, grid paper

MODEL

Step 1	Step 2
Fold a sheet of paper in half. On one half of the paper, draw a figure against the fold. Cut it out.	Unfold the figure. One side is like a mirror image of the other side. The right side is a flip over the fold of the other side.

Record

Draw the line of symmetry. Is the left half of
your figure congruent with the right half?
Explain how you know.

▶ TRY THIS

1. Fold a sheet of grid paper in half.
   Copy the figure at the right,
   or make one of your own.
   Then complete it so that
   when you unfold the
   paper, the figure has
   a line of symmetry.

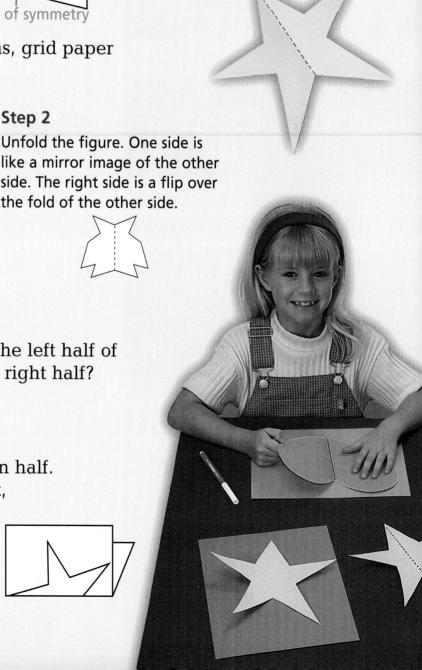

2. How do you know your figure has a line of symmetry?

3. Is the left half of your figure congruent with the right half? How do you know?

▶ PRACTICE

4. Find a picture in a newspaper or magazine that has a line of symmetry. Cut out the picture, and paste it onto a sheet of notebook paper. Draw and label the line of symmetry.

5. How do you know your picture has a line of symmetry?

6. Are the two halves of your picture congruent with each other? Explain.

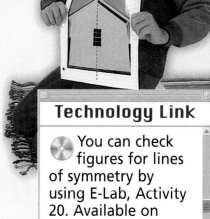

Technology Link

You can check figures for lines of symmetry by using E-Lab, Activity 20. Available on CD-ROM and on the Internet at www.hbschool.com/elab

Is the blue line a line of symmetry? Write *yes* or *no*.

7.

8.

9.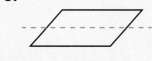

Problem Solving • Mixed Applications

10. **Calendar** On June 21, Erin came home from 6 days at the beach. Before that, she had spent 1 week at her grandparents' house. On what date did Erin go to see her grandparents?

11. **Logic** In a game, Brian scored 32 more points than Carl. Carl scored 15 fewer points than Ethan. Ethan scored 24 points. How many points did Brian and Carl each score?

12. There were 28 books on the New Arrivals shelf. Students checked out 9 of the books. How many books were left?

13. Sarah shared a package of 30 crackers with 4 friends. How many crackers did each person get?

14. ◁▷ **Write About It** Make a list of objects that have a line of symmetry.

More About Symmetry

Why learn this? You will be able to recognize symmetry in nature, in art, and in common objects and symbols.

Plane figures may have one or more lines of symmetry.

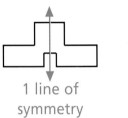
1 line of symmetry

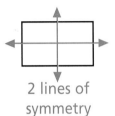
2 lines of symmetry

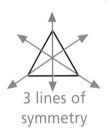
3 lines of symmetry

Many objects in nature have symmetry.

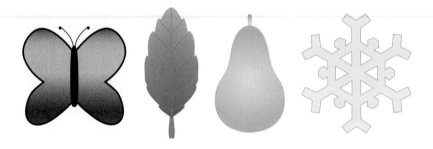

- Find the line or lines of symmetry in each object above.

Some letters and numbers have symmetry, too.

 M 3

A E H M 8 3

- Which letters or numbers above have more than one line of symmetry? Why?

ART LINK

Artists who work with stained glass often make colorful symmetrical designs. How many lines of symmetry can you find in this stained glass design?

▶ CHECK

Is the blue line a line of symmetry? Write *yes* or *no*.

1.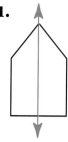

2.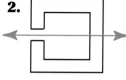

3.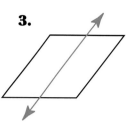

▶ PRACTICE

Is the blue line a line of symmetry? Write *yes* or *no*.

4.

5.

6.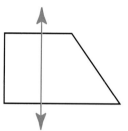

Trace each figure. Draw the line or lines of symmetry. How many lines of symmetry does each figure have?

7.

8.

9.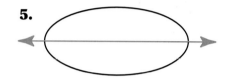

Problem Solving • Mixed Applications

10. Compare Stacy got a 79 on her math test last week. This week, she got a 92. How much higher was her score this week?

11. ▱ **Write About It** Draw a plane figure with one or more lines of symmetry. Label the lines of symmetry.

Mixed Review and Test Prep

Choose the missing factor for each number sentence. (pages 230–231)

12. $4 \times \underline{\ ?\ } = 20$

13. $\underline{\ ?\ } \times 6 = 36$

14. $8 \times \underline{\ ?\ } = 72$

Choose the letter that shows the number of angles. (pages 332–333)

15.
  A 2
  B 6
  C 8
  D 3

16.
  F 2
  G 3
  H 4
  J 5

17.
  A 4
  B 7
  C 3
  D 6

MORE PRACTICE page H102

Symmetric Patterns

Why learn this? You will see how symmetric designs are like a flip, or a mirror image.

Symmetry is like a mirror image. If you place half of a symmetric figure or pattern against a mirror along its line of symmetry, the reflection shows the other half, so that you see the whole figure or pattern.

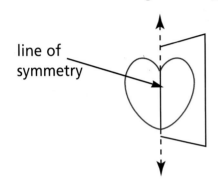

line of symmetry

- What would you see if you placed each of these figures against a mirror along the figure's line of symmetry?

 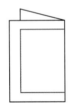   

You can use dot paper to complete the other half of a symmetric figure.

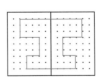

▶ CHECK

Trace and complete each drawing to make a symmetric figure.

 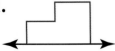 **1.**

 **2.**

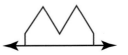 **3.**

 **4.**

▶ PRACTICE

Trace and complete each drawing to make a symmetric figure.

5. 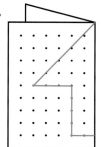 **6.** 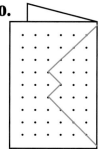 **7.** 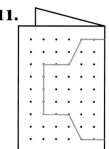 **8.**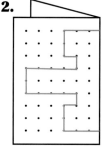

For each figure, fold a sheet of dot paper in half and copy the figure. Then unfold the paper and draw the other half to make a symmetric figure.

9. **10.** **11.** **12.**

Problem Solving • Mixed Applications

13. Estimation Cathy's family is taking a 700-mile trip by car. They have already traveled 482 miles. About how many more miles do they have to travel?

14. Mental Math Meg, her sister, and her brother are doing chores at home. They each have 4 chores to do. How many chores do they have to do in all?

15. Time Perry's school begins at 8:15. Lunch is served 3 hours and 45 minutes later. At what time is lunch served?

16. Visual Thinking Draw the next two figures in the pattern.

17. Logical Reasoning There were 17 dogs in a pet shop. During the month, 12 of the dogs were sold. There were 8 new dogs brought to the pet shop. How many dogs were in the pet shop at the end of the month?

18. Time After a power failure, the clock reads 10:15. It should read 2:30. For how long was the power off?

19. ✎ Write About It Draw half of a figure on dot paper. Exchange with a classmate. Complete the other half of each other's figures to make symmetric figures.

Problem–Solving Strategy: Draw a Picture

▶ **THE PROBLEM** Cheryl made a design with pattern blocks. She told Scott that it was only half of the picture, and challenged him to draw the other half. How will the picture look when Scott completes it?

REMEMBER:
UNDERSTAND
PLAN
SOLVE
LOOK BACK

UNDERSTAND

• What are you asked to find?

• What information will you use?

• Is there information you will not use? If so, what?

PLAN

• What strategy can you use?

You can *draw a picture* to show how the complete picture will look.

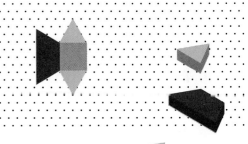

SOLVE

• How can you solve the problem?

You can complete Cheryl's picture.

Get triangle dot paper and pattern blocks.

Find the pattern blocks that Cheryl used, and trace them on the paper.

Then place another set of the same blocks across from the first set, in opposite positions.

You will see the completed picture.

Trace the blocks and label the lines of symmetry.

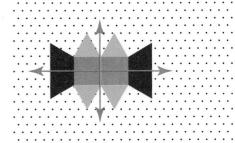

LOOK BACK

• How can you decide if your answer makes sense?

• What other strategy could you use?

▶ PRACTICE

Draw a picture to solve.

1. Alec made this design with pattern blocks. Gena matched it to make the other half. How did the design look when Gena completed it?

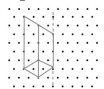

2. Carol is sitting next to Randy. Jay is between Carol and Pam. Martha is beside Randy. Pam is at the far right. From left to right, in what order are they sitting?

3. Elaine lives several houses from the corner. She went for a walk around the square block. How many right-hand turns did she make before she was back where she started from?

4. Hunter covered a wall with 1-foot mirror squares. The wall is 6 feet wide and 7 feet high. How many 1-foot squares did he use?

Mixed Applications

Solve.

CHOOSE a strategy and a tool.	
• Draw a Picture • Act It Out • Find a Pattern • Make a Model • Guess and Check	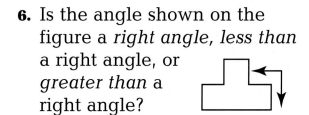 Paper/Pencil Calculator Hands-On Mental Math

5. There are 10 people in a line. Bob is at the front of the line. There are 4 people between Bob and Almir. What is Almir's position in line?

6. Is the angle shown on the figure a *right angle, less than* a right angle, or *greater than* a right angle?

7. Michelle drew a design. Tony matched it to make the other half. How does the complete design look?

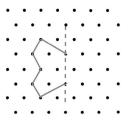

8. Amy spent $4 more at the fair than Tasha. Together, they spent $22. How much did each girl spend?

MORE PRACTICE ⋯⋯ page H103

► CHECK Understanding

VOCABULARY

1. An imaginary line that divides a figure in half is a __?__ . (page 350)

2. __?__ is like a mirror image. (page 354)

Tell what kind of motion was used to move each plane figure. Write *slide, flip,* or *turn.* (pages 348–349)

3.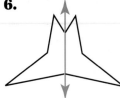

4.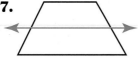

5.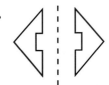

► CHECK Skills

Is the blue line a line of symmetry? Write *yes* or *no.* (pages 352–353)

6.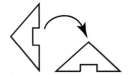

7.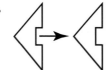

Trace the figure. Draw the line or lines of symmetry. How many lines of symmetry does the figure have? (pages 352–353)

8.

► CHECK Problem Solving

Solve. (pages 356–357)

CHOOSE a strategy and a tool.
- Draw a Picture • Make a Model • Act It Out
- Find a Pattern • Use a Graph

Paper/Pencil   Calculator   Hands-On   Mental Math

9. A remote-control car costs $9.58. Jamal has one $5 bill, two $1 bills, seven quarters, and six nickels. How much more money does he need?

10. Nick divided his collection of 27 stamps into 3 groups. How many stamps did he put into each group?

11. Copy and complete the other half of this picture to the right. Label the line or lines of symmetry.

Test Prep

Choose the best answer.

1. This table shows the birthday months of third-grade students.

THIRD-GRADE BIRTHDAYS	
Month	**Students**
Jan, Feb, Mar	4
Apr, May, Jun	7
Jul, Aug, Sep	6
Oct, Nov, Dec	5

How many students are in the third grade?

A 22   **B** 13

C 7   **D** 4

2. These two figures are congruent. Which of the following is *not* true?

F One is upside down.

G Both are the same size and shape.

H Both are triangles.

J One is larger.

3. Look at how this plane figure was moved.

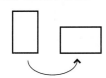

What kind of motion was used to move it?

A slide   **B** flip

C turn   **D** line of symmetry

4. The town planted trees, using a grid.

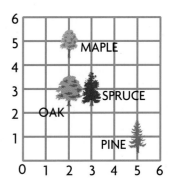

At which ordered pair are the spruce trees?

F (5,2)   **G** (2,3)

H (3,3)   **J** (2,5)

5. What is the other half of this symmetric figure?

A ⊖   **B** ⊏⊐

C ⊽   **D** ▱

6. Daniel has 3 quarters, 2 dimes, and 8 pennies. How much more money does he need to have $1.25?

F $1.03   **G** $1.25

H $0.25   **J** $0.22

7. Sam put 45 snowballs into 5 piles. Then 16 of the snowballs melted. Which shows how many snowballs are left?

A $45 \div 5 = \underline{}$

B $45 + 16 = \underline{}$

C $16 - 5 = \underline{}$

D $45 - 16 = \underline{}$

MATH FUN!

TREASURE LINE HUNT

PURPOSE To be able to recognize line segments and angles

YOU WILL NEED paper and pencil, a way to time 3 minutes

Play a game with a small group. Set the timer for 3 minutes. Each of you hunts near you for things that have line segments and angles. Draw the outside of each

shape, showing the segments and angles. Switch papers and see if you can identify items from the drawings. You get one point for each correct answer.

HOME NOTE Play this game at home with your family. Are they as good as you are at identifying things around your house?

WHAT IS IT?

PURPOSE To practice locating points on a grid

Copy the grid on a piece of paper. Locate the points on the grid. Connect the lines as you find the points. When you are finished, you should find something you might see in the spring. Color it and add the missing parts.

GRID POINTS

(3,0)	(3,6)
(3,2)	(4,5)
(2,3)	(5,6)
(1,4)	(5,4)
(1,6)	(4,3)
(2,5)	(3,2)

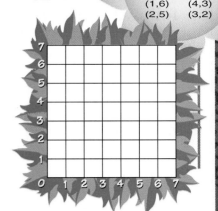

TANGRAM IT

PURPOSE To practice recognizing congruent figures

YOU WILL NEED paper and pencil, set of tangrams

Make figures with the tangrams. Which pieces are congruent? How many figures can you make using two congruent pieces? Is there

another pair of congruent pieces you can use to make more figures? Are these figures different from or the same as the first ones? Draw them and compare them with your classmates' drawings.

Congruence: Slides, Flips and Turns

Carey is creating a page border for the school newsletter. Using a drawing program on the computer, she is designing a border for the page. Carey created shapes for the border. What color is the shape that shows a slide? a flip? a turn?

MATERIALS
ALDUS® SuperPaint® or any other drawing program

EXAMPLE

Carey's drawing progam has a **Transform** menu that lets her flip and turn shapes.

She makes a shape and clicks on it to select it. Then she copies and pastes the shape using the **Edit** menu.

> To *flip* the shape, she chooses Flip Horizontal or Flip Vertical from the **Transform** menu.

> To *turn* the shape she chooses Rotate Left or Rotate Right from the **Transform** menu.

> She *slides* each shape by clicking on and dragging it to place it in her design.

Transform

Transform
Scale Selection . . .
Rotate Selection . . .
Flip Horizontal
Flip Vertical
Rotate Left
Rotate Right

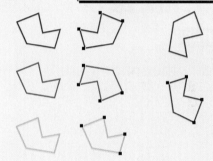

▶ PRACTICE

1. Draw each shape showing a flip, a turn, and a slide.

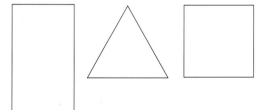

2. **Using the Computer** Use a computer drawing program to design a greeting card for a classmate or relative using only 3 shapes. Make the shapes look different by flipping, turning, and sliding them.

Study Guide and Review

Vocabulary Check

Choose a term from the box to complete the sentence.

VOCABULARY
angle
face
line of symmetry
line segment
plane

1. A flat surface of a solid figure is a(n) __?__.
   (page 316)

2. A flat surface that goes on and on is a(n) __?__.
   (page 322)

3. A(n) __?__ is formed where two line segments cross or meet. (page 332)

4. A(n) __?__ is straight and is the part of a line between two endpoints. (page 332)

5. An imaginary line that divides a figure in half is a(n) __?__. (page 350)

Study and Solve

CHAPTER 18

EXAMPLE

Identify the solid figure.

cone

For Problems 6–9, identify the solid figure. Write *a*, *b*, *c*, or *d*. (pages 316–317)

    a. cube   b. cylinder
    c. sphere   d. square pyramid

6.

7.

8.

9.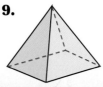

For Problems 10–13, use the figure.
(pages 316–319, 322–323)

Raisins

10. Is the figure a solid figure or a plane figure?

11. How many faces does it have?

12. How many edges does it have?

13. How many corners does it have?

For Problems 14–15, use the figure.
(pages 322–323)

14. Is the figure a solid figure or a plane figure?

15. Is the figure formed by straight lines, curved lines, or both?

CHAPTER 19

EXAMPLE

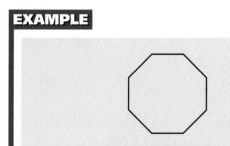

How many line segments are in the figure? 8 line segments

For Problems 16–17, use the figure.
(pages 332–333)

16. How many line segments are in the figure?

17. How many angles are in the figure?

18. Is the angle shown a *right angle, less than* a right angle, or *greater than* a right angle?
(pages 332–333)

19. Are these two solid shapes congruent? Why or why not?
(pages 342–343)

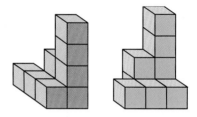

CHAPTER 20

EXAMPLE

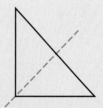

How many lines of symmetry does the figure have? 1 line

20. How many lines of symmetry does the figure have?
(pages 352–353)

Performance Assessment

Tasks: Show What You Know

1. Use 12 pattern blocks in three or four different shapes to show a pattern. Record your pattern on paper and then extend the pattern by drawing the next three shapes in the pattern. Describe the repeating part of your pattern and explain how it repeats. (pages 324–327)

2. Draw two figures on grid paper that are congruent. Explain how you know they are congruent. (pages 336–337)

3. Write your first and last name with all capital letters. Tell which letters have lines of symmetry. Draw the lines of symmetry. Explain how you know the letters have lines of symmetry. (pages 352–353)

Problem Solving

Solve. Explain your method.

CHOOSE a strategy and a tool.
- Find a Pattern
- Make a Table
- Act It Out
- Draw a Picture
- Make a List
- Make a Model

Paper/Pencil   Calculator   Hands-On   Mental Math

4. Draw the missing shapes in the following pattern. (pages 326–327)

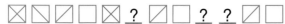

5. Are these two solid shapes congruent? Explain why or why not. (pages 356–357)

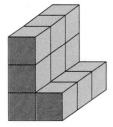 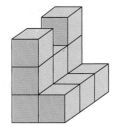

6. Half of this figure is missing. Draw the whole figure on dot paper. (pages 356–357)

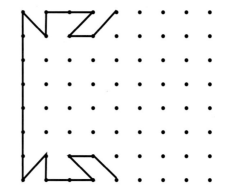

Cumulative Review

Solve the problem. Then write the letter of the correct answer.

1. 59
       +44

A. 15
B. 93
C. 102
D. 103

(pages 22–23)

2. Find the ending time.
starting time: 5:30 elapsed time: 2 hr 15 min

A. 6:45   B. 7:15
C. 7:30   D. 7:45

(pages 90–91)

3. Write the value of the blue digit.

84,230

A. 8   B. 800
C. 8,000   D. 80,000

(pages 144–145, 150–153)

4. The answer to a multiplication problem is the __?__.

A. divisor   B. factor
C. product   D. quotient

(pages 188–189)

5. $32 \div 8 =$ __?__

A. 3   B. 4
C. 6   D. 24

(pages 250–251)

6. $54 \div 9 =$ __?__

A. 6   B. 7
C. 8   D. 9

(pages 250–251)

For Problems 7–8, use the survey results in the tally table.

FAVORITE COLOR	
Color	Votes
Blue	~~||||~~ ~~||||~~
Purple	~~||||~~	
Red	~~||||~~ |||
Yellow	||

7. How many people answered the survey?

A. 14 people B. 26 people
C. 30 people D. 31 people

8. What is the favorite color of the people surveyed?

A. blue   B. purple
C. red   D. yellow

(pages 272–273)

9. What is the name of the solid figure?

A. cube
B. cylinder
C. square pyramid
D. sphere

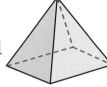

(pages 316–317)

10. Which solid figure has a circle as a face?

A. cone
B. rectangular prism
C. square pyramid
D. cube

(pages 320–321)

21 FRACTIONS: PARTS OF A WHOLE

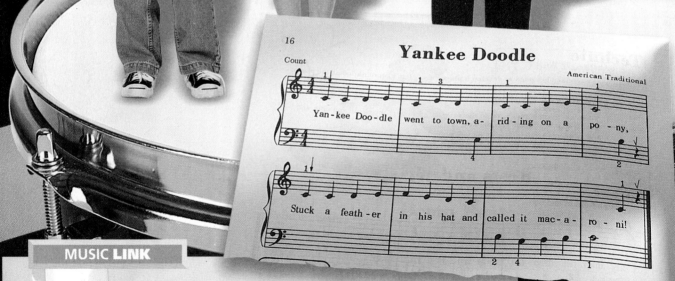

MUSIC **LINK**

Musical notes are based on the number of beats to a measure. A time signature at the beginning of a song tells how to count the beats. In $\frac{4}{4}$ time, there are 4 beats to a measure.

Music Fractions

"Yankee Doodle" is a traditional American song written in the 1700's. It became the theme song of the Continental Army in the Revolutionary War.

Look at the notes, and write the fraction sentence for each measure. A vertical line shows the end of a measure. Use the table to decode the notes and make a "Yankee Doodle" poster.

YOU WILL NEED: fraction bars or strips that show eighths, quarters, halves, and a whole

- Copy the chart, and finish naming the fractions that make a whole.

- Write addition sentences, using fractions for each of the 8 measures of "Yankee Doodle" given here. Each fraction sentence should add up to one whole.

- Illustrate your poster.

DID YOU

☑ finish the fraction equations?

☑ write 8 addition sentences for the 8 measures of "Yankee Doodle"?

☑ make and illustrate a poster?

Music Notation		
Whole Note	o	$1 = 1$
Half Note	♩ or ⌐	$\frac{1}{2} + ? = 1$
Quarter Note	♩ or ⌐	$\frac{1}{4} + \frac{1}{4} + \frac{1}{4} + ? = 1$
Rest	𝄽	$\frac{1}{4}$ count rest

Modeling Parts of a Whole

Why learn this? You can see how a whole can be divided into different numbers of parts as in a puzzle.

You can use paper folding to explore equal parts.

Cut four strips of paper the same size.

- Fold one strip into 2 equal parts. Color 1 part blue.

- Fold one strip into 4 equal parts. Color 1 part green.

- Fold one strip into 8 equal parts. Color 1 part red.

- Fold one strip into 16 equal parts. Color 3 parts yellow.

Talk About It

- In the strip with the green color, how many parts are in the whole? How many of those parts are green?

- In the strip with the red color, how many parts are in the whole? How many of those parts are red?

CRITICAL THINKING   Which paper strip has the largest parts? the smallest parts? Why?

▶ CHECK

Tell how many parts make up the whole figure. Then tell how many parts are shaded.

1.   **2.**    **3.**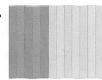

Tell how many parts make up the whole. Then tell how many parts are shaded.

4.

5.

6.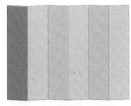

7.

8.

9.

Problem Solving • Mixed Applications

10. **Calendar** Judy started a 2-week sewing class on March 15. On what date was the last class?

11. **Time** Jacob practiced playing his trumpet for 14 minutes more than Stacy. Together, they spent 56 minutes practicing their trumpets. How many minutes did they each spend practicing?

12. **Measurement** Don, John, and Ron divide a piece of rope so they each get the same length. How many parts are there? How many parts does Ron get?

13. ▣ **Write About It** Janine folded one paper strip into 6 parts and another paper strip of equal size into 10 parts. Which strip has larger parts? Tell how you know.

Mixed Review and Test Prep

Write how many hundreds, tens, and ones. (pages 144–145)

14. 249   15. 384   16. 492   17. 891   18. 908

Name the solid figure that each looks like. Choose the letter of the correct answer. (pages 316–317)

19.
A cube
B rectangular prism
C sphere
D cylinder

20.
F cone
G sphere
H cube
J cylinder

21.
A cube
B sphere
C cone
D cylinder

Other Ways to Model Fractions

VOCABULARY
fraction
numerator
denominator

Why learn this? You can use fractions to share fairly.

Yvette and Gary share a sandwich equally. What fraction of the sandwich does Yvette eat?

A **fraction** is a number that names part of a whole.

Use fraction bars to show how 1 whole can be divided into 2 equal parts.

1	
$\frac{1}{2}$	$\frac{1}{2}$

The **numerator** tells how many parts are being used.

The **denominator** tells how many equal parts are in the whole.

Yvette's part → **1**
Equal parts in all → **2**

Read: one half
one out of two
one divided by two

Write: $\frac{1}{2}$

So, Yvette eats $\frac{1}{2}$ of the sandwich.

Here are some other fractions.

1 out of 4 is shaded.
One fourth is shaded.

$\frac{1}{4}$

5 out of 6 are shaded.
Five sixths are shaded.

$\frac{5}{6}$

3 out of 8 are shaded.
Three eighths are shaded.

$\frac{3}{8}$

CRITICAL THINKING Why can you describe $\frac{1}{4}$ as "1 divided by 4"?

Using a number line is another way to show parts of a whole. These number lines from 0 to 1 represent a whole. The whole line can be divided into any number of equal parts.

Find $\frac{1}{2}$ on number line A.

- What is another name for $\frac{2}{2}$ on this number line?

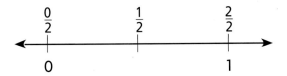

Find $\frac{1}{4}$ on number line B.

- What is another name for $\frac{2}{4}$ on this number line?

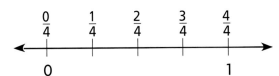

Look at number line C.

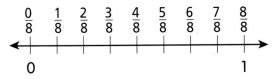

- What is another name for $\frac{1}{2}$ on this number line?

Talk About It

- Which number line above shows a whole divided into 4 equal parts?

- Into how many equal parts is a whole divided in number line C?

- Where would $\frac{1}{4}$ be located on number line A above?

▶ CHECK

Write the fraction that names the point of each letter on the number line.

1.

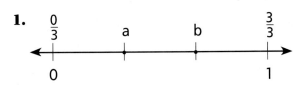

2.

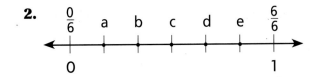

3. How does a number line help you find parts of a whole?

MORE PRACTICE page H103

LESSON
CONTINUES

Tell the part that is shaded. Write your answer using numbers and words.

4.

5.

6.

7.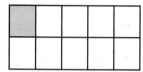

8.

9.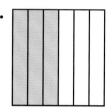

Write the fraction that names the point of each letter on the number line.

10.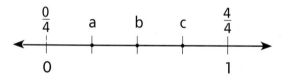

11.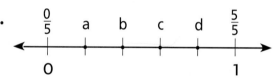

Write the fraction, using numbers.

12. five eighths

13. nine out of ten

14. seven ninths

15. one divided by six

16. four divided by seven

17. two out of eleven

18. two sixths

19. four fifths

20. five out of six

Problem Solving • Mixed Applications

21. Reasoning Ms. Haines is planning a 100th-day party in her class. Today is the 82nd day of school. In how many school days is the 100th-day party?

22. Money Gary spent $3.95 on a sandwich, $2.25 on fries, and $1.25 on a drink. How much did the sandwich and fries cost?

23. Visual Thinking How much of the pie was eaten?

24. ✏️ **Write a problem** using the picture shown.

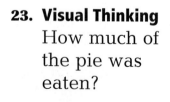

One of the ways people use fractions is in preparing food. Sandwiches for a family may use $\frac{1}{4}$ of a loaf of bread. A cookie recipe may call for $\frac{3}{4}$ of a cup of milk. One half of a pizza crust may be covered with vegetables.

Calcium keeps your bones strong. One cup of milk has $\frac{1}{3}$ of the calcium needed daily by an adult. How many cups of milk would provide all the calcium needed by an adult in one day?

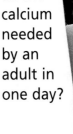

25. Suppose you and 3 friends share equal pieces of a loaf of French bread. What fraction describes your part?

26. Reasoning You buy frozen cookie dough and divide it into 5 parts. You put nuts in 1 part, sprinkles in 1 part, and raisins in 3 parts. What fraction describes the number of parts into which you put raisins?

27. Money One pizza shop cuts each pizza into 8 equal pieces. Each piece sells for $1.50. How many pieces could you get for $3.00?

28. Consumer Nancy bought a dozen eggs. She used 5 eggs while baking. What part of the dozen did she use?

Mixed Review and Test Prep

Use patterns of hundreds or thousands to find the sum or difference. (pages 148–149)

29. $200 + 743$ **30.** $349 - 100$ **31.** $9,374 - 3,000$

32. $441 + 300$ **33.** $887 - 200$ **34.** $7,217 - 1,000$

35. $601 + 300$ **36.** $792 - 400$ **37.** $3,463 + 1,000$

Round each number to the nearest ten or ten dollars. Choose the letter of the correct answer. (pages 174–175)

38. $59   **A** $40   **39.** $97   **F** $80   **40.** 93   **A** 80
        B $90   **G** $70   **B** 90
        C $60   **H** $100   **C** 10
        D $70   **J** $200   **D** 200

Counting Parts to Make a Whole

Why learn this? You can count parts when each member of your group has a part to complete.

These children are making a flag. Each child is making $\frac{1}{4}$ of the flag. How many children are needed to make the whole flag?

$\frac{1}{4}$ $\frac{2}{4}$ $\frac{3}{4}$ $\frac{4}{4}$ $\frac{4}{4} = 1$ whole

You can count by fourths. $\frac{1}{4}, \frac{2}{4}, \frac{3}{4}, \frac{4}{4}$

$\frac{4}{4}$ make 1 whole.

So, 4 children are needed to make the whole flag.

Talk About It

• How many parts make up the whole flag?

• What if the flag had three parts? What fractional part would describe each part?

Wholes can have any number of pieces.

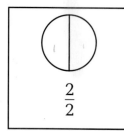

$\frac{2}{2}$

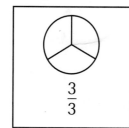

$\frac{3}{3}$

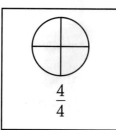

$\frac{4}{4}$

▶ CHECK

1. How many parts would make up each whole?

2. Tell about the numbers that name a whole fraction.

▶ PRACTICE

Write a fraction to describe each shaded part.

3.

4.

5. ○ ○ ○ ○

Write a fraction that names the shaded part.

6.   **7.**   **8.**

Problem Solving • Mixed Applications

For Problems 9–10, use the cube train.

9. Visual Thinking What fractional part of the cube train is red?

10. What fractional part of the cube train is red and blue?

11. Time Sasha started her homework at 4:00. She was finished a half hour later. What time was it then?

12. ✏️ **Write About It** How many twentieths will you need to count to make one whole? Explain.

Mixed Review and Test Prep

Compare the numbers. Write <, >, or = for each ●. (pages 164–165)

13. 87 ● 78   **14.** 110 ● 101   **15.** 317 ● 317   **16.** 889 ● 898

Choose the letter of the correct quotient. (pages 250–251)

17. 56 ÷ 7 = _?_   **A** 8   **B** 9   **C** 7   **D** 5

18. 72 ÷ 8 = _?_   **F** 8   **G** 6   **H** 9   **J** 7

19. 63 ÷ 9 = _?_   **A** 7   **B** 6   **C** 8   **D** 9

Comparing Fractions

Why learn this? You can compare fractional amounts when building or cooking.

You can compare fractions by using fraction bars.

A. Compare $\frac{1}{4}$ and $\frac{2}{4}$.

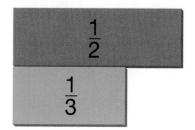

Record: $\frac{1}{4} < \frac{2}{4}$, or $\frac{2}{4} > \frac{1}{4}$.

B. Compare $\frac{1}{2}$ and $\frac{1}{3}$.

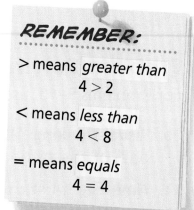

Record: $\frac{1}{2} > \frac{1}{3}$, or $\frac{1}{3} < \frac{1}{2}$.

Talk About It CRITICAL THINKING

- In A, how can you compare the fractions that have the same denominators but different numerators?

- In B, how can you compare the fractions that have the same numerators but different denominators?

- What happens to the size of the pieces as the denominator gets larger?

REMEMBER:

> means *greater than*
  $4 > 2$

< means *less than*
  $4 < 8$

= means *equals*
  $4 = 4$

▶ CHECK

Compare. Write $<$, $>$, or $=$ for each ●. You may use fraction bars to help you.

1.

$\frac{1}{3}$	
$\frac{1}{3}$	$\frac{1}{3}$

$\frac{1}{3}$ ● $\frac{2}{3}$

2.

$\frac{1}{4}$	$\frac{1}{4}$
$\frac{1}{6}$	$\frac{1}{6}$

$\frac{2}{4}$ ● $\frac{2}{6}$

3.

$\frac{1}{8}$	$\frac{1}{8}$	$\frac{1}{8}$	$\frac{1}{8}$
$\frac{1}{5}$	$\frac{1}{5}$	$\frac{1}{5}$	$\frac{1}{5}$

$\frac{4}{8}$ ● $\frac{4}{5}$

▶ PRACTICE

Compare. Write $<$, $>$, or $=$ for ●.

4.

$$\frac{3}{4} \bullet \frac{1}{4}$$

5.

$$\frac{7}{8} \bullet \frac{7}{8}$$

6.

$$\frac{3}{6} \bullet \frac{3}{4}$$

7.

$$\frac{1}{4} \bullet \frac{1}{2}$$

8.

$$\frac{3}{8} \bullet \frac{3}{12}$$

9.

$$\frac{4}{10} \bullet \frac{4}{5}$$

10.

$$\frac{1}{4} \bullet \frac{3}{8}$$

11.

$$\frac{4}{5} \bullet \frac{11}{12}$$

12.

$$\frac{3}{4} \bullet \frac{2}{3}$$

Problem Solving • Mixed Applications

13. Data The numbers on an eight-section spinner are the odd numbers between 4 and 20. What are the numbers?

14. Art A marker box holds 8 markers. How many boxes are needed to hold 48 markers?

15. Money Luca gave the clerk a $1 bill. The clerk gave Luca 1 quarter and a penny in change. How much change did Luca get? How much was the purchase?

16. Number Sense Merri has about $50 in her bank account. What is the least amount she could have? What is the greatest amount?

17. Time Eduardo started playing ball at 2:30 and played for 45 minutes. Then he ate lunch for 35 minutes. What time is it now?

18. ✏ **Write About It** Two pies are equal in size. One is cut into sixths, the other into eighths. Which pie has the larger pieces? Explain.

LESSON
CONTINUES

MORE PRACTICE page H104

Problem–Solving Strategy: Draw a Picture

REMEMBER:
UNDERSTAND
PLAN
SOLVE
LOOK BACK

▶ **THE PROBLEM** Lisa and two classmates ran in a race to raise money for a school food drive. Lisa ran $\frac{3}{4}$ mile, Jeff ran $\frac{5}{8}$ mile, and Melissa ran $\frac{1}{2}$ mile. Who ran the farthest?

UNDERSTAND

- What are you asked to find?

- What information will you use?

- Is there any information you will not use? If so, what?

PLAN

- What strategy can you use to solve the problem?

  You can *draw a picture* to show what part of a mile each person ran.

SOLVE

- How can you solve the problem?

  Cut three fraction strips the same length.

  Shade $\frac{3}{4}$ of one strip, $\frac{5}{8}$ of a second strip, and $\frac{1}{2}$ of a third strip.

  Compare the strips. Find the strip that has the largest shaded part.

  Since $\frac{3}{4} > \frac{5}{8} > \frac{1}{2}$, Lisa ran the farthest.

Lisa $\frac{3}{4}$
Jeff $\frac{5}{8}$
Melissa $\frac{1}{2}$

LOOK BACK

- How can you decide if your answer makes sense?

- What other strategy could you use to solve the problem?

▶ PRACTICE

Draw a picture to solve.

1. Sonu's team won $\frac{1}{2}$ of its games. Ed's team won $\frac{2}{3}$ of its games. Which team won more of its games?

2. Gigi spent $\frac{4}{10}$ of her allowance on stickers and $\frac{3}{5}$ on a magazine. On which item did Gigi spend more?

3. Noe began making a shape using 1 triangle and 3 squares.

He repeated these figures three more times until he used a total of 16 figures. How many squares did Noe use in all?

4. Mr. May tiled his basement floor. He used 9 rows of tiles with 8 tiles in each row. How many tiles did Mr. May use?

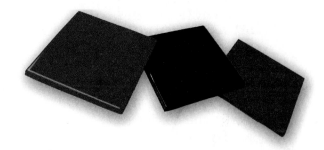

Mixed Applications

Solve.

CHOOSE a strategy and a tool.					
• Draw a Picture • Act It Out • Make a Model • Write a Number Sentence	 Paper/Pencil	 Calculator	 Hands-On	 Mental Math	

5. There were 56 pennies in a jar. Bill took out 25 pennies. The next day, he dropped in 12 pennies. How many pennies are in the jar now?

6. Carol, Mo, and Jen measured their heights. Carol was taller than Mo. Jen was taller than Carol. Order their heights from shortest to tallest.

7. Joseph has baseball practice at 4 o'clock. Practice lasts for $1\frac{1}{2}$ hours. Will Joseph make it home in time to eat dinner at 5 o'clock?

8. Ronnie ordered a pizza. He ate $\frac{1}{2}$ of it at lunch and $\frac{1}{4}$ of it after school. At which time did he eat a larger part of the pizza?

9. A new President is elected every four years. Presidents were elected in 1992 and 1996. What are the next two presidential election years?

10. Terry baked this pan of fruit bars. His family ate $\frac{1}{2}$ of them. How many fruit bars did they eat?

Equivalent Fractions

VOCABULARY

equivalent fractions

You will investigate equivalent fractions.

Equivalent fractions are two or more fractions that name the same amount.

▶ EXPLORE

Use fraction bars to model other fractions that name $\frac{1}{2}$.

MATERIALS: fraction bars

MODEL

Step 1	Step 2	Step 3
Start with the bar for 1 whole. Line up the bar for $\frac{1}{2}$.	Use $\frac{1}{4}$ pieces to form a bar the same size as $\frac{1}{2}$ the bar.	Use $\frac{1}{6}$ to form a bar the same size as $\frac{1}{2}$.

Record

Write the fractions you found that are equivalent to $\frac{1}{2}$. Make more fractions equivalent to $\frac{1}{2}$ using eighths, tenths, and twelfths. Record the fractions you find.

▶ TRY THIS

Find an equivalent fraction for each. Use fraction bars to help you.

1.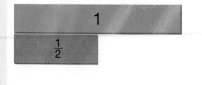

2.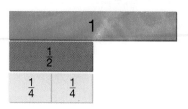

3. How can you tell by looking at the models that they are equivalent?

Technology Link

 In *Mighty Math Number Heroes,* the game *Fraction Fireworks* will challenge you to create fireworks to show equivalent fractions. Use Grow Slide Levels H and R.

4. ✏ **Write About It** Explain how to make a model to decide if $\frac{3}{4}$ and $\frac{2}{3}$ are equivalent.

Technology Link

💿 You can name equivalent fractions by using E-Lab, Activity 21. Available on CD-ROM and on the Internet at www.hbschool.com/elab

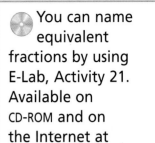

▶ PRACTICE

Find an equivalent fraction for each. Use fraction bars to help you.

5. | 1 |
   | $\frac{1}{4}$ | $\frac{1}{4}$ | $\frac{1}{4}$ |

6. | 1 |
   | $\frac{1}{6}$ |

7. | 1 |
   | $\frac{1}{10}$ | $\frac{1}{10}$ | $\frac{1}{10}$ | $\frac{1}{10}$ | $\frac{1}{10}$ |

8. $\frac{1}{2} = \frac{?}{4}$

9. $\frac{2}{3} = \frac{?}{12}$

10. $\frac{4}{5} = \frac{?}{10}$

11. $\frac{10}{10} = \frac{?}{8}$

12. $\frac{2}{3} = \frac{?}{6}$

13. $\frac{3}{4} = \frac{?}{8}$

Problem Solving • Mixed Applications

Using Data For Problems 14–15, use the recipe.

14. **Reasoning** Bonnie has only a $\frac{1}{4}$-cup measure. How many $\frac{1}{4}$-cup measures should she use to measure the peanuts? to measure the raisins?

Trail Mix Ingredients
$\frac{1}{2}$ cup peanuts
$\frac{3}{4}$ cup raisins
$\frac{1}{4}$ cup carob chips

15. **Number Sense** Order the ingredients in amounts from least to greatest.

16. **Compare** Lucy ate $\frac{2}{8}$ of a pizza. Linda ate $\frac{1}{4}$ of the pizza. Who ate less pizza?

17. **Compare** Yoko ate $\frac{3}{4}$ of her cupcake. Matt ate $\frac{2}{3}$ of his cupcake. Who ate more?

18. On Monday $\frac{1}{4}$ of the class went to the library. On Tuesday $\frac{1}{3}$ of the class went. On which day did more students go to the library?

19. **Number Sense** Fran used $\frac{1}{2}$ of a dozen eggs in her recipe. Name two other fraction names for the same amount.

20. **Mental Math** Ben and Teri made 6 kites. They put 4 bows on each tail. How many bows did they put on the kite tails?

21. **Measurement** Mark is 52 inches tall. His father is 67 inches tall. How much taller than Mark is Mark's father?

▶ CHECK Understanding

VOCABULARY

1. A __?__ is a number that names part of a whole. (page 370)

2. In a fraction, the __?__ tells how many parts are being used. (page 370)

3. In a fraction, the __?__ tells how many equal parts in the whole. (page 370)

4. __?__ are two or more fractions that name the same amount. (page 380)

Tell the part that is shaded. Write your answer using numbers and words. (pages 370–373)

Write the fraction that names the point of each letter on the number line. (pages 370–373)

5.

6.

7.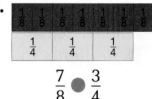

▶ CHECK Skills

Compare. Write < , > , or = for ●. (pages 376–377)

8.

$\frac{1}{4}$ ● $\frac{2}{4}$

9.

$\frac{1}{3}$ ● $\frac{1}{6}$

10.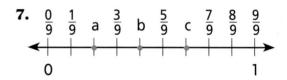

$\frac{7}{8}$ ● $\frac{3}{4}$

▶ CHECK Problem Solving

Solve. (pages 378–379)

CHOOSE a strategy and a tool.

- Draw a Picture
- Make a Model
- Act It Out
- Write a Number Sentence

 Paper/Pencil   Calculator   Hands-On   Mental Math

11. Ray's pizza is $\frac{1}{2}$ mushroom and $\frac{1}{3}$ pepperoni. Does more of the pizza have mushrooms or pepperoni?

12. A drink cost 55¢. Nate paid for it with 4 coins. What were the coins?

Test Prep

Choose the best answer.

1. How does this figure look after it is flipped?

A   **B**

C **D**

2. Tim planted a garden. At which ordered pair is the corn?

F (5,3) **G** (2,3)

H (4,5) **J** (3,3)

3. Jon and 3 friends shared a whole pizza. Each boy got an equal part. How much of the pizza did each boy eat?

A $\frac{1}{3}$ **B** $\frac{1}{5}$

C $\frac{1}{6}$ **D** $\frac{1}{4}$

4. Which circle has the smallest parts?

F   **G**

H   **J**

5. 63 ÷ 9 = ___?___

A 9 **B** 7

C 1 **D** 8

6. What is the product of 9 × 5?

F 45 **G** 3

H 54 **J** 63

7. Joanne put zero flowers in 6 vases. How many flowers did she put in each vase?

A 24 **B** 0

C 1 **D** 6

8. Which fraction tells how much is shaded?

F $\frac{2}{5}$ **G** $\frac{1}{6}$

H $\frac{3}{8}$ **J** $\frac{2}{3}$

9. 272
    −116

A 166 **B** 388

C 176 **D** 156

10. Jean put 47 crayons in one bag and 34 in another bag. She put 17 crayons on the table. How many crayons did Jean have?

F 88 **G** 79

H 98 **J** 99

22 PARTS OF A GROUP

LANGUAGE ARTS LINK

Every year, a book award called the Newbery Medal is given for that year's best piece of children's literature. The book is selected by a committee of librarians (the group), each of whom has one vote (the parts).

Eight Say *Great!*

Find out what eight classmates say is great. Make a survey to ask a *who, what,* or *where* question about something your friends say is great.

YOU WILL NEED: inch grid paper, crayons, paper and pencil

Make a survey question to get information.

- Ask eight classmates the question, and record their answers with tally marks on scratch paper.

- Use the tally marks to make a bar graph on inch grid paper; use the same color crayon for the same answers.

- Write sentences about the results, telling about the question as the whole and the answers as parts.

- Share your bar graph and results with the class.

DID YOU

✓ take a survey of eight classmates?

✓ record the answers with tally marks, and then make a bar graph with crayons?

✓ write sentences about the results?

✓ share your graph and results with the class?

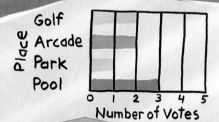

Where is a great place to go for a birthday?

Place: Golf, Arcade, Park, Pool
Number of Votes: 0 1 2 3 4 5

"The question is where is a great place for a birthday? The whole is 8 of 8. The parts are $\frac{2}{8}, \frac{2}{8}, \frac{1}{8},$ and $\frac{3}{8}$."

Part of a Group

You will investigate how to model and describe equal parts of a group.

Use a fraction to name part of a group.
Use tiles to show 4 equal parts with 1 part green.

This group has 4 tiles. There are 4 equal parts. The green tile shows 1 part.

This group has 8 tiles. There are 4 equal parts. The green tiles show 1 part.

Both groups show 4 equal parts with 1 part green.

▶ EXPLORE

Use color tiles to show equal parts of a group.

MATERIALS: color tiles

A. Use tiles. Make 3 equal parts with 1 part red.

B. Use tiles. Make 2 equal parts with 1 part yellow.

Record

Draw and color both tile models. Explain how many tiles you put in each group and what colors you used for the parts.

• Compare your groups with a classmate's groups. How are they alike? How are they different?

Now investigate using tiles to make other models to show equal parts of a group.

▶ TRY THIS

Draw and color both tile models.

1. 1 part green of 3 equal parts

2. 1 part blue of 4 equal parts

3. How did you decide on the number of tiles to put in the group?

4. Why is it possible to use different numbers of tiles for a group?

5. **Write About It** How is part of a group different from part of a whole? Draw an example of each.

▶ PRACTICE

Use tiles to show equal parts of the group. Draw a picture of your model.

6. Make 2 equal parts with 1 part blue.

7. Make 4 equal parts with 1 part red.

Look at each picture. Find the number of equal parts that are green.

8.

9.

Problem Solving • Mixed Applications

10. **Visual Thinking** Thalia wants to save 3 of the brownies for her family. What fraction names the part of the pan of brownies Thalia wants to save?

11. **Probability** Ron puts the tiles into a bag. Without looking, he pulls out a tile. Which color is he more likely to get? Explain.

12. **Logical Reasoning** The sum of the facing page numbers in the book is 25. What two pages is the book opened to?

Fractions of a Group

Why learn this? You can use fractions when you share food with friends.

Patti put the fruit she bought on two plates. Plate A holds 4 kinds of fruit. Plate B holds 2 kinds of fruit. What fraction of the fruit on each plate are apples?

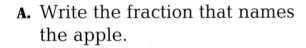

A. Write the fraction that names the apple.

part that is the apple → 1 ← numerator
total parts → 4 ← denominator

Read: one fourth or one out of four

Write: $\frac{1}{4}$

So, $\frac{1}{4}$ of the fruit on the first plate are apples.

B. Write the fraction that names the apples.

part that is apples → 1 ← numerator
total parts → 2 ← denominator

Read: one half or one out of two

Write: $\frac{1}{2}$

So, $\frac{1}{2}$ of the fruit on the second plate are apples.

CRITICAL THINKING   What is alike about each fraction of the fruit that are apples? What is different?

▶ CHECK

1. Suppose there are an apple, an orange, and a pear on a plate. What fraction of the fruit is the orange? Explain.

2. Draw 4 circles. Shade 1 circle. Write the fraction that names the shaded part of the circles.

3. Draw a picture that shows 6 fruits in 2 equal groups. Write a fraction that names the fruit that is in one group.

Technology Link

In **Mighty Math Number Heroes**, the game *Fraction Fireworks* challenges you to create fireworks as you learn about fractions. Use Grow Slide Levels H and R.

▶ PRACTICE

Write the fraction that names the part of the group shown.

4. 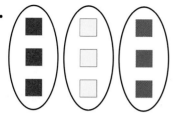 yellow tiles

5.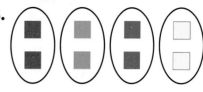

   green tiles

6.

   red tiles

7.

   blue tiles

Draw the picture. Use numbers and words to describe the part that is shaded.

8. Draw 5 circles. Shade 1 circle.

9. Draw 6 squares. Shade 1 square.

10. Draw 3 stars. Shade 1 star.

11. Draw 8 triangles. Make 2 equal groups. Shade 1 group.

12. Draw 10 circles. Make 5 equal groups. Shade 1 group.

13. Draw 12 squares. Make 6 equal groups. Shade 1 group.

Problem Solving • Mixed Applications

14. **Number Sense** Omar put 12 balloons into 2 equal parts. He gave 1 part to Tim. What part of the balloons did Omar give to Tim?

15. **Visual Thinking** What part of the circle is shaded? What part of the circle is not shaded?

16. ⬛▷ **Write a problem** about the hats, for which you need to name a fraction of a group.

Mixed Review and Test Prep

Find the product. (pages 212–213)

17. $3 \times 8 = \underline{\ ?\ }$ 18. $8 \times 5 = \underline{\ ?\ }$ 19. $6 \times 8 = \underline{\ ?\ }$ 20. $8 \times 7 = \underline{\ ?\ }$

Use patterns of hundreds or thousands to find the sum or difference. Choose the letter of the correct answer. (pages 148–149)

21. $1,623 - 1,000$ **A** 1,000   **B** 1,523   **C** 623   **D** 523

22. $4,925 + 5,000$ **F** 5,925   **G** 9,000   **H** 9,825   **J** 9,925

More About Fractions of a Group

Why learn this? You can use parts that make a whole when you share markers or toys with classmates.

Fractions of a group can name more than 1 part. Counting parts of a group makes a pattern.

Model	⬜⬜⬜ ⬜⬜⬜	⬛⬜⬜ ⬜⬜⬜	⬛⬛⬜ ⬜⬜⬜	⬛⬛⬛ ⬜⬜⬜	⬛⬛⬛ ⬛⬜⬜	⬛⬛⬛ ⬛⬛⬜	⬛⬛⬛ ⬛⬛⬛
Number of parts	6	6	6	6	6	6	6
Number of blue parts	0	1	2	3	4	5	6
Fraction of blue parts	$\frac{0}{6}$	$\frac{1}{6}$	$\frac{2}{6}$	$\frac{3}{6}$	$\frac{4}{6}$	$\frac{5}{6}$	$\frac{6}{6}$

Talk About It [CRITICAL THINKING]

- How many equal parts are in the group of counters?

- How can you tell when the blue counters in the group are the same as 1 whole?

▶ CHECK

Use the pattern to complete the table.

1.	Model	⬭⬭⬭⬭	⬭⬤⬭⬭	⬤⬤⬭⬭	⬤⬤⬤⬭	?
2.	Number of parts	4	4	?	4	4
3.	Number of blue parts	?	1	2	3	4
4.	Fraction of blue parts	$\frac{0}{4}$	$\frac{1}{4}$	$\frac{2}{4}$	?	$\frac{4}{4}$

5. For this pattern, how many counters are in each equal part?

▶ PRACTICE

Use a pattern to complete the table.

	Model	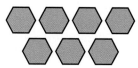	?	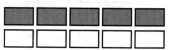			
6.							
7.	Number of parts	5	5	5	?	5	5
8.	Number of blue parts	0	1	?	3	4	5
9.	Fraction of blue parts	$\frac{0}{5}$	$\frac{1}{5}$	$\frac{2}{5}$	$\frac{3}{5}$	$\frac{4}{5}$	?

Write a fraction to describe the shaded part.

10.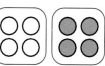

11.

12.

13.

14.

15.

Problem Solving • Mixed Applications

16. What part of the checkers is black?

17. Money Wes gave the clerk a quarter for a 13¢ toy. What coins could he receive in change?

18. Visual Thinking What part of the cards does each child have?

19.

Logical Reasoning If the parts are cut along each fold, how many pieces will there be?

20. ✏️ **Write About It** How are the two pictures alike? How are they different?

LESSON CONTINUES ➔

Problem–Solving Strategy: Draw a Picture

▶ **THE PROBLEM** Each student is decorating 2 eggs. Students will fill egg cartons with 12 decorated eggs. What part of a carton will each student make? How many students' eggs are needed to fill each egg carton?

REMEMBER:

UNDERSTAND
PLAN
SOLVE
LOOK BACK

UNDERSTAND

- What are you asked to do?

- What information will you use?

- Is there any information you will not use? If so, what?

PLAN

- What strategy can you use to solve the problem?

  You can *draw a picture.*

SOLVE

- How can you use the strategy to solve the problem?

  You can draw 12 circles to show the egg carton.

  Draw rings around groups of 2 eggs to show the part each student makes.

  Each student fills $\frac{1}{6}$ of an egg carton.

  So, 6 students' eggs are needed to fill a whole egg carton.

CULTURAL LINK

People in the Ukraine make decorated eggs called *pysanky*. No design is used twice. First the eggs are covered with wax. Then a design is drawn on part of the egg, and the egg is dipped into a dye. Suppose 2 out of 10 eggs have been decorated. What part of the whole group still needs decoration?

LOOK BACK

- How can you decide if your answer makes sense?

- What other strategy could you use to solve the problem?

Draw a picture to solve.

1. Each student pours batter into one cup of a 6-cup muffin tin. What part of the tin will each student fill? How many students will pour batter?

2. Randi and her two friends will share 15 baseball cards. What part of the cards will each person get?

3. Josh's mother bought a carton of 8 juice boxes. She planned for her 4 children to share them equally. How many boxes did each child get? What part of the carton did each child share?

4. Emma bakes one sheet of cookies at a time. Each sheet holds $\frac{1}{4}$ batch. What part of the batch is made by baking 3 sheets? 4 sheets?

Mixed Applications

Solve.

CHOOSE a strategy and a tool.	
• Make a Model • Guess and Check • Act It Out • Draw a Picture • Write a Number Sentence	 Paper/Pencil Calculator Hands-On Mental Math

5. Jeff has $5.37. He needs $7.50 to buy a trading card case. How much more money does he need?

6. How many sticks are needed to make 4 triangles?

7. Robbie has a bag of 10 marbles. He likes the 2 red marbles best. What part of his marbles are red?

8. Each day Ashley sews $\frac{1}{10}$ of a quilt. After four days, how much has she sewn?

9. There were 357 people in line for lunch. All but 75 people wanted a hot lunch. How many hot lunches were sold?

10. Sean cuts the pizza into 8 equal pieces. He and 3 friends each get 2 pieces. How much of the pizza does each get?

11. Lois bought 12 apples. She shared them equally with 5 friends. How many apples did each one get?

12. Jerry had 9 nickels. He spent 35¢. How much money does Jerry have left?

Comparing Parts of a Group

Why learn this? You can compare parts of groups when you compare collections.

Tory and Courtney each have 5 fish in their aquariums. In Tory's aquarium, $\frac{2}{5}$ of the fish are goldfish. In Courtney's aquarium, $\frac{4}{5}$ of the fish are goldfish. Who has more goldfish?

Compare $\frac{2}{5}$ and $\frac{4}{5}$.

You can use tiles to compare parts of a group. Use yellow tiles to show goldfish.

REMEMBER:

You can use *fraction bars* to compare fractions.

$\frac{2}{3} > \frac{1}{3}$ or $\frac{1}{3} < \frac{2}{3}$

Tory   Courtney

☐☐☐☐☐   ☐☐☐☐☐

$\frac{2}{5}$ < $\frac{4}{5}$

So, Courtney has more goldfish in her aquarium.

Talk About It [CRITICAL THINKING]

• How are the fractions $\frac{2}{5}$ and $\frac{4}{5}$ alike?

• How are the fractions different?

• How can you find out which fraction is greater?

▶ CHECK

Compare the parts of each group that are red. Write <, >, or = for the ●. You may use tiles to help you.

1. ☐☐☐
   ☐☐☐

   $\frac{2}{3}$ ● $\frac{1}{3}$

2. ☐☐☐☐☐☐☐☐
   ☐☐☐☐☐☐☐☐

   $\frac{5}{8}$ ● $\frac{3}{8}$

3. ☐☐☐☐☐☐
   ☐☐☐☐☐☐

   $\frac{4}{6}$ ● $\frac{4}{6}$

SCIENCE LINK

There are more than 100 kinds of goldfish. Most have two sets of paired fins and three single fins, or 7 fins in all. Goldfish have very large eyes and a good sense of smell and hearing. Suppose an aquarium has 2 kinds of goldfish. Of the goldfish, 3 are of one type, and 2 are of another type. Compare the two groups of goldfish by using fractions.

Compare the part of each group that is blue.
Write $<$, $>$, or $=$ for the ●.

4.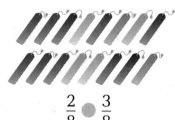

$\frac{2}{8}$ ● $\frac{3}{8}$

5.

$\frac{1}{6}$ ● $\frac{3}{6}$

6.

$\frac{3}{7}$ ● $\frac{3}{7}$

7.

$\frac{4}{10}$ ● $\frac{6}{10}$

8.

$\frac{2}{3}$ ● $\frac{1}{3}$

9.

$\frac{4}{4}$ ● $\frac{3}{4}$

Problem Solving • Mixed Applications

10. **Compare** A florist makes two bunches of flowers. One bunch is $\frac{5}{7}$ roses and the other is $\frac{4}{7}$ roses. Which bunch has more roses?

11. **Money** Ali buys 2 packs of cards and a game book. How much do they cost?

12. **Number Sense** The 32 students in Yana's class work in groups of four. How many groups are there?

13. ✏ **Write About It** Tell how comparing fractional parts of a whole is like comparing fractional parts of a group.

Mixed Review and Test Prep

Read each event. Tell if the event is *certain* or *impossible* to happen. (pages 296–297)

14. You will go to the sun tomorrow.

15. An ice cube will melt in hot water.

16. Touching a very hot pan will burn you.

Choose the letter of the correct product. (pages 198–201)

17. $4 \times 7 =$ ___?___   **A** 26 **B** 21
   C 14 **D** 28

18. $4 \times 8 =$ ___?___   **F** 32 **G** 34
   H 35 **J** 38

19. $4 \times 9 =$ ___?___   **A** 18 **B** 36
   C 54 **D** 45

20. $4 \times 6 =$ ___?___   **F** 24 **G** 12
   H 18 **J** 32

► CHECK Understanding

Find the number of equal parts that are orange. (pages 386–387)

1. ⬭⬭⬭⬭
   ⬭⬭⬭⬭

2. ⬭⬭⬭⬭⬭

3. ⬭⬭⬭⬭⬭⬭
   ⬭⬭⬭⬭⬭⬭

Use the pattern to complete the table. (pages 390–391)

4.	Model	⬭⬭⬭ ⬭⬭⬭	⬭⬭⬭ ⬭⬭⬭	⬭⬭⬭ ⬭⬭⬭	⬭⬭⬭ ⬭⬭⬭	⬭⬭⬭ ⬭⬭⬭	⬭⬭⬭ ⬭⬭⬭	?
5.	Number of parts	6	?	6	6	6	6	6
6.	Number of blue parts	0	1	2	?	4	5	6
7.	Fraction of blue parts	$\frac{0}{6}$	$\frac{1}{6}$	$\frac{2}{6}$	$\frac{3}{6}$	$\frac{4}{6}$	?	$\frac{6}{6}$

► CHECK Skills

Draw the picture. Use numbers and words to describe the part that is shaded. (pages 388–389)

8. Draw 6 triangles. Shade 1.

9. Draw 8 circles. Make 2 equal groups. Shade 1 group.

Compare the parts of each group that are green.
Write < , > , or = for the ●. (pages 394–395)

10. △△△△△
    △△△△△
    $\frac{3}{5}$ ● $\frac{2}{5}$

11. ▪▪▪▪□□
    ▪▪▪▪□□
    $\frac{4}{6}$ ● $\frac{4}{6}$

12. ●●●●○○○○
    ●●●●○○○○
    $\frac{3}{8}$ ● $\frac{4}{8}$

► CHECK Problem Solving

Solve. (pages 392–393)

CHOOSE a strategy and a tool.

- Draw a Picture
- Write a Number Sentence
- Act It Out
- Make a Model

 Paper/Pencil   Calculator   Hands-On   Mental Math

13. Three students have 18 cookies to share equally. What fraction will each one get?

14. Roni's necklace has 20 beads. Of those, 15 are silver. How many are not silver?

Test Prep

Choose the best answer.

1. How much of the pie has been eaten?

  A $\frac{1}{2}$ **B** $\frac{1}{3}$ **C** $\frac{1}{4}$ **D** $\frac{1}{5}$

2. Compare the figures. Which pair is congruent?

3. This plane figure was moved by flipping.

What did it look like before it was flipped?

  A **B**

  C **D**

4. How do these fraction bars compare?

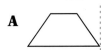

  F $\frac{2}{3} > \frac{3}{4}$ **G** $\frac{2}{3} < \frac{3}{4}$

  H $\frac{2}{3} = \frac{3}{4}$ **J** $\frac{1}{4} = \frac{1}{5}$

5. What fraction names the part that is purple?

  A $\frac{3}{4}$ **B** $\frac{1}{2}$ **C** $\frac{1}{4}$ **D** $\frac{4}{4}$

6. Mr. James gave red pens to 10 students, blue pens to 5 students, and green pens to 8 students. How many pens did Mr. James give to students?

  F 13   **G** 15   **H** 23   **J** 18

7. What part of this muffin tin is filled?

  A $\frac{1}{6}$ **B** $\frac{3}{6}$ **C** $\frac{4}{6}$ **D** $\frac{5}{6}$

8. A pizza was cut into 6 equal pieces. What is one part of the whole pizza?

  F $\frac{3}{6}$

  G $\frac{1}{6}$

  H $\frac{2}{6}$

  J $\frac{6}{6}$

9. What fraction names the part of the group that is green?

  A $\frac{1}{3}$ **B** $\frac{2}{3}$ **C** $\frac{2}{8}$ **D** $\frac{4}{6}$

23 DECIMALS

HEALTH **LINK**

About seven-tenths of the average adult-size body is made up of water. We can write this fact in different ways that say the same thing. Both $\frac{7}{10}$ and 0.7 are read "seven tenths."

Problem-Solving Activity

Estimating Decimal Volume

Learn how fractions and decimals are related.

Use two empty two-liter soda bottles marked with tenths. Fill each bottle to a different mark.

YOU WILL NEED: empty two-liter soda bottles, 10-inch tagboard strip, tape, paper funnel, salt or sand, marker

- Take the label off the bottle.

- Mark the tagboard strip in tenths and tape it to the bottle.

- Choose a mark, and fill your bottle to that mark with sand or salt. Work over a bucket or tub.

- Make a display, organizing bottles from least full to fullest.

- Record how full each bottle is to the closest tenth.

DID YOU

☑ tape a tenths strip to your bottle?

☑ choose a mark and fill your bottle to it?

☑ organize bottles from least full to fullest?

☑ record about how full each bottle is to the nearest tenth?

Tenths

VOCABULARY

decimal
tenths

Why learn this? You can use decimals to name fractional amounts of tenths such as parts of 10 parking spaces.

A **decimal** is a number that uses place value and a decimal point to show amounts that are less than one, such as **tenths**.

Suppose a parking lot has 10 parking spaces and there are cars in 4 of the spaces. Four tenths, or four out of the ten parking spaces, are filled.

Four tenths can be written as a fraction, $\frac{4}{10}$, or as a decimal, 0.4.

Write: $\frac{4}{10}$ **Write**: 0.4   **Read**: four tenths

Use decimal squares to model tenths.

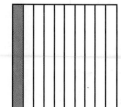

This square is divided into 10 equal parts. One **tenth**, or one of the ten parts, is shaded.

Read: one tenth
Write: 0.1, or $\frac{1}{10}$

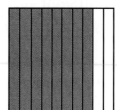

This square is also divided into 10 equal parts. Eight tenths, or eight of the ten parts, are shaded.

Read: eight tenths
Write: 0.8, or $\frac{8}{10}$

Talk About It

• How are fractions and decimals alike?

• What decimal number shows $\frac{2}{10}$?

• How can you use a decimal square to show $\frac{5}{10}$?

• How can you write seven tenths as a decimal and a fraction?

CRITICAL THINKING What coin is 0.1, or $\frac{1}{10}$, of a dollar?

SCIENCE LINK

You can use a fraction and a decimal to describe the part of a vegetable that contains water. Lettuce is about $\frac{9}{10}$ water. What decimal can you use to name the part of lettuce that contains water?

▶ CHECK

Write the decimal for the shaded part.

1.    **2.**   **3.**   **4.**

Calculator Activities page H67

► PRACTICE

Write the decimal and the fraction for the shaded part.

5.
6.
7.
8.

Write each fraction as a decimal.

9. $\frac{5}{10}$ **10.** $\frac{7}{10}$ **11.** $\frac{4}{10}$ **12.** $\frac{8}{10}$ **13.** $\frac{3}{10}$ **14.** $\frac{1}{10}$

Write each decimal as a fraction.

15. 0.9   **16.** 0.5   **17.** 0.3   **18.** 0.6   **19.** 0.2   **20.** 0.8

Problem Solving • Mixed Applications

21. Money Ice skates cost $25.00. Joe has $13.50. How much more money does he need in order to buy the skates?

22. Time A soccer game started at 3:30 and lasted 1 hour 15 minutes. At what time was the game over?

23. Science Tomatoes are in three tenths of a garden. Write a fraction and a decimal to show the part that is planted with tomatoes.

24. ✐ **Write a problem** about this decimal square.

Mixed Review and Test Prep

Draw the picture. Use numbers and words to describe the part that is shaded. (pages 388–389)

25. Draw 4 circles. Shade 1 circle.

26. Draw 6 squares. Make 2 equal groups. Shade 1 group.

27. Draw 9 stars. Make 3 equal groups. Shade 1 group.

Choose the letter of the correct product. (pages 208–211)

28. $7 \times 5 = \underline{?}$
A 30
B 35
C 40
D 45

29. $7 \times 8 = \underline{?}$
F 50
G 48
H 54
J 56

30. $6 \times 7 = \underline{?}$
A 49
B 54
C 42
D 56

Hundredths

VOCABULARY
hundredths

You will investigate decimal numbers called hundredths.

Hundredths are decimals that show small amounts. There are 100 hundredths in one whole just as there are 100 pennies in one dollar.

▶ EXPLORE

You can use unit cubes, and a decimal square to show hundredths.

MATERIALS: unit cubes, decimal squares, markers

* Place two unit cubes on a decimal square.

* Decide how many unit cubes the square can hold.

* Decide what part of the square is covered with unit cubes.

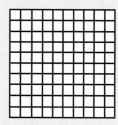

decimal square

Record

Cut and paste a decimal model on your paper. Shade where you placed the unit cubes. Write the fraction and the decimal that name the shaded part. (Hint: Decimals are written like money amounts.) Explain how you decided how many unit cubes the decimal square can hold.

Now investigate other hundredths models.

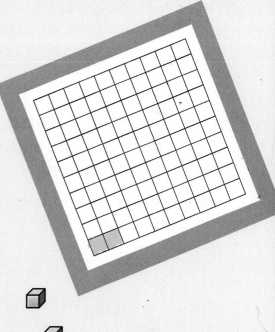

▶ TRY THIS

1. Cut, paste, and shade two more models.

   * seven hundredths

   * twenty-five hundredths

2. Write the fraction and the decimal that name the shaded part of each.

Talk About It

3. Look at your models. How many parts are shaded out of the total number?

4. How can you model 0.15 on a decimal square?

5. How can you write 15¢ as a decimal part of a dollar?

Technology Link

You can model tenths and hundredths by using E-Lab, Activity 23. Available on CD-ROM and on the Internet at www.hbschool.com/elab

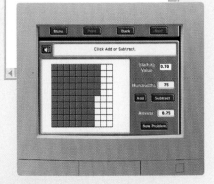

▶ PRACTICE

Shade decimal squares to show each amount. Write the decimal number that names the shaded part.

6. three hundredths

7. eight hundredths

8. eleven hundredths

9. sixteen hundredths

10. twenty hundredths

11. forty-two hundredths

For Exercises 12–14, use the mosaic tile design.

12. What decimal describes the yellow tiles?

13. What decimal describes the blue tiles?

14. What decimal describes the red tiles?

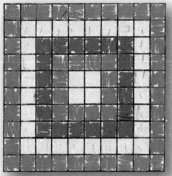

Problem Solving • Mixed Applications

15. Angie put 5 unit cubes on her decimal square. What decimal number describes the part covered by unit cubes?

16. **Visual Thinking** There are 86 green tiles in a 100-tile design. What decimal number describes the green tiles?

17. **Money** Felicia bought a drink for 65¢. She gave the clerk a $1 bill. What three coins did she receive as change?

18. Will's book has 100 pages. He has read 72 pages. How many more pages does he have to read to finish the book?

19. How many unit cubes would be needed to show 0.08 on a decimal square?

20. **Time** Will read from 9:30 until 10:15 and from 2:20 until 2:45. How long did Will read?

21. ▣▷ **Write a problem** using this information. Rosa has 56 pennies.

Reading and Writing Hundredths

Why learn this? You can use decimals to describe parts of a whole, such as parts of a carton.

Two classes are selling cookies. Each class has been given 100 boxes to sell. They are recording their sales on decimal squares. What part of their boxes did each class sell so far?

Write: 0.20
Read: twenty hundredths

One class sold 0.20, or twenty hundredths, of their boxes.

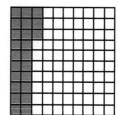

Write: 0.23
Read: twenty-three hundredths

The other class sold 0.23, or twenty-three hundredths, of their boxes.

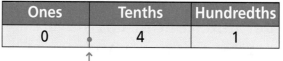

Place-value charts help you understand decimals.

Ones	Tenths	Hundredths
0	3	0

↑
decimal point

Ones	Tenths	Hundredths
0	4	1

↑
decimal point

Write: 0.30
Read: thirty hundredths

Write: 0.41
Read: forty-one hundredths

A **decimal point** separates a whole number from a fractional part of a number.

▶ CHECK

1. On the place-value chart, how many places to the right of the decimal point is tenths? hundredths?

Record how you read and write the decimal name for
each shaded part.   Example: Read: two tenths
Write: 0.2

2.    **3.** 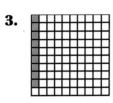   **4.** 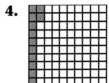   **5.**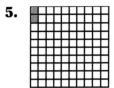

6. 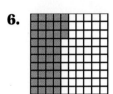   **7.** 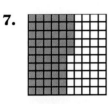   **8.** 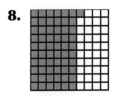   **9.**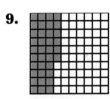

10. 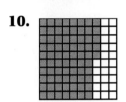   **11.** 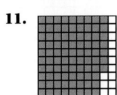   **12.** 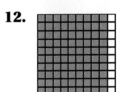   **13.**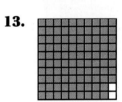

Problem Solving • Mixed Applications

14. Number Sense There were 100 students trying out for a play. Of those, 42 students were chosen. What decimal describes the students that were chosen?

15. Time Abby is in a school play in 4 days. Today is March 25. What is the date of Abby's play?

16. Money George has 5 coins that are worth 86¢ in all. What coins might George have?

17. ✏ **Write a problem** using decimals in hundredths.

Mixed Review and Test Prep

Compare the numbers. Write <, >, or = for each ●. (pages 164–167)

18. 65 ● 73   **19.** 212 ● 122   **20.** 743 ● 734   **21.** 972 ● 982

Choose the letter of the correct product. (pages 214–215)

22. 9 × 5 = __?__   **A** 50   **23.** 3 × 9 = __?__   **F** 27   **24.** 9 × 1 = __?__   **A** 0

B 63   **G** 34   **B** 1

C 40   **H** 32   **C** 9

D 45   **J** 48   **D** 8

VOCABULARY

mixed
decimal

Decimals Greater Than 1

Why learn this? You can understand how to use decimal numbers or money amounts greater than 1.

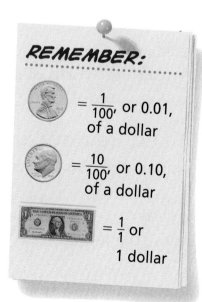

John bought 3 sheets of 100 stamps and 25 more stamps. What decimal shows the number of stamps that John bought?

A **mixed decimal** is a number that is made up of a whole number and a decimal.

Use decimal squares to show John's stamps.

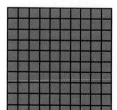 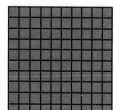 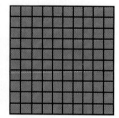 

Write: 3.25   **Read:** three and twenty-five hundredths

Hint: Say *and* when you read the decimal point.
So, John has 3.25 sheets of stamps.

• Where should you place the decimal point in two and fifteen hundredths? Why?

Write money amounts greater than one dollar by using a decimal point and a dollar sign.

Write: $1.25   **Read:** one dollar and twenty-five cents

▶ CHECK

1. What decimal number and money amount are represented by 1 dollar, 5 dimes, and 4 pennies?

2. What decimal number and money amount are represented by 2 dollars, 7 dimes, and 4 pennies?

REMEMBER:

$= \frac{1}{100}$, or 0.01, of a dollar

$= \frac{10}{100}$, or 0.10, of a dollar

$= \frac{1}{1}$ or 1 dollar

Write the mixed decimal the model shows.

3. 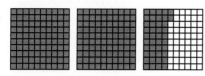   **4.**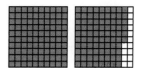

Write as a mixed decimal.

5. two and three tenths

6. eighteen and four tenths

7. six and twenty-three hundredths

8. five and twelve hundredths

Write each mixed decimal in words.

9. 8.05   **10.** 15.87   **11.** 9.2

12. 4.48   **13.** 10.16   **14.** 11.1

Problem Solving • Mixed Applications

15. Money Cal gave the cashier $1.70. How many dollars, dimes, and pennies is that?

16. Consumer Hans spent $4.53 for milk and eggs. The eggs cost $1.49. How much did the milk cost?

17. Sports Chris won 6 out of 10 games in a tennis match. What decimal describes the part of the games that Chris won?

18. ◁▣▷ **Write About It** Tell how you know that 1¢ is the same as 0.01.

Mixed Review and Test Prep

Write the numbers in order from *greatest* to *least*.

(pages 168–169)

19. 34, 68, 82   **20.** 332, 374, 347   **21.** 620, 586, 623

Choose the letter that shows the fraction using numbers.

(pages 370–373)

22. two thirds   **A** $\frac{2}{5}$ **23.** five out of nine   **F** $\frac{5}{9}$ **24.** seven tenths   **A** $\frac{10}{10}$

B $\frac{3}{2}$ **G** $\frac{4}{9}$ **B** $\frac{5}{10}$

C $\frac{1}{3}$ **H** $\frac{1}{5}$ **C** $\frac{10}{7}$

D $\frac{2}{3}$ **J** $\frac{9}{5}$ **D** $\frac{7}{10}$

Comparing Decimal Numbers

Why learn this? You can compare data used in games.

Batter up

Mitch and Mallory took 10 turns in the batting cage. Mallory hit the ball 7 out of 10 times. Mitch hit the ball 5 out of 10 times. Who hit the ball more often?

Use decimal squares to compare the scores.

Mallory's score   Mitch's score

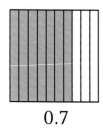   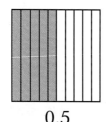

0.7   0.5

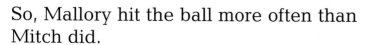

0.7 > 0.5

So, Mallory hit the ball more often than Mitch did.

———————

Which granola bar weighs more?

Use a place-value chart to compare weights.

Place-Value Chart	
ones	tenths
2	5
2	2

Look at the ones.
Then look at the tenths.

2.5 > 2.2

So, the Razzle granola bar weighs more.

CRITICAL THINKING How can you use decimal squares to compare decimals?

► CHECK

Compare. Use < or > for each ●.

1.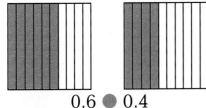

0.6 ● 0.4

2.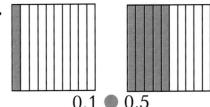

0.1 ● 0.5

► PRACTICE

Compare. Use < or > for each ●.

3.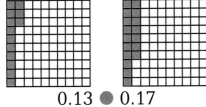

0.13 ● 0.17

4.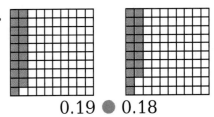

0.19 ● 0.18

5.
Ones	Tenths
0	3
0	5

0.3 ● 0.5

6.
Ones	Tenths
0	9
0	6

0.9 ● 0.6

7.
Ones	Tenths
2	4
2	7

2.4 ● 2.7

Problem Solving • Mixed Applications

8. **Measurement** Tricia rode her bicycle 2.3 miles on Wednesday and 1.4 miles on Thursday. Which day did she ride farther?

9. **Consumer** Which costs more?

10. **Reasoning** Sally lives 2.3 miles from school. Larry lives 2.1 miles from school. Who lives closer?

11. Greg had 100 stickers. He put 48 of them in a book. How many stickers does he have left to put in a book?

12. **Money** Jan spent $3.64 for milk and eggs. The milk cost $2.70. How much were the eggs?

13. **Compare** Art walks $\frac{4}{6}$ mile. Ben walks $\frac{3}{6}$ mile. Who walks farther?

14. ✏ **Write About It** How can you compare 0.9 and 1.0? Which is greater?

LESSON
CONTINUES

Problem–Solving Strategy: Draw a Picture

▶ **THE PROBLEM** On Field Day in the standing long jump, Brett jumped 0.8 meter. Kathy jumped 0.6 meter. Who jumped farther?

REMEMBER:
UNDERSTAND
PLAN
SOLVE
LOOK BACK

UNDERSTAND

• What are you asked to find?

• What information will you use?

• Is there information you will not use? If so, what?

PLAN

• What strategy can you use to solve the problem?

  You can draw a picture to show and compare the decimal amounts.

SOLVE

• How can you use the strategy to solve the problem?

  Shade 0.8 of one decimal square and 0.6 of the other. Compare them.

Brett's Jump   **Kathy's Jump**

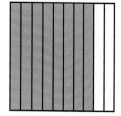   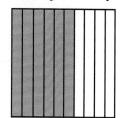

$$0.8 > 0.6$$

So, Brett jumped farther than Kathy.

LOOK BACK

• Why is it helpful to draw a picture?

• What other strategy could you use?

410 Chapter 23

▶ PRACTICE

Draw a picture to solve.

1. Christy lives 0.5 mile from school. Greg lives 0.3 mile from school. Who lives closer to school?

2. Meg ate $\frac{7}{10}$ of a granola bar. Paul ate $\frac{5}{10}$ of a granola bar of the same size. Who ate more?

3. Todd saved $\frac{4}{6}$ of his allowance and spent $\frac{2}{6}$ of it. Did he save or spend more of his allowance?

4. Julie jogged 3.6 miles on Friday and 3.8 miles on Saturday. On which day did she jog farther?

Mixed Applications

Solve.

CHOOSE a strategy and a tool.
- Draw a Picture
- Act It Out
- Find a Pattern
- Make a Model
- Write a Number Sentence

 Paper/Pencil   Calculator   Hands-On   Mental Math

5. Juan wants to buy a game that costs $26. He has saved $18 so far. How much more money does he need to buy the game?

6. A paper chain has 91 red strips and 88 yellow strips. Are there more red strips or yellow strips in the chain?

7. There are 13 people waiting in line at the movie. There are 4 people in front of Rhea. How many people are behind her?

8. Each section of the cafeteria has 9 tables. A table seats 8 students. How many seats are in each section of the cafeteria?

9. Thanksgiving is the fourth Thursday in November. November 16 is the third Thursday this year. What date is Thanksgiving?

10. Ben made this design. What decimal describes the red section?

11. Tyrone walked 1.4 miles to baseball practice. Will walked 1.6 miles to baseball practice. Who walked farther?

MORE PRACTICE page H108

▶ CHECK Understanding

VOCABULARY

1. A __?__ is a number that uses place value and a decimal point to show amounts that are less than one. (page 400)

2. A __?__ separates a whole number from a fractional part of a number. (page 404)

3. There are 100 __?__ in a whole. (page 402)

4. A __?__ means one of ten equal parts. (page 400)

5. A __?__ is a number that is made up of a whole number and a decimal. (page 406)

Write the decimal and fraction for the part that is shaded. (pages 400–401)

Write the mixed decimal the model shows. (pages 406–407)

6.   7.

8.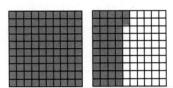

▶ CHECK Skills

Compare. Use < or > for each ●. (pages 408–409)

9.

0.7 ● 0.8

10.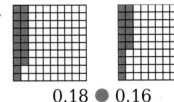

0.18 ● 0.16

Write as a mixed decimal. (pages 406–407)

11. three and five tenths

12. five and two hundredths

▶ CHECK Problem Solving

Solve. (pages 410–411)

CHOOSE a strategy and a tool.
- Draw a Picture   • Act It Out
- Make a Model   • Write a Number Sentence

 Paper/Pencil   Calculator   Hands-On   Mental Math

13. Mia has 0.3 yd of ribbon. Kim has 0.5 yd of ribbon. Who has more ribbon?

14. Neri has 35 cookies to share with 4 friends. How many cookies will each person get?

Test Prep

Choose the best answer.

1. Which part of the figure is shaded?

A $\frac{7}{10}$ **B** $\frac{3}{10}$

C $\frac{4}{5}$ **D** $\frac{3}{8}$

2. In Tabitha's bag, $\frac{3}{10}$ of the marbles are red. In Jenny's bag, $\frac{4}{10}$ are red. Which number sentence shows who has more red marbles?

F $\frac{3}{10} > \frac{4}{10}$ **G** $\frac{4}{10} > \frac{3}{10}$

H $\frac{3}{10} = \frac{4}{10}$ **J** $\frac{2}{10} = \frac{4}{10}$

3. Use the picture to compare fractions.

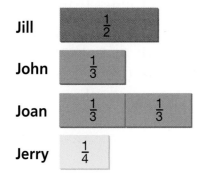

Whose fraction pieces shows the greatest amount?

A Joan **B** Jill

C Jerry **D** John

4. $8 \times 9 = $ ___?___

F 63 **G** 72 **H** 81 **J** 54

5. What is the decimal for the part that is shaded?

A 0.40 **B** 0.04

C 40.0 **D** 4.0

6. Which statement is true about the angle shown below?

F It is a right angle.

G It is less than a right angle.

H It is greater than a right angle.

J The figure is a circle.

7. Which is the same as twelve and seven hundredths?

A 12.7 **B** 0.127

C 12.07 **D** 0.07

8. Which number tells how much is shaded?

F 0.06 **G** 6.0

H 0.6 **J** 60.00

MATH FUN!

THE 'WHOLE' TRUTH

PURPOSE To practice naming fractions that make a whole

YOU WILL NEED set of fraction bars

Play this game in a small group. Place the fraction bars face down. On your turn, pick up two fraction bars. If you do not have enough to make one whole, draw more bars from the pile.

If you go over one whole, you are out. Play until all the fraction bars are used. The winner is the one with the most whole bars.

 Make a set of fraction bars, using colored construction paper, and play the game with members of your family.

THE BIGGER, THE BETTER

PURPOSE To practice comparing fractions

YOU WILL NEED fraction cards for twelfths, sixths, fourths, thirds, and halves

Play this game with a partner. Turn three fraction cards face up. Place the others in a pile face down. On your turn take one card from the pile and compare it with the cards facing up. Take any card that is less than the one you are holding. If none are less, place your card face up with the others. Take turns. If you take all the cards facing up, replace three from the pile. Play until there are no more cards in the pile. The player with more cards wins.

CONCENTRATION

PURPOSE To understand the relationship between fractions and decimals

YOU WILL NEED decimal squares, index cards

Play this game with a small group. First, make cards for 0.1, 0.01, 0.5, 0.05, 0.25, 0.75, 0.2, 0.02, 0.3, 0.03; $\frac{1}{10}$, $\frac{1}{100}$, $\frac{5}{10}$, $\frac{5}{100}$, $\frac{25}{100}$, $\frac{75}{100}$, $\frac{2}{10}$, $\frac{2}{100}$, $\frac{3}{10}$, $\frac{3}{100}$.

Lay the cards face down in a 4-by-5 array. Now, follow the rules for the game of Concentration®.

Comparing Decimals on a Bar Graph

<table>
<tr><td>MATERIALS
Graph Links Plus or any other graphing program</td></tr>
</table>

For his science project, Eric compared the growth of three bean plants using three different brands of plant food. He measured the height of each plant after three weeks. Then he made this bar graph by using a computer graphing program. How tall was the tallest bean plant?

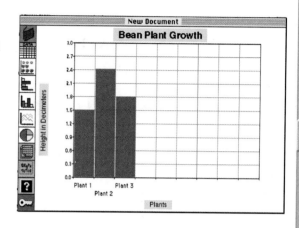

EXAMPLE

You can show decimals with some graphing programs.

In *Graph Links Plus*, choose Preferences from the **Options** menu.

In the Preferences window, click On for Decimal Point. Now you can enter decimals in the Data Center.

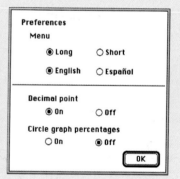

▶ PRACTICE

1. Drake measured the lengths of 5 different insects in centimeters. Make a bar graph to compare their lengths.

Ant	0.8
Ladybug	0.9
Bumblebee	2.1
Horsefly	1.8
Mosquito	1.1

2. **Using the Computer** Zoe compared the heights of the people in her family. Her mother is 1.8 meters tall. Her father is 2.1 meters tall. Her sister is 1.1 meter. Her brother is 1.5 meter. Zoe is 1.4 meter. Use a graphing program to make a bar graph of this data.

Study Guide and Review

Vocabulary Check

Choose a term from the box to complete the sentence.

VOCABULARY

decimal
decimal point
denominator
fraction
mixed decimal
numerator

1. A number that names part of a whole is a _?_.
   (page 370)

2. In a fraction, the _?_ tells how many equal parts are in the whole. (page 370)

3. In a fraction, the _?_ tells how many parts are being used. (page 370)

4. A number that uses place value and a decimal point to show an amount that is less than one, such as tenths, is a _?_. (page 400)

5. A _?_ separates the whole number from the decimal part of a number. (page 404)

6. A _?_ is a number that is made up of a whole number and a decimal. (page 406)

Study and Solve

CHAPTER 21

EXAMPLE

Compare. Write <, >, or = for ●.

$\frac{1}{3}$	$\frac{1}{3}$	$\frac{1}{3}$

$\frac{1}{3}$	$\frac{1}{3}$	$\frac{1}{3}$

$\frac{1}{3}$ ● $\frac{2}{3}$ $\frac{1}{3} < \frac{2}{3}$

For Problems 7–8, tell the part that is shaded. Write your answer using numbers and words. (pages 370–373)

7.

8.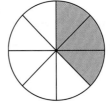

For Problems 9–10, compare. Write <, >, or = for ●. (pages 376–377)

9.

$\frac{1}{8}$ ● $\frac{1}{4}$

10.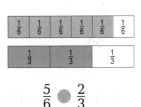

$\frac{5}{6}$ ● $\frac{2}{3}$

Write a fraction to describe the shaded part. Then find an equivalent fraction. Use fraction bars to help you. (pages 374–375, 380–381)

11.

Solve. (pages 378–379)

12. Joe ate $\frac{1}{6}$ of a pie. Lonnie ate $\frac{1}{3}$ of the pie. Who ate more?

CHAPTER 22

EXAMPLE

Look at the picture. Find the number of equal parts that are red.

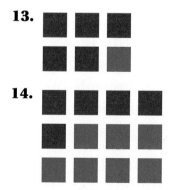

Because 4 out of 5 tiles are red, $\frac{4}{5}$ of the tiles are red.

For Problems 13–14, look at the pictures. Find the number of equal parts that are blue. (pages 386–387)

13.

14.

Draw the picture. Use numbers and words to describe the part that is shaded. (pages 388–389)

15. Draw 7 triangles. Shade 3.

CHAPTER 23

EXAMPLE

Write as a mixed decimal.

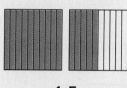

1.5

Write the decimal and the fraction for the part that is shaded. (pages 400–401)

16.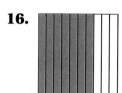

Write the decimal and fraction for the part that is shaded. (pages 404–405)

17.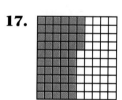

For Problems 18–19, write as a mixed decimal. (pages 406–407)

18. two and seven tenths

19. one and twenty-three hundredths

Solve. (pages 408–409)

20. Billy lives 0.7 mile from his school and 0.3 mile from the park. How much closer does he live to the park than to the school?

Performance Assessment

Tasks: Show What You Know

1. Fold a sheet of paper into eight equal parts. Color three parts blue. Tell what fraction of the paper is blue. Explain how you know what fraction is blue. (pages 368–373)

2. Compare fractions of groups. Use two-color counters to show each part of the group named. Draw their picture. Then write $<$, $>$, or $=$ for each ●. (pages 394–395)

$$\frac{3}{7} \bullet \frac{5}{7} \qquad \frac{4}{5} \bullet \frac{3}{5}$$

3. Use two whole decimal squares divided into 100 equal parts. Shade one whole square and 45 parts of another. Explain how to read and write the decimal name for each shaded part. (pages 406–407)

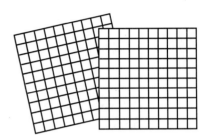

Problem Solving

Solve. Explain your method.

CHOOSE a strategy and a tool.
- Find a Pattern
- Act It Out
- Draw a Picture
- Make a Table
- Make a Model

Paper/Pencil   Calculator   Hands-On   Mental Math

4. Mrs. Fong's class is selling candy. Each student was given the same number of boxes to sell. Walter sold $\frac{1}{6}$ of his candy, Jill sold $\frac{1}{3}$, and Paul sold $\frac{1}{2}$. Who sold the most candy? Explain how you know. (pages 378–379)

5. Tim picked 12 flowers. He gave $\frac{8}{12}$ of the flowers to Mother and $\frac{4}{12}$ of the flowers to Grandmother. How many flowers did he give to Mother? How many did he give to Grandmother? (pages 392–393)

6. Lily and Eli are reading the same book. Lily has read 0.7 of the book. Eli has read 0.6 of his book. Who has read more? Explain. (pages 410–411)

Cumulative Review

Solve the problem. Then write the letter of the correct answer.

1.
   A. 16   **B.** 24
   C. 26   **D.** 36

(pages 38–43)

2. Count the money.

   A. $4.26   **B.** $8.25
   C. $8.26   **D.** $8.35

(pages 106–107)

3. How many hundreds, tens, and ones are in 635?

   A. 3 hundreds, 6 tens, 5 ones
   B. 5 hundreds, 3 tens, 6 ones
   C. 6 hundreds, 3 tens, 5 ones
   D. 6 hundreds, 5 tens, 3 ones

(pages 144–145)

For Problems 4–5, use the spinner.

4. Which is *not* a possible outcome of spinning the pointer on this spinner?

   A. spinning a 1
   B. spinning a 2
   C. spinning a 3
   D. spinning a 4

5. Is the spinner fair or unfair?

   A. fair   **B.** unfair

(pages 296–299, 304–305)

6. A __?__ is a flat surface that goes on and on.

   A. corner   **B.** plane
   C. edge   **D.** solid

(page 322)

7. What kind of motion was used to move the figure?

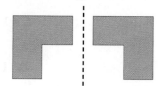

   A. flip   **B.** slide
   C. turn   **D.** tessellate

(pages 348–349)

8. Compare.

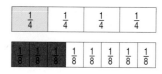

$$\frac{1}{4} \bullet \frac{3}{8}$$

   A. <   **B.** >   **C.** =

(pages 376–377)

9. What is the decimal for the part that is shaded?

   A. 0.01   **B.** 0.09
   C. 0.9   **D.** 0.91

(pages 400–401)

10. What is the mixed decimal for five and six hundredths?

   A. 5.06   **B.** 5.6
   C. 6.05   **D.** 605

(pages 406–407)

24 MEASUREMENT: CUSTOMARY UNITS

0 1 2 3 4 5 6 7 8

Before there were rulers and yardsticks people used body parts to measure length. An inch was the width of a man's thumb, and a foot was the length of a man's foot. Since people vary in size, these measurements were not all alike.

1 yard
1 inch
1 foot

Measurement Marathon

Rulers are convenient tools to measure things. Make your own ruler and then measure three objects.

YOU WILL NEED: 2 strips of paper, 1" × 12"; pencil and paper

- Make your own ruler and recording chart.

- Find and measure three or more objects.

- List each object on your recording sheet.

- Measure each object as exactly as you can and record your findings.

- Compare results with those of a classmate to decide whose measure is more exact.

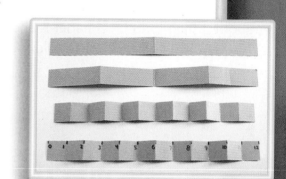

DID YOU

☑ make a ruler with 12 equal sections marked from zero to 12?

☑ make a recording chart?

☑ measure three objects and record your measures?

☑ compare measures with a classmate?

Inch, Foot, Yard, and Mile

Why learn this? You can measure the lengths of objects or distances such as feet or miles.

The customary system of measurement is used widely in the United States. The **inch (in.)**, the **foot (ft)**, the **yard (yd)**, and the **mile (mi)** are the units that are used to measure length or distance.

A paper clip is about 1 **inch** long.

A piece of notebook paper is about 1 **foot** long.

A baseball bat is about 1 **yard** long.

You can walk 1 **mile** in about 20 minutes.

Talk About It CRITICAL THINKING

- How can you decide which customary unit to use when measuring something?

- Suppose you want to measure the length of a crayon. Which unit would you use? Explain.

- What might you measure in your classroom by using inches? by using feet?

▶ CHECK

Choose the unit that you would use to measure each. Write *inch*, *foot*, *yard*, or *mile*.

1. the length of a marker

2. the length of a desk

3. the distance between school and your home

4. the length of the playground

5. the length of your shoe

SCIENCE LINK

Walruses are large sea mammals. Their protective skin is about 1 inch thick. Their foreflippers are about 1 foot to 2 feet long. Their tusks grow to be about 1 yard long. Make a list of other items that are about an inch, a foot, or a yard.

▶ PRACTICE

Choose the unit that you would use to measure each.
Write *inch, foot, yard,* or *mile.*

6. the length of a leaf

7. the length of your leg

8. the distance you could walk in an hour

9. the distance between your classroom and the gym

Choose the better unit of measure. Write *inches, feet, yards,* or *miles.*

10. Your bicycle is about 4 _?_ long.

11. The door of your classroom is about 1 _?_ wide.

12. Your shoe is about 7 _?_ long.

13. A shoelace is about 24 _?_ long.

14. A jet flew 1,217 _?_ .

15. A football player ran 50 _?_ to score the touchdown.

Problem Solving • Mixed Applications

16. Reasoning Which unit of measure would you use to describe the distance you travel to a shopping mall?

17. Compare Ann's handspan is 8 inches. Mel's handspan is 13 inches. How much shorter is Ann's handspan than Mel's?

18. Science Janet wants to find out how much her plant grew last week. Which unit of measure should she use? Explain.

19. ✏️ **Write a problem** about an item that can be measured using inches, feet, or yards. Ask what unit of measure should be used.

Mixed Review and Test Prep

List the possible outcomes of each event. (pages 298–299)

20. flipping a counter with a red side and yellow side

21. flipping a penny and a nickel at the same time

22. rolling a number cube

Round each number to the nearest hundred. Choose the letter of the correct estimate. (pages 172–173)

23. 206 **A** 100
      B 200
      C 300
      D 400

24. 397 **F** 390
      G 307
      H 300
      J 400

25. 583 **A** 580
      B 590
      C 600
      D 700

26. 911 **F** 900
      G 700
      H 1,000
      J 800

Estimating and Comparing Length

You will investigate how to estimate length and to check your estimate by measuring to the nearest inch.

An estimate is an answer that is close to the actual answer. Estimate the length of the red ribbon by using paper clips or your knuckle, or by looking at it. Tell about how many inches long you think it is.

▶ EXPLORE

Use a ruler to find the actual measurement of the red ribbon. Measure to the nearest inch.

MATERIALS: ruler

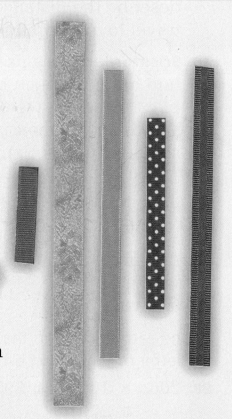

REMEMBER:

To use a *ruler*:

• line up one end of the object with the zero mark.

• find the inch mark closest to the object's other end. The ribbon is about 2 inches long.

Record

Copy the table. Record your estimate and actual measurement for the red ribbon.

Color	Estimate	Measure
red		

• How does your estimate compare with your actual measurement?

Now, investigate estimating and measuring other ribbons.

▶ TRY THIS

1. Estimate and measure the other ribbons.

2. Record your estimates and measurements in the table.

3. How did you estimate the length of each ribbon?

4. ◁▷ **Write About It** How do your estimates compare with your actual measurements? Give examples.

Technology Link

 You can measure length to the nearest inch by using E-Lab, Activity 24. Available on CD-ROM and on the Internet at www.hbschool.com/elab

▶ PRACTICE

Estimate the length of each key. Then use a ruler to measure to the nearest inch.

5.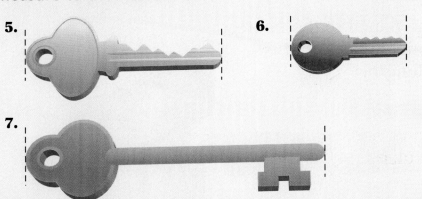

6.

7.

8.

List two things in your classroom that measure about each given length.

9. 1 inch　　　**10.** 6 inches　　　**11.** 12 inches

Problem Solving • Mixed Applications

12. Visual Thinking Without using a ruler, draw a line about 6 inches long. Then measure. Tell what happened.

13. Reasoning Meg's pencil box is about 10 inches long. She wants to put a 12-inch ruler in it. Will it fit? Explain.

14. Money George buys a $0.69 toy. He pays with $1.00. How much change should he receive? What coins might his change be?

15. ◁▷ **Write About It** Explain how you can estimate the length of this piece of yarn.

Measuring to the Nearest Half Inch

Why learn this? You can measure an object, such as a pencil, when the length falls between two inch marks on the ruler.

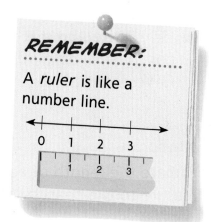

Sometimes you need to measure to the nearest half inch.

To find the length of the pencil to the nearest half inch, look for the $\frac{1}{2}$-inch mark that is nearest to the pencil's length.

So, the pencil is $7\frac{1}{2}$ inches, to the nearest half inch.

Talk About It CRITICAL THINKING

- How do you know where to find the $\frac{1}{2}$-inch marks on the ruler?

- Which straw is longer, one that measures about 3 inches or one that measures about $2\frac{1}{2}$ inches? Explain.

▶ CHECK

Measure the length to the nearest half inch.

1. |⊢————————————|

2. |⊢————————————|

3. |⊢————————————————————|

4. |⊢——————————|

5. |⊢————|

6. |⊢——————————————|

7. |⊢————————————————————————|

Measure the length to the nearest half inch.

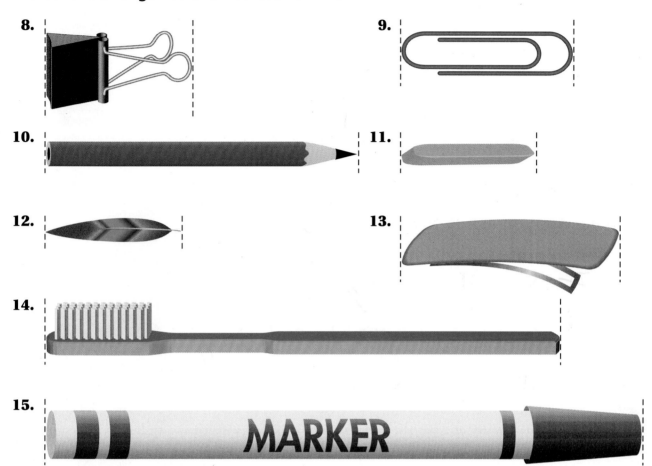

8.

9.

10.

11.

12.

13.

14.

15. **MARKER**

Problem Solving • Mixed Applications

16. **Visual Thinking** Laura's wood strip was 27 inches long. She cut off a 6-inch piece to use for a project. Then she cut three times that length to use on another project. How much wood is left?

17. **Reasoning** The museum has a doll collection. Of the 358 dolls in the collection, 79 are baby dolls. How many of the museum's dolls are not baby dolls?

18. **Number Sense** A comb measures $5\frac{1}{2}$ inches to the nearest half inch. Between which two inch marks does the edge of the comb lie?

19. **Write About It** Would measuring to the nearest inch or to the nearest half inch be closer to an object's actual measurement? Explain.

LESSON CONTINUES

Problem–Solving Strategy: Make a Model

REMEMBER:

UNDERSTAND

PLAN

SOLVE

LOOK BACK

▶ **THE PROBLEM** Your class is learning about the bald eagle. You decide to find out how your armspan compares with the eagle's wingspan. How can you measure and compare your armspan with the wingspan of an eagle?

UNDERSTAND

• What are you asked to do?

• What information will you use?

• Is there any information you will not use? If so, what?

PLAN

• What strategy can you use?

You can *make a model* to measure and compare your partner's armspan with the wingspan of an eagle.

SOLVE

• How can you solve the problem?

Use string to measure the length of the eagle's wingspan and cut.

Use string to measure the length of your partner's armspan and cut.

Use a yardstick to find the length of each string piece to the nearest half inch. Compare.

So, your armspan is less than the eagle's wingspan.

SOCIAL STUDIES LINK

The bald eagle is the national bird of the United States. Its wingspan is about 72 in. About how many yards is the length of the wingspan of a bald eagle?

LOOK BACK

• Why is it helpful to make a model?

• What other strategy could you use?

▶ PRACTICE

Make a model to solve.

1. Suppose you want to make an ankle bracelet. How can you measure your ankle to find its length? Measure to the nearest half inch. Tell how long your ankle bracelet will be.

2. Drew wants to cut a pan of cornbread into 4 equal pieces. In how many ways can she do this? Show how each cut pan would look.

3. There are 7 feet between the door and the pencil sharpener. There are 4 times as many feet between the pencil sharpener and the chalkboard. How far away is the pencil sharpener from the chalkboard?

4. Yuri and his dad put 4 rows of 8 cork squares on his bedroom wall for a bulletin board. How many cork squares did they put up?

Mixed Applications

Solve.

CHOOSE a strategy and a tool.
- Draw a Picture • Act It Out • Find a Pattern
- Make a Model • Write a Number Sentence

Paper/Pencil   Calculator   Hands-On   Mental Math

5. It will take Hannah 45 minutes to do her homework and 30 minutes to eat her lunch. At what time will she finish her homework and lunch?

6. At the end of the day, a restaurant has $\frac{1}{4}$ of an apple pie and $\frac{3}{4}$ of a cherry pie left. Which pie has more left?

7. Emily wants to make a belt. How can she measure her waist to find the length for the belt?

8. How many tulip bulbs are in 5 packages?

9. The numbers of the first three homes on Anita's street are 2600, 2604, 2608. Anita's is the fifth house. What is her house number?

MORE PRACTICE page H109

Estimating and Comparing Capacity

Why learn this? You can decide which customary units to use when measuring liquids.

Capacity is the amount of liquid a container can hold when filled. The customary units for measuring capacity are **cup**, **pint**, **quart**, and **gallon**.

cup (c)

pint (pt)

quart (qt)

gallon (gal)

Fill a measuring cup with water, beans, or rice.

Count the number of cups it takes to fill the pint, quart, and gallon containers. Copy the table and record what you find.

	Pint	Quart	Gallon
Cups			
Pints			
Quarts			

Talk About It

• How many pint containers does it take to fill a quart? a gallon? How many quart containers does it take to fill a gallon? Add your findings to the table.

CRITICAL THINKING Look at the two quart containers in the Remember box. How can you prove that both containers have the same capacity?

▶ CHECK

1. Did it take more cups, pints, or quarts to fill a gallon container? Explain.

2. Suppose you want to measure the amount of water in a bathtub. Which unit would you use? Explain.

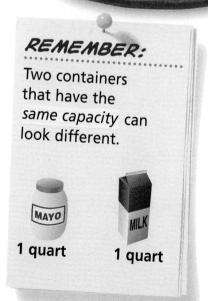

REMEMBER:
Two containers that have the same capacity can look different.

1 quart   1 quart

▶ PRACTICE

Choose the better estimate.

3.  8 pints or
8 gallons

4.  2 cups or
2 quarts

Choose the unit that you would use to measure each.
Write *cup, pint, quart,* or *gallon.*

5. a mug of tea

6. the gas in a car's tank

7. a bowl of soup

8. a container of ice cream

Write the greater amount.

9. 1 cup or 2 pints

10. 1 gallon or 3 quarts

11. 3 pints or 1 quart

12. 4 pints or 7 cups

Problem Solving • Mixed Applications

13. Time Mayta can write her
name 5 times in 1 minute.
How many times can Mayta
write her name in 9 minutes?

14. Consumer Sally mixes 3
cups of fruit juice and 1 pint
of sherbet. How many cups
did Sally mix?

15. Career A toy maker got a
shipment of 32 wheels. How
many 4-wheel toy cars can
the toy maker build with the
new wheels?

16. ✏ **Write About It** How can
two containers with different
shapes hold the same
capacity?

Mixed Review and Test Prep

Tell whether each event is *certain* or *impossible.* (pages 296–297)

17. choosing a penny
from a bag of
dimes

18. getting wet when
jumping into a
lake

19. spinning green
on an all-yellow
spinner

Choose the letter of the correct fraction written as
a number. (pages 370–373)

20. one fourth

   A $\frac{4}{4}$ **B** $\frac{3}{4}$

   C $\frac{4}{1}$ **D** $\frac{1}{4}$

21. five divided by nine

   F $\frac{9}{5}$ **G** $\frac{5}{9}$

   H $\frac{4}{9}$ **J** $\frac{9}{4}$

22. eight out of ten

   A $\frac{8}{10}$ **B** $\frac{10}{8}$

   C $\frac{2}{10}$ **D** $\frac{10}{2}$

MORE PRACTICE page H109

Estimating and Comparing Weight

Why learn this? You can decide which customary units to use to find out how much food and other objects weigh.

The customary units for measuring weight are **ounce (oz)** and **pound (lb)**.

These things weigh about 1 **ounce**.

These things weigh about 1 **pound**.
1 pound = 16 ounces

Place 9 pennies in a plastic cup. The 9 pennies weigh about 1 ounce. Find two things in your classroom that weigh about 1 ounce each.

Place 144 pennies in a second plastic cup. The 144 pennies weigh about 1 pound. Find two things in your classroom that weigh about 1 pound each.

Talk About It

- Which objects did you find that weigh about 1 ounce? that weigh about 1 pound?

- Would you use pounds or ounces to weigh light objects? to weigh heavy objects?

CRITICAL THINKING   Is a larger item always heavier? Why or why not?

▶ CHECK

Choose the unit that you would use to weigh each. Write *ounce* or *pound*.

1.
2.
3.

SCIENCE **LINK**

Some swans weigh as much as 50 pounds. They have long, strong feathers to help them fly. Their outer wing feathers are up to 18 inches long, but two together weigh only 1 ounce. How many of these swan feathers would weigh 1 pound?

Choose the unit that you would use to weigh each.
Write *ounce* or *pound*.

4.

5.

6.

7.

8.

9.

Choose the better estimate.

10.    5 ounces or
5 pounds

11.    9 ounces or
9 pounds

Problem Solving • Mixed Applications

12. Money Lee needs $3.00 to buy new tennis balls. He has $2.89. Does he have enough? Explain.

13. Reasoning Pam has about 800 tickets. She needs 725 tickets to get a stuffed animal. Does she have enough? Explain.

14. Compare A baseball glove weighs about 14 ounces. Is this more than or less than a pound? How much more or less?

15. ✏️ **Write About It** Is a bigger item always a heavier item? Give an example.

Mixed Review and Test Prep

Draw the picture. Use numbers and words to describe
the part that is shaded. (pages 388–389)

16. Draw 6 circles. Shade 1 circle.

17. Draw 5 squares. Shade 1 square.

18. Draw 10 stars. Make 2 equal groups. Shade 1 group.

Choose the letter that names the point on the number line. (pages 370–373)

19. $\frac{0}{5}$? $\frac{5}{5}$ **A** $\frac{1}{5}$ **B** $\frac{2}{5}$
    0   1   **C** $\frac{4}{5}$ **D** $\frac{3}{5}$

20. $\frac{0}{8}$? $\frac{8}{8}$ **F** $\frac{6}{8}$ **G** $\frac{5}{8}$
    0   1   **H** $\frac{1}{8}$ **J** $\frac{3}{8}$

▶ CHECK Understanding

VOCABULARY

1. The customary units used to measure length or distance are __?__, __?__, __?__, and __?__. (page 422)

2. The customary units used to measure capacity are __?__, __?__, __?__, and __?__. (page 430)

3. The amount of liquid a container can hold when filled is its __?__. (page 430)

4. The customary units used to measure weight are __?__ and __?__. (page 432)

▶ Check Skills

Choose the best estimate. (pages 422–425; 430–433)

5.
6 in. or 6 ft

6. 1 pt or 1 gal

7. 1 oz or 1 lb

8. 2 oz or 2 lb

9. 25 in. or 25 ft

10. 1 c or 1 qt

▶ Check Problem Solving

Solve. (pages 428–429)

CHOOSE a strategy and a tool.

• Draw a Picture • Act It Out • Find a Pattern
• Make a Model • Write a Number Sentence

 Paper/Pencil   Calculator   Hands-On   Mental Math

11. Iris is making slacks. How might she find out her waist measurement?

12. How could the Smiths complete their garden so it is symmetrical?

13. Tony's baseball glove weighs 16 ounces. What is another name for the amount Tony's baseball glove weighs?

14. Joan poured 2 quarts of water into a bucket. How many more quarts of water would she have to add for it to have 1 gallon of water in it?

Test Prep

Choose the best answer.

1. Round 837 to the nearest hundred.

   A 900

   B 800

   C 600

   D 700

2. This table shows the distance some children ride to school.

   Who rides the farthest?

RIDE TO SCHOOL	
Student	Miles
Anna	0.9
Miguel	1.3
Tory	1.1
Tyrone	0.8

   F Anna   G Miguel

   H Tory   J Tyrone

3. A pencil measures $6\frac{1}{2}$ inches. Between which two inch marks on a ruler is the point of the pencil?

   A between 5 and 6 inches

   B between 7 and 8 inches

   C between 6 and 7 inches

   D between 4 and 5 inches

4. Which shows the numbers in order from *greatest* to *least*?

   F 415, 377, 395

   G 395, 377, 415

   H 415, 395, 377

   J 377, 395, 415

5. There were 100 students who tried out for a play. Of these, 56 students were chosen. What decimal describes the students that were chosen?

   A 0.1   B 5.6

   C 0.65   D 0.56

6. There are 32 students in the third grade. They work in groups of 4. How many groups are there?

   F 128

   G 6

   H 28

   J 8

7. Dillon weighed 10 math books. Which is the better unit of measure?

   A ounce

   B pound

   C inch

   D yard

8. Use this table to compare weights.

COMPARING WEIGHTS	
Object	Weight
lamp	6 pounds
book	1 pound
dog	30 pounds
fruit	18 ounces

   Which weighs the most?

   F dog   G book

   H lamp   J fruit

25 MEASUREMENT: METRIC UNITS

There are two systems of measuring temperatures. In the customary system, you measure with a Fahrenheit scale, in which normal body temperature is about 98.6°F.

Problem-Solving Activity

Use a Thermometer

Record the temperature for one week in and around your classroom. Read a Fahrenheit thermometer and a Celsius thermometer two times every day. Make observations about the temperatures and the location of the thermometers.

YOU WILL NEED: 2 thermometers, 1 of each scale; tape; paper and pencil

• Decide on a location for the two thermometers and attach them side by side with tape.

• Make a recording chart for each thermometer.

• Set two times a day to record the temperature, once near the beginning of the day and once near the end.

• Record the results for one week.

• Share your results with your class.

DID YOU

☑ place the thermometers in two locations and record the results for one week?

☑ share your results and the locations of the thermometers with your class?

Temperatures		Celsius	
Fahrenheit		9:30 A.M.	2:30 P.M.
9:30 A.M.	2:30 P.M.	11°C	17°C
Mon 52°F	63°F	12°C	17°C
Tue 54°F	62°F	12°C	19°C
Wed 54°F	67°F	16°C	20°C
Thu 60°F	68°F	14°C	19°C
Fri 58°F	66°F		

Centimeter, Decimeter, Meter

Why learn this? You can measure items in your classroom using different units of measure.

The metric system of measurement is used in many countries around the world. **Centimeter (cm)**, **decimeter (dm)**, and **meter (m)** are the units used to measure length or distance.

A *centimeter* is about the width of your index finger.

A *decimeter* is about the width of an adult's hand.

1 dm = 10 cm

Your armspan is about 1 *meter* long.

1 m = 10 dm, or 100 cm

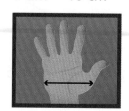

Talk About It CRITICAL THINKING

- How can you decide which metric unit to use to measure something?

- Suppose you want to measure the length of a paper clip. Which unit would you use? Explain.

- What might you measure in your classroom using centimeters? using meters?

▶ CHECK

Choose the unit that you would use to measure each. Write *cm*, *dm*, or *m*.

1. a fingernail

2. a notebook

3. the distance between your desk and the teacher's desk

4. a glue stick

CULTURAL LINK

In 1791, French scientists invented a system of measuring based on the meter and called it the metric system. The metric system uses place value based on ten, just like our number system. Each larger unit is made up of ten smaller ones.

Examples

1 dm = 10 cm

1 m = 10 dm

How many centimeters are in 1 meter?

▶ PRACTICE

Choose the unit that you would use to measure each.
Write *cm*, *dm*, or *m*.

5. a whistle

6. a paintbrush

7. your height

8. the distance you could walk in one minute

9. the distance around a cup

10. the distance you can throw a ball

Choose the unit that was used to measure each.
Write *cm*, *dm*, or *m*.

11. Your math book is about 3 _?_ long.

12. A glue stick is about 12 _?_ long.

13. The classroom door is about 1 _?_ wide.

14. Maria ran about 400 _?_ in 5 minutes.

15. A computer disk is about 9 _?_ wide.

16. A ballpoint pen is about 2 _?_ long.

Problem Solving • Mixed Applications

17. Number Sense The morning temperature was 18°C. In the afternoon it was 33°C. How much warmer was it in the afternoon?

18. Compare Ann's shoes are 19 cm long. Jesse's shoes are 8 cm longer. How long are Jesse's shoes?

19. Elapsed Time Mrs. Green gave her class 3 weeks to prepare a book report. The book report was due on May 25. When did she tell the class about it?

20. ▥ **Write About It** Does it take more centimeter units or more decimeter units to measure the same object? Explain.

Mixed Review and Test Prep

Write the fraction by using numbers. (pages 370–373)

21. three fourths

22. one divided by six

23. seven out of eight

Choose the letter of the correct product. (pages 208–211)

24. $5 \times 7 = $ _?_   **A** 35   **B** 70   **C** 40   **D** 56

25. $7 \times 2 = $ _?_   **F** 7   **G** 10   **H** 9   **J** 14

26. $9 \times 7 = $ _?_   **A** 72   **B** 36   **C** 63   **D** 54

MORE PRACTICE page H110

Estimating and Comparing Length

You will investigate how to estimate, compare, and measure metric length.

▶ EXPLORE

Estimate and measure the length of the objects shown. Use centimeters, decimeters, and meters as units of measure.

MATERIALS: centimeter ruler, meterstick, classroom objects shown

Record

Copy the table. Record your estimate. Then measure to the nearest whole unit and record.

Object	Unit	Estimate	Measurement
pencil	dm		
paper clip	cm		
chalk	cm		
scissors	cm		
pen	dm		
door	m		
desk	m		

Now investigate sorting objects by length. Use the objects from the chart.

► TRY THIS

1. Which objects are less than 1 dm long? greater than 1 dm long? greater than 1 m long?

2. How did you estimate the length of each object?

3. 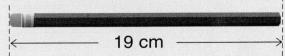 **Write About It** Could the length of a crayon be 1 dm or 10 cm? Explain.

► PRACTICE

Estimate and measure each object. Use the unit of measure given.

4. the length of a chalkboard eraser (cm)

5. the length of your math book (dm)

6. the length of a small paper clip (cm)

7. the height of your chair (m)

List two things that measure about as long as these measurements.

8. 1 centimeter   9. 1 decimeter   10. 1 meter

Technology Link

You can estimate metric length by using E-Lab, Activity 25. Available on CD-ROM and on the Internet at www.hbschool.com/elab

Problem Solving • Mixed Applications

11. **Number Sense** William cut a 100-cm rope into 2 pieces. One piece is 63 cm. How long is the other piece?

12. **Reasoning** Patti is 82 cm tall. Rose is 8 dm tall. Meg is 9 dm tall and Yolanda is 89 cm tall. Who is tallest? Explain.
    HINT: 1 dm = 10 cm

13. **Mental Math** The third-grade class is running a 15-yard relay. A marker is placed every 3 yards after the starting line. How many markers are used?

14. **Geometry** The swimming pool is 37 feet long and 18 feet wide. What is the perimeter of the pool?

15. **Money** Carol has 6 quarters, 10 dimes, and a penny. Does she have enough to buy a key chain for $3.00? Explain.

16. 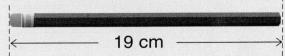 **Write a problem** using the information shown.

19 cm

MORE PRACTICE page H110

Measuring and Drawing Length

Why learn this? You can draw lines to a given length or find the length of an object in centimeters.

Marc needs to draw a 15-cm line to begin the sketch of the bridge he is building. How can you help him measure and draw the 15-cm line?

MODEL

Step 1	Step 2	Step 3
Place the ruler where you want to draw the line.	Draw a dot by the left edge, or zero mark. Draw another dot above the 15 mark on the ruler.	Draw a line connecting the two dots.
	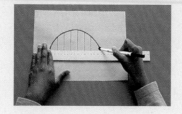	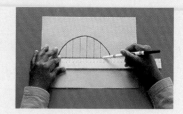

So, Marc can use a centimeter ruler to measure and draw a line of a given length.

To check his work, Marc can use the ruler to measure the line he drew.

So, Marc's line is 15 cm long.

▶ CHECK

1. Describe how Marc could draw a line measuring 21 cm.

2. How are drawing a line and measuring a line alike?

Measure each object or line.

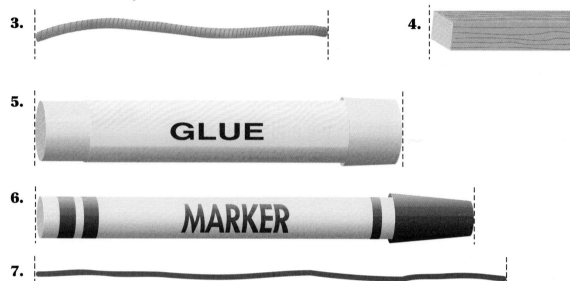

3.

4.

5. GLUE

6. MARKER

7.

Draw a line of the given length.

8. 7 cm **9.** 16 cm **10.** 22 cm

Problem Solving • Mixed Applications

11. Compare Rita's pencil is 4 cm longer than Judd's pencil. Judd's pencil is 1 dm long. How long is Rita's pencil?

12. Estimation One paper clip is about 3 cm long. About how long would a 5-clip chain be?

13. Logic Hope scored 15 points. Ruth scored 3 less than Hope. Kendra scored 2 points. Sara scored 3 times as many as Kendra. Louisa scored 1 less than Hope. How many points did Ruth, Sara, and Louisa score?

14. Time Andrew worked on his model plane for 16 minutes more than Justin. Together, they spent 54 minutes on their planes. How many minutes did each boy spend on his plane?

15. Visual Thinking Tab thought that he drew a 7-cm line, but now it measures 9 cm. What could have happened?

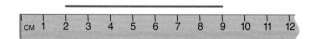

16. ✏ **Write About It** Cal wants to draw a line between 8 and 12 cm long. Draw a line for Cal. Tell its length to the nearest cm. Then tell how you drew the line. LESSON CONTINUES

Problem–Solving Strategy: Work Backward

▶ **THE PROBLEM** Marc spent 3 days building a 52-cm bridge out of straws and craft sticks. He built 15 cm of the bridge on Tuesday and 18 cm on Wednesday. He used 50 straws and 25 craft sticks for the project. How much of the bridge did he build on Monday?

REMEMBER:
UNDERSTAND
PLAN
SOLVE
LOOK BACK

UNDERSTAND

- What are you asked to do?

- What information will you use?

- Is there any information you will not use? If so, what?

PLAN

- What strategy can you use to solve the problem?

  You can *work backward* to find the length of the bridge part built on Monday.

SOLVE

- How can you work backward to solve the problem?

  Add the lengths of the parts built on Tuesday and Wednesday.

$$
\begin{array}{r} 15 \\ +18 \\ \hline 33 \end{array}
\qquad
\begin{array}{r} 52 \\ -33 \\ \hline 19 \end{array}
$$

  Subtract that sum from the total length.

  So, Marc built 19 cm of the bridge on Monday.

LOOK BACK

- Why is it helpful to work backward?

- What other strategy could you use?

SCIENCE LINK

The Golden Gate Bridge, which is in San Francisco, California, is one of the longest bridges of its kind. It measures 2,737 meters. Use a calculator to find out how many centimeters long the Golden Gate Bridge is.

Work backward to solve.

1. James spent 4 days building an 84-cm bridge. He built 16 cm on Thursday, 23 cm on Friday, and 37 cm on Saturday. How much of the bridge did James build on Wednesday?

2. Mr. Ho sells birds. He sold 8 birds and then bought 4 more. Now he has 14 birds. How many birds did he have to begin with?

3. Boris bought a pack of postcards. A friend gave him 8 postcards. Boris used 18 postcards. He has 6 left. How many postcards were in the pack Boris bought?

4. Kara has 57 animal stickers and 12 fuzzy stickers in her 100-sticker collection. How many stickers in Kara's collection are not animal or fuzzy stickers?

Mixed Applications

Solve.

CHOOSE a strategy and a tool.
- Draw a Picture • Act It Out • Find a Pattern
- Make a Model • Work Backward

Paper/Pencil   Calculator   Hands-On   Mental Math

5. Shawn's party is now over. It lasted for 3 hours. When did it start?

6. Cathy has 20 photos in her scrapbook. She has 8 family photos and 3 dog photos. The rest are photos of her friends. How many of Cathy's photos are of her friends?

7. Kim did 2 sit-ups the first week, 4 the second week, and 6 the third week. If this pattern continues, how many sit-ups will Kim do the tenth week?

8. Which would cost less, 4 small stickers or 3 large stickers?

9. In the row of lockers, Carlos has the middle locker. There are 12 lockers to the right of Carlos's locker. How many lockers are in the row?

Estimating and Comparing Capacity

Why learn this? You can decide which metric units to use when measuring liquids.

Capacity is the amount a container will hold when it is filled. Capacity can be measured by using metric units such as **milliliter (mL)**, and **liter (L)**.

A medicine dropper has a capacity of about 1 mL.

1 mL

A water glass has a capacity of about 250 mL.

250 mL

A water bottle has a capacity of about 1,000 mL, or 1 L.

1,000 mL, or 1 L

Ms. West told the students that they should drink 2,000 mL of water a day. How many 1-L sipper bottles of water should each student drink?

Pour water, rice, or beans from mL containers to L containers to help you find the answer.

1,000 mL = 1 L, so 2,000 mL = 2 L.

So, each of Ms. West's students should drink two 1-L sipper bottles of water each day.

Talk About It

• What are two things that are measured in milliliters?

• What are two things that are measured in liters?

▶ CHECK

1. What metric unit would you use to measure the amount of water a spoon holds?

2. Is a liter closer to a quart or a gallon?

Choose the better estimate. Write *mL* or *L*.

3.

250 mL or 250 L

4.

2 mL or 2 L

5.

5 mL or 5 L

6.

3 mL or 3L

7.

5 mL or 5 L

8.

500 mL or 500 L

Choose the unit you would use to measure each.
Write *mL* or *L*.

9. a mug of soup

10. a tank of gasoline

11. a jug of cider

12. a bottle of syrup

Problem Solving • Mixed Applications

13. Logic Shelby wants to add 3,000 mL of water to the fish tank. How many times will she have to fill a 1-L container to do this?

14. Tess filled her dog's 500-mL water dish. Now the dish has 175 mL of water. How much water is gone?

15. Reasoning An 8-L pot of soup is divided equally into 4 bowls. How much soup does each bowl hold?

16. ✏️ **Write About It**
Make a list of household items that come in containers that hold about 1 L.

Mixed Review and Test Prep

Choose the unit that you would use to measure each.
Write *cup, pint, quart,* or *gallon.* (pages 430–431)

17. glass of water

18. a bathtub full of water

19. a small container of ice cream

Choose the letter of the correct mixed decimal. (pages 406–407)

20. one and sixth tenths   **A** 6.2 **B** 6.1 **C** 1.6 **D** 1.5

21. four and five hundredths   **F** 4.50 **G** 4.05 **H** 5.40 **J** 5.50

22. seven and thirteen hundredths   **A** 7.13 **B** 7.31 **C** 1.13 **D** 7.03

Estimating and Comparing Mass

Why learn this? You can decide which metric units to use to find the mass, or amount of matter in, an object.

The metric units for measuring mass are **gram (g)** and **kilogram (kg)**.

1g   1 kg = 1,000 g   1,000 g = 1 kg

These things have a mass of about 1 gram.   These things have a mass of about 1 kilogram.

You can use a simple balance to find mass.

• Place a book that has a mass of about 1 kilogram on one side of a simple balance. Place one classroom object at a time on the other side. List the objects that have a mass of about 1 kilogram.

• Place one paper clip on one side of a simple balance. Place one classroom object at a time on the other side. List the objects that have a mass of about 1 gram.

• How does the simple balance help you decide if an object has a mass of about 1 kilogram or 1 gram?

▶ CHECK

1. Which unit is used to find the mass of small items?

2. Suppose you wanted to find your mass. Would you use grams or kilograms?

Choose the better estimate. Write *g* or *kg*.

3.

1 g or 1 kg

4.

1 g or 1 kg

5.

7 g or 7 kg

6.

20 g or 20 kg

7.

10 g or 10 kg

8.

2 g or 2 kg

9.

10 g or 10 kg

10.

12 g or 12 kg

11.

20 g or 20 kg

Choose the unit you would use to measure each.
Write *g* or *kg*.

12. a marking pen

13. a dictionary

14. an index card

15. a television set

16. a bowling ball

17. a tennis ball

Problem Solving • Mixed Applications

18. Career The veterinarian is finding the mass of Sharon's dog. Will the doctor use g or kg?

19. Logic Jed gained 2 kg this year. His mass is 41 kg now. What was his mass last year?

20. Compare A stapler has a mass of about 800 g. A tape holder has a mass of about 1 kg. Which has a greater mass?

21. **Write a problem** about the picture.

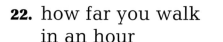

Mixed Review and Test Prep

Choose the unit that you would use to measure each. Write *inch, foot, yard,* or *mile*. (pages 422–423)

22. how far you walk in an hour

23. the length of your arm

24. the length of a marker

Choose the letter of each decimal written as a fraction. (pages 400–401)

25. 0.1 **A** $\frac{1}{0}$ **B** $\frac{1}{10}$

 C $\frac{0}{1}$ **D** $\frac{10}{1}$

26. 0.4 **F** $\frac{1}{4}$ **G** $\frac{1}{14}$

 H $\frac{3}{4}$ **J** $\frac{4}{10}$

27. 0.2 **A** $\frac{2}{1}$ **B** $\frac{12}{10}$

 C $\frac{2}{10}$ **D** $\frac{11}{10}$

▶ CHECK Understanding

VOCABULARY

1. The metric units used to measure length or distance are __?__, __?__, and __?__. (page 438)

2. The amount a container will hold when it is filled is its __?__. (page 446)

3. Capacity can be measured by using metric units such as __?__ and __?__. (page 446)

4. The metric units for measuring mass are __?__ and __?__. (page 448)

▶ CHECK Skills

Choose the better estimate. (pages 440–441, 446–449)

5.

8 cm or 8 dm

6.

2 mL or 2 L

7.

1 g or 1 kg

8.

10 g or 10 kg

9.

25 dm or 25 m

10.

250 mL or 250 L

▶ Check Problem Solving

Solve. (pages 444–445)

CHOOSE a strategy and a tool.

- Draw a Picture
- Act It Out
- Find a Pattern
- Make a Model
- Work Backward

 Paper/Pencil Calculator Hands-On Mental Math

11. Izzy works 20 hours each week. He worked 8 hours on Saturday and 4 hours on Sunday. How many hours does he still have to work?

12. A class of 30 students went on a field trip. Each carpool driver could drive 4 students. How many carpool drivers did the class need?

13. Ms. Gerber lost 5 markers. Her class used up 9 more. There are 10 markers left. How many markers were there to begin with?

14. Jeff jogged 6 kilometers each day for 7 days. How many kilometers did he jog?

Test Prep

Choose the best answer.

1. Which unit should be used to measure the distance around the classroom?

   A kilogram
   B liter
   C meter
   D gram

2. Which unit is the smallest?

   F quart
   G pint
   H gallon
   J cup

3. Tell which event is impossible to happen?

   A choosing a penny from a bag of mixed coins

   B spinning green on an all yellow spinner

   C getting wet when walking in the rain

   D playing a game with a friend

4. Which unit could be used to weigh a cat?

   F inch
   G cup
   H mile
   J pound

5. $8 \times 9 = \underline{\ ?\ }$

   A 74   B 72
   C 81   D 76

6. Susan earned $45 cutting lawns. She cut one lawn each day for 5 days. How much money did she earn for each lawn?

   F $5
   G $40
   H $6
   J $9

7. Use numbers to write the fraction *one fourth*.

   A $\frac{1}{3}$ B $\frac{1}{4}$
   C $\frac{1}{2}$ D $\frac{4}{8}$

8. Which unit could be used to measure the mass of a lunch box?

   F liter
   G milliliter
   H kilogram
   J centimeter

9. Use this table to compare the mass of some objects.

MEASURING MASS	
Object	**Mass**
TV	12 kg
floppy disk	2 g
telephone	7 kg
stepladder	36 kg

Which has the greatest mass?

A TV   B stepladder
C floppy disk   D telephone

26 MEASURING PLANE FIGURES

Butterflies like bright-colored flowers and drink their nectar. Butterflies like warm, sunny gardens. Large rocks give them a warm place to sit in the sun. A birdbath or a puddle is a source of water.

PERENNIAL
BUTTERFLY WEED
ASCLEPIAS
$1.69

PLANTER MIXED COLORS
ZINNIA

PERENNIAL
MARMALADE
RUDBECKIA

Problem-Solving Activity

Plan a Butterfly Garden

Suppose that you could design a butterfly garden. Your garden can be no larger than 10 feet by 8 feet in size.

Plan a flower garden for butterflies that includes bright flowers, parsley for caterpillars, some large rocks, and a birdbath.

YOU WILL NEED: inch grid paper; pencil, crayons, or markers; books, magazines, or seed catalogs

- Draw the outline of your garden on inch grid paper.

- Show where you would put flowers, parsley, large rocks, and a birdbath.

- Find the number of squares within your garden to find its area.

- Write number sentences that show the length around your garden and its area.

DID YOU

- ☑ draw a plan for a butterfly garden?

- ☑ find the length around your garden and the area inside your garden?

- ☑ write number sentences?

grass rock rock
parsley bird bath
cosmos nasturtium
impatiens sunflowers

length around = 6 + 10 + 6 + 10 = 32 feet
area = 6 × 10 = 60 square feet

VOCABULARY
perimeter

Finding Perimeter

Why learn this? You can compare distances around plane figures such as posters.

Joseph wants to glue ribbon around the outside of his poster. How much ribbon will he need?

Joseph uses connecting cubes to measure each side of the poster. Then he counts the cubes.

So, the poster is about 52 cubes around. The distance around a plane figure is its **perimeter**.

CRITICAL THINKING How could you find the number of cubes without counting each one? Explain.

Use connecting cubes to find the perimeter of your math book. Be sure one side of each cube fits along the side of your book.

MODEL

Step 1	**Step 2**
Make lines of cubes to show the length of each side.	Count or add the cubes to find how many in all.

▶ CHECK

1. How many cubes form the distance around your math book?

2. Suppose you used large paper clips to measure your math book. Would you need more or fewer clips than cubes? Explain.

3. How can you find the perimeter of a 3-sided figure?

Technology Link

In *Mighty Math Carnival Countdown*, the game *Pattern Block Roundup* challenges you to find the perimeter of figures. Use Grow Slide Levels N and O.

Find the perimeter of each figure in cubes.

4.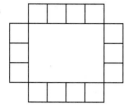

5.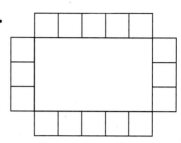

Use unit cubes. Find the perimeter of each figure.

6.

7.

8.

9.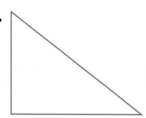

Problem Solving • Mixed Applications

10. Measurement Lois made a square that measures 3 cubes on each side. What was the perimeter of the square?

11. Number Sense A box of 24 pencils is shared equally among 4 students. How many pencils does each student get?

12. Money Ed buys a pack of clay for 74¢. He pays with a $1 bill. What are the fewest coins he will receive in change?

13. ✏️ **Write a problem** using perimeter and this drawing.

Mixed Review and Test Prep

Write the number. Tell whether it is *odd* or *even*. (pages 132–133)

14. 12 **15.** 35 **16.** 27 **17.** 48 **18.** 100

Choose the letter that shows the value of the blue digit. (pages 144–145)

19. 485
 A 8 ones
 B 8 tens
 C 8 hundreds
 D 8 thousands

20. 263
 F 3 ones
 G 3 tens
 H 3 hundreds
 J 3 thousands

21. 15,935
 A 5 tens
 B 5 hundreds
 C 5 thousands
 D 5 hundred thousands

More About Perimeter

Why learn this? You can find the distance around something, such as a picture frame.

Suppose you want to frame a classmate's photo with ribbon. How much ribbon would you need to go around the outside of a classmate's photo?

Measure the perimeter of the photo to find out.

Use a ruler to find the length of each side. Then add the lengths to find how much ribbon is needed.

$6 + 9 + 6 + 9 = 30$, or 30 cm

So, 30 cm of ribbon is needed to go around the outside of the photo.

CRITICAL THINKING   Would the perimeter change if the sides were added in a different order? Explain.

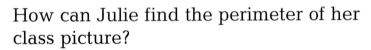

How can Julie find the perimeter of her class picture?

She can add the measurements for each side.

So, the perimeter of her class picture is 24 inches.

▶ CHECK

1. How would you find the perimeter of a triangle with sides measuring 6, 8, and 10 inches?

2. How can you find the perimeter of an object if the measure of its sides is not shown?

▶ PRACTICE

Use your centimeter ruler to find the perimeter.

3.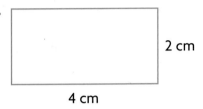

4.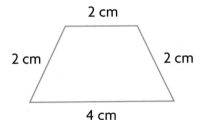

Find the perimeter of each figure.

5.
2 cm
4 cm

6.
2 cm
2 cm   2 cm
4 cm

7.
3 cm
1 cm   1 cm
3 cm

8.
1 cm
6 cm

Problem Solving • Mixed Applications

9. Compare Mario has $\frac{2}{4}$ yard of red ribbon and $\frac{1}{4}$ yard of blue ribbon. Of which color does he have more?

10. There were 17 birds in a tree. Then 6 more birds flew to the tree, and 9 flew away. How many birds are in the tree?

11. Measurement Rick is gluing ribbon around a picture frame. The frame is 5 inches long and 4 inches wide. How many inches of ribbon does Rick need?

12.  **Write About It** Explain how you can find the perimeter of your favorite photo.

Mixed Review and Test Prep

Tell whether the two figures are congruent. Write *yes* or *no*. (pages 336–337)

13.    **14.**   **15.**

Choose the letter of the correct unit of measure. (pages 438–439)

16. an eraser   **A** centimeter   **B** decimeter   **C** meter   **D** liter

17. a book   **F** gram   **G** decimeter   **H** meter   **J** liter

18. length of a bus   **A** centimeter   **B** gram   **C** meter   **D** liter

Finding Area

You will investigate finding the area of a plane figure.

Area is the number of square units needed to cover a flat surface. You can use square tiles to find the area of your math book.

▶ EXPLORE

Use tiles. Cover the front of your math book. Try to cover the whole surface.

MATERIALS: tiles, math book, index card, calculator, crayon box

Record

Draw a picture to show what you did.

Write the number of tiles you used to cover the book. Your number tells the book's area in square units.

Now investigate finding the area of other objects.

▶ TRY THIS

1. Cover each object with tiles. Tell its area in square units.

   A. an index card   **B.** a calculator   **C.** a crayon box

2. How did you find out how many tiles were needed to cover each object?

3. ✏️ **Write About It** How can you find the area using the number of tiles in one row and the total number of rows?

▶ PRACTICE

Use square tiles to make each figure. Draw the figures. Write the area in square units.

4. 3 rows of tiles, 2 tiles in each row

5. 4 rows of tiles, 3 tiles in each row

6. 5 rows of tiles, 3 tiles in each row

7. 3 rows of tiles, 3 tiles in each row

Technology Link

You can find the area of plane figures by using E-Lab, Activity 26. Available on CD-ROM and on the Internet at www.hbschool.com/elab

Find the area of each figure. Label the answer in square units.

8.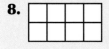

9.

10.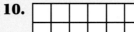

11.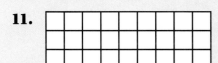

Problem Solving • Mixed Applications

12. A tile floor has 6 rows with 4 tiles in each row. How many tiles are used to make the floor?

13. Visual Thinking A square floor tile is 4 inches on each side. What is its perimeter?

14. Estimation Sam estimated that 300 tiles would be needed for a classroom floor. Jeff estimated the amount to be 400 tiles. There were 387 tiles used. Whose estimate was closer?

15. Patterns Ellen is making a quilt, using a row of print fabric squares and then a row of solid squares. If she continues this pattern and begins with print squares, will the 12th row be solid or print squares?

16. Mental Math James used square tiles to make a hot plate for his mother. He used 8 tiles in each row. He made 9 rows. What is the area of the hot plate?

17. ✏️ **Write a problem** about the figure using area.

Perimeter and Area

Why learn this? You can predict what will happen to a garden's perimeter and area when you change its shape.

Lauren has enough fencing to put around the perimeter of a 16-square-foot garden plot. She wants to use as little fencing as possible. How can she find the smallest perimeter for a 16-square-foot figure?

Make all the rectangles you can with an area of 16 square feet.

Rectangle A	Rectangle B	Rectangle C

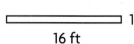 1 ft
16 ft

□ 2 ft
8 ft

□ 4 ft
4 ft

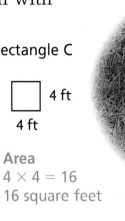

Area
16 × 1 = 16
16 square feet

Area
8 × 2 = 16
16 square feet

Area
4 × 4 = 16
16 square feet

Find the perimeter of each rectangle.

Rectangle A	Rectangle B	Rectangle C

1 ft
16 ft

2 ft
8 ft

4 ft
4 ft

Perimeter
16 + 1 + 16 + 1 = 34
34 feet

Perimeter
8 + 2 + 8 + 2 = 20
20 feet

Perimeter
4 + 4 + 4 + 4 = 16
16 feet

So, the 16-square-foot garden plot with the smallest perimeter is Rectangle C.

▶ CHECK

1. What is the shape of the garden plot with the largest perimeter? the smallest perimeter?

2. Describe the changes in perimeters when figures with the same area change shape from long and thin to square.

Find the area and perimeter of the figure.

3. 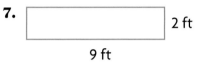 1 ft
   8 ft

4. 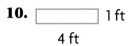 2 ft
   6 ft

5.  3 ft
   4 ft

6. ☐ 1 ft
   12 ft

7. ☐ 2 ft
   9 ft

8. ☐ 3 ft
   6 ft

9. ☐ 2 ft
   5 ft

10. ☐ 1 ft
   4 ft

11. ☐ 3 ft
   3 ft

Problem Solving • Mixed Applications

12. Visual Thinking Suppose a pair of picture frames have the same area. Which frame uses more wood? Explain.

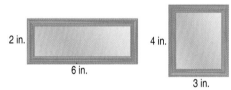

2 in. 6 in. 4 in. 3 in.

13. Reasoning A tile design is 6 feet long and 6 feet wide. How can the 1-foot squares be moved so that the area stays the same but the perimeter changes?

14. Measurement Joe is making a dog pen that is 14 feet long by 10 feet wide. How many feet of fencing does Joe need to buy?

15. Mental Math Rhonda's blanket is 7 feet wide and 9 feet long. What is the area of the blanket?

16. Money Ethan bought 2 hot dogs for $2.25 each and a drink for $1.75. How much did he spend?

17. ✏️ **Write About It** Suppose a flower bed has an area of 9 square feet. Could its perimeter be 12 feet? Explain.

LESSON CONTINUES ⇨

Problem–Solving Strategy: Act It Out

▶ **THE PROBLEM** A toymaker wants you to design a gameboard made up of tiles 1 inch square. Its perimeter must be 24 inches and its area 32 square inches. What will the gameboard look like? How long will it be? How wide will it be?

REMEMBER:
- UNDERSTAND
- PLAN
- SOLVE
- LOOK BACK

UNDERSTAND

- What are you asked to do?

- What information will you use?

- Is there any information you will not use? If so, what?

PLAN

- What strategy can you use to solve the problem?

  Act it out to find the length and width of the gameboard.

SOLVE

- How can you act it out to solve the problem?

  Use tiles 1 inch square to make all the rectangles you can with an area of 32 square inches.

  Find the perimeter of each rectangle. Look for a perimeter of 24 inches.

  So, the gameboard is a rectangle that is 8 inches long and 4 inches wide.

2 in.
16 in.
A = 32 sq in.
P = 36 in.

4 in.
8 in.
A = 32 sq in.
P = 24 in.

32 in.
A = 32 sq in.
P = 66 in.

LOOK BACK

- Why is it helpful to act out a problem?

- What other strategy could you use?

► PRACTICE

Act it out to solve.

1. You are making a gameboard with tiles 1 inch square. It has a perimeter of 30 inches and an area of 54 square inches. Draw what the gameboard looks like. How long will it be? How wide?

2. Peter is putting wood trim around a window in a hallway. The window is 36 inches wide and 60 inches long. How much wood trim does Peter need to buy?

3. Kim is putting lace around a card. The card is a rectangle, 7 inches long and 5 inches wide. How many inches of lace does Kim need?

4. Denise wants to put a frame around a rectangular picture that is 14 inches long and 9 inches wide. How much wood does Denise need?

Mixed Applications

Solve.

CHOOSE a strategy and a tool.
- Draw a Picture • Act It Out • Guess and Check
- Work Backward • Write a Number Sentence

Paper/Pencil   Calculator   Hands-On   Mental Math

---

5. Sam has $8, Ana has $9, Jan has $12, and Faye has $7. Which two students could put their money together and have a total of $21?

6. Roz eats 1 sandwich and 2 pieces of fruit each day at lunch. How many pieces of fruit does she eat in 5 days?

7. Gwen buys 24 cookies. She buys twice as many oatmeal cookies as raisin cookies. How many of each does Gwen buy?

8. This collection of coins was worth 50¢ before one coin rolled away. What coin was it?

9. A quilt is made of pieces 1 foot square. It has an area of 35 square feet and a perimeter of 24 feet. How many rows of squares are in the quilt? How many squares are in each row?

10. Allen has $63 in his bank. Last week he earned $20 and spent $12. He put the rest in his bank. How much money did he have at the beginning of last week?

MORE PRACTICE page H113

▶ CHECK Understanding

VOCABULARY

1. The distance around a plane figure is the __?__ . (page 454)

2. The number of square units needed to cover a flat surface is the __?__ . (page 458)

3. Can two figures have the same area but different perimeters? Draw pictures to show your answer. (pages 460–461)

▶ CHECK Skills

Find the perimeter. (pages 454–457)

4.

12 cm 20 cm
16 cm

5.

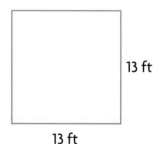

13 ft
13 ft

6.

12 in.
15 in.

Find the perimeter and area. (pages 460–461)

7.

4 cm
9 cm

8.

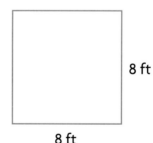

8 ft
8 ft

9.

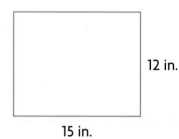

6 in.
7 in.

▶ CHECK Problem Solving

Solve. (pages 462–463)

CHOOSE a strategy and a tool.

• Draw a Picture • Act It Out • Make a Model
• Work Backward • Find a Pattern

 Paper/Pencil   Calculator   Hands-On   Mental Math

10. Louise can fit 5 apples in one basket. How many baskets will she need if she wants to put 28 apples in baskets?

11. A floor has an area of 72 square feet and a perimeter of 34 feet. What are the length and width of the floor?

Test Prep

Choose the best answer.

1. Which unit should you use to measure the length of your hand?

   A inch
   B foot
   C yard
   D mile

2. Which is the largest unit to measure capacity?

   F cup
   G pint
   H quart
   J gallon

3. Which decimal is equal to $\frac{8}{10}$?

   A 0.08
   B 0.18
   C 8.08
   D 0.8

4. Tom started his homework at 5:00. He finished 45 minutes later. At what time did he finish his homework?

   F 5:30   **G** 4:45
   H 5:45   **J** 4:15

5. Which fraction describes the green part?

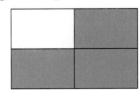

   A $\frac{3}{6}$ **B** $\frac{4}{5}$
   C $\frac{3}{4}$ **D** $\frac{3}{8}$

6. Brandi and her two friends will share 18 crayons. What part of the crayons will each person get?

   F $\frac{1}{3}$ **G** $\frac{1}{4}$
   H $\frac{1}{5}$ **J** $\frac{1}{6}$

7. What is the area of this figure?

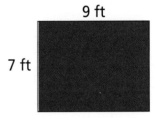

9 ft

7 ft

   A 63 square feet
   B 32 square feet
   C 16 square feet
   D 72 square feet

8. What is the perimeter of this square?

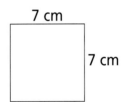

7 cm

7 cm

   F 14 centimeters
   G 24 centimeters
   H 28 centimeters
   J 49 centimeters

9. $9 \times 8 = \underline{\ ?\ }$

   A 78   **B** 72
   C 81   **D** 91

MATH FUN!

DO I MEASURE UP?

PURPOSE To practice estimating, comparing, and measuring customary lengths

YOU WILL NEED paper and pencil, yardstick, customary tape measure

Work with a partner to estimate the customary lengths of parts of your body. Include your height and at least four other body parts. Make a chart to show your estimates. Then use a yardstick and a tape measure to get exact measurements. Compare results.

HOME NOTE Ask family members to estimate your body measurements. How close were their estimates? Ask family members to measure themselves.

CIRCLE JUMP

PURPOSE To practice measuring and drawing metric lengths

YOU WILL NEED 2 number cubes, centimeter ruler, pencil and paper

Play with a partner. On a large piece of paper, draw six circles that are not near one another. Take turns rolling the number cubes. Use your centimeter ruler to draw a line as many centimeters long as the number you rolled. Begin on any circle. Begin all other moves at the point where you stopped. You must draw a line on every turn, and you may land on each circle only once. The winner is the first one who lands on all six circles.

WHAT'S THE PERIMETER

PURPOSE To practice finding the perimeter of objects

YOU WILL NEED customary tape measure, paper and pencil

Work with a partner to find the perimeter of objects. Use your tape measure to find the lengths of the sides. Then add the lengths to find the perimeter. Make a chart like this one.

Object	Lengths of Sides	Perimeter
1. pencil box	4 + 8 + 4 + 8	24 inches
2.		

Perimeter and Area

MATERIALS
ALDUS® SuperPaint® or any other drawing program

Keisha is making cards for a math game using a computer drawing program. The cards are 6 centimeters wide by 4 centimeters long. She can fit 3 cards across the page and 6 cards down.

- What will be the perimeter of the array of cards? the area? (Hint: Use a calculator to help you.)

- If she needs 25 cards for her game, will one page of cards be enough?

EXAMPLE

A ruler across the top and along the left side of the drawing window allows you to draw shapes with the exact measurements you want.

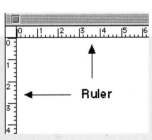

Most drawing programs can show measurements in inches, centimeters, or other units. Keisha chose Grid & Rulers from the **Options** menu. In the Grid & Rulers window, she selected Centimeters.

▶ PRACTICE

1. Angela made an array of rectangles 3 cm wide and 6 cm long. She fit 8 rows of 3 rectangles on a page. Make a model of her array. What is its perimeter?

2. **Using the Computer** How many 4 cm by 4 cm squares can you fit on a page? Use a computer drawing program to make the array. What is the perimeter? the area? (Hint: Use a calculator to help you.)

Study Guide and Review

Vocabulary Check

Choose a term from the box to complete the sentence.

VOCABULARY
area
cup, pint, quart, and gallon
centimeter, decimeter, and meter
capacity
gram and kilogram
inch, foot, yard, and mile
milliliter and liter
ounce and pound
perimeter

1. The customary units used to measure length or distance are __?__. (page 422)

2. The customary units used to measure capacity are __?__. (page 430)

3. The amount of liquid a container can hold when filled is its __?__. (pages 430, 446)

4. The customary units used to measure weight are __?__. (page 432)

5. The metric units used to measure length or distance are __?__. (page 438)

6. Capacity can be measured by using metric units such as __?__. (page 446)

7. The metric units for measuring mass are __?__. (page 448)

8. The distance around a plane figure is the __?__. (page 454)

9. The number of square units needed to cover a flat surface is its __?__. (page 458)

Study and Solve

CHAPTER 24

EXAMPLE

Choose the better estimate.

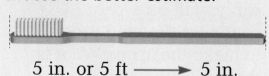

5 in. or 5 ft ⟶ 5 in.

For Problems 10–13, choose the better estimate. (pages 422–425, 430–433)

10.

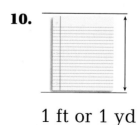

1 ft or 1 yd

11.

1 pt or 1 gal

12.

4 oz or 4 lb

13.

9 pt or 9 gal

Measure the line segment to the nearest inch. (pages 424–425)

14. _____

For Problems 15–16, measure the line segment to the nearest half inch. (pages 426–427)

15. _____

16. _____

Solve. (pages 422–423)

17. Julie is planning a trip to another city. Will she measure the distance in feet or miles?

CHAPTER 25

EXAMPLE

Choose the better estimate.

5 cm or 5 dm ⟶ 5 cm

Choose the better estimate. (pages 440–441)

18.

4 m or 4 cm

Solve. (pages 444–445)

19. Juan and Rina spent 3 days building a 48-m racetrack. They built 15 m on Monday and 23 m on Tuesday. How much of the racetrack did they build on Wednesday?

CHAPTER 26

EXAMPLE

Find the perimeter.

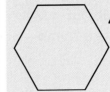

4 cm Add all sides.
4 + 4 + 4 +
4 + 4 + 4 = 24 cm

For Problems 20–21, find the perimeter. (pages 454–457)

20.

10 ft

12 ft

21.

5 units

Solve. (pages 460–461)

22. Doreen's kitchen is 8 feet by 9 feet. What is the area of the kitchen?

Performance Assessment

Tasks: Show What You Know

1. Choose a pencil, crayon, or marker from your desk. Explain each step as you measure the object to the nearest half inch. (pages 426–427)

2. Name or draw a picture of something in your classroom or your community that you would measure with each unit: centimeter, decimeter, meter. Explain how many centimeters equal 1 decimeter. How many decimeters equal 1 meter? (pages 438–439)

3. Explain each step as you use a centimeter ruler to measure the perimeter of your math book cover. (pages 454–457)

Problem Solving

Solve. Explain your method.

CHOOSE a strategy and a tool.
- Find a Pattern
- Act It Out
- Make a Model
- Work Backward
- Write a Number Sentence

 Paper/Pencil   Calculator   Hands-On   Mental Math

4. Draw 3 squares that are the same size on dot paper. Show 3 different ways to shade $\frac{1}{2}$ of the area of the square. (pages 428–429)

5. Becky planted a seed three weeks ago. Today her plant is 24 cm tall. The first week it grew 10 cm. The second week it grew 8 cm. How much did the plant grow in the third week? (pages 444–445)

6. Jim is making a hot plate pad using 1-inch square tiles. The pad has a perimeter of 36 inches and an area of 80 square inches. Draw what the pad will look like. How long will it be? How wide will it be? (pages 462–463)

Cumulative Review

Solve the problem. Then write the letter of the correct answer.

1. $4.55
   +5.45
   - **A.** $1.10
   - **B.** $9.00
   - **C.** $9.90
   - **D.** $10.00

   (pages 52–53, 114–115)

2. $22.95
   + 15.15
   - **A.** $7.80
   - **B.** $37.80
   - **C.** $38.00
   - **D.** $38.10

3. Compare the numbers.

   98 ● 101

   - **A.** <
   - **B.** >
   - **C.** =
   - **D.** −

   (pages 164–167)

4. 63 ÷ 7 = __?__
   - **A.** 8
   - **B.** 9
   - **C.** 70
   - **D.** 763

   (pages 248–249, 250–251)

5. The __?__ at the bottom of a pictograph tells how many each picture stands for.
   - **A.** label
   - **B.** key
   - **C.** scale
   - **D.** interval

   (page 280)

6. A(n) __?__ is straight and does not end.
   - **A.** angle
   - **B.** edge
   - **C.** line
   - **D.** line segment

   (page 332)

7. How many lines of symmetry does the figure have?

   - **A.** 1 line of symmetry
   - **B.** 2 lines of symmetry
   - **C.** 3 lines of symmetry
   - **D.** 4 lines of symmetry

   (pages 352–353)

8. Write a fraction to describe the shaded part.

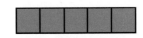

   - **A.** $\frac{0}{5}$
   - **B.** $\frac{1}{5}$
   - **C.** $\frac{5}{10}$
   - **D.** $\frac{5}{5}$

   (pages 374–375)

9. Compare the part of each group that is red.

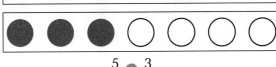

   $\frac{5}{7}$ ● $\frac{3}{7}$

   - **A.** <
   - **B.** >
   - **C.** =
   - **D.** +

   (pages 394–395)

10. The amount of liquid in a medicine dropper can be measured in __?__.
    - **A.** milliliters
    - **B.** liters
    - **C.** quarts
    - **D.** gallons

    (page 446)

27 MULTIPLYING BY ONE-DIGIT NUMBERS

The Inuit used to carve domino stones out of walrus tusks. People have played dominoes in many lands for hundreds of years.

You can play dominoes with double-sixes, double-nines, and double-twelves.

472

Making Double-Six Dominoes

Make a 28-tile set of dominoes to play at school or home. Decide how many dot stickers you need for one set before making the dominoes.

YOU WILL NEED: a set of double-six or double-nine dominoes; 28 unruled index cards, 1 for each double tile; paper dots

- Look at a classroom set of 28 domino tiles and count how many times each array of dots appears.

- Figure out how many dots you need to make your own set of 28 domino tiles.

- Get the number of dots you need from your teacher.

- Make your own set of dominoes.

- Play dominoes with a friend.

HOW TO MAKE A SET OF DOMINOES

- Fold each index card in half and mark a pencil line in the fold.

- Glue dots just like the ones you see in a domino game.

- Use a classroom set of dominoes to copy the patterns.

DID YOU

☑ count how many times each array of dots appears in a set?

☑ find the product and get the dots from your teacher?

☑ make and play dominoes?

Arrays with Tens and Ones

Why learn this? You can multiply to find the number of eggs in several cartons.

Anna bought 4 egg cartons. There were 12 eggs in each carton. How many eggs did Anna buy?

$$4 \times 12 = \underline{\ ?\ }$$

Make an array using base-ten blocks.

Show 4×10 and 4×2 with tens and ones.

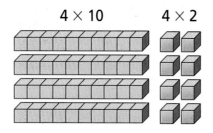

Put the 4 tens and 8 ones together to make a rectangle. Draw the rectangle on grid paper. Count the squares in the array.

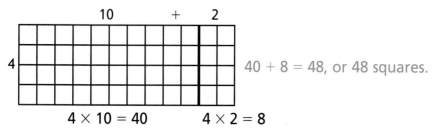

40 + 8 = 48, or 48 squares.

So, Anna bought 48 eggs.

EXAMPLE

$$5 \times 18 = \underline{\ ?\ }$$

50 + 40 = 90, or 90 squares.

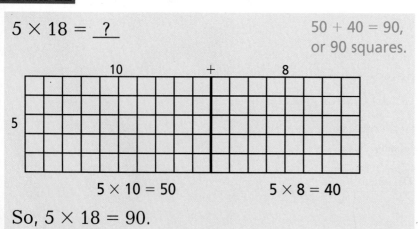

So, $5 \times 18 = 90$.

SCIENCE LINK

Some chickens lay white eggs, some lay brown eggs, and others lay speckled eggs. The color depends on the kind of chicken. The color of the shell doesn't change the taste of the eggs. If you buy one dozen brown eggs and one dozen white eggs, what is the total number of eggs purchased?

▶ CHECK

Put the tens and ones together. Name the factors of the new rectangle.

1.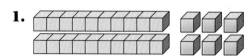

2.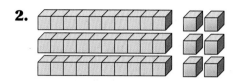

▶ PRACTICE

Use the array. Add the two products to find the answer. Complete the multiplication sentence.

3.

$5 \times 15 =$ _?_

4.

$4 \times 17 =$ _?_

Draw each array on grid paper. Show how you found the product.

5. $6 \times 13 =$ _?_

6. $5 \times 12 =$ _?_

7. $7 \times 14 =$ _?_

8. $4 \times 15 =$ _?_

9. $8 \times 12 =$ _?_

10. $9 \times 13 =$ _?_

Problem Solving • Mixed Applications

11. Reasoning Tammy is buying cupcakes for the third-grade party. Each package contains 12 cupcakes. There are 65 third graders at her school. Will 6 packages be enough? Explain.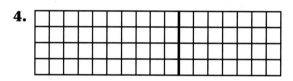

12. Time Rodney took 4 minutes more to solve the puzzle than Kenny. Together they spent 18 minutes working on the puzzle. How many minutes did each boy spend on the puzzle?

13. Money Rhonda gave the clerk $7.00 for a domino game that cost $6.28. How much change did she receive?

14. ▦ **Write a problem** using this information: Ian is filling 3 ice-cube trays with water. Each tray makes 14 ice cubes.

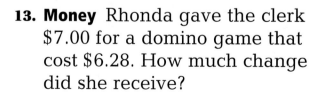

LESSON CONTINUES ⟹

MORE PRACTICE page H113

Problem–Solving Strategy: Make a Model

▶ **THE PROBLEM** Brianna is sewing squares of fabric together to make a quilt. The quilt will have 6 rows of squares. It will have 14 squares in each row. What will be the area of Brianna's quilt?

REMEMBER:

UNDERSTAND
PLAN
SOLVE
LOOK BACK

UNDERSTAND

• What are you asked to find?

• What information will you use?

• Is there information you will not use? If so, what?

PLAN

• What strategy can you use?
  You can *make a model* to find the area.

SOLVE

• How can you make a model of the quilt? Draw a rectangle on grid paper that shows 6 rows of squares with 14 squares in each row. Use the model to find 6 × 14.

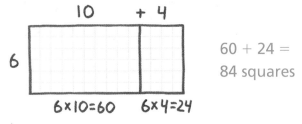

60 + 24 =
84 squares

So, Brianna's quilt will have an area of 84 square units.

LOOK BACK

• How can you decide if your answer makes sense?

• How else could you solve this problem?

Make a model to solve.

1. Mr. Patterson is laying square tiles on the floor of a bathroom. He will lay 5 rows with 18 tiles in each row. What is the area of the floor?

2. Jeremy arranged number cards in 4 rows. He put 13 cards in each row. How many cards did he use?

3. There are 12 windows across the front of a building on each floor. The building has 6 floors. How many windows are across the front of the building?

4. Seletha put her shell collection onto a board. She arranged the shells in 3 rows. There are 15 shells in each row. How many shells does she have?

Mixed Applications

Solve.

CHOOSE a strategy and a tool.
- Find a Pattern
- Guess and Check
- Work Backward
- Write a Number Sentence
- Make a Model

 Paper/Pencil   Calculator   Hands-On   Mental Math

5. Nancy is reading a book that is 185 pages long. She read 24 pages the first day. She read 19 pages the second day and 21 pages the third day. How many pages does she have left to read?

6. Tickets for the play cost $4 for adults and $3 for children. Mr. Whitman paid $23 for 7 people. For how many adults did he pay? For how many children?

7. At the craft fair, there are 8 rows of tables with 14 tables in each row. How many tables of crafts are at the fair?

8. Are these two figures congruent? Explain your answer.

9. Suppose you want to put a border around a table in your classroom. Your teacher has some border left over from another table. How can you find out how much more border you will need?

Modeling Multiplication

You will investigate using base-ten blocks to help you multiply.

Use base-ten blocks to find equal groups.

In Frank's school, there are 3 third-grade classes. In each class there are 28 students. How many third-grade students are in Frank's school?

$$3 \times 28 = \underline{\ ?\ }$$

▶ EXPLORE

Use base-ten blocks to make a model of the problem. Find the product.

MATERIALS: base-ten blocks

MODEL

Step 1	Step 2
Model 3 groups of 28.	Combine the tens and combine the ones. Regroup the ones.

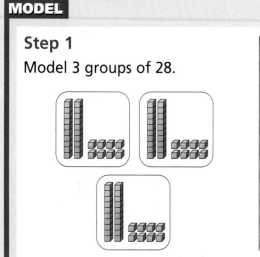

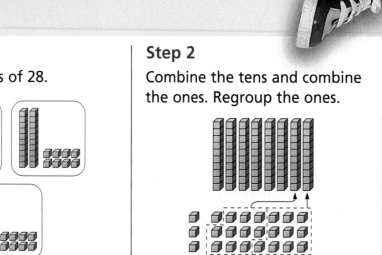

Record

Write how you found the product, and the answer to the question.

Now investigate making a model of a number of fourth-grade students.

▶ TRY THIS

1. In Frank's school, there are 4 fourth-grade classes. There are 24 students in each class. Make a model and find the total number of fourth-grade students.

2. Why were the ones regrouped in both problems?

3. ✏️ **Write About It** Explain how you found the total number of fourth graders.

Technology Link

You can solve multiplication problems by using E-Lab, Activity 27. Available on CD-ROM and on the Internet at www.hbschool.com/elab

▶ PRACTICE

Use base-ten blocks to find each product.

4. Each student in Julie's class brought 2 cans of juice for Field Day. How many cans did the 26 students bring?

5. There are 5 classes signed up for the tug-of-war. Each class has 24 students. How many students are in the tug-of-war?

6. $2 \times 14 = \underline{\ ?\ }$ 7. $3 \times 41 = \underline{\ ?\ }$ 8. $4 \times 34 = \underline{\ ?\ }$ 9. $6 \times 14 = \underline{\ ?\ }$

10. $4 \times 38 = \underline{\ ?\ }$ 11. $5 \times 26 = \underline{\ ?\ }$ 12. $2 \times 45 = \underline{\ ?\ }$ 13. $3 \times 31 = \underline{\ ?\ }$

Problem Solving • Mixed Applications

14. **Number Sense** On Monday, 425 hot lunches were sold. On Tuesday, 87 fewer hot lunches were sold. How many lunches were sold on Tuesday?

15. **Money** Brian sold 5 calendars for his club. Allen sold 8 calendars. Each calendar cost $2. How much did Allen and Brian make in all?

16. **Mental Math** Josh put the chairs in 9 rows. There are 9 chairs in each row. How many chairs are there?

17. **Time** Sheila worked on her bicycle for 1 hour and 45 minutes. She started at 12:30. At what time did she stop?

Recording Multiplication

Why learn this? You can multiply without using base-ten blocks to find the total number of comic books.

Brandon has 3 boxes of comic books. There are 36 comic books in each box. How many comic books does Brandon have?

$$\begin{array}{r} 36 \\ \times\,3 \\ \hline \end{array}$$

Use base-ten blocks to model the problem. Use paper and pencil to record what you did.

MODEL

Step 1

Model 3 groups of 36.

Tens	Ones
3	6
×	3

Step 2

Multiply the ones. Record the product.

Multiply the tens. Record the product.

Add the two products.

Hundreds	Tens	Ones	
	3	6	
×		3	
	1	8	(3 × 6)
+	9	0	(3 × 30)
1	0	8	

CRITICAL THINKING   How does knowing basic multiplication facts help you multiply with paper and pencil?

▶ CHECK

1. What place value was multiplied first? multiplied next?

2. When do you regroup?

3. Why are there hundreds in the product of 36 × 3?

4. What addition problem is the same as finding 3 × 36?

5. How can you use base-ten blocks to find 3 × 26 = _?_?

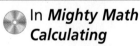

Technology Link

In *Mighty Math Calculating Crew*, the game *Intergalactic Trader* challenges you to multiply by 1-digit numbers. Use Grow Slide Level L.

Find each product. Use base-ten blocks to help you.

6.	21	7.	19	8.	12	9.	34	10.	17
	× 4		× 2		× 3		× 2		× 4

11.	25	12.	13	13.	16	14.	28	15.	15
	× 3		× 5		× 5		× 3		× 5

16.	12	17.	44	18.	61	19.	39	20.	58
	× 8		× 5		× 4		× 6		× 5

21.	62	22.	23	23.	14	24.	33	25.	82
	× 4		× 5		× 6		× 3		× 4

26. **Patterns** Lisa and Vicky played a number game. When Lisa said 2, Vicky said 6. When Lisa said 8, Vicky said 24. What did Vicky say when Lisa said 14?

27. **Measurement** Laura glued lace around the perimeter of a picture frame. The frame is 7 inches long and 5 inches wide. What is the perimeter of the frame?

28. **Money** Debbie has $8 in her purse. She earned $6 baby-sitting. Then she spent $3. How much money did she have before she baby-sat?

29. ▣ **Write About It** Is it always necessary to regroup to find a product? Explain why or why not. Give an example.

Mixed Review and Test Prep

Write each fraction as a decimal. (pages 400–401)

30. $\frac{2}{10}$ 31. $\frac{6}{10}$ 32. $\frac{1}{10}$ 33. $\frac{5}{10}$ 34. $\frac{9}{10}$

Choose the letter for the correct mixed decimal. (pages 406–407)

35. one and four tenths   **A** 1.04   **B** 1.4   **C** 4.01   **D** 0.4

36. six and five tenths   **F** 5.6   **G** 6.05   **H** 5.06   **J** 6.5

37. seven and nine hundredths   **A** 7.09   **B** 7.90   **C** 79   **D** 9.70

38. five and eight hundredths   **F** 8.5   **G** 8.05   **H** 5.08   **J** 58

Practicing Multiplication

Why learn this? You can multiply more quickly to find how many students went on a field trip.

Students at Karen's school went on a field trip to a planetarium. The students rode in 5 buses. There were 33 students in each bus. How many students went on the field trip?

$5 \times 33 = \underline{\ ?\ }$ Rewrite as: $\begin{array}{r} 33 \\ \times\ 5 \\ \hline \end{array}$

MODEL

Step 1
Multiply the ones. $5 \times 3 = 15$ ones
Regroup 15 ones as 1 ten 5 ones.

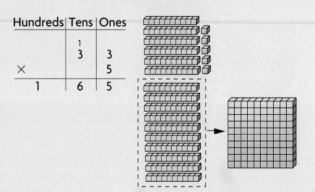

Step 2
Multiply the tens. $5 \times 3 = 15$ tens
Add the 1 ten you regrouped.
$15 + 1 = 16$ tens
Regroup 16 tens as 1 hundred 6 tens.

Talk About It
- In Step 1, why were the ones regrouped? How were they regrouped?
- In the written multiplication problem, what happened to the regrouped ten?
- In Step 2, why were the tens regrouped? How were they regrouped?

CRITICAL THINKING In the written multiplication problem, what happened to the regrouped hundred?

SCIENCE LINK
A planetarium shows a starry sky and the movement of the planets through space. If 3 star panels each have 15 stars, what is the total number of stars?

Calculator Activities page H61

► **CHECK**

Find the product. Use base-ten blocks to help you.

1. 62	**2.** 54	**3.** 24	**4.** 51	**5.** 12
× 4	× 6	× 2	× 4	× 7

6. In which of the Exercises 1–5 did you need to regroup?

► **PRACTICE**

Find the product.

7. 13	**8.** 71	**9.** 39	**10.** 14	**11.** 43
× 3	× 9	× 4	× 6	× 2
12. 82	**13.** 31	**14.** 92	**15.** 23	**16.** 17
× 4	× 5	× 8	× 5	× 5

Problem Solving • Mixed Applications

17. Estimation Mrs. Wood's car gets about 28 miles for each gallon of gasoline. She used 6 gallons. About how many miles did she travel?

18. Money Lynn earns $7 an hour at her job. Last week she worked 32 hours. How much money did she earn?

19. Logical Reasoning The sum of the digits in Mr. Keller's age is 9. The ones digit is twice as much as the tens digit. How old is Mr. Keller?

20. ✏️ **Write a problem** in which the ones and tens must be regrouped to find the product. Exchange with a classmate and solve.

Mixed Review and Test Prep

Write the greater amount. (pages 430–431)

21. 3 cups or 1 pint   **22.** 7 pints or 1 gallon   **23.** 5 pints or 5 quarts

Choose the letter of the correct mixed decimal. (pages 406–407)

24. 3.21

  A three and twenty-one hundredths

  B three and two tenths

  C three and twenty tenths

  D twenty-one and three tenths

25. 20.07

  F twenty and seven tenths

  G twenty and zero hundredths

  H seven hundredths

  J twenty and seven hundredths

► CHECK Understanding

Use the array. Add the two products to find the answer. Complete the multiplication sentence. (pages 474–475)

1.

$4 \times 15 = \underline{?}$

2.

$5 \times 13 = \underline{?}$

Copy. Fill in the blanks. (pages 480–481)

3.

Tens	Ones	
1	4	
	4	
1	6	← $\underline{?} \times \underline{?}$
+ 4	0	← $\underline{?} \times \underline{?}$
5	6	

4.

	Tens	Ones	
	1	5	
×		3	
		$\underline{?}$	← 3×5
		$\underline{?}$	← 3×10
		$\underline{?}$	

► CHECK Skills

Find the product. Use base-ten blocks to help you. (pages 478–483)

5. 34
    × 2

6. 27
    × 2

7. 45
    × 3

8. 22
    × 5

9. 16
    × 3

10. 56
     × 3

11. 41
     × 8

12. 29
     × 6

13. 52
     × 4

14. 63
     × 7

► CHECK Problem Solving

Solve. (pages 476–477)

CHOOSE a strategy and a tool.

- **Guess and Check**
- **Write a Number Sentence**
- **Act It Out**
- **Make a Model**

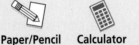 Paper/Pencil   Calculator   Hands-On   Mental Math

15. A pillow has 9 rows of squares. There are 11 squares in each row. How many squares are on the pillow?

16. A window has 6 rows of panes with 16 panes in each row. How many panes make up the window?

17. One factor is 1 less than the other. The product is 42. What are the factors?

18. A mirror is 4 feet wide and 3 feet high. What is the perimeter of the mirror?

Test Prep

Choose the best answer.

1. What decimal is equal to $\frac{5}{10}$?

   A 0.4 **B** 0.5 **C** 0.7 **D** 0.05

2. Amy put 18 balloons into 2 equal groups. She gave 1 group to Todd. What part of the balloons did Amy give to Todd?

   F $\frac{1}{4}$ **G** $\frac{1}{2}$ **H** 9 **J** $\frac{1}{9}$

3. Toby earns $5 an hour bagging groceries. He works 9 hours each week. How much does he earn in one week?

   A $15 **B** $55
   C $45 **D** $35

4. Mr. Rodriguez is putting a wallpaper border around a room. The room is 9 feet wide and 12 feet long. How many feet of border does he need?

   F 21 feet **G** 108 feet
   H 42 feet **J** 84 feet

5. Angela's soccer practice begins at 3:45. Practice is over at 5:00. How long is Angela's soccer practice?

   A 1hr 5 min **B** 1 hr 15 min
   C 1 hr 30 min **D** 1 hr 10 min

6. What is the area of the figure?

   7 ft ▭
   10 ft

   F 17 square feet
   G 34 square feet
   H 70 square feet
   J 80 square feet

7. What is the product of this array?

   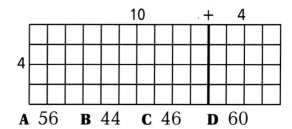

   A 56 **B** 44 **C** 46 **D** 60

8. There are 35 students in a city-wide spelling contest. An equal number are from 5 different schools. How many students are from each school?

   F 6 **G** 165 **H** 30 **J** 7

9. Charlotte plants seeds in 5 flower pots. Each flower pot holds 18 ounces of soil. How much soil does she need to fill all 5 flower pots?

   A 100 ounces
   B 40 ounces
   C 23 ounces
   D 90 ounces

28 DIVIDING BY ONE-DIGIT NUMBERS

Mercury

Venus

Earth

Mars

Asteroid Belt

Jupiter

Comet

Saturn

Uranus

Neptune

Pluto

SCIENCE LINK

Our solar system is huge! The distance from Earth to the sun is about 93 million miles. The farthest planet, Pluto, is about 3,697 million miles from the sun.

Travel the Solar System

Design a board game to travel through the solar system. Start on Earth and advance by solving a division problem that has a remainder. The remainder is your rocket fuel.

YOU WILL NEED: large drawing paper, index cards, counters or markers

- Make a gameboard that includes the planets in the order shown. Include extra spaces for moons and comets.

- Make game cards by copying the division problems shown; shuffle the cards and place them face down.

- Play the game.

How to Play the Game

1. Take turns drawing a card and solving the problem.

2. If the division problem has a remainder, move forward that number of planets.

3. If you land on the same planet as an opponent, the opponent must move back to the sun.

4. If you solve a problem without a remainder, move back one planet.

5. The winner is the first rocket to reach Pluto.

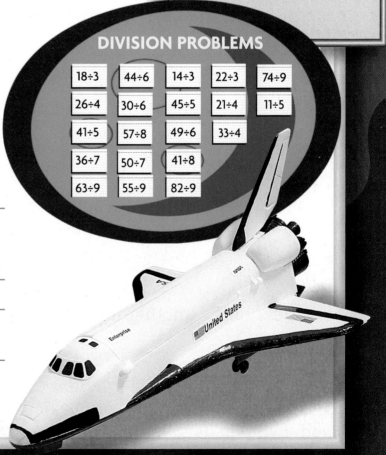

DIVISION PROBLEMS

18÷3	44÷6	14÷3	22÷3	74÷9
26÷4	30÷6	45÷5	21÷4	11÷5
41÷5	57÷8	49÷6	33÷4	
36÷7	50÷7	41÷8		
63÷9	55÷9	82÷9		

DID YOU

- ☑ make a gameboard showing the planets in their order from the sun?

- ☑ make game cards?

- ☑ play the game by solving division problems?

Dividing with Remainders

You will investigate using counters to model division with a remainder.

In division, the amount left over is called the **remainder**.

▶ EXPLORE

Make a model to show 17 divided by 3.

MATERIALS: counters

MODEL

Step 1	**Step 2**
Use 17 counters.	Draw 3 circles. Divide the 17 counters into 3 equal groups by putting them in the circles.

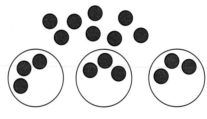

Record

Explain how you found the quotient of 17 ÷ 3 using the counters.

Talk About It

- How many counters are in each group? How many counters are left over?

- What do you call the 2 counters that are left over?

Now model finding another quotient.

▶ TRY THIS

1. Use counters to find the quotient of 23 ÷ 4. Draw a picture of the model you made.

2. ✏️ **Write About It** Explain how you used the counters to find the quotient and the remainder.

▶ PRACTICE

Use counters to find the quotient and remainder.

3. $18 \div 4 = \underline{\ ?\ }$ **4.** $16 \div 3 = \underline{\ ?\ }$ **5.** $14 \div 4 = \underline{\ ?\ }$

6. $11 \div 3 = \underline{\ ?\ }$ **7.** $13 \div 2 = \underline{\ ?\ }$ **8.** $21 \div 4 = \underline{\ ?\ }$

9. $12 \div 5 = \underline{\ ?\ }$ **10.** $10 \div 3 = \underline{\ ?\ }$ **11.** $15 \div 2 = \underline{\ ?\ }$

Use the model to find the quotient and remainder.

12. $21 \div 4 = \underline{\ ?\ }$

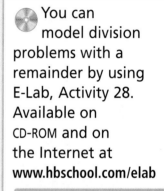
MODEL

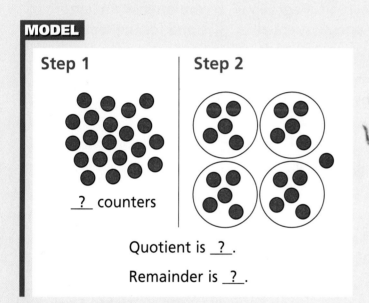

Step 1 | Step 2

$\underline{\ ?\ }$ counters

Quotient is $\underline{\ ?\ }$.

Remainder is $\underline{\ ?\ }$.

Find the quotient and remainder. You may use counters to help you.

13. $9 \div 4 = \underline{\ ?\ }$ **14.** $11 \div 2 = \underline{\ ?\ }$

15. $13 \div 3 = \underline{\ ?\ }$ **16.** $18 \div 4 = \underline{\ ?\ }$ **17.** $23 \div 5 = \underline{\ ?\ }$

18. $29 \div 3 = \underline{\ ?\ }$ **19.** $35 \div 4 = \underline{\ ?\ }$ **20.** $31 \div 6 = \underline{\ ?\ }$

Problem Solving • Mixed Applications

21. Science In science class Lisa read 15 pages about planets. She read 5 pages each day. How many days did she read about planets?

22. ✏️ **Write a problem** using division, about 13 books and 4 shelves. Exchange with a classmate and solve.

Modeling Division

Why learn this? You can divide to find the number of chairs in each row.

Mrs. Frye, the music teacher, is putting the chairs in 4 rows. There are 51 chairs. How many chairs will she put in each row?

$$51 \div 4 = \underline{\ ?\ }$$

MODEL

Step 1	**Step 2**	**Step 3**
Model 51 with tens and ones. To divide by 4, draw 4 circles. Begin with the tens. Put equal numbers of tens in each circle.	One ten is left. Regroup it as 10 ones. Put equal groups of ones in each circle.	You can use the letter *r* to stand for the remainder. So, 51 ÷ 4 = 12 r3.

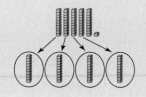
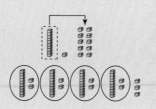

Talk About It CRITICAL THINKING

- How many tens and ones went into each circle? How many ones were left over? What is the quotient of 51 ÷ 4?

- In Step 2, why did the one ten have to be regrouped into ones?

- Why is there a remainder?

So, Mrs. Frye put 12 chairs in each row. There were 3 chairs left over.

▶ **CHECK**

Write the letter of the number sentence which matches the model.

1.

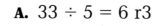

A. 33 ÷ 5 = 6 r3

B. 33 ÷ 6 = 5 r3

Technology Link

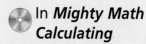

In *Mighty Math Calculating Crew*, the game *Intergalactic Trader* challenges you to divide by one-digit numbers. Use Grow Slide Level P.

Use the model to find the quotient and remainder.

2.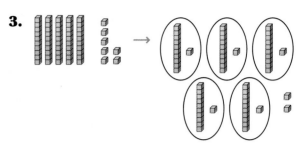

___?___ tens ___?___ ones $28 \div 3 =$ ___?___

3.

___?___ tens ___?___ ones $57 \div 5 =$ ___?___

Find the quotient. Use base-ten blocks to help you.

4. $41 \div 4 =$ ___?___   **5.** $53 \div 3 =$ ___?___   **6.** $47 \div 4 =$ ___?___   **7.** $38 \div 3 =$ ___?___

8. $49 \div 3 =$ ___?___   **9.** $19 \div 2 =$ ___?___   **10.** $36 \div 2 =$ ___?___   **11.** $60 \div 5 =$ ___?___

Problem Solving • Mixed Applications

12. At Mega Videos, there is a special display of 63 comedy videos. They are arranged on 3 shelves. How many comedy videos are on each shelf?

13. **Time** Melissa spent 33 minutes on homework. She spent 3 more minutes doing math than doing science. How long did she spend on each subject?

14. **Logic** Alex got through 4 levels during the 31 minutes he played a video game. He spent the same amount of time at each level except the last. How long did he spend at the first three levels?

15. ✏ **Write About It** Explain how you know when to stop putting ones into the circles when you are using base-ten blocks to divide.

Mixed Review and Test Prep

Draw a line of the given length. (pages 442–443)

16. 6 cm   **17.** 8 cm   **18.** 11 cm   **19.** 12 cm

Trace each figure. Draw the line or lines of symmetry. Choose the letter that shows how many lines of symmetry each figure has. (pages 352–353)

20.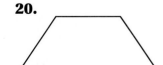
A 2
B 0
C 1
D 3

21.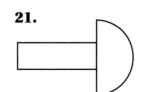
F 2
G 1
H 4
J 3

22.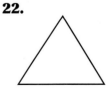
A 3
B 1
C 4
D 2

Recording Division

Why learn this? You can divide to find the number of muffins that will go into each of several boxes.

Jody baked 46 muffins. She put them into 3 boxes. How many muffins did she put into each box? How many were left?

$$46 \div 3 = \underline{\ ?\ }$$

Write: $3\overline{)46}$ **Read:** 46 divided by 3

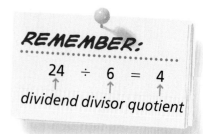

REMEMBER:
$$24 \div 6 = 4$$
dividend divisor quotient

MODEL

Step 1

Model 46 with base-ten blocks. Draw 3 circles. Begin with the tens. Put an equal number of tens in each circle.

Tens	Ones	
1		← 1 ten in each group
3)4	6	
− 3		← 3 tens used
1		← 1 ten left

Step 2

There is 1 ten to regroup. Regroup the ten as 10 ones to make 16 ones. Put an equal number of ones in each circle.

Tens	Ones	
1	5	← 5 ones in each group
3)4	6	
− 3	↓	← Bring down the ones.
1	6	

Step 3

There is 1 ten 5 ones in each group. There is a remainder of 1.

Tens	Ones	
1	5 r1	
3)4	6	
− 3		
1	6	
1	5	← 15 ones used
	1	← 1 one left

Step 4

Check your answer by multiplying.

$$\begin{array}{r} 15 \leftarrow \text{in each group} \\ \times\ 3 \leftarrow \text{groups} \\ \hline 45 \end{array} \qquad \begin{array}{r} 45 \\ +\ 1 \leftarrow \text{Add the remainder.} \\ \hline 46 \end{array}$$

This number should equal the dividend.

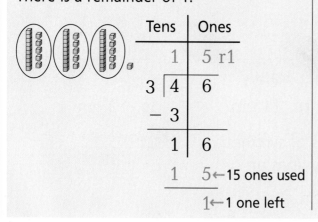

So, Jody put 15 muffins into each box and 1 muffin was left.

▶ CHECK

Find the quotient. You may wish to use base-ten blocks.

1. $27 \div 2 = \underline{\ ?\ }$ **2.** $25 \div 3 = \underline{\ ?\ }$ **3.** $39 \div 2 = \underline{\ ?\ }$ **4.** $45 \div 4 = \underline{\ ?\ }$

▶ PRACTICE

Find the quotient. Then check each answer.

5. $56 \div 3 = \underline{\ ?\ }$ **6.** $31 \div 2 = \underline{\ ?\ }$ **7.** $52 \div 4 = \underline{\ ?\ }$ **8.** $64 \div 5 = \underline{\ ?\ }$

9. $75 \div 4 = \underline{\ ?\ }$ **10.** $66 \div 3 = \underline{\ ?\ }$ **11.** $36 \div 5 = \underline{\ ?\ }$ **12.** $47 \div 3 = \underline{\ ?\ }$

13. $6\overline{)37}$ **14.** $4\overline{)23}$ **15.** $7\overline{)54}$ **16.** $6\overline{)51}$

17. $5\overline{)43}$ **18.** $8\overline{)62}$ **19.** $6\overline{)40}$ **20.** $9\overline{)32}$

Problem Solving • Mixed Applications

21. Mrs. Roberts has 63 marbles to put into 3 bags. If she puts the same number in each bag, how many will that be? Will there be any marbles left over?

22. Visual Thinking Megan's painting is the middle one. There are 9 paintings to the right of Megan's painting. How many paintings are in the display?

23. Money Ramon gave the clerk a $5 bill. The clerk gave Ramon a $1 bill, 6 dimes, and 3 pennies. How much change did Ramon get? How much was his purchase?

24. ✏️ **Write About It** Explain why the remainder cannot be greater than the divisor in a division problem.

Mixed Review and Test Prep

Choose the unit you would use to measure each.
Write *mL* or *L*. (pages 446–447)

25. a large container of ice cream

26. a glass of juice

27. a kitchen sink full of water

Choose the letter of the correct product. (pages 480–481)

28. $\begin{array}{r} 12 \\ \times\ 3 \\ \hline \end{array}$ **A** 35   **B** 42   **C** 15   **D** 36

29. $\begin{array}{r} 39 \\ \times\ 2 \\ \hline \end{array}$ **F** 59   **G** 78   **H** 45   **J** 68

30. $\begin{array}{r} 56 \\ \times\ 4 \\ \hline \end{array}$ **A** 112   **B** 240   **C** 224   **D** 226

31. $\begin{array}{r} 24 \\ \times\ 3 \\ \hline \end{array}$ **F** 67   **G** 74   **H** 62   **J** 72

Practicing Division

Why learn this? You can divide to find the number of cars in each case by using only paper and pencil.

Roger has 64 Matchbox® cars. He stores them in 5 cases. How many Matchbox cars are in each case? Are there any cars left over?

$$64 \div 5 = \underline{\ ?\ }$$

Write: $5\overline{)64}$ **Read:** 64 divided by 5

MODEL

What is $64 \div 5$?

Step 1

Divide the tens. There is an equal number of tens in each group. Five tens are used. One ten is left.

$$\begin{array}{r} 1 \\ 5\overline{)64} \\ -5 \\ \hline 1 \end{array}$$

Step 2

Regroup the leftover ten as 10 ones to make 14 ones. Divide the 14 ones by 5. There are 2 ones in each group. Ten ones are used and 4 ones are left.

$$\begin{array}{r} 12 \text{ r}4 \\ 5\overline{)64} \\ -5\downarrow \\ \hline 14 \\ -10 \\ \hline 4 \end{array}$$

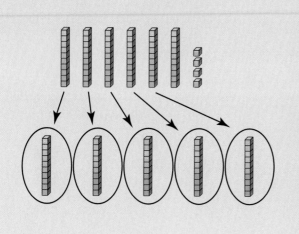

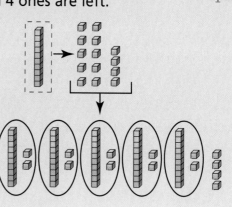

So, there are 12 Matchbox cars in each case and 4 cars are left over.

Talk About It [CRITICAL THINKING]

• Why was the ten regrouped in Step 2?

• What did subtracting 10 from 14 show?

• How can you check the answer?

▶ CHECK

Find the quotient, using only paper and pencil.

1. $39 \div 4 = \underline{\quad?\quad}$ **2.** $28 \div 6 = \underline{\quad?\quad}$ **3.** $41 \div 3 = \underline{\quad?\quad}$ **4.** $54 \div 5 = \underline{\quad?\quad}$

▶ PRACTICE

Find the quotient. Check each answer by using multiplication.

5. $29 \div 5 = \underline{\quad?\quad}$ **6.** $63 \div 4 = \underline{\quad?\quad}$ **7.** $48 \div 4 = \underline{\quad?\quad}$ **8.** $73 \div 3 = \underline{\quad?\quad}$

9. $61 \div 4 = \underline{\quad?\quad}$ **10.** $56 \div 6 = \underline{\quad?\quad}$ **11.** $79 \div 5 = \underline{\quad?\quad}$ **12.** $88 \div 4 = \underline{\quad?\quad}$

13. $9\overline{)83}$ **14.** $8\overline{)51}$ **15.** $7\overline{)59}$ **16.** $6\overline{)55}$

17. $7\overline{)66}$ **18.** $9\overline{)48}$ **19.** $8\overline{)68}$ **20.** $9\overline{)28}$

Problem Solving • Mixed Applications

21. Logic Five friends are in line. Sue is ahead of Lynn. Joe is behind Eric. Sue is behind Joe. Lynn is ahead of Pam. Who is second in line?

22. Mrs. Gray has 50 roses to put into 4 vases. How many roses will she put in each if she divides them equally?

23. Visual Thinking A solid figure has 5 faces, 8 edges, and 5 corners. What solid figure is it?

24. ▨ **Write a problem** about 3 orange trees that have 42 oranges.

Mixed Review and Test Prep

Compare the numbers. Write $<$, $>$, or $=$ for each ●. (pages 164–167)

25.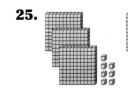

307 ● 297

26.

431 ● 431

27.

218 ● 219

Choose the letter of the correct unit you would use to measure each. (pages 448–449)

28. a large dog
A gram
B kilogram
C centimeter
D liter

29. pencil
F kilogram
G liter
H gram
J meter

30. your desk
A milliliter
B kilogram
C liter
D gram

Choosing Whether to Multiply or Divide

Why learn this? You can choose the correct operation to solve a problem such as how many books are on each shelf.

In order to solve a problem, you must choose an operation, such as multiplication or division.

Use multiplication

- when all the groups are the same size.

- when you know the size of the groups and the number of groups.

- when you need to find the total.

Use division

- when you know the total and all the groups are the same size.

- when you know the number of groups and you need to find the number in each group.

- when you know the number in each group and you need to find the number of groups.

Read the problems. Decide whether you would multiply or divide to solve each problem.

A. Mrs. O'Brien is putting 48 math books in a bookcase. She will put the same number of books on each shelf. There are 3 shelves. How many books will she put on each shelf?

B. Lori swims 25 laps each morning. She does this 5 mornings a week. How many laps does Lori swim in one week?

Talk About It

- What is asked for in Problem A? Should you multiply or divide? Explain.

- What is asked for in Problem B? Should you multiply or divide? Explain.

▶ CHECK

1. What multiplication or division sentence would you use to solve each problem?

▶ PRACTICE

Write whether you should multiply or divide.
Solve each problem.

2. Craig scored 64 points. He scored the same number of points in each of 4 games. How many points did he score in each game?

3. Allison ate 5 crackers. Each cracker had 28 calories. How many calories were in the 5 crackers?

4. Mr. Simms spent $56 on paint. He used the same amount of paint for each of 4 rooms. What did it cost to paint each room?

5. Tom bought 4 pairs of pants. Each pair cost $18. How much did Tom spend?

Problem Solving • Mixed Applications

6. **Career** The clerk has 68 new sweaters to display on 6 racks. She wants an equal number on each rack. How many sweaters will she put on each rack?

7. **Time** It takes Carol 12 minutes to get to her friend's house. It takes her 4 times as long to get to her grandmother's house. How long does it take to get to her grandmother's?

8. **Money** Sylvia bought a purse for $10.96, a wallet for $5.46, and a necklace for $8.26. How much money did she spend?

9. **Consumer** Neil bought a CD on sale for $8.79. The original price was $14.50. How much money did Neil save?

10. **Elapsed Time** Dan's football practice begins in 2 weeks. Today is February 3. When does Dan's football practice begin?

11. Talia bought 15 bulbs. She planted the same number of bulbs in 3 different flower beds. How many bulbs did she plant in each bed?

12. ✏ **Write About It** How are multiplication and division different?

MORE PRACTICE page H116

Problem–Solving Strategy: Write a Number Sentence

▶ **THE PROBLEM** There were 51 students at the first meeting of the Science Club. Mr. Wilson wanted to put them into groups of 4. How many groups of students did he make? Were all the students in a group of 4?

REMEMBER:

UNDERSTAND
PLAN
SOLVE
LOOK BACK

UNDERSTAND

- What are you asked to find?

- What information will you use?

- Is there information you will not use? If so, what?

PLAN

- What strategy can you use to solve the problem?

  You can *write a number sentence* to find the number of groups. Since Mr. Wilson wants to divide the number of students into groups of 4, write a division number sentence to find how many groups are formed.

  $$51 \div 4 = \underline{\ ?\ }$$

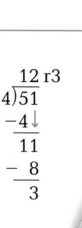

SOLVE

- How will you divide?

  Write the problem as $4\overline{)51}$.

  Then divide.

  So, there were 12 groups of students, with 3 students left over. Mr. Wilson can form 13 groups, with 3 students in one of the groups.

$$
\begin{array}{r}
12\ \text{r}3 \\
4\overline{)51} \\
-4\downarrow \\
\hline
11 \\
-\ 8 \\
\hline
3
\end{array}
$$

LOOK BACK

- How can you decide if your answer makes sense?

- How else could you solve this problem?

Write a number sentence to solve.

1. Mrs. Klein put the 38 students in groups of 3 for their first project. How many groups were there? Were any students left over?

2. Matt and 2 classmates each have 75 baseball cards. How many cards do the three students have in all?

3. The plant nursery has a display of herbs. There are 6 shelves with 15 herbs on each shelf. How many herbs are in the display?

4. Julie took 46 photos. She put 6 photos on each page of her album. How many pages did she use? How many photos are left over?

Mixed Applications

Solve.

CHOOSE a strategy and a tool.
- Act It Out
- Use a Table
- Draw a Picture
- Write a Number Sentence

 Paper/Pencil   Calculator   Hands-On   Mental Math

5. Which of these spinners is fair? Why? Write A or B.
   A.   B.

6. Jenny walks 0.8 mile to school. Bobby walks 0.5 mile to school. Who walks the greater distance to school?

7. Sammy is putting a border around the bulletin board. The bulletin board is 36 inches wide and 48 inches long. How much border does Sammy need?

8. Allison took a survey of students' favorite music. She found that 8 students like country, 11 like soul, and 18 like rock. How many students did she ask in her survey?

9. Vince did his math homework before he did his spelling. He did his reading homework after he did his spelling. He did his science homework before his math. Which homework did he do last?

10. Janice has 8 CDs and Danielle has 13. Bill has 16 CDs and Michael has 11. How many more CDs do Bill and Michael have than Janice and Danielle?

▶ CHECK Understanding

1. **VOCABULARY** In division, the amount left over is called the __?__. (page 488)

Use the model to find the quotient and remainder. (pages 488–491)

2. 13 ÷ 3 = __?__

MODEL

Step 1	Step 2
	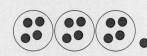
__?__ counters	Quotient is __?__. Remainder is __?__.

3. 9 ÷ 2 = __?__

MODEL

Step 1	Step 2
	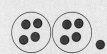
__?__ counters	Quotient is __?__. Remainder is __?__.

4.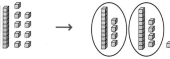

__?__ tens __?__ ones   29 ÷ 2 = __?__

5.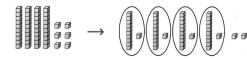

__?__ tens __?__ ones   46 ÷ 4 = __?__

▶ CHECK Skills

Find the quotient. Check each answer by using multiplication. (pages 492–495)

6. 27 ÷ 5 = __?__   7. 53 ÷ 6 = __?__   8. 36 ÷ 3 = __?__   9. 45 ÷ 4 = __?__

10. 3)‾64   11. 4)‾71   12. 5)‾58   13. 4)‾37

▶ CHECK Problem Solving

Solve. (pages 496–499)

CHOOSE a strategy and a tool.
- Work Backward
- Guess and Check
- Write a Number Sentence
- Make a Model

 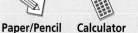

Paper/Pencil   Calculator   Hands-On   Mental Math

14. Students in the Math Club were put into groups of 4. There were 33 students in the club. How many groups were there? Were all students in a group of 4?

15. Laura's doll collection is displayed on 4 shelves. There are 14 dolls on each shelf. How many dolls are in Laura's collection?

Test Prep

Choose the best answer.

1. There are 29 chairs that need to be put into 3 rows. If the same number are put in each row, how many chairs will be left over?

   A 3
   B 4
   C 2
   D 26

2. Jean baked 48 muffins. Each pan holds 6 muffins. How many pans did she fill?

   F 7
   G 8
   H 9
   J 6

3. John earns $10 for each lawn he cuts. He cut 12 lawns. How much did he earn?

   A $10   B $25
   C $120   D $110

4. $19 \div 4 = $ ___?___

   F 4 r1
   G 4 r3
   H 5
   J 76

5. Molly has soccer practice from 4:30 until 5:45 on Tuesdays and Thursdays. For how long does Molly practice each week?

   A 1 hr 30 min B 2 hr 15 min
   C 2 hr 45 min D 2 hr 30 min

6. Which number sentence matches this model?

   F $11 \div 3 = $ ___?___
   G $11 \times 3 = $ ___?___
   H $9 \times 3 = $ ___?___
   J $9 \div 3 = $ ___?___

7. Mr. Adams bought 6 cans of paint. Each can cost $13. How much did he spend?

   A $78   B $36
   C $7   D $68

8. It rained 24 inches in one year. The next year it rained 28 inches. The third year it rained 26 inches. How much did it rain in the three years?

   F 62 inches G 78 inches
   H 74 inches J 72 inches

9. Ms. Yanis's singing class has 48 students. She puts them in 4 groups. How many students are in each group?

   A $48 \times 4 = 192$
   B $48 - 4 = 44$
   C $48 \div 4 = 12$
   D $48 + 4 = 52$

10. $\begin{array}{r} 741 \\ -372 \\ \hline \end{array}$

    F 369   G 269
    H 469   J 431

MATH FUN!

180	104	100
95	315	135
56	165	216

258	104	100
33	63	82
78	280	230

Player 1   **Player 2**

MULTI-SCORE

PURPOSE To practice multiplication skills

YOU WILL NEED 3 number cubes, 18 counters, paper and pencil

Play with a partner. Copy the gameboards shown. On your turn, roll the three cubes and put two of them together to form a two-digit number.

Multiply that number by the third one. If your product is on the board, put a counter on that space. The first player to cover three spaces in a row is the winner of the round. See who can win more rounds.

PRODUCE THE QUOTIENT

PURPOSE To practice division skills, using paper and pencil

YOU WILL NEED 3 number cubes, paper and pencil

Play this game with a small group. On your turn, throw three cubes. Use two of them to form a two-digit number

and divide that number by the third cube. Record the quotient and remainder.

CHINESE STICK MULTIPLICATION

PURPOSE To practice finding products

Find these products. Then see if you can do them by using Chinese stick numerals.

$14 \times 5 = \underline{?}$ $41 \times 2 = \underline{?}$

$27 \times 3 = \underline{?}$ $35 \times 8 = \underline{?}$

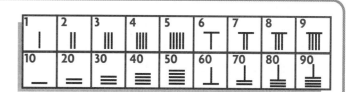

1	2	3	4	5	6	7	8	9
I	II	III	IIII	IIIII	T	T	III	III
10	20	30	40	50	60	70	80	90

 HOME NOTE Make a copy of the Chinese stick numerals to take home. See if members of your family can use it to solve problems.

Changing the Scale on a Bar Graph

VOCABULARY

interval

MATERIALS
Graph Links Plus or any other graphing program

The third grade class sold boxes of candles. Each box holds 25 candles. The bar graph shows the number of candles each class sold.

The scale of the bar graph has **intervals** of 20 (20, 40, 60, ...). Would it be easier if the scale had intervals of 25 (25, 50, 75, ...)?

In some graphing programs, such as *Graph Links Plus,* you can change the intervals of a bar graph's scale.

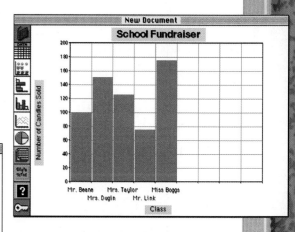

Choose Range/Interval from the Options menu. Click Manual Range and then click Set Intervals. Change 20 to 25 and click OK.

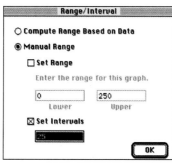

Compare the two graphs.

• Why is an interval of 25 better than 20?

• Why is it easier to read the graph with intervals of 25?

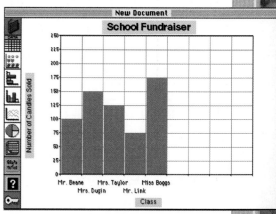

▶ PRACTICE

1. Frozen yogurt cups come in cartons of 50. The table shows the number of cartons sold each week. Make a bar graph showing the total cups sold each week.

FROZEN YOGURT SALES	
Week	Cartons Sold
1	6
2	8
3	7
4	7

2. **Using the Computer** Diskettes come in boxes of 15. Ellen bought 5 boxes. Troy bought 3 boxes. Lee bought 6 boxes. Laurie bought 8 boxes. Use a graphing program to make a bar graph showing the number of diskettes each person bought.

Study Guide and Review

Study and Solve

CHAPTER 27

EXAMPLE

$$
\begin{array}{r}
\overset{1}{4}2 \\
\times\ 8 \\
\hline
336
\end{array}
$$

Multiply ones. $8 \times 2 = 16$
Regroup 16 as 1 ten 6 ones.
Multiply tens. $8 \times 4 = 32$
Add the 1 ten. $32 + 1 = 33$
33 tens = 3 hundreds 3 tens

Use the array. Add the two products to find the answer. Complete the multiplication sentence. (pages 474–475)

1.

$3 \times 13 =$ ___?___

2.

$6 \times 12 =$ ___?___

For Problems 3–6, use base-ten blocks to find each product. (pages 478–479)

3. $3 \times 44 =$ ___?___

4. $2 \times 48 =$ ___?___

5. $5 \times 23 =$ ___?___

6. $4 \times 37 =$ ___?___

For Problems 7–16, find the product.
(pages 480–483)

7.
$$
\begin{array}{r}
36 \\
\times\ 6 \\
\hline
\end{array}
$$

8.
$$
\begin{array}{r}
45 \\
\times\ 4 \\
\hline
\end{array}
$$

9.
$$
\begin{array}{r}
23 \\
\times\ 7 \\
\hline
\end{array}
$$

10.
$$
\begin{array}{r}
53 \\
\times\ 2 \\
\hline
\end{array}
$$

11.
$$
\begin{array}{r}
21 \\
\times\ 3 \\
\hline
\end{array}
$$

12.
$$
\begin{array}{r}
39 \\
\times\ 5 \\
\hline
\end{array}
$$

13.
$$
\begin{array}{r}
55 \\
\times\ 4 \\
\hline
\end{array}
$$

14.
$$
\begin{array}{r}
46 \\
\times\ 2 \\
\hline
\end{array}
$$

15. $48 \times 6 =$ ___?___

16. $27 \times 5 =$ ___?___

Solve. (pages 476–477)

17. Pete lays 9 rows of carpet squares. Each row has 13 squares. How many carpet squares does he need?

18. Ms. Gomez has 28 students. Each student turned in 4 papers. How many papers does she have to grade?

19. Sarah's quilt has 8 rows of 18 squares. How many squares are in Sarah's quilt?

CHAPTER 28

EXAMPLE

$$
\begin{array}{r}
12 \text{ r3} \\
6\overline{)75} \\
-6 \\
\hline
15 \\
-12 \\
\hline
3
\end{array}
$$

Divide tens. $7 \div 6$
Multiply. $6 \times 1 = 6$
Subtract. $7 - 6 = 1$
Divide ones. $15 \div 6$
Repeat steps as needed.
Write 3 as remainder.

Use the counters to find the quotient and remainder. (pages 488–489)

20. $16 \div 3 = \underline{}$

Step 1

$\underline{}$ counters

Step 2

Quotient is $\underline{}$.
Remainder is $\underline{}$.

Use the base-ten blocks to find the quotient. (pages 490–493)

21. $33 \div 2 = \underline{}$

Step 1

$\underline{}$ tens
$\underline{}$ ones

Step 2

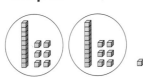

Quotient is
$\underline{}$

For Problems 22–32, find the quotient. Check each answer by using multiplication. (pages 494–495)

22. $5\overline{)26}$ **23.** $6\overline{)52}$

24. $2\overline{)24}$ **25.** $3\overline{)34}$

26. $4\overline{)54}$ **27.** $7\overline{)38}$

28. $65 \div 3 = \underline{}$

29. $62 \div 5 = \underline{}$

30. $44 \div 2 = \underline{}$

31. $80 \div 7 = \underline{}$

32. $83 \div 9 = \underline{}$

Solve. (pages 496–499)

33. Mrs. Williams had 42 cookies. She divided them evenly among 8 children. How many cookies did each child get? How many cookies were left?

34. Tony put 6 cookies in each bag. He filled 15 bags. How many cookies did Tony put in bags?

35. There are 64 ounces in a bottle of juice. How many 8-ounce glasses can be filled with juice?

36. Tracy has 58 marbles. She put them in 6 equal piles. How many are in each pile? How many marbles are left over?

Performance Assessment

Tasks: Show What You Know

1. Show and explain each step as you find the product for 4×37. Use base-ten blocks to help you. (pages 474–475, 480–483)

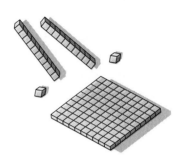

2. Show and explain each step as you find the quotient for $51 \div 4$. Use base-ten blocks to help you. (pages 490–495)

Problem Solving

Solve. Explain your method.

CHOOSE a strategy and a tool.
- Find a Pattern
- Make a Table
- Draw a Picture
- Act It Out
- Write a Number Sentence
- Make a Model

Paper/Pencil   Calculator   Hands-On   Mental Math

3. Bessie is making a poster with photos of everyone in her grade. She puts 8 photos in each row, and there are 14 rows in all. How many students are in Bessie's grade? (pages 476–477)

4. There were 35 players at the tennis camp. The coach put them into groups of 4. How many groups did he make? Were all the players in a group? (pages 498–499)

Cumulative Review

Solve the problem. Then write the letter of the correct answer.

1. 521
    −436

    A. 85
    B. 95
    C. 115
    D. 957

    (pages 56–57, 62–65)

2. $40.00
    − 35.97

    A. $4.03
    B. $4.13
    C. $5.13
    D. $5.97

    (pages 114–115)

3. Round $86 to the nearest ten dollars.

    A. $10   **B.** $80
    C. $90   **D.** $100

    (pages 174–175)

4. 6
    ×7

    A. 13
    B. 32
    C. 36
    D. 42

    (pages 208–215)

5. What solid figure is shown?

    A. circle
    B. cube
    C. sphere
    D. cylinder

    (pages 316–317)

6. Compare.

ones	tenths
1	4

ones	tenths
1	5

    1.4 ● 1.5

    A. <   **B.** >
    C. =   **D.** −

    (pages 408–409)

7. What is the best estimate of the width?

    A. 60 dm   **B.** 60 cm
    C. 60 m   **D.** 60 g

    (pages 438–439)

8. 54
    × 6

    A. 9
    B. 304
    C. 324
    D. 424

    (pages 480–483)

9. 48 ÷ 4 = ?
    A. 9 r12   **B.** 11
    C. 12   **D.** 192

    (pages 494–495)

10. 4)85
    A. 20 r5   **B.** 21 r1
    C. 21 r5   **D.** 111 r1

    (pages 494–495)

STUDENT HANDBOOK

1 ▸ Troubleshooting Lessons H2

Before you begin a new topic, it often helps to review things that you learned earlier. These lessons will help you get ready to learn new topics in math.

2 ▸ Extension Lessons H32

You can challenge yourself to learn new and interesting things when you try these Extension lessons.

Using the Addition Table

Why learn this? An addition table can help you remember facts that you may have forgotten.

Randy ate 9 green grapes and 4 red grapes. How many grapes did Randy eat?

You can use an addition table to find the sum.

$9 + 4 = \underline{\ ?\ }$

Find the column for 9 across the top.
Find the row for 4 down the left side.
The sum for 9 + 4 is where the row and column meet.

$9 + 4 = 13$

So, Randy ate 13 grapes.

You can use the addition table to find a difference.

$16 - 7 = \underline{\ ?\ }$

Find the column for 7 and move down the column to find 16. Look for the number of the row (9) to find the difference.

So, $16 - 7 = 9$

Addition Table

Column ↓

Row →

+	0	1	2	3	4	5	6	7	8	9
0	0	1	2	3	4	5	6	7	8	9
1	1	2	3	4	5	6	7	8	9	10
2	2	3	4	5	6	7	8	9	10	11
3	3	4	5	6	7	8	9	10	11	12
4	4	5	6	7	8	9	10	11	12	13
5	5	6	7	8	9	10	11	12	13	14
6	6	7	8	9	10	11	12	13	14	15
7	7	8	9	10	11	12	13	14	15	16
8	8	9	10	11	12	13	14	15	16	17
9	9	10	11	12	13	14	15	16	17	18

CRITICAL THINKING How can you use the addition table to find 6 + 7? to find 11 − 5?

▶ CHECK

Use the addition table to find the sum or difference.

1. $4 + 7 = \underline{\ ?\ }$
2. $8 - 6 = \underline{\ ?\ }$
3. $9 + 5 = \underline{\ ?\ }$
4. $7 + 9 = \underline{\ ?\ }$
5. $13 - 8 = \underline{\ ?\ }$
6. $14 - 6 = \underline{\ ?\ }$

Use the addition table to find the sum or difference.

7. 4 +5	**8.** 8 −3	**9.** 6 +2	**10.** 8 +4	**11.** 7 −1
12. 5 −5	**13.** 7 +3	**14.** 3 +8	**15.** 9 −4	**16.** 6 +7
17. 6 +6	**18.** 12 − 3	**19.** 9 +9	**20.** 8 +7	**21.** 14 − 6

22. $3 + 9 = \underline{\ ?\ }$ **23.** $6 + 8 = \underline{\ ?\ }$ **24.** $17 - 9 = \underline{\ ?\ }$ **25.** $4 + 4 = \underline{\ ?\ }$

26. $14 - 7 = \underline{\ ?\ }$ **27.** $5 + 7 = \underline{\ ?\ }$ **28.** $9 + 6 = \underline{\ ?\ }$ **29.** $18 - 9 = \underline{\ ?\ }$

Problem Solving • Mixed Applications

30. Mental Math Sabrina saw 8 ducks in the lake. She saw 4 more ducks swimming toward them. How many ducks did Sabrina see in the lake?

31. There were 12 squirrels eating acorns on the ground. Suddenly, 4 of them ran up a tree. How many squirrels were left eating acorns?

32. Nicky has 9 goldfish in his fish tank. Charlie has 6 goldfish in his fish tank. How many more goldfish does Nicky have than Charlie?

33. Reading Ed checked out 8 animal books at the library. Beth checked out 7 animal books. How many animal books did Ed and Beth check out at the library?

34. Carol has 6 baby rabbits. She gave 4 baby rabbits to her friends. How many baby rabbits does Carol still have?

35. Reasoning Hussan saw 6 gerbils in one cage. He saw 11 gerbils in a second cage. How many more gerbils are in the second cage?

36. Logic Joan counted 5 birds sitting on the fence. A few minutes later, the 5 birds were still on the fence. How many birds had flown away?

37. ✏ **Write a problem** about adding the numbers 5 and 7.

Names for Numbers

Why learn this? You can add numbers with sums greater than 9.

Bill saw 6 birds in his front yard. He saw 7 birds in the yard next door. How many birds did Bill see in all?

$$6 + 7 = \underline{\ ?\ }$$

Add the ones.

Regroup the 13 ones as 1 ten 3 ones.

6 + 7

6 + 7 = 13

So, Bill saw 13 birds.

REMEMBER:

10 ones = 1 ten

Talk About It CRITICAL THINKING

- How do you know when to regroup the ones as tens? Explain.

- How would you regroup 15 ones as tens and ones?

- How can regrouping ones as tens and ones help you add two-digit numbers?

► CHECK

Regroup the ones. Write the number of tens and ones.

Example: 13 ones = 1 ten 3 ones

1. 12 ones = __?__

2. 18 ones = __?__

3. 16 ones = __?__

SCIENCE LINK

Bald eagles sometimes use the same nest year after year. They add more twigs and branches each year. One nest weighed more than 2 tons. That is about as much as an elephant weighs!

Male bald eagles weigh about 9 pounds. Females weigh about 12 pounds. About how much would a male and female weigh together?

Regroup the ones. Write the number of tens and ones.

4.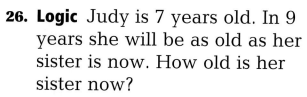

5.

6.

11 ones = __?__

19 ones = __?__

17 ones = __?__

7. 16 ones   8. 14 ones   9. 9 ones   10. 15 ones

11. 8 ones   12. 12 ones   13. 13 ones   14. 18 ones

Find the sum.

15. 6
    +8

16. 5
    +7

17. 8
    +4

18. 5
    +9

19. 7
    +7

20. 8
    +8

21. 4
    +9

22. 8
    +7

23. 3
    +9

24. 5
    +6

Problem Solving • Mixed Applications

25. Mary collects pictures of dogs. She had 16 pictures. She sent 6 pictures to her grandmother. How many pictures of dogs does Mary still have?

26. **Logic** Judy is 7 years old. In 9 years she will be as old as her sister is now. How old is her sister now?

27. Tom's dog has 8 puppies. Four of the puppies are sleeping. How many of the puppies are not sleeping?

28. **Reasoning** James saw 8 squirrels playing by the oak tree. They all ran away. How many squirrels are still playing by the tree?

29. **Consumer** There were 5 cans of soup in the cabinet. Tony's father put in 4 more cans of soup. How many cans of soup are in the cabinet now?

30. ▱ **Write a problem** where the answer is 15.

Regrouping Numbers

Why learn this? You will be able to recognize when regrouping is needed.

Andy and his dad went to the movies. There were 34 people in line. Then 16 people went inside. How many people were still in line?

$$34 - 16 = \underline{\ ?\ }$$

MODEL

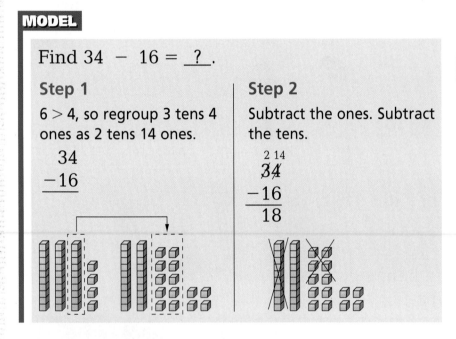

Find $34 - 16 = \underline{\ ?\ }$.

Step 1

$6 > 4$, so regroup 3 tens 4 ones as 2 tens 14 ones.

$$\begin{array}{r} 34 \\ -16 \\ \hline \end{array}$$

Step 2

Subtract the ones. Subtract the tens.

$$\begin{array}{r} {}^{2\ 14} \\ \cancel{34} \\ -16 \\ \hline 18 \end{array}$$

So, 18 people were still in line.

Talk About It CRITICAL THINKING

• In Step 1, where did the 14 ones come from?

• When do you regroup numbers?

▶ CHECK

Regroup. Write the number of tens and ones.
Example: 3 tens 5 ones = 2 tens 15 ones

1.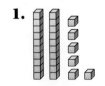

2 tens 6 ones = _?_

2.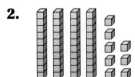

4 tens 8 ones = _?_

3.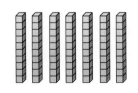

7 tens = _?_

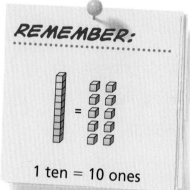

REMEMBER:

1 ten = 10 ones

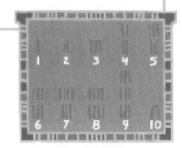

SOCIAL STUDIES LINK

Early Egyptians used numbers based on 10. The numbers 1–9 were single marks, such as $|, ||$, and $|||$.

The number 10 was an arch, $\cap$.

What number was $\cap|||$?

▶ PRACTICE

Regroup. Write the number of tens and ones.

4.

3 tens 2 ones = ?

5.

5 tens 1 one = ?

6.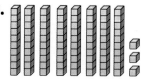

8 tens 3 ones = ?

Regroup the tens and ones.
Example: 13 = 0 tens 13 ones

7. 16   **8.** 34   **9.** 42   **10.** 55   **11.** 20

12. 56   **13.** 40   **14.** 65   **15.** 87   **16.** 98

Find the difference.

17. 24
       − 9

18. 27
       − 18

19. 42
       − 25

20. 33
       − 19

21. 54
       − 27

22. 62
       − 16

23. 84
       − 49

24. 91
       − 35

25. 83
       − 59

26. 71
       − 52

27. 65
       − 48

28. 81
       − 42

29. 28
       − 19

30. 73
       − 58

31. 45
       − 27

Problem Solving • Mixed Applications

32. During May and June, 64 Boy Scouts went camping. In May 36 of the Boy Scouts went camping. How many Boy Scouts went camping in June?

33. Reasoning There are 35 spaces on the gameboard. Brooke has moved 16 spaces. How many more spaces does she need to move to get to the end of the board?

34. Sports Tara's basketball team scored 32 points. Jordan's team scored 28 points. How many points did the two teams score in all?

35. ⬤ **Write a problem** using the following information. Mark had a box of 36 crayons. He gave 18 crayons to Rod.

Using a Calendar

Why learn this? You can find days and dates on a calendar.

Calendars are tables that show the days, weeks, and months of a year in order. One way to use calendars is to record special days.

EXAMPLE

Carol's birthday is on Tuesday, October 16.

Write: October 16   **Read:** October sixteenth

Look at this calendar for October.

Notice that

⇨ there are 31 days in October.

⇨ October begins on a Monday and ends on a Wednesday in this year.

October

Sun	Mon	Tue	Wed	Thu	Fri	Sat
	1	2	3	4	5	6
7	8	9	10	11	12	13
14	15	16	17	18	19	20
21	22	23	24	25	26	27
28	29	30	31			

Saturday and Sunday are *weekend* days. The other days of the week are *weekdays*.

Talk About It CRITICAL THINKING

- What is the date of the third Sunday in the calendar above?

- In the calendar above, on what day of the week is the last day of September? the first day of November?

- How can you use a calendar to find the day of the week for a given date?

▶ CHECK

For Exercises 1–4, use the June calendar.

1. How many Mondays are there in June?

2. On what day is the last day of May?

3. On what day is the first day of July?

4. How many weekdays are there in June?

June

Sun	Mon	Tue	Wed	Thu	Fri	Sat
					1	2
3	4	5	6	7	8	9
10	11	12	13	14	15	16
17	18	19	20	21	22	23
24	25	26	27	28	29	30

▶ PRACTICE

For Exercises 5–7, use the March calendar.
Write the day of the week.

March						
Sun	Mon	Tue	Wed	Thu	Fri	Sat
	1	2	3	4	5	6
7	8	9	10	11	12	13
14	15	16	17	18	19	20
21	22	23	24	25	26	27
28	29	30	31			

5. March 5

6. March 28

7. March 13

For Exercises 8–10, use the March calendar. Write the date.

8. the second Monday   9. the third Thursday   10. the fourth Tuesday

For Exercises 11–14, use the November calendar.

November						
Sun	Mon	Tue	Wed	Thu	Fri	Sat
			1	2	3	4
5	6	7	8	9	10	11
12	13	14	15	16	17	18
19	20	21	22	23	24	25
26	27	28	29	30		

11. How many Fridays are in this month?

12. On what day does the month end?

13. On what day of the week is the last day of October? the first day of December?

14. What is the date of the third Saturday in November?

Problem Solving • Mixed Applications

For Problems 15–18, use the calendars shown.

15. Melinda's party is in 14 days. Today is March 9. What is the date of Melinda's party?

16. **Elapsed Time** Today is November 22. Karen went to Mead Park two weeks ago. On what day and date did Karen go to the park?

17. Joel is going to camp from June 23 through June 30. Today is June 8. How many days are there until he leaves for camp? How long will he be gone?

18. ✏ **Write About It** Look at the calendars above. What pattern do you notice in the dates of each Monday? Do the other days of the week follow the same pattern?

Counting Coins

Why learn this? You can count the money you have in your pocket or purse.

Janell used these coins to pay for a bag of chips. How much money did she spend?

Sort and count the coins in order from the ones with the greatest value to the ones with the least value.

Count: 25¢   50¢   60¢   65¢   66¢   67¢   68¢

Write: 68¢   **Read:** sixty-eight cents

So, Janell spent 68¢.

Evan puts 76¢ in his pocket. What is one combination of coins he can use to make this amount?

Count: 25¢   50¢   60¢   70¢   75¢   76¢

Write: 76¢   **Read:** seventy-six cents

So, Evan can use 2 quarters, 2 dimes, 1 nickel, and 1 penny to make 76¢.

▶ CHECK

Write the amount.

1.

List the coins you could use to make each amount.

2. 22¢   **3.** 64¢

▶ PRACTICE

Write each amount as you would write it and read it.

4.

5.

6.

Write the total amount.

7. 1 quarter,
3 dimes,
6 pennies

8. 2 quarters,
1 dime, 3 nickels,
7 pennies

9. 3 quarters,
4 nickels,
3 pennies

10. 2 quarters,
2 dimes,
2 pennies

11. 1 quarter,
3 dimes,
6 nickels

12. 5 dimes,
4 nickels,
3 pennies

13. 3 quarters,
3 nickels,
3 pennies

14. 4 dimes,
5 nickels,
9 pennies

15. 2 quarters,
5 nickels,
5 pennies

List the coins you could use to make each amount.

16. 39¢

17. 53¢

18. 84¢

19. 65¢

20. 31¢

21. 89¢

22. 29¢

23. 72¢

24. 99¢

25. 46¢

26. 57¢

27. 68¢

Problem Solving • Mixed Applications

28. Angela has 2 quarters, 1 dime, 1 nickel, and 3 pennies. How much money does she have?

29. Alex has 1 quarter, 1 dime, 1 nickel, and 1 penny. How much more money does he need to have 50¢?

30. Flora has 27¢ in her hand and 36¢ in her purse. How much money does she have in all?

31. ✏️ **Write a problem** about the 4 coins in Keiko's pocket. (HINT: What do they equal?)

Place Value

Why learn this? You regroup when you trade 10 pennies for a dime or 10 dimes for a dollar.

Mae spills a handful of blocks on the table. How can she group the blocks so she can count them easily?

Each time Mae has 10 blocks, she regroups them for a ten.

So, Mae has 3 tens 7 ones, or 37.

Record:

Tens	Ones
3	7

Jed has 10 tens 18 ones. How can he regroup the blocks so he can count them easily? How many blocks does Jed have?

So, Jed has 1 hundred, 1 ten, 8 ones, or 118.

Record:

Hundreds	Tens	Ones
1	1	8

REMEMBER:

10 ones = 1 ten

10 tens = 1 hundred

Talk About It

- How do you know when you need to regroup?

- How would you regroup 12 tens 19 ones? What number is this?

You can trade coins and bills by using what you know about regrouping ones and tens.

4 dimes, 15 pennies = __?__

5 dimes, 5 pennies = 55¢

13 dimes, 19 pennies = __?__

1 dollar, 4 dimes, 9 pennies = $1.49

- How would you use what you know about regrouping to trade 15 dimes? How much money is this?

▶ CHECK

Regroup ones for tens or tens for hundreds. Write how many hundreds, tens, and ones you can make. Then write the number.

1.

2.

3.

4. 5 tens, 15 ones

5. 7 tens, 23 ones

6. 2 tens, 31 ones

7. 18 tens, 3 ones

8. 15 tens, 2 ones

9. 10 tens, 9 ones

▶ PRACTICE

Copy and complete each place-value chart to show regrouping.

10.

Hundreds	Tens	Ones
	4	12
	?	?

11.

Hundreds	Tens	Ones
	1	22
	?	?

12.

Hundreds	Tens	Ones
	8	19
	?	?

13.

Hundreds	Tens	Ones
	9	13
	?	?

14.

Hundreds	Tens	Ones
	15	10
	?	?

15.

Hundreds	Tens	Ones
	12	14
	?	?

Tell the value of each coin collection.

16. 11 dimes, 2 pennies

17. 12 dimes, 4 pennies

18. 15 dimes, 9 pennies

19. 10 dimes, 15 pennies

20. 14 dimes, 6 pennies

21. 9 dimes, 19 pennies

Problem Solving • Mixed Applications

22. **Mental Math** Julie has 43 loose pens. How many ten-pen packs can she fill? How many single pens will be left?

23. **Reasoning** I have no tens yet. If you trade 20 of my ones for tens, you will have 2 tens and 5 ones. What's my number?

24. Yana came home from the peanut hunt with 21 peanuts. She ate 5 peanuts when she got home. How many peanuts does Yana have left?

25. ▭ **Write a problem** about Hal's baseball cards. Hal adds 2 ten-packs of baseball cards to his collection of 17 cards.

Rounding on a Number Line

Why learn this? You can use rounding to estimate when you do not need an exact amount.

A small bus holds 18 people. To the nearest ten, about how many people does the bus hold?

Use a number line to help you find out.

Think: Is 18 closer to 10 or to 20?

18 is closer to 20 than to 10.
So, the bus holds about 20 people.

Talk About It

- Between which two tens is 18?

- Which digit helps you find the tens the number is between?

- Which digit helps you find the closer ten?

- To which ten would you round the number 15? 14? Why?

- What number line would you draw to help you round 25 to the nearest ten?

▶ CHECK

Tell which two tens the number is between. Then round the number to the nearer ten. Use the number line to help you.

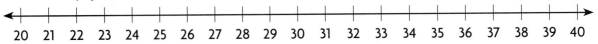

1. 23	**2.** 38	**3.** 27	**4.** 24
5. 39	**6.** 31	**7.** 22	**8.** 36
9. 37	**10.** 33	**11.** 32	**12.** 26
13. 29	**14.** 22	**15.** 35	**16.** 34

▶ PRACTICE

Tell which two tens the number is between. Then round the number to the nearest ten. Use the number line to help you.

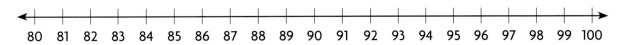

80 81 82 83 84 85 86 87 88 89 90 91 92 93 94 95 96 97 98 99 100

17. 88 **18.** 93 **19.** 82 **20.** 91

21. 87 **22.** 94 **23.** 92 **24.** 85

Round the number to the nearest ten.

25. 43 **26.** 56 **27.** 73 **28.** 91

29. 17 **30.** 25 **31.** 49 **32.** 51

Write three numbers that round to each number.

33. 30 **34.** 80 **35.** 40 **36.** 10

Problem Solving • Mixed Applications

Using Data Use the toys and their prices to solve.

37. Money Lila has 50¢ to spend at the toy store. Which toy costs about 50¢?

38. Order the toys from least expensive to most expensive.

39. Consumer Carl bought two books and a robot. How much did he spend?

40. Estimation Janice bought a pen and a book. To the nearest 10¢, about how much did she spend?

41. Compare Manny buys a book and a pen. Rita buys a stuffed toy. Who spends more? How much more? Explain.

42. ▥ **Write About It** Mr. Abram says that he sold about 20 robots last week. How can you find the number of robots Mr. Abram sold?

Skip Counting

Why learn this? When you have equal groups of toys, skip counting will help you quickly find how many in all.

When objects are in equal groups, you can find how many in all by

- counting them one by one.

- skip counting them.

These cubes are in groups of 2. Count them one by one.

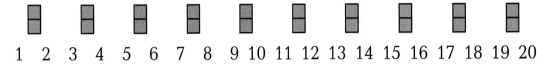

1 2 3 4 5 6 7 8 9 10 11 12 13 14 15 16 17 18 19 20

Skip count by twos.

  2   4   6   8   10   12   14   16   18   20

When you have equal groups, how does skip counting help you find the total?

▶ CHECK

1. Copy and complete. Skip count by fives.

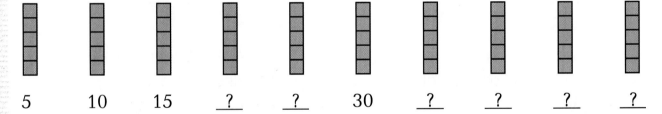

5   10   15   ?   ?   30   ?   ?   ?   ?

2. Copy and complete. Skip count by tens.

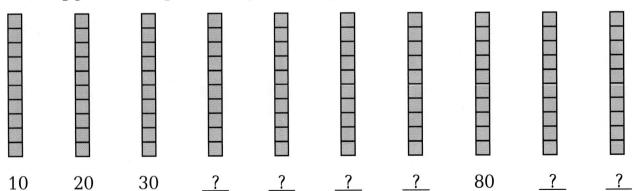

10   20   30   ?   ?   ?   ?   80   ?   ?

3. Skip count by twos.

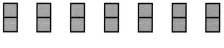

2 4 6 _?_ _?_ _?_ _?_

4. Skip count by fives.

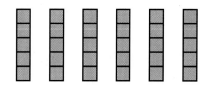

5 10 15 _?_ _?_ _?_

5. Skip count by tens.

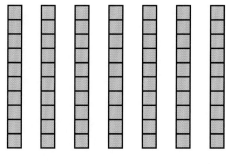

10 20 30 _?_ _?_ _?_ _?_

6. Skip count by threes.

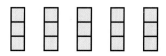

3 6 9 _?_ _?_

Skip count to complete the pattern.

7. 2, _?_, 6, 8, _?_, _?_

8. 5, 10, _?_, 20, _?_, _?_

Count by twos, fives, and tens.

9. 2, 4, 6, _?_, _?_, _?_, 14, 16, _?_, _?_

10. 5, 10, _?_, _?_

11. 10, _?_

Problem Solving • Mixed Applications

12. Money Josh put his pennies in 6 stacks with 5 pennies in each stack. How many pennies does Josh have?

13. Consumer At the garage sale, Ronnie bought 8 Matchbox® cars. Each car cost one nickel. How much did Ronnie spend?

14. Compare Tom has 6 bags of marbles with 2 marbles in each bag. Jen has 2 bags of marbles with 5 marbles in each bag. Who has more marbles?

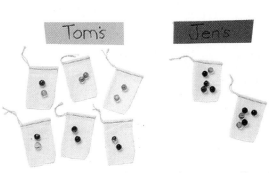

Equal Groups

Why learn this? You can use division to share things equally with classmates.

Use division when you want to separate objects into groups of equal size.

Hillary baked 24 cookies for her school lunches. She put 4 cookies into each bag. How many bags of cookies did Hillary have?

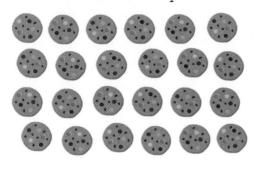

$$24 \div 4 = \underline{\ ?\ }$$

Talk About It CRITICAL THINKING

- How many cookies are there in all?

- Use 24 counters. How many groups of 4 can you make using all the counters?

- What division sentence tells what you did?

So, Hillary had 6 bags of cookies.

▶ CHECK

Use the pictures to answer the questions.

1.

How many squares are there in all?
How many equal groups are there?
How many are in each group?

$$10 \div 2 = \underline{\ ?\ }$$

2.

How many triangles are there?
How many equal groups?
How many are in each group?

$$4 \div 1 = \underline{\ ?\ }$$

Use the pictures to answer the questions.

3.

4.

5.

How many are there in all?

How many groups are there?

How many are in each group?

$12 \div 3 = $?

How many are there in all?

How many groups are there?

How many are in each group?

$8 \div 4 = $?

How many are there in all?

How many groups are there?

How many are in each group?

$12 \div 2 = $?

Copy and complete the table.

	How many in all?	How many equal groups?	How many in each group?
6.	10	2	?
7.	15	?	3
8.	8	2	?
9.	12	?	3

Problem Solving • Mixed Applications

10. An-Mei baked 24 cookies. She put an equal number of cookies on each of 3 baking sheets. How many cookies did she put on each sheet?

11. Kofi used 2 eggs in each batch of cookies he made. He used 8 eggs in all. How many batches of cookies did he make?

12. Money Jay has $5.00. He needs to buy eggs, margarine, and raisins to make cookies. Does he have enough money?

$1.05 $2.19 $1.69

13. Gregory, Daniel, and Ira have 9 cookies to share equally. How many cookies will each boy get?

14. Mental Math Toby put 3 cookies in each bag. She filled 9 bags. How many cookies did she have?

15. ✏️ **Write a problem** that uses division to solve. Write about a food you like to share with friends.

Fact Families

Why learn this? You will know when to use multiplication or division to solve problems.

Alex collects stamps. This is a page from his stamp collection. You can use multiplication and division to tell about his stamps.

Use multiplication to put the stamps together.

3 × 4 = 12 or 4 × 3 = 12

Use division to separate the stamps into equal groups.

12 ÷ 3 = 4 or 12 ÷ 4 = 3

A *fact family* is a set of related multiplication and division sentences using the same numbers. It shows how multiplication and division are related.

Fact Family for 3, 4, 12

| Multiplication | | | | Division | | |
factor	factor	product		dividend	divisor	quotient
3 ×	4 =	12		12 ÷	3 =	4
4 ×	3 =	12		12 ÷	4 =	3

▶ CHECK

1. What are the other three number sentences that belong in the fact family for 5 × 6 = 30?

2. What are the other three number sentences that belong in the fact family for 3 × 9 = 27?

3. What other fact belongs in the fact family with 4 × 4 = 16?

4. Why are there only two number sentences in the fact family for 4, 4, 16?

▶ PRACTICE

Write the other three sentences that belong in the fact family.

5. $8 \times 2 = 16$

6. $3 \times 5 = 15$

7. $7 \times 5 = 35$

8. $6 \times 4 = 24$

9. $8 \times 4 = 32$

10. $6 \times 3 = 18$

11. $8 \times 5 = 40$

12. $9 \times 5 = 45$

13. $8 \times 3 = 24$

14. $6 \times 9 = 54$

15. $6 \times 7 = 42$

16. $7 \times 8 = 56$

Write the fact family for each set of numbers.

17. 2, 4, 8

18. 5, 2, 10

19. 3, 7, 21

20. 2, 7, 14

21. 7, 4, 28

22. 5, 5, 25

23. 4, 5, 20

24. 4, 9, 36

25. 2, 9, 18

26. 9, 3, 27

27. 5, 6, 30

28. 6, 2, 12

Problem Solving • Mixed Applications

Using Data For Problems 29 and 35, use the table.

29. Brandi used 8 of each type of sea object to decorate a mirror. How many objects are on the mirror?

BRANDI'S COLLECTION	
Starfish	Sand Dollar
Conch	Periwinkle

30. Science Brandi has 12 starfish, 15 sand dollars, 24 conchs, and 45 periwinkles. How many objects are in Brandi's collection?

31. Mental Math Brandi put her 15 sand dollars into 5 rows. How many of her sand dollars are in each row?

32. Mental Math Brandi put her 24 conch shells into 3 boxes. How many of her conch shells are in each box?

33. Brandi put her 12 starfish on 2 tables. How many of her starfish are on each table?

34. Brandi has 45 periwinkles. She wants to use the shells for 5 projects. How many periwinkles can she use in each project?

35. ▭ **Write a problem** about the number of objects in Brandi's collection. Use multiplication.

Understanding Pictographs

Why learn this? You can use data in graphs to compare things, such as how the number of dog pets compare to the number of cat pets.

Michael's class wants to know what kinds of pets their classmates have. The students surveyed their classmates and made this tally table.

OUR PETS	
Pet	**Tallies**
Dogs	||||| |||||
Cats	|||||	
Gerbils	||||
Hamsters	||||| |||||
Rabbits	||

Then the students decided to make a graph to show what they found out. They made a pictograph.

OUR PETS	
Dogs	🐾 🐾 🐾 🐾 🐾
Cats	🐾 🐾 🐾
Gerbils	🐾 🐾
Hamsters	🐾 🐾 🐾 🐾 🐾
Rabbits	🐾

Key: Each 🐾 = 2 students.

Notice that

⇨ in the key, each picture stands for 2 students.

▶ CHECK

1. How is the pictograph like the tally table? How is it different?

2. How do you read the data for dogs in the pictograph?

▶ PRACTICE

For Problems 3–7, use the pictograph.

BOOKS READ THIS MONTH	
Karen	📗📗📗📗📗📗
Roger	📗📗📗📗
Tina	📗📗📗📗📗📗📗
Amber	📗📗📗
Daniel	📗📗📗📗

Key: Each 📗 = 2 books.

3. How many books does each picture stand for?

4. How many books did each student read?

5. Who read the most books? the fewest?

6. How many more books did Karen read than Daniel?

7. Suppose *Kendall* is added to the pictograph. Kendall read 12 books. How many pictures will be in her row?

Problem Solving • Mixed Applications

8. A pictograph shows the number of students who brought lunch. In the key, each picture stands for 3 students. There are 4 pictures in the row for Mrs. Tong's class. How many students in Mrs. Tong's class brought lunch?

9. **Sports** In the football game, Roy made 7 points in the first half and 14 points in the second half. Jeff made a total of 28 points in the game. Who made more points?

10. **Mental Math** Joe bought 6 folders. He bought 3 times as many markers. How many markers did he buy?

11. **Money** Brad bought a gift for $7.79. He gave the clerk a $10 bill. How much change did he receive?

12. **Logic** Pat has the same number of pennies as nickels. The nickels are worth 20 cents. How many pennies does she have?

13. **Time** Lisa and Melanie went to a movie at 12:45. The movie was over at 2:45. How long was the movie?

14. Summer vacation begins in three weeks. Today is May 7. When does summer vacation begin?

15. ⬛▶ **Write a problem** using the pictograph at the top of the page.

Open and Closed Figures

Why learn this? You can recognize open and closed figures in patterns of drapes, wallpaper, and paintings.

Figures with ends that do not touch are *open* figures. These are open figures.

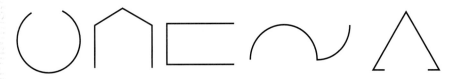

Figures that begin and end at the same point are *closed* figures. These are closed figures.

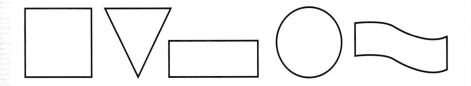

A style of painting called Cubism began in the early 1900's. Cubist artists used flat shapes and figures in their paintings of people, musical instruments, and other objects. Here is a Cubist painting of Pablo Picasso, an artist. Find two open and closed figures in this painting.

Talk About It `CRITICAL THINKING`

• Is the letter O an open or a closed figure? the letter Z? the letter E?

• Is the number 3 an open or a closed figure? the number 8? the number 5?

• Give other examples of an open letter and number and a closed letter and number.

• How do you know if a figure is open or closed?

▶ CHECK

Tell if each picture suggests an open or a closed figure. Write *open* or *closed*.

1. **2.** **3.**

Tell if each figure is open or closed.

4.   **5.**   **6.**    **7.**

8.   **9.**   **10.**   **11.**

12. Use the letters below. Make a table that shows if each letter is open or closed.

B C D L M N O X Y Z

Problem Solving • Mixed Applications

13. Time Kerry took her dog for a 35-minute walk. Then she spent 25 minutes giving her dog a bath. How long did she spend with her dog in all?

14. Logic Frank wrote down three numbers in a row. The numbers are between 1 and 10. Their sum is 12. What are the three numbers?

15. Money Nathan has six one-dollar bills, 2 quarters, 8 dimes, and 7 nickels. Does he have enough money to buy a tape costing $8.00? Explain.

16. Elapsed Time Anne Marie's science project is due in three weeks. Today is January 11. When is Anne Marie's science project due?

17. Mental Math Craft sticks are on sale for 9¢ a box. How much will 9 boxes cost?

18. Reasoning I am a solid figure with zero faces, zero edges, and zero corners. What am I?

19. Measurement Jerry rode 6.3 miles in the morning and 5.9 miles in the afternoon. How far did Jerry ride in all?

20. ✏ **Write About It** Suppose you use a piece of string to show a closed figure. Explain how you know the figure you made is closed.

Using a Ruler

Why learn this? You can find the measure of an object.

You can use a ruler to measure objects up to 12 inches. How long is a new crayon?

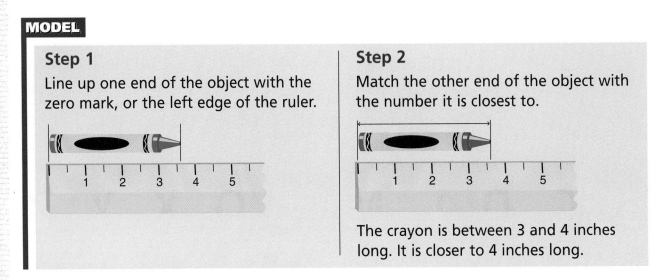

MODEL

Step 1

Line up one end of the object with the zero mark, or the left edge of the ruler.

Step 2

Match the other end of the object with the number it is closest to.

The crayon is between 3 and 4 inches long. It is closer to 4 inches long.

So, a new crayon is about 4 inches long.

Talk About It CRITICAL THINKING

- How did you decide between which two inches the crayon measured?

- How did you decide if the crayon was closer to 3 inches or to 4 inches?

▶ CHECK

Tell between which two inch marks the object measures. Then tell the length to the nearest inch.

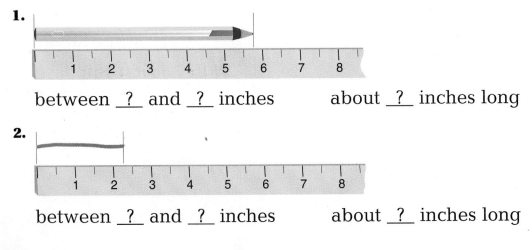

1.

between __?__ and __?__ inches   about __?__ inches long

2.

between __?__ and __?__ inches   about __?__ inches long

Tell between which two inch marks the object measures.
Then tell the length to the nearest inch.

3.

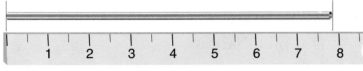

between __?__ and __?__ inches   about __?__ inches long

4.

between __?__ and __?__ inches   about __?__ inches long

5.

between __?__ and __?__ inches   about __?__ inches long

Problem Solving • Mixed Applications

Using Data For Problems 6–8 and 12, use the drawing.

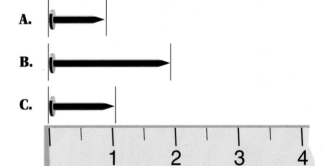

6. Which nail is about 2 inches long?

7. Between which two measurements is nail A?

8. Which two nails are the same length, to the nearest inch?

9. Mental Math Habib ordered 12 brownies and shared them with two friends. How many brownies did each person get?

10. Reasoning Pat is making a felt flag 8 inches long. One piece is 5 inches long and another is almost 2 inches long. Does Pat have enough felt? Explain.

11. Sharon wants to measure her pencil. Which unit of measure should she use?

12. ✐ **Write a problem** about the measurements of the nails shown in the drawing.

Multiplication Facts

Why learn this? You will be able to find the product of any two numbers.

Michael has filled 9 pages of his baseball-card-collection book. Each page holds 6 baseball cards. How many baseball cards are in Michael's book?

$$9 \times 6 = \underline{\ ?\ }$$

To help you find a product, you can make an array. Then you can break the larger array into smaller arrays to help you find the product.

MODEL

What is 9×6?

Step 1

Make an array that shows 9 rows of 6.

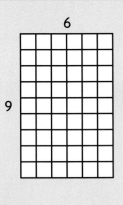

Step 2

You can break the array into 2 smaller arrays in different ways.
Multiply 9×3 and 9×3.
Or, multiply 4×6 and 5×6.

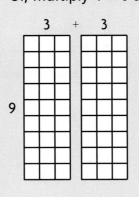

Step 3

Then add the products of the two arrays.

```
  27
 +27
 ---
  54

  or

  24
 +30
 ---
  54
```

So, there are 54 baseball cards in Michael's book.

▶ CHECK

1. Name two other smaller arrays that you could use to find $9 \times 6 = \underline{\ ?\ }$.

2. Describe an array that shows 7×9. What smaller arrays could you use to find the product?

Break the array into two smaller arrays to find each product.

3. 5
4
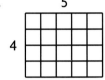

4. 7
3
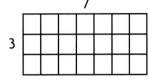

5. 8
6
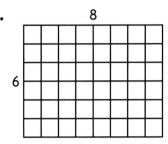

Complete the tables.

6.

×	2	3	4	5
8	?	?	?	?

7.

×	4	5	6	7
7	?	?	?	?

8.

×	1	2	3	4
9	?	?	?	?

9.

×	3	4	5	6
5	?	?	?	?

10.

×	5	6	7	8
6	?	?	?	?

11.

×	6	7	8	9
4	?	?	?	?

Find the product.

12. $8 \times 6 =$? **13.** $5 \times 9 =$? **14.** $7 \times 6 =$? **15.** $9 \times 9 =$?

16. $8 \times 5 =$? **17.** $4 \times 6 =$? **18.** $3 \times 8 =$? **19.** $7 \times 7 =$?

20. $9 \times 6 =$? **21.** $8 \times 2 =$? **22.** $5 \times 6 =$? **23.** $8 \times 8 =$?

24. $8 \times 9 =$? **25.** $7 \times 3 =$? **26.** $6 \times 8 =$? **27.** $3 \times 6 =$?

28. $9 \times 5 =$? **29.** $8 \times 7 =$? **30.** $9 \times 7 =$?

Problem Solving • Mixed Applications

31. Sports The coach bought 8 packages of baseballs for the team. There were 3 baseballs in each package. How many baseballs did he buy?

32. Time Brett's baseball game starts in 1 hour and 15 minutes. It is now 5:10. At what time does the game start?

33. Money Tim went to a garage sale and bought a baseball glove for $9.75 and a bat for $8.59. How much money did he spend in all?

34. ✏️ **Write a problem** about a baseball team that plays 9 ball games a month.

Division Facts

Why learn this? You can quickly find a quotient.

There are 12 swings at the park. There are 4 swings on each swing set. How many swing sets are there?

$$12 \div 4 = \underline{\ ?\ }$$

To recall a division fact, think of the related multiplication fact.

$$4 \times \underline{\ ?\ } = 12$$

Fact families can help you remember multiplication and division facts.

You know that $4 \times 3 = 12$. So, $12 \div 4 = 3$. So, there are 3 swing sets at the park.

Here is the fact family for 4, 3, 12.

factor	factor	product	dividend	divisor	quotient
4 × 3	=	12	12 ÷ 4	=	3
3 × 4	=	12	12 ÷ 3	=	4

Talk About It CRITICAL THINKING

- Suppose you want to find the quotient $18 \div 2 = \underline{\ ?\ }$. What related multiplication fact would you use to help you?

- What multiplication and division sentences make up the fact family for 4, 6, 24?

► CHECK

Write the multiplication sentence you would use to help you recall each division fact. Solve.

1. $35 \div 5 = \underline{\ ?\ }$ **2.** $40 \div 8 = \underline{\ ?\ }$ **3.** $16 \div 4 = \underline{\ ?\ }$ **4.** $42 \div 7 = \underline{\ ?\ }$

5. $25 \div 5 = \underline{\ ?\ }$ **6.** $24 \div 3 = \underline{\ ?\ }$ **7.** $18 \div 2 = \underline{\ ?\ }$ **8.** $30 \div 6 = \underline{\ ?\ }$

▶ PRACTICE

Write the other three number sentences that belong in the fact family.

9. $2 \times 5 = 10$ **10.** $7 \times 3 = 21$ **11.** $20 \div 5 = 4$

12. $4 \times 8 = 32$ **13.** $36 \div 4 = 9$ **14.** $28 \div 7 = 4$

Write the fact family for each set of numbers.

15. 2, 4, 8   **16.** 8, 7, 56   **17.** 3, 9, 27

18. 9, 6, 54   **19.** 3, 8, 24   **20.** 7, 2, 14

Find the quotient.

21. $16 \div 2 = \underline{\ ?\ }$ **22.** $20 \div 4 = \underline{\ ?\ }$ **23.** $36 \div 6 = \underline{\ ?\ }$ **24.** $45 \div 5 = \underline{\ ?\ }$

25. $18 \div 3 = \underline{\ ?\ }$ **26.** $16 \div 8 = \underline{\ ?\ }$ **27.** $28 \div 4 = \underline{\ ?\ }$ **28.** $56 \div 7 = \underline{\ ?\ }$

Problem Solving • Mixed Applications

29. Consumer Anita has 3 trays. She puts 6 sandwiches on each tray. How many sandwiches does she put on the trays?

30. Mental Math Becky arranged her stickers in 7 rows of 4. How many stickers does Becky have?

31. Money Jeremy counted his change. He had 5 quarters, 3 dimes, and 7 nickels. How much change did he have?

32. Reading Andy has read 14 books during the past 7 weeks. He has read the same number of books each week. How many books did he read each week?

33. Time It took Ron 4 hours and 45 minutes to put his model airplane together. He started on it at 1:30. At what time did he finish it?

34. Measurement The school bus driver drove 206 miles during one week. The next week she drove 275 miles. How many miles did she drive during the two weeks?

35. Logic Nicole is thinking of a product. One of the factors is 6. It is 2 less than the other factor. What is the product?

36. ✏ **Write About It** Explain how fact families can help you recall division facts.

Computing Distances

Why learn this? You can use large numbers to solve problems about distances.

Alaska is the largest state in the United States. It has about 5,580 miles of coastline along the Pacific Ocean. It has about 1,060 miles of coastline along the Arctic Ocean. About how many miles of coastline does Alaska have in all?

Add.

$$
\begin{array}{r}
\overset{1}{5,5\,8\,0} \\
+\,1,0\,6\,0 \\
\hline
6,6\,4\,0
\end{array}
$$

So, Alaska has about 6,640 miles of coastline.

_____

About how many more miles of Alaska's coastline are along the Pacific Ocean than along the Arctic Ocean?

Subtract.

$$
\begin{array}{r}
5,5\,8\,0 \\
-\,1,0\,6\,0 \\
\hline
4,5\,2\,0
\end{array}
$$

So, Alaska has about 4,520 more miles of coastline along the Pacific Ocean.

_____

A calculator can help you add and subtract large numbers.

 Press

▶ CHECK

1. Which keys would you press to find 1,483 + 2,789?

2. In what order should you enter the numbers to subtract 407 from 1,633?

▶ PRACTICE

Find the sum or difference. You may wish to use a calculator.

3. 4,216
    +3,582

4. 5,365
    −2,104

5. 5,673
    +1,294

6. 8,907
    −5,605

7. 3,345
    +2,438

8. 9,437
    −6,420

9. 7,116
    +2,597

10. 7,884
    −3,082

11. 6,459
    +1,642

12. 8,932
    −4,613

13. 5,951
    +5,148

14. 4,507
    −1,602

15. 3,169
    +9,350

16. 9,294
    −2,156

17. 5,459
    +4,541

Problem Solving • Applications

For Problems 18–19, use the drawing.

18. The red boat and the blue boat sailed with passengers to Alaska. How many passengers were on the boats?

19. Marion went to Alaska on the red boat. Eli went to Alaska on the yellow boat. How many more passengers were on Marion's boat?

20. Alexis flew 2,451 miles from New York to Los Angeles. Then she flew 1,542 miles to Mexico City. How many miles in all did Alexis fly?

21. The Rio Grande is 1,885 miles long. The Ohio River is 981 miles long. What is the difference in miles in the two rivers' lengths?

22. ✏ **Write a problem** about the Mississippi River, which is 2,348 miles long, and the Yukon River, which is 1,979 miles long.

NUMBER of PASSENGERS

1,494
960
1,070

SOCIAL STUDIES **LINK**

Alaska is more than twice the size of Texas, the second largest state. Alaska became the 49th state in 1959. Its capital is Juneau. For how many years has Alaska been a state?

Time Before the Hour

Why learn this? You might want to know how long it is until the next hour if your favorite show is on.

Darrell is having a birthday party at 2:00. The clocks show the time it is now. How many minutes are there until Darrell's birthday party?

analog clock

1:42
digital clock

SCIENCE LINK

A sundial is the oldest kind of clock. It uses the sun and shadows to show the time. Why is using an analog or a digital clock a better way to tell time?

When a clock shows 31 or more minutes *after* the hour, the time can also be said as time *before* the hour.

5 minutes
10 minutes
15 minutes
16 minutes
17 minutes
18 minutes

To find the number of minutes before the hour, count back from the 12 by fives and ones to where the minute hand is pointing.

Read: 18 minutes before two
Write: 1:42

So, there are 18 minutes until Darrell's birthday party.

▶ CHECK

1. How would you read the time shown as time *after* the hour?

2. How would you read 9:37 as time *before* the hour?

▶ PRACTICE

Write how many minute marks the minute hand is before the 12.

3.

4.

5.

6.

Tell how you would read each time *before* the hour. Write the time.

7.

8.

9.

10.

Problem Solving • Applications

11. Celenia has band practice before the game. Her father dropped her off at 4:50. How many minutes is that before 5:00?

12. Craig was at the football field 20 minutes before the game started. It started at 6:00. At what time did Craig get there?

13. Shannon was home at 17 minutes before eight. It took her 20 minutes to get home. When did Shannon leave?

14. The Jets got the ball at 7:30, and scored 12 minutes later. How many minutes before eight was it when they scored?

15. The third quarter of the game began at 7:20. It ended 32 minutes later. At what time did the quarter end? How many minutes is that before 8:00?

16. The snack stand closes at 20 minutes before eight. How many minutes after seven will it be when the snack stand closes?

17. Joey has to leave at 8:00. His watch shows that it is 7:37. In how many minutes does Joey have to leave?

18. ▭▶ **Write a problem** about an after-school game that begins before the hour.

Making a Time Line

Why learn this? You can use a time line to show events in the order they happened.

A *time line* can be used to look at events that happen in history. Important events in Florida's history are shown on the time line below. Between which years did Walt Disney World open?

- 1958 *Explorer I* was launched from Cape Canaveral
- 1961 The first American in space launched from Cape Canaveral
- 1969 The first man to land on the moon was launched from Cape Canaveral
- 1971 Walt Disney World opened

Walt Disney World opened in 1971.

Since 1971 is between 1970 and 1975, Walt Disney World opened between 1970 and 1975.

CRITICAL THINKING How is a time line the same as and different from a number line?

▶ CHECK

1. Between which years was *Explorer 1* launched from Cape Canaveral?

2. What event happened in Florida between 1960 and 1965?

3. Where does the first man to land on the moon appear on the time line?

4. How would you change the time line to show that a new state capitol building was completed in 1977?

SCIENCE LINK

During the first moon landing, rocks were collected and brought back to Earth. They were studied under special lights and microscopes. The rocks were named or grouped. Moon samples and rocks were collected during six moon landings. The last was in 1972. Find that year on the time line.

For Exercises 5–18, use the time line.

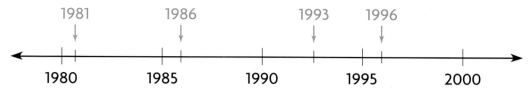

- 1981 Carrie is born in Shady Grove Hospital
- 1986 Carrie starts kindergarten
- 1993 Carrie starts middle school
- 1996 Carrie becomes a high-school cheerleader

5. How many years are between each date shown?

6. Between what years is Carrie born?

7. What happens between 1985 and 1990?

8. Between what years does Carrie start middle school?

9. What happens between 1995 and 2000?

10. How would you change the time line to include Carrie's first full-time job in 2005?

Decide if each year can be put on the time line. Write *yes* or *no*.

11. 1971

12. 1982

13. 1991

14. 2001

15. 1785

16. 1893

17. 1999

18. 2010

Problem Solving • Applications

19. Gerald wants to make a time line to show his life. He was born in 1989. Should his time line begin with 1985 or 1990? Tell why you think so.

20. Suppose you made a time line of the years 1992, 1996, and 2000. Where would you place an event that happened in 1994?

21. Robyn's time line shows only the odd years between 1988 and 1998. What years are on her time line?

22. Stacy made a time line of every 10 years between 1950 and 2000. What years are on her time line?

23. Liz made a time line of the years 1985, 1995, and 2005. Where would she place an event that happened in 1991?

24. ◼▷ **Write an event** that could be added to the time line above. Tell where it would appear on the time line.

Using Arrays to Find Square Numbers

Why learn this? Knowing about square numbers can help you make designs and measure squares.

Erin bought 3 cans of tennis balls. There are 3 balls in each can. How many tennis balls did Erin buy?

$$3 \times 3 = \underline{\ ?\ }$$

You can make an array with square tiles to solve the problem.

When both factors are the same, the product is called a *square* number.

$$3 \times 3 = 9$$

Both factors are 3, so 9 is a square number. Erin bought 9 tennis balls.

_____

Use square tiles or pieces of paper. Make an array with 4 rows and 4 columns.

Talk About It

• What multiplication fact does your array show?

• What shape is your array? Why?

CRITICAL THINKING When the factors are not the same, what do you notice about the shape of the array?

▶ CHECK

Write the multiplication fact for each array. Write *yes* or *no* to tell if the product is a square number.

1.

2.

3.

4.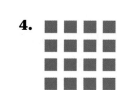

Write the multiplication fact for each array. Write *yes* or *no* to tell if the product is a square number.

5.    6. 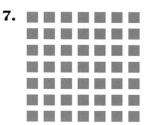   7. 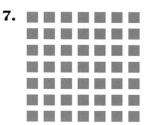   8.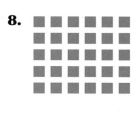

Draw each array and find the product. Write *yes* or *no* to tell which products are square numbers.

9. 8
  ×8

10. 7
  ×6

11. 7
  ×7

12. 9
  ×8

13. 9
  ×9

14. 5
  ×5

15. 5
  ×6

16. 7
  ×5

17. 9
  ×6

18. 6
  ×6

19. 8
  ×4

20. 4
  ×4

21. 7
  ×9

22. 3
  ×3

23. 8
  ×5

Problem Solving • Applications

For Problems 24–28, use the drawing.

24. Hector's garden is divided into sections. Which section of the garden has the most plants?

25. Write a number sentence to show how many lettuce plants are in the garden.

26. Is the product for the number of bean plants a square number? Explain.

27. How many more herb plants than lettuce plants are there?

28. Write a number sentence to show how many plants in all are in Hector's garden. Is the product a square number?

29. 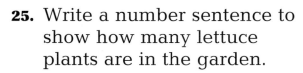 **Write About It** Draw square arrays for the products 1, 4, 9, 16, and 25. Describe the pattern you see in the arrays.

Making a Survey

Why learn this? You can use surveys to find out what people think about different things.

Mr. Turner asked the students in his class to make a survey. He gave them these rules to follow for making their surveys:

- Keep your questions clear and simple.

- Ask the question only once of each person.

- Use tally marks as you are taking the survey. Afterward, use the results to make a frequency table.

- Let each person know all the choices before he or she answers.

April's survey asked students to name their favorite subject in school.

Then April put her survey results into a frequency table.

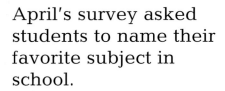

April
Survey:
What is your favorite
school subject?
Math IIII IIII
Reading IIII II
P.E. IIII IIII
Social Studies IIII
Science IIII III
Art IIII IIII II

Favorite Subjects	
Subject	Votes
Math	9
Reading	7
P.E.	10
Social Studies	4
Science	8
Art	12

▶ CHECK

1. How many students did April survey?

2. Was April's question clear and simple?

3. Why is it important to ask each person only once?

▶ PRACTICE

Change the survey below into a frequency table. Then use the survey to answer Problems 4–8.

4. What was the question in the survey? Was it clear and simple?

5. How many students did Chad survey?

6. Which fruit did the most students like best?

7. Which fruit was the least favorite?

8. How many students liked apples?

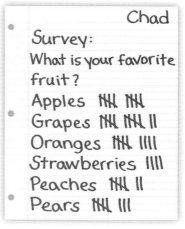

Chad
Survey:
What is your favorite fruit?
Apples ||||| |||||
Grapes ||||| ||||| ||
Oranges ||||| ||||
Strawberries ||||
Peaches ||||| ||
Pears ||||| |||

Make a survey about each question below. Survey your classmates or students from another class. Then make a frequency table of the data.

9. What is your favorite television show to watch?

10. What is your favorite game to play?

Problem Solving • Applications

11. How many students did you survey for Problem 6? Problem 7?

12. Which television show was the favorite of the most students? Which game? Which television show was the least favorite? Which game?

13. In Jeremy's survey, 7 students named *All in a Day's Play* as their favorite television show. There were 3 times as many students who named *Space Travelers*. How many students named *Space Travelers* as their favorite show?

14. ✏ **Write About It** Design a survey to give your family about their favorite dinners. What questions can you ask in the survey? What did you find to be the hardest thing about taking a survey? What did you find to be the most interesting thing about taking a survey?

Predicting Outcomes

Why learn this? You can tell what may happen in experiments, such as with spinners or coins.

Mrs. Archer's students are doing experiments. In one experiment, they predict the number of times they will spin each color on this spinner if they spin 20 times.

Bryan said that each color has an *equally likely* chance of being spun since each section is of equal size. He predicted that he would spin each color 5 times, since 20 divided by 4 equals 5.

In another experiment, students toss a coin. They toss the coin 20 times and record the results.

- Predict how many times the coin will land heads up. How many times will it land tails up? Explain.

▶ CHECK

1. Predict how many times you would spin each color if you spun the spinner 40 times in the experiment above. Explain.

2. Suppose you spun the pointer on the spinner at the right 20 times. Predict how many times you would spin each color. What do you predict would happen if you spun 40 times?

3. A spinner has 6 equal sections. Each is a different color. For an experiment, you are to spin 30 times. Predict how many times you would spin each color.

► PRACTICE

For each spinner below, predict the number of times you would spin each color in the given number of spins.

4. 20 spins

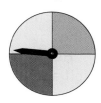

5. 25 spins

6. 30 spins

7. 40 spins

For Exercises 8–10, suppose you pulled and replaced a block from the bag at the right a given number of times. Predict how many times you would pull each color if you did this.

8. 10 times

9. 20 times

10. 30 times

Problem Solving • Applications

11. Melanie is rolling a number cube for an experiment. The number cube is labeled with numbers 1 through 6. Predict how many times she will roll each number if she rolls 60 times.

12. A bag contains 4 red marbles, 4 orange marbles, and 8 green marbles. You are to pull a marble from the bag 20 times and replace it. Predict how many times you would pull a green marble.

13. A coin is tossed 50 times. It lands heads up 21 times. How many times does it land tails up?

14. A spinner with 4 equal sections has 2 purple sections, 1 green section, and 1 red section. Predict how many times you will spin purple if you spin 40 times.

15. In Exercises 4–7 above, which spinner would be fair to use in a game?

16. ✏️ **Write About It** Will experiments always turn out the way you predict? Explain why or why not.

Figures That Tessellate

Why learn this? You can make and find these special figures in pictures and on clothing.

Figures *tessellate* if they cover a surface without overlapping or leaving any space between them, when placed side by side.

Here are some figures that do tessellate. The designs they form with repeating patterns are called *tessellations*.

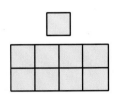 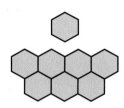 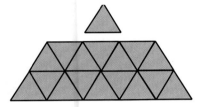

Here are some figures that do not tessellate.

Talk About It CRITICAL THINKING

- What is the difference between figures that tessellate and figures that do not tessellate?

- Does a figure have to remain in one position in order for it to tessellate? Explain.

- Do circles tessellate? Explain.

▶ CHECK

1. Choose one of the figures below. Trace the figure and cut it out. Then use it to make a tessellation.

   a.   **b.**

ART LINK

M.C. Escher was a Dutch artist famous for his drawings of tessellations. He taught himself about math and science. He used what he learned in his drawings. He did several animal drawings, including this one titled "Swans." Find the tessellating pattern.

▶ PRACTICE

Tell if each figure will tessellate. Write *yes* or *no*.

2.

3.

4.

5.

6.

7.

8.

9.

Trace and cut out each figure. Use each figure to make a tessellation.

10.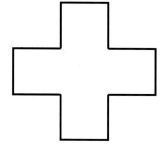

11.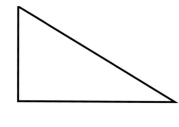

12.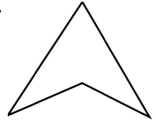

Problem Solving • Applications

13. In Exercises 2 through 9 above, how did you determine which figures would tessellate?

14. Which figures in Exercises 10 through 12 needed to be flipped or turned in order to make a tessellation?

15. Show two ways you could make a tessellation with this figure.

16. Is this a tessellation? Explain why or why not.

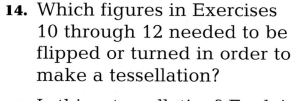

17. Will this figure tessellate? Without tracing and cutting it out, explain why you think it will or will not tessellate.

18. ✏ **Write About It** Find a tessellation in your classroom. Where did you find it? Draw the figure in the tessellation. Was the figure flipped or turned to make the tessellation?

Symmetry by Turning

Why learn this? You will see examples of point symmetry in flowers, plane figures, and objects.

You can turn a plane figure about a center point. If the shape of the figure looks exactly the same with each turn, the figure has *point symmetry*.

This flower shape has point symmetry. The shading on the one petal helps you see that the figure has been turned and traced. Each new figure is the same as the one in the first position.

- How can you find out if the figure in each position is congruent with the figure in the first position?

Trace this figure and cut it out. Shade one part of it. Trace the figure onto your paper, and then turn and trace it as many times as you can so that each time it is in a different position. Copy the shading each time you trace the figure.

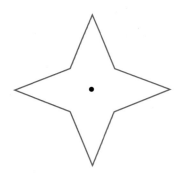

- Why do you need to shade each time you trace the figure?

▶ CHECK

1. How many times did you trace and turn the figure?

2. Does the figure have point symmetry? Explain how you know.

▶ PRACTICE

Trace each figure and cut it out. Use the method on page H46 to find out if it has point symmetry. Write *yes* or *no*.

3.

4.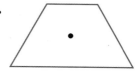

5.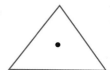

6.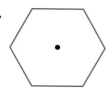

7.

8.

Problem Solving • Applications

9. In your own words, explain how you can find out if a figure has point symmetry.

10. Which figures in Exercises 3–8 have one or more lines of symmetry?

11. How many times did you trace and turn the hexagon in Exercise 3 to find out if it had point symmetry? the clover in Exercise 6? the star in Exercise 7?

12. Explain how you know this figure has point symmetry.

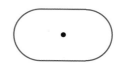

13. Draw a figure of your own that has point symmetry. Explain how you know that it has point symmetry.

14. Explain how you know that the figure in Exercise 8 does not have point symmetry.

15. Draw a rectangle. Explain how you know it has point symmetry.

16. ✏️ **Write About It** Explain the difference between point symmetry and line symmetry.

Mixed Numbers

Why learn this? You can use mixed numbers to name amounts made up of wholes and parts.

Kristelle is hungry! How many pieces of French toast does she plan to eat?

A *mixed number* is made up of a whole number and a fraction.

To write a mixed number, think:

* How many wholes?

* How many parts of a whole?

Kristelle plans to eat 1 whole piece and $\frac{1}{2}$ piece of French toast.

So, Kristelle plans to eat $1\frac{1}{2}$ pieces of French toast.

Talk About It CRITICAL THINKING

* Can a whole number tell how many pieces of French toast Kristelle plans to eat? Explain.

* Between what two numbers is the amount of French toast that Kristelle plans to eat?

* Suppose Kristelle plans to eat $1\frac{2}{2}$ pieces of French toast. Could that amount be written another way? Explain.

► CHECK

Write a mixed number for the part that is shaded.

1.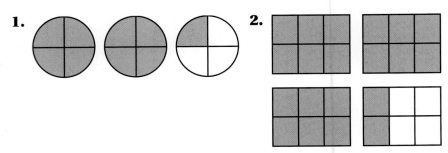
2.

HEALTH LINK

For good nutrition, you should eat 6 servings of breads, cereals, rice, or pasta each day. One serving is equal to one slice of bread or $\frac{1}{2}$ cup of cooked cereal, rice, or pasta. How many cups of rice does it take to equal 6 servings?

Write a mixed number for the part that is shaded.

3.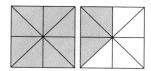

4.

5.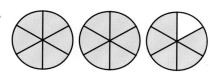

6.

7. Draw 2 squares. Color $1\frac{1}{2}$ green.

8. Draw 3 rectangles. Color $2\frac{3}{4}$ red.

9. Draw 4 circles. Color $3\frac{7}{8}$ blue.

10. Draw 3 squares. Color $2\frac{1}{3}$ orange.

11. Draw 5 circles. Color $3\frac{1}{4}$ brown.

12. Draw 4 triangles. Color $2\frac{1}{2}$ pink.

Describe the pattern and complete.

13. $\frac{1}{2}$, 1, $1\frac{1}{2}$, 2, $2\frac{1}{2}$, __?__, __?__, __?__

14. $\frac{1}{4}$, $\frac{2}{4}$, $\frac{3}{4}$, 1, $1\frac{1}{4}$, $1\frac{2}{4}$, __?__, __?__, __?__

15. $\frac{1}{3}$, $\frac{2}{3}$, 1, $1\frac{1}{3}$, $1\frac{2}{3}$, 2, $2\frac{1}{3}$, __?__, __?__, __?__

16. $\frac{1}{6}$, $\frac{2}{6}$, $\frac{3}{6}$, $\frac{4}{6}$, $\frac{5}{6}$, 1, $1\frac{1}{6}$, __?__, __?__, __?__

17. $\frac{1}{8}$, $\frac{2}{8}$, $\frac{3}{8}$, $\frac{4}{8}$, $\frac{5}{8}$, $\frac{6}{8}$, $\frac{7}{8}$, 1, $1\frac{1}{8}$, __?__, __?__, __?__

Problem Solving • Applications

18. Candi counted quarters until she reached $1.00. How many quarters did she count? What fractional part of $1.00 is each quarter?

19. A recipe calls for $3\frac{3}{4}$ cups of sugar. Mary has 4 cups of sugar. Does she have enough? Explain.

20. Caryn's mother made three and one-half batches of cookies for the school fair. Write this amount as a mixed number.

21. ✏ **Write About It** How do you think *mixed number* got its name?

Fraction of a Number

Why learn this? You can find what your share of objects such as toys, treats, or supplies will be.

Each group of 4 students is making 12 greeting cards. Each student makes $\frac{1}{4}$ of the cards. How many cards are made by each student?

What is $\frac{1}{4}$ of 12?

$\frac{1}{4}$ of 12 = ___?___

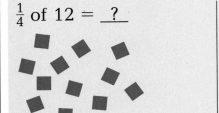

First, model the number 12.

Since you want to find $\frac{1}{4}$, divide 12 into 4 equal groups.

Count the number of tiles in one group.

So, $\frac{1}{4}$ of 12 = 3.

Each student will make 3 greeting cards.

Talk About It CRITICAL THINKING

- Which part of the fraction tells how many equal parts to divide the group into?

- Which part of the fraction tells how many of those parts to use?

▶ CHECK

Make a model to answer the questions.

1. To find $\frac{3}{4}$ of 12, how many equal parts is the group of 12 divided into?

2. How many equal parts should you use?

3. What is $\frac{3}{4}$ of 12?

ART LINK

One way to make several cards that have the same design is to make stencils. Fold a piece of thin plastic, cardboard, or heavy paper. Cut designs along the fold. Put the stencil design over a blank card and shade in the designs using paint, markers, or colored pencils. Suppose you stenciled 8 cards and gave $\frac{1}{4}$ of them away. How many cards would you give away?

▶ PRACTICE

Use the picture to complete the number sentence.

4.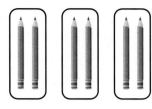

$\frac{1}{3}$ of 6 = __?__

5.

$\frac{1}{2}$ of 8 = __?__

6.

$\frac{2}{3}$ of 9 = __?__

7.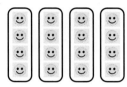

$\frac{3}{4}$ of 16 = __?__

8.

$\frac{5}{6}$ of 12 = __?__

9.

$\frac{2}{5}$ of 10 = __?__

Draw the picture. Shade the number of groups given.
Complete the number sentence.

10. Draw 6 circles.
Make 3 groups.
Shade 2 groups.
$\frac{2}{3}$ of 6 = __?__

11. Draw 12 squares.
Make 4 groups.
Shade 1 group.
$\frac{1}{4}$ of 12 = __?__

12. Draw 3 triangles.
Make 3 groups.
Shade 2 groups.
$\frac{2}{3}$ of 3 = __?__

13. Draw 10 stars.
Make 5 groups.
Shade 4 groups.
$\frac{4}{5}$ of 10 = __?__

14. Draw 14 circles.
Make 2 groups.
Shade 1 group.
$\frac{1}{2}$ of 14 = __?__

15. Draw 16 squares.
Make 8 groups.
Shade 5 groups.
$\frac{5}{8}$ of 16 = __?__

Problem Solving • Applications

16. Bonnie baked 12 muffins. Of these, $\frac{2}{3}$ had nuts. How many of the muffins had nuts?

17. Kreg had $15. He spent $\frac{1}{3}$ of his money on art supplies. How much did Kreg spend on art supplies?

18. Roger had 15 pictures. He gave $\frac{3}{5}$ of them to his family. How many pictures did he give away?

19. ✏ **Write About It** Tell how you would find $\frac{2}{3}$ of 30.

Adding and Subtracting Decimals

Why learn this? You can add and subtract distances.

Melissa walked 0.2 mile to Paul's house and 0.5 mile to the library. How far did she walk?

Add. 0.2 + 0.5

MODEL

Step 1	**Step 2**
Shade 0.2 of one decimal square and 0.5 of another.	Cut out each part and combine the two parts.

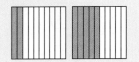

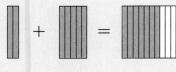

0.2 + 0.5 = 0.7

So, Melissa walked 0.7 mile.

Melissa and Paul are walking to the park, which is 0.6 mile away. They have walked 0.4 mile so far. How much farther do they have to go?

Subtract. 0.6 − 0.4

MODEL

Step 1	**Step 2**	**Step 3**
Shade 0.6 of a decimal square.	Cut out the shaded part. Then cut away 0.4 of the shaded part.	Count to find the difference.

0.6 − 0.4 = 0.2

So, Melissa and Paul have 0.2 mile left to walk.

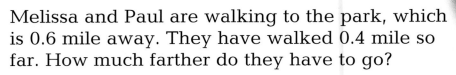

- How is adding and subtracting decimals different from adding and subtracting whole numbers?

► CHECK

Write a number sentence for the decimal squares.

1.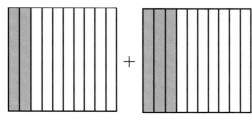

2.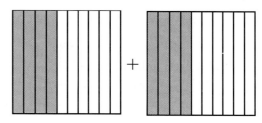

3.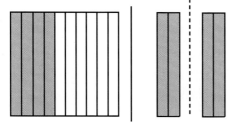

4.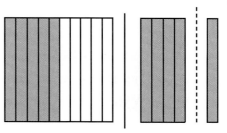

► PRACTICE

Write a number sentence and solve. You may wish to use decimal squares.

5. three tenths + one tenth = ___?___   **6.** two tenths + six tenths = ___?___

7. six tenths − three tenths = ___?___   **8.** nine tenths − one tenth = ___?___

9. four tenths + two tenths = ___?___   **10.** eight tenths − five tenths = ___?___

Find the sum or difference.

11. $0.7 + 0.2 = $ ___?___   **12.** $0.1 + 0.8 = $ ___?___   **13.** $0.3 + 0.5 = $ ___?___

14. $0.8 - 0.2 = $ ___?___   **15.** $0.9 - 0.4 = $ ___?___   **16.** $0.7 - 0.6 = $ ___?___

17. $0.6 + 0.3 = $ ___?___   **18.** $0.5 - 0.4 = $ ___?___   **19.** $0.2 + 0.5 = $ ___?___

Problem Solving • Applications

20. Allison cut a 0.2-meter piece of wood from a 0.9-meter strip. How much of the strip of wood is left?

21. Jason lives 0.4 mile from Maury and 0.3 mile from Dan. How much closer does Jason live to Dan than to Maury?

22. Joan walked 2.3 miles on Friday and 1.5 miles on Saturday. How far did she walk in all?

23. If you add 0.1 to me, you get 0.5. What number am I?

24. ✏️ **Write a problem** about adding or subtracting decimals.

Measuring Greater Lengths

Why learn this? You can use rulers to measure longer objects or greater distances than the ruler.

Tom wants to measure his desk, but his desk is longer than his ruler. How can Tom use the ruler to measure his desk?

MODEL

Step 1	**Step 2**
Line up the zero mark of the centimeter ruler with the left edge of your desk. 	At the other end of the ruler, make a chalk mark on the desk. Record "30 cm" on a sheet of paper. 
Step 3	**Step 4**
Move the ruler to the right. Line up the left side of the centimeter ruler with the chalk mark. 	Mark and move the ruler until you reach the other edge of the desk. Add the numbers of centimeters you recorded to find the measurement. 

So, the desk is about 85 cm long.

▶ CHECK

1. Why do you add 30 each time you move the ruler?

2. Suppose that to find the width of your desk, you marked off 30 cm and then measured another 22 cm. What would the desk's width be?

3. Why is it important to mark before you move the ruler again?

Use a centimeter ruler to find the length of each object. Use the mark-and-move method to help you.

4.

5.

6.

7.

8.

9.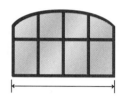

For Exercises 10–13, use a meterstick or a ruler and the mark-and-move method to measure. Round measurements to the nearest meter.

10. the length of your classroom

11. the width of your classroom

12. the width of the longest chalkboard in your classroom

13. the length of the longest bulletin board in your classroom

14. What number did you record when you marked off each meter? Explain.

Problem Solving • Applications

For Problems 15 and 16, use Nancy's recording sheet.

15. How long was the object Nancy measured?

16. How many times did Nancy need to mark and move her ruler?

30 cm + 30 cm + 15 cm

17. Rosa's ruler is only 15 cm long. When she marks and moves, what number should she record? Explain.

18. ✏️ **Write About It** Why do you think this method of measuring is called mark-and-move?

Multiplying to Find Area

Why learn this? You can find the number of tiles for a table.

Bob and Lynne are making a tile top for their kitchen table. Each tile covers 1 square foot of the table. The table is 5 feet long and 3 feet wide. How many tiles are needed to cover the table?

You can multiply the table's length by its width to find the number of tiles needed to cover it.

The table is 5 feet long.

The table is 3 feet wide.

$$\text{length} \times \text{width} = \text{area (square units)}$$
$$\downarrow \qquad \downarrow \qquad \downarrow$$
$$5 \quad \times \quad 3 \quad = \quad 15$$

The area of the table is 15 square feet.
So, 15 tiles are needed to cover the table.

Talk About It [CRITICAL THINKING]

- What do you need to know to find the area of the table?

- How does multiplication help you find the area?

▶ CHECK

Multiply to find the area of the figure. Write a number sentence to show what you did.

1.
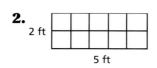
3 ft
4 ft

2.
2 ft
5 ft

3.
4 ft
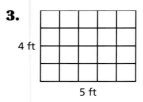
5 ft

4. Explain how the array in Exercise 1 shows what you need to multiply to find the area.

REMEMBER:

An array shows objects in rows and columns.

$3 \times 4 = 12$

ART LINK

"The Four Seasons" is a giant outdoor mosaic in the city of Chicago created by Marc Chagall. It covers a rectangular prism 70 ft long by 14 ft high by 10 ft wide. Use a calculator to help you find the area of one side (70 ft × 14 ft) of "The Four Seasons."

Multiply to find the area of the figure. Write a number sentence to show what you did.

5.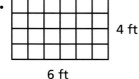
6 ft · 4 ft

6.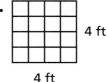
4 ft · 4 ft

7.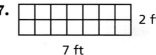
7 ft · 2 ft

8.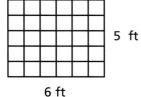
6 ft · 5 ft

9.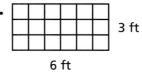
6 ft · 3 ft

10.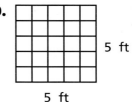
5 ft · 5 ft

11. 2 ft · 3 ft

12. 7 ft · 4 ft

13. 7 ft · 7 ft

14. 3 ft · 4 ft

15. 6 ft · 2 ft

16. 5 ft · 3 ft

Problem Solving • Applications

17. Ms. Lee is tiling her kitchen floor. The floor is 8 feet long and 6 feet wide. How many tiles 1 foot square will she need?

18. Susan wants to cover her dresser top with felt. Her dresser top is 4 feet long and 2 feet wide. What is the area of Susan's dresser top?

19. Wayne's picnic blanket is 9 feet long and 5 feet wide. Jerry's picnic blanket is 8 feet long and 6 feet wide. Whose picnic blanket covers a larger area? Explain.

20. ▭ **Write About It** Describe how you would use multiplication to find the area of your desk.

CALCULATOR Activities

MISSION NOT-SO-IMPOSSIBLE
Skip Counting and Patterns

Mission: To find the number of favors to be given out at Jane's party.

- There will be 7 people at Jane's birthday party.
- Each person will get a bag of party favors.
- Each bag will have 5 party favors in it.

Using the Calculator

Press these keys on the *TI-108*:

0.	5.	5.	5.	10.	15.	20.	25.	30.	35.
ON/C	5	+	5	=	=	=	=	=	=

Press these keys on the *Casio SL-450*:

0.	5.	5.+	5.+	10.+	15.+	20.+	25.+	30.+	35.+
AC	5	+	+	=	=	=	=	=	=

So, there will be 35 party favors handed out at Jane's party.

▶ PRACTICE

Use your calculator in the same way.

1. Tom bought 8 bags of balloons for his party. Each bag has 12 balloons in it. Skip count to find the number of balloons Tom bought.
2. Jerry's mother baked 48 cookies. Each student in Jerry's class will receive 2 cookies. How many students will each receive 2 cookies?

ARE WE THERE YET?

Addition of Whole Numbers

Philadelphia to Dean's Diesel	150 miles
Dean's Diesel to Evergreen Rest Stop	170 miles
Evergreen Rest Stop to Route 87 Diner	60 miles
Route 87 Diner to Canadian border	120 miles
Canadian border to Montreal	60 miles

REMEMBER:
You can use addition to calculate distances between several points on a map.

Look at the sign. Can you figure out how many miles Randi's family drove from the beginning of their trip to the Evergreen Rest Stop?

Using the Calculator

Press these keys on the *TI-108*:

Press these keys on the *Casio SL-450*:

So, Randi's family drove 320 miles.

▶ PRACTICE

Use your calculator and the sign above to answer each question.

1. How many miles did Randi's family drive from the beginning of their trip to the Route 87 Diner?
2. How many miles did Randi's family drive from the beginning of their trip to the Canadian border?
3. What's the distance between Philadelphia and Montreal?

Use your calculator to solve.

4. 732 + 847 + 953 = _?_
5. 247 + 398 + 66 = _?_

SUBTRACTION PATHS
Subtraction of Whole Numbers

Using subtraction, find a path that starts at 18 and finishes at 2. You may have to try several paths before you find the correct one.

START	18	7	9	
	20	4	16	
	0	5	2	FINISH

REMEMBER:
When you subtract, you take a lesser number from a greater one.

$$5 - 3 = 2$$
↑ ↑
greater lesser

Using the Calculator
Using the *TI-108*, press the following keys:

Using the *Casio SL-450*, press the following keys:

So, you start with 18, subtract 7, then subtract 4, and then subtract 5.

▶ PRACTICE

Use your calculator.
Figure out these subtraction paths if they are possible.

1.
START	10	12	11	
	2	16	6	
	3	2	3	FINISH

2.
START	6	8	16	
	1	12	3	
	2	5	9	FINISH

3.
START	65	29	92	46	
	12	8	10	1	
	53	23	8	14	
	0	4	11	0	FINISH

Solve.

4. $67 - 49 = $ _?_

5. $99 - 64 = $ _?_

6. $476 - 387 - 61 = $ _?_

7. $85 - 16 - 9 = $ _?_

8. $754 - 525 - 29 = $ _?_

9. $462 - 144 - 100 = $ _?_

10. $943 - 315 - 128 = $ _?_

11. $5,865 - 3,976 - 889 = $ _?_

CASHING IN
Multiplication of Whole Numbers

Zach makes $5 an hour at The Ramp, an in-line skate and skateboard shop. His time card lists the number of hours he works every week. How much did he make for week 1?

> **REMEMBER:**
> Multiplication is a shortcut for addition.
>
> Using addition:
> $3 + 3 + 3 + 3 = 12$
>
> Using multiplication:
> $4 \times 3 = 12$

Using the Calculator

Press these keys on the *TI-108*:

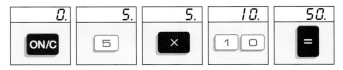

The Ramp Time Card	
Name: Zach	
Week	Hours worked
1	10
2	15
3	8
4	6
5	12
6	10

Press these keys on the *Casio SL-450*:

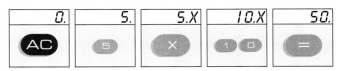

So, Zach earned $50 for week 1.

▶ PRACTICE

Use your calculator to solve.

1. How much did Zach earn for week 2?
2. How much did Zach earn for week 3?
3. How much did Zach earn for week 4?
4. Starting Zach's fifth week of work, his boss gave him a raise. He is now making $6 an hour. What will his paycheck be if he works 12 hours in one week?
5. During week 6, Zach worked 10 hours. When he got his paycheck, it was for $50. What mistake was made on his paycheck? How much should the check be for?
6. $189 \times 73 = $ ___?___
7. $6,441 \times 24 = $ ___?___

 **NOW, *THAT'S* FAST!**
Division of Whole Numbers

Have you ever tried flipping a pancake in a pan? It's not an easy thing to do. Imagine being able to flip a pancake 348 times in 2 minutes. That's exactly what Dean Gould did in 1995 when he broke the world's record for pancake flipping. About how many flips could this world record holder complete in 1 minute?

Using the Calculator

If you are using the *TI-108*, press these keys:

If you are using the *Casio SL-450*, press these keys:

So, Mr. Gould flipped a pancake about 174 times in 1 minute.

▶ PRACTICE

Use your calculator to solve.

1. The pancake-flipping record holder also holds the needle-threading record. Dean Gould can thread 3,848 needles in 2 hours. About how many needles can he thread in 1 hour?

2. Why is the answer to Problem 1 an estimate?

3. $81 \div 9 =$ _?_

4. $1,000 \div 10 =$ _?_

5. $1,000 \div 100 =$ _?_

6. $246 \div 2 =$ _?_

7. $168 \div 8 =$ _?_

8. $732 \div 3 =$ _?_

 **TEXAS TWO-STEP**
Two-Step Problems

The memory keys store, compute, and recall numbers. The M+ key stores numbers to be added. The M- key stores numbers to be subtracted. The MRC or MR key computes and recalls the numbers in memory as one number.

Last night at Ranchers Dance Hall, there were 30 couples dancing. Then 10 couples got tired and sat down. There are 2 people to a couple. How many *people* were still dancing?

Using the Calculator

Using the *TI-108*, press these keys:

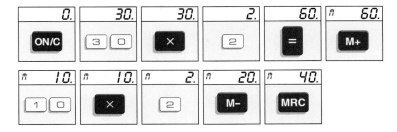

Using the *Casio SL-450*, press these keys:

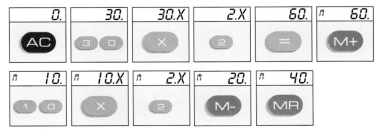

So, 40 *people*, or 20 couples, were still dancing.

▶ PRACTICE

Use your calculator to solve.

1. Each case of oranges had 12 oranges. Ali sold 8 cases and Jason sold 3 cases. How many more *oranges* did Ali sell than Jason?

2. Jerome wants to buy a game that costs $25. During three weeks Jerome saved $3, $8, and $7. How much more money does he need?

HOW CORNY CAN YOU GET? (PART 1)
Decimal Addition

What is the sum on the chart for C?

A	B	C	D	E	F
1.5 + 5.3	0.5 + 0.8	1.2 + 2.59	3.1 + 3.1	7.2 + 9.2	1.1 + 2.1
6.8	1.3		6.2		3.2
G	H	I	J	K	L
2.04 + 0.03	6.3 + 0.9	1.4 + 0.7	8.21 + 0.1	0.04 + 0.08	0.61 + 1
			8.31		1.61
M	N	O	P	Q	R
4.02 + 0.02	2.4 + 6	0.1 + 0.1	0.45 + 0.45	9 + 0.5	9.1 + 0
4.04	8.4	0.2		9.5	9.1
S	T	U	V	W	X
6.9 + 0.1	0.02 + 0.02	4.51 + 5.06	0.75 + 1	1.75 + 2	0.3 + 0.3
7.0			1.75	3.75	0.6
Y	Z				
7.3 + 0.04	0.5 + 0.5				
7.34					

Using the Calculator

Using the *TI-108*, press these keys:

Using the *Casio SL-450*, press these keys:

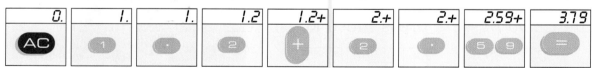

So, C = 3.79.

▶ PRACTICE

Use your calculator.

1. Find the sums for E, G, H, I, K, P, T, U, and Z.
2. Use the chart to solve the riddle. Match the letters to each decimal sum. What did the mother tomato say to the lazy baby tomato?

0.12	16.4	0.04	3.79	7.2	9.57	0.9

3. Jake earns $10.00 a week for baby-sitting and $5.25 a week on his paper route. He gets $2.50 a week for an allowance. How much money does Jake get each week?

HOW CORNY CAN YOU GET? (PART 2)

Decimal Subtraction

What is the difference on the chart for A?

A 19.4-8.8	B 3.3-0.3 3	C 0.5-0.25	D 10.5-10 0.5	E 13.5-4.5	F 4.31-0.25
G 16.45-2.05	H 19.2-8.4 10.8	I 8.4-3.3	J 1.76-0.36 1.4	K 5.25-1.2 4.05	L 12.3-4.3 8
M 8.14-0.2	N 0.72-0.36	O 10.9-4.1	P 10.5-10.5 0	Q 19.00-18.02 0.98	R 0.08-0.02 0.06
S 15.75-0.25 15.5	T 9.3-6.1	U 9.2-7.3 1.9	V 1.02-0.52 0.5	W 3.88-2.08	X 17.98-0.98 17
Y 12.10-0.85 11.25	Z 1.1⁻0.1 1				

REMEMBER:

Enter the decimal point on the calculator after you enter the whole number and before you enter the decimal parts.

Using the Calculator

Using the *TI-108*, press the following keys:

Using the *Casio SL-450*, press these keys:

So, A = 10.6.

▶ PRACTICE

Use your calculator.

1. Find the differences for C, E, F, G, I, M, N, O, T, and W.
2. Use the chart to solve the riddle. Match the letters to their differences.

   What time was it when the elephant sat on the fence?

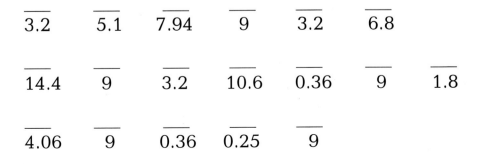

___	___	___	___	___	___
3.2	5.1	7.94	9	3.2	6.8

___	___	___	___	___	___	___
14.4	9	3.2	10.6	0.36	9	1.8

___	___	___	___	___
4.06	9	0.36	0.25	9

 **ALL THUMBS**
Fixing Input Errors

Adam, was working on his third-grade calculator exercises. He entered 19 + 39 + 43 + 109 + 78. He quickly realized that for the last number, he needed to enter 76. Can he fix his mistake without starting all over again? What is the sum?

Using the Calculator

If you have the *TI-108*, press these keys:

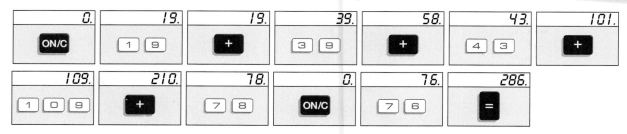

If you have the *Casio SL-450*, press these keys:

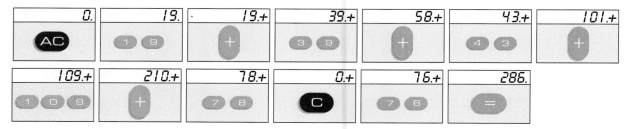

Yes, he can fix his mistake without starting from the beginning. Adam can press **ON/C** on the *TI-108* or **C** on the *Casio SL-450*, re-enter 76, and then press the = key. The answer to the problem is 286.

▶ PRACTICE

Use your calculator to solve. Input the correct number in brackets after you have entered the wrong number.

1. 12 + 14 [15] + 49 = _?_

2. 375 + 674 + 358 [35] + 34 = _?_

3. 56 [65] + 67 = _?_

BATTER UP!
Fractions—Changing Fractions to Decimals

Shannon usually gets about 3 hits for every 10 times she is at bat, or gets a hit $\frac{3}{10}$ of the time. What decimal number shows how often she gets a hit?

Using the Calculator
Using the *TI-108*, press these keys:

Using the *Casio SL-450*, press these keys:

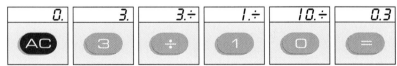

So, Shannon gets a hit 0.3 of the time.

▶ PRACTICE

Use your calculator to solve.

1. What decimal can you write for a ball player who gets a hit 2 times out of 10 times at bat?

2. What decimal can you write for a ball player who gets a hit 1 time out of 10 times at bat?

Use your calculator to change these fractions to decimals.

3. $\frac{1}{2}$ 4. $\frac{3}{4}$ 5. $\frac{2}{5}$

6. $\frac{1}{4}$ 7. $\frac{3}{5}$ 8. $\frac{4}{5}$

9. $\frac{2}{4}$ 10. $\frac{1}{5}$ 11. $\frac{5}{5}$

More Practice
CHAPTER 1

Lesson 1.1 (pages 2–3)

Find the sum.

1. $\begin{array}{r} 4 \\ +5 \\ \hline \end{array}$	2. $\begin{array}{r} 9 \\ +6 \\ \hline \end{array}$	3. $\begin{array}{r} 6 \\ +2 \\ \hline \end{array}$	4. $\begin{array}{r} 5 \\ +3 \\ \hline \end{array}$	5. $\begin{array}{r} 7 \\ +6 \\ \hline \end{array}$	6. $\begin{array}{r} 3 \\ +6 \\ \hline \end{array}$
7. $\begin{array}{r} 8 \\ +3 \\ \hline \end{array}$	8. $\begin{array}{r} 6 \\ +7 \\ \hline \end{array}$	9. $\begin{array}{r} 7 \\ +4 \\ \hline \end{array}$	10. $\begin{array}{r} 5 \\ +7 \\ \hline \end{array}$	11. $\begin{array}{r} 8 \\ +6 \\ \hline \end{array}$	12. $\begin{array}{r} 9 \\ +7 \\ \hline \end{array}$

13. $8 + 4 = \underline{\ ?\ }$ 14. $4 + 9 = \underline{\ ?\ }$ 15. $6 + 9 = \underline{\ ?\ }$ 16. $5 + 6 = \underline{\ ?\ }$

17. $4 + 6 = \underline{\ ?\ }$ 18. $8 + 5 = \underline{\ ?\ }$ 19. $9 + 3 = \underline{\ ?\ }$ 20. $7 + 3 = \underline{\ ?\ }$

Lesson 1.2 (pages 4–5)

Find the sum.

1. $\begin{array}{r} 6 \\ +6 \\ \hline \end{array}$	2. $\begin{array}{r} 5 \\ +4 \\ \hline \end{array}$	3. $\begin{array}{r} 4 \\ +4 \\ \hline \end{array}$	4. $\begin{array}{r} 3 \\ +2 \\ \hline \end{array}$	5. $\begin{array}{r} 7 \\ +8 \\ \hline \end{array}$	6. $\begin{array}{r} 2 \\ +2 \\ \hline \end{array}$
7. $\begin{array}{r} 5 \\ +5 \\ \hline \end{array}$	8. $\begin{array}{r} 5 \\ +6 \\ \hline \end{array}$	9. $\begin{array}{r} 9 \\ +7 \\ \hline \end{array}$	10. $\begin{array}{r} 8 \\ +8 \\ \hline \end{array}$	11. $\begin{array}{r} 6 \\ +9 \\ \hline \end{array}$	12. $\begin{array}{r} 4 \\ +7 \\ \hline \end{array}$

13. $9 + 9 = \underline{\ ?\ }$ 14. $6 + 5 = \underline{\ ?\ }$ 15. $7 + 8 = \underline{\ ?\ }$ 16. $3 + 3 = \underline{\ ?\ }$

17. $3 + 4 = \underline{\ ?\ }$ 18. $5 + 4 = \underline{\ ?\ }$ 19. $9 + 8 = \underline{\ ?\ }$ 20. $8 + 6 = \underline{\ ?\ }$

Lesson 1.3 Part 1 (pages 6–7)

Find the sum.

1. $\begin{array}{r} 7 \\ +6 \\ \hline \end{array}$	$\begin{array}{r} 6 \\ +7 \\ \hline \end{array}$	2. $\begin{array}{r} 4 \\ +3 \\ \hline \end{array}$	$\begin{array}{r} 3 \\ +4 \\ \hline \end{array}$	3. $\begin{array}{r} 5 \\ +7 \\ \hline \end{array}$	$\begin{array}{r} 7 \\ +5 \\ \hline \end{array}$	4. $\begin{array}{r} 8 \\ +3 \\ \hline \end{array}$	$\begin{array}{r} 3 \\ +8 \\ \hline \end{array}$
5. $\begin{array}{r} 2 \\ +9 \\ \hline \end{array}$	$\begin{array}{r} 9 \\ +2 \\ \hline \end{array}$	6. $\begin{array}{r} 4 \\ +8 \\ \hline \end{array}$	$\begin{array}{r} 8 \\ +4 \\ \hline \end{array}$	7. $\begin{array}{r} 5 \\ +6 \\ \hline \end{array}$	$\begin{array}{r} 6 \\ +5 \\ \hline \end{array}$	8. $\begin{array}{r} 8 \\ +9 \\ \hline \end{array}$	$\begin{array}{r} 9 \\ +8 \\ \hline \end{array}$

9. $1 + 0 = \underline{\ ?\ }$ 10. $4 + 5 = \underline{\ ?\ }$ 11. $5 + 0 = \underline{\ ?\ }$ 12. $4 + 0 = \underline{\ ?\ }$

13. $0 + 3 = \underline{\ ?\ }$ 14. $5 + 4 = \underline{\ ?\ }$ 15. $3 + 5 = \underline{\ ?\ }$ 16. $5 + 3 = \underline{\ ?\ }$

17. $3 + 3 = \underline{\ ?\ }$ 18. $9 + 0 = \underline{\ ?\ }$ 19. $3 + 8 = \underline{\ ?\ }$ 20. $0 + 0 = \underline{\ ?\ }$

Lesson 1.3 Part 2 (pages 8–9)

Make a table to solve.

1. Malcolm has 113 baseball cards, 98 basketball cards, and 141 football cards. Order the number of cards from least to greatest.

2. Ms. Kauffman's class is collecting cans for a canned-food drive. On Monday they collected 98 cans. Tuesday they collected 77 cans, and Wednesday they collected 105 cans. Order the number of cans from greatest to least.

Lesson 1.4 (pages 10–11)

Find the difference.

1. $\begin{array}{r} 8 \\ -0 \\ \hline \end{array}$ 2. $\begin{array}{r} 9 \\ -3 \\ \hline \end{array}$ 3. $\begin{array}{r} 4 \\ -1 \\ \hline \end{array}$ 4. $\begin{array}{r} 6 \\ -5 \\ \hline \end{array}$ 5. $\begin{array}{r} 7 \\ -7 \\ \hline \end{array}$ 6. $\begin{array}{r} 4 \\ -0 \\ \hline \end{array}$

7. $4 - 4 = \underline{\ ?\ }$ 8. $8 - 6 = \underline{\ ?\ }$ 9. $5 - 2 = \underline{\ ?\ }$ 10. $7 - 3 = \underline{\ ?\ }$

Lesson 1.5 (pages 12–13)

Write the missing number to complete each fact in the fact family.

1. $5 + \underline{\ ?\ } = 11$ $6 + \underline{\ ?\ } = 11$ $11 - \underline{\ ?\ } = 6$ $11 - \underline{\ ?\ } = 5$

2. $6 + \underline{\ ?\ } = 9$ $3 + \underline{\ ?\ } = 9$ $9 - \underline{\ ?\ } = 6$ $9 - \underline{\ ?\ } = 3$

Write the fact family for each set of numbers.

3. 3, 9, 12   4. 4, 4, 8   5. 4, 8, 12   6. 5, 8, 13

7. 2, 7, 9   8. 6, 8, 14   9. 5, 7, 12   10. 4, 9, 13

CHAPTER 2

Lesson 2.1 (pages 18–19)

Find the sum.

1. $1 + (3 + 9) = \underline{\ ?\ }$ 2. $3 + (9 + 3) = \underline{\ ?\ }$ 3. $(9 + 2) + 4 = \underline{\ ?\ }$

4. $(2 + 8) + 5 = \underline{\ ?\ }$ 5. $4 + (3 + 7) = \underline{\ ?\ }$ 6. $6 + (3 + 4) = \underline{\ ?\ }$

Group the addends. Then find the sum.

7. $6 + 2 + 5$ 8. $5 + 7 + 3$ 9. $2 + 6 + 4$

10. $7 + 2 + 6$ 11. $5 + 5 + 6$ 12. $7 + 8 + 4$

Lesson 2.2 (pages 20–21)

Find the sum.

1.	26 +18	**2.**	42 +15	**3.**	39 +21	**4.**	56 +23	**5.**	27 +25
6.	64 +34	**7.**	52 +36	**8.**	72 +47	**9.**	68 +39	**10.**	96 +74

Lesson 2.3 (pages 22–23)

Find the sum.

1.	18 +36	**2.**	42 +21	**3.**	32 +32	**4.**	25 +32	**5.**	38 +29
6.	49 +36	**7.**	47 +51	**8.**	64 +52	**9.**	83 +74	**10.**	87 +64

Lesson 2.4 (pages 24–27)

Estimate each sum or difference by rounding.

1.	36 −11	**2.**	58 −23	**3.**	36 +28	**4.**	26 +37	**5.**	82 −19
6.	53 +48	**7.**	568 +242	**8.**	598 −212	**9.**	473 +385	**10.**	679 +192

Lesson 2.5 Part 1 (pages 28–29)

Tell if you need to *add* or *subtract*. Solve.

1. Christina drove 23 miles to get to the beach, and Vanessa drove 39 miles to get to the beach. How many more miles did Vanessa drive?

2. Natalie spent 29 minutes on the computer, and then Quinton used the computer for 37 minutes. How long did Natalie and Quinton use the computer in all?

3. Jack has 45 marbles. Carl has 15 fewer marbles. How many marbles does Carl have?

4. There were some cookies on a plate. Lois put 12 more cookies on the plate. Now there are 29 cookies. How many cookies were on the plate to begin with?

Lesson 2.5 Part 2 (pages 30–31)

Write a number sentence to solve.

1. Taylor skated for 4 miles on Monday, 5 miles on Wednesday, and 9 miles on Friday. How many miles did Taylor skate in the three days?

2. Ethan backpacked 8 miles on a trail that is 39 miles long. How many more miles does Ethan need to backpack to finish the trail?

3. Ruben and his family went to Sea Land. They saw 16 sharks and 7 dolphins. How many more sharks than dolphins did they see?

4. Mimi sold candy bars to raise money for her school. She sold 6 on Monday, 11 on Tuesday, 9 on Wednesday, and 13 on Thursday. How many candy bars did Mimi sell in the four days?

CHAPTER 3

Lesson 3.1 (pages 36–37)

Find the difference. You may wish to use base-ten blocks.

1. $26 - 15$
2. $35 - 13$
3. $42 - 32$
4. $46 - 35$
5. $57 - 24$

6. $61 - 28$
7. $72 - 56$
8. $57 - 35$
9. $49 - 38$
10. $52 - 34$

11. $43 - 24$
12. $58 - 43$
13. $45 - 36$
14. $61 - 15$
15. $51 - 22$

Lesson 3.2 (pages 38–39)

Find the difference. Regroup if needed.

1. $23 - 17$
2. $42 - 23$
3. $37 - 14$
4. $33 - 24$
5. $45 - 26$

6. $37 - 29$
7. $46 - 38$
8. $61 - 29$
9. $79 - 34$
10. $95 - 62$

11. $65 - 23$
12. $52 - 14$
13. $73 - 36$
14. $91 - 67$
15. $45 - 18$

Lesson 3.3 (pages 40–41)

Find the difference.

1. 50
    −17

2. 70
    −56

3. 40
    −28

4. 30
    −17

5. 20
    −13

6. 80
    −42

7. 60
    −49

8. 40
    −35

9. 70
    −52

10. 60
    −32

Lesson 3.4 (pages 42–43)

Find the difference.

1. 46
    −29

2. 80
    −43

3. 46
    −16

4. 56
    −32

5. 52
    −37

6. 72
    −36

7. 43
    −19

8. 82
    −53

9. 50
    −31

10. 85
    −67

Lesson 3.5 Part 1 (pages 44–45)

Find the sum or difference.

1. 17
    +26

2. 34
    −21

3. 40
    −18

4. 29
    +17

5. 52
    +38

6. 91
    −34

7. 80
    −52

8. 33
    +42

9. 76
    −29

10. 32
    +31

11. 76
    +17

12. 43
    −37

13. 52
    −24

14. 73
    −17

15. 16
    +49

Lesson 3.5 Part 2 (pages 46–47)

Work backward to solve.

1. Denzel had some baseball cards. He gave 8 to Mark. Joe gave Denzel 12 more cards. Now Denzel has 43 cards. How many baseball cards did he have to begin with?

2. Ansley drew pictures on Friday, and 11 more on Saturday. She gave 3 pictures to her mom. Now Ansley has 13 pictures. How many pictures did she draw on Friday?

CHAPTER 4

Lesson 4.1 (pages 52–53)

Find the sum.

1. 118 $+113$	**2.** 213 $+136$	**3.** 293 $+146$	**4.** 492 $+313$	**5.** 632 $+243$
6. 536 $+293$	**7.** 491 $+432$	**8.** 432 $+383$	**9.** 736 $+211$	**10.** 692 $+123$
11. 206 $+134$	**12.** 738 $+217$	**13.** 46 $+622$	**14.** 224 $+671$	**15.** 167 $+258$

Lesson 4.2 (pages 54–55)

Find the sum.

1. 172 283 $+113$	**2.** $\$2.19$ 2.48 $+\ 1.72$	**3.** 342 149 $+364$	**4.** 326 473 $+728$	**5.** 234 457 $+148$
6. 429 333 $+418$	**7.** $\$5.62$ 4.19 $+\ 3.43$	**8.** 562 391 $+239$	**9.** 729 645 $+128$	**10.** $\$9.11$ 3.42 $+\ 2.36$
11. 518 128 $+\ 76$	**12.** 38 328 $+375$	**13.** 765 28 $+\ 96$	**14.** 954 742 $+471$	**15.** 429 905 $+867$

Lesson 4.3 Part 1 (pages 56–57)

Find the difference.

1. 354 -126	**2.** 268 -179	**3.** 523 -133	**4.** 736 -214	**5.** 463 -234
6. 924 -734	**7.** 684 -316	**8.** 836 -217	**9.** 792 -563	**10.** 393 -265
11. 916 -345	**12.** 874 -389	**13.** 289 -190	**14.** 738 -282	**15.** 743 -376
16. 674 -248	**17.** 725 -142	**18.** 438 -356	**19.** 815 -492	**20.** 635 -257

Lesson 4.3 Part 2 (pages 58–59)

Use guess and check to solve.

1. Two numbers have a sum of 22. Their difference is 4. What are the two numbers?

2. Zachary and his mom made 70 cookies. They made 30 more cookies on Saturday than on Friday. How many cookies did they make each day?

3. Todd and Frank have 11 toy cars in all. Todd has 3 more than Frank has. How many toy cars does each boy have?

4. Sue and Lisa spent $15 altogether at the card shop. Sue spent $5 more than Lisa did. How much money did each girl spend?

Lesson 4.4 (pages 60–61)

Regroup. Write another name for each.

1. 602   2. 40   3. 304   4. 200

5. 407   6. 903   7. 705   8. 808

Use base-ten blocks to find the difference.

9. $\begin{array}{r} 300 \\ -162 \\ \hline \end{array}$ 10. $\begin{array}{r} 602 \\ -426 \\ \hline \end{array}$ 11. $\begin{array}{r} 500 \\ -321 \\ \hline \end{array}$ 12. $\begin{array}{r} 207 \\ -132 \\ \hline \end{array}$ 13. $\begin{array}{r} 909 \\ -333 \\ \hline \end{array}$

14. $\begin{array}{r} 709 \\ -569 \\ \hline \end{array}$ 15. $\begin{array}{r} 800 \\ -563 \\ \hline \end{array}$ 16. $\begin{array}{r} 700 \\ -342 \\ \hline \end{array}$ 17. $\begin{array}{r} 407 \\ -138 \\ \hline \end{array}$ 18. $\begin{array}{r} 803 \\ -526 \\ \hline \end{array}$

Lesson 4.5 (pages 62–65)

Find the difference.

1. $\begin{array}{r} 400 \\ -234 \\ \hline \end{array}$ 2. $\begin{array}{r} 200 \\ -136 \\ \hline \end{array}$ 3. $\begin{array}{r} 600 \\ -326 \\ \hline \end{array}$ 4. $\begin{array}{r} 700 \\ -419 \\ \hline \end{array}$ 5. $\begin{array}{r} \$8.00 \\ -\ 4.72 \\ \hline \end{array}$

6. $\begin{array}{r} 500 \\ -181 \\ \hline \end{array}$ 7. $\begin{array}{r} \$4.00 \\ -\ 2.63 \\ \hline \end{array}$ 8. $\begin{array}{r} 300 \\ -137 \\ \hline \end{array}$ 9. $\begin{array}{r} 800 \\ -213 \\ \hline \end{array}$ 10. $\begin{array}{r} 900 \\ -717 \\ \hline \end{array}$

11. $\begin{array}{r} 700 \\ -426 \\ \hline \end{array}$ 12. $\begin{array}{r} 300 \\ -123 \\ \hline \end{array}$ 13. $\begin{array}{r} \$4.00 \\ -\ 3.19 \\ \hline \end{array}$ 14. $\begin{array}{r} 600 \\ -431 \\ \hline \end{array}$ 15. $\begin{array}{r} 800 \\ -623 \\ \hline \end{array}$

16. $\begin{array}{r} 600 \\ -541 \\ \hline \end{array}$ 17. $\begin{array}{r} 500 \\ -237 \\ \hline \end{array}$ 18. $\begin{array}{r} 400 \\ -315 \\ \hline \end{array}$ 19. $\begin{array}{r} 200 \\ -157 \\ \hline \end{array}$ 20. $\begin{array}{r} 800 \\ -369 \\ \hline \end{array}$

CHAPTER 5

Lesson 5.1 (pages 76–77)

Tell how you would read each time. Write the time.

1.

2.

3.

4.

5.

6.

7.

8.

Lesson 5.2 (pages 78–79)

Choose the better estimate of time.

1. take a nap   1 minute or 1 hour

2. watch show on television   30 hours or 30 minutes

3. vacuum the house   25 minutes or 25 hours

Decide if the estimated time makes sense. Write *yes* or *no*.

4. It takes about 3 hours to brush your teeth.

5. It takes about 10 minutes to fold a load of laundry.

6. It takes about 1 hour to write your full name.

Lesson 5.3 (pages 80–81)

Write each time.

1.

2.

3.

4.

5.

6.

7.

8.

Lesson 5.4 Part 1 (pages 82–83)

Write the two ways you would read each time.

1.

2.

3.

4.

Write each time.

5.

6.

7.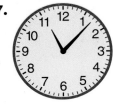

8.

Lesson 5.4 Part 2 (pages 84–85)

Act it out to solve.

1. Cheerleading practice starts at 4:00. It is over at 5:17. Where are the hands on the clock when cheerleading practice is over?

2. Mrs. Marshall leaves for the grocery store at two o'clock. She gets home 47 minutes after two. Where are the hands on the clock when Mrs. Marshall gets home?

CHAPTER 6

Lesson 6.1 (pages 90–91)

Find the elapsed time.

1. **start:** 1:30
   end: 1:45

2. **start:** 3:15
   end: 4:15

3. **start:** 4:30
   end: 5:00

4. **start:** 12:00
   end: 12:45

5. **start:** 2:15
   end: 3:00

6. **start:** 8:30
   end: 9:15

7. **start:** 11:00
   end: 12:00

8. **start:** 5:15
   end: 5:30

Find the ending time.

9. **start:** 5:15
   elapsed:
   1 hour

10. **start:** 9:00
    elapsed:
    1 hour and
    15 min

11. **start:** 11:00
    elapsed:
    30 min

12. **start:** 3:30
    elapsed:
    30 min

Lesson 6.2 (pages 92–93)

For Problems 1–5, use the schedule.

1. At what time does the pottery class begin? When does it end?

2. In which room is the sculpture class being held?

3. Which classes are held in Room B?

4. How long is the painting class?

5. If Amad takes pottery class, will he be out in time to take drawing class?

ART CLASS SCHEDULE		
Class	Time	Room
Pottery	1:00–1:45	A
Painting	1:00–1:45	B
Sculpture	2:00–2:45	A
Drawing	2:00–2:30	B
Cartooning	3:00–3:30	A

Lesson 6.3 (pages 94–95)

Copy and complete the schedule.

	BASKETBALL PRACTICE SCHEDULE		
	Activity	Time	Elapsed Time
1.	Warm-up	3:00–3:15	?
2.	Free Throw Practice	3:15–3:45	?
3.	Passing Practice	?	30 min
4.	Practice Game	?	45 min

For Problems 5–6, use the schedule you made.

5. How much longer is the practice game than passing practice?

6. How much time is spent at basketball practice?

Lesson 6.4 (pages 96–97)

For Problems 1–5, use the schedule.

1. On what day of the week is football practice?

2. Patricia goes to practice on Monday. Which sport is she involved in?

3. How much time is spent at soccer practice?

4. How much time is spent at basketball practice?

INTRAMURAL SPORT SCHEDULE		
Sport	Day	Time
Soccer	Mon	3:00–4:15
Baseball	Tues	3:30–4:30
Basketball	Wed	3:45–4:45
Football	Thurs	3:00–4:30
Softball	Fri	3:15–4:30

5. How much longer is softball practice than basketball practice?

Lesson 6.5 Part 1 (pages 98–99)

For Exercises 1–14, use your six month calendar.
Write the date 4 weeks later.

1. May 12
2. June 2
3. April 4
4. March 30
5. February 4
6. January 15
7. May 9
8. April 12

Write the number of weeks.

9. from February 14 to March 14
10. from May 11 to June 15
11. from April 4 to May 23
12. from January 6 to January 27
13. from March 19 to April 30
14. from April 1 to June 3

Lesson 6.5 Part 2 (pages 100–101)

Work backward to solve. Use your six month calendar.

1. The date on Hunter's calendar is June 30. He just spent 3 days at his grandparents' house. Before that, he was on a 2–week vacation. On what date did Hunter leave for vacation?

2. The date on Felicia's calendar is June 14. She just spent 5 days at the beach. Before that, she was at soccer camp for a week. On what date did Felicia leave for soccer camp?

CHAPTER 7

Lesson 7.1 (pages 106–107)

Count the money and write the amount.

1.

2.

3.

4.

Lesson 7.2 (pages 108–109)

Make three equivalent sets for each amount. List how
many of each bill and coin you used.

1. $3.29
2. $5.76
3. $7.11
4. $9.35

5. $1.42
6. $4.26
7. $8.36
8. $2.56

9. $4.31
10. $9.55
11. $2.14
12. $7.09

Lesson 7.3 (pages 110–111)

Compare the amounts of money. Write the letter of the greater amount.

1. a.    b.

2. a.    b.

3. a.   b.

4. a.     b.

Lesson 7.4 (pages 112–113)

List the coins you would get as change from a $1 bill.

1. $0.42
2. $0.23
3. $0.51
4. $0.37
5. $0.33

6. $0.86
7. $0.72
8. $0.65
9. $0.94
10. $0.61

11. $0.96
12. $0.68
13. $0.54
14. $0.79
15. $0.48

Lesson 7.5 Part 1 (pages 114–115)

Find the sum.

1. $1.43
    + 2.19

2. $3.17
    + 1.56

3. $2.56
    + 4.19

4. $6.45
    + 4.73

5. $8.74
    + 5.26

Find the difference.

6. $2.86
    − 1.42

7. $3.52
    − 1.37

8. $7.82
    − 5.93

9. $4.93
    − 1.45

10. $9.00
    − 3.47

Lesson 7.5 Part 2 (pages 116–117)

Write a number sentence to solve.

1. Tatiana buys a poster for $1.75, a CD for $13.25, and a T-shirt for $14.15. How much does she spend in all? How much change will she get from $30.00?

2. Dustin buys a hamburger for $2.49, french fries for $1.67, and a drink for $1.45. How much does Dustin spend in all? How much change will he get from $10.00?

CHAPTER 8

Lesson 8.1 (pages 128–129)

For Exercises 1–5, use the words TEACHERS ARE GREAT! Answer each question. If your answer is a number, tell if it is a cardinal or an ordinal number.

TEACHERS ARE GREAT!

1. How many letters are in the third word?

2. What is the third letter in the first word?

3. What is the second letter in the second word?

4. In TEACHERS, in which position is the letter T?

5. In GREAT, in which position is the letter E?

Lesson 8.2 (pages 130–131)

Write true or false. Change words in the false sentences to make them true.

1. There are 10 ones in ten.

2. There are 10 dimes in 1 dollar.

3. There are 10 ones in 1 hundred.

4. There are 10 pennies in 1 dollar.

Lesson 8.3 (pages 132–133)

Answer each question. Use a hundred chart to help you.

1. Skip count by twos. Move 3 skips. Where are you?

2. Skip count by twos. Move 12 skips. Where are you?

3. Skip count by threes. Move 5 skips. Where are you?

4. Skip count by fives. Move 7 skips. Where are you?

5. Skip count by threes. Move 6 skips. Where are you?

6. Skip count by fives. Move 5 skips. Where are you?

Write the number. Tell whether it is *odd* or *even*.

7. 16
8. 21
9. 43
10. 154
11. 1,617
12. 519
13. 1,072
14. 529
15. 766
16. 2,033
17. 6,923
18. 359

Lesson 8.4 (pages 134–135)

Use patterns of tens to find the sum or difference.

1. $52 + 10 + 10$
2. $16 + 10 + 10$
3. $29 + 10 + 10$
4. $43 + 20$
5. $61 + 30$
6. $17 + 40$
7. $37 - 10$
8. $75 - 10 - 10$
9. $62 - 10 - 10$
10. $95 - 30$
11. $89 - 40$
12. $57 - 30$
13. $76 - 40$
14. $32 + 40$
15. $43 + 30$

Lesson 8.5 Part 1 (pages 136–137)

Estimate the number of beans in each jar. Use Jars A and B on page 136 as benchmarks.

1.

13, 56, or 102

2.

7, 31, or 90

3.

12, 57, or 89

4.

11, 32, or 93

5.

5, 24, or 88

6.

10, 25, or 45

Lesson 8.5 Part 2 (pages 138–139)
Make a model to solve.

1. Jerome has 8 coins in his hand. He tells Holly the coins are worth $0.73. How can Holly find out which coins Jerome is holding?

2. Victoria is estimating the number of pennies in a large jar. She can hold about 20 pennies in her hand. About how many pennies are in 5 handfuls?

3. Margaret's vacation begins in 3 weeks. Today is June 1. On what date does Margaret's vacation begin?

4. Ivan added 4 tens to a set of 7 tens and 5 ones. What number do the tens and ones show?

CHAPTER 9

Lesson 9.1 (pages 144–145)
Write how many hundreds, tens, and ones.

1. 492
2. 673
3. 584
4. 167
5. 219
6. 934

Write the value of the blue digit.

7. 439
8. 721
9. 396
10. 567
11. 128
12. 899
13. 428
14. 370

Lesson 9.2 (pages 146–147)
Look in your book of 1,000 squares. Write the page number on which each number is found.

1. 91
2. 311
3. 790
4. 106
5. 567
6. 419
7. 175
8. 891

Lesson 9.3 (pages 148–149)
Use patterns of hundreds or thousands to find the sum or difference.

1. 753 + 200
2. 342 + 100
3. 523 + 300
4. 493 − 100
5. 973 − 300
6. 546 − 400
7. 2,493 + 1,000
8. 3,924 + 2,000
9. 6,729 + 3,000
10. 6,429 − 2,000
11. 7,243 − 1,000
12. 9,329 − 3,000

Lesson 9.4 (pages 150–153)

Write each number in standard form.

1. 40,000 + 1,000 + 500 + 2

2. 200,000 + 6,000 + 700 + 50 + 6

3. 50,000 + 5,000 + 500 + 50 + 5

4. 80,000 + 9,000 + 800 + 10 + 4

5. four hundred sixty-five thousand, nine hundred forty-two

6. three hundred eighty thousand, four hundred fifty-three

7. forty-two thousand, seven hundred sixty-one

8. fifteen thousand, six hundred twenty-nine

Write the value of the blue digit.

9. 19,319

10. 27,496

11. 373,153

12. 81,329

13. 29,548

14. 56,258

15. 86,457

16. 99,568

Lesson 9.5 Part 1 (pages 154–155)

Choose a benchmark of 1,000 or 10,000 to estimate or count each number.

1. 6,716

2. 17,973

3. 12,735

4. 20,936

5. 4,362

6. 5,123

7. 4,692

8. 87,142

9. 2,499

10. 8,742

11. 12,881

12. 26,902

Lesson 9.5 Part 2 (pages 156–157)

Use the table to solve.

1. For every 1,000 tickets sold, a free ticket is given away. How many tickets were given away in April? Explain.

2. The theater opens the balcony when there are more than 10,000 patrons in one month. In which month did the theater open the balcony?

Movie Theater Ticket Sales	
January	6,142
February	10,329
March	7,319
April	4,902
May	3,998

3. The theater hires extra ushers when there are more than 5,000 patrons in one month. For which months did the theater hire extra ushers?

4. To the nearest thousand, how many tickets were sold each month?

CHAPTER 10

Lesson 10.1 (pages 162–163)

Draw base-ten blocks to show your models. Circle the picture that shows the greater number.

1. 62 and 74   **2.** 93 and 78   **3.** 100 and 113

4. 123 and 101   **5.** 317 and 329   **6.** 285 and 263

7. 136 and 142   **8.** 373 and 415   **9.** 309 and 294

Lesson 10.2 (pages 164–167)

Compare the numbers. Write $<$, $>$, or $=$ for each ●.

1.

63 ● 58

2.

126 ● 128

3.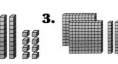

237 ● 311

4.

122 ● 145

5.

326 ● 258

6.

256 ● 251

7. 76 ● 62   **8.** 42 ● 51   **9.** 62 ● 64

10. 112 ● 152   **11.** 4,109 ● 3,102 **12.** 4,132 ● 4,132

13. 492 ● 493   **14.** 201 ● 210   **15.** 432 ● 423

16. 4,562 ● 4,566 **17.** 129 ● 129   **18.** 1,732 ● 1,731

Lesson 10.3 Part 1 (pages 168–169)

Write the numbers in order from greatest to least.

1. 47, 39, 51   **2.** 77, 89, 10   **3.** 103, 92, 423

4. 97, 113, 103   **5.** 621, 719, 536   **6.** 175, 793, 419

Write the numbers in order from least to greatest.

7. 34, 92, 29   **8.** 43, 64, 53   **9.** 14, 92, 32

10. 132, 123, 133 **11.** 109, 107, 110 **12.** 181, 118, 148

Lesson 10.3 Part 2 (pages 170–171)

Draw a picture to solve.

1. Anita wants 3 books. The prices are $3.75, $7.79, and $2.19. Order the books from most expensive to least expensive.

2. Ed has 56 stickers, Amanda has 61 stickers, and Whitney has 39 stickers. Put the number of stickers in order from least to greatest.

3. Liz guessed there are 747 pennies in a jar. Richard's guess was 695 pennies. There are 725 pennies in the jar. Whose guess is closer?

4. Morgan estimated it was 275 miles from Clarksville to Riverside. Dante estimated 310 miles. It is actually 296 miles. Whose estimate is closer?

Lesson 10.4 (pages 172–173)

Round each number to the nearest hundred. You may wish to use a number line.

1. 429   2. 319   3. 563   4. 872

5. 194   6. 632   7. 411   8. 699

9. 727   10. 946   11. 872   12. 333

13. 749   14. 678   15. 921   16. 857

Tell which two tens or two hundreds each number is between. Then tell what the number rounds to.

17. 56   18. 129   19. 687

20. 372   21. 417   22. 323

Lesson 10.5 (pages 174–175)

Round to the nearest ten or ten dollars.

1. 52   2. 39   3. 45   4. $21   5. $89

6. 26   7. 72   8. $82   9. $17   10. $66

Round to the nearest hundred or hundred dollars.

11. 239   12. 476   13. 189   14. $651   15. $539

16. 391   17. 727   18. $821   19. $933   20. $265

CHAPTER 11

Lesson 11.1 (pages 186–187)

Look at the pictures. Write how many there are in all.

1.   **2.**   **3.**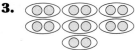

3 groups of 4 = _?_   2 groups of 5 = _?_   4 groups of 2 = _?_

Lesson 11.2 Part 1 (pages 188–189)

Write the addition sentence and a multiplication sentence for each.

1.   **2.**   **3.**

Find the product. You may wish to draw a picture.

4. $9 \times 2 = $ _?_   **5.** $1 \times 5 = $ _?_   **6.** $6 \times 2 = $ _?_   **7.** $3 \times 5 = $ _?_

8. $5 \times 8 = $ _?_   **9.** $2 \times 5 = $ _?_   **10.** $4 \times 2 = $ _?_   **11.** $5 \times 4 = $ _?_

Lesson 11.2 Part 2 (pages 190–191)

Draw a picture to solve.

1. In Mrs. Carol's class 7 students each wrote 3 poems. How many poems were written in all?

2. In Michelle's flower garden are 4 rows of rose bushes. There are 6 rose bushes in each row. How many rose bushes are in her garden?

Lesson 11.3 (pages 192–195)

Complete the multiplication sentence for each number line.

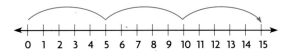

1. $3 \times 5 = $ _?_

2. $5 \times 3 = $ _?_

Use the number line. Find the product.

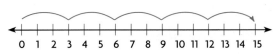

3. $3 \times 1 = $ _?_   **4.** $3 \times 4 = $ _?_   **5.** $6 \times 2 = $ _?_   **6.** $7 \times 3 = $ _?_

7. $9 \times 3 = $ _?_   **8.** $5 \times 4 = $ _?_   **9.** $4 \times 7 = $ _?_   **10.** $3 \times 8 = $ _?_

Lesson 11.4 (pages 196–197)

Find the product.

1. $1 \times 0 = \underline{}$ 2. $0 \times 5 = \underline{}$ 3. $2 \times 1 = \underline{}$ 4. $6 \times 1 = \underline{}$

5. $9 \times 0 = \underline{}$ 6. $1 \times 3 = \underline{}$ 7. $6 \times 2 = \underline{}$ 8. $0 \times 4 = \underline{}$

9. $7 \times 2 = \underline{}$ 10. $8 \times 3 = \underline{}$ 11. $5 \times 5 = \underline{}$ 12. $4 \times 2 = \underline{}$

Lesson 11.5 (pages 198–201)

Find the product. You may wish to use a multiplication table.

1. $\begin{array}{r} 4 \\ \times 1 \\ \hline \end{array}$ 2. $\begin{array}{r} 3 \\ \times 5 \\ \hline \end{array}$ 3. $\begin{array}{r} 9 \\ \times 1 \\ \hline \end{array}$ 4. $\begin{array}{r} 4 \\ \times 4 \\ \hline \end{array}$ 5. $\begin{array}{r} 3 \\ \times 4 \\ \hline \end{array}$ 6. $\begin{array}{r} 5 \\ \times 2 \\ \hline \end{array}$

7. $\begin{array}{r} 4 \\ \times 5 \\ \hline \end{array}$ 8. $\begin{array}{r} 2 \\ \times 4 \\ \hline \end{array}$ 9. $\begin{array}{r} 4 \\ \times 3 \\ \hline \end{array}$ 10. $\begin{array}{r} 8 \\ \times 4 \\ \hline \end{array}$ 11. $\begin{array}{r} 7 \\ \times 4 \\ \hline \end{array}$ 12. $\begin{array}{r} 6 \\ \times 5 \\ \hline \end{array}$

13. $6 \times 4 = \underline{}$ 14. $7 \times 5 = \underline{}$ 15. $4 \times 0 = \underline{}$ 16. $9 \times 4 = \underline{}$

CHAPTER 12

Lesson 12.1 (pages 206–207)

Find the product.

1. $5 \times 4 = \underline{}$ 2. $6 \times 6 = \underline{}$ 3. $5 \times 6 = \underline{}$

4. $6 \times 2 = \underline{}$ 5. $9 \times 6 = \underline{}$ 6. $8 \times 6 = \underline{}$

7. $3 \times 6 = \underline{}$ 8. $4 \times 6 = \underline{}$ 9. $7 \times 6 = \underline{}$

Write the multiplication fact that is shown by each array.

10.    11.    12.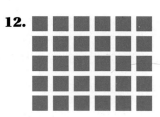

Name all the arrays you can make with each set of tiles.

13. 4 tiles   14. 16 tiles   15. 18 tiles

16. 20 tiles   17. 24 tiles   18. 30 tiles

Lesson 12.2 (pages 208–211)

Find the product.

1. $3 \times 7 = \underline{\ ?\ }$ 2. $5 \times 7 = \underline{\ ?\ }$ 3. $1 \times 7 = \underline{\ ?\ }$ 4. $5 \times 6 = \underline{\ ?\ }$

5. $7 \times 0 = \underline{\ ?\ }$ 6. $2 \times 7 = \underline{\ ?\ }$ 7. $9 \times 7 = \underline{\ ?\ }$ 8. $4 \times 7 = \underline{\ ?\ }$

9. $6 \times 7 = \underline{\ ?\ }$ 10. $7 \times 8 = \underline{\ ?\ }$ 11. $7 \times 7 = \underline{\ ?\ }$ 12. $8 \times 7 = \underline{\ ?\ }$

Lesson 12.3 (pages 212–213)

Find the product.

1. $3 \times 8 = \underline{\ ?\ }$ 2. $2 \times 6 = \underline{\ ?\ }$ 3. $2 \times 8 = \underline{\ ?\ }$ 4. $8 \times 8 = \underline{\ ?\ }$

5. $4 \times 8 = \underline{\ ?\ }$ 6. $0 \times 8 = \underline{\ ?\ }$ 7. $3 \times 4 = \underline{\ ?\ }$ 8. $7 \times 8 = \underline{\ ?\ }$

9. $6 \times 8 = \underline{\ ?\ }$ 10. $5 \times 8 = \underline{\ ?\ }$ 11. $8 \times 1 = \underline{\ ?\ }$ 12. $9 \times 8 = \underline{\ ?\ }$

Lesson 12.4 Part 1 (pages 214–215)

Find the product.

1. $\begin{array}{r} 6 \\ \times 9 \\ \hline \end{array}$ 2. $\begin{array}{r} 9 \\ \times 1 \\ \hline \end{array}$ 3. $\begin{array}{r} 5 \\ \times 5 \\ \hline \end{array}$ 4. $\begin{array}{r} 2 \\ \times 9 \\ \hline \end{array}$ 5. $\begin{array}{r} 9 \\ \times 0 \\ \hline \end{array}$

6. $\begin{array}{r} 5 \\ \times 9 \\ \hline \end{array}$ 7. $\begin{array}{r} 9 \\ \times 9 \\ \hline \end{array}$ 8. $\begin{array}{r} 3 \\ \times 9 \\ \hline \end{array}$ 9. $\begin{array}{r} 7 \\ \times 9 \\ \hline \end{array}$ 10. $\begin{array}{r} 4 \\ \times 9 \\ \hline \end{array}$

11. $8 \times 9 = \underline{\ ?\ }$ 12. $6 \times 5 = \underline{\ ?\ }$ 13. $9 \times 2 = \underline{\ ?\ }$ 14. $9 \times 5 = \underline{\ ?\ }$

15. $9 \times 7 = \underline{\ ?\ }$ 16. $6 \times 9 = \underline{\ ?\ }$ 17. $9 \times 9 = \underline{\ ?\ }$ 18. $9 \times 8 = \underline{\ ?\ }$

Lesson 12.4 Part 2 (pages 216–217)

Make a model to solve.

1. Candace planted a garden of 4 rows with 3 plants in each row. How many plants are in Candace's garden?

2. Coach Riley has his team in 6 rows of 4 players each. How many players are on Coach Riley's team?

3. Mrs. Johnson hung her students' poems on a bulletin board. The bulletin board has 7 poems across and 4 poems down. How many poems are hanging on the bulletin board?

4. Jenna tiled her bathroom floor. She put down 6 rows of tiles. There are 8 tiles in each row. How many tiles are on the bathroom floor?

Lesson 12.5 (pages 218–221)

Use the multiplication table to find the products.

1. $\begin{array}{r} 5 \\ \times 4 \\ \hline \end{array}$	**2.** $\begin{array}{r} 9 \\ \times 3 \\ \hline \end{array}$	**3.** $\begin{array}{r} 7 \\ \times 5 \\ \hline \end{array}$	**4.** $\begin{array}{r} 4 \\ \times 0 \\ \hline \end{array}$	**5.** $\begin{array}{r} 7 \\ \times 7 \\ \hline \end{array}$
6. $\begin{array}{r} 7 \\ \times 2 \\ \hline \end{array}$	**7.** $\begin{array}{r} 3 \\ \times 2 \\ \hline \end{array}$	**8.** $\begin{array}{r} 9 \\ \times 8 \\ \hline \end{array}$	**9.** $\begin{array}{r} 6 \\ \times 4 \\ \hline \end{array}$	**10.** $\begin{array}{r} 9 \\ \times 5 \\ \hline \end{array}$
11. $\begin{array}{r} 6 \\ \times 0 \\ \hline \end{array}$	**12.** $\begin{array}{r} 7 \\ \times 4 \\ \hline \end{array}$	**13.** $\begin{array}{r} 5 \\ \times 6 \\ \hline \end{array}$	**14.** $\begin{array}{r} 8 \\ \times 7 \\ \hline \end{array}$	**15.** $\begin{array}{r} 9 \\ \times 3 \\ \hline \end{array}$

CHAPTER 13

Lesson 13.1 (pages 226–227)

Copy and complete the table. Use counters to help you.

	Counters	How many groups?	How many in each group?
1.	10	5	?
2.	12	?	6
3.	16	4	?
4.	25	?	5
5.	27	3	?
6.	32	?	4

Lesson 13.2 (pages 228–229)

Show how you can use subtraction to solve.

1. $15 \div 5 = \underline{\ ?\ }$ **2.** $24 \div 6 = \underline{\ ?\ }$ **3.** $20 \div 5 = \underline{\ ?\ }$

4. $16 \div 8 = \underline{\ ?\ }$ **5.** $12 \div 3 = \underline{\ ?\ }$ **6.** $6 \div 2 = \underline{\ ?\ }$

Write the division sentence shown by the repeated subtraction.

7.
$$\begin{array}{r}35 \\ -7 \\ \hline 28 \end{array} \quad \begin{array}{r}28 \\ -7 \\ \hline 21 \end{array} \quad \begin{array}{r}21 \\ -7 \\ \hline 14 \end{array} \quad \begin{array}{r}14 \\ -7 \\ \hline 7 \end{array} \quad \begin{array}{r}7 \\ -7 \\ \hline 0 \end{array}$$

8.
$$\begin{array}{r}42 \\ -6 \\ \hline 36 \end{array} \quad \begin{array}{r}36 \\ -6 \\ \hline 30 \end{array} \quad \begin{array}{r}30 \\ -6 \\ \hline 24 \end{array} \quad \begin{array}{r}24 \\ -6 \\ \hline 18 \end{array} \quad \begin{array}{r}18 \\ -6 \\ \hline 12 \end{array} \quad \begin{array}{r}12 \\ -6 \\ \hline 6 \end{array} \quad \begin{array}{r}6 \\ -6 \\ \hline 0 \end{array}$$

9.
$$\begin{array}{r}25 \\ -5 \\ \hline 20 \end{array} \quad \begin{array}{r}20 \\ -5 \\ \hline 15 \end{array} \quad \begin{array}{r}15 \\ -5 \\ \hline 10 \end{array} \quad \begin{array}{r}10 \\ -5 \\ \hline 5 \end{array} \quad \begin{array}{r}5 \\ -5 \\ \hline 0 \end{array}$$

10.
$$\begin{array}{r}32 \\ -8 \\ \hline 24 \end{array} \quad \begin{array}{r}24 \\ -8 \\ \hline 16 \end{array} \quad \begin{array}{r}16 \\ -8 \\ \hline 8 \end{array} \quad \begin{array}{r}8 \\ -8 \\ \hline 0 \end{array}$$

Lesson 13.3 (pages 230–231)

Write the missing factor or quotient for each number sentence.

1. $7 \times \underline{\ ?\ } = 28$ $28 \div 7 = \underline{\ ?\ }$ 2. $9 \times \underline{\ ?\ } = 72$ $72 \div 9 = \underline{\ ?\ }$

3. $4 \times \underline{\ ?\ } = 24$ $24 \div 4 = \underline{\ ?\ }$ 4. $8 \times \underline{\ ?\ } = 48$ $48 \div 8 = \underline{\ ?\ }$

5. $6 \times \underline{\ ?\ } = 54$ $54 \div 6 = \underline{\ ?\ }$ 6. $5 \times \underline{\ ?\ } = 35$ $35 \div 5 = \underline{\ ?\ }$

Check each division with multiplication. Show your work.

7. $40 \div 8 = \underline{\ ?\ }$ 8. $36 \div 6 = \underline{\ ?\ }$ 9. $63 \div 9 = \underline{\ ?\ }$ 10. $56 \div 7 = \underline{\ ?\ }$

11. $45 \div 5 = \underline{\ ?\ }$ 12. $54 \div 9 = \underline{\ ?\ }$ 13. $28 \div 7 = \underline{\ ?\ }$ 14. $24 \div 4 = \underline{\ ?\ }$

Lesson 13.4 (pages 232–233)

Write the fact family for each set of numbers.

1. 2, 8, 16   2. 3, 4, 12   3. 5, 6, 30

4. 6, 7, 42   5. 7, 7, 49   6. 6, 9, 54

7. 7, 8, 56   8. 7, 9, 63   9. 8, 8, 64

Lesson 13.5 (pages 234–235)

Write the multiplication fact you can use to find each quotient. Write the quotient.

1. $10 \div 2 = \underline{\ ?\ }$ 2. $18 \div 3 = \underline{\ ?\ }$ 3. $15 \div 5 = \underline{\ ?\ }$ 4. $40 \div 5 = \underline{\ ?\ }$

5. $21 \div 3 = \underline{\ ?\ }$ 6. $24 \div 4 = \underline{\ ?\ }$ 7. $25 \div 5 = \underline{\ ?\ }$ 8. $35 \div 5 = \underline{\ ?\ }$

9. $32 \div 4 = \underline{\ ?\ }$ 10. $45 \div 5 = \underline{\ ?\ }$ 11. $28 \div 4 = \underline{\ ?\ }$ 12. $36 \div 4 = \underline{\ ?\ }$

13. $30 \div 5 = \underline{\ ?\ }$ 14. $18 \div 2 = \underline{\ ?\ }$ 15. $20 \div 4 = \underline{\ ?\ }$ 16. $16 \div 2 = \underline{\ ?\ }$

Lesson 13.6 Part 1 (pages 236–237)

Write a or b to show which number sentence you would use to solve each problem.

1. Barry walks 2 miles a day. How many miles does Barry walk in 9 days?
   a. $18 \div 2 = 9$
   b. $9 \times 2 = 18$

2. Mrs. Rogers put her 24 students into 6 groups. How many students are in each group?
   a. $24 \div 6 = 4$
   b. $6 \times 4 = 24$

Lesson 13.6 Part 2 (pages 238–239)

Write a number sentence to solve.

1. In Mr. Brawner's class there are 28 students in 4 rows. How many students are in each row?

2. Clarissa does aerobics 3 times a week. How many times does she do aerobics in 5 weeks?

3. Amanda walks 6 miles a day. How many miles does Amanda walk in 1 week?

4. Connor invites 15 friends to his birthday party. For a party game they must get into 5 teams. How many friends are on each team?

CHAPTER 14

Lesson 14.1 (pages 244–245)

Write the division sentence. You may wish to use square tiles.

1. How many groups of 5 are in 25?

2. How many groups of 4 are in 28?

3. How many groups of 6 are in 18?

4. How many groups of 7 are in 35?

5. How many groups of 8 are in 32?

6. How many groups of 9 are in 54?

7. How many groups of 9 are in 81?

8. How many groups of 7 are in 63?

9. How many groups of 8 are in 56?

10. How many groups of 6 are in 48?

Lesson 14.2 (pages 246–247)

Find the quotient.

1. $6 \div 6 = \underline{\ ?\ }$

2. $0 \div 3 = \underline{\ ?\ }$

3. $3 \div 1 = \underline{\ ?\ }$

4. $4 \div 1 = \underline{\ ?\ }$

5. $2 \div 2 = \underline{\ ?\ }$

6. $0 \div 7 = \underline{\ ?\ }$

7. $8 \div 1 = \underline{\ ?\ }$

8. $0 \div 1 = \underline{\ ?\ }$

9. $9 \div 1 = \underline{\ ?\ }$

10. $4 \div 4 = \underline{\ ?\ }$

11. $7 \div 1 = \underline{\ ?\ }$

12. $5 \div 5 = \underline{\ ?\ }$

13. $8 \div 8 = \underline{\ ?\ }$

14. $6 \div 1 = \underline{\ ?\ }$

15. $7 \div 7 = \underline{\ ?\ }$

16. $9 \div 9 = \underline{\ ?\ }$

17. $0 \div 8 = \underline{\ ?\ }$

18. $1 \div 1 = \underline{\ ?\ }$

Lesson 14.3 (pages 248-249)

Use the multiplication table on page 248 to find each quotient.

1. $24 \div 4 = \underline{\ ?\ }$ **2.** $18 \div 6 = \underline{\ ?\ }$ **3.** $35 \div 7 = \underline{\ ?\ }$

4. $30 \div 5 = \underline{\ ?\ }$ **5.** $28 \div 4 = \underline{\ ?\ }$ **6.** $63 \div 9 = \underline{\ ?\ }$

7. $36 \div 9 = \underline{\ ?\ }$ **8.** $21 \div 7 = \underline{\ ?\ }$ **9.** $64 \div 8 = \underline{\ ?\ }$

10. $28 \div 7 = \underline{\ ?\ }$ **11.** $54 \div 6 = \underline{\ ?\ }$ **12.** $36 \div 6 = \underline{\ ?\ }$

13. $56 \div 8 = \underline{\ ?\ }$ **14.** $24 \div 6 = \underline{\ ?\ }$ **15.** $54 \div 9 = \underline{\ ?\ }$

16. $63 \div 7 = \underline{\ ?\ }$ **17.** $48 \div 8 = \underline{\ ?\ }$ **18.** $27 \div 3 = \underline{\ ?\ }$

19. $42 \div 6 = \underline{\ ?\ }$ **20.** $36 \div 4 = \underline{\ ?\ }$ **21.** $72 \div 9 = \underline{\ ?\ }$

Lesson 14.4 Part 1 (pages 250-251)

Copy and complete the tables.

1.

÷	25	30	35	40	45
5	?	?	?	?	?

2.

÷	24	32	40	48	56
8	?	?	?	?	?

3.

÷	24	30	36	42	48
6	?	?	?	?	?

4.

÷	27	36	45	54	63
9	?	?	?	?	?

Find the quotient.

5. $48 \div 8 = \underline{\ ?\ }$ **6.** $63 \div 7 = \underline{\ ?\ }$ **7.** $45 \div 9 = \underline{\ ?\ }$

8. $42 \div 6 = \underline{\ ?\ }$ **9.** $54 \div 9 = \underline{\ ?\ }$ **10.** $48 \div 6 = \underline{\ ?\ }$

11. $28 \div 7 = \underline{\ ?\ }$ **12.** $36 \div 6 = \underline{\ ?\ }$ **13.** $72 \div 8 = \underline{\ ?\ }$

14. $56 \div 8 = \underline{\ ?\ }$ **15.** $36 \div 9 = \underline{\ ?\ }$ **16.** $64 \div 8 = \underline{\ ?\ }$

Lesson 14.4 Part 2 (pages 252-253)

Make a table to solve.

1. Craig has 3 water bottles. The blue bottle holds 16 ounces of water. The red bottle holds 24 ounces of water. The green bottle holds 32 ounces of water. How many 8-ounce servings are in each bottle?

2. The fair offers 7-minute pony rides. The ride operates for 35 minutes in the morning, 49 minutes during lunch, and 56 minutes in the afternoon. How many rides can be taken during each time?

Lesson 14.5 (pages 254–255)

Write *a* or *b* to show which number sentence you would use to solve each problem.

1. On Monday morning, there were 12 puppies in the pet store window. Then 3 were sold. How many were left?
   a. $12 \div 3 = 4$ **b.** $12 - 3 = 9$

2. Mr. Wong has 3 children. He gives 2 cookies to each of his children. What is the least number of cookies he could have started with?
   a. $3 \times 2 = 6$ **b.** $3 + 2 = 5$

CHAPTER 15

Lesson 15.1 (pages 266–267)

Kenneth did an experiment with his hamsters. He put them in a maze and recorded which hamster reached the end first. Change Kenneth's tally table into a frequency table. Then answer the questions.

KENNETH'S HAMSTERS	
Hamster	**Wins**
Fluffy	IIII
Buttercup	llll II
Dan	II

1. Which hamster won the most times?

2. How many times did Kenneth run his hamsters through the maze?

3. How many more times did Buttercup win than Fluffy?

Lesson 15.2 Part 1 (pages 268–269)

For Problems 1–2, tell what kind of table should be used. Write *tally table* or *frequency table*.

1. Deepa is getting ready to do an experiment with a coin. She will record which side the coin lands on each time she flips it.

2. Bryan wants to show his friends what happened in his experiment with a number cube.

Lesson 15.2 Part 2 (pages 270–271)

Solve.

1. Subeer flipped a coin 40 times and recorded which side it landed on each time. Make a table about his experiment.

2. Jon rolled a number cube 15 times and recorded the number. Make a table about his experiment.

Lesson 15.3 (pages 272–273)

For Problems 1–4, use the survey results in the tally table.

FAVORITE PETS	
Pets	**Tallies**
Fish	卌 l
Dogs	卌 卌 lll
Cats	卌 llll
Birds	卌

1. For which animal did most people vote?

2. How many more people voted for cats than birds?

3. How many people answered the survey?

4. How many more people voted for dogs than fish?

Lesson 15.4 (pages 274–275)

For Problems 1–4, use the table.

CHORUS MEMBERS			
	Third Grade	**Fourth Grade**	**Fifth Grade**
Boys	5	7	7
Girls	9	6	8

1. How many chorus members are third-grade girls?

2. How many fourth graders are chorus members?

3. Which grade has 14 students in the chorus?

4. How many students are in the chorus in all?

CHAPTER 16

Lesson 16.1 (pages 280–281)

For Problems 1–6, use the pictograph.

OUR FAVORITE COLOR	
blue	▮▮▮▮▮
green	▮▮▮
yellow	▯
red	▮▮

Key: Each ▮ stands for 3 students.

1. Which color is liked best by the most students?

2. How many more students like green better than yellow?

3. How many students like red?

4. How many students like blue better than green?

5. How many students answered the survey?

6. If 3 more students choose red, how should the pictograph change?

Lesson 16.2 (pages 282–283)

Make a pictograph to show the number of students
who buy lunch at Lily Pond Elementary School. Decide
on a symbol and key for the graph. Include a title and
labels.

NUMBER OF SCHOOL LUNCHES BOUGHT	
Day	**Number of Students**
Monday	20
Tuesday	40
Wednesday	10
Thursday	30
Friday	50

Lesson 16.3 (pages 284–285)

For Problems 1–4, use the bar graph.

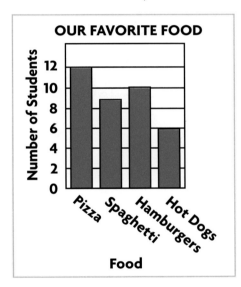

1. What food is liked best by the most
students?

2. How many students like hamburgers
the best?

3. How many more students like spaghetti
better than hot dogs?

4. How many students took part in the food
survey?

Lesson 16.4 (pages 286–287)

Make a bar graph of the data in the table showing how
students get to school. Use a scale numbered by twos
(0, 2, 4, 6, 8, 10). Remember to title and label the graph.

HOW WE GET TO SCHOOL	
Way	**Number of Students**
Bus	9
Car	6
Bicycle	3
Walking	4

Lesson 16.5 Part 1 (pages 288–289)

For Problems 1–3, use the pictograph.

CLASS HAMSTERS

Third Grade	● ● ● ● ● ●
Fourth Grade	● ●
Fifth Grade	● ● ●

Key: Each ● stands for 4 hamsters.

1. Which class has the most hamsters? the fewest?

2. How many hamsters does the fifth grade class have?

3. How many more hamsters does the third-grade class have than the fifth-grade class?

Lesson 16.5 Part 2 (pages 290–291)

For Problems 1–4, use the graph.

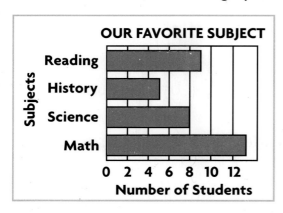

1. What is the favorite subject of the most students?

2. How many more students like reading better than history?

3. How many students voted?

4. How many more students like math better than reading?

CHAPTER 17

Lesson 17.1 (pages 296–297)

Read each event. Tell whether the event is *certain* or *impossible* to happen.

1. You will climb to the moon on a ladder made of cheese.

2. You will pull a circle out of a bag of these figures.

3. The sun will rise tomorrow.

4. Touching an ice cube will make your finger cold.

5. You will not fall asleep during the next week.

Lesson 17.2 Part 1 (pages 298–299)

List the possible outcomes of each event.

1. answering a math problem

2. flipping a coin

Which outcome is most likely to happen?

3. You pull a figure from the bag.

Lesson 17.2 Part 2 (pages 300–301)

Make a list to solve.

1. Kelly and Sandra are doing an experiment. They are spinning the pointer of a spinner and flipping a coin. What are all the possible outcomes for spinning the pointer on this spinner and flipping a coin?

Lesson 17.3 (pages 302–303)

Mr. Ricci's class did an experiment. The students put cubes, marbles, and small rubber balls into a bag. Mr. Ricci pulled one object from the bag, recorded it, and then replaced the object. He pulled 30 times. Use the table to decide which kind of toy is most likely to be pulled in one pull.

MR. RICCI'S BAG	
Object	**Number of Times Pulled**
Rubber Ball	16
Marble	8
Cube	6

Lesson 17.4 (pages 304-305)

Choose the spinner that is fair. Write *A* or *B*.

1.

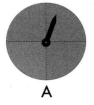

A   B

2.

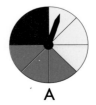

A   B

CHAPTER 18

Lesson 18.1 (pages 316–317)

Name the solid figure that each looks like.

1.

2.

3.

4.

Lesson 18.2 (pages 318–319)

Eric had a box. He cut along the edges of his box and flattened it. Use the picture of the flattened box to answer the questions.

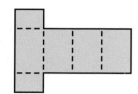

1. How many edges did Eric's box have?

2. How many faces did Eric's box have?

3. Was Eric's box a rectangular prism or a cube?

4. Was his box a solid or a plane figure?

5. How is a rectangular prism different from a cube?

Lesson 18.3 (pages 320–321)

Tell which solid figure has each set of faces. Write *a*, *b*, or *c*.

1.

   a. cube

   b. rectangular prism

   c. square pyramid

2.

   a. rectangular prism

   b. cone

   c. cube

3.

   a. square pyramid

   b. cube

   c. rectangular prism

Lesson 18.4 (pages 322–323)

Tell if each figure is formed by only straight lines, only curved lines, or both straight and curved lines.

1.    **2.**    **3.**

4. Draw a figure that is formed by only curved lines.

5. Draw a figure that is formed by both curved and straight lines.

Lesson 18.5 Part 1 (pages 324–325)

Draw the next two shapes in each pattern.

1.

2.

Tell what shapes are missing in each pattern.

3.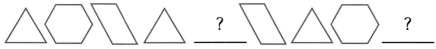

Lesson 18.5 Part 2 (pages 326–327)

Find a pattern to solve.

1. Jerry is playing with her baby brother's blocks. What will be the next three shapes in her pattern?

2. Tito sees a pattern in the set of numbers 9, 12, 15, 18. He wants to write the next three numbers. What numbers will he write?

3. David sees a pattern in the set of numbers 7, 14, 21, 28. He wants to write the next three numbers. What numbers will he write?

CHAPTER 19

Lesson 19.1 (pages 332–333)

Write the number of line segments in each figure.

1.

2.

Write the number of angles in each figure.

3.

4.

Lesson 19.2 (pages 334–335)

Use a grid. Make a map of the garden. Use the ordered pairs below to place flowers on your map. Record the first letter of the flower's name on the correct point.

1. daisies (4,3)

2. roses (2,1)

3. bluebells (1,4)

Lesson 19.3 (pages 336–337)

Tell whether the two figures are congruent. Write *yes* or *no*.

1.

2.

3.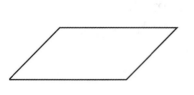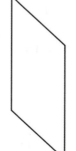

4.

Lesson 19.4 (pages 338–339)

Trace and cut out each figure. Use each cutout figure
to find the number of congruent figures in the design.
Record your findings in a table.

1.   **2.**

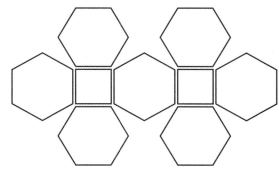

Lesson 19.5 Part 1 (pages 340–341)

For Exercises 1–2, use cubes to build each figure. Tell how
many cubes make up each figure.

1.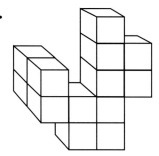

2.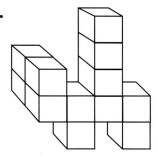

Lesson 19.5 Part 2 (pages 342–343)

Make a list to solve.

1. Jane built a solid figure with
blocks. She used 6 blocks in
the first layer, 2 blocks in the
second layer, 1 block in the
third layer, and 1 block in the
fourth layer. Could the solid
figure below be the one that
Jane built? Explain.

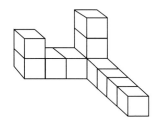

2. Jon and his friend wanted to
build a solid figure using
8 blocks in the first layer,
6 blocks in the second layer,
5 blocks in the third layer,
2 blocks in the fourth layer,
and 1 block in the fifth layer.
Could this be the figure they
built? Explain.

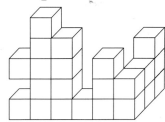

CHAPTER 20

Lesson 20.1 (pages 348–349)

Tell what kind of motion was used to move each plane figure. Write *slide*, *flip*, or *turn*.

1.

2.

3.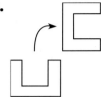

4.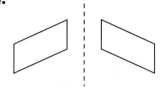

Lesson 20.2 (pages 350–351)

Copy each figure. Write whether it has a line of symmetry. If the answer is *yes*, draw and label the line of symmetry.

1.

2.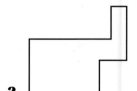

3.

Lesson 20.3 (pages 352–353)

Is the blue line a line of symmetry? Write *yes* or *no*.

1.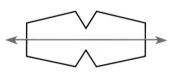

2.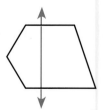

3.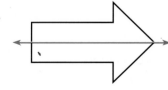

Trace each figure. Draw the line or lines of symmetry. How many lines of symmetry does each figure have?

4.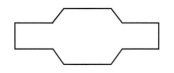

5.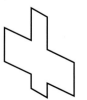

6.

Lesson 20.4 Part 1 (pages 354–355)

Trace and complete each drawing to make a symmetric figure.

1.    **2.** 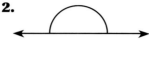   **3.**    **4.**

Lesson 20.4 Part 2 (pages 356–357)

Draw a picture to solve.

1. Mr. Russell is covering a floor with tiles. Each tile is 2 feet square. The floor is 8 feet long and 4 feet wide. How many 2-foot tiles will he use?

2. The school track has 6 sides. Carla starts in the middle of one side. How many corners does she run around before she is where she started?

CHAPTER 21

Lesson 21.1 (pages 368–369)

Tell how many parts make up the whole. Then tell how many parts are shaded.

1.   **2.** 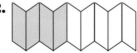   **3.** 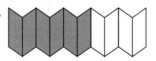   **4.**

Lesson 21.2 (pages 370–373)

Tell the part that is shaded. Write your answer using numbers and words.

1.   **2.**   **3.**

Write the fraction using numbers.

4. four sixths   **5.** seven ninths   **6.** two fourths

7. Write the fraction that names the points on the number line.

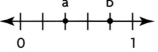

Lesson 21.3 (pages 374–375)

Write a fraction to describe each shaded part.

1.
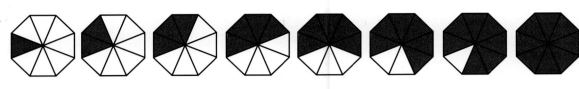

Write a fraction that names the shaded part.

2.   **3.**   **4.**

Lesson 21.4 Part 1 (pages 376–377)

Compare. Write $<$, $>$, or $=$ for ●.

1.

$\frac{1}{6}$	$\frac{1}{6}$	$\frac{1}{6}$

$\frac{1}{4}$	$\frac{1}{4}$	$\frac{1}{4}$

$\frac{3}{6}$ ● $\frac{3}{4}$

2.

$\frac{1}{5}$	$\frac{1}{5}$	$\frac{1}{5}$	$\frac{1}{5}$

$\frac{1}{5}$	$\frac{1}{5}$

$\frac{4}{5}$ ● $\frac{2}{5}$

Lesson 21.4 Part 2 (pages 378–379)

Draw a picture to solve.

1. Genny and Raul each had the same number of blocks. Genny used $\frac{2}{8}$ of her blocks to build a castle. Raul used $\frac{3}{5}$ of his blocks to build a car. Who used more blocks?

2. Ted rode his bike $\frac{3}{4}$ mile. Seema rode her bike $\frac{5}{6}$ mile. Judy rode her bike $\frac{1}{2}$ mile. Who rode the farthest?

Lesson 21.5 (pages 380–381)

Find an equivalent fraction. Use fraction bars to help you.

1. $\frac{6}{8} = \frac{?}{4}$ **2.** $\frac{3}{6} = \frac{?}{2}$ **3.** $\frac{2}{5} = \frac{?}{10}$ **4.** $\frac{1}{2} = \frac{?}{4}$

5. $\frac{2}{6} = \frac{?}{3}$ **6.** $\frac{1}{4} = \frac{?}{8}$ **7.** $\frac{3}{6} = \frac{?}{4}$ **8.** $\frac{4}{5} = \frac{?}{10}$

CHAPTER 22

Lesson 22.1 (pages 386–387)

Use tiles to show equal parts of the group. Draw a picture of your model.

1. Make 5 equal parts, with 1 part green.

2. Make 3 equal parts, with 1 part yellow.

3. Make 7 equal parts, with 1 part purple.

Lesson 22.2 (pages 388–389)

Write the fraction that names the part of the group shown.

1. 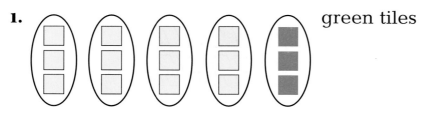 green tiles

2. purple triangles

Draw the picture. Use numbers and words to describe the part that is shaded.

3. Draw 7 rectangles. Shade 1 rectangle.

4. Draw 16 circles. Make 4 equal groups. Shade 1 group.

Lesson 22.3 Part 1 (pages 390–391)

Write a fraction to describe the shaded part.

1.

2.

3.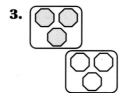

4.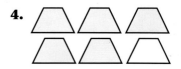

Lesson 22.3 Part 2 (pages 392–393)

Draw a picture to solve.

1. Selene has 30 marbles. She wants to share them equally with herself and 4 of her friends. What part of the marble collection will each friend get? How many marbles will each friend get?

2. Pedro feeds his goldfish 1 ounce of food every day. One package of food lasts a week. How many ounces are in a package? What part of the package do the goldfish eat each day?

Lesson 22.4 (pages 394–395)

Compare the parts of each group that are blue. Write < , > , or = for each ●.

1.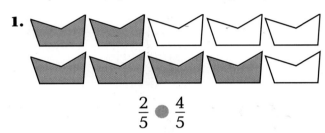

$$\frac{2}{5} \quad ● \quad \frac{4}{5}$$

2.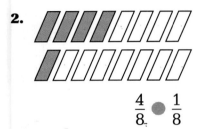

$$\frac{4}{8} \quad ● \quad \frac{1}{8}$$

3.

$$\frac{6}{12} \quad ● \quad \frac{6}{12}$$

CHAPTER 23

Lesson 23.1 (pages 400–401)

Write the decimal and the fraction for the part that is shaded.

1.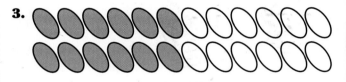

2.

3.

4.

Write each decimal as a fraction.

5. 0.6   6. 0.1   7. 0.3   8. 0.2

9. 0.5   10. 0.8   11. 0.4   12. 0.7

Lesson 23.2 (pages 402–403)

Shade decimal squares to show each amount. Write the
decimal number that names the shaded part.

1. thirty-two hundredths

2. fifteen hundredths

3. ninety-nine hundredths

4. seven hundredths

Lesson 23.3 (pages 404–405)

Record how you read and write the decimal name for
each shaded part.

1.

2.

3.

4.

5.

6.

Lesson 23.4 (pages 406–407)

Write the mixed decimal the model shows.

1.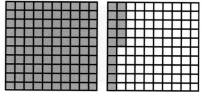

2.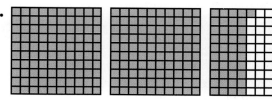

Write as a mixed decimal.

3. four and eight tenths

4. ten and two hundredths

5. eleven and five tenths

6. fifteen and three hundredths

Write each mixed decimal in words.

7. 3.42

8. 16.01

9. 21.55

10. 8.08

11. 6.12

12. 20.01

13. 13.51

14. 36.06

Lesson 23.5 Part 1 (pages 408–409)

Compare. Use < or > for each ●.

1.

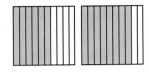

0.6 ● 0.8

2.

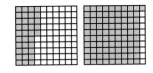

0.35 ● 0.91

3.

Ones	Tenths
0	8
0	6

0.8 ● 0.6

4.

Ones	Tenths
1	9
1	5

1.9 ● 1.5

Lesson 23.5 Part 2 (pages 410–411)

Draw a picture to solve.

1. Shana and her sister, Shari, are sharing crayons. Shana has $\frac{3}{5}$ of the crayons and Shari has $\frac{2}{5}$ of the crayons. Which sister has more crayons?

2. Kevin swam 1.4 miles on Monday and 3.2 miles on Wednesday. On which day did he swim farther?

CHAPTER 24

Lesson 24.1 (pages 422–423)

Choose the unit that you would use to measure each. Write *inch, foot, yard* or *mile*.

1. the distance between your bedroom and your kitchen

2. the distance between your school and your house

3. the length of your finger

4. the height of your desk

Lesson 24.2 (pages 424–425)

Estimate the length of each key. Then use a ruler to measure to the nearest inch.

1.

2.

Lesson 24.3 Part 1 (pages 426–427)

Measure the length to the nearest half inch.

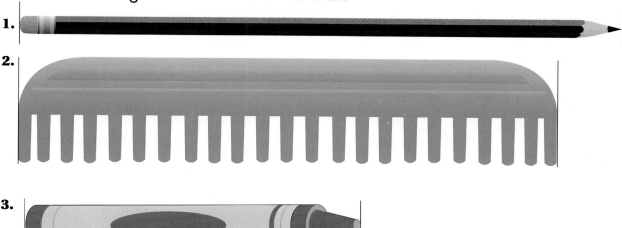

1.

2.

3.

Lesson 24.3 Part 2 (pages 428–429)

Make a model to solve.

1. Kisha's desk is 2 yards from the door. Lola's desk is 3 times as far from the door. How far is Lola's desk from the door?

2. Ricki wants to tile a wall that is 8 feet tall. He has 32 one-foot-square tiles. How many feet wide can the tiled part of the wall be?

3. Cathy and June have 14 gerbils. Cathy has 2 more gerbils than June. How many gerbils does each girl have?

4. Tim has 14 cubes in his train. There are 4 more red cubes than green cubes. How many cubes of each color are there?

Lesson 24.4 (pages 430–431)

Choose the unit that you would use to measure each. Write *cup, pint, quart,* or *gallon.*

1. the water in a swimming pool

2. a glass of juice

3. half-and-half cream

4. juice in a juice box

5. a large container of milk

6. a container of yogurt

Write the greater amount.

7. 5 pints or 2 quarts

8. 1 gallon or 6 quarts

9. 3 cups or 1 pint

10. 6 cups or 6 quarts

11. 3 quarts or 5 pints

12. 4 gallons or 4 pints

Lesson 24.5 (pages 432–433)

Choose the unit that you would use to weigh each.
Write *ounce* or *pound*.

1. feathers
2. cookie
3. jar of cookies
4. dog

Choose the better estimate.

5. a banana

    3 ounces
    or 3 pounds

6. a cat

    10 ounces
    or 10 pounds

7. a skateboard

    5 ounces
    or 5 pounds

CHAPTER 25

Lesson 25.1 (pages 438–439)

Choose the unit that you would use to measure each.
Write *cm, dm,* or *m.*

1. a paper clip
2. the length of your backpack
3. the length of a soccer field
4. a hairbrush

Choose the unit that was used to measure each.
Write *cm, dm,* or *m.*

5. Manuel can swim 100 _?_ in 2 minutes.

6. Fara's rabbit's ears are 12 _?_ long.

7. Todd's sneakers are 28 _?_ long.

8. Jody's baseball bat is 7 _?_ long.

9. Matt's fishing pole is 2 _?_ long.

10. Mia's skateboard is about 4 _?_ long.

Lesson 25.2 (pages 440–441)

List two things that measure about as long as these measurements.

1. 5 centimeters
2. 15 decimeters
3. 3 meters
4. 10 meters
5. 2 decimeters
6. 30 meters
7. 2 centimeters
8. 1 meter
9. 20 centimeters

Lesson 25.3 Part 1 (pages 442–443)

Draw a line of the given length.

1. 3 cm

2. 9 cm

3. 27 cm

4. 19 cm

5. 12 cm

6. 16 cm

Lesson 25.3 Part 2 (pages 444–445)

Work backward to solve.

1. Donna likes to watch the rabbits at the park. She saw 18 black rabbits and 23 brown rabbits. There are 55 rabbits in all. How many of the rabbits are not black or brown?

2. Luis is painting a 20-yard pole. He painted 6 yards yesterday and 9 yards today. How many yards will he have to paint tomorrow to finish painting the pole?

3. Darrell rode his bike 5 miles uphill and 4 miles downhill. He rode 13 miles in all. How many of the miles were not uphill or downhill?

4. Jeremy had 15 friends over for a party. During the party, 8 of his friends were swimming and 4 were playing cards. How many of his friends were not swimming or playing cards?

Lesson 25.4 (pages 446–447)

Choose the unit you would use to measure each.
Write *mL* or *L*.

1. a can of soda

2. a squirt bottle of soap

3. a small pool

4. a large bottle of water

5. water in a bucket

6. juice in a cup

7. glue in a bottle

8. water in a fish tank

9. drop of rain

Lesson 25.5 (pages 448–449)

Choose the unit you would use to measure each.
Write *g* or *kg*.

1. a light bulb

2. a car

3. a bicycle

4. a teddy bear

5. a letter

6. a suitcase

7. a button

8. a dictionary

9. a watermelon

CHAPTER 26

Lesson 26.1 (pages 454–455)

Find the perimeter of each figure in cubes.

1.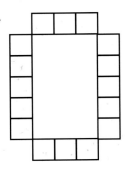

2.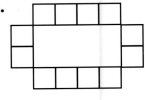

3.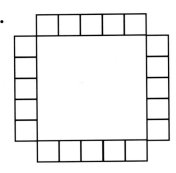

Lesson 26.2 (pages 456–457)

Use your centimeter ruler to measure. Find the perimeter of each figure.

1.

2.

Find the perimeter of each figure.

3.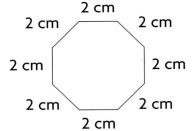

2 cm
2 cm   2 cm
2 cm   2 cm
2 cm   2 cm
2 cm   2 cm
2 cm

4.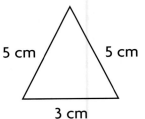

5 cm   5 cm
3 cm

5.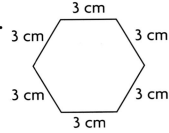

3 cm
3 cm   3 cm
3 cm   3 cm
3 cm

Lesson 26.3 (pages 458–459)

Use square tiles to make each figure. Draw the figures. Write the area in square units.

1. 7 rows of tiles, 3 tiles in each row

2. 4 rows of tiles, 8 tiles in each row

Find the area of each figure. Label the answer in square units.

3.

4.

5.

Lesson 26.4 Part 1 (pages 460–461)

Find the area and perimeter of the figure.

1.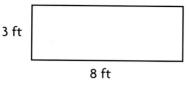

3 ft

8 ft

2.

10 ft

1 ft

3.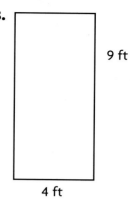

9 ft

4 ft

Lesson 26.4 Part 2 (pages 462–463)

Act it out to solve.

1. Ms. Brugler wants to put a fence around the edge of her rectangular garden. The garden is 8 feet long and 4 feet wide. How many feet of fence does Ms. Brugler need?

2. Balanca wants pink carpet in her bedroom. Her room is a square, 9 feet on one side. How much carpet does Balanca need?

3. Ahmit wants to put wallpaper on a wall. The wall is 8 feet tall and 6 feet wide. How much wallpaper does Ahmit need? He also wants to put a border all around the edge of the wall. How many feet will he need of the border?

CHAPTER 27

Lesson 27.1 Part 1 (pages 474–475)

Put the tens and ones together. Name the factors of the new rectangle.

1.

2.

Draw each array on grid paper. Show how you found the product.

3. $3 \times 16 =$ __?__

4. $8 \times 11 =$ __?__

5. $2 \times 13 =$ __?__

6. $4 \times 15 =$ __?__

7. $4 \times 12 =$ __?__

8. $3 \times 14 =$ __?__

Lesson 27.1 Part 2 (pages 476–477)

Make a model to solve.

1. Joanne put her books into a bookcase. She put 16 books on each shelf. The bookcase had 7 shelves. How many books did Joanne have?

2. Mr. Ivey's third-grade class had its picture taken. For the picture, 13 students stood in each row. There were 3 rows. How many students are in Mr. Ivey's class?

Lesson 27.2 (pages 478–479)

Use base-ten blocks to find each product.

1. Warren and two of his friends are sharing building blocks. Each one has 25 blocks. How many blocks do they have in all?

2. A squirrel family is saving nuts for the winter. There are 5 squirrels in the family. Each squirrel finds 42 nuts. How many nuts does the family have?

3. $5 \times 16 = $?

4. $8 \times 22 = $?

5. $3 \times 36 = $?

6. $6 \times 24 = $?

7. $7 \times 41 = $?

8. $8 \times 27 = $?

Lesson 27.3 (pages 480–481)

Find each product. Use base-ten blocks to help you.

1. $\begin{array}{r} 32 \\ \times\ 4 \\ \hline \end{array}$

2. $\begin{array}{r} 11 \\ \times\ 7 \\ \hline \end{array}$

3. $\begin{array}{r} 25 \\ \times\ 5 \\ \hline \end{array}$

4. $\begin{array}{r} 37 \\ \times\ 4 \\ \hline \end{array}$

5. $\begin{array}{r} 18 \\ \times\ 9 \\ \hline \end{array}$

6. $\begin{array}{r} 54 \\ \times\ 5 \\ \hline \end{array}$

7. $\begin{array}{r} 79 \\ \times\ 2 \\ \hline \end{array}$

8. $\begin{array}{r} 52 \\ \times\ 6 \\ \hline \end{array}$

9. $\begin{array}{r} 14 \\ \times\ 6 \\ \hline \end{array}$

10. $\begin{array}{r} 29 \\ \times\ 4 \\ \hline \end{array}$

11. $\begin{array}{r} 23 \\ \times\ 2 \\ \hline \end{array}$

12. $\begin{array}{r} 31 \\ \times\ 5 \\ \hline \end{array}$

13. $\begin{array}{r} 33 \\ \times\ 4 \\ \hline \end{array}$

14. $\begin{array}{r} 71 \\ \times\ 5 \\ \hline \end{array}$

15. $\begin{array}{r} 52 \\ \times\ 4 \\ \hline \end{array}$

16. $\begin{array}{r} 83 \\ \times\ 2 \\ \hline \end{array}$

17. $\begin{array}{r} 16 \\ \times\ 5 \\ \hline \end{array}$

18. $\begin{array}{r} 35 \\ \times\ 2 \\ \hline \end{array}$

19. $\begin{array}{r} 28 \\ \times\ 3 \\ \hline \end{array}$

20. $\begin{array}{r} 49 \\ \times\ 6 \\ \hline \end{array}$

21. $\begin{array}{r} 57 \\ \times\ 6 \\ \hline \end{array}$

22. $\begin{array}{r} 39 \\ \times\ 4 \\ \hline \end{array}$

23. $\begin{array}{r} 62 \\ \times\ 5 \\ \hline \end{array}$

24. $\begin{array}{r} 71 \\ \times\ 7 \\ \hline \end{array}$

Lesson 27.4 (pages 482–483)

Find the product. Use base-ten blocks to help you.

1. $95 \times 3 = $?
2. $24 \times 6 = $?
3. $69 \times 4 = $?
4. $23 \times 8 = $?

CHAPTER 28

Lesson 28.1 (pages 488–489)

Use counters to find the quotient and remainder.

1. $25 \div 4 = $?
2. $42 \div 5 = $?
3. $41 \div 7 = $?
4. $86 \div 9 = $?
5. $52 \div 7 = $?
6. $37 \div 4 = $?

Lesson 28.2 (pages 490–491)

Use the model to find the quotient and remainder.

1. $34 \div 4 = $?

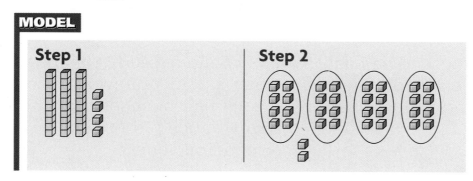

2. $67 \div 7 = $?

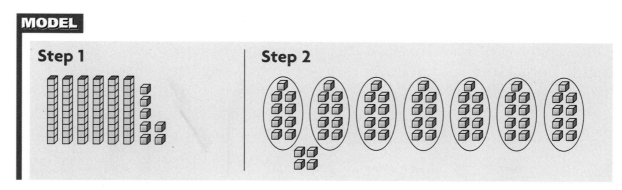

Lesson 28.3 (pages 492–493)

Find the quotient. Show the division problem on paper.
Then check each answer.

1. $38 \div 7 = $?
2. $49 \div 5 = $?
3. $18 \div 3 = $?
4. $55 \div 9 = $?
5. $37 \div 4 = $?
6. $49 \div 8 = $?

Lesson 28.4 (pages 494–495)

Find the quotient, using only paper and pencil. Check
each answer by using multiplication.

1. $59 \div 8 =$ __?__

2. $43 \div 6 =$ __?__

3. $31 \div 5 =$ __?__

4. $68 \div 8 =$ __?__

5. $20 \div 4 =$ __?__

6. $19 \div 2 =$ __?__.

7. $44 \div 5 =$ __?__

8. $62 \div 7 =$ __?__

9. $37 \div 4 =$ __?__

10. $33 \div 2 =$ __?__

11. $79 \div 6 =$ __?__

12. $92 \div 8 =$ __?__

Lesson 28.5 Part 1 (pages 496–497)

Decide whether to multiply or divide. Solve each problem.

1. Mr. Sherard bought a box of 12 doughnuts for his children. He has 4 children. Each child ate the same number of doughnuts. How many doughnuts did each child eat?

2. Brett has 3 dogs. He spends $21 each week on dog food. Each dog eats the same amount. How much does Brett spend on each dog per week?

3. Devon plays 3 sports. She has 3 uniforms for each sport. How many uniforms does she have?

4. Michelle saved her money to buy 2 pairs of new shoes. Each pair of shoes costs $15. How much did Michelle spend on shoes?

Lesson 28.5 Part 2 (pages 498–499)

Write a number sentence to solve.

1. Mrs. Fathid has 3 flower beds. There are 32 flowers in each bed. How many flowers does Mrs. Fathid have?

2. After the party, Victor and his 3 sisters had 38 pieces of candy. They divided the candy equally. How many pieces of candy did each person have? Was there any candy left over?

3. Carlos wants to give each of his friends a card for Valentine's Day. Each card costs $1. Carlos has 6 friends. How much will he spend?

4. Mr. Ling has 88 crayons. Each student in his class will get 4 crayons. How many students does Mr. Ling have in his class?

Be a Good TEST TAKER

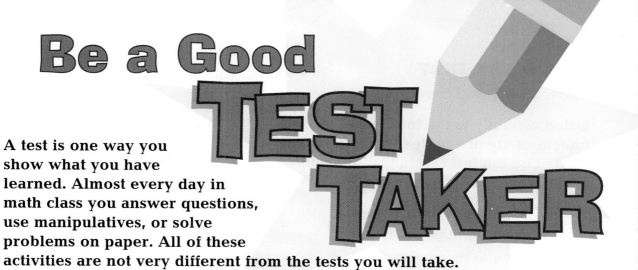

A test is one way you show what you have learned. Almost every day in math class you answer questions, use manipulatives, or solve problems on paper. All of these activities are not very different from the tests you will take. So, you are getting ready for tests every day.

THE TIPS ON THESE PAGES WILL HELP YOU BECOME A BETTER TEST TAKER.

GETTING READY FOR A TEST

What you do at home the night before the test and the morning of the test is very important. Follow these tips:

- GET A GOOD NIGHT'S SLEEP.

- EAT A GOOD BREAKFAST.

- DO NOT WORRY AND GET UPSET.

- DO THE VERY BEST YOU CAN DURING THE TEST.

TAKING THE TEST

Understand the Directions

Listen carefully to the teacher when the directions are given. Read the directions printed on the test carefully. Ask yourself these questions:

- Do I have pencils and a good eraser?
- Can I write on the test itself?
- Do I have to mark an answer sheet?
- How many questions are on the test?
- How long can I work on the test?

**Ask your teacher for help if you do not understand the directions.
Follow all test directions carefully.**

Answer the Questions

Read each question slowly.

If you don't know a word, try to figure it out by reading the rest of the sentence or problem.

Some questions have answer choices. Follow these tips to help you choose the correct answer:

- Read the question carefully.

- Study each answer choice.

- Cross out the answers that look wrong to you.

- Then choose the correct one from the answer choices you did not cross out.

- Skip the question if all the answers seem right to you.

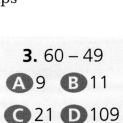

3. 60 − 49

A 9   **B** 11

C 21   **D** 109

Answer A could not be right because the difference between 60 and 49 is more than 10. Answer D could not be right because the problem is subtraction. The answer must be less than 60. Answer B is correct because you have to regroup 6 tens 0 ones as 5 tens 10 ones. So, the answer is 11, not 21.

Mark Your Answers

Sometimes you will use a separate answer sheet. This answer sheet may be scored by a machine. You must mark only in the space for the answer you choose.

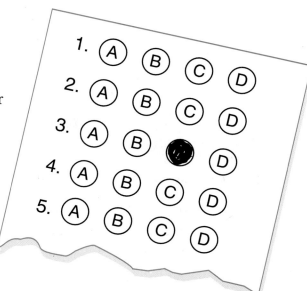

Study the answer sheet carefully. Find out which way the numbers go. Sometimes the numbers go down a column. Sometimes the numbers go across the answer sheet.

Keep your place on the answer sheet. Make sure you mark the answer for each question on a choice for the right question number.

Erase an answer cleanly if you want to change it.

Keep Track of Time

Some tests you take will be timed tests. Your teacher will tell you how long you have to finish the test.

Your teacher will tell you how much time you have left as you are taking the test.

If you don't have many minutes left, try to work faster. But don't work so fast that you make careless mistakes.

If you know that you can't answer all the questions that are left, look at them to find the easiest ones. Answer those and skip the rest.

REVIEWING YOUR RESULTS

If you finish before the time is up, look over your answer sheet. Erase any stray marks you see.

Use any time you have left to check your answers.

Be sure that you have marked each answer in the correct place on the answer sheet.

YOU CAN BE A
GOOD TEST TAKER.
REMEMBER THESE TIPS.
THEY WILL HELP YOU DO
WELL ON EVERY TEST!

"WE ARE GOOD TEST TAKERS."

ADDITION FACTS TEST

	K	L	M	N	O	P	Q	R
A	3 + 8	2 + 9	6 + 4	8 + 7	3 + 4	7 + 7	1 + 8	4 + 5
B	4 + 9	9 + 2	7 + 5	6 + 0	9 + 3	5 + 4	6 + 3	9 + 7
C	8 + 8	1 + 9	6 + 2	5 + 8	8 + 0	7 + 6	7 + 1	6 + 9
D	5 + 5	4 + 3	9 + 4	8 + 6	6 + 5	0 + 9	5 + 6	7 + 9
E	4 + 7	9 + 1	8 + 5	7 + 0	7 + 2	8 + 3	4 + 8	7 + 3
F	5 + 2	6 + 8	1 + 7	2 + 3	4 + 4	5 + 3	9 + 9	3 + 6
G	0 + 8	7 + 4	8 + 2	1 + 6	8 + 4	5 + 1	3 + 3	2 + 7
H	9 + 8	2 + 6	9 + 5	8 + 1	3 + 9	5 + 7	4 + 2	6 + 6
I	3 + 7	7 + 8	9 + 0	4 + 6	2 + 8	6 + 7	9 + 6	3 + 5
J	0 + 7	8 + 9	2 + 5	6 + 1	5 + 9	2 + 4	0 + 6	3 + 2

SUBTRACTION FACTS TEST

	K	L	M	N	O	P	Q	R
A	16 − 7	9 − 0	14 − 8	8 − 3	12 − 5	5 − 5	17 − 8	12 − 7
B	13 − 8	8 − 6	9 − 4	6 − 2	12 − 6	14 − 7	10 − 6	7 − 4
C	8 − 2	13 − 7	9 − 8	15 − 9	5 − 4	14 − 5	9 − 3	11 − 6
D	10 − 8	5 − 3	11 − 4	8 − 0	14 − 6	6 − 6	10 − 7	12 − 4
E	11 − 3	14 − 9	10 − 5	12 − 9	13 − 5	7 − 6	12 − 3	11 − 2
F	7 − 5	13 − 6	8 − 4	15 − 7	11 − 8	9 − 6	6 − 0	17 − 9
G	10 − 9	7 − 3	11 − 9	16 − 9	8 − 5	10 − 3	7 − 7	9 − 2
H	18 − 9	15 − 8	8 − 1	12 − 8	9 − 5	11 − 7	8 − 7	15 − 6
I	6 − 5	16 − 8	8 − 8	10 − 2	6 − 3	9 − 7	11 − 5	7 − 1
J	13 − 4	9 − 9	7 − 0	13 − 9	7 − 2	6 − 4	10 − 4	9 − 1

MULTIPLICATION FACTS TEST

	K	L	M	N	O	P	Q	R
A	6 ×2	6 ×5	8 ×7	9 ×0	5 ×8	2 ×8	9 ×9	6 ×7
B	8 ×8	9 ×1	4 ×9	5 ×6	5 ×2	8 ×4	0 ×5	5 ×4
C	9 ×5	4 ×8	2 ×6	8 ×9	8 ×0	9 ×6	3 ×3	5 ×7
D	5 ×5	6 ×4	8 ×5	4 ×2	7 ×3	0 ×8	3 ×4	8 ×6
E	4 ×7	7 ×8	2 ×4	3 ×7	7 ×2	7 ×4	3 ×9	3 ×6
F	3 ×8	7 ×1	1 ×5	5 ×3	6 ×0	2 ×9	7 ×6	1 ×9
G	6 ×9	4 ×3	7 ×9	2 ×5	9 ×7	1 ×7	9 ×4	0 ×7
H	4 ×4	9 ×8	1 ×6	3 ×2	4 ×6	0 ×9	3 ×5	6 ×8
I	6 ×3	7 ×0	5 ×1	4 ×5	6 ×1	2 ×3	7 ×5	2 ×2
J	5 ×9	7 ×7	9 ×3	8 ×3	9 ×2	6 ×6	0 ×6	2 ×7

DIVISION FACTS TEST

	K	L	M	N	O	P	Q	R
A	$9\overline{)45}$	$6\overline{)42}$	$6\overline{)12}$	$8\overline{)64}$	$1\overline{)9}$	$5\overline{)0}$	$8\overline{)16}$	$1\overline{)8}$
B	$6\overline{)6}$	$7\overline{)35}$	$5\overline{)15}$	$6\overline{)18}$	$8\overline{)72}$	$2\overline{)6}$	$2\overline{)18}$	$7\overline{)56}$
C	$9\overline{)81}$	$4\overline{)16}$	$1\overline{)7}$	$7\overline{)21}$	$2\overline{)8}$	$9\overline{)54}$	$1\overline{)3}$	$5\overline{)45}$
D	$2\overline{)10}$	$4\overline{)28}$	$8\overline{)0}$	$9\overline{)36}$	$4\overline{)20}$	$9\overline{)72}$	$3\overline{)27}$	$9\overline{)27}$
E	$7\overline{)49}$	$2\overline{)12}$	$8\overline{)40}$	$5\overline{)10}$	$8\overline{)48}$	$1\overline{)4}$	$5\overline{)35}$	$4\overline{)12}$
F	$3\overline{)9}$	$6\overline{)36}$	$4\overline{)4}$	$8\overline{)24}$	$2\overline{)14}$	$8\overline{)32}$	$1\overline{)5}$	$7\overline{)63}$
G	$5\overline{)25}$	$4\overline{)36}$	$9\overline{)18}$	$3\overline{)6}$	$7\overline{)14}$	$4\overline{)24}$	$5\overline{)20}$	$3\overline{)0}$
H	$7\overline{)28}$	$3\overline{)18}$	$6\overline{)54}$	$7\overline{)0}$	$4\overline{)8}$	$6\overline{)48}$	$4\overline{)32}$	$9\overline{)9}$
I	$3\overline{)15}$	$9\overline{)63}$	$3\overline{)21}$	$2\overline{)16}$	$5\overline{)30}$	$7\overline{)42}$	$6\overline{)30}$	$6\overline{)18}$
J	$6\overline{)24}$	$3\overline{)24}$	$8\overline{)56}$	$3\overline{)12}$	$5\overline{)40}$	$1\overline{)6}$	$2\overline{)4}$	$1\overline{)1}$

TABLE OF MEASURES

METRIC	CUSTOMARY
Length	
1 centimeter (cm) = 10 millimeters (mm)	1 foot (ft) = 12 inches (in.)
1 decimeter (dm) = 10 centimeters	1 yard (yd) = 3 feet, or 36 inches
1 meter (m) = 100 centimeters	1 mile (mi) = 1,760 yards, or 5,280 feet
1 kilometer (km) = 1,000 meters	
Weight	
1 kilogram (kg) = 1,000 grams (g)	1 pound (lb) = 16 ounces (oz)
Capacity	
1 liter (L) = 1,000 milliliters (mL)	1 pint (pt) = 2 cups (c)
	1 quart (qt) = 2 pints
	1 gallon (gal) = 4 quarts

TIME

1 minute (min) = 60 seconds (sec)	1 week (wk) = 7 days
1 hour (hr) = 60 minutes	1 year (yr) = 12 months (mo), or
1 day = 24 hours	52 weeks, or 365 days

MONEY

1 penny = 1 cent (¢)	1 quarter = 25 cents
1 nickel = 5 cents	1 half dollar = 50 cents
1 dime = 10 cents	1 dollar ($) = 100 cents

SYMBOLS

$<$ is less than	°F degrees Fahrenheit
$>$ is greater than	°C degrees Celsius
$=$ is equal to	

GLOSSARY

addend Any of the numbers that are added *(page 2)*
Example: $2 + 3 = 5$
The addends are 2 and 3.

addition The process of finding the total number of items when two groups of items are joined; the opposite operation of subtraction *(page 2)*

analog clock A clock that shows time on the hour when the minute hand is on the 12 *(page 76)*

angle A figure formed where two line segments cross or meet *(page 332)*
Example:

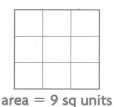

area The number of square units needed to cover the surface of a figure *(page 458)*
Example:

area = 9 sq units

array An arrangement that shows objects in rows and columns *(pages 206, H28, H56)*
Example:

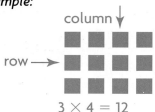

column ↓
row →

$3 \times 4 = 12$

bar graph A way to show information that uses bars to stand for data *(page 284)*
Example:

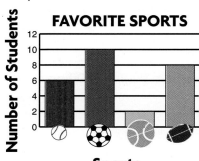

FAVORITE SPORTS
Number of Students
Sports

benchmark number Numbers like 10, 25, 50, or 100 that are used to help make estimates *(page 136)*

capacity The amount a container can hold when filled *(pages 430, 446)*

cardinal number A number that tells how many items are in a group *(page 128)*

centimeter (cm) A metric unit that is used to measure length;
100 centimeters = 1 meter *(page 438)*
Example:

1 cm

certain Something that will always happen *(page 296)*

closed figure A figure that begins and ends at the same point *(page 322)*
Examples:

cone A solid, pointed figure that has a flat, round base *(page 316)*
Example:

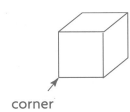

congruent figures Figures that are the same size and shape *(page 336)*
Example:

corner The place where 2 or more edges meet *(page 316)*
Example:

corner

counting back The way to find the difference when you subtract 1, 2, or 3 *(page 10)*
Example: $7 - 3 = \underline{?}$
Count: 7 ... 6, 5, 4

counting on The way to find the sum when one of the addends is 1, 2, or 3 *(page 2)*
Example: $4 + 2 = \underline{?}$
Count: 4 ... 5, 6

counting up The way to find the difference by beginning with the smaller number *(page 10)*
Example: $6 - 3 = \underline{?}$
Count: 3 ... 4, 5, 6

cube A solid figure with six congruent square faces *(page 316)*
Example:

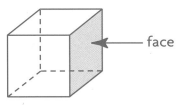

face

cup (c) A customary unit used to measure capacity *(page 430)*
Example:

cylinder A solid or hollow object that is shaped like a can *(page 316)*
Example:

D

data Information collected about people or things *(page 266)*

decimal A number that uses place value and a decimal point to show tenths, hundredths, and so on *(page 400)*

decimal point A period that separates the whole numbers from the fractional part of a number; or that separates dollars from cents *(pages 106, 404)*
Example:

0.1

decimal point

decimeter A metric unit that is used to measure length;
10 decimeters = 1 meter
(page 438)

denominator The number below the bar in a fraction. It tells the total number of equal parts or groups into which the whole or group has been divided. *(page 370)*

Example: $\frac{3}{4}$ ← denominator

difference The answer in a subtraction problem *(page 10)*
Example: $8 - 5 = 3$ ← difference

digit Any one of the ten symbols 0, 1, 2, 3, 4, 5, 6, 7, 8, or 9 used to write numbers *(page 144)*

digital clock A clock that shows time on the hour when the minutes show 00 *(page 76)*

dividend The number that is to be divided in a division problem *(page 230)*
Example: $35 \div 5$
The dividend is 35.

division The process of sharing a number of items to find how many groups can be made or how many items will be in a group; the opposite operation of multiplication *(page 228)*

divisor The number that divides the dividend *(page 230)*
Example: $18 \div 3$
The divisor is 3.

doubles When both addends are the same number *(page 4)*

doubles minus one When one addend is one less than the other *(page 4)*

doubles plus one When one addend is one more than the other *(page 4)*

E ▶

edge The line segment where two faces of a solid figure meet *(page 316)*
Example:

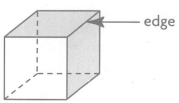

elapsed time The time that passes from the start of an activity to the end of that activity *(page 90)*

equally likely Outcomes that have the same chance of happening *(page H42)*

equivalent Two or more sets that name the same amount *(page 108)*

equivalent fractions Two or more fractions that name the same amount *(page 380)*
Example:

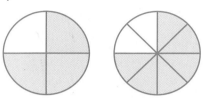

$\frac{3}{4}$ and $\frac{6}{8}$ name the same amount.

estimate Rounding numbers to find *about* how many *(page 24)*

even number A whole number that has 0, 2, 4, 6, or 8 in the ones place *(page 132)*

event The action that happens in an experiment that brings about an outcome *(page 296)*

expanded form A way to write numbers by showing the value of each digit *(page 144)*
Example: $241 = 200 + 40 + 1$

experiment A test that is done in order to find out something *(page 268)*

F ▶

face A flat surface of a solid figure *(page 316)*
Example:

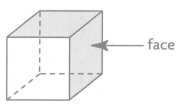

fact family A set of related addition and subtraction or multiplication and division number sentences *(pages 12, 232)*
Examples:

$$2 + 4 = 6 \qquad 6 - 4 = 2$$
$$4 + 2 = 6 \qquad 6 - 2 = 4$$
$$\text{or } 3 \times 6 = 18 \qquad 18 \div 6 = 3$$
$$6 \times 3 = 18 \qquad 18 \div 3 = 6$$

factor A number that is multiplied by another number to find a product *(page 188)*
Example: $4 \times 7 = 28$
The factors are 4 and 7.

fair When every outcome has an equal chance of happening *(page 304)*

flip A move that involves flipping a figure across a line *(page 348)*
Example:

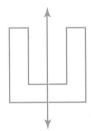

foot (ft) A customary unit used to measure length or distance
1 foot = 12 inches
(page 422)

fraction A number that names part of a whole or part of a group *(page 370)*
Examples:

$$\frac{1}{3}$$

frequency table A way to organize data that uses numbers to show how often something happens *(page 266)*

G

gallon (gal) A customary unit used to measure capacity *(page 430)*

gram (g) A metric unit that is used to measure mass. A paper clip has a mass of about 1 gram. *(page 448)*

greater than (>) A symbol used to compare two numbers, with the greater number given first *(page 164)*
Example: $8 > 6$

grid A map divided into equally spaced squares *(page 334)*
Example:

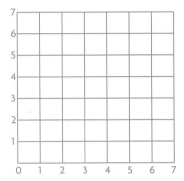

H

horizontal bar graph A bar graph that has bars going across from left to right *(page 284)*

hours (hr) Hours measure long amounts of time. An hour is made up of 60 minutes. There are 24 hours in one day. *(page 78)*

hour hand The short hand on a clock *(page 76)*
Example:

hundredth One of one hundred equal parts *(page 402)*
Example:

I ◤

impossible Something that will never happen *(page 296)*

inch (in.) A customary unit used to measure length *(page 422)*
Example:

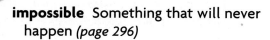

interval The distance between two numbers on the scale of a graph *(page 503)*

inverse operations Operations that undo each other. Addition and subtraction are opposite operations, and so are multiplication and division. *(page 230)*
Examples:
$5 + 4 = 9$, so $9 - 4 = 5$.
$6 \times 3 = 18$, so $18 \div 3 = 6$.

K ◤

key Used on a pictograph to tell how many each picture stands for *(page 280)*

kilogram (kg) A metric unit that is used to measure mass;
1,000 grams = 1 kilogram
(page 448)

L ◤

least likely An event that has a lesser chance of happening compared to other events *(page 298)*

less than (<) A symbol used to compare two numbers, with the lesser number given first *(page 164)*
Example: $6 < 8$

line A straight path extending in both directions with no endpoints *(page 332)*
Example:

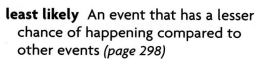

line of symmetry A line that divides a figure into two congruent parts *(page 350)*
Example:

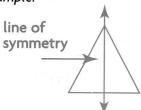
line of symmetry

line segment Part of a line, with two endpoints *(page 332)*
Example:

liter (L) A metric unit that is used to measure capacity;
1,000 milliliters = 1 liter
(page 446)

M ◤

make a ten The way to find the sum when one of the addends is close to 10 *(page 2)*
Example: $9 + 6 = \underline{?}$
$9 + 1 = 10$ and $10 + 5 = 15$

mass The amount of matter in an object. Matter is what all objects are made of. *(page 448)*

meter (m) A metric unit that is used to measure length or distance;
100 centimeters = 1 meter
(page 438)

mile (mi) A customary unit used to measure length or distance;
1 mile = 5,280 feet
(page 422)

milliliter (mL) A metric unit that is used to measure capacity. A small spoon holds about 5 milliliters. *(page 446)*

minutes (min) Minutes measure short amounts of time. There are 60 minutes in one hour. *(page 78)*

minute hand The long hand on a clock *(page 76)*
Example:

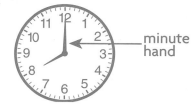
minute hand

mixed decimal A number that is made up of a whole number and a decimal *(page 406)* *Example:* 3.7

mixed number A number that has a whole number and a fraction *(page H48)* *Example:* $2\frac{1}{2}$

most likely An event that has a greater chance of happening compared to other events *(page 298)*

multiplication The process of finding the total number of items made up of equal-size groups, or of finding the total number of items in a given number of groups. Each group contains the same number of items. It is the opposite operation of division. *(page 188)*

number line A line with equally spaced ticks named by numbers *(page 24)*

Example:

numerator The number above the bar in a fraction. It tells how many of the equal parts of the whole or group are being considered. *(page 370)*

Example: $\frac{2}{3}$ ← numerator

odd number A whole number that has 1, 3, 5, 7, or 9 in the ones place *(page 132)*

open figure A figure that does not begin and end at the same point *(page H24)* *Examples:*

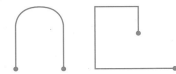

opposite operations Operations that undo each other. Addition and subtraction are opposite operations, and so are multiplication and division. *(page 12)*
Examples: $6 + 3 = 9$, so $9 - 3 = 6$.
$9 \times 3 = 27$, so $27 \div 3 = 9$.

Order Property of Multiplication Two numbers can be multiplied in any order and the product is the same *(page 192)*
Example: $3 \times 2 = 6$
$2 \times 3 = 6$

ordered pair A pair of numbers used to locate a point on a grid. The first number tells the left-right position and the second number tells the up-down position. *(page 334)*

ordinal number A number telling order or position *(page 128)*
Examples: first, second

ounce (oz) A customary unit used to measure weight *(page 432)*

perimeter The distance around a figure *(page 454)*
Example:

pictograph A graph that uses pictures to show and compare information *(page 280)*
Example:

HOW WE GET TO SCHOOL	
Walk	✺✺✺
Ride a Bike	✺✺✺✺✺
Ride a Bus	✺✺✺✺✺✺
Ride in a Car	✺✺
Key: Each ✺ = 10 students.	

pint (pt) A customary unit used to measure capacity *(page 430)*

plane A flat surface that goes on and on *(page 322)*
Example:

part of a plane

plane figure A closed figure in a plane that is formed by lines that are curved, straight, or both *(page 322)*
Example:

point symmetry When a figure can be turned about a central point and still look the same *(page H46)*
Example:

possible outcome Something that has a chance of happening in an experiment *(page 298)*

pound (lb) A customary unit used to measure weight *(page 432)*

product The answer in a multiplication problem *(page 188)*
Example: $6 \times 2 = 12$
The product is 12.

quart (qt) A customary unit used to measure capacity *(page 430)*

quotient The answer in a division problem *(page 230)*
Example: $27 \div 3 = 9$
The quotient is 9.

rectangle A plane figure with opposite sides that are equal and four right angles *(pages 320, 332)*

rectangular prism A solid figure in which all six faces are rectangles *(page 316)*
Example:

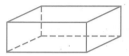

regroup To exchange amounts of equal value to rename a number *(page 32)*
Example: 23 = 2 tens 3 ones
or 1 ten 13 ones

remainder The number that is left over after dividing *(page 488)*
Example:

$$5)\overline{19} \quad 3 \text{ r}4 \leftarrow \text{remainder}$$

results Data from conducting a survey or an experiment *(page 272)*

right angle A right angle is a special angle. The corners of a sheet of paper are at right angles. *(page 332)*
Example:

round When you round a number to the nearest ten, you find the ten that is closest. *(page 24)*

sames Two numbers that are alike. When you subtract sames, the difference is zero. *(page 10)*

scale The numbers on a bar graph that help you read the number each bar shows *(page 284)*

schedule A table that lists activities and the times they happen *(page 92)*

slide A movement of a figure to a new position without turning or flipping it *(page 348)*
Example:

sphere Any round object whose curved surface is the same distance from the center to all its points *(page 316)*
Example:

square A plane figure with four equal sides and four right angles *(pages 322, 332)*

square number A product of two factors that are the same *(page H38)*
Example: $3 \times 3 = 9$; 9 is a square number.

square pyramid A solid figure with a base that is a square and four faces that are triangles with a common point *(page 316)*
Example:

standard form A way to write numbers by using the digits 0–9, with each digit having a place value *(page 144)*
Example: 2,394

subtraction The process of finding how many are left when a number of items are taken away from a group of items; the process of finding the difference when two groups are compared; the opposite operation of addition *(page 10)*

sum The answer to an addition problem *(page 2)*
Example: $12 + 7 = 19$
The sum is 19.

survey A set of questions that a group of people are asked *(page 272)*

symmetry When one half of a figure looks like the mirror image of the other half *(page 354)*
Example:

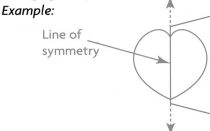

Line of symmetry

T

tally table A way to organize data that uses tally marks to show how often something happens *(page 266)*

tangram A puzzle made up of seven pieces—5 triangles, 1 square, and 1 parallelogram *(page 330)*

tenth One of ten equal parts *(page 400)*

tessellation A repeating pattern of closed figures that covers a surface with no gaps and no overlaps *(page H44)*
Example:

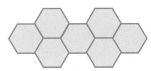

time line A way to look at events that happen in history *(page H36)*

triangle A plane figure with three sides *(page 320)*

turn A move that involves rotating a figure *(page 348)*
Example:

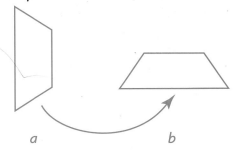

a   b

vertical bar graph A bar graph that has
bars going up from the bottom
(page 284)

yard (yd) A customary unit used to
measure length or distance
1 yard = 3 feet *(page 422)*

Zero Property When adding zero to or
subtracting zero from a number, the
result is that number. When multiplying
by zero, the result is zero. You cannot
divide by zero. *(pages 6, 10, 196, and 246)*
Example: $4 + 0 = 4$
$4 - 0 = 4$
$4 \times 0 = 0$

INDEX

O

Odd numbers, 132–133, 153, 235, 297, 455
Ones. *See* Place value
Open figures, H24–H25
Operations. *See* Addition; Division; Multiplication; Subtraction
Opposite operations. *See* Inverse operations
Order
of addends, 6–7, 456
of factors, 192, 193, 194
property, 6–7, 8–9, 18–19, 23, 192–195
See also Comparing; Ordering numbers
Ordered pairs, 334–335
Ordering numbers, 13, 65, 161, 168–169, 197, 233, 407
Ordinal numbers, 128–129
Organize data. *See* Data
Ounces, 432–433
Outcomes
certain, 296–297
equally likely, H42–H43
impossible, 296–297
possible, 298–299
predicting, H42–H43
recording, 302–303

P

Parentheses, 18–19, 32, 95, 129, 131
Parts of a whole, 368–369, 374–375
Patterns
in a hundred chart, 132–133, 134–135
of hundred thousands, 150–153
of hundreds, 148–149, 235
number, 3, 5, 132–133, 134–135, 148–149, 167, 173, 195, 217, 235, 297, 317, 373
and number relationships, 326–327
with plane figures, 324–325, 354–355
in problem solving, 326–327
of ten thousands, 150–153
of tens, 134–135, 140, 149, 173
of thousands, 148–149, 235
Pennies, 106–107, 108–113, 300–301, H10–H11
Perimeters, 454–455, 456–457, 460–461, 467
Physical Education Link, 188
Pictographs, 200, 259, 280–281, 282–283, 289, H22–H23
Pints, 430–431
Place value
charts, 150
hundred thousands, 150–153
hundreds, 144–145
hundredths, 402–403, 404–405
ones, 144–145, H12–H13
practice and review, 131, 145, 147, 149, 152, 173, 175, 201, 211, 213, 221, 229, 281, 305, 317, 321, 335, 337, 369, 455, H17
ten thousands, 150–153
tens, 130–131, 144–145, H12–H13
tenths, 399, 400–401
thousands, 146–147
Plane, defined, 322
Plane figures. *See* Geometry
Points
decimal, 106–107, 400–401, 404–410
endpoints, 332–333
on grids, 334–335
Polygons. *See* Geometry, plane figures
Pounds, 432–433

Practice and review

addition, 3, 5, 7, 9, 19, 21, 23, 26–27, 29, 53, 55, 65, 77, 79, 117, 129, 131, 135, 149, 167, 173, 195, 201, 213, 235, 273, 275, 297, 317, 321, 389, H3, H5, H33
basic facts, 19, 23, 27, 107, 111, 145, 229, 231, 255, 273, 275, 281, 285, 305, 335, 375, 389, 401, 405, 439
benchmark numbers, 221, 333
certain and impossible events, 431
choosing
operations, 29, 237, 255, 497
units of customary measurement, 447, 449, 483
units of metric measurement, 457, 491, 493, 495
comparing numbers, 11, 43, 197, 231, 375, 405, 495
congruent figures, 457
counting
angles in plane figures, 353
line segments in plane figures, 349
money, 43, 249, H10
skip, 3, 5, 39, 173, H17
decimals, 447, 449, 481, 483
division, 227, 229, 231, 233, 234–235, 237, 240, 245, 247, 249, 251, 273, 275, 285, 375, 489, 491, 493, 494–495, H21, H31
draw a picture, 357, 379
estimation, 41, 53
even and odd numbers, 153, 235, 297, 455
fact families, 39, 107, 153, 233, 247, 335, 349, H20–H21
fractions, 369, 373, 375, 377, 379, 381, 387, 389, 391, 395, 431, 433, 439, H49, H51
hands-on, 21, 37, 61, 81, 91, 109, 113, 163, 187, 207, 227, 245, 303, 319, 339, 341, 351, 381, 387, 403, 425, 440, 459, 479, 489
measurement, 77, 79, 81, 83, 85, 86, 91, 97, 99, 101, 423, 425, 427, 431, 433, 434, 439, 441, 447, 449, 457, 483, 491, 493, 495, H11, H13, H55
missing factors, 255, 353
money concepts and applications, 43, 107, 109, 113, 115, 213, 249, 321
more practice, H68–H116
motion of plane figures, 349
multiplication, 187, 189, 191, 193, 197, 199, 207, 210, 213, 215, 219, 229, 231, 249, 255, 273, 275, 281, 285, 305, 333, 389, 401, 405, 439, 475, 477, 479, 481, 482–483, 493, H29
number patterns, 3, 5, 149, 167, 173, 195, 235, 297, 317, 323, 373
odd and even numbers, 153, 235, 297, 455
ordering numbers, 13, 65, 197, 233, 407
place value, 131, 145, 147, 149, 152, 173, 175, 201, 211, 213, 221, 227, 281, 305, 317, 321, 335, 337, 369, 455, H13
possible outcomes, predicting, 337, 423
repeated subtraction, 285
rounding to the nearest 10 or 100, 53, 173, 211, 373, 423
skip counting, 3, 5, 39, 173, 188–189, H17
solid figures, identifying, 369
standard notation, 175, 233
subtraction, 11, 13, 37, 39, 41, 42–43, 57, 61, 62–65, 115, 117, 153, 173, H7, H33
symmetry, 351, 353, 355, 491
telling time, 77, 79, 81, 83, 85, 86, 91, 145, 149, H34
using tables, 253

Predicting outcomes, H42–H43
See also Events; Probability
Prisms, 316–321
Probability
events
certain, 296–297
equally likely, H42–H43
impossible, 296–297
possible, 298–299
predicting, H42–H43
recording, 302–303
fair games, 304–305
practice and review, 297, 299, 301, 305, 337, 423, H43
Problem solving
with calculators. *See* choose a strategy
check, 14, 32, 48, 66, 86, 102, 118, 140, 158, 176, 202, 222, 240, 256, 276, 292, 306, 328, 344, 358, 382, 396, 434, 450, 464, 484, 500
choose a method (pencil/paper, mental math, hands-on, calculator), 9, 31, 47, 59, 85, 101, 117, 139, 157, 171, 191, 217, 239, 253, 271, 291, 301, 327, 343, 357, 379, 393, 411, 429, 445, 463, 477, 499
choose a strategy, 9, 14, 31, 47, 48, 59, 66, 72, 85, 86, 101, 102, 117, 118, 124, 139, 140, 157, 158, 171, 176, 182, 191, 202, 217, 222, 239, 240, 253, 256, 262, 271, 276, 291, 292, 301, 306, 312, 328, 343, 344, 357, 358, 364, 379, 382, 393, 396, 411, 418, 429, 434, 445, 450, 463, 464, 470, 477, 484, 499, 500, 506
choose the operation, 28–29, 236–237, 254–255, 496–497
Problem Solving • Mixed Applications, 3, 5, 7, 9, 11, 13, 19, 21, 23, 26, 29, 31, 37, 39, 41, 43, 45, 47, 53, 55, 57, 59, 61, 64, 77, 79, 81, 83, 85, 91, 93, 95, 97, 99, 101, 107, 109, 111, 113, 115, 117, 129, 131, 133, 135, 137, 139, 145, 147, 149, 152, 155, 157, 163, 166, 169, 171, 173, 175, 187, 189, 191, 194, 197, 200, 207, 210, 213, 215, 217, 220, 227, 229, 231, 233, 235, 237, 239, 245, 247, 249, 251, 253, 255, 267, 269, 271, 273, 275, 281, 283, 285, 287, 289, 291, 297, 299, 301, 303, 305, 317, 319, 321, 323, 325, 327, 333, 335, 337, 339, 341, 343, 349, 351, 353, 355, 357, 369, 372, 375, 377, 379, 381, 387, 389, 391, 393, 395, 401, 403, 405, 407, 409, 411, 423, 425, 427, 429, 431, 433, 439, 441, 443, 445, 447, 449, 455, 457, 459, 461, 463, 475, 477, 479, 483, 489, 491, 493, 495, 497, 499, H3, H5, H7, H9, H11, H13, H15, H17, H19, H21, H23, H25, H27, H29, H31, H33, H35, H37, H39, H41, H43, H45, H47, H49, H51, H53, H55, H57
Problem-Solving Activity
American Tall Tales and Legends, 51
Anytown, U.S.A., 315
The Census, 143
Clothes Then and Now, 105
Collecting Pennies, 279
Counting the Minutes, 75
Decorate with Designs, 347
Eight Say *Great!*, 385
Estimating Decimal Volume, 399
Exercise Routines, 127
Fantastic Fruits, 1
Great Inventions, 161
Greeting Card Assembly Line, 35
Legs and More Legs, 185
The Lunch List, 295
Making Double-Six Dominoes, 473

Photo Credits

Page Placement Key: (t)-top (c)-center (b)-bottom (l)-left (r)-right (fg)-foreground (bg)-background (i)-inset

Harcourt Brace & Company:

Page: iv (t) Eric Camden; v (t) Ron Kunzman; v (c) Sheri O'Neal; v (b) Ron Kunzman; vi (t) Harcourt Brace & Company; vi (c), vi (b) Victoria Bowen; vii, viii (t) Eric Camden; viii (b) Greg Leary; ix (t) Weronica Ankarorn; ix (b) Sheri O'Neal; x (t) Allan Landau; x (b) Sheri O'Neal; xi (t) Victoria Bowen; xi (b) Sheri O'Neal; xii (t) Ed McDonald; xii (b), xiii Eric Camden; xiv Victoria Bowen; xv (t) Harcourt Brace & Company; xv (b) Britt Runion; xvi (t) Weronica Ankarorn; xvi (b) Victoria Bowen; xvii (t) Eric Camden; xvii (b) Harcourt Brace & Company; xviii, xix (t) Sheri O'Neal; xix (c) Ron Kunzman; xix (b) Eric Camden; xxi Ron Kunzman; xxvi-1 (bg), xxvi (ti), xxvi (ci) Eric Camden; xxvi (bi) Weronica Ankarorn; 1 (i) Eric Camden; 2 (t) Harcourt Brace & Company; 2 (c) Don Couch; 6 Sheri O'Neal; 7 Rich Franco; 8 (r) Sheri O'Neal; 8 (b) Harcourt Brace & Company; 9 Weronica Ankarorn; 10 Sheri O'Neal; 13 Weronica Ankarorn; 15 Harcourt Brace & Company; 16 (ti), 17 (i) Eric Camden; 18, 19, 20, 22, 23, 26, 29, 30, 31 Sheri O'Neal; 34-35 (bg), 34 (ti) Ed McDonald; 35 (i) Eric Camden 36, 38, 39, 41, 42 (t) Ron Kunzman; 43 Harcourt Brace & Company; 45, 46 Ron Kunzman; 47 Harcourt Brace & Company; 50 (ti), 51 (i) Eric Camden; 52, 53 Weronica Ankarorn; 54 Harcourt Brace & Company; 55, 56, 57, 58 Victoria Bowen; 60, 62 Victoria Bowen; 68 Ed McDonald; 74-75 (bg) Harcourt Brace & Company; 74-75 (bg clock), 74 (ti), 74 (ci) Ed McDonald; 75 (i), 76, 78 Eric Camden; 79 (t) Ed McDonald; 79 (c), 80, 82, 83, 84, 88-89 (all photos) Eric Camden; 90 Victoria Bowen; 91 Eric Camden; 92, 93, 96 (t), 97, 100 Victoria Bowen; 104-105 (bg) Weronica Ankarorn; 105 (i) Eric Camden; 106, 107 (t) Harcourt Brace & Company; 107 (b) Greg Leary; 108 (t) Harcourt Brace & Company; 108 (b) Greg Leary; 109 Harcourt Brace & Company; 110 (tr) Greg Leary; 110, 111 Harcourt Brace & Company; 112 (tl) Greg Leary; 112 (tr) Weronica Ankarorn; 112 (b), 113, 114, 116, 117 Greg Leary; 118, 119, 123, 125 Harcourt Brace & Company; 126-127 (all photos) Eric Camden; 128 Greg Leary; 128 (b), 131 (t) Harcourt Brace & Company; 131 (b) Greg Leary; 132, 133 Sheri O'Neal; 134, 135, 136 Greg Leary; 136 (bg) Harcourt Brace & Company; 137, 138 (t) Greg Leary; 138 (b) Sheri O'Neal; 139 Greg Leary; 142 (i), 143 (i) Eric Camden; 145 Rich Franco; 146 Sheri O'Neal; 147, 148, 149 Rich Franco; 160 (i) Weronica Ankarorn; 161 (i) Eric Camden; 162, 163, 166, 169, 170, 171, 172, 173, 174 Sheri O'Neal; 182 Harcourt Brace & Company; 184 (li) Eric Camden; 185 (b), 186, 188 (t) Allen Landau; 188 (b) Harcourt Brace & Company; 190, 192, 194, 196 (t) Allen Landau; 196 (b), 197 Harcourt Brace & Comapny; 198 Allen Landau; 200 Harcourt Brace & Company; 201 Weronica Ankarorn; 204 (ti), 205 (ti), 205 (bi) Eric Camden; 206 Ed McDonald; 207 (bl) Harcourt Brace & Company; 207 (br) Timothy Fuller; 208 Ed McDonald; 211 Weronica Ankarorn; 212 (t) Ed McDonald; 215 Victoria Bowen; 216 Ed McDonald; 217 (l) Harcourt Brace & Company; 217 (r), 218, 220 Ed McDonald; 226 Sheri O'Neal; 227, 228, 229, 230, 231, 232, 233, 234 (t), 235, 236 (t), 238 Victoria Bowen; 242-243 (bg), 242 (ti), 243 (i) Eric Camden; 244 Sheri O'Neal; 245 Harcourt Brace & Company; 246, 248, 249 (c) Sheri O'Neal; 249 (b) Harcourt Brace & Company; 250, 252, 253, 254, 255 Sheri O'Neal; 264-265 (bg), 265 (ti), 265 (bi), 266, 267 (b), 268, 269, 270, 271, 272, 273, 274, 275, 278-279 (bg), 279 (ti), 279 (bi) Eric Camden; 280 (b), 282, 283, 285, 286, 287, 289, 290 Britt Runion; 294-295 (all photos), 296 Eric Camden; 298, 299 Ed McDonald; 300 (t) Harcourt Brace & Company; 300 (b), 302 Ed McDonald; 303 (b), 304, 305 Ed McDonald; 308 Victoria Bowen; 314-315 (bg), 314 (ti), 314 (li) Ed McDonald; 315 (i) Eric Camden; 317, 318, 319, 321, 322, 323, 324 Don Couch; 326 Timothy Fuller; 330-331 (bg) Eric Camden; 330 (bi) Weronica Ankarorn; 331 (ti), 331 (bi) Eric Camden; 332 Victoria Bowen; 334, 335, 336 Britt Runion; 338 Victoria Bowen; 340 Britt Runion; 341 Weronica Ankarorn; 342 Britt Runion; 346-347 (i) Ed McDonald; 348, 350, 351, 352 (t), 354, 357, 360 Victoria Bowen; 366-367 (all photos) Ed McDonald; 368, 369, 370 Victoria Bowen; 371 Harcourt Brace & Company; 372 Victoria Bowen; 373 Harcourt Brace & Company; 374, 375, 376, 377, 378 (t) Victoria Bowen; 378 (b) Weronica Ankarorn; 379, 380, 381 Victoria Bowen; 384 (ti) Ed McDonald; 384 (bi) Harcourt Brace & Company; 385 (ti), 385 (bi) Ed McDonald; 386, 388, 390, 391, 392 (t), 393 Don Couch; 399 (i) Ed McDonald; 402, 404, 406 (t) Eric Camden; 406 (b) Harcourt Brace & Company; 407, 408, 410, 411 Eric Camden; 414 Victoria Bowen; 419 Harcourt Brace & Company; 420-421 (all photos) Ed McDonald; 422 (t), 423, 424, 426, 427, 428 (t) Ron Kunzman; 429 (t) Sheri O'Neal; 429 (b), 430, 431, 432 (t) Ron Kunzman; 436 (ci) Ed McDonald; 436 (bi) Terry Sinclair; 437 (t) Harcourt Brace & Company; 437 (b) Ed McDonald; 438, 439, 440, 441, 442, 443, 444 (b), 445 (c), 446, 447, 448, 449 Sheri O'Neal; 452-453 (bg) Ed McDonald; 452 (i) Weronica Ankarorn; 453 (bi) Ed McDonald; 454, 455, 456 (t) Eric Camden; 456 (b) Harcourt Brace & Company; 457, 458, 460, 461, 462, 463 Eric Camden; 466 Victoria Bowen; 472-473 (bg), 473 (bi) Ed McDonald; 474 (t) Ron Kunzman; 475 Bartlett Digital Photography; 476, 478, 479, 480, 481 Ron Kunzman; 482 (t) Weronica Ankarorn; 487 (bi) Ed McDonald; 488, 490, 492, 493, 494, 495, 496, 497, 498, 499 Britt Runion; 502 Victoria Bowen; 506 Harcourt Brace & Company; Facing H1 (t) Eric Camden; Facing H1 (c) Victoria Bowen; Facing H1 (b) Greg Leary; H1 (tl) Ron Kunzman; H1 (tr) Harcourt Brace & Company; H1 (bl) Greg Leary; H1 (br) Ron Kunzman; H4 (t) Sheri O'Neal; H8 Victoria Bowen; H12 (t) Greg Leary; H13, H18 Victoria Bowen; H20 Sheri O'Neal; H28 Ron Kunzman; H22, H23, H30, H33 Britt Runion; H34 (b) Ed McDonald; H40, H41 Eric Camden; H48 Victoria Bowen; H50 Don Couch; H52 Victoria Bowen; H56 (t) Eric Camden; H58, H61, H66, H67 Harcourt Brace & Company; H119 Sheri O'Neal.

Other: Cover: Daniel J. Cox/Tony Stone Images

Page: iv (b) Doug Perrine/Innerspace Visions; 3 Steve Maslowski/Photo Researchers; 4 Gordon Lansbury/Bruce Coleman, Inc.; 10 Peter Christopher/Masterfile; 12 Rosemary Calvert/Tony Stone Images; 16-17 (bg) Tom Campbell/Innerspace Visions; 16 (bi) David Hall/Innerspace Visions; 24 Andrew J. Martinez/Photo Researchers; 25, 27 Doug Perrine/Innerspace Visions; 28 Tom & Pat Leeson/Photo Researchers; 34 The Granger Collection, New York; 40 (t) Richard Hutchings/Photo Researchers; 40 (b) The Granger Collection, New York; 42 (b) Phil A. Wever; 50 (bi) Dave La Fleur/United States Postal Service; 63 Jeff Greenberg/PhotoEdit; 64 Craig Tuttle/The Stock Market; 65 Marshall Chamber of Commerce; 74 (bi) Pat Lanza/Bruce Coleman, Inc.; 77 Martin Barraud/Tony Stone Images; 85 Walter Chandoha; 95 Will Ryan/The Stock Market; 96 (b) National Baseball Library, Cooperstown, N.Y.; 99 Comstock; 104 (ti) Yeadon Archive/Archive Photos; 104 (bi) Art Resource; 115 Royal Canadian Mint; 129 Long Photography, Inc.; 142-143 (bg) Superstock; 144 (t) SPL/Photo Researchers; 144 (b) A. Gragera, Latin Stock/SPL/Photo Researchers; 150 (t) Bill Tucker/International Stock Photography; 150 (tc) Nancy Sheehan/PhotoEdit; 150 (bc) Barbara Campbell/Gamma Liaison; 150 (b) Brent Jones; 153 Richard Martin/Agence Vandystadt/Allsport; 154 Michael Lustbader/Photo Researchers; 156 Lewis Kemper/Tony Stone Images; 160-161 (bg) Flip Chalfant/The Image Bank; 164 Superstock; 165 Woody Woodpecker® Walter Lantz Productions, Inc. © Universal Studios Florida. A Universal Studios/Rank Group Joint Venture. All Rights Reserved. © 1998 UCSI; 167 John Elk/Tony Stone Images; 168 Peter Krinninger/International Stock Photography; 184-185 (bg) Corel Professional Photos; 184 (tr) J.A.L. Cooke/Animals Animals; 184 (tr), 184 (bg) Metatools Inc.; 184 (br) Maria Zorn/Animals Animals; 185 (t) Ralph A. Reinhold/Animals Animals; 185 (ctl) Patti Murray/Animals Animals; 185 (ctr) Akira Maroba/Animals Animals; 185 (cl) London Scientific Films; 185 (cr) Superstock; 185 (cbl) Zig Leszczynski/Animals Animals; 185 (cbr) G.I. Bernard/Animals Animals; 195 James P. Blair/National Geographic Image Collection; 204-205 (bg), 204 (bi) Superstock; 212 (b) Charles Benes/The Stockhouse; 214 Jon Lamar/The Stock Market; 224 (i) Derek Berwin/The Image Bank; 234 (b) F. Stuart Westmorland/Photo Researchers; 236 (b) Hans Reinhard/Tony Stone Images; 242 (bi) Peter Gridley/FPG International; 251 Peter Langone/International Stock Photography; 264 (b) Dwight R. Kuhn/Bruce Coleman, Inc.; 267 (t) Bob Thomason/Tony Stone Images; 272 (b) Don Mason/The Stock Market; 278 (bi) The Granger Collection, New York; 280 (t) Archive Photos; 281 Superstock; 284 Renee Lynn/Photo Researchers; 288 Jose Fuste Raga/The Stock Market; 315 (ri) The Granger Collection, New York; 320 (b) "African Face" 1985 by sculptor Eamon Hamilton; 346-347 (bg) Michael Heron/The Stock Market; 352 (b) Bohdan Hrynewych/Stock, Boston; 392 (b) Steven L. Raymer/National Geographic Image Collection; 394 Steinhart Aquarium, Tom McHugh/Photo Researchers; 394 (b) Dr. Paul A. Zahl/Photo Researchers; 422 (b) Johnny Johnson/Alaska Stock Images; 428 (b) Daniel J. Cox/Natural Selection Stock Photography; 432 Superstock; 436-437 (bg) Jean Paul Nacivet/FPG International; 436 (ti) D. Robert Franz/Masterfile; 444 (c) Glen Allison/Tony Stone Images; 445 (t) M. Mastrorillo/The Stock Market; 453 (ti) 94 Zefa Germany/The Stock Market; 472 (bi) J. Pickerell/FPG International; 474 (t) Animals Animals; 477 Aaron Rezny/The Stock Market; 482 Superstock; H3 Steve Maslowski/Photo Researchers; H4 (tc) Daniel Wray/Natural Selection Stock Photography; H4 (bc) Superstock; H24 Juan Gris (Jose Victoriano Gonzalez), Spanish, 1887-1927, Portrait of Pablo Picasso, oil on canvas, 1912, 74.1x93 cm, Gift of Leigh B. Block, 1958.525 photograph 1996, The Art Institute of Chicago; H33 Johnny Johnson/Alaska Stock Images; H34 (t) Runk/Schoenberger/Grant Heilman Photography; H36 (t) Archive Photos; H36 (b) The Stockhouse; H44 M.C. Escher's "Swans" ©1997 Cordon Art-Baarn-Holland. All rights reserved.; H56 (b) Cathlyn Melloan/Tony Stone Images; H120 Superstock.